# DEATH NOTE

## Black Edition

# I

Story by Tsugumi Ohba     Art by Takeshi Obata

# Original Graphic Novel Edition
## Volume 1

# Original Graphic Novel Edition
## Volume 2

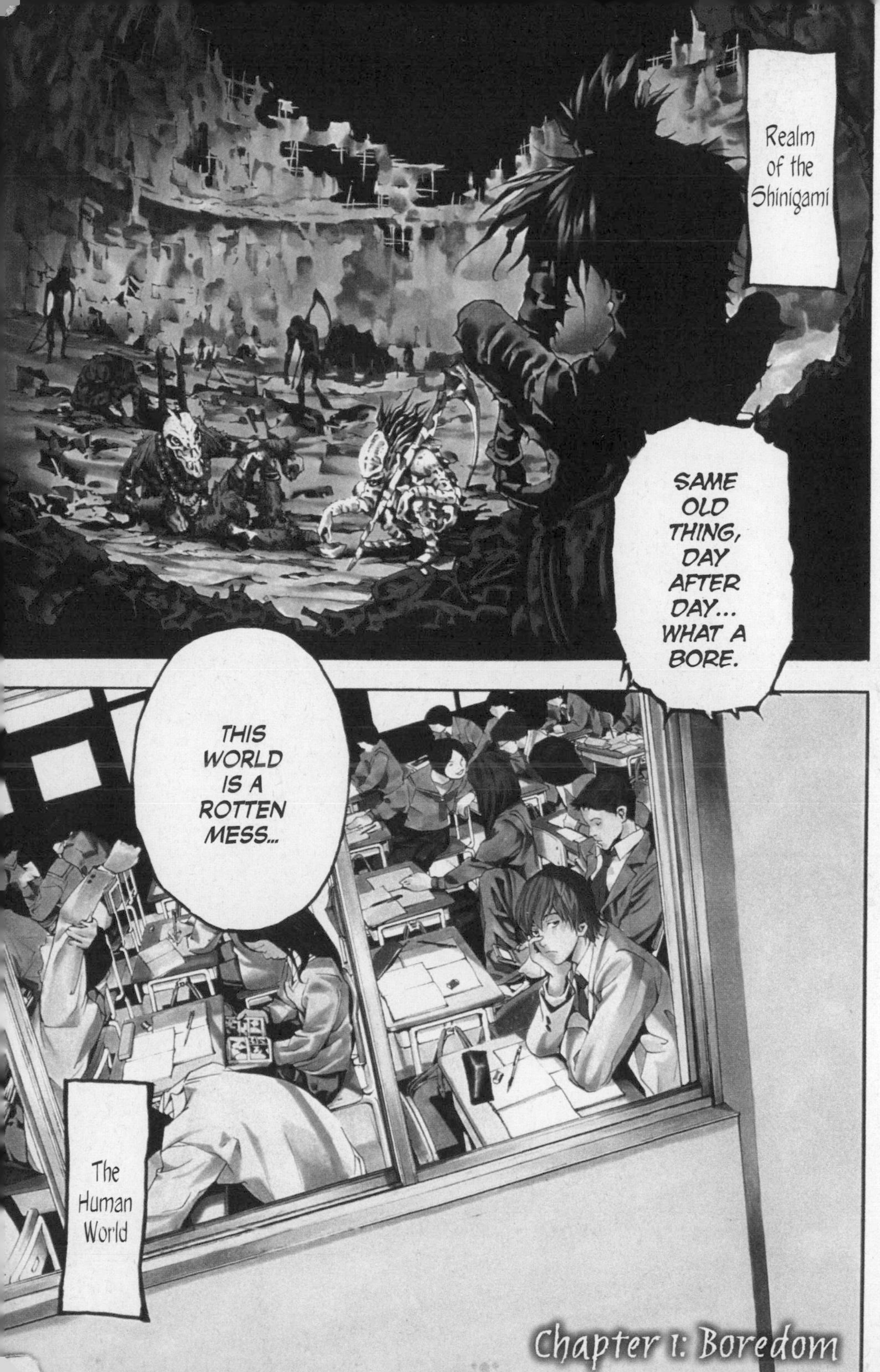
Realm of the Shinigami
SAME OLD THING, DAY AFTER DAY... WHAT A BORE.
THIS WORLD IS A ROTTEN MESS...
The Human World
Chapter 1: Boredom

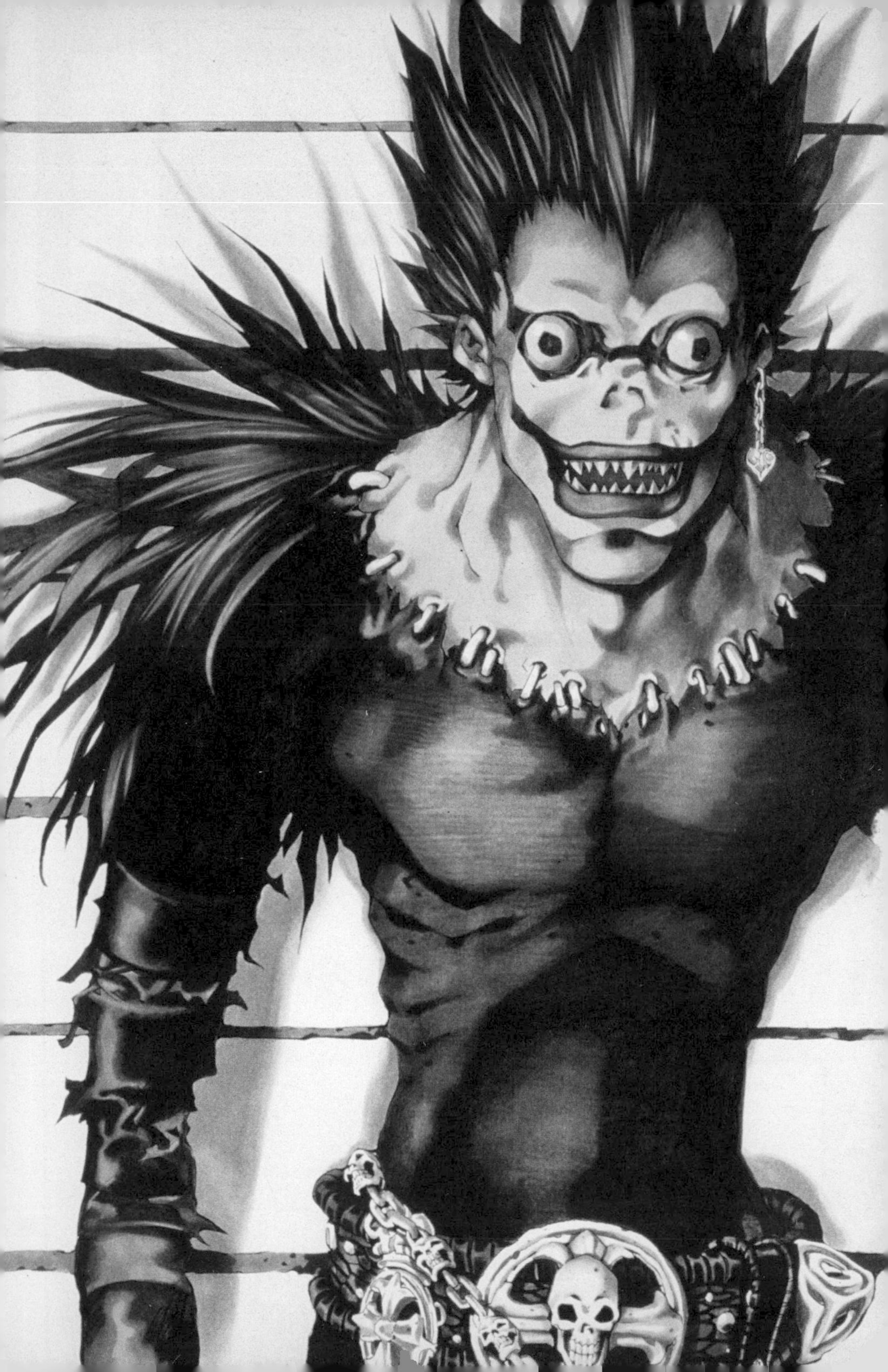

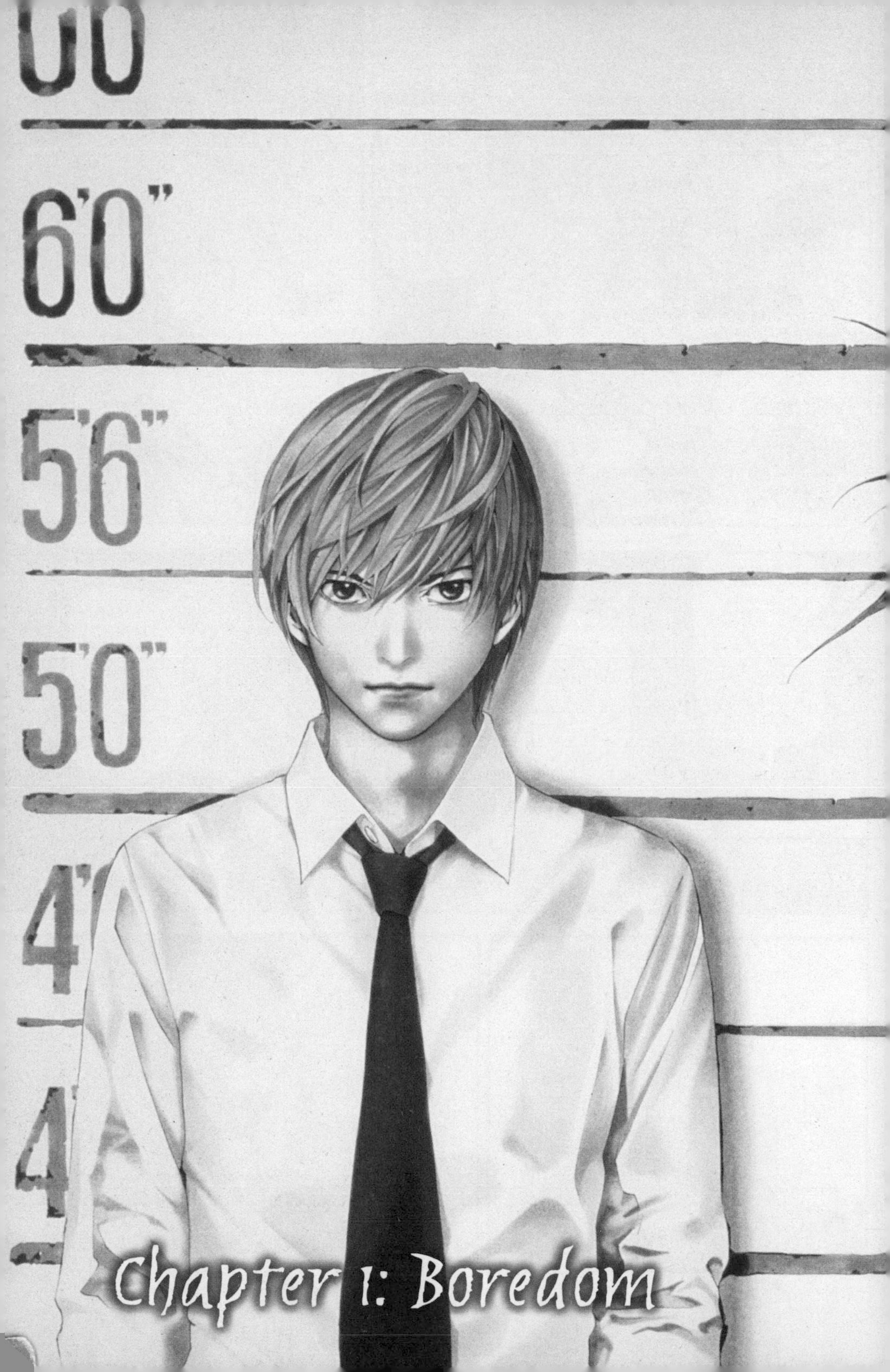
6'0"
5'6"
5'0"
Chapter 1: Boredom

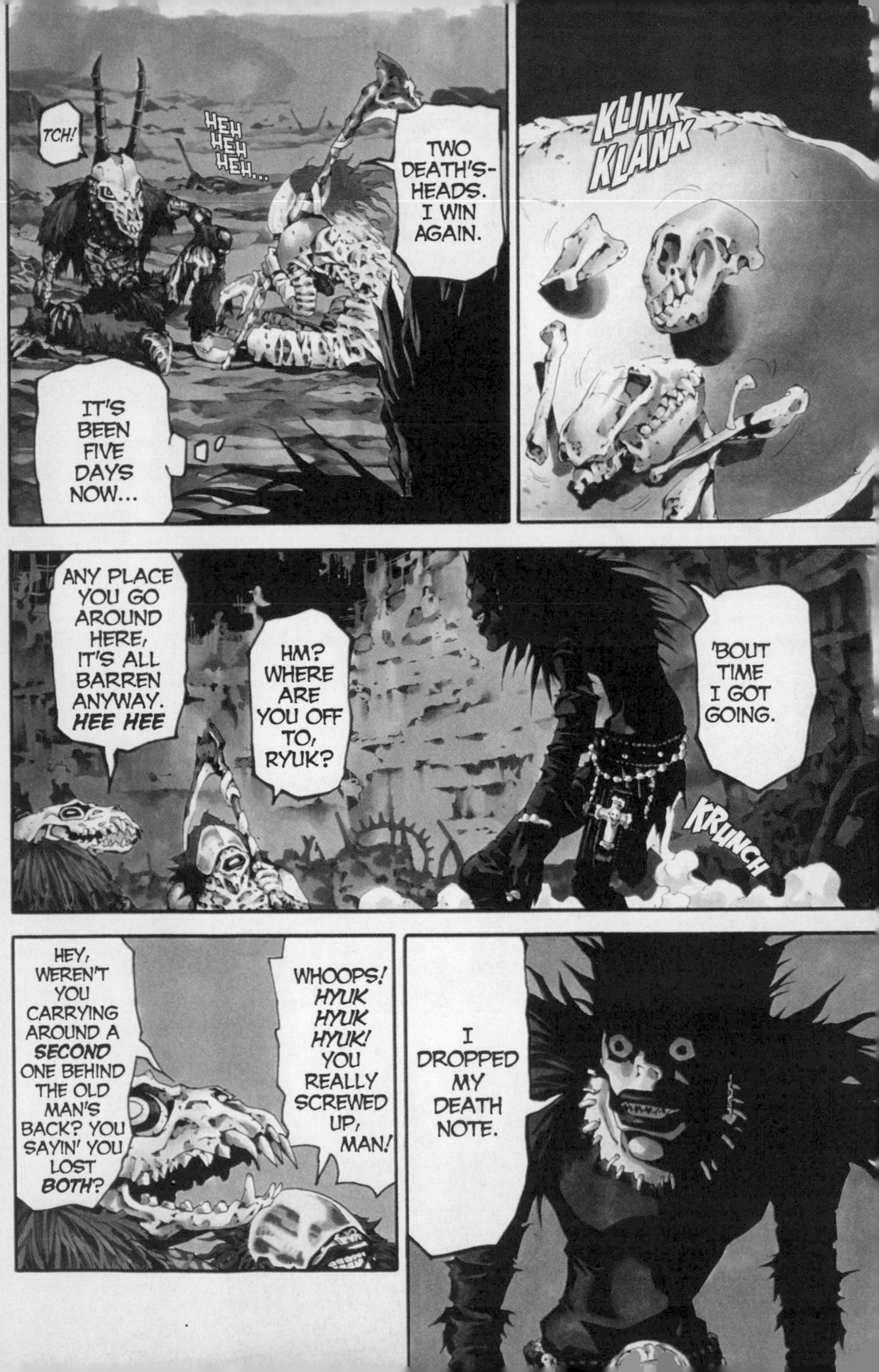
KLINK KLANK
TWO DEATH'S-HEADS. I WIN AGAIN.
HEH HEH HEH...
TCH!
IT'S BEEN FIVE DAYS NOW...
'BOUT TIME I GOT GOING.
KRUNCH
HM? WHERE ARE YOU OFF TO, RYUK?
ANY PLACE YOU GO AROUND HERE, IT'S ALL BARREN ANYWAY. HEE HEE
I DROPPED MY DEATH NOTE.
WHOOPS! HYUK HYUK HYUK! YOU REALLY SCREWED UP, MAN!
HEY, WEREN'T YOU CARRYING AROUND A SECOND ONE BEHIND THE OLD MAN'S BACK? YOU SAYIN' YOU LOST BOTH?

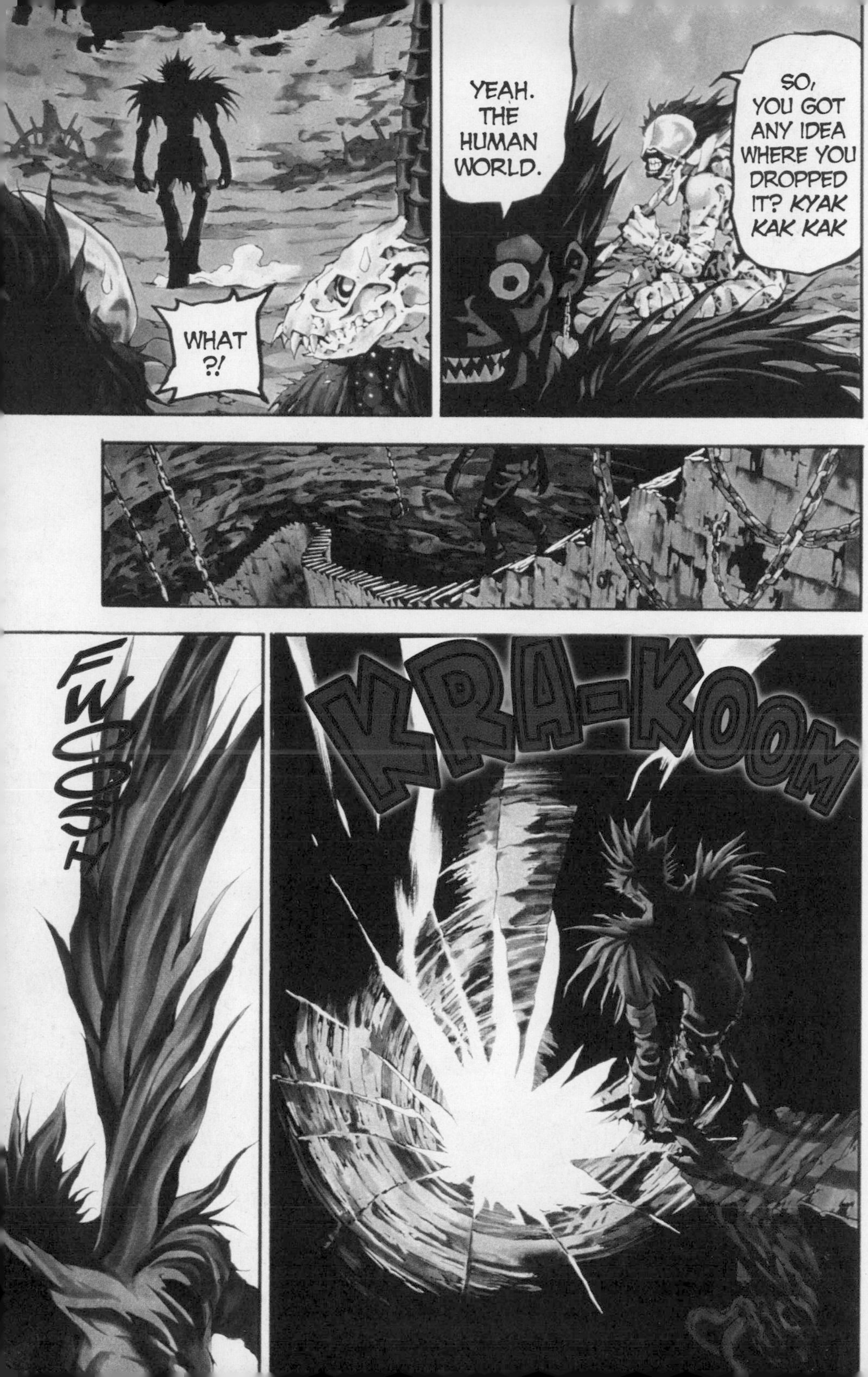
SO, YOU GOT ANY IDEA WHERE YOU DROPPED IT? *KYAK KAK KAK*
YEAH. THE HUMAN WORLD.
WHAT ?!
KRA-KOOM
FWOOOSH

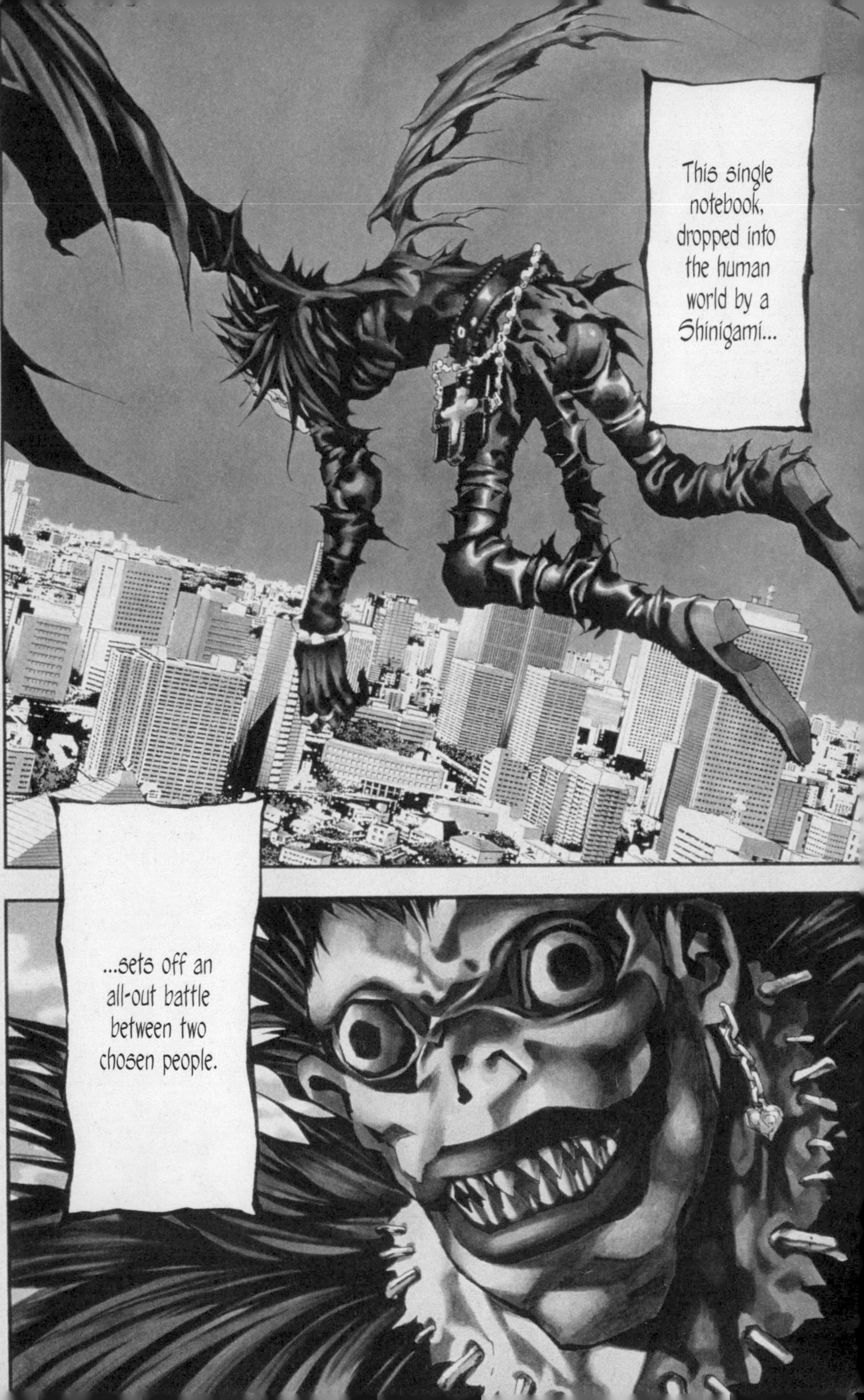
This single notebook, dropped into the human world by a Shinigami...
...sets off an all-out battle between two chosen people.

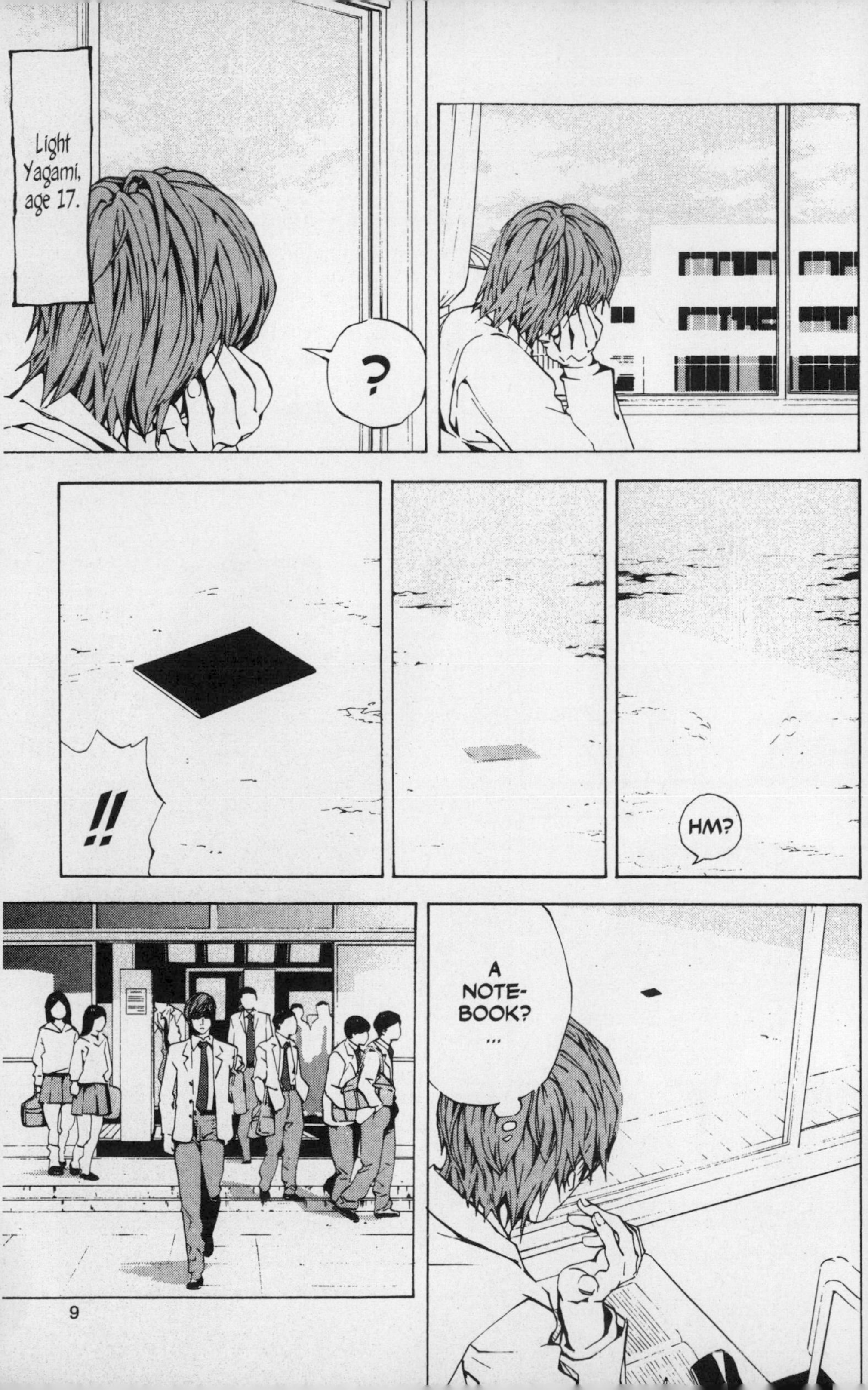
Light Yagami, age 17.
?
HM?
!!
A NOTE-BOOK? ...

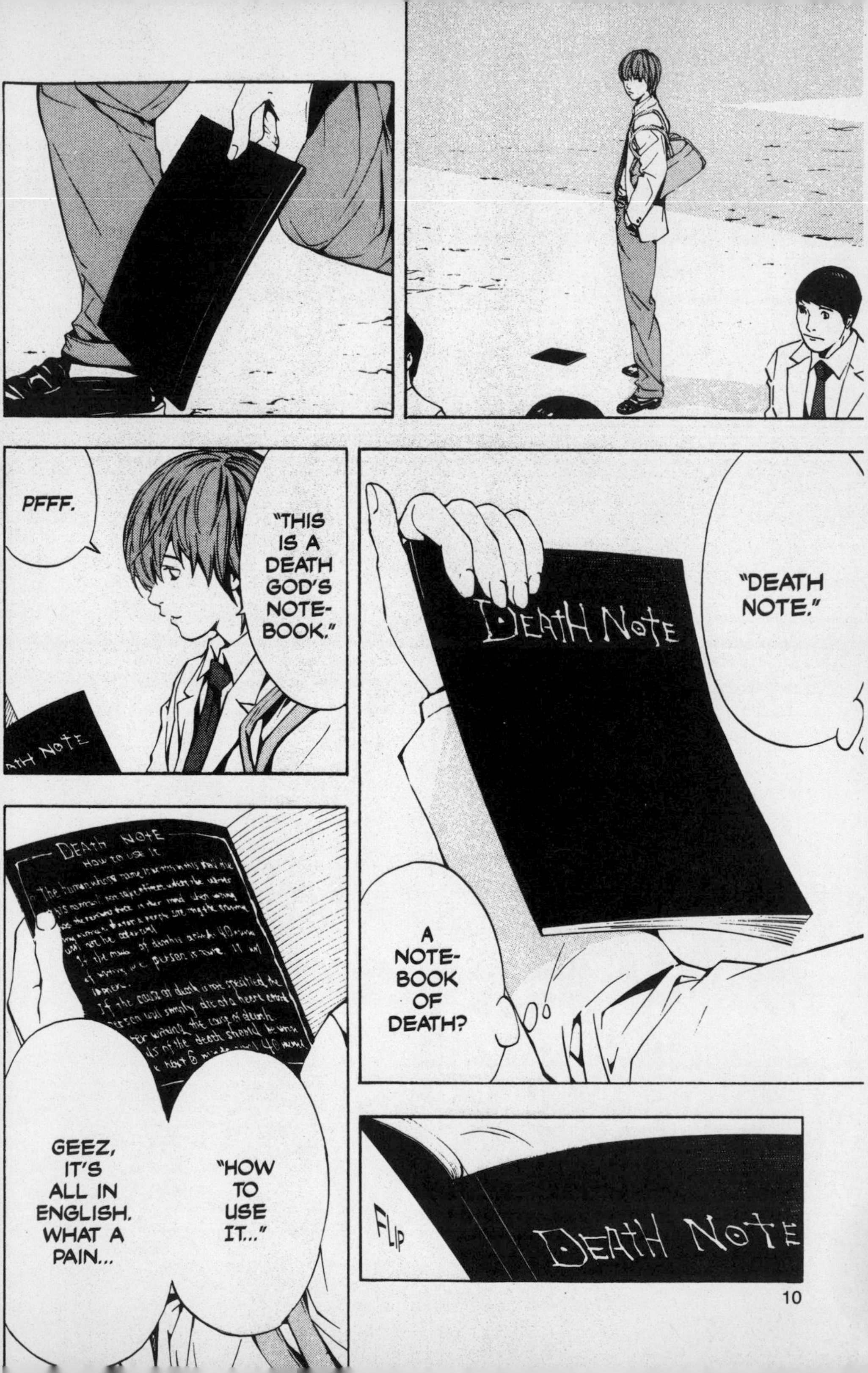
"DEATH NOTE."
DEATH NOTE
A NOTE-BOOK OF DEATH?
"THIS IS A DEATH GOD'S NOTE-BOOK."
PFFF.
FLIP
DEATH NOTE
DEATH NOTE
HOW TO USE IT
"HOW TO USE IT..."
GEEZ, IT'S ALL IN ENGLISH. WHAT A PAIN...

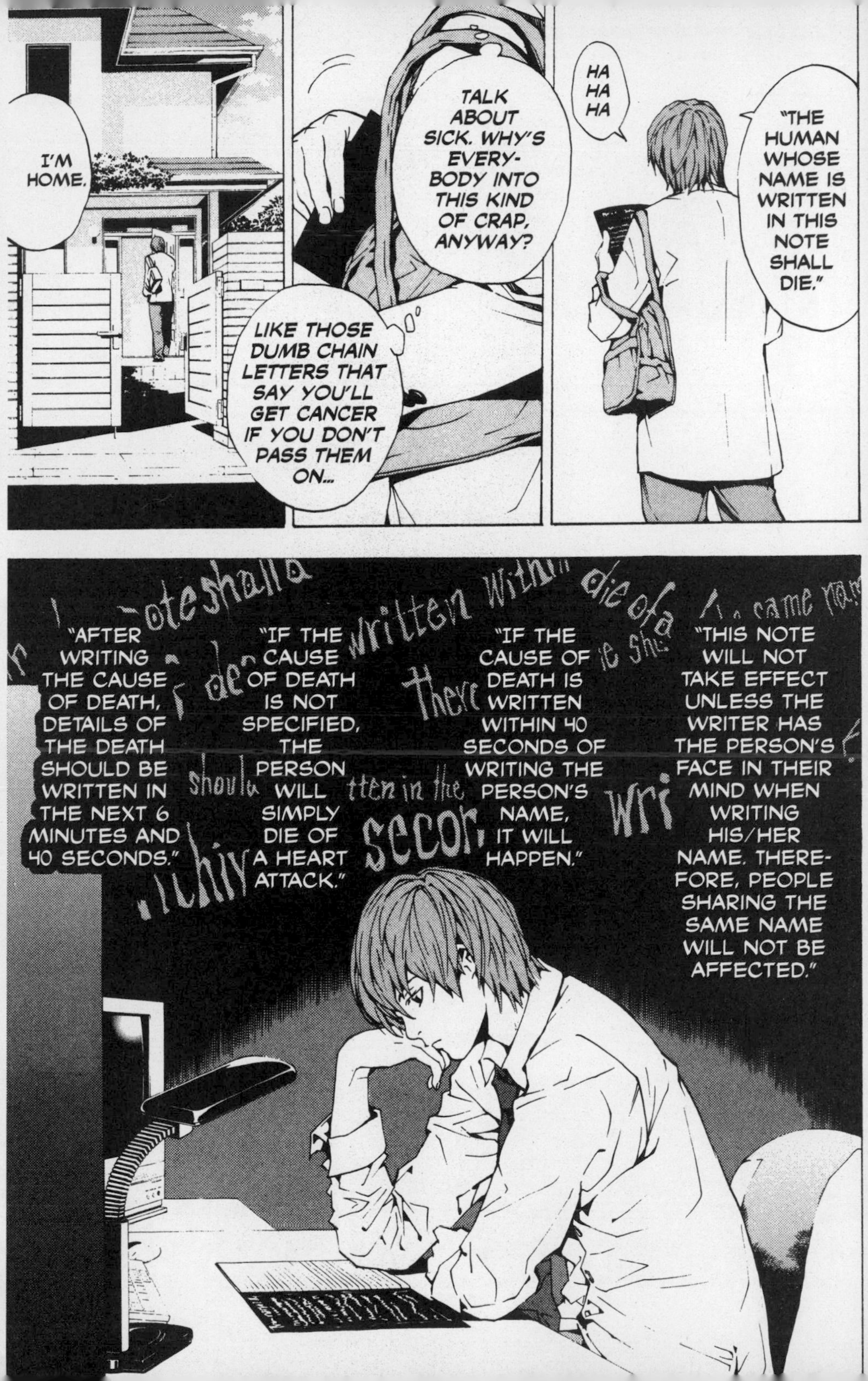
"THE HUMAN WHOSE NAME IS WRITTEN IN THIS NOTE SHALL DIE."
HA HA HA
TALK ABOUT SICK. WHY'S EVERYBODY INTO THIS KIND OF CRAP, ANYWAY?
LIKE THOSE DUMB CHAIN LETTERS THAT SAY YOU'LL GET CANCER IF YOU DON'T PASS THEM ON...
I'M HOME.
"THIS NOTE WILL NOT TAKE EFFECT UNLESS THE WRITER HAS THE PERSON'S FACE IN THEIR MIND WHEN WRITING HIS/HER NAME. THEREFORE, PEOPLE SHARING THE SAME NAME WILL NOT BE AFFECTED."
"IF THE CAUSE OF DEATH IS WRITTEN WITHIN 40 SECONDS OF WRITING THE PERSON'S NAME, IT WILL HAPPEN."
"IF THE CAUSE OF DEATH IS NOT SPECIFIED, THE PERSON WILL SIMPLY DIE OF A HEART ATTACK."
"AFTER WRITING THE CAUSE OF DEATH, DETAILS OF THE DEATH SHOULD BE WRITTEN IN THE NEXT 6 MINUTES AND 40 SECONDS."

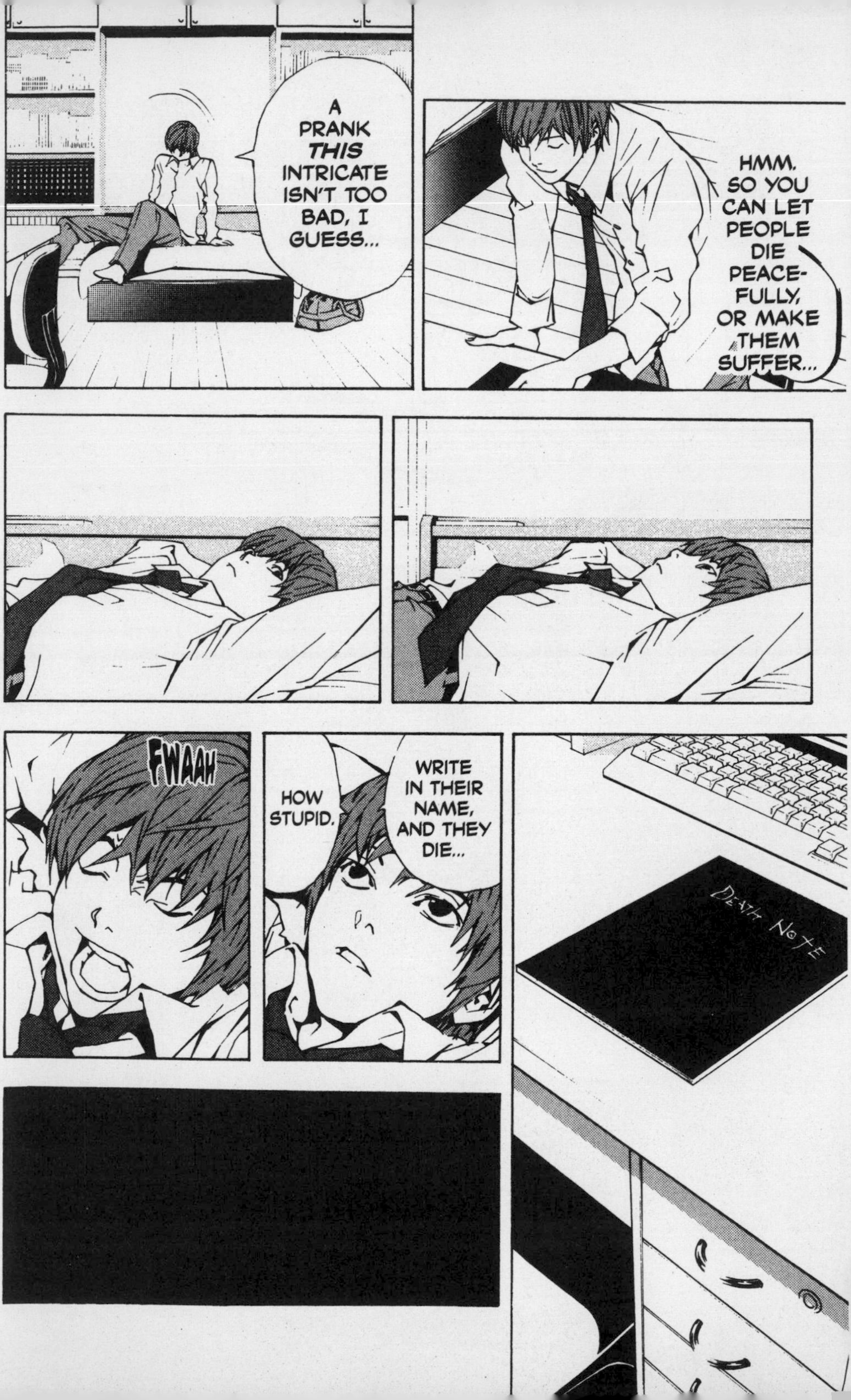
HMM. SO YOU CAN LET PEOPLE DIE PEACE-FULLY, OR MAKE THEM SUFFER...
A PRANK *THIS* INTRICATE ISN'T TOO BAD, I GUESS...
DEATH NOTE
WRITE IN THEIR NAME, AND THEY DIE...
HOW STUPID.
FWAAH

READ THIS WAY

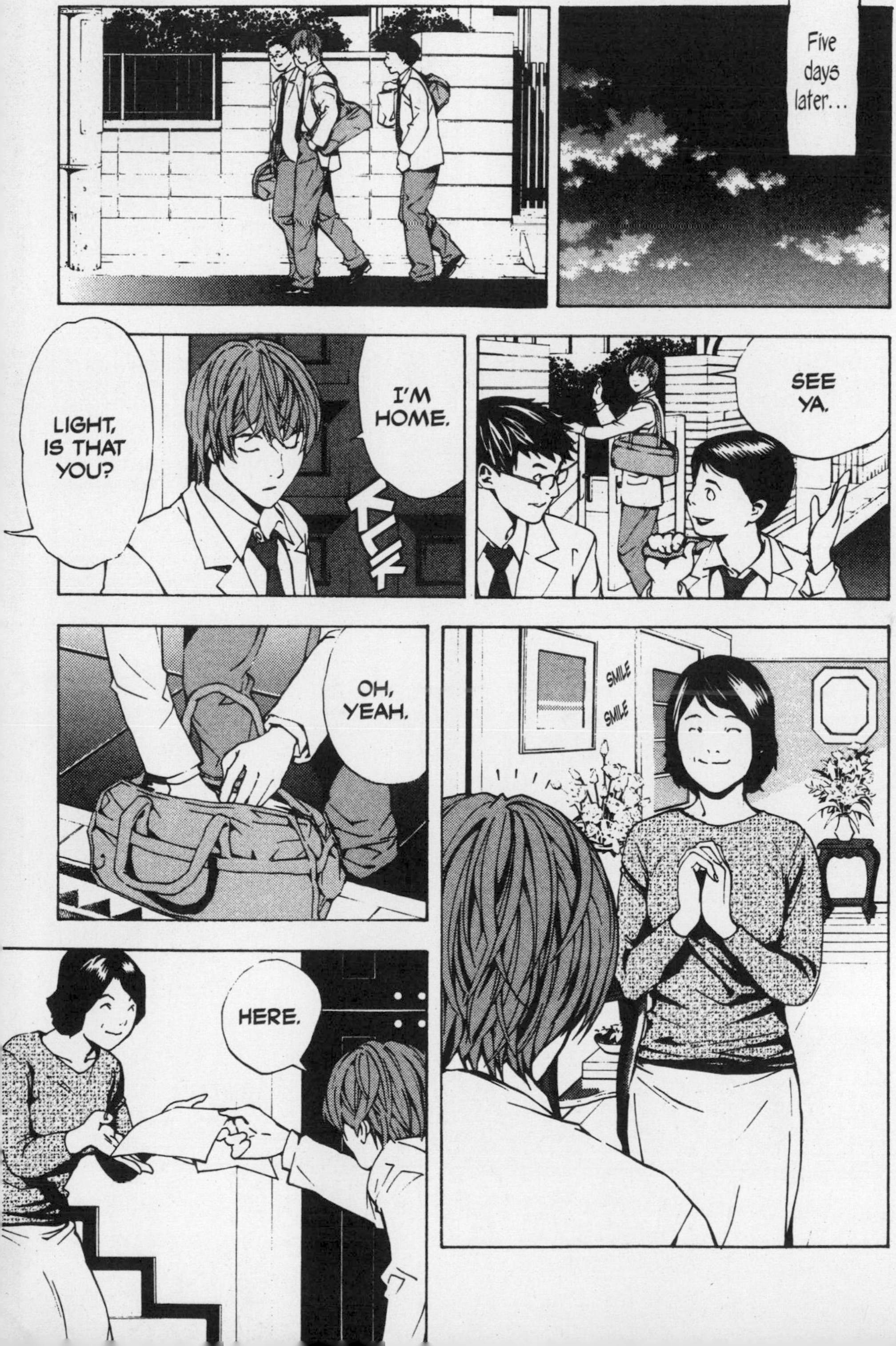

Five days later…
SEE YA.
I'M HOME.
KLIK
LIGHT, IS THAT YOU?
SMILE
SMILE
OH, YEAH.
HERE.

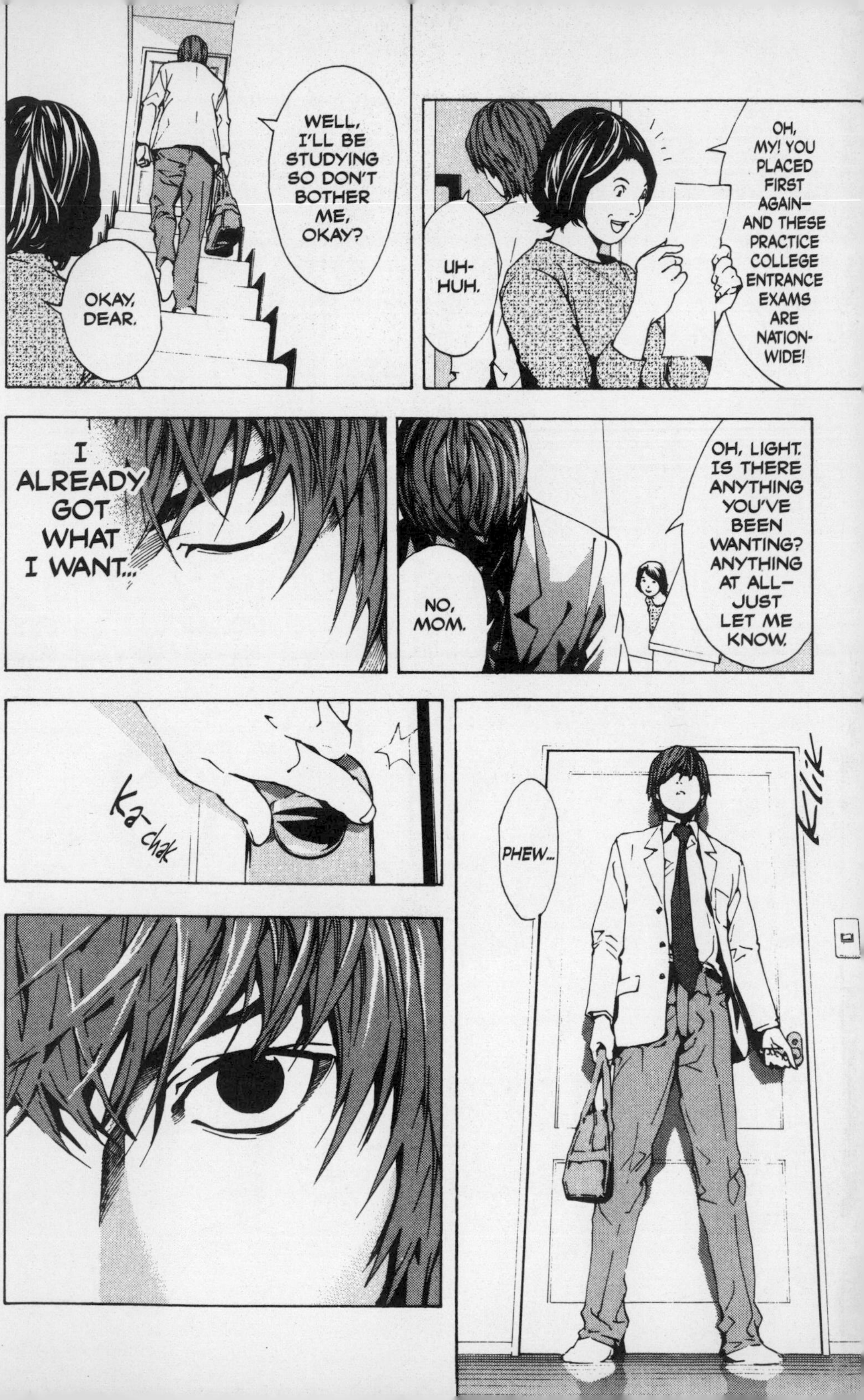
OH, MY! YOU PLACED FIRST AGAIN—AND THESE PRACTICE COLLEGE ENTRANCE EXAMS ARE NATION-WIDE!
UH-HUH.
WELL, I'LL BE STUDYING SO DON'T BOTHER ME, OKAY?
OKAY, DEAR.
OH, LIGHT. IS THERE ANYTHING YOU'VE BEEN WANTING? ANYTHING AT ALL—JUST LET ME KNOW.
NO, MOM.
I ALREADY GOT WHAT I WANT...
Klik
PHEW...
Ka-chak

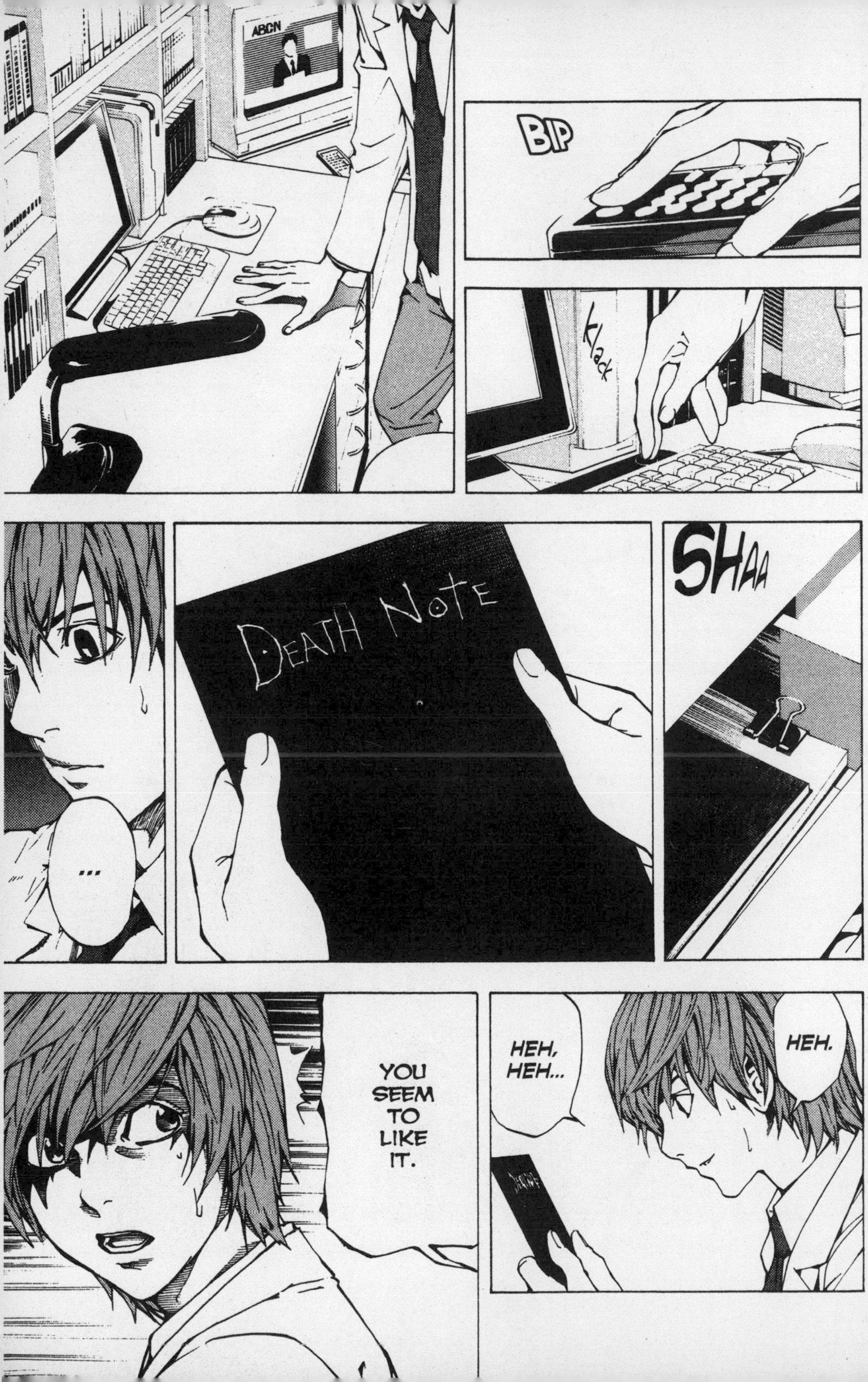
BIP
klack
ABCN
SHAA
DEATH NOTE
...
HEH.
HEH, HEH...
YOU SEEM TO LIKE IT.

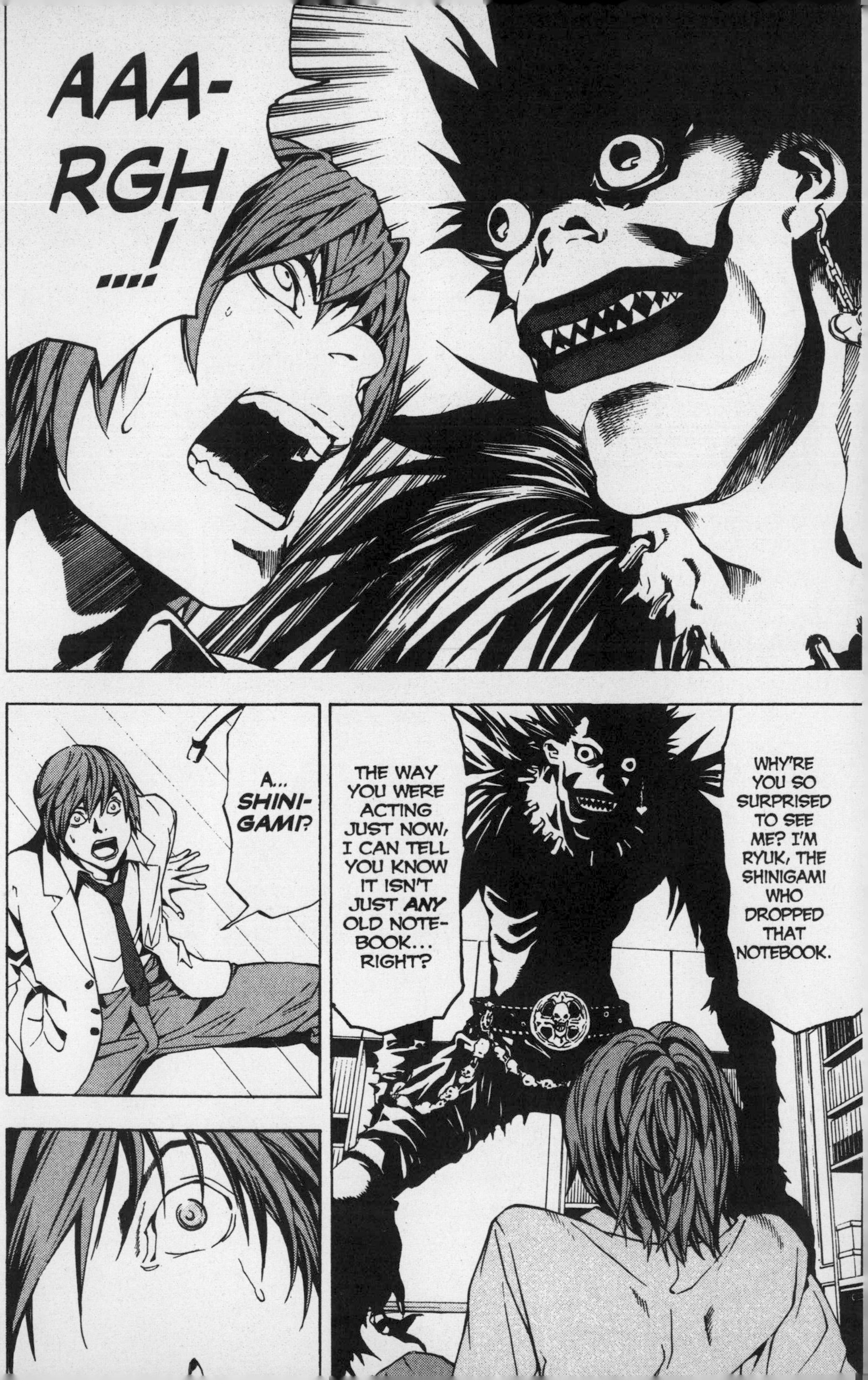
AAA-RGH...!
WHY'RE YOU SO SURPRISED TO SEE ME? I'M RYUK, THE SHINIGAMI WHO DROPPED THAT NOTEBOOK.
THE WAY YOU WERE ACTING JUST NOW, I CAN TELL YOU KNOW IT ISN'T JUST ANY OLD NOTE-BOOK... RIGHT?
A... SHINI-GAMI!?

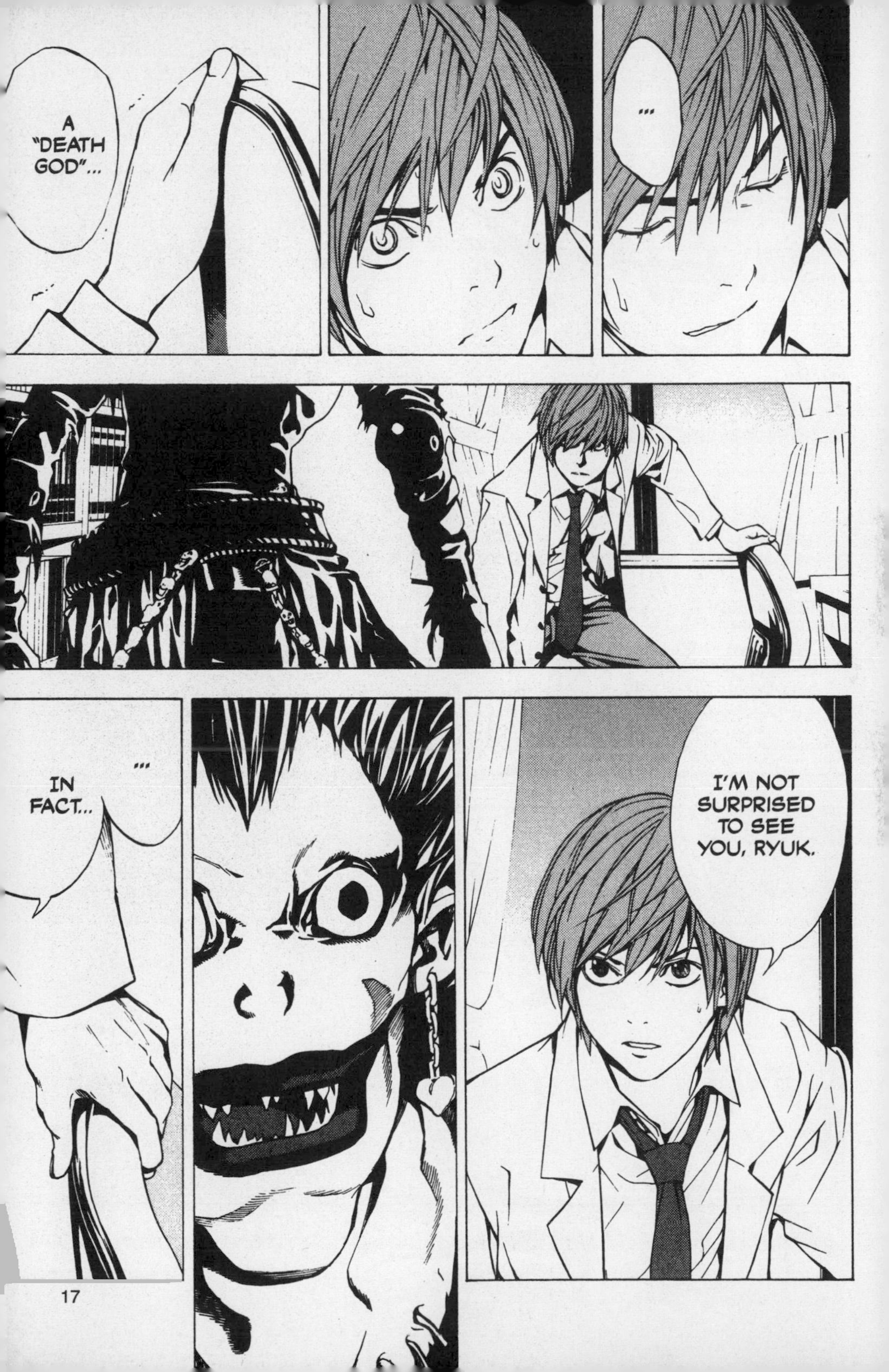
...
A "DEATH GOD"...
I'M NOT SURPRISED TO SEE YOU, RYUK.
...
IN FACT...

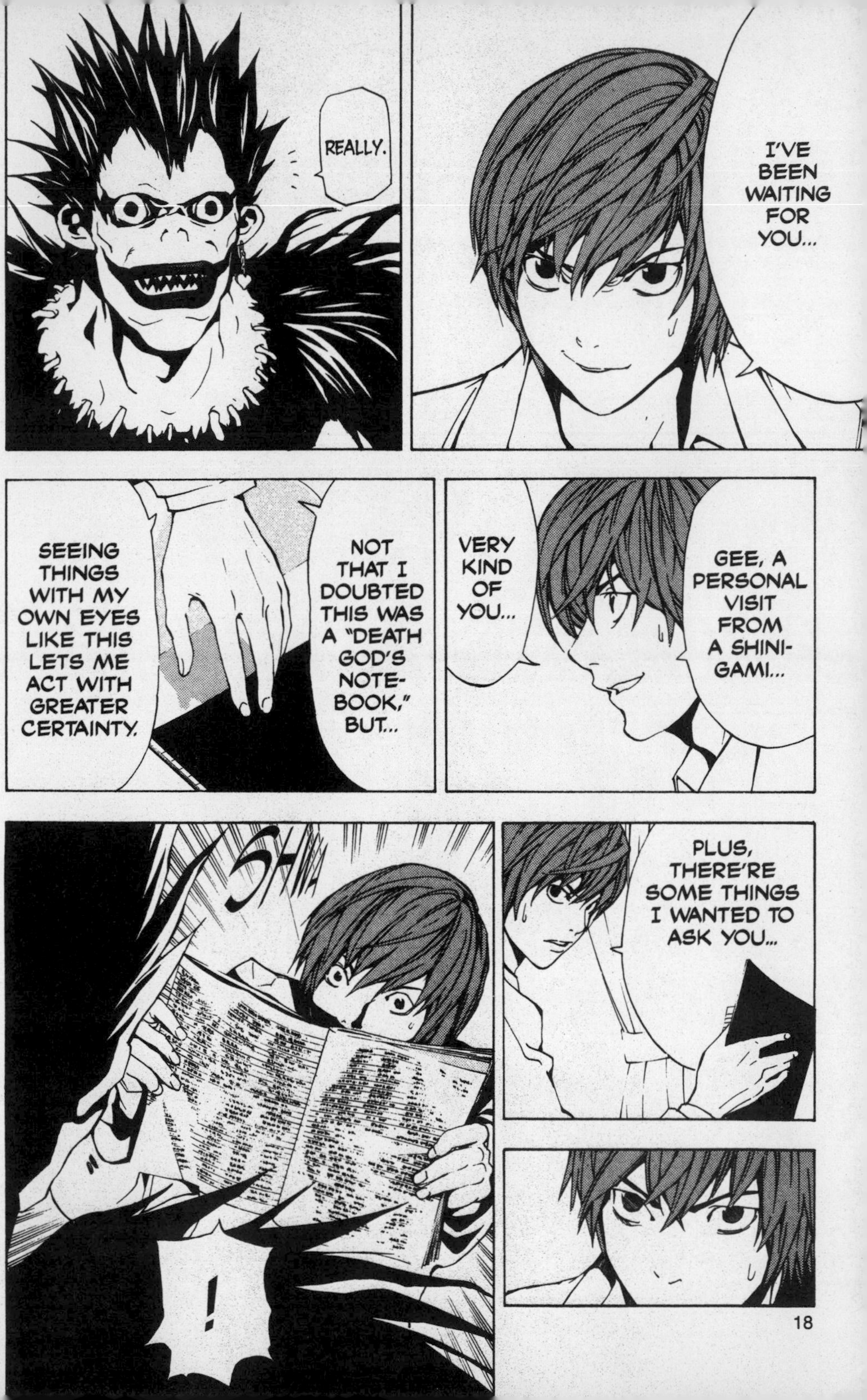
I'VE BEEN WAITING FOR YOU...
REALLY.
GEE, A PERSONAL VISIT FROM A SHINI-GAMI...
VERY KIND OF YOU...
NOT THAT I DOUBTED THIS WAS A "DEATH GOD'S NOTE-BOOK," BUT...
SEEING THINGS WITH MY OWN EYES LIKE THIS LETS ME ACT WITH GREATER CERTAINTY.
PLUS, THERE'RE SOME THINGS I WANTED TO ASK YOU...
!

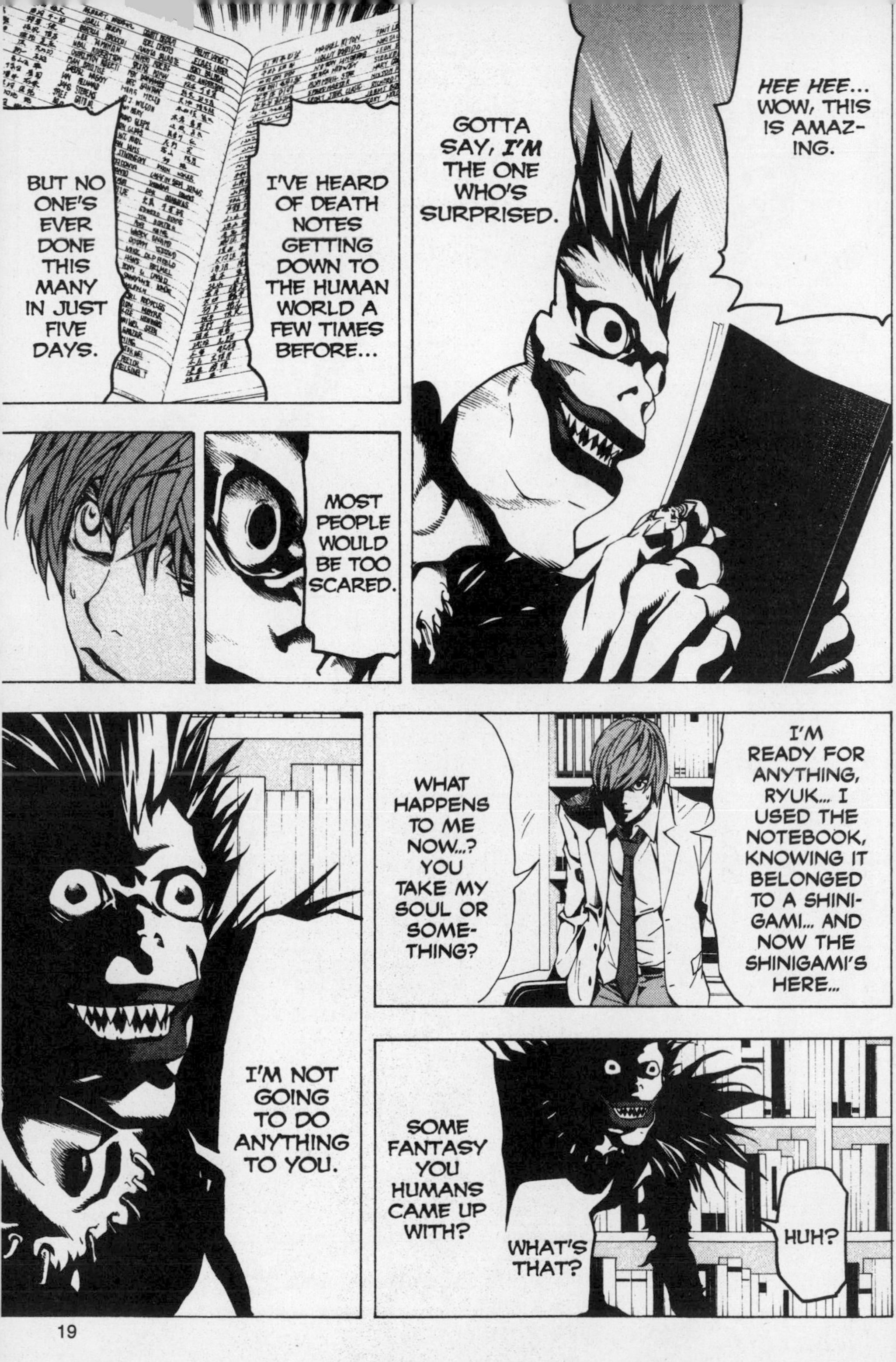
HEE HEE... WOW, THIS IS AMAZ-ING.
GOTTA SAY, *I'M* THE ONE WHO'S SURPRISED.
I'VE HEARD OF DEATH NOTES GETTING DOWN TO THE HUMAN WORLD A FEW TIMES BEFORE...
BUT NO ONE'S EVER DONE THIS MANY IN JUST FIVE DAYS.
MOST PEOPLE WOULD BE TOO SCARED.
I'M READY FOR ANYTHING, RYUK... I USED THE NOTEBOOK, KNOWING IT BELONGED TO A SHINI-GAMI... AND NOW THE SHINIGAMI'S HERE...
WHAT HAPPENS TO ME NOW...? YOU TAKE MY SOUL OR SOME-THING?
HUH?
WHAT'S THAT?
SOME FANTASY YOU HUMANS CAME UP WITH?
I'M NOT GOING TO DO ANYTHING TO YOU.

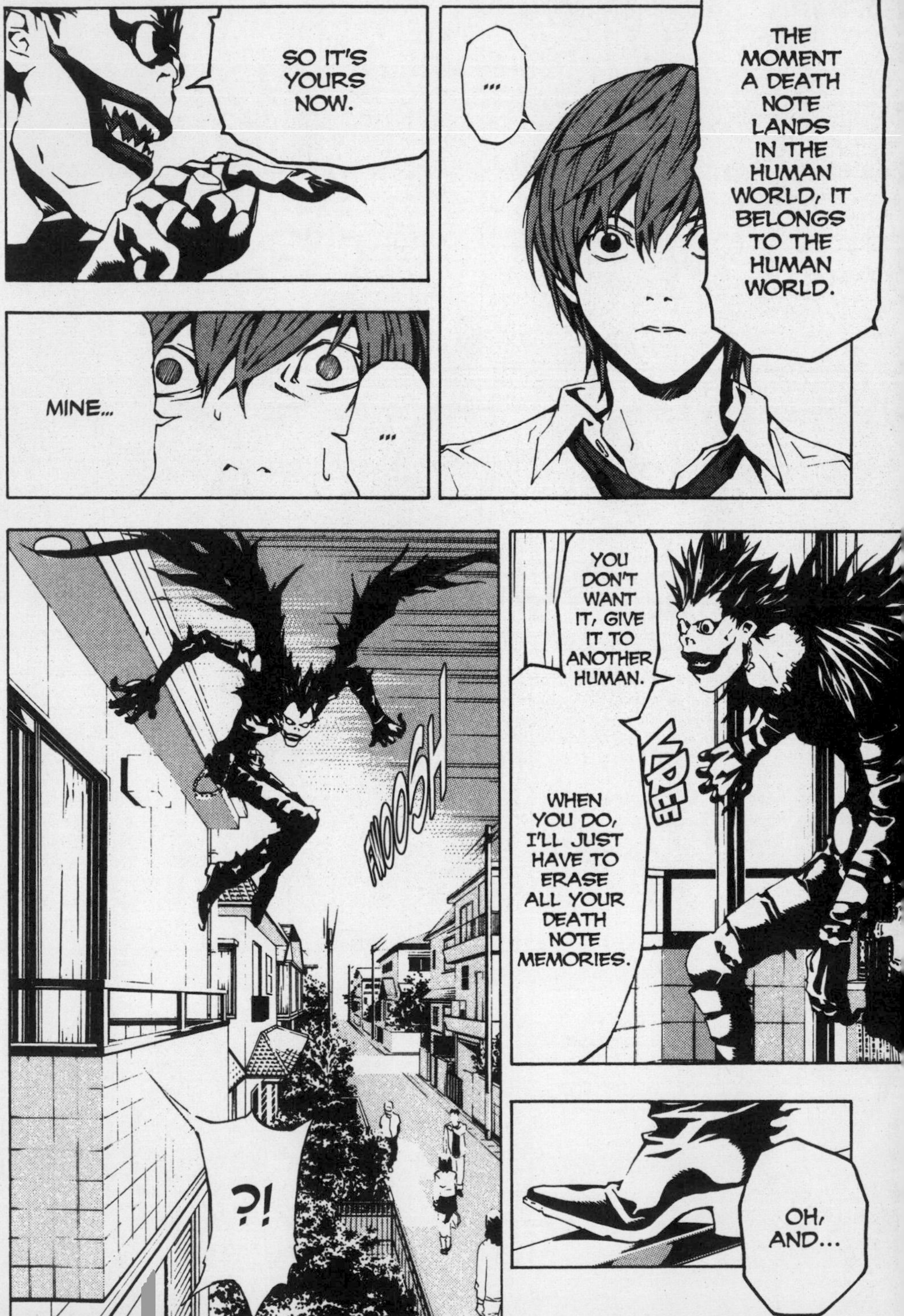
THE MOMENT A DEATH NOTE LANDS IN THE HUMAN WORLD, IT BELONGS TO THE HUMAN WORLD.
...
SO IT'S YOURS NOW.
MINE...
...
YOU DON'T WANT IT, GIVE IT TO ANOTHER HUMAN.
VREE
WHEN YOU DO, I'LL JUST HAVE TO ERASE ALL YOUR DEATH NOTE MEMORIES.
OH, AND...
FWOOSH
?!

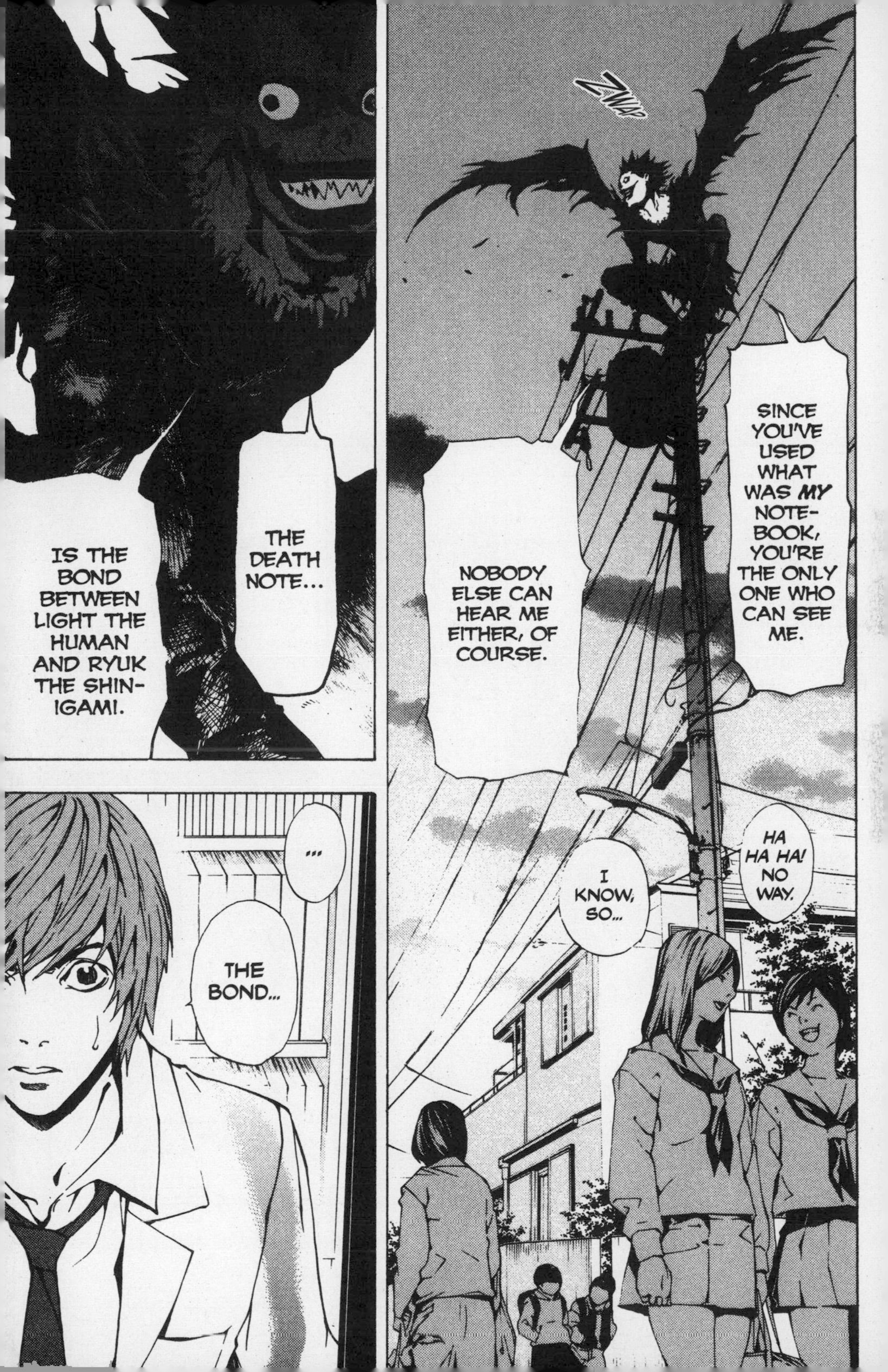
ZWAP
SINCE YOU'VE USED WHAT WAS *MY* NOTEBOOK, YOU'RE THE ONLY ONE WHO CAN SEE ME.
NOBODY ELSE CAN HEAR ME EITHER, OF COURSE.
*HA HA HA!* NO WAY.
I KNOW, SO...
THE DEATH NOTE...
IS THE BOND BETWEEN LIGHT THE HUMAN AND RYUK THE SHINIGAMI.
...
THE BOND...

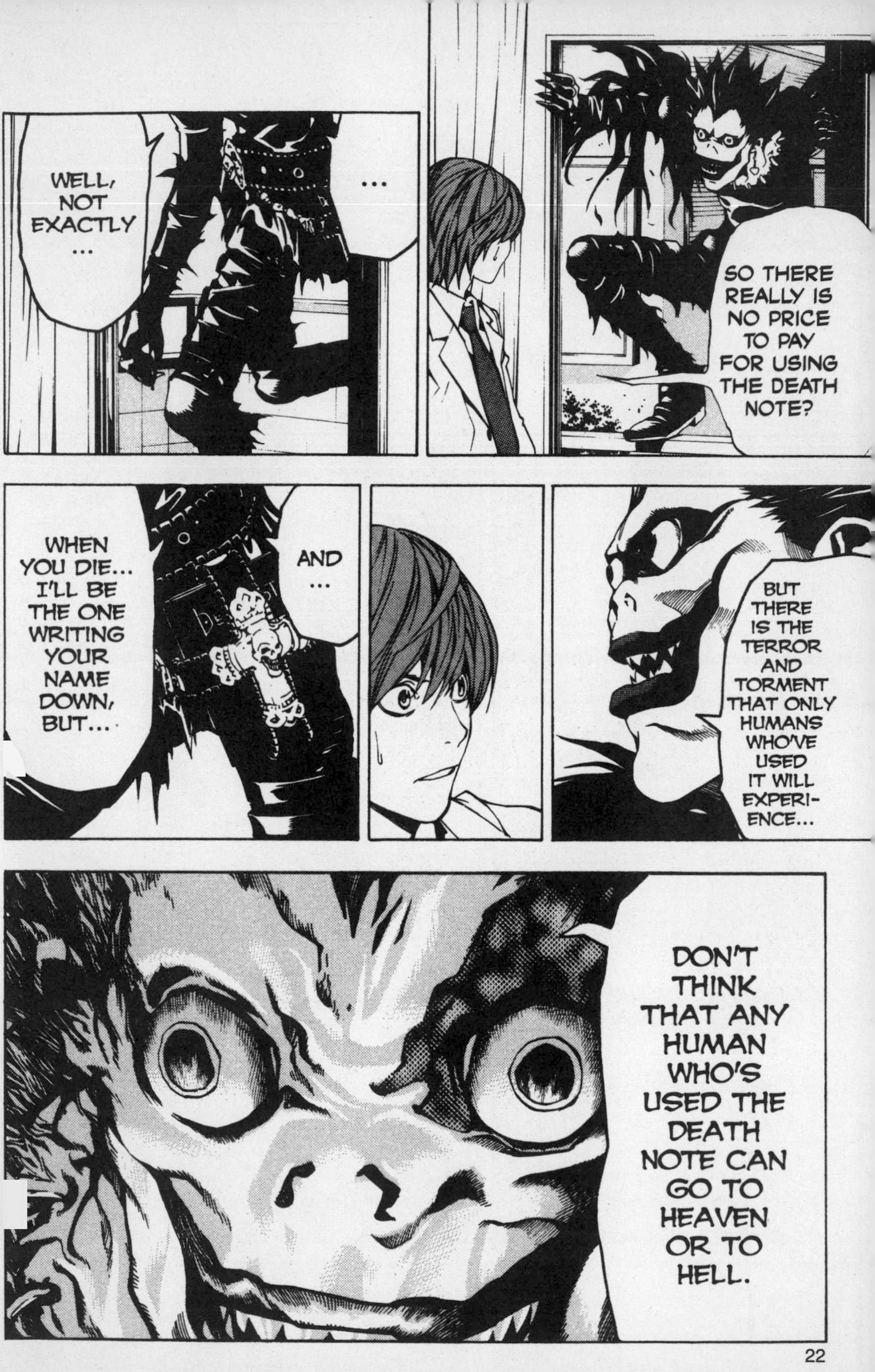
SO THERE REALLY IS NO PRICE TO PAY FOR USING THE DEATH NOTE?
...
WELL, NOT EXACTLY ...
BUT THERE IS THE TERROR AND TORMENT THAT ONLY HUMANS WHO'VE USED IT WILL EXPERIENCE...
AND ...
WHEN YOU DIE... I'LL BE THE ONE WRITING YOUR NAME DOWN, BUT...
DON'T THINK THAT ANY HUMAN WHO'S USED THE DEATH NOTE CAN GO TO HEAVEN OR TO HELL.

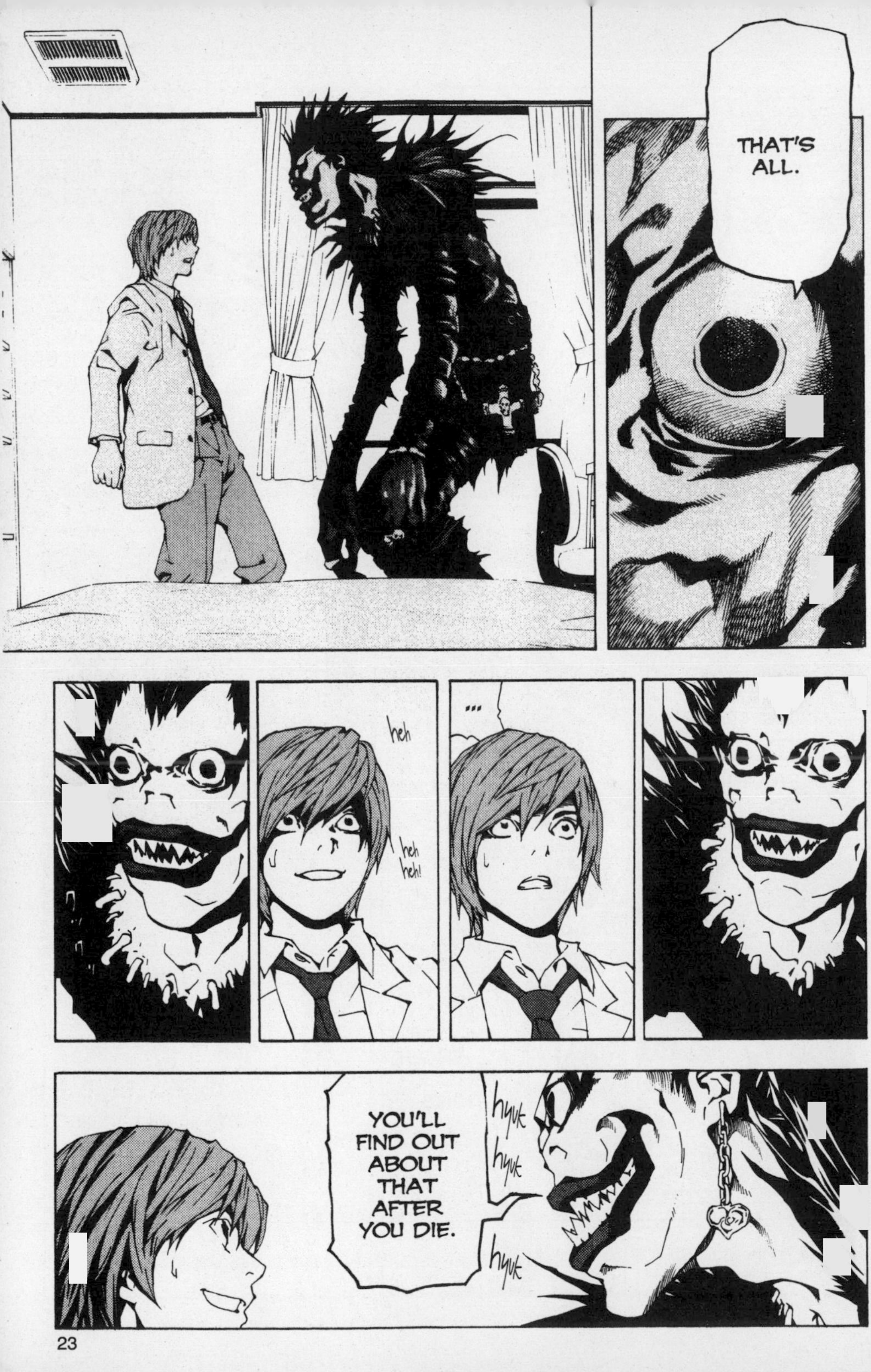
THAT'S ALL.
...
heh
heh heh!
hyuk hyuk hyuk
YOU'LL FIND OUT ABOUT THAT AFTER YOU DIE.

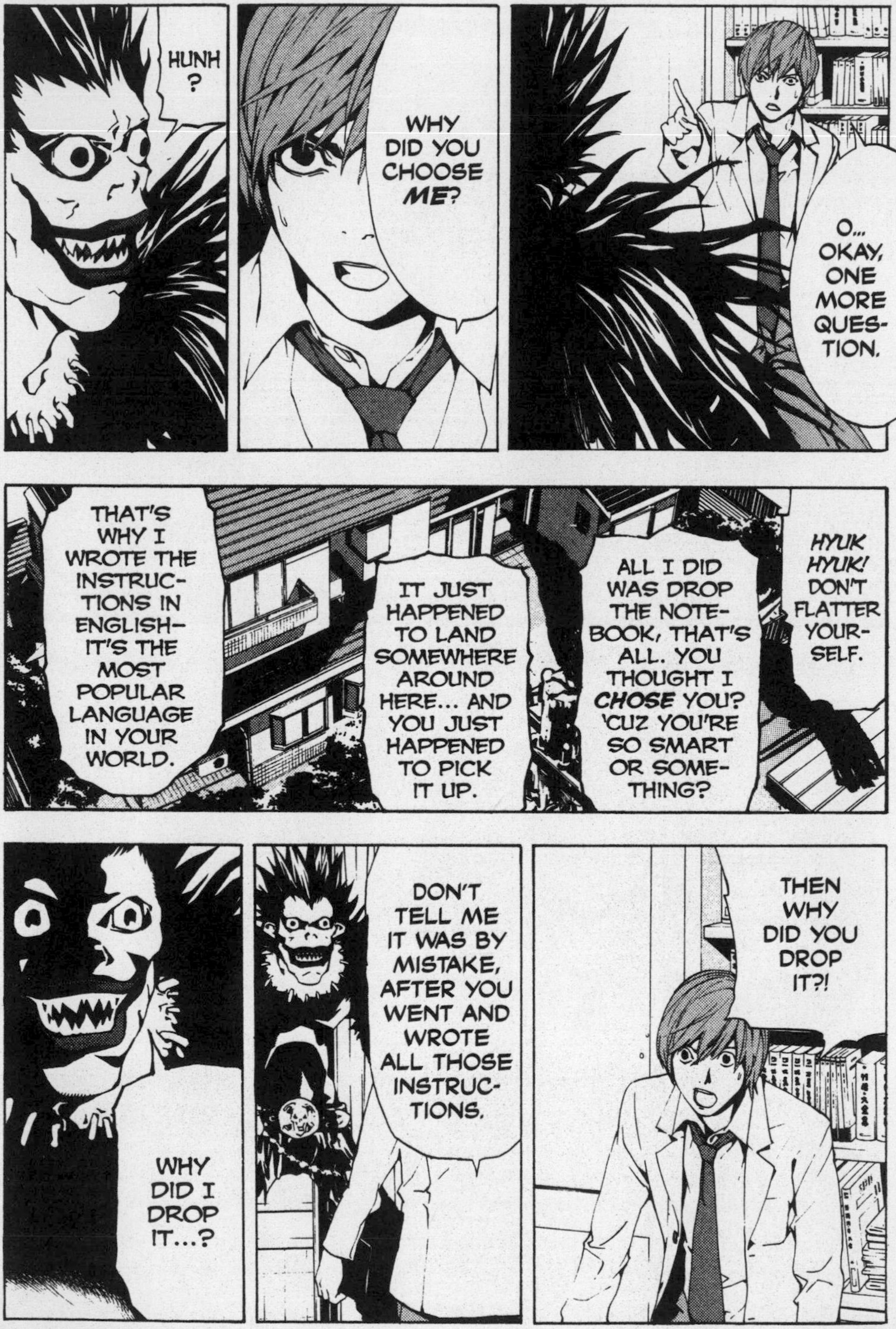
O... OKAY, ONE MORE QUES-TION.
WHY DID YOU CHOOSE *ME*?
HUNH?
*HYUK HYUK!* DON'T FLATTER YOUR-SELF.
ALL I DID WAS DROP THE NOTE-BOOK, THAT'S ALL. YOU THOUGHT I *CHOSE* YOU? 'CUZ YOU'RE SO SMART OR SOME-THING?
IT JUST HAPPENED TO LAND SOMEWHERE AROUND HERE... AND YOU JUST HAPPENED TO PICK IT UP.
THAT'S WHY I WROTE THE INSTRUC-TIONS IN ENGLISH— IT'S THE MOST POPULAR LANGUAGE IN YOUR WORLD.
THEN WHY DID YOU DROP IT?!
DON'T TELL ME IT WAS BY MISTAKE, AFTER YOU WENT AND WROTE ALL THOSE INSTRUC-TIONS.
WHY DID I DROP IT...?

READ THIS WAY

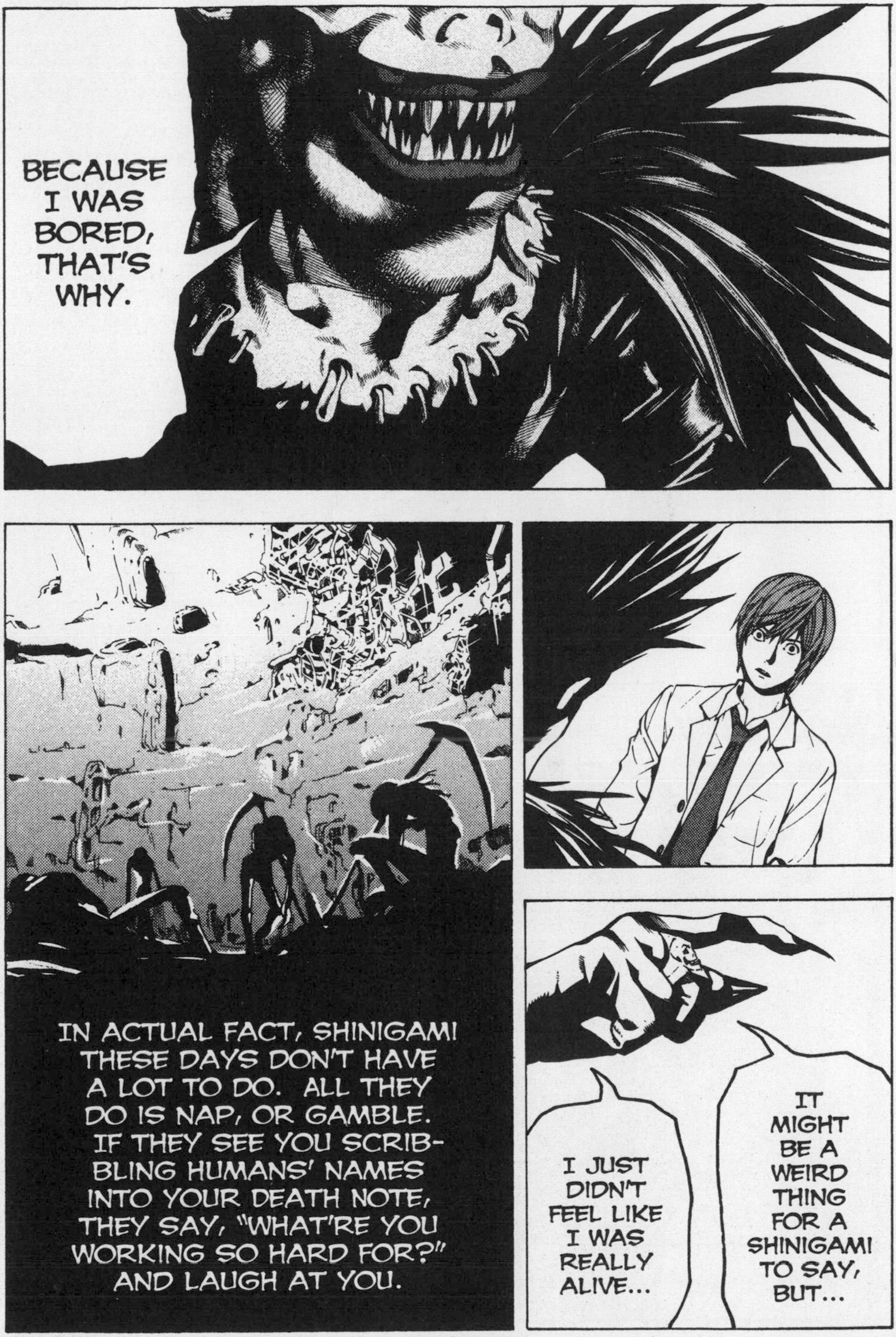
BECAUSE I WAS BORED, THAT'S WHY.
IT MIGHT BE A WEIRD THING FOR A SHINIGAMI TO SAY, BUT...
I JUST DIDN'T FEEL LIKE I WAS REALLY ALIVE...
IN ACTUAL FACT, SHINIGAMI THESE DAYS DON'T HAVE A LOT TO DO. ALL THEY DO IS NAP, OR GAMBLE. IF THEY SEE YOU SCRIB-BLING HUMANS' NAMES INTO YOUR DEATH NOTE, THEY SAY, "WHAT'RE YOU WORKING SO HARD FOR?" AND LAUGH AT YOU.

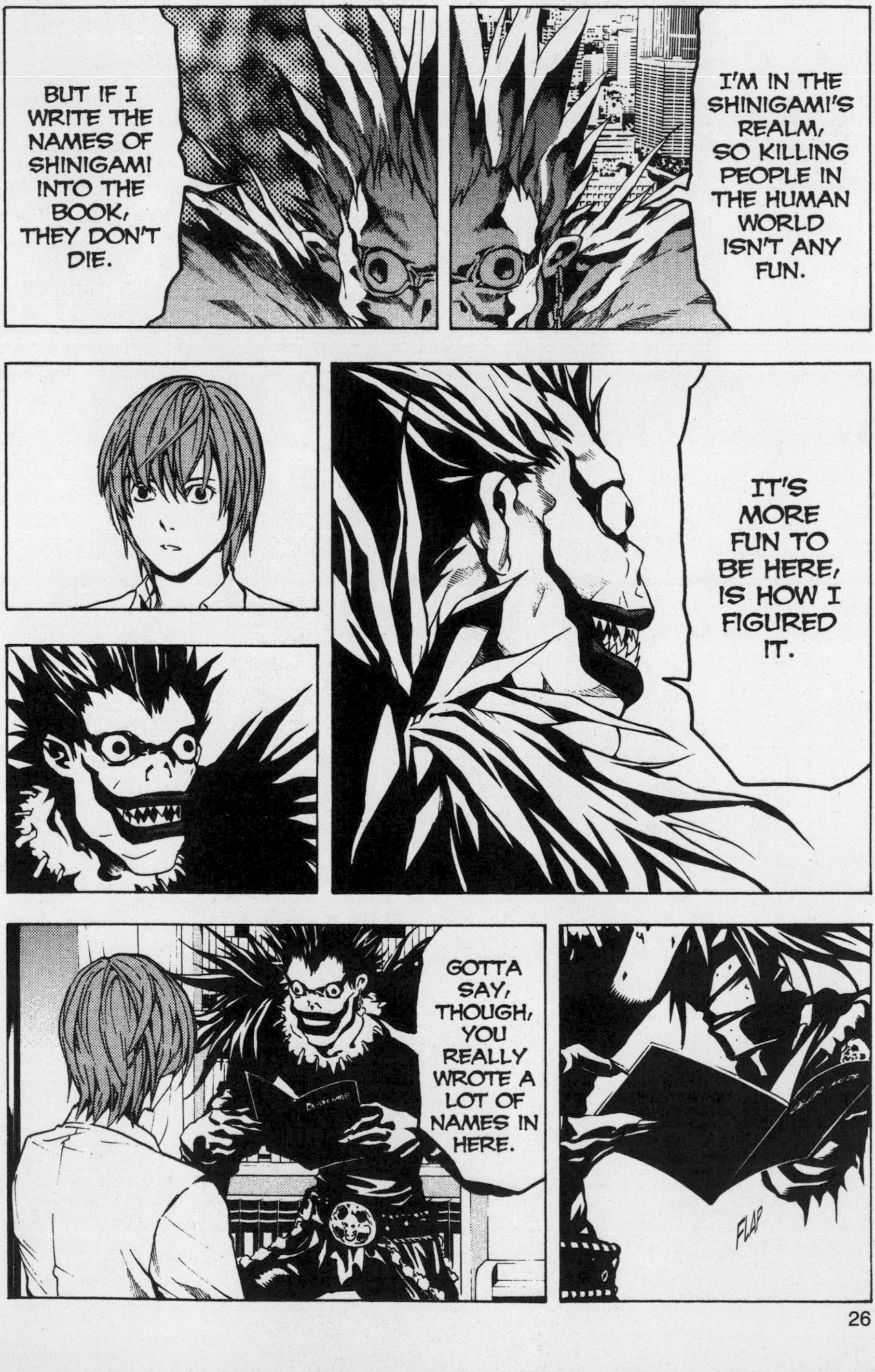
I'M IN THE SHINIGAMI'S REALM, SO KILLING PEOPLE IN THE HUMAN WORLD ISN'T ANY FUN.
BUT IF I WRITE THE NAMES OF SHINIGAMI INTO THE BOOK, THEY DON'T DIE.
IT'S MORE FUN TO BE HERE, IS HOW I FIGURED IT.
FLAP
GOTTA SAY, THOUGH, YOU REALLY WROTE A LOT OF NAMES IN HERE.

READ THIS WAY

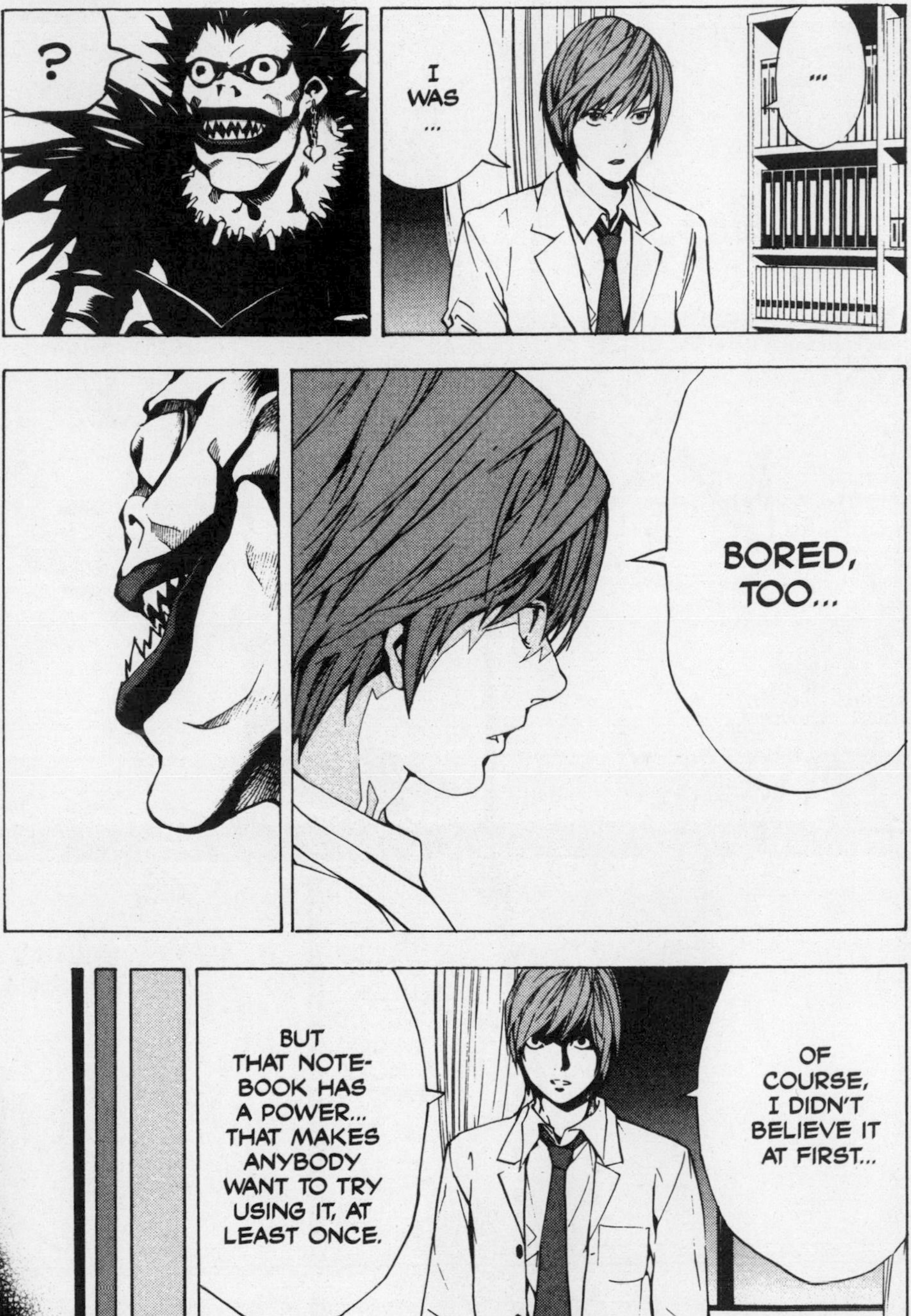
...
I WAS ...
?
BORED, TOO...
OF COURSE, I DIDN'T BELIEVE IT AT FIRST...
BUT THAT NOTE-BOOK HAS A POWER... THAT MAKES ANYBODY WANT TO TRY USING IT, AT LEAST ONCE.

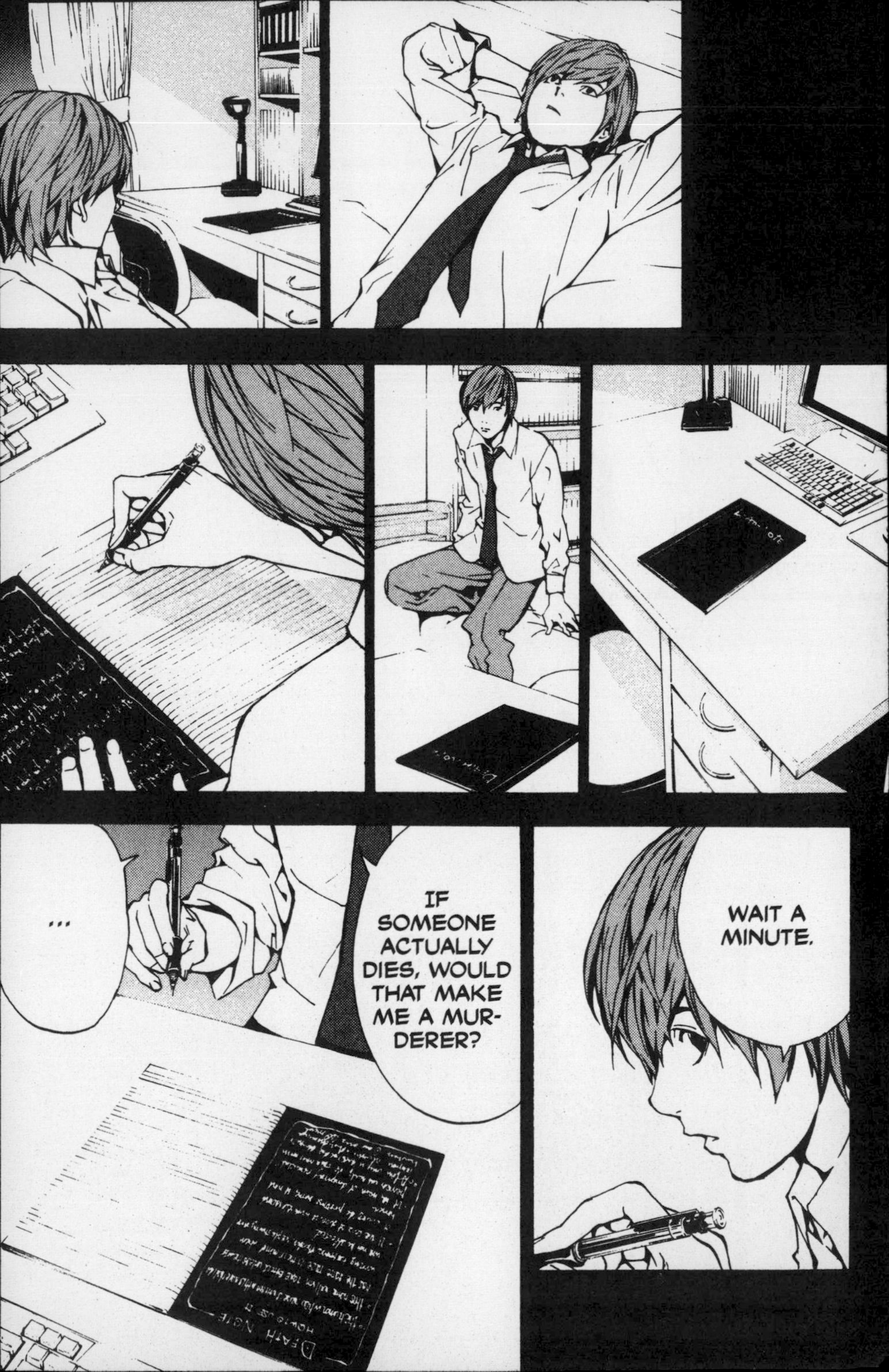
WAIT A MINUTE.
IF SOMEONE ACTUALLY DIES, WOULD THAT MAKE ME A MURDERER?
...

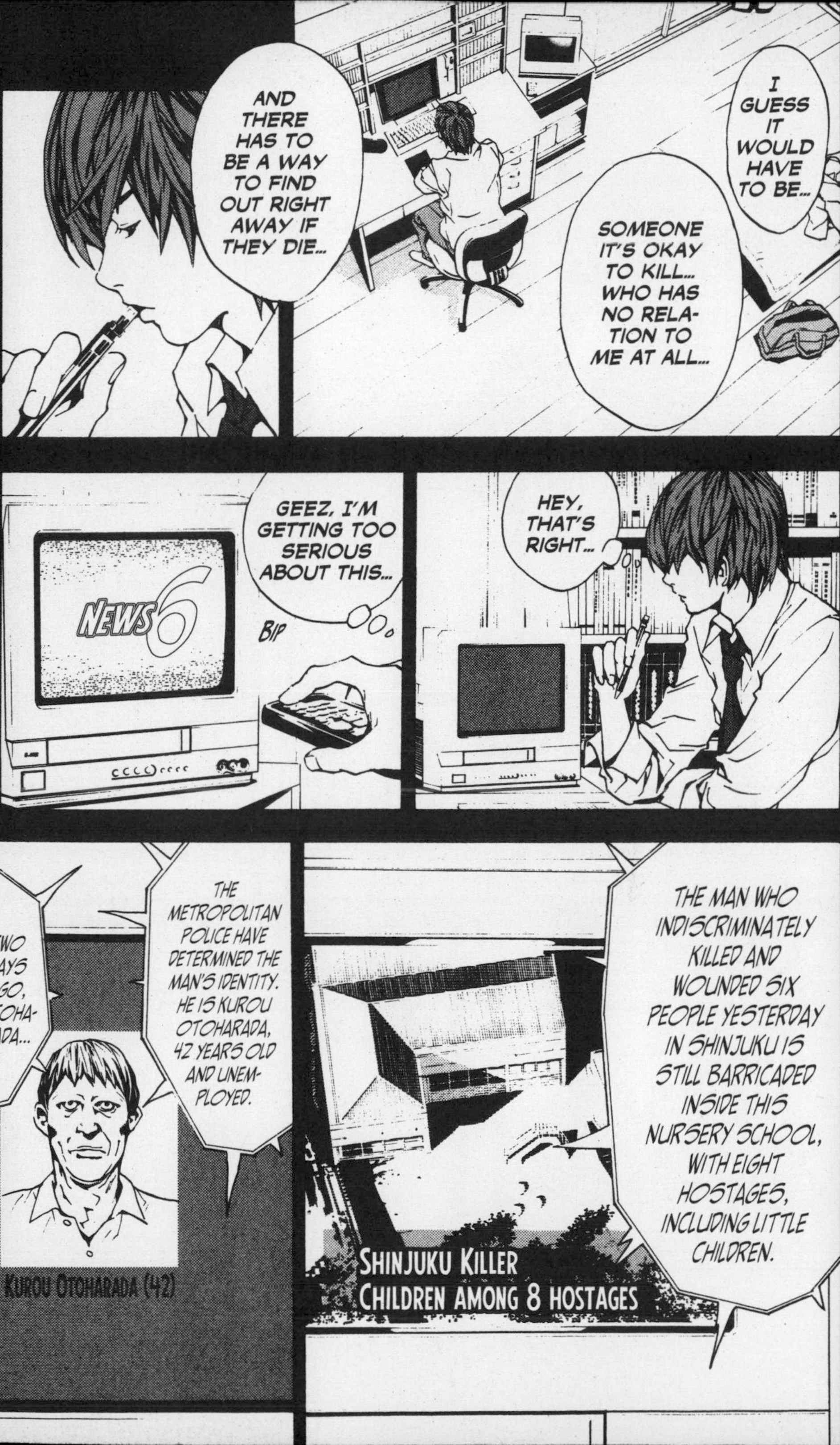
I GUESS IT WOULD HAVE TO BE...
SOMEONE IT'S OKAY TO KILL... WHO HAS NO RELATION TO ME AT ALL...
AND THERE HAS TO BE A WAY TO FIND OUT RIGHT AWAY IF THEY DIE...
HEY, THAT'S RIGHT...
GEEZ, I'M GETTING TOO SERIOUS ABOUT THIS...
BIP
NEWS 6
THE MAN WHO INDISCRIMINATELY KILLED AND WOUNDED SIX PEOPLE YESTERDAY IN SHINJUKU IS STILL BARRICADED INSIDE THIS NURSERY SCHOOL, WITH EIGHT HOSTAGES, INCLUDING LITTLE CHILDREN.
SHINJUKU KILLER
CHILDREN AMONG 8 HOSTAGES
THE METROPOLITAN POLICE HAVE DETERMINED THE MAN'S IDENTITY. HE IS KUROU OTOHARADA, 42 YEARS OLD AND UNEMPLOYED.
TWO DAYS AGO, OTOHARADA...
KUROU OTOHARADA (42)

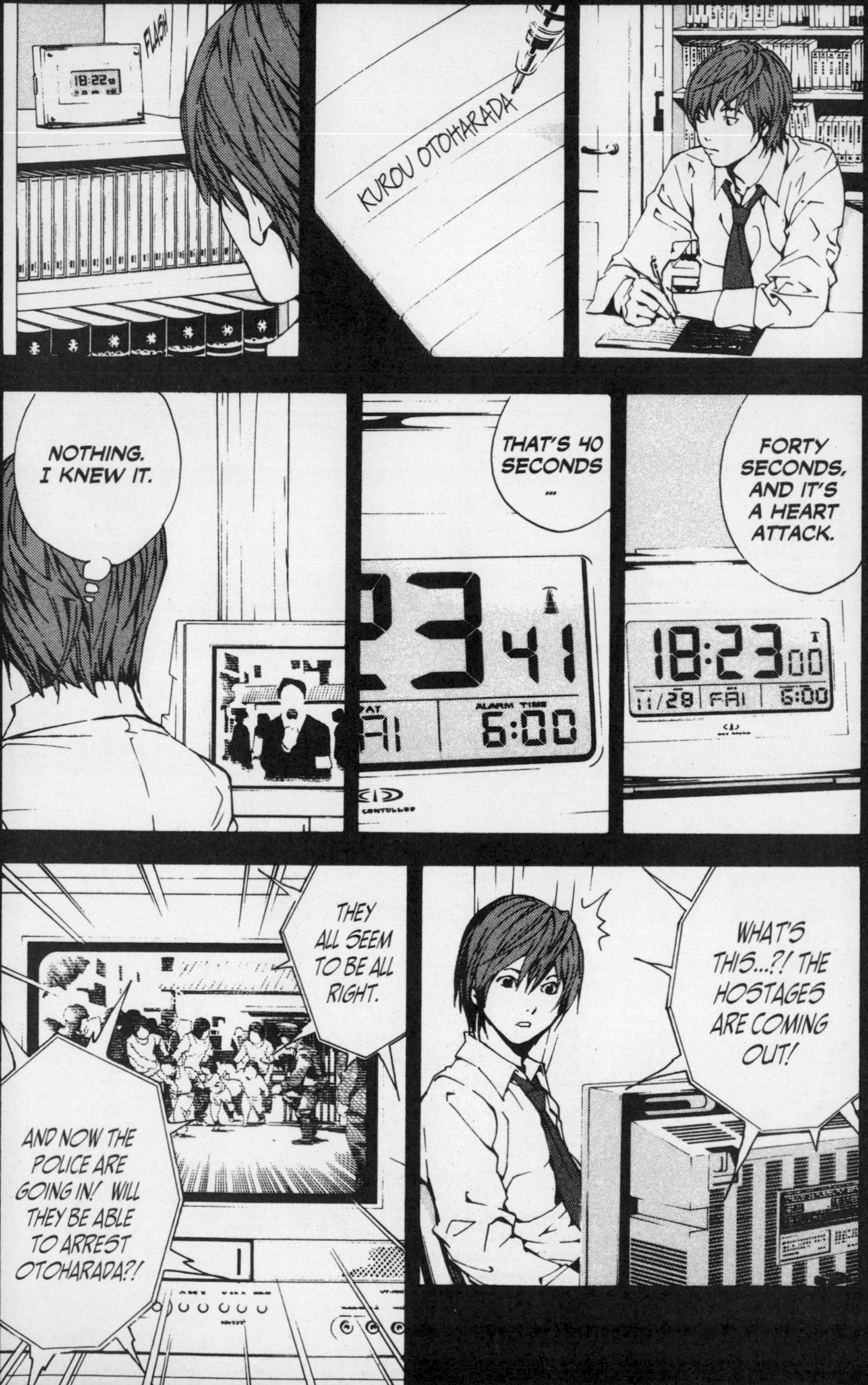
KUROU OTOHARADA
FLASH
18:22
FORTY SECONDS, AND IT'S A HEART ATTACK.
18:23 00
6:00
THAT'S 40 SECONDS ...
6:00
NOTHING. I KNEW IT.
WHAT'S THIS...?! THE HOSTAGES ARE COMING OUT!
THEY ALL SEEM TO BE ALL RIGHT.
AND NOW THE POLICE ARE GOING IN! WILL THEY BE ABLE TO ARREST OTOHARADA?!

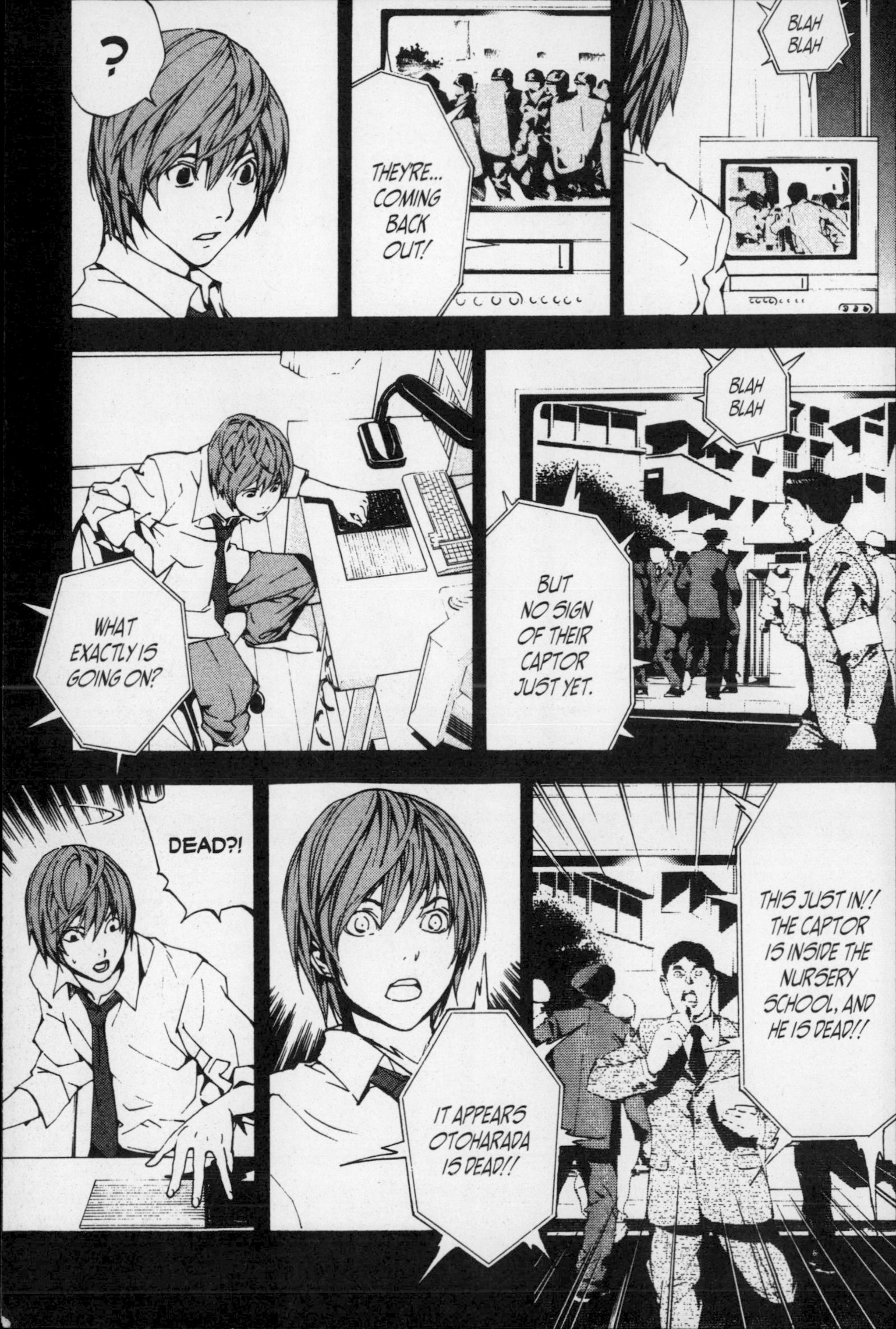
BLAH BLAH
THEY'RE... COMING BACK OUT!
?
BLAH BLAH
BUT NO SIGN OF THEIR CAPTOR JUST YET.
WHAT EXACTLY IS GOING ON?
THIS JUST IN!! THE CAPTOR IS INSIDE THE NURSERY SCHOOL, AND HE IS DEAD!!
IT APPEARS OTOHARADA IS DEAD!!
DEAD?!

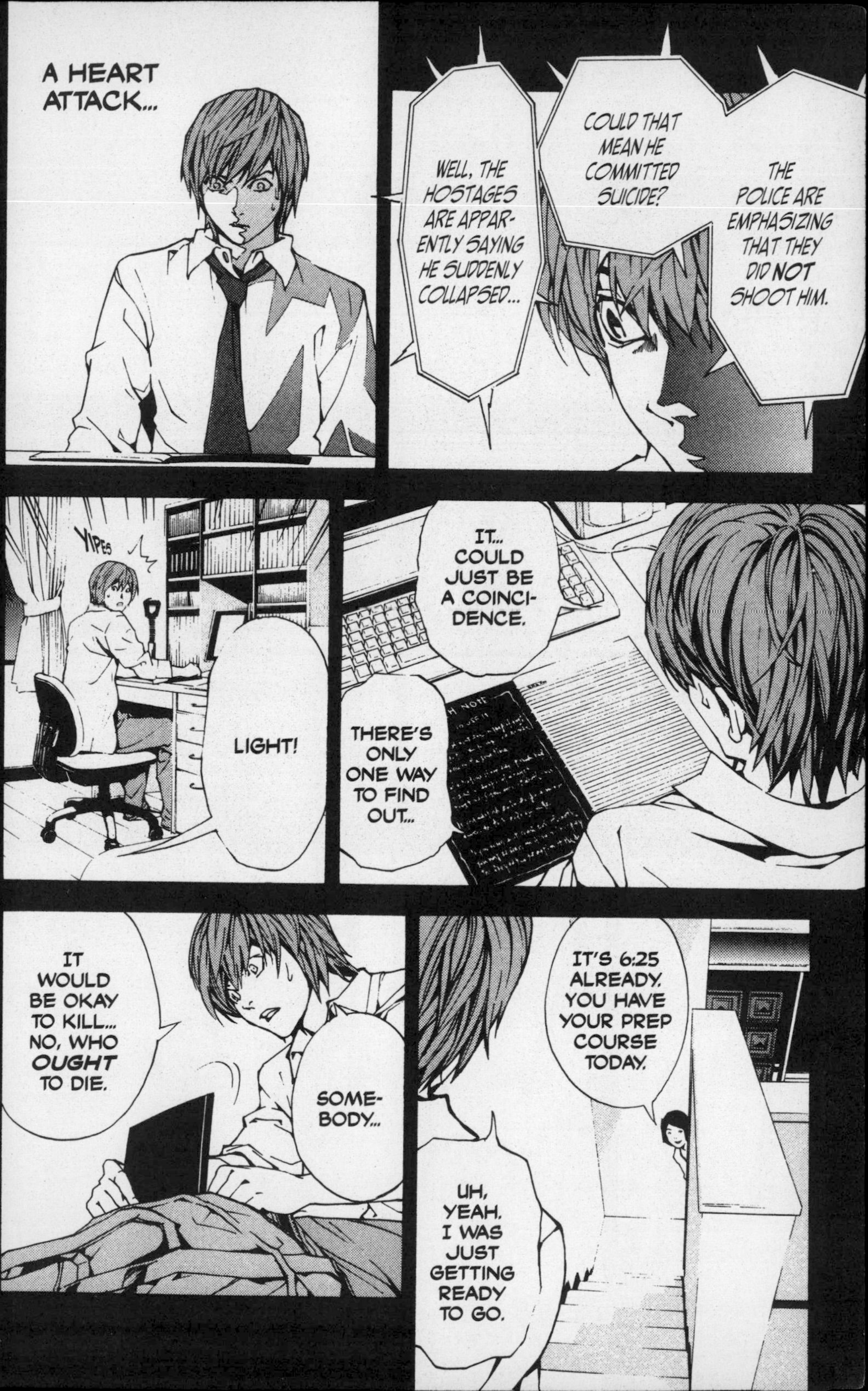
THE POLICE ARE EMPHASIZING THAT THEY DID NOT SHOOT HIM.
COULD THAT MEAN HE COMMITTED SUICIDE?
WELL, THE HOSTAGES ARE APPARENTLY SAYING HE SUDDENLY COLLAPSED...
A HEART ATTACK...
IT... COULD JUST BE A COINCIDENCE.
THERE'S ONLY ONE WAY TO FIND OUT...
LIGHT!
YIPES
IT'S 6:25 ALREADY. YOU HAVE YOUR PREP COURSE TODAY.
UH, YEAH. I WAS JUST GETTING READY TO GO.
SOME-BODY...
IT WOULD BE OKAY TO KILL... NO, WHO OUGHT TO DIE.

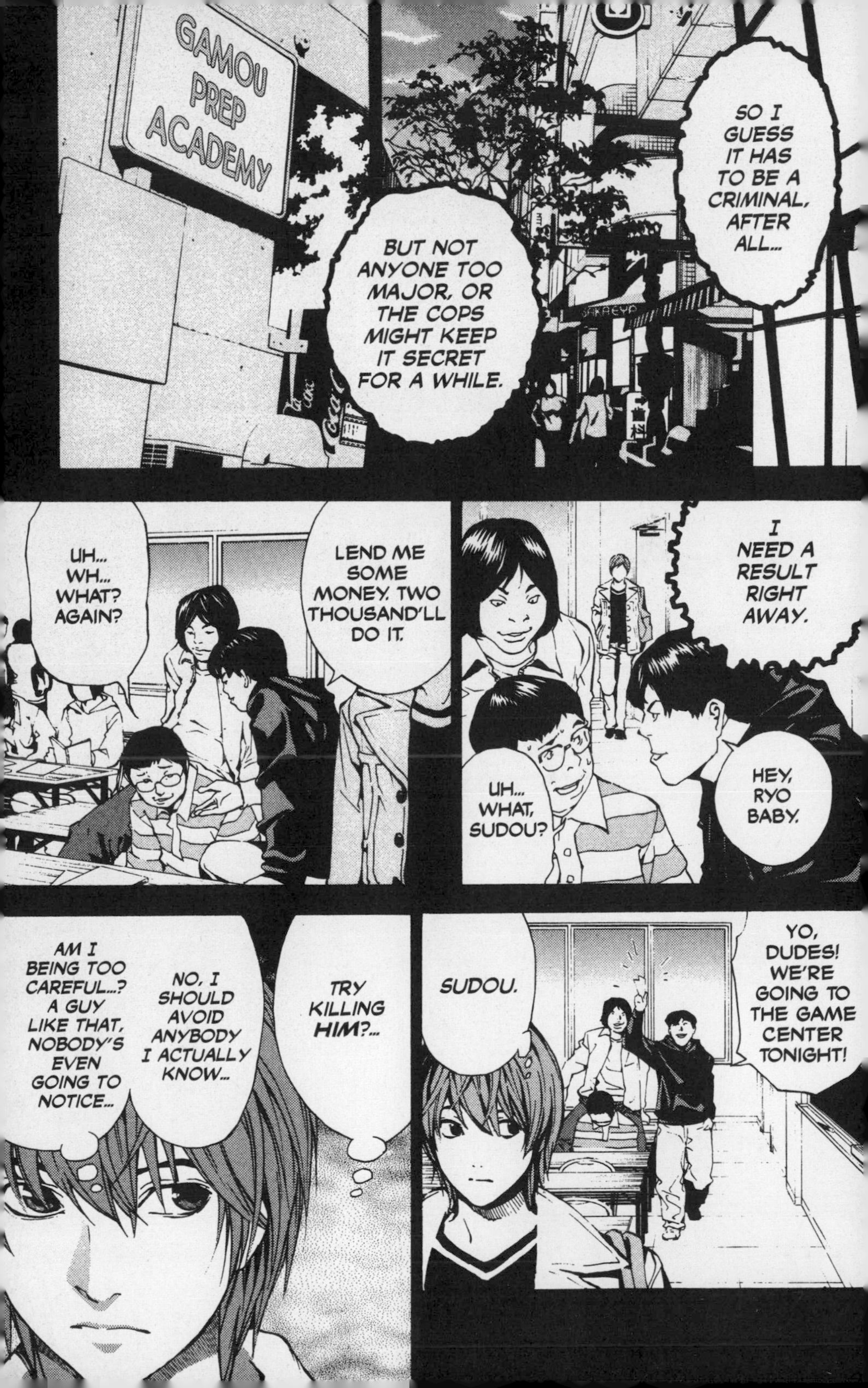
SO I GUESS IT HAS TO BE A CRIMINAL, AFTER ALL...
BUT NOT ANYONE TOO MAJOR, OR THE COPS MIGHT KEEP IT SECRET FOR A WHILE.
GAMOU PREP ACADEMY
I NEED A RESULT RIGHT AWAY.
HEY, RYO BABY.
UH... WHAT, SUDOU?
LEND ME SOME MONEY. TWO THOUSAND'LL DO IT.
UH... WH... WHAT? AGAIN?
YO, DUDES! WE'RE GOING TO THE GAME CENTER TONIGHT!
SUDOU.
TRY KILLING **HIM**?...
NO, I SHOULD AVOID ANYBODY I ACTUALLY KNOW...
AM I BEING TOO CAREFUL...? A GUY LIKE THAT, NOBODY'S EVEN GOING TO NOTICE...

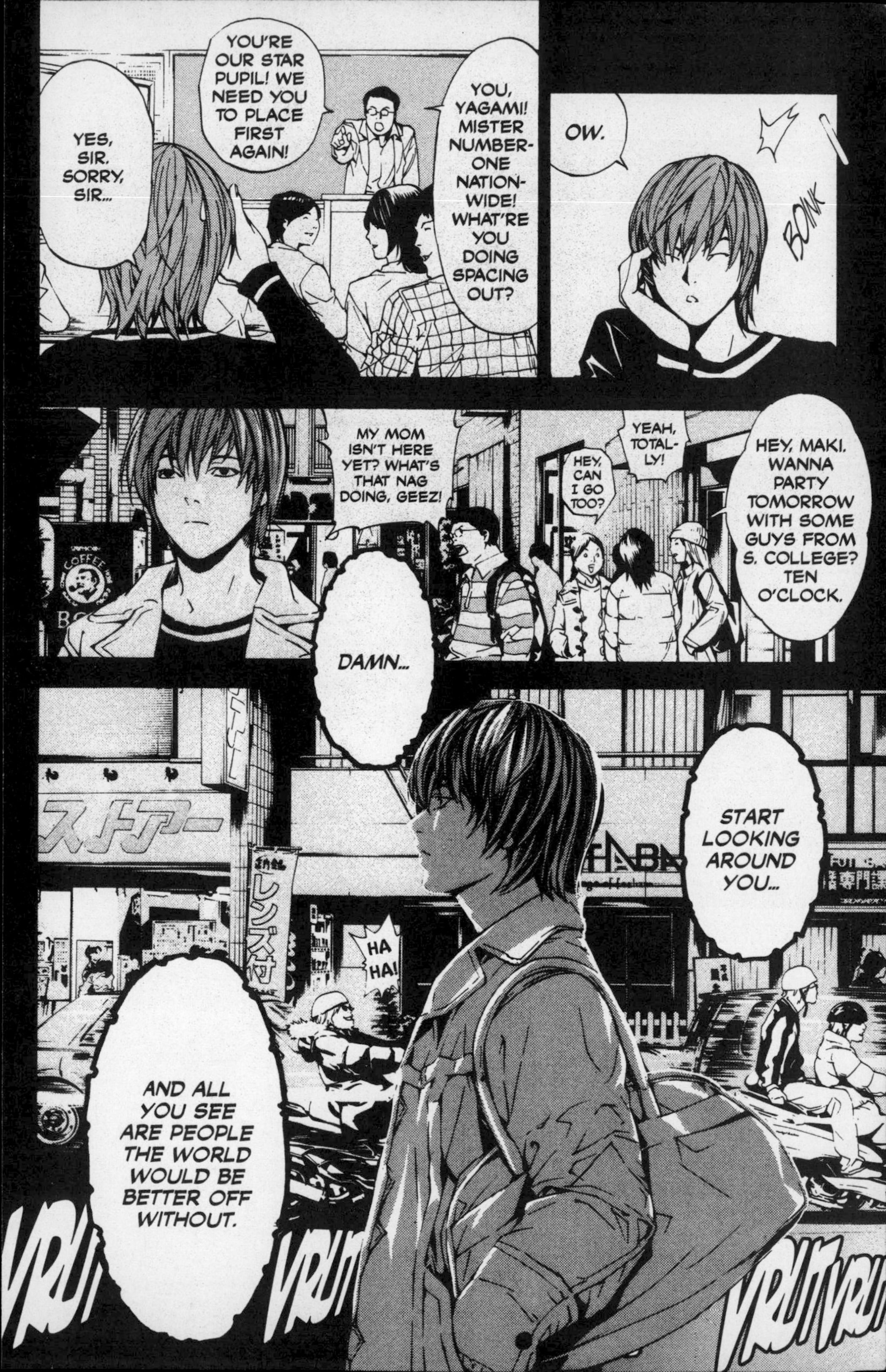
OW.
BOINK
YOU, YAGAMI! MISTER NUMBER-ONE NATION-WIDE! WHAT'RE YOU DOING SPACING OUT?
YOU'RE OUR STAR PUPIL! WE NEED YOU TO PLACE FIRST AGAIN!
YES, SIR. SORRY, SIR...
HEY, MAKI. WANNA PARTY TOMORROW WITH SOME GUYS FROM S. COLLEGE? TEN O'CLOCK.
YEAH, TOTAL-LY!
HEY, CAN I GO TOO?
MY MOM ISN'T HERE YET? WHAT'S THAT NAG DOING, GEEZ!
DAMN...
START LOOKING AROUND YOU...
HA HA!
AND ALL YOU SEE ARE PEOPLE THE WORLD WOULD BE BETTER OFF WITHOUT.

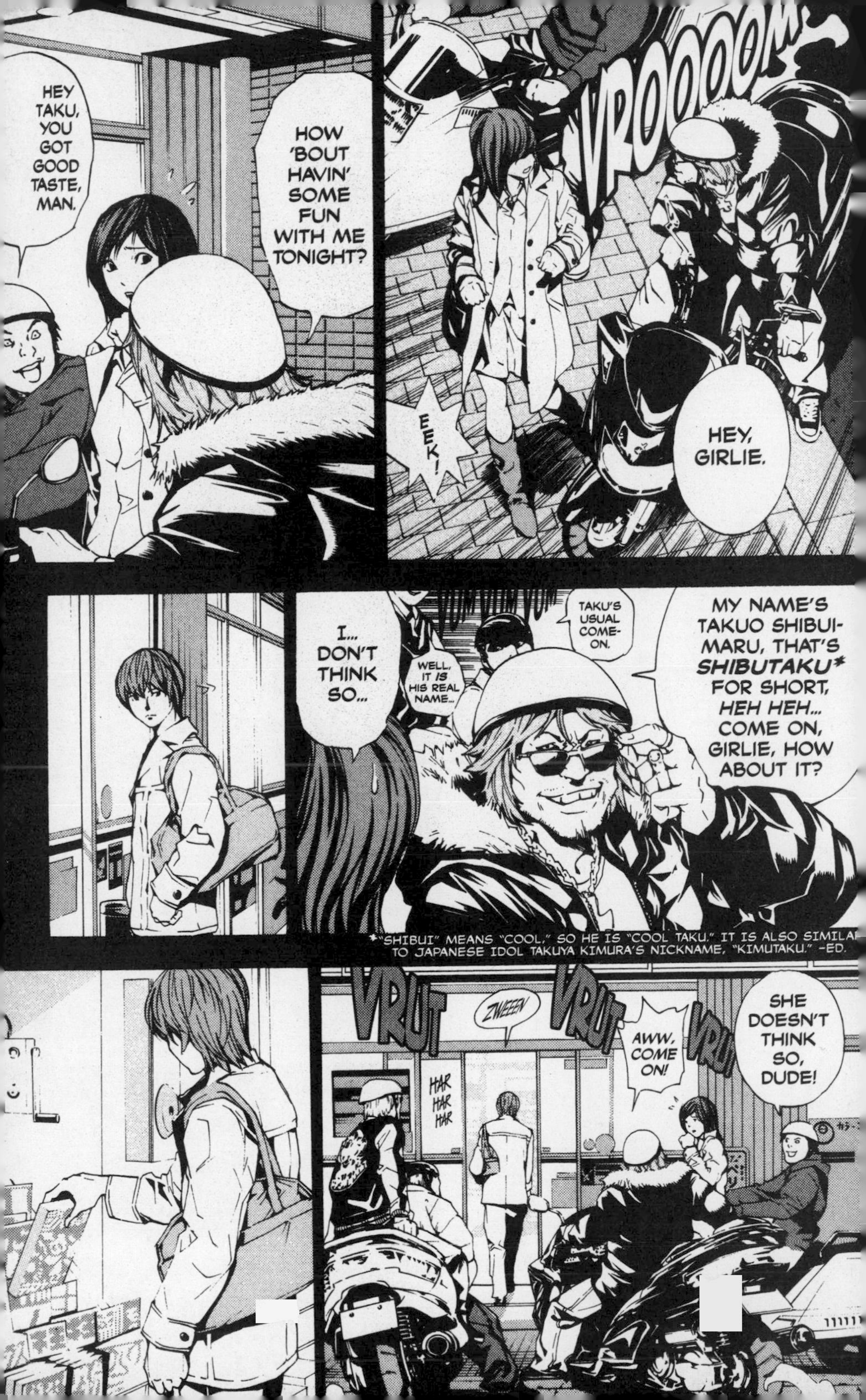
VROOOOM
HEY, GIRLIE.
EEK!
HOW 'BOUT HAVIN' SOME FUN WITH ME TONIGHT?
HEY TAKU, YOU GOT GOOD TASTE, MAN.
MY NAME'S TAKUO SHIBUI-MARU, THAT'S *SHIBUTAKU** FOR SHORT, *HEH HEH...* COME ON, GIRLIE, HOW ABOUT IT?
TAKU'S USUAL COME-ON.
VOM VOM VOM
WELL, IT *IS* HIS REAL NAME...
I... DON'T THINK SO...
SHE DOESN'T THINK SO, DUDE!
VRUT
AWW, COME ON!
VRUT
ZWEEEN
VRUT
HAR HAR HAR

*"SHIBUI" MEANS "COOL," SO HE IS "COOL TAKU." IT IS ALSO SIMILAR TO JAPANESE IDOL TAKUYA KIMURA'S NICKNAME, "KIMUTAKU." -ED.

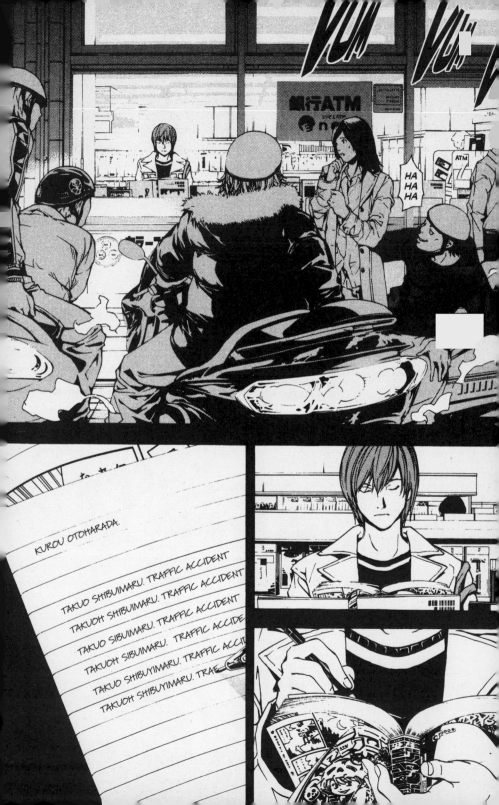

KUROU OTOHARADA.

TAKUO SHIBUIMARU. TRAFFIC ACCIDENT

TAKUOH SHIBUIMARU. TRAFFIC ACCIDENT

TAKUO SIBUIMARU. TRAFFIC ACCIDENT

TAKUOH SIBUIMARU. TRAFFIC ACCIDE

TAKUO SHIBUYIMARU. TRAFFIC ACCI

TAKUOH SHIBUYIMARU. TRAF

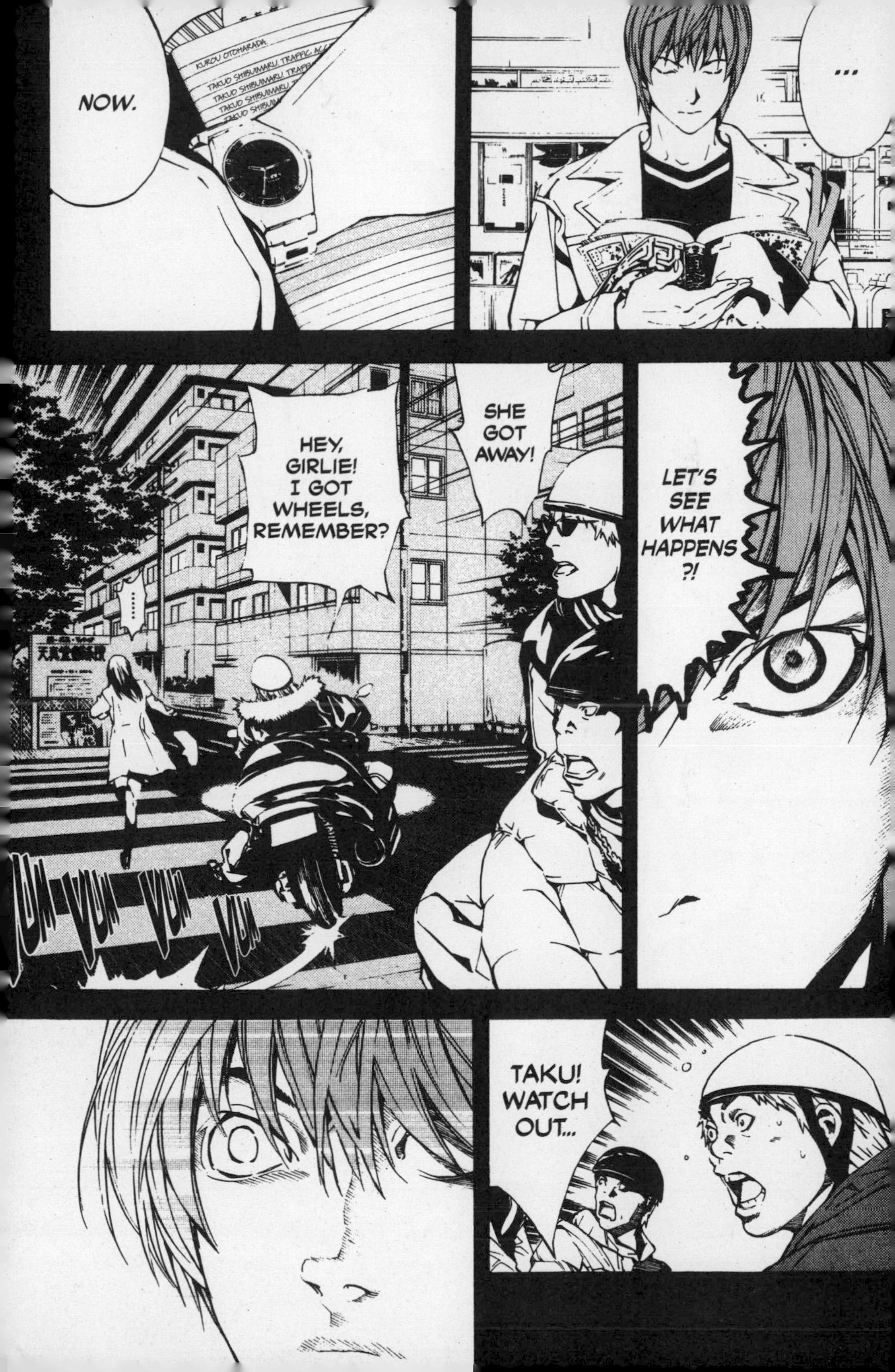
...
NOW.
KUROU OTOHARADA
LET'S SEE WHAT HAPPENS?!
SHE GOT AWAY!
HEY, GIRLIE! I GOT WHEELS, REMEMBER?
TAKU! WATCH OUT...

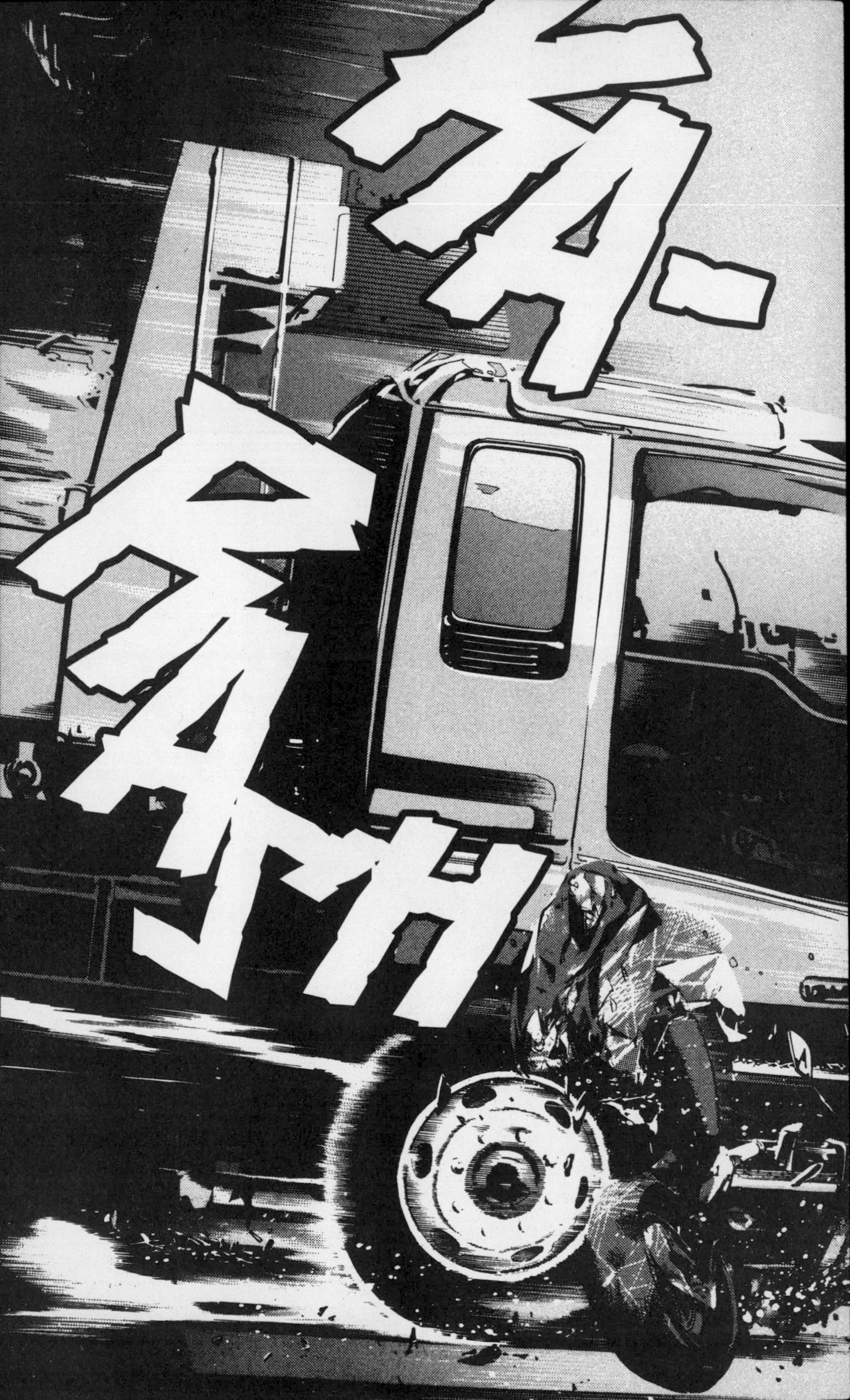

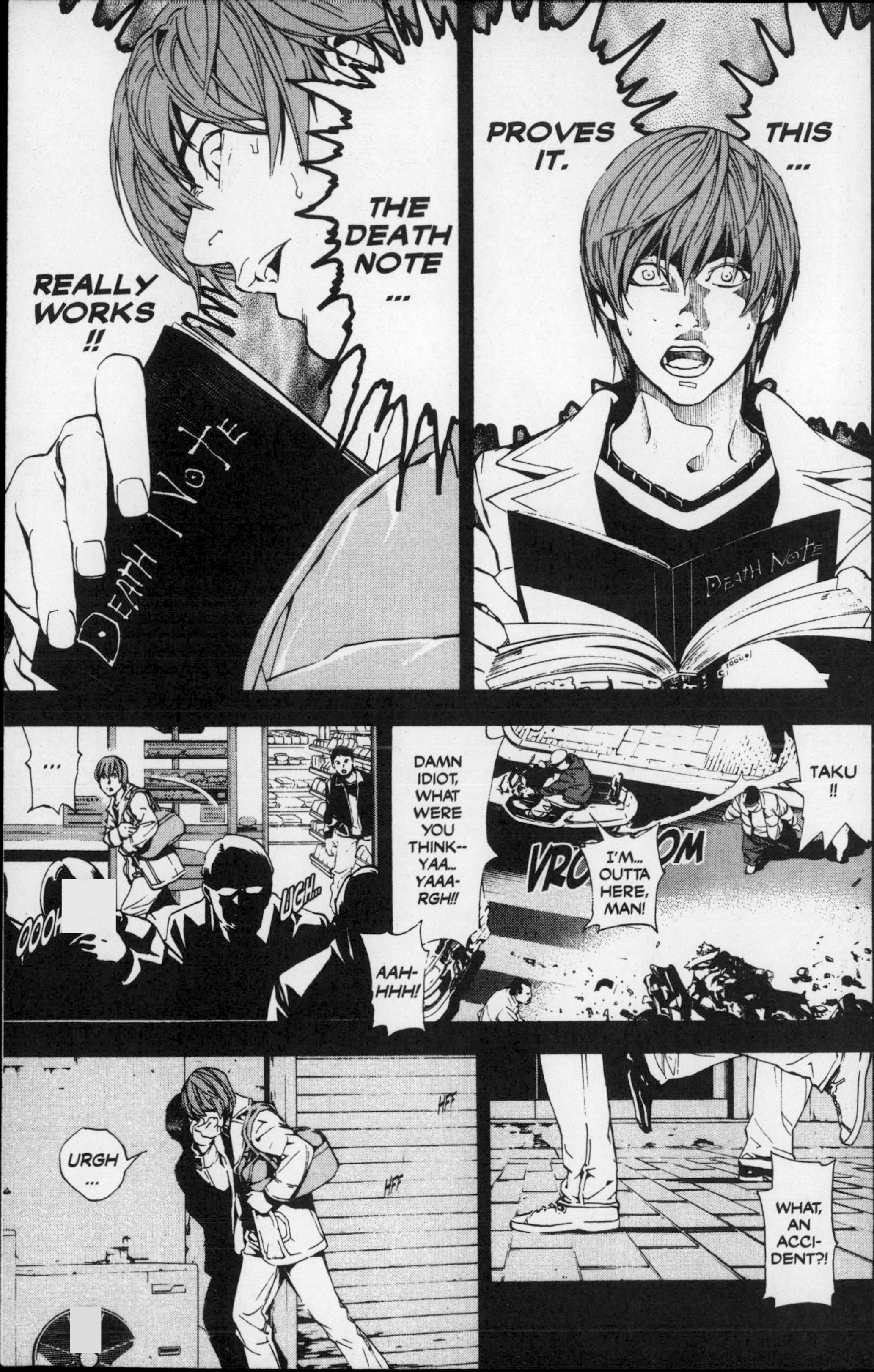
THIS ...
PROVES IT.
THE DEATH NOTE ...
REALLY WORKS !!
TAKU !!
I'M... OUTTA HERE, MAN!
DAMN IDIOT, WHAT WERE YOU THINK-- YAA... YAAA-RGH!!
AAH-HHH!
...
UGH...
OOOH
WHAT, AN ACCI-DENT?!
HFF
URGH ...
HFF

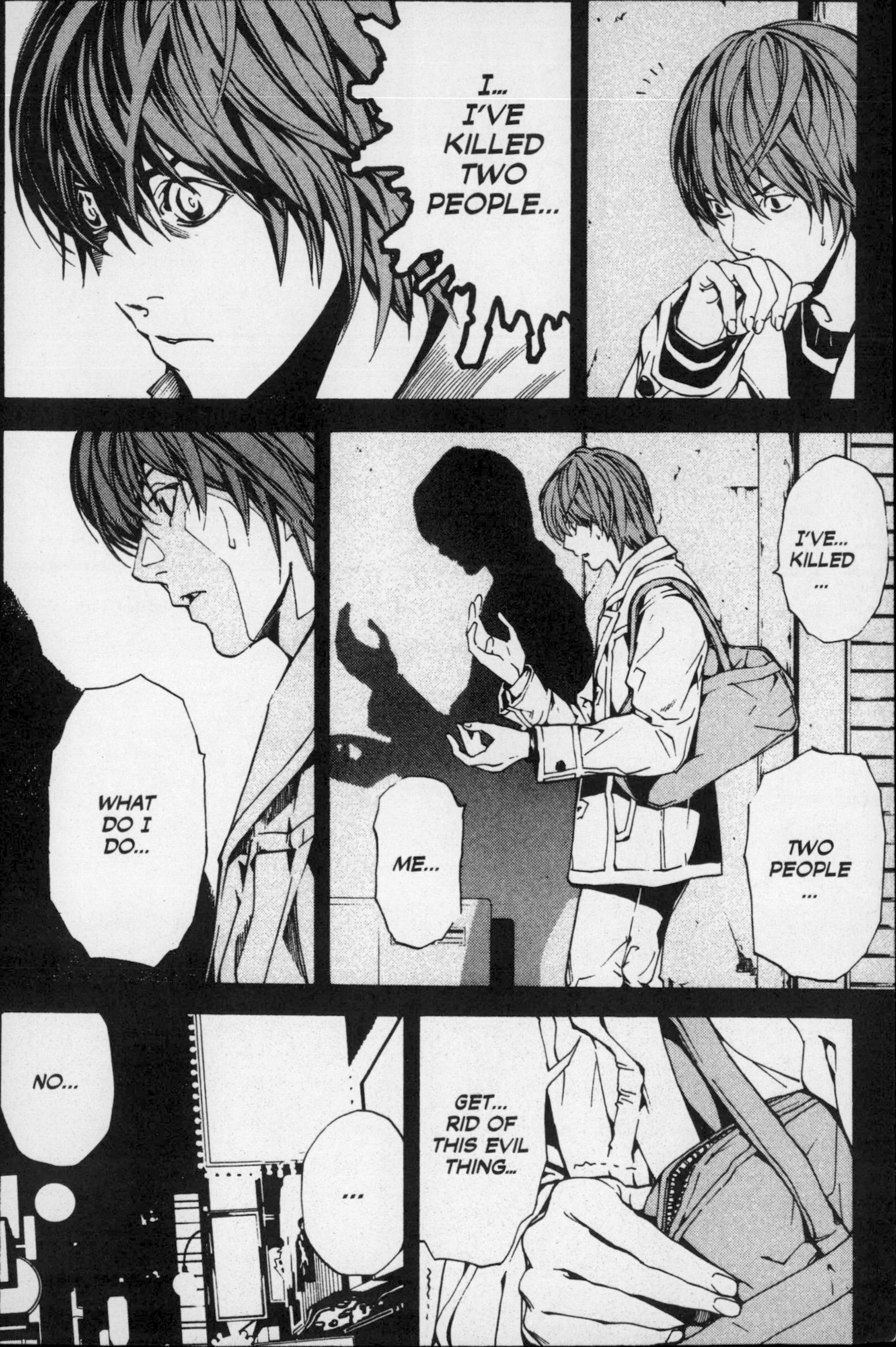
I... I'VE KILLED TWO PEOPLE...
I'VE... KILLED ...
TWO PEOPLE ...
ME...
WHAT DO I DO...
GET... RID OF THIS EVIL THING...
NO...
...

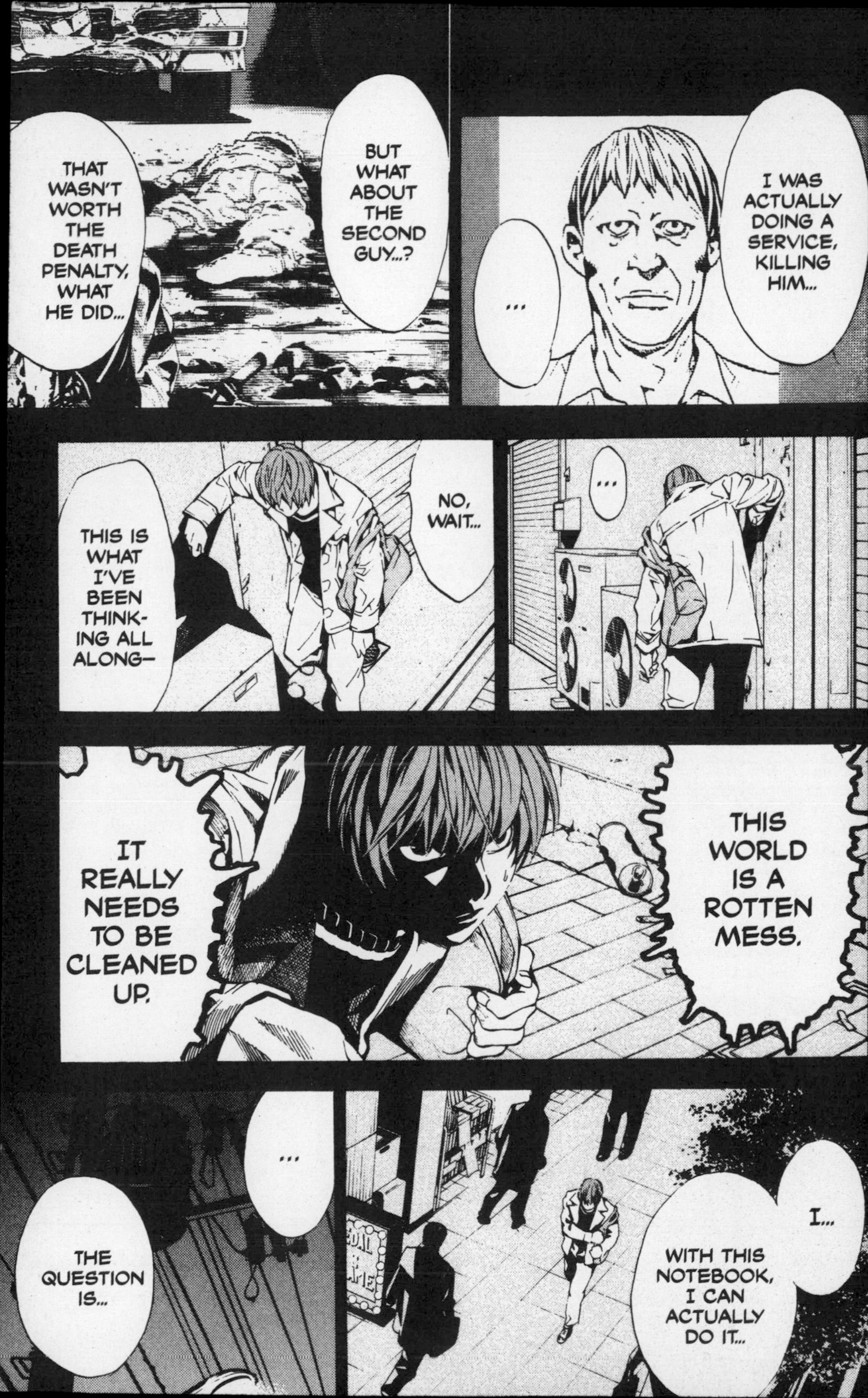
I WAS ACTUALLY DOING A SERVICE, KILLING HIM...
...
BUT WHAT ABOUT THE SECOND GUY...?
THAT WASN'T WORTH THE DEATH PENALTY, WHAT HE DID...
...
NO, WAIT...
THIS IS WHAT I'VE BEEN THINKING ALL ALONG—
THIS WORLD IS A ROTTEN MESS.
IT REALLY NEEDS TO BE CLEANED UP.
I...
WITH THIS NOTEBOOK, I CAN ACTUALLY DO IT...
...
THE QUESTION IS...

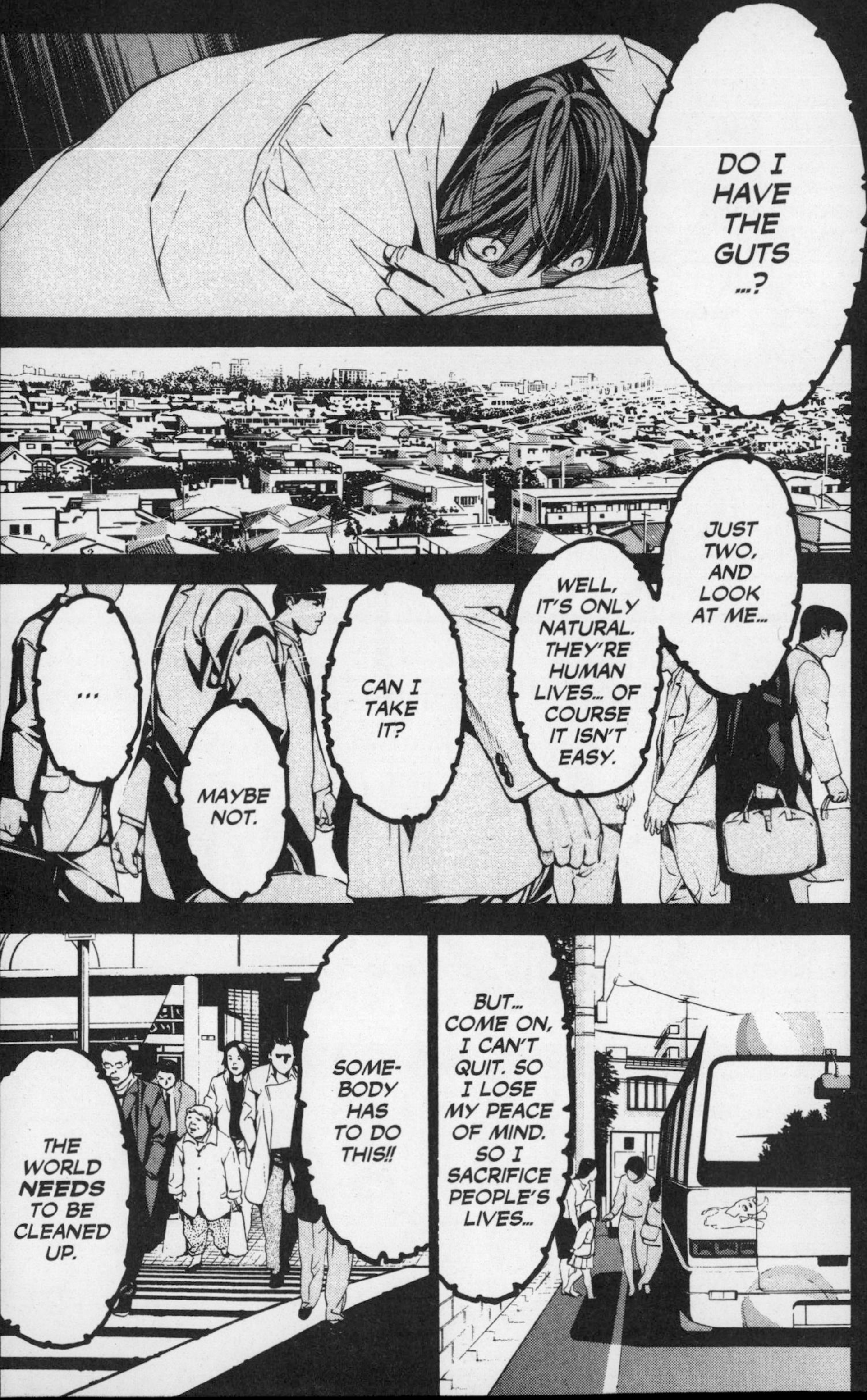
DO I HAVE THE GUTS ...?
JUST TWO, AND LOOK AT ME...
WELL, IT'S ONLY NATURAL. THEY'RE HUMAN LIVES... OF COURSE IT ISN'T EASY.
CAN I TAKE IT?
MAYBE NOT.
...
BUT... COME ON, I CAN'T QUIT. SO I LOSE MY PEACE OF MIND. SO I SACRIFICE PEOPLE'S LIVES...
SOME-BODY HAS TO DO THIS!!
THE WORLD **NEEDS** TO BE CLEANED UP.

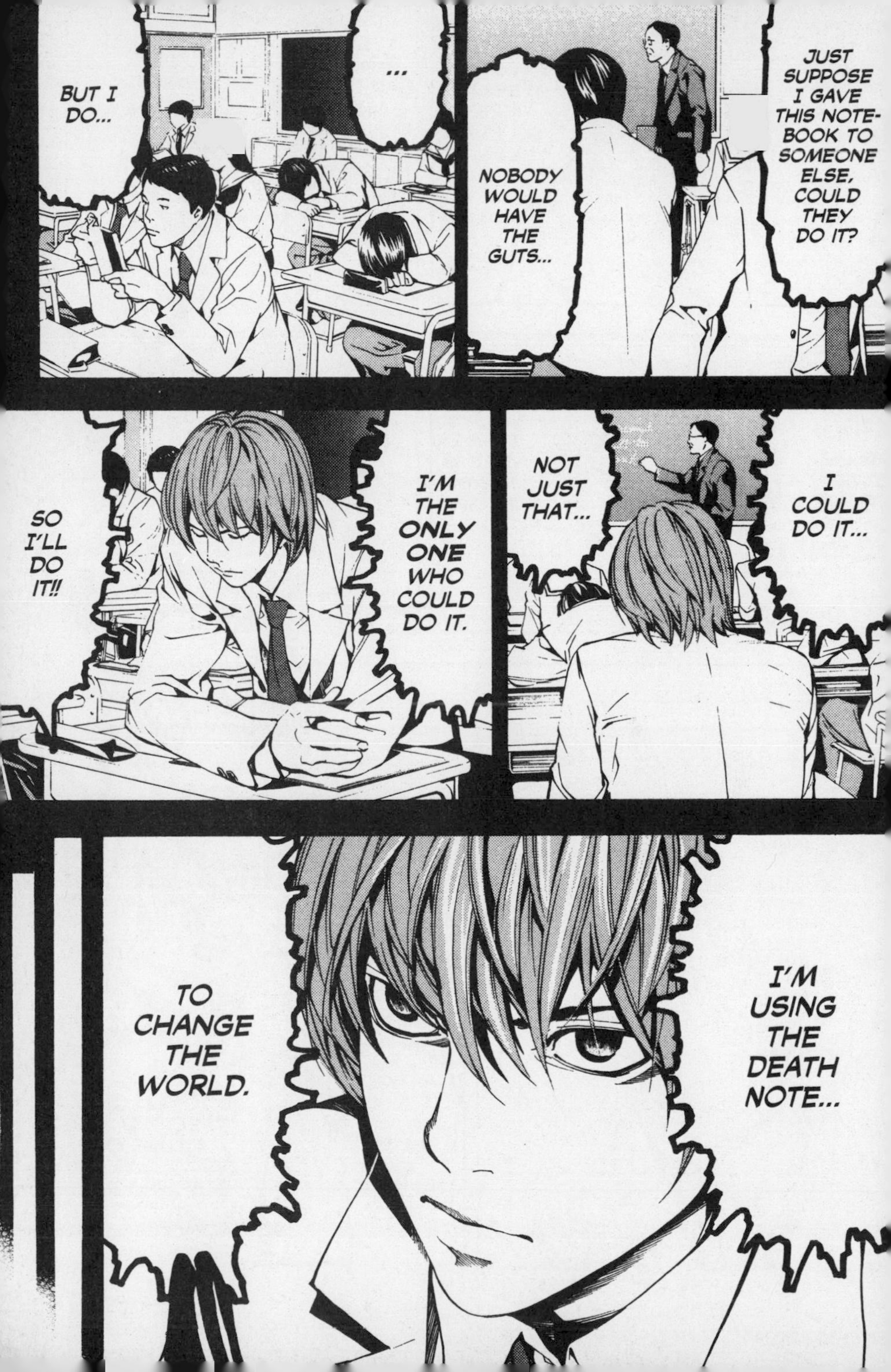
JUST SUPPOSE I GAVE THIS NOTE-BOOK TO SOMEONE ELSE, COULD THEY DO IT?
NOBODY WOULD HAVE THE GUTS...
...
BUT I DO...
I COULD DO IT...
NOT JUST THAT...
I'M THE ONLY ONE WHO COULD DO IT.
SO I'LL DO IT!!
I'M USING THE DEATH NOTE...
TO CHANGE THE WORLD.

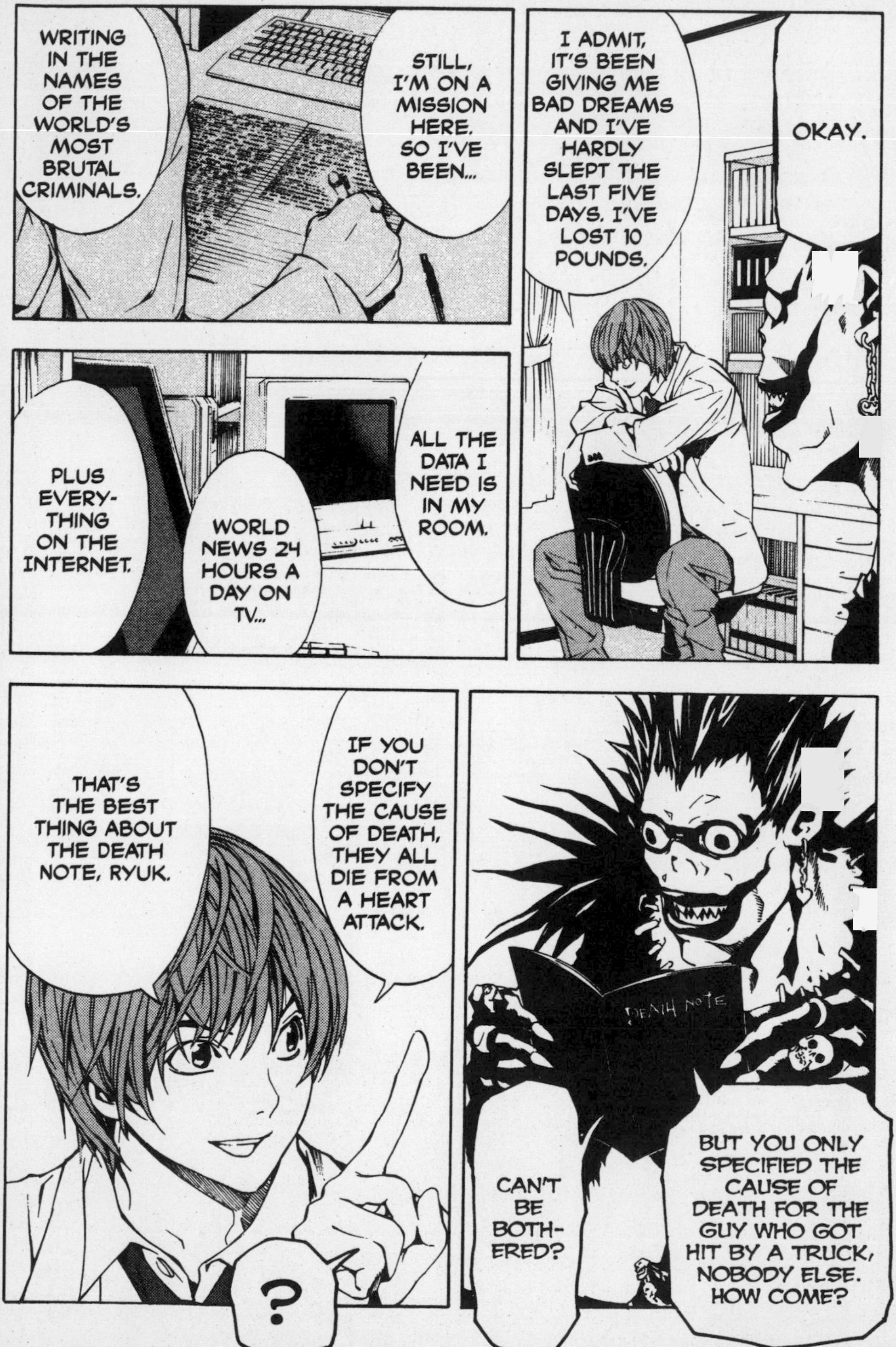
OKAY.
I ADMIT, IT'S BEEN GIVING ME BAD DREAMS AND I'VE HARDLY SLEPT THE LAST FIVE DAYS. I'VE LOST 10 POUNDS.
STILL, I'M ON A MISSION HERE. SO I'VE BEEN...
WRITING IN THE NAMES OF THE WORLD'S MOST BRUTAL CRIMINALS.
ALL THE DATA I NEED IS IN MY ROOM.
WORLD NEWS 24 HOURS A DAY ON TV...
PLUS EVERY-THING ON THE INTERNET.
DEATH NOTE
BUT YOU ONLY SPECIFIED THE CAUSE OF DEATH FOR THE GUY WHO GOT HIT BY A TRUCK, NOBODY ELSE. HOW COME?
CAN'T BE BOTH-ERED?
IF YOU DON'T SPECIFY THE CAUSE OF DEATH, THEY ALL DIE FROM A HEART ATTACK.
THAT'S THE BEST THING ABOUT THE DEATH NOTE, RYUK.
?

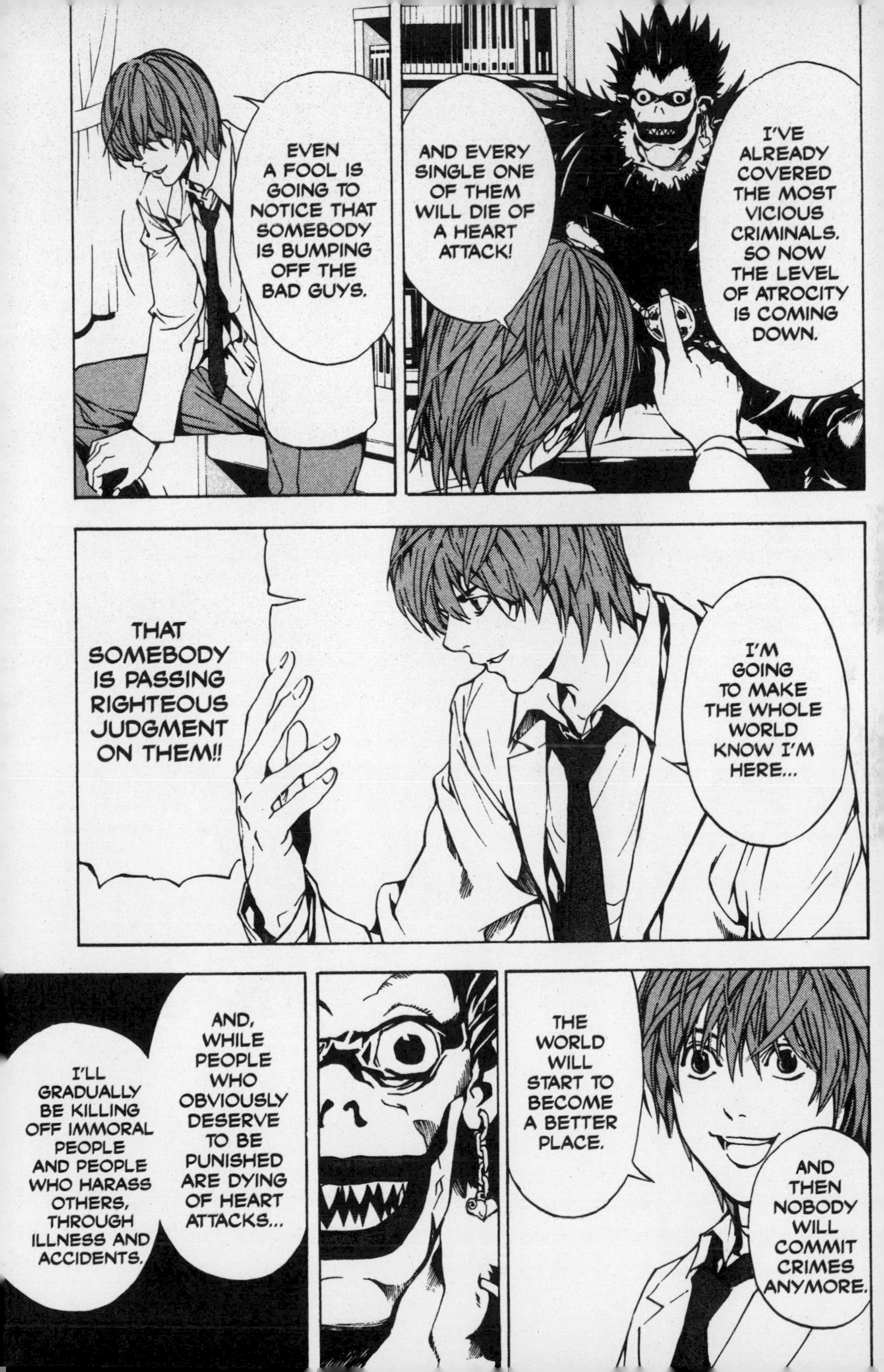
I'VE ALREADY COVERED THE MOST VICIOUS CRIMINALS. SO NOW THE LEVEL OF ATROCITY IS COMING DOWN.
AND EVERY SINGLE ONE OF THEM WILL DIE OF A HEART ATTACK!
EVEN A FOOL IS GOING TO NOTICE THAT SOMEBODY IS BUMPING OFF THE BAD GUYS.
I'M GOING TO MAKE THE WHOLE WORLD KNOW I'M HERE...
THAT SOMEBODY IS PASSING RIGHTEOUS JUDGMENT ON THEM!!
THE WORLD WILL START TO BECOME A BETTER PLACE.
AND THEN NOBODY WILL COMMIT CRIMES ANYMORE.
AND, WHILE PEOPLE WHO OBVIOUSLY DESERVE TO BE PUNISHED ARE DYING OF HEART ATTACKS...
I'LL GRADUALLY BE KILLING OFF IMMORAL PEOPLE AND PEOPLE WHO HARASS OTHERS, THROUGH ILLNESS AND ACCIDENTS.

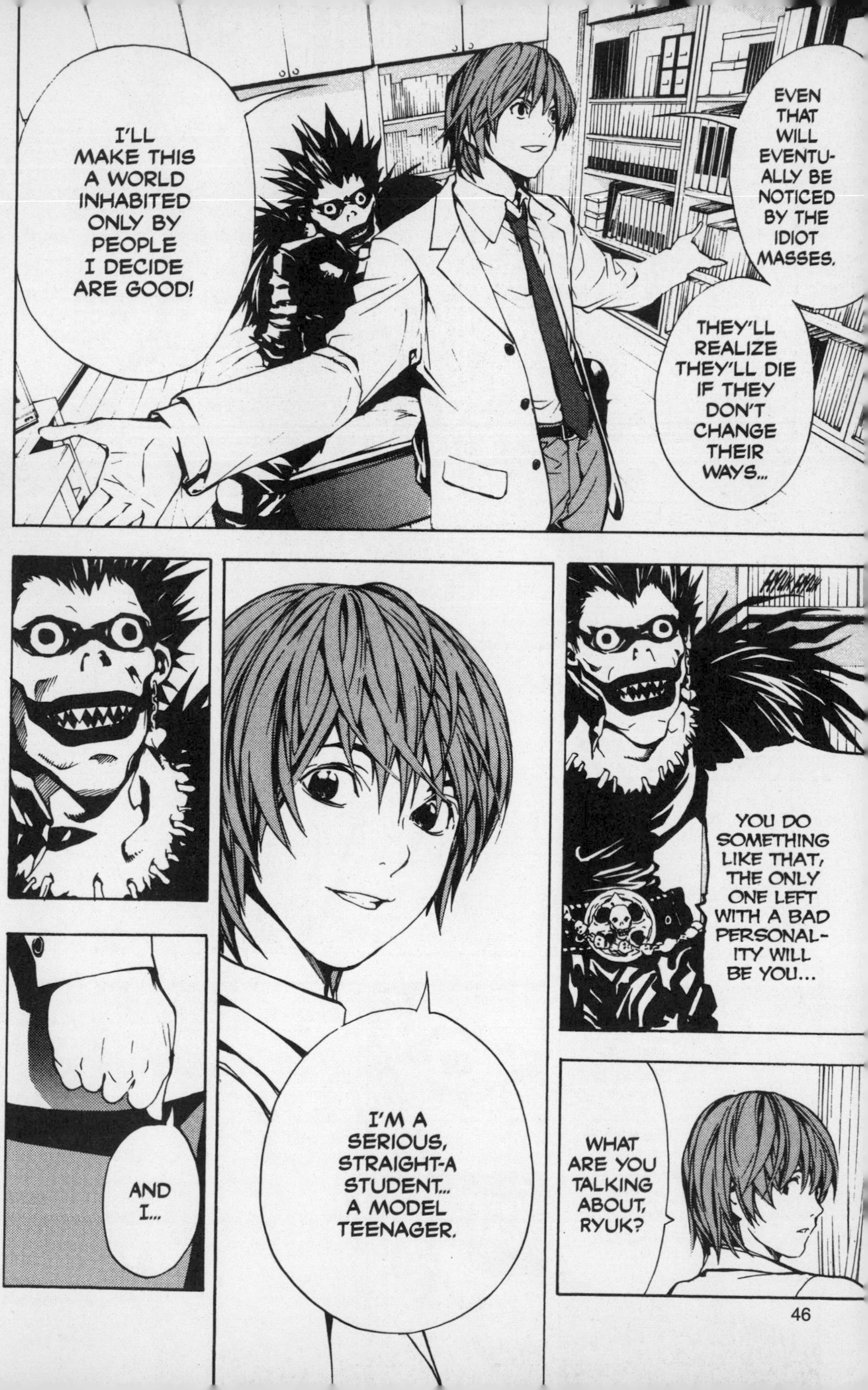
EVEN THAT WILL EVENTUALLY BE NOTICED BY THE IDIOT MASSES.
THEY'LL REALIZE THEY'LL DIE IF THEY DON'T CHANGE THEIR WAYS...
I'LL MAKE THIS A WORLD INHABITED ONLY BY PEOPLE I DECIDE ARE GOOD!
HYUK HYUK
YOU DO SOMETHING LIKE THAT, THE ONLY ONE LEFT WITH A BAD PERSONALITY WILL BE YOU...
WHAT ARE YOU TALKING ABOUT, RYUK?
AND I...
I'M A SERIOUS, STRAIGHT-A STUDENT... A MODEL TEENAGER.

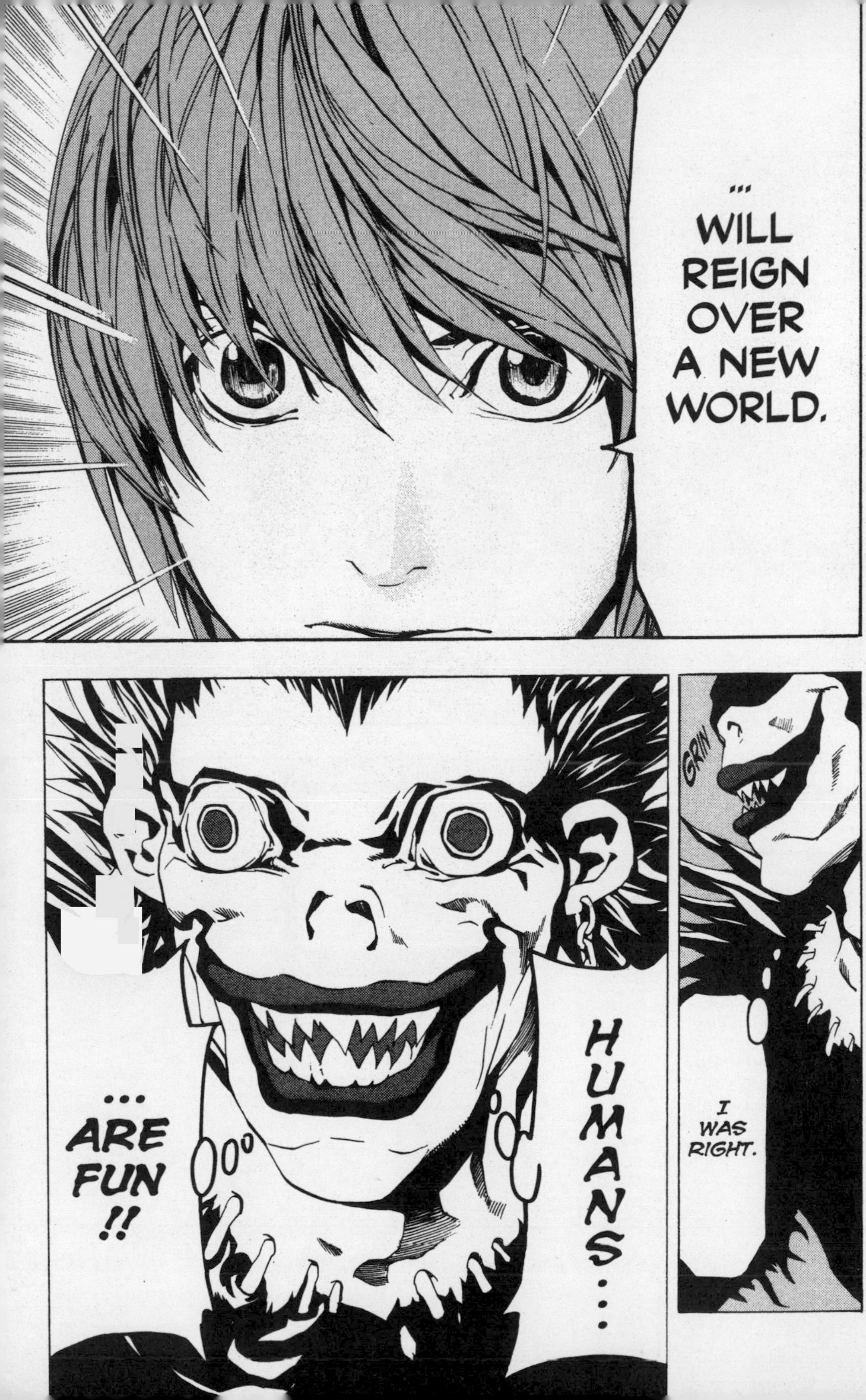
...
WILL REIGN OVER A NEW WORLD.
GRIN
I WAS RIGHT.
HUMANS...
... ARE FUN!!

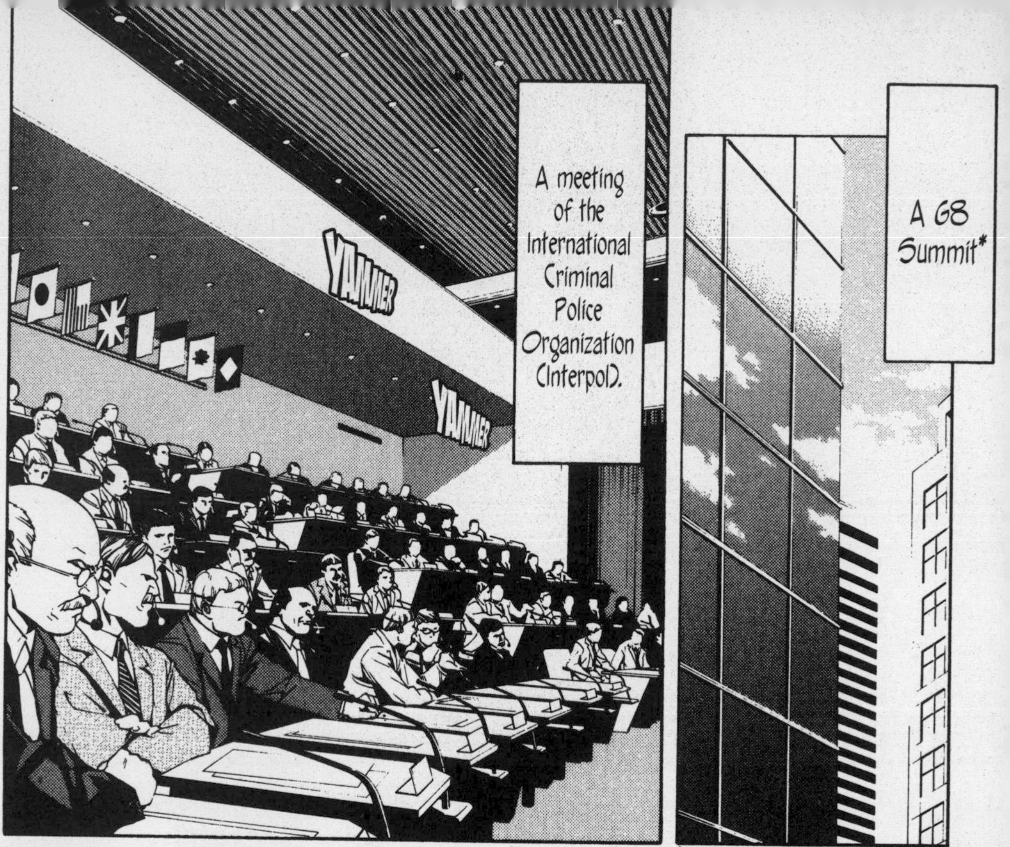
A G8 Summit*
A meeting of the International Criminal Police Organization (Interpol).
YAMMER
YAMMER

*G8 STANDS FOR GROUP OF EIGHT, WHICH IS MADE UP OF THE WORLD'S LEADING NATIONS.

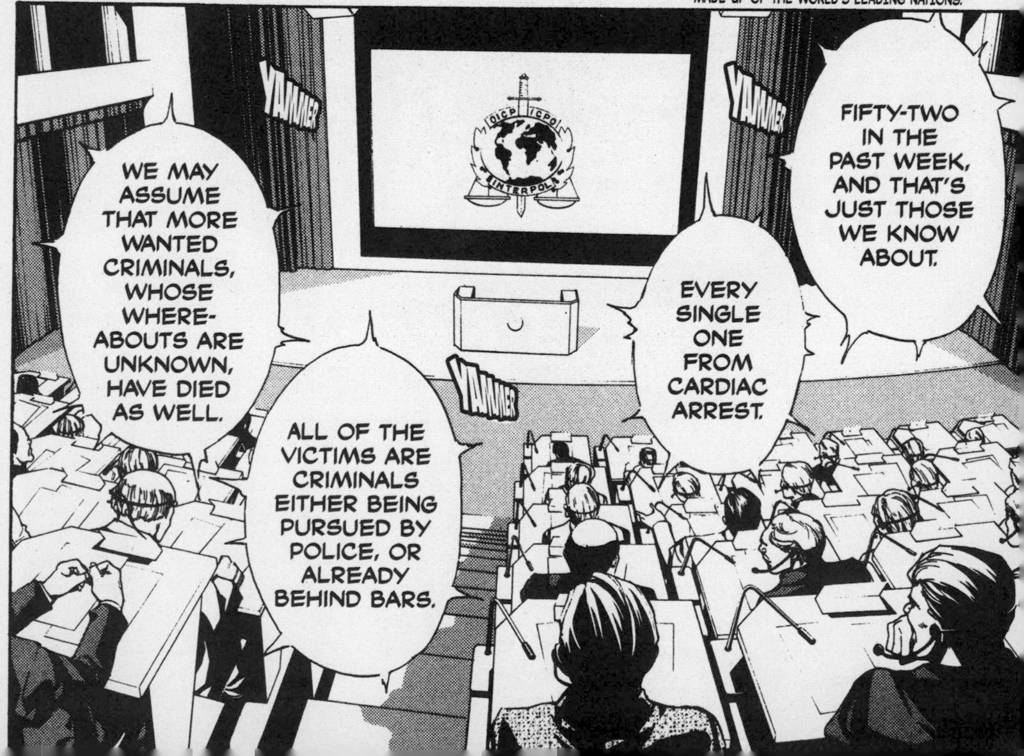
YAMMER
YAMMER
FIFTY-TWO IN THE PAST WEEK, AND THAT'S JUST THOSE WE KNOW ABOUT.
EVERY SINGLE ONE FROM CARDIAC ARREST.
YAMMER
ALL OF THE VICTIMS ARE CRIMINALS EITHER BEING PURSUED BY POLICE, OR ALREADY BEHIND BARS.
WE MAY ASSUME THAT MORE WANTED CRIMINALS, WHOSE WHERE-ABOUTS ARE UNKNOWN, HAVE DIED AS WELL.

READ THIS WAY

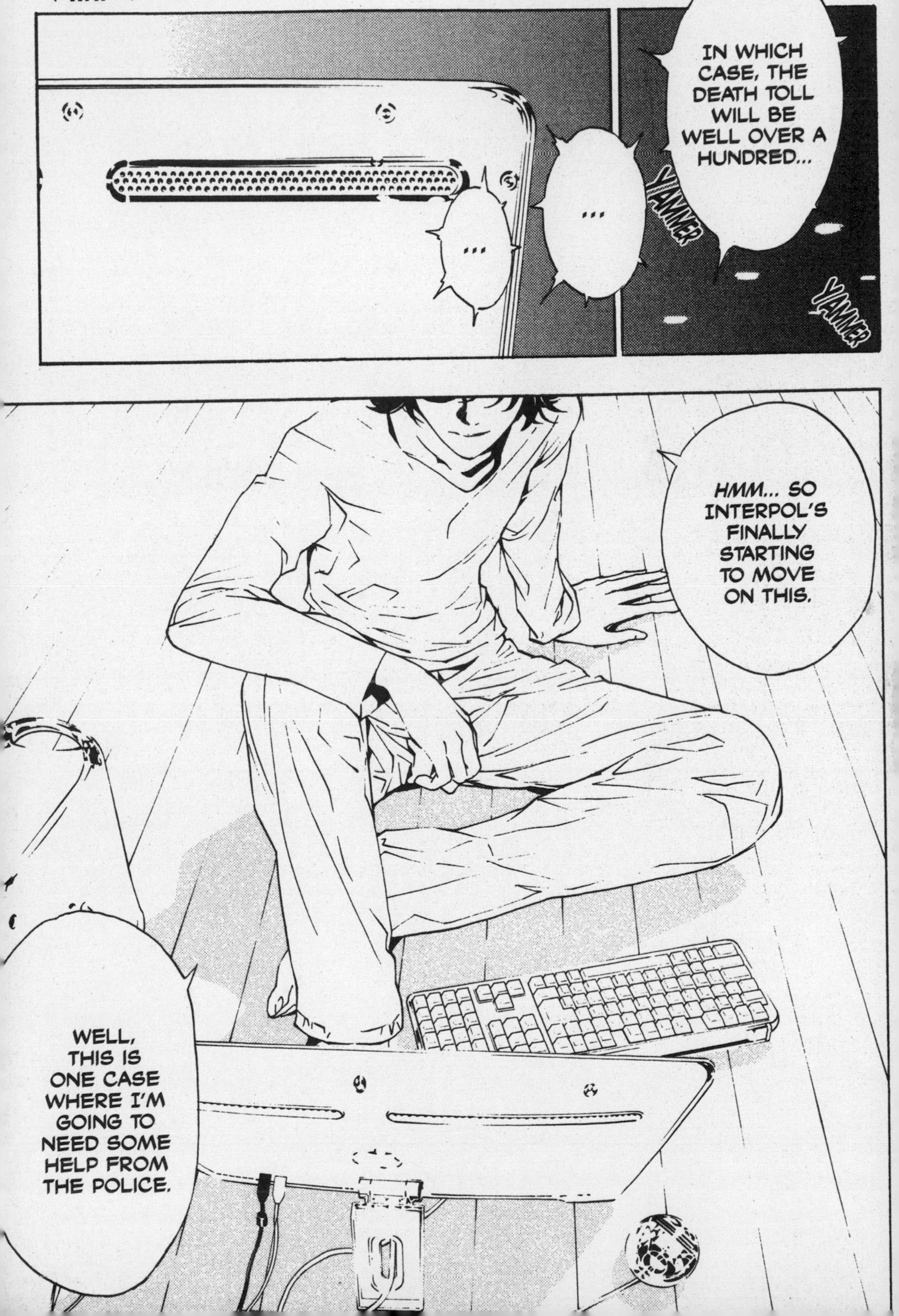
IN WHICH CASE, THE DEATH TOLL WILL BE WELL OVER A HUNDRED...
YAMMER
YAMMER
...
...
*HMM...* SO INTERPOL'S FINALLY STARTING TO MOVE ON THIS.
WELL, THIS IS ONE CASE WHERE I'M GOING TO NEED SOME HELP FROM THE POLICE.

# DEATH NOTE
## How to use it
### I

○ The human whose name is written in this note shall die.

　このノートに名前を書かれた人間は死ぬ。

○ This note will not take effect unless the writer has the person's face in their mind when writing his/her name. Therefore, people sharing the same name will not be affected.

　書く人物の顔が頭に入っていないと効果はない。
　ゆえに同姓同名の人物に一遍に効果は得られない。

○ If the cause of death is written within 40 seconds of writing the person's name, it will happen.

　名前の後に人間界単位で40秒以内に死因を書くと、その通りになる。

○ If the cause of death is not specified, the person will simply die of a heart attack.

　死因を書かなければ全てが心臓麻痺となる。

○ After writing the cause of death, details of the death should be written in the next 6 minutes and 40 seconds.

　死因を書くと更に6分40秒、詳しい死の状況を記載する時間が与えられる。

# chapter 2 L

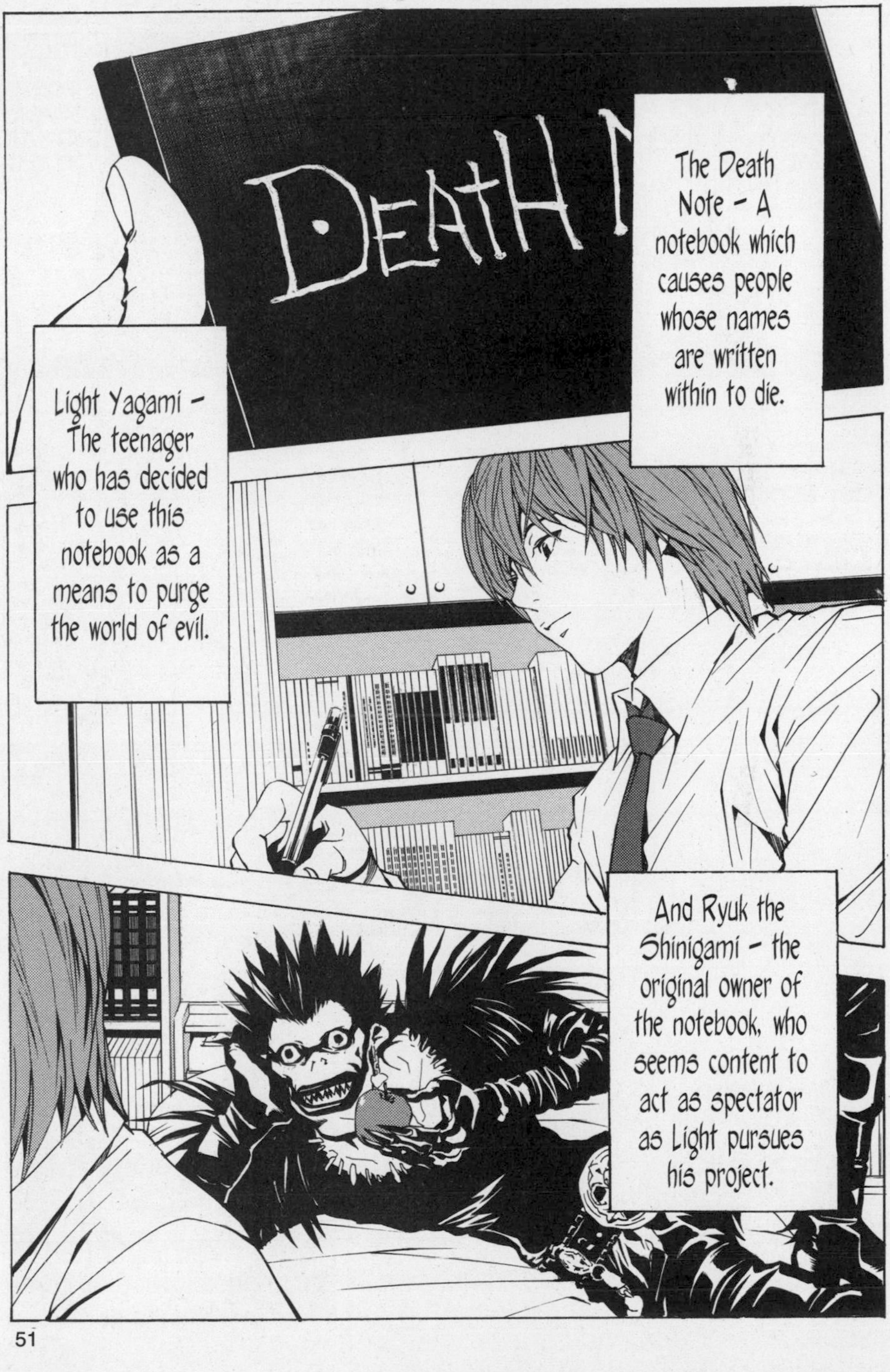
DEATH N
The Death Note – A notebook which causes people whose names are written within to die.
Light Yagami – The teenager who has decided to use this notebook as a means to purge the world of evil.
And Ryuk the Shinigami – the original owner of the notebook, who seems content to act as spectator as Light pursues his project.

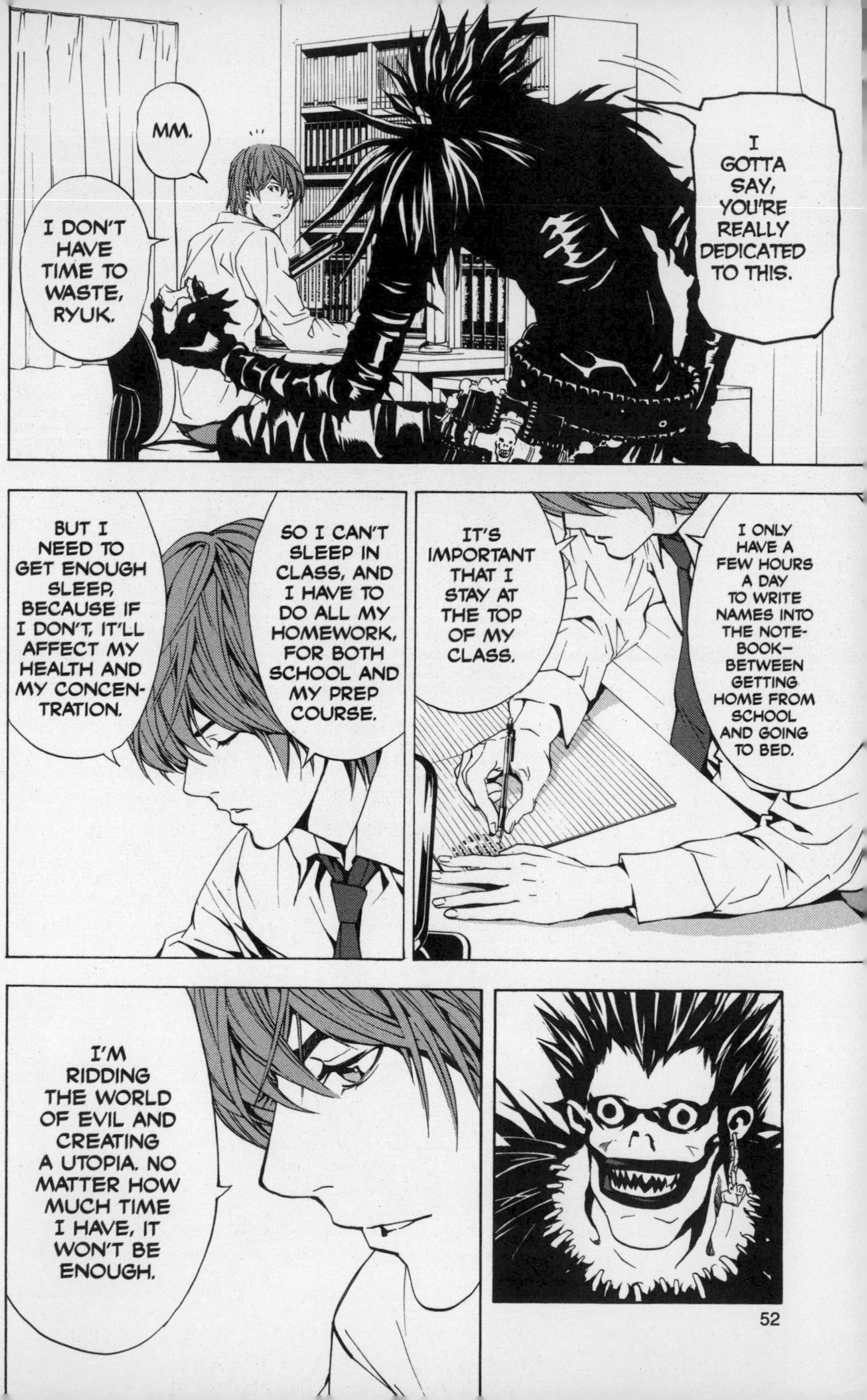
I GOTTA SAY, YOU'RE REALLY DEDICATED TO THIS.
MM.
I DON'T HAVE TIME TO WASTE, RYUK.
I ONLY HAVE A FEW HOURS A DAY TO WRITE NAMES INTO THE NOTE-BOOK—BETWEEN GETTING HOME FROM SCHOOL AND GOING TO BED.
IT'S IMPORTANT THAT I STAY AT THE TOP OF MY CLASS.
SO I CAN'T SLEEP IN CLASS, AND I HAVE TO DO ALL MY HOMEWORK, FOR BOTH SCHOOL AND MY PREP COURSE.
BUT I NEED TO GET ENOUGH SLEEP, BECAUSE IF I DON'T, IT'LL AFFECT MY HEALTH AND MY CONCEN-TRATION.
I'M RIDDING THE WORLD OF EVIL AND CREATING A UTOPIA. NO MATTER HOW MUCH TIME I HAVE, IT WON'T BE ENOUGH.

# chapter 2 L

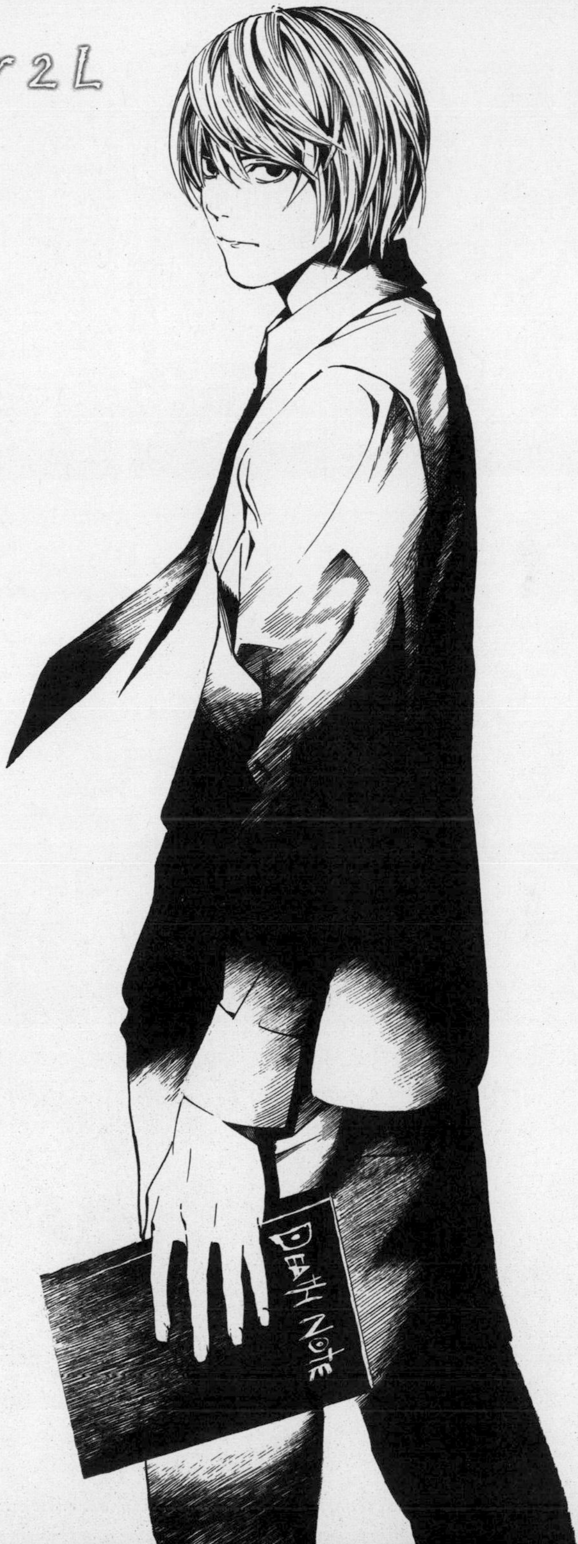
DEATH NOTE

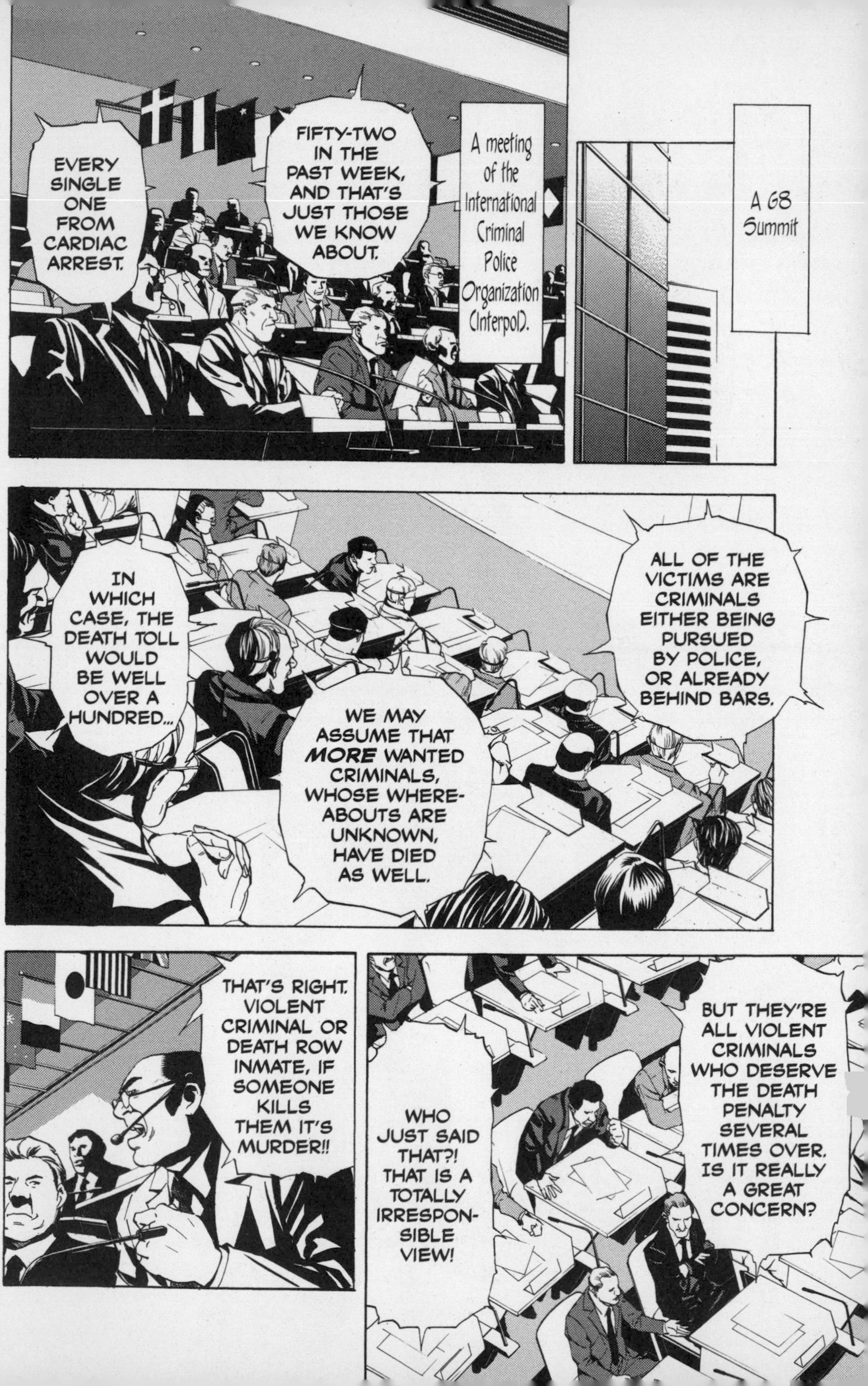
A G8 Summit
A meeting of the International Criminal Police Organization (Interpol).
FIFTY-TWO IN THE PAST WEEK, AND THAT'S JUST THOSE WE KNOW ABOUT.
EVERY SINGLE ONE FROM CARDIAC ARREST.
ALL OF THE VICTIMS ARE CRIMINALS EITHER BEING PURSUED BY POLICE, OR ALREADY BEHIND BARS.
WE MAY ASSUME THAT *MORE* WANTED CRIMINALS, WHOSE WHERE-ABOUTS ARE UNKNOWN, HAVE DIED AS WELL.
IN WHICH CASE, THE DEATH TOLL WOULD BE WELL OVER A HUNDRED...
BUT THEY'RE ALL VIOLENT CRIMINALS WHO DESERVE THE DEATH PENALTY SEVERAL TIMES OVER. IS IT REALLY A GREAT CONCERN?
WHO JUST SAID THAT?! THAT IS A TOTALLY IRRESPON-SIBLE VIEW!
THAT'S RIGHT. VIOLENT CRIMINAL OR DEATH ROW INMATE, IF SOMEONE KILLS THEM IT'S MURDER!!

READ THIS WAY

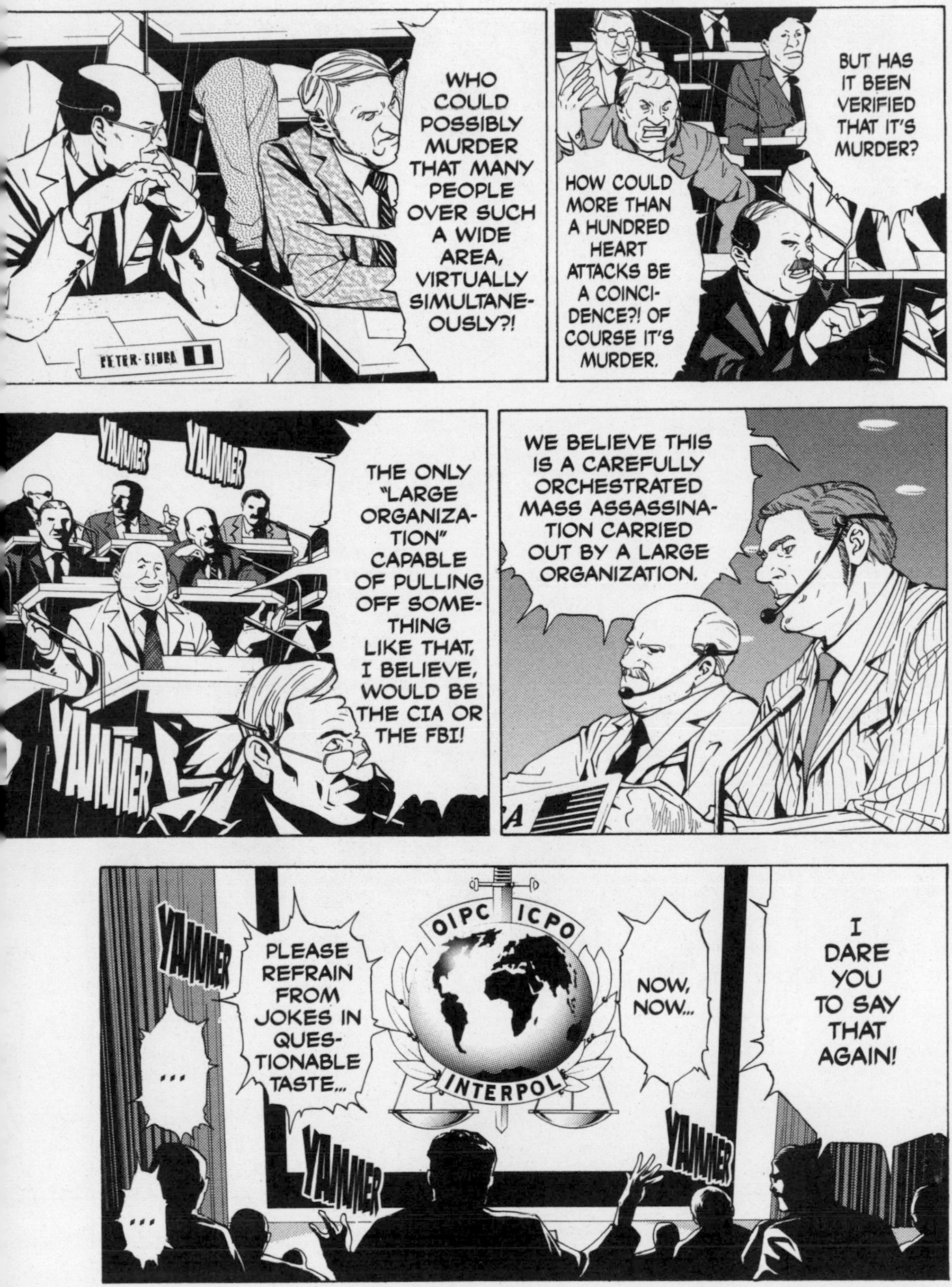
BUT HAS IT BEEN VERIFIED THAT IT'S MURDER?
HOW COULD MORE THAN A HUNDRED HEART ATTACKS BE A COINCIDENCE?! OF COURSE IT'S MURDER.
WHO COULD POSSIBLY MURDER THAT MANY PEOPLE OVER SUCH A WIDE AREA, VIRTUALLY SIMULTANEOUSLY?!
WE BELIEVE THIS IS A CAREFULLY ORCHESTRATED MASS ASSASSINATION CARRIED OUT BY A LARGE ORGANIZATION.
YAMMER
YAMMER
THE ONLY "LARGE ORGANIZATION" CAPABLE OF PULLING OFF SOMETHING LIKE THAT, I BELIEVE, WOULD BE THE CIA OR THE FBI!
YAMMER
I DARE YOU TO SAY THAT AGAIN!
NOW, NOW...
YAMMER
OIPC ICPO
INTERPOL
PLEASE REFRAIN FROM JOKES IN QUESTIONABLE TASTE...
YAMMER
YAMMER
...
...

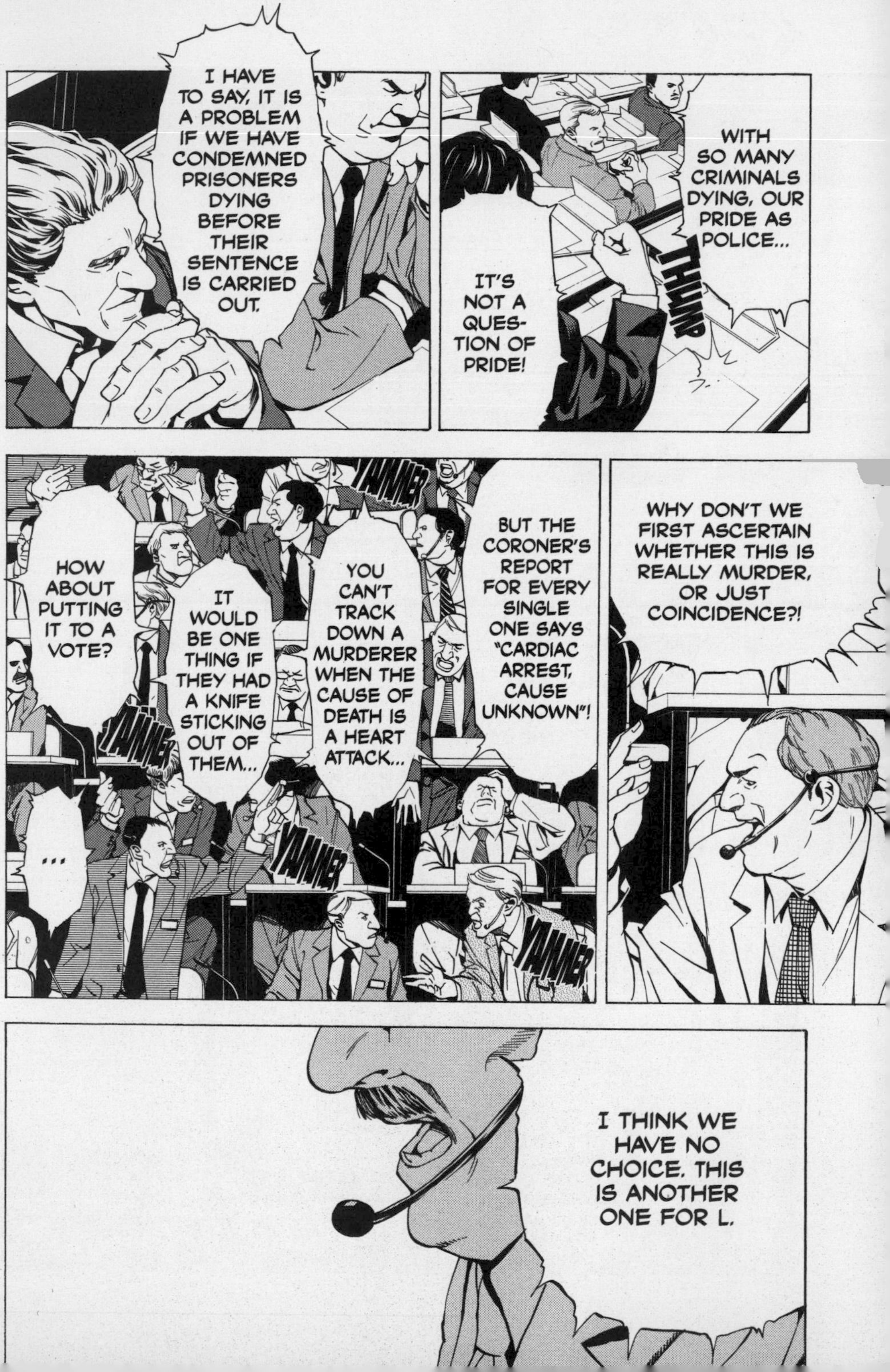
WITH SO MANY CRIMINALS DYING, OUR PRIDE AS POLICE...
THUMP
IT'S NOT A QUES-TION OF PRIDE!
I HAVE TO SAY, IT IS A PROBLEM IF WE HAVE CONDEMNED PRISONERS DYING BEFORE THEIR SENTENCE IS CARRIED OUT.
WHY DON'T WE FIRST ASCERTAIN WHETHER THIS IS REALLY MURDER, OR JUST COINCIDENCE?!
YAMMER
BUT THE CORONER'S REPORT FOR EVERY SINGLE ONE SAYS "CARDIAC ARREST, CAUSE UNKNOWN"!
YOU CAN'T TRACK DOWN A MURDERER WHEN THE CAUSE OF DEATH IS A HEART ATTACK...
IT WOULD BE ONE THING IF THEY HAD A KNIFE STICKING OUT OF THEM...
HOW ABOUT PUTTING IT TO A VOTE?
YAMMER
YAMMER
YAMMER
...
I THINK WE HAVE NO CHOICE. THIS IS ANOTHER ONE FOR L.

READ THIS WAY

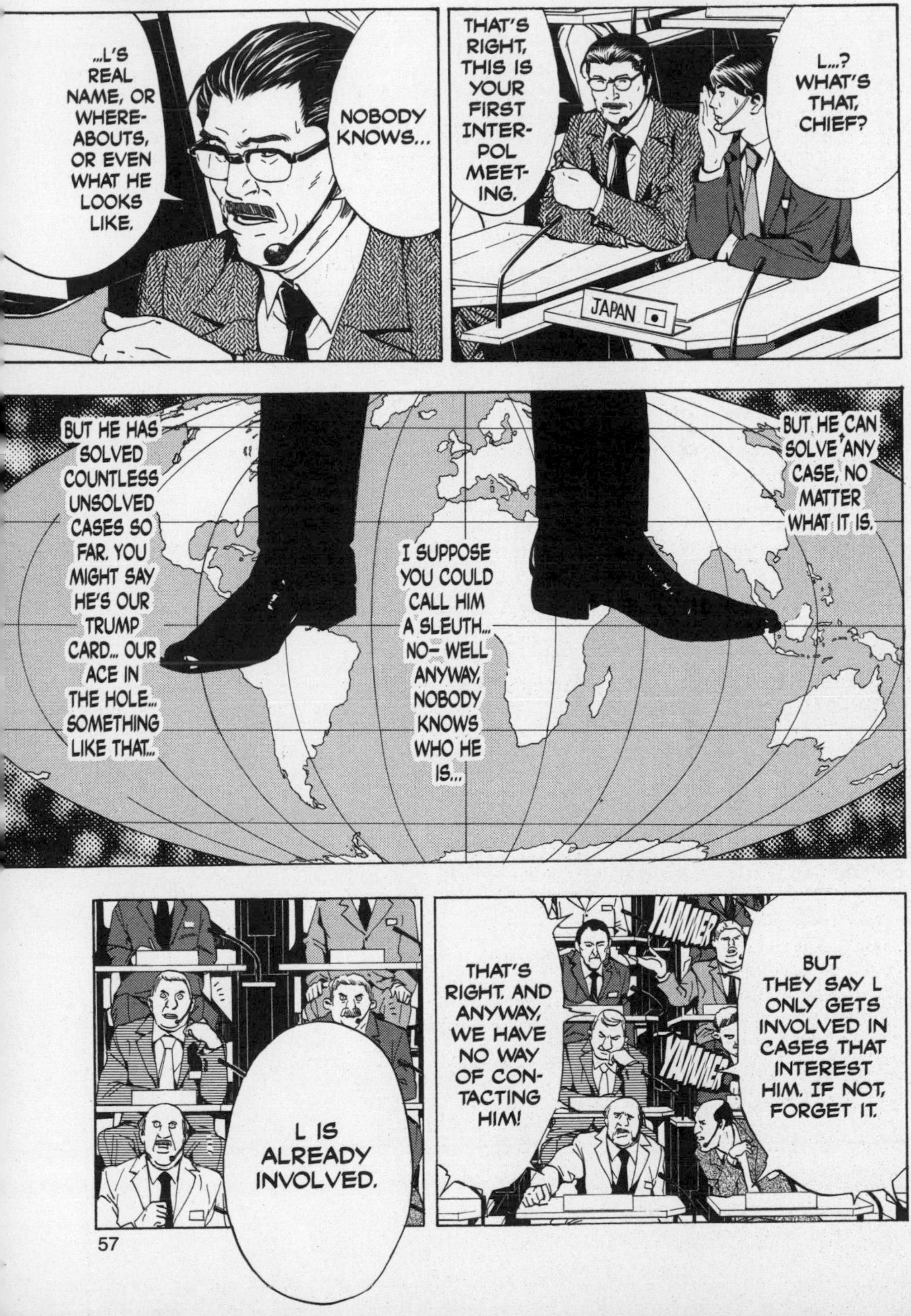

L...? WHAT'S THAT, CHIEF?
THAT'S RIGHT, THIS IS YOUR FIRST INTERPOL MEETING.
JAPAN
NOBODY KNOWS...
...L'S REAL NAME, OR WHEREABOUTS, OR EVEN WHAT HE LOOKS LIKE.
BUT HE CAN SOLVE ANY CASE, NO MATTER WHAT IT IS.
I SUPPOSE YOU COULD CALL HIM A SLEUTH... NO-- WELL ANYWAY, NOBODY KNOWS WHO HE IS...
BUT HE HAS SOLVED COUNTLESS UNSOLVED CASES SO FAR. YOU MIGHT SAY HE'S OUR TRUMP CARD... OUR ACE IN THE HOLE... SOMETHING LIKE THAT...
BUT THEY SAY L ONLY GETS INVOLVED IN CASES THAT INTEREST HIM. IF NOT, FORGET IT.
YAMMER
YAMMER
THAT'S RIGHT. AND ANYWAY, WE HAVE NO WAY OF CONTACTING HIM!
L IS ALREADY INVOLVED.

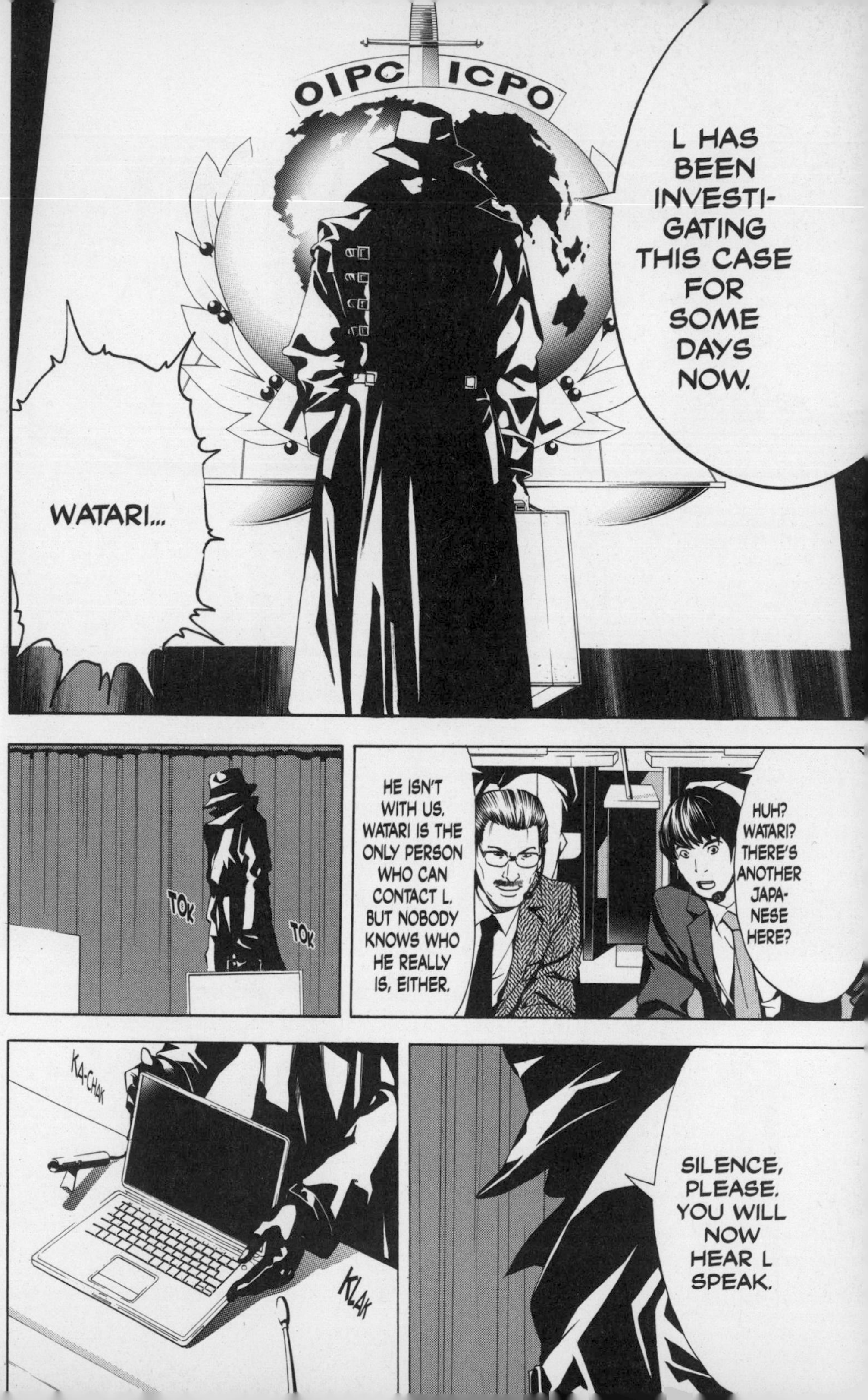
L HAS BEEN INVESTIGATING THIS CASE FOR SOME DAYS NOW.
OIPC ICPO
WATARI...
HUH? WATARI? THERE'S ANOTHER JAPANESE HERE?
HE ISN'T WITH US. WATARI IS THE ONLY PERSON WHO CAN CONTACT L. BUT NOBODY KNOWS WHO HE REALLY IS, EITHER.
TOK
TOK
SILENCE, PLEASE. YOU WILL NOW HEAR L SPEAK.
KA-CHAK
KLAK

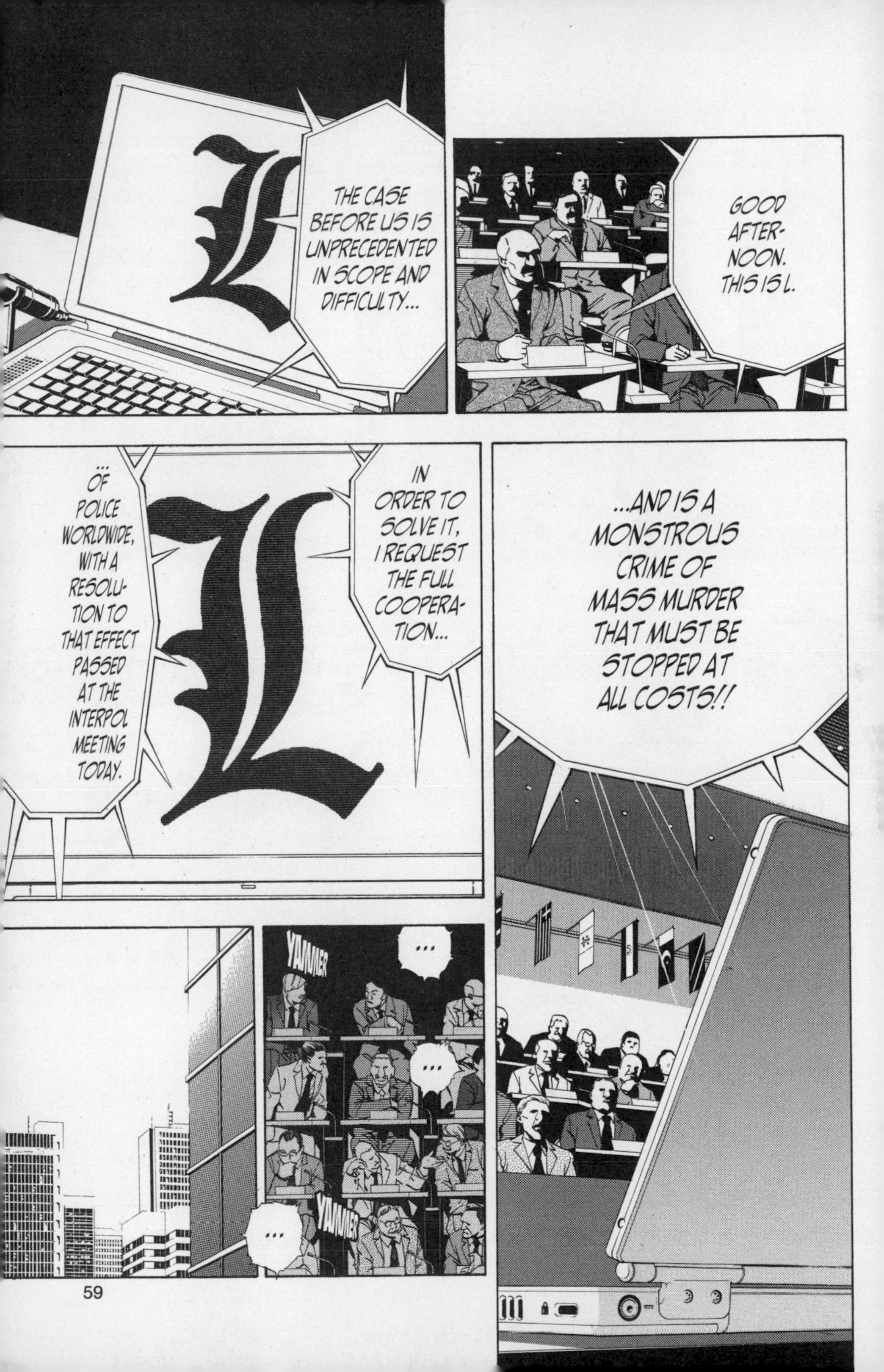
GOOD AFTERNOON. THIS IS L.
THE CASE BEFORE US IS UNPRECEDENTED IN SCOPE AND DIFFICULTY...
...AND IS A MONSTROUS CRIME OF MASS MURDER THAT MUST BE STOPPED AT ALL COSTS!!
IN ORDER TO SOLVE IT, I REQUEST THE FULL COOPERATION...
...OF POLICE WORLDWIDE, WITH A RESOLUTION TO THAT EFFECT PASSED AT THE INTERPOL MEETING TODAY.
YAMMER
...
...
YAMMER
...

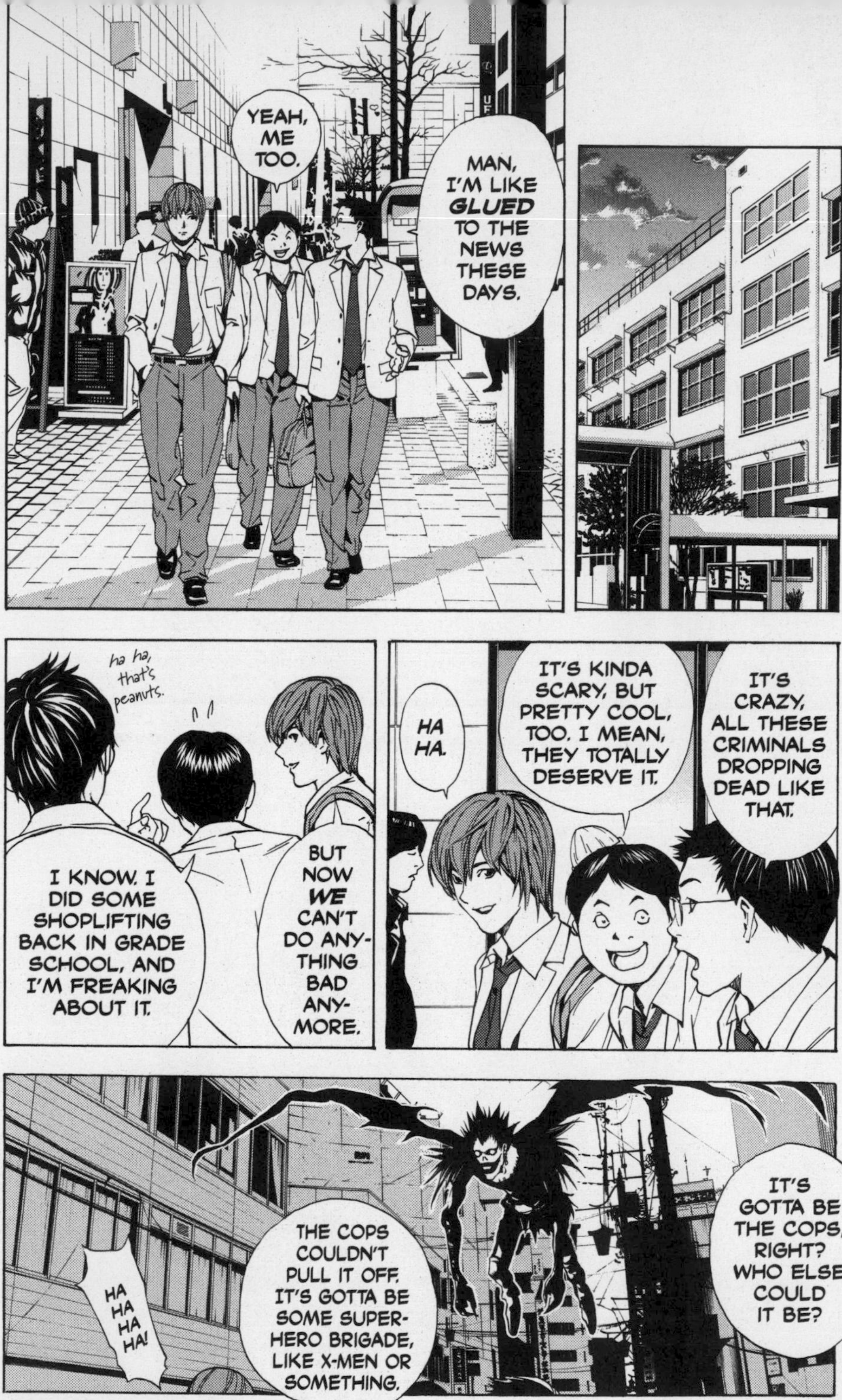
MAN, I'M LIKE GLUED TO THE NEWS THESE DAYS.
YEAH, ME TOO.
IT'S CRAZY, ALL THESE CRIMINALS DROPPING DEAD LIKE THAT.
IT'S KINDA SCARY, BUT PRETTY COOL, TOO. I MEAN, THEY TOTALLY DESERVE IT.
HA HA.
BUT NOW WE CAN'T DO ANY-THING BAD ANY-MORE.
I KNOW. I DID SOME SHOPLIFTING BACK IN GRADE SCHOOL, AND I'M FREAKING ABOUT IT.
ha ha, that's peanuts.
IT'S GOTTA BE THE COPS, RIGHT? WHO ELSE COULD IT BE?
THE COPS COULDN'T PULL IT OFF. IT'S GOTTA BE SOME SUPER-HERO BRIGADE, LIKE X-MEN OR SOMETHING.
HA HA HA HA!

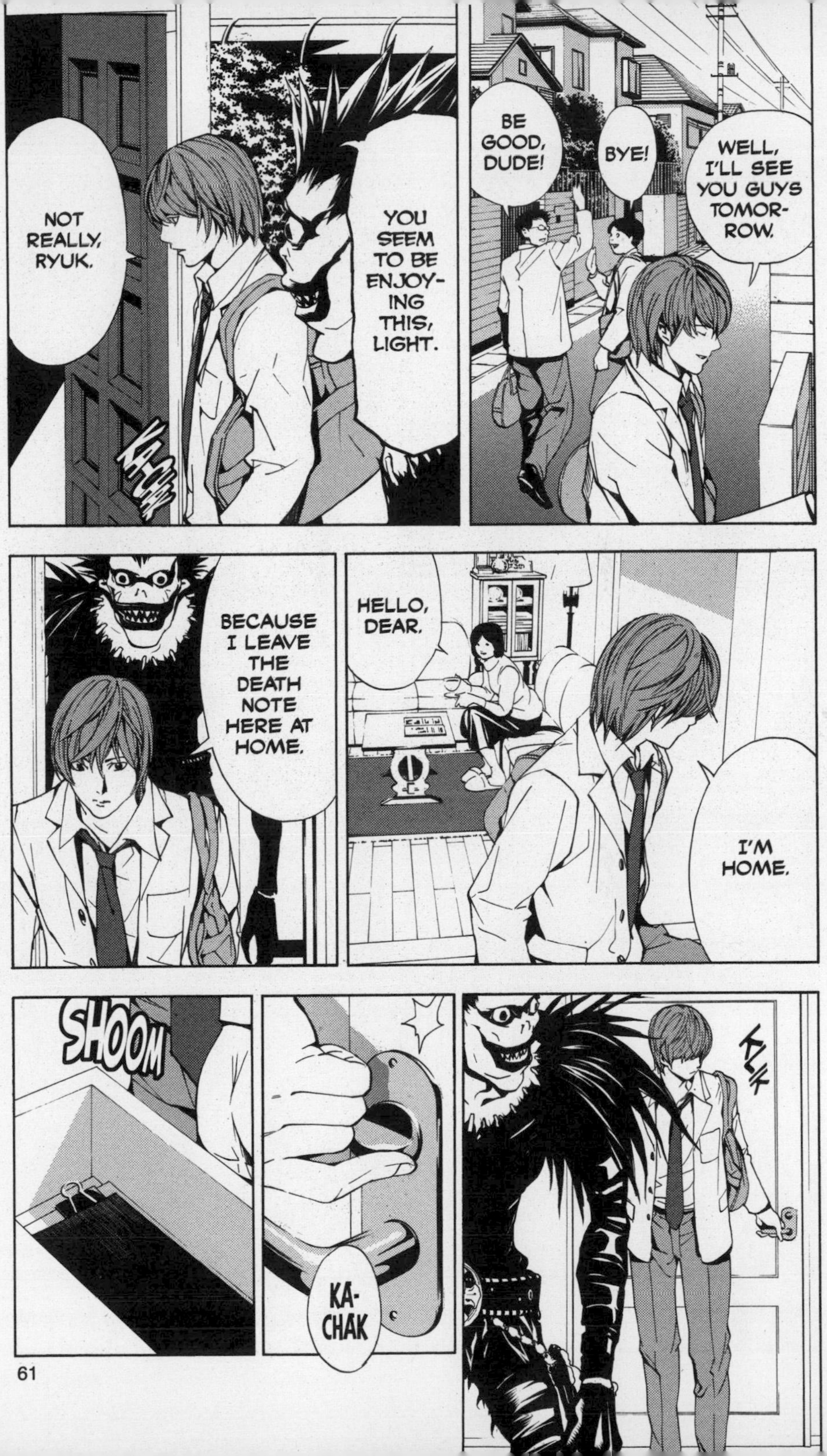
WELL, I'LL SEE YOU GUYS TOMORROW.
BYE!
BE GOOD, DUDE!
YOU SEEM TO BE ENJOYING THIS, LIGHT.
NOT REALLY, RYUK.
KACHAK
I'M HOME.
HELLO, DEAR.
BECAUSE I LEAVE THE DEATH NOTE HERE AT HOME.
KLIK
KA-CHAK
SHOOM

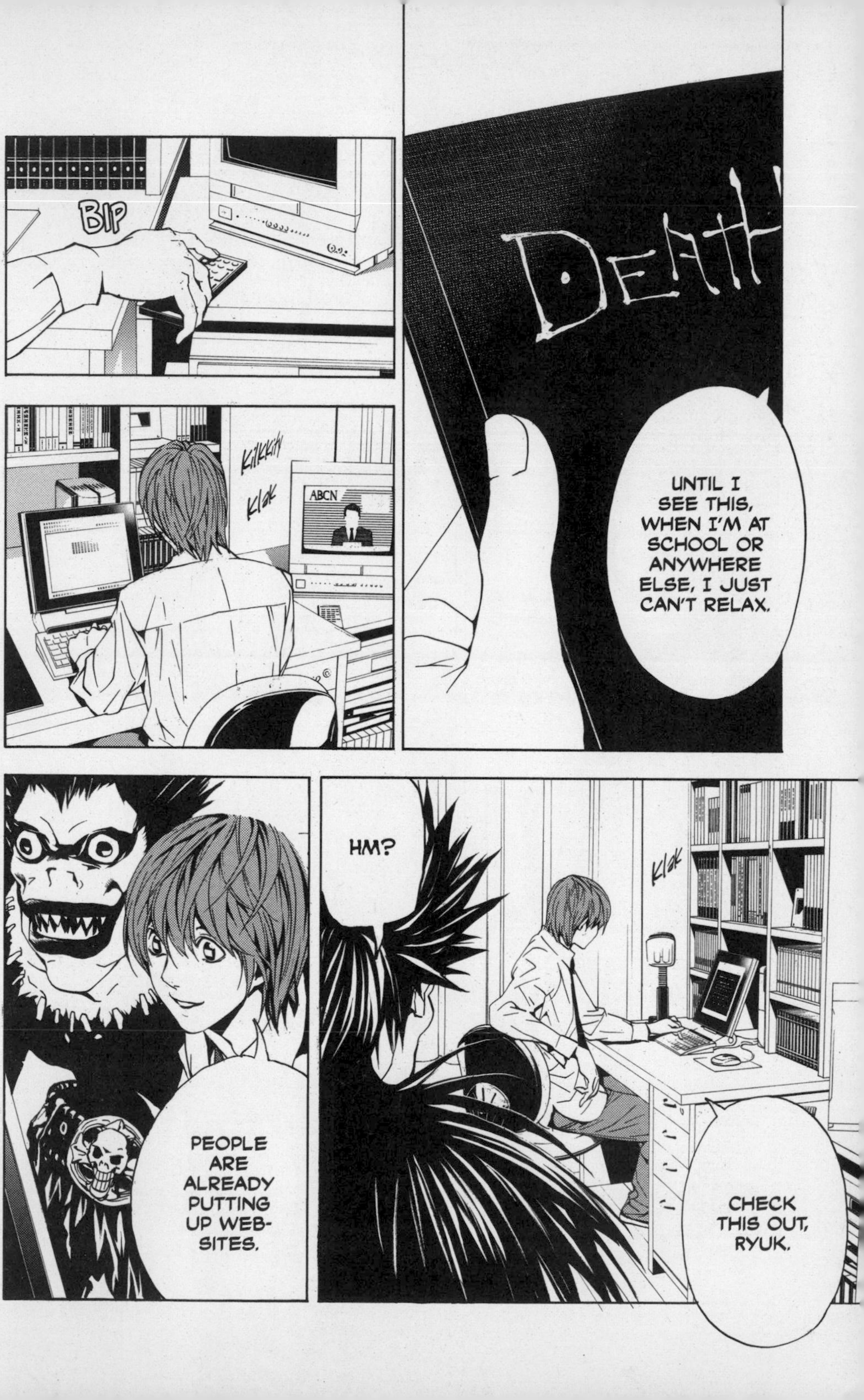
DEATH
UNTIL I SEE THIS, WHEN I'M AT SCHOOL OR ANYWHERE ELSE, I JUST CAN'T RELAX.
BIP
Kilkkity
Klak
ABCN
Klak
HM?
CHECK THIS OUT, RYUK.
PEOPLE ARE ALREADY PUTTING UP WEB-SITES.

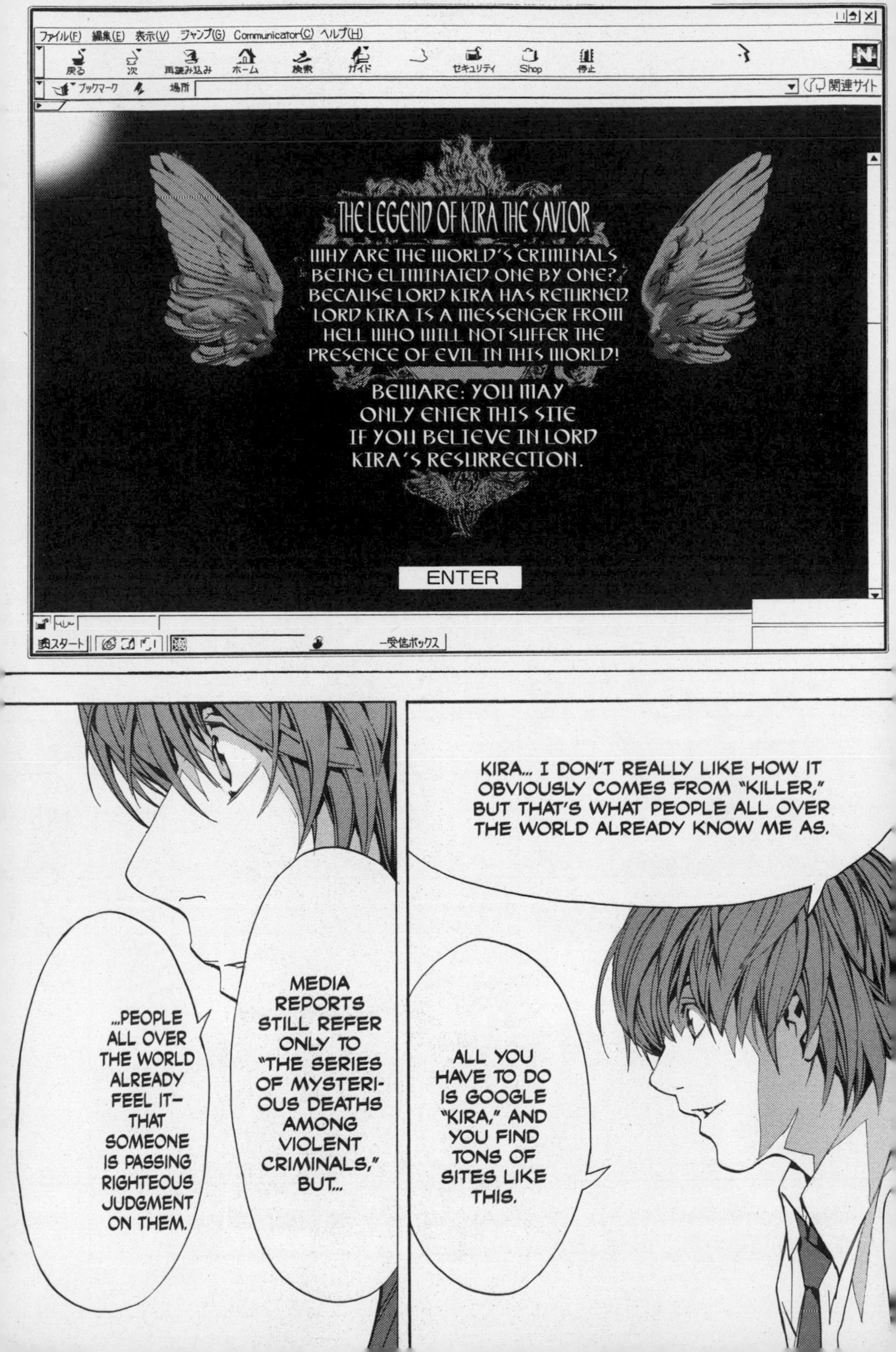
THE LEGEND OF KIRA THE SAVIOR
WHY ARE THE WORLD'S CRIMINALS BEING ELIMINATED ONE BY ONE? BECAUSE LORD KIRA HAS RETURNED. LORD KIRA IS A MESSENGER FROM HELL WHO WILL NOT SUFFER THE PRESENCE OF EVIL IN THIS WORLD!
BEWARE: YOU MAY ONLY ENTER THIS SITE IF YOU BELIEVE IN LORD KIRA'S RESURRECTION.
ENTER
KIRA... I DON'T REALLY LIKE HOW IT OBVIOUSLY COMES FROM "KILLER," BUT THAT'S WHAT PEOPLE ALL OVER THE WORLD ALREADY KNOW ME AS.
ALL YOU HAVE TO DO IS GOOGLE "KIRA," AND YOU FIND TONS OF SITES LIKE THIS.
MEDIA REPORTS STILL REFER ONLY TO "THE SERIES OF MYSTERIOUS DEATHS AMONG VIOLENT CRIMINALS," BUT...
...PEOPLE ALL OVER THE WORLD ALREADY FEEL IT—THAT SOMEONE IS PASSING RIGHTEOUS JUDGMENT ON THEM.

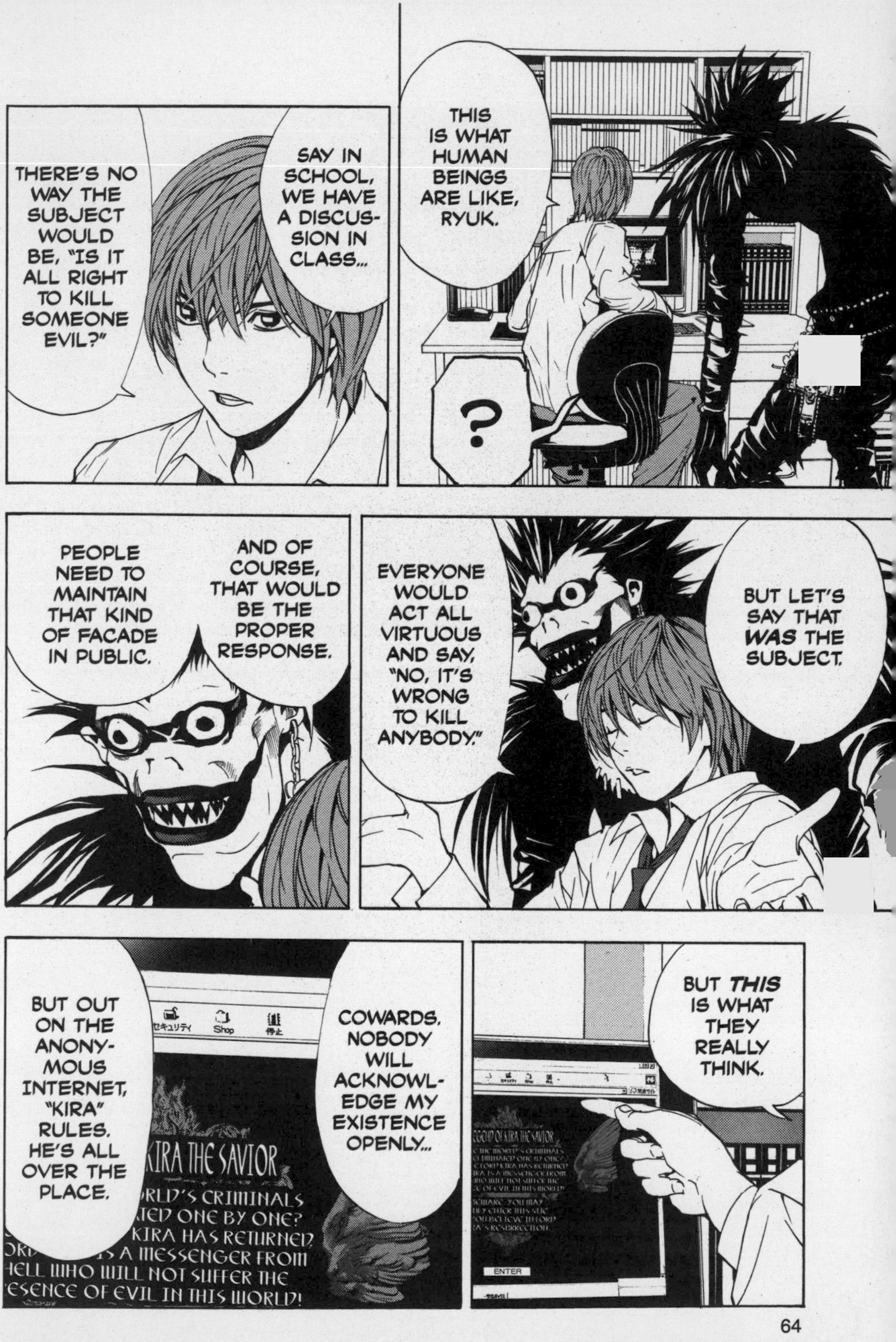
THIS IS WHAT HUMAN BEINGS ARE LIKE, RYUK.
?
SAY IN SCHOOL, WE HAVE A DISCUSSION IN CLASS...
THERE'S NO WAY THE SUBJECT WOULD BE, "IS IT ALL RIGHT TO KILL SOMEONE EVIL?"
BUT LET'S SAY THAT *WAS* THE SUBJECT.
EVERYONE WOULD ACT ALL VIRTUOUS AND SAY, "NO, IT'S WRONG TO KILL ANYBODY."
AND OF COURSE, THAT WOULD BE THE PROPER RESPONSE.
PEOPLE NEED TO MAINTAIN THAT KIND OF FACADE IN PUBLIC.
BUT *THIS* IS WHAT THEY REALLY THINK.
ENTER
COWARDS, NOBODY WILL ACKNOWLEDGE MY EXISTENCE OPENLY...
BUT OUT ON THE ANONYMOUS INTERNET, "KIRA" RULES. HE'S ALL OVER THE PLACE.
Shop
KIRA THE SAVIOR
KIRA HAS RETURNED
HELL WHO WILL NOT SUFFER THE

READ THIS WAY

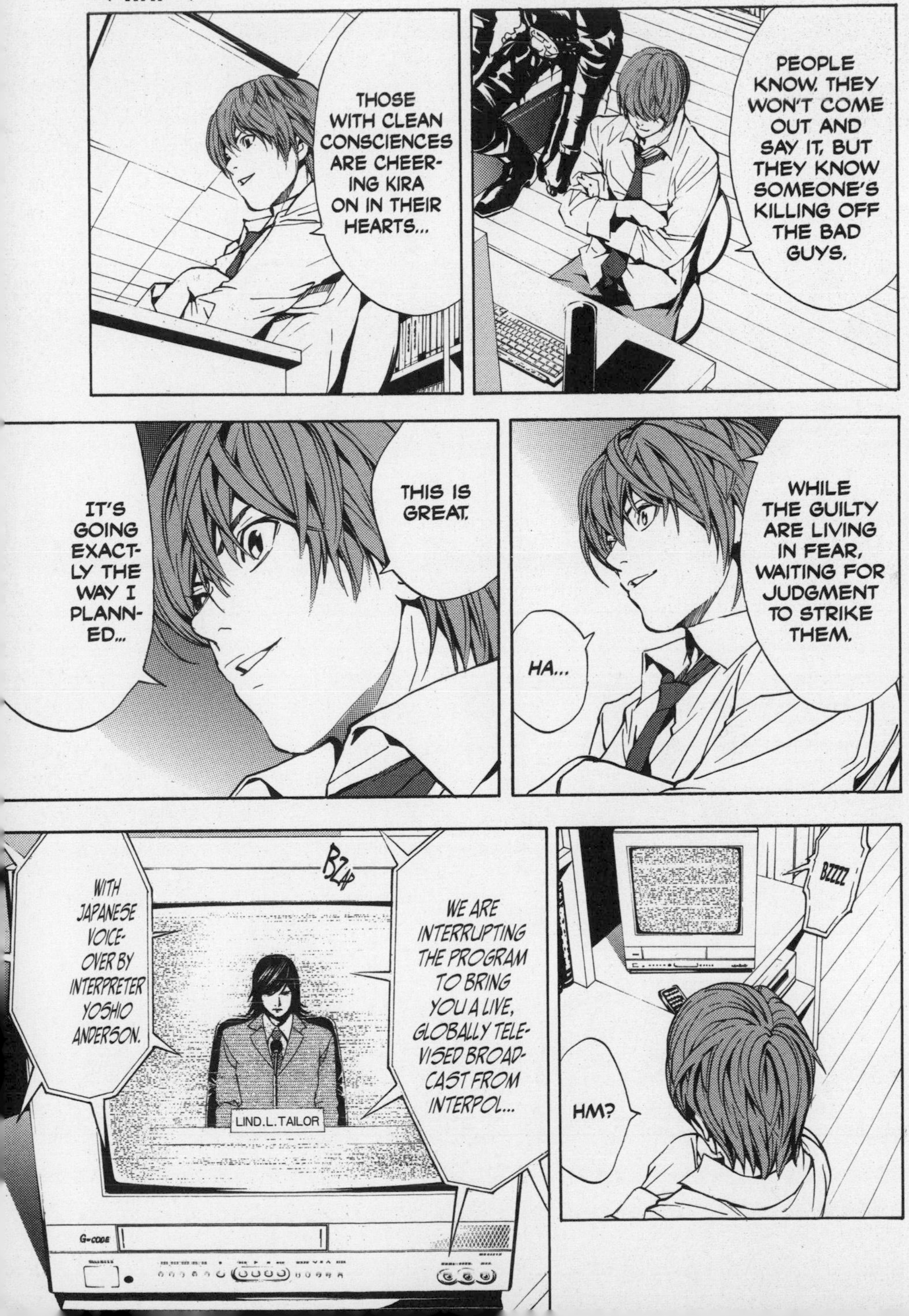
PEOPLE KNOW. THEY WON'T COME OUT AND SAY IT, BUT THEY KNOW SOMEONE'S KILLING OFF THE BAD GUYS.
THOSE WITH CLEAN CONSCIENCES ARE CHEERING KIRA ON IN THEIR HEARTS...
WHILE THE GUILTY ARE LIVING IN FEAR, WAITING FOR JUDGMENT TO STRIKE THEM.
HA...
THIS IS GREAT.
IT'S GOING EXACTLY THE WAY I PLANNED...
BZZZZ
HM?
BZAP
WE ARE INTERRUPTING THE PROGRAM TO BRING YOU A LIVE, GLOBALLY TELEVISED BROADCAST FROM INTERPOL...
WITH JAPANESE VOICE-OVER BY INTERPRETER YOSHIO ANDERSON.
LIND.L.TAILOR
G-CODE

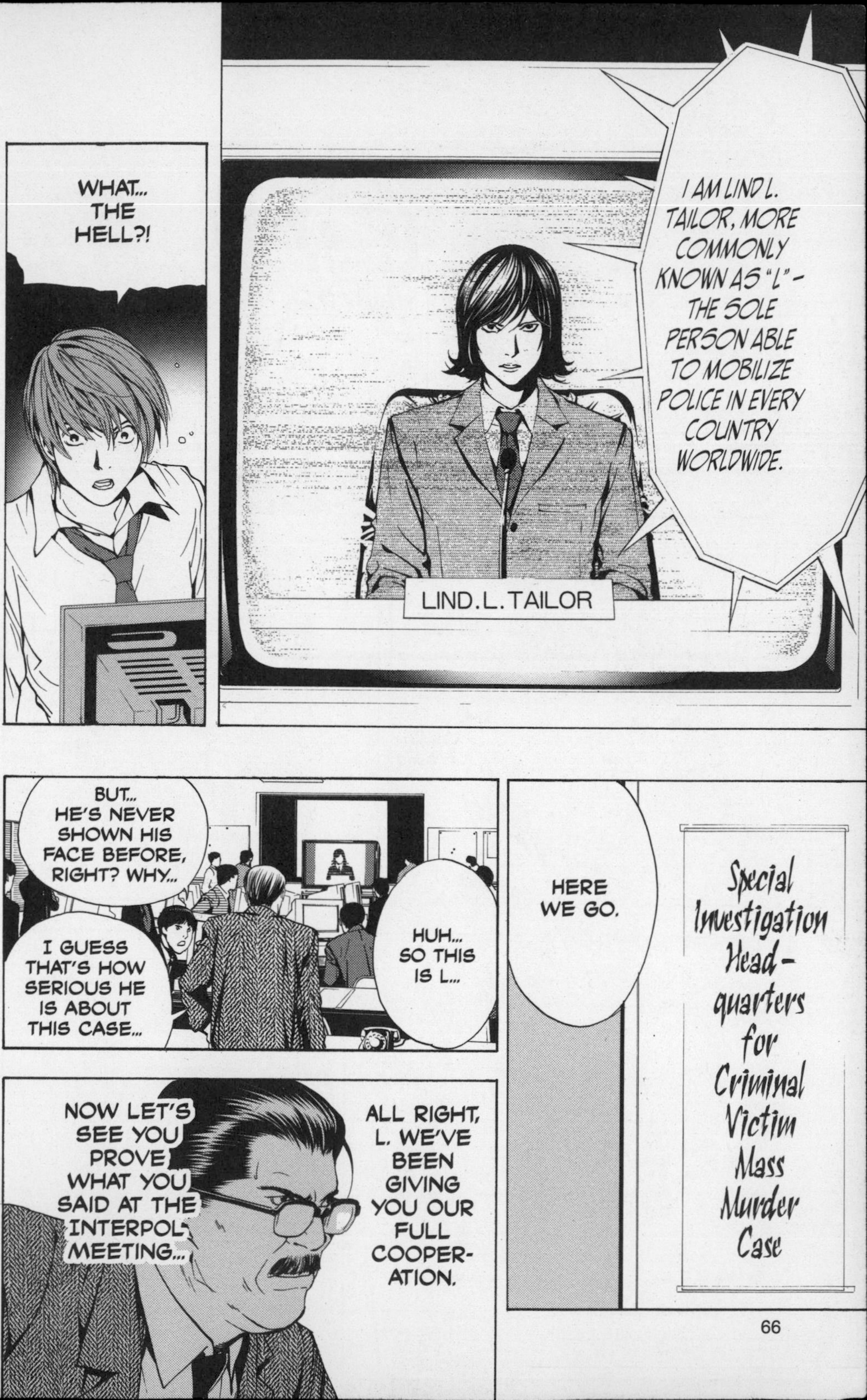
I AM LIND L. TAILOR, MORE COMMONLY KNOWN AS "L" - THE SOLE PERSON ABLE TO MOBILIZE POLICE IN EVERY COUNTRY WORLDWIDE.
LIND.L.TAILOR
WHAT... THE HELL?!
Special Investigation Head-quarters for Criminal Victim Mass Murder Case
HERE WE GO.
HUH... SO THIS IS L...
BUT... HE'S NEVER SHOWN HIS FACE BEFORE, RIGHT? WHY...
I GUESS THAT'S HOW SERIOUS HE IS ABOUT THIS CASE...
ALL RIGHT, L. WE'VE BEEN GIVING YOU OUR FULL COOPER-ATION.
NOW LET'S SEE YOU PROVE WHAT YOU SAID AT THE INTERPOL MEETING...

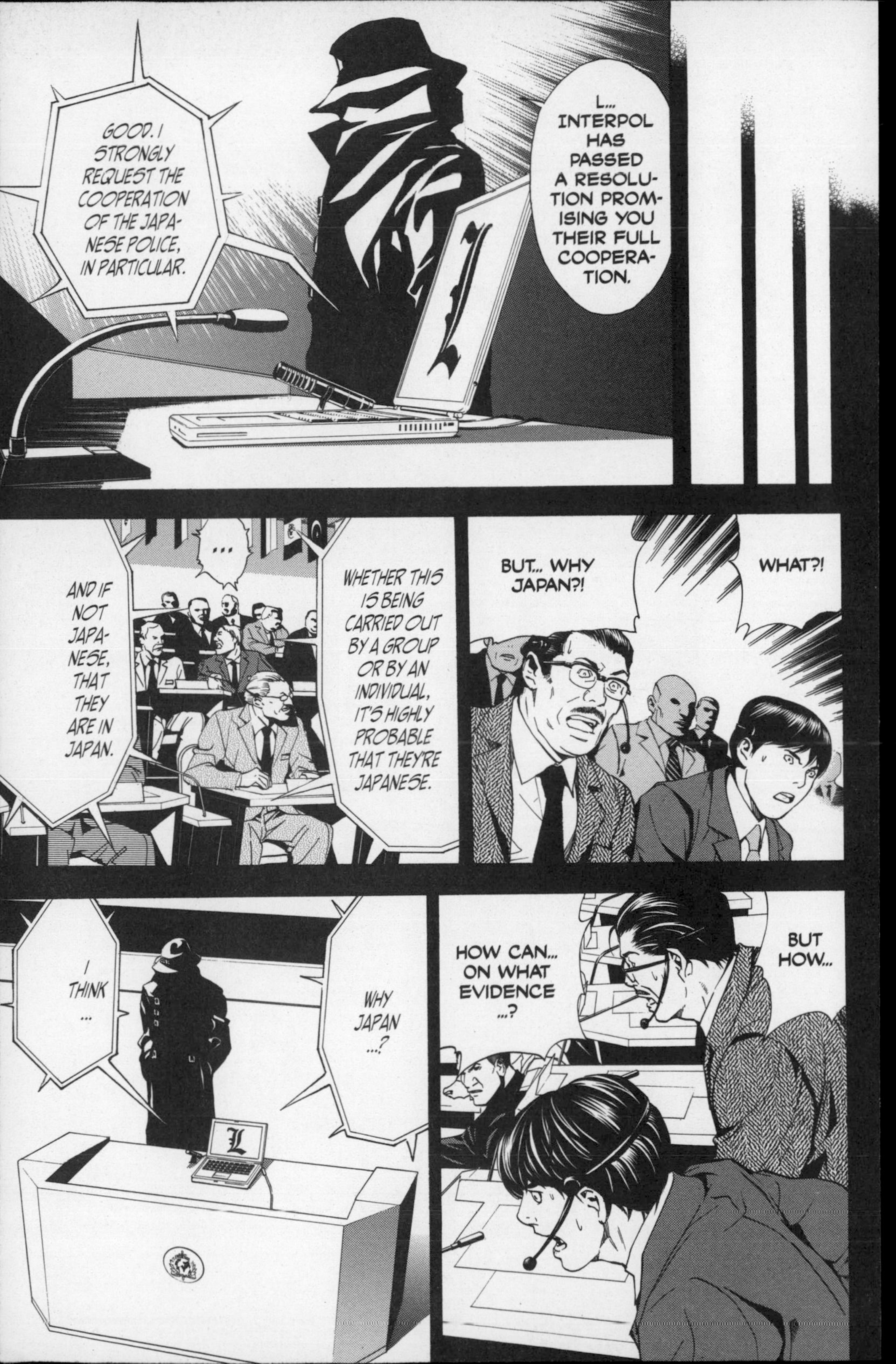
L... INTERPOL HAS PASSED A RESOLUTION PROMISING YOU THEIR FULL COOPERATION.
GOOD. I STRONGLY REQUEST THE COOPERATION OF THE JAPANESE POLICE, IN PARTICULAR.
WHAT?!
BUT... WHY JAPAN?!
...
WHETHER THIS IS BEING CARRIED OUT BY A GROUP OR BY AN INDIVIDUAL, IT'S HIGHLY PROBABLE THAT THEY'RE JAPANESE.
AND IF NOT JAPANESE, THAT THEY ARE IN JAPAN.
BUT HOW...
HOW CAN... ON WHAT EVIDENCE ...?
WHY JAPAN ...?
I THINK ...

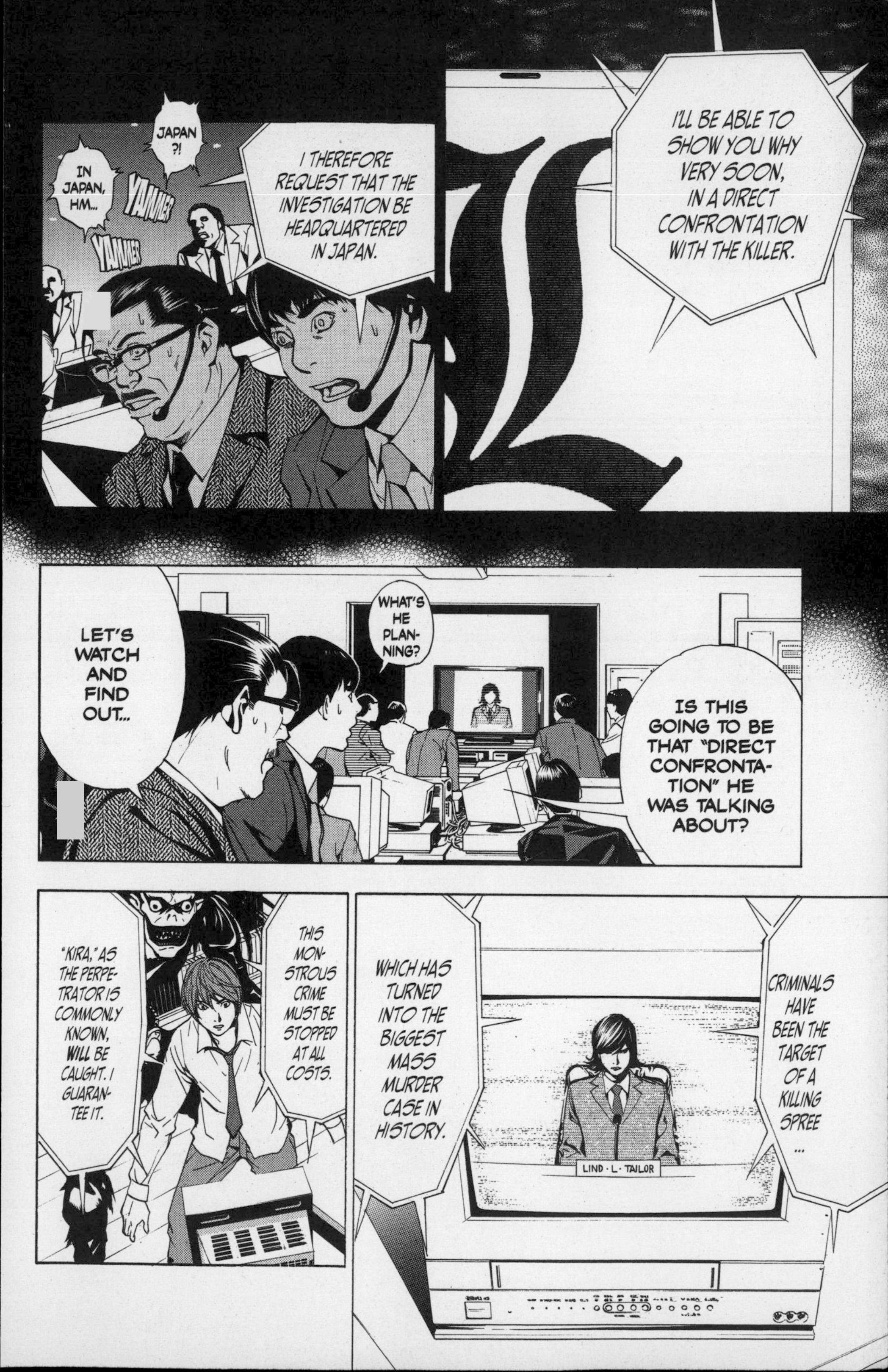
I'LL BE ABLE TO SHOW YOU WHY VERY SOON, IN A DIRECT CONFRONTATION WITH THE KILLER.
I THEREFORE REQUEST THAT THE INVESTIGATION BE HEADQUARTERED IN JAPAN.
JAPAN ?!
YAMMER
IN JAPAN, HM...
YAMMER
IS THIS GOING TO BE THAT "DIRECT CONFRONTATION" HE WAS TALKING ABOUT?
WHAT'S HE PLANNING?
LET'S WATCH AND FIND OUT...
CRIMINALS HAVE BEEN THE TARGET OF A KILLING SPREE...
WHICH HAS TURNED INTO THE BIGGEST MASS MURDER CASE IN HISTORY.
LIND · L · TAILOR
THIS MONSTROUS CRIME MUST BE STOPPED AT ALL COSTS.
"KIRA," AS THE PERPETRATOR IS COMMONLY KNOWN, **WILL** BE CAUGHT. I GUARANTEE IT.

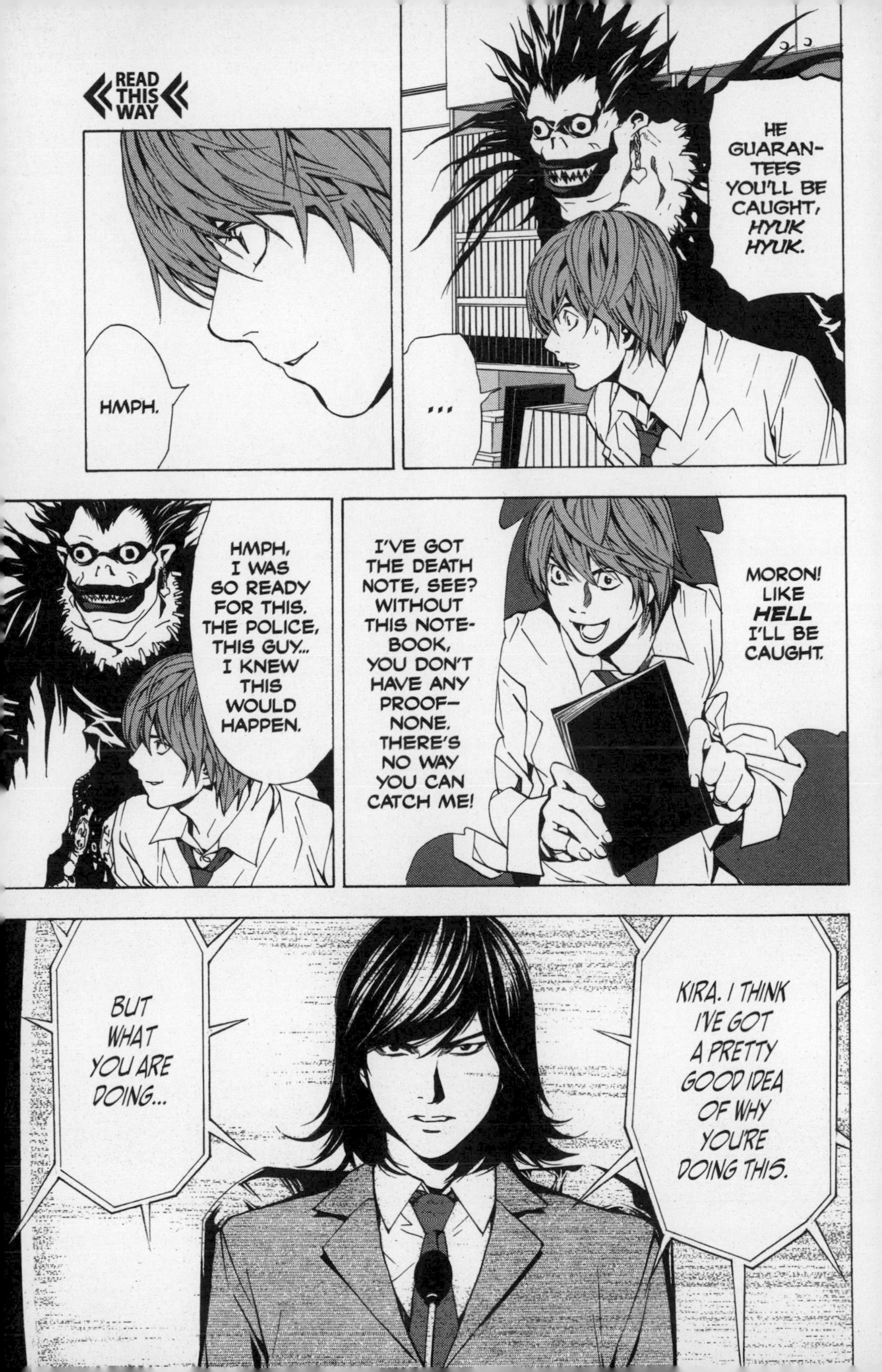
READ THIS WAY
HE GUARANTEES YOU'LL BE CAUGHT, *HYUK HYUK*.
...
HMPH.
MORON! LIKE *HELL* I'LL BE CAUGHT.
I'VE GOT THE DEATH NOTE, SEE? WITHOUT THIS NOTEBOOK, YOU DON'T HAVE ANY PROOF—NONE. THERE'S NO WAY YOU CAN CATCH ME!
HMPH, I WAS SO READY FOR THIS. THE POLICE, THIS GUY... I KNEW THIS WOULD HAPPEN.
KIRA. I THINK I'VE GOT A PRETTY GOOD IDEA OF WHY YOU'RE DOING THIS.
BUT WHAT YOU ARE DOING...

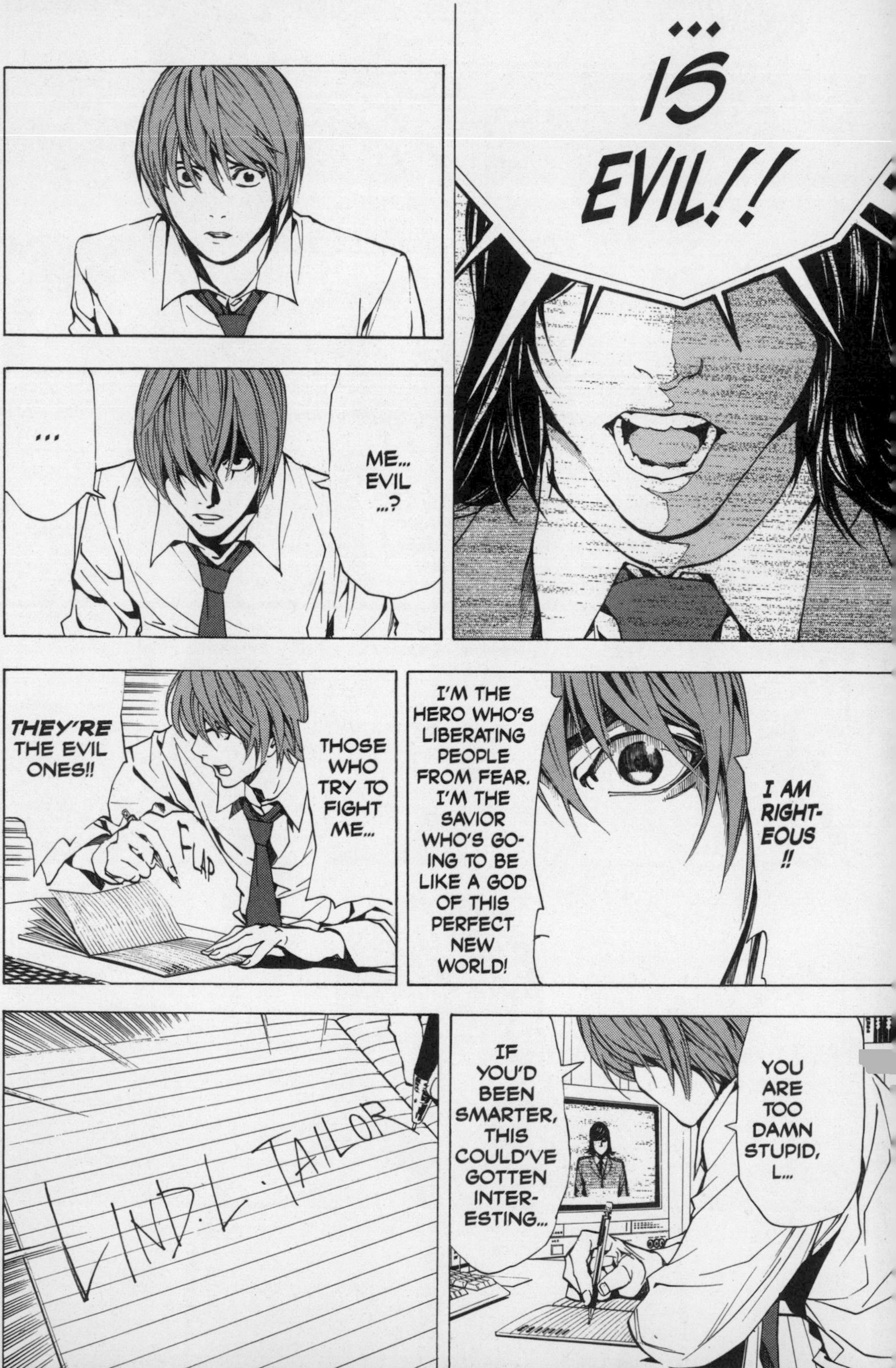
...IS EVIL!!
ME... EVIL ...?
...
I AM RIGHTEOUS!!
I'M THE HERO WHO'S LIBERATING PEOPLE FROM FEAR. I'M THE SAVIOR WHO'S GOING TO BE LIKE A GOD OF THIS PERFECT NEW WORLD!
THOSE WHO TRY TO FIGHT ME...
THEY'RE THE EVIL ONES!!
FLAP
YOU ARE TOO DAMN STUPID, L...
IF YOU'D BEEN SMARTER, THIS COULD'VE GOTTEN INTERESTING...
LIND L. TAILOR

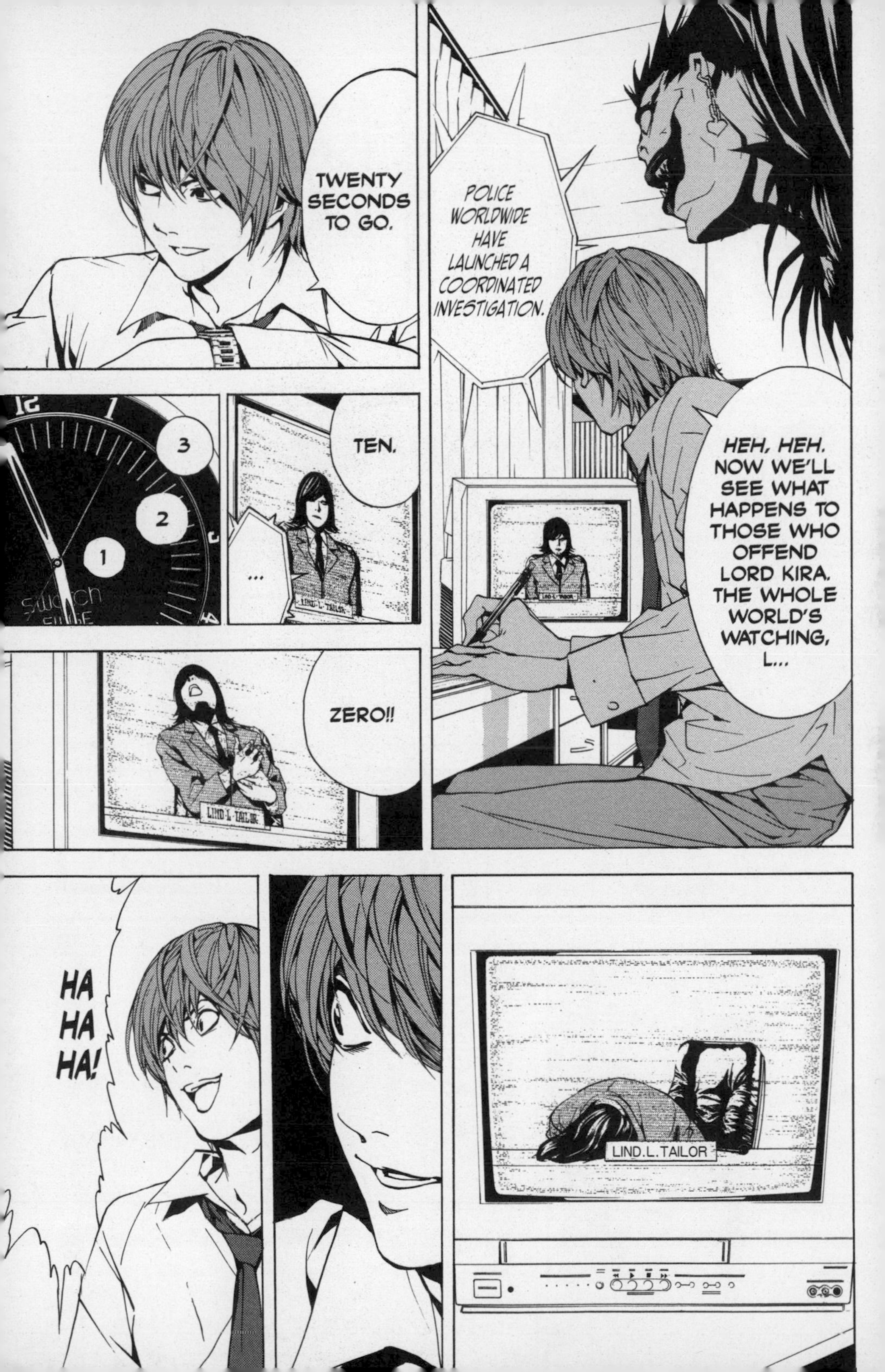
POLICE WORLDWIDE HAVE LAUNCHED A COORDINATED INVESTIGATION.
LIND.L.TAILOR
HEH, HEH. NOW WE'LL SEE WHAT HAPPENS TO THOSE WHO OFFEND LORD KIRA. THE WHOLE WORLD'S WATCHING, L...
TWENTY SECONDS TO GO.
TEN.
...
LIND.L.TAILOR
3
2
1
ZERO!!
LIND.L.TAILOR
LIND.L.TAILOR
HA HA HA!

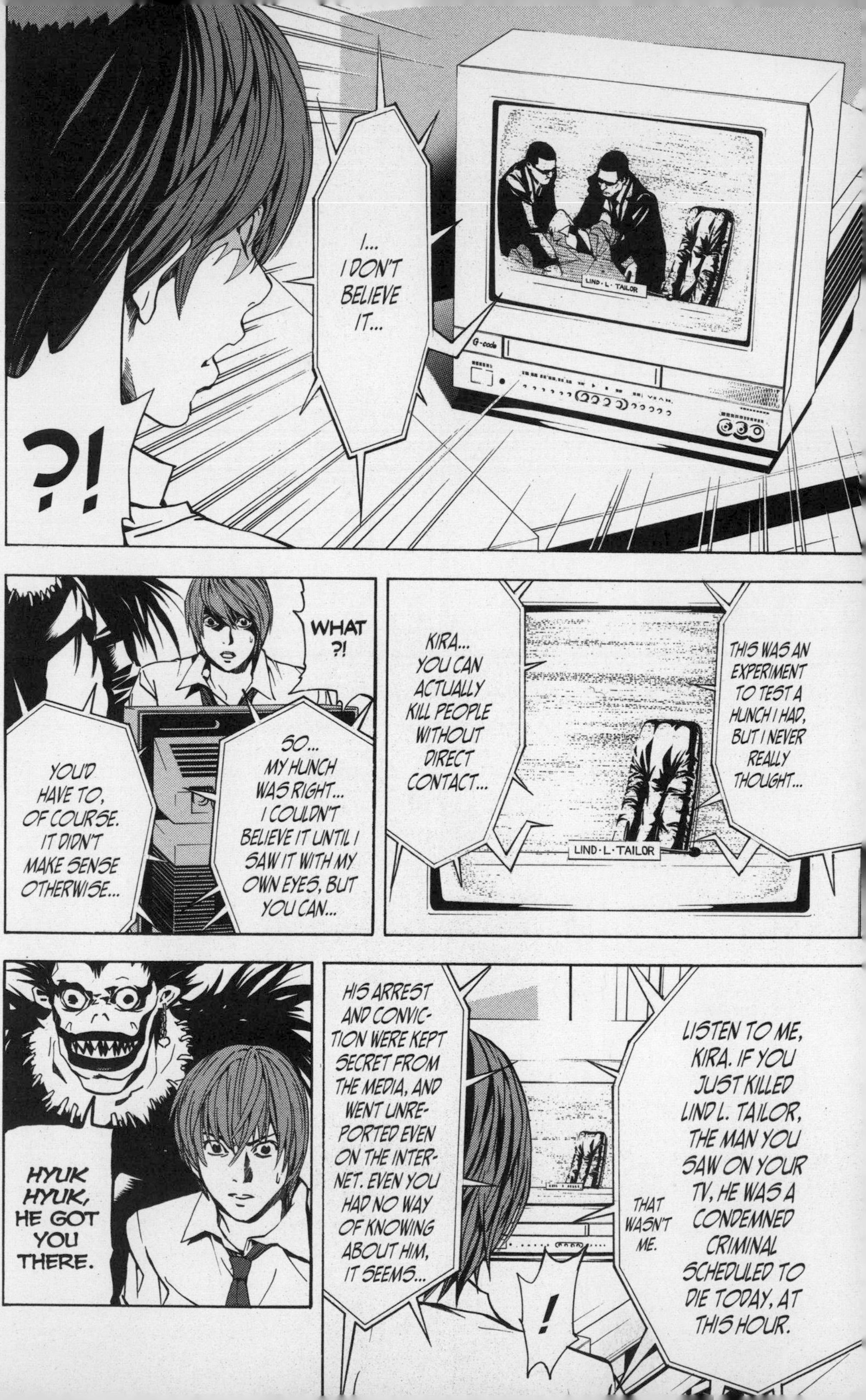
G-code
LIND · L · TAILOR
I... I DON'T BELIEVE IT...
?!
THIS WAS AN EXPERIMENT TO TEST A HUNCH I HAD, BUT I NEVER REALLY THOUGHT...
KIRA... YOU CAN ACTUALLY KILL PEOPLE WITHOUT DIRECT CONTACT...
LIND · L · TAILOR
WHAT ?!
SO... MY HUNCH WAS RIGHT... I COULDN'T BELIEVE IT UNTIL I SAW IT WITH MY OWN EYES, BUT YOU CAN...
YOU'D HAVE TO, OF COURSE. IT DIDN'T MAKE SENSE OTHERWISE...
LISTEN TO ME, KIRA. IF YOU JUST KILLED LIND L. TAILOR, THE MAN YOU SAW ON YOUR TV, HE WAS A CONDEMNED CRIMINAL SCHEDULED TO DIE TODAY, AT THIS HOUR.
THAT WASN'T ME.
HIS ARREST AND CONVICTION WERE KEPT SECRET FROM THE MEDIA, AND WENT UNREPORTED EVEN ON THE INTERNET. EVEN YOU HAD NO WAY OF KNOWING ABOUT HIM, IT SEEMS...
!
HYUK HYUK, HE GOT YOU THERE.

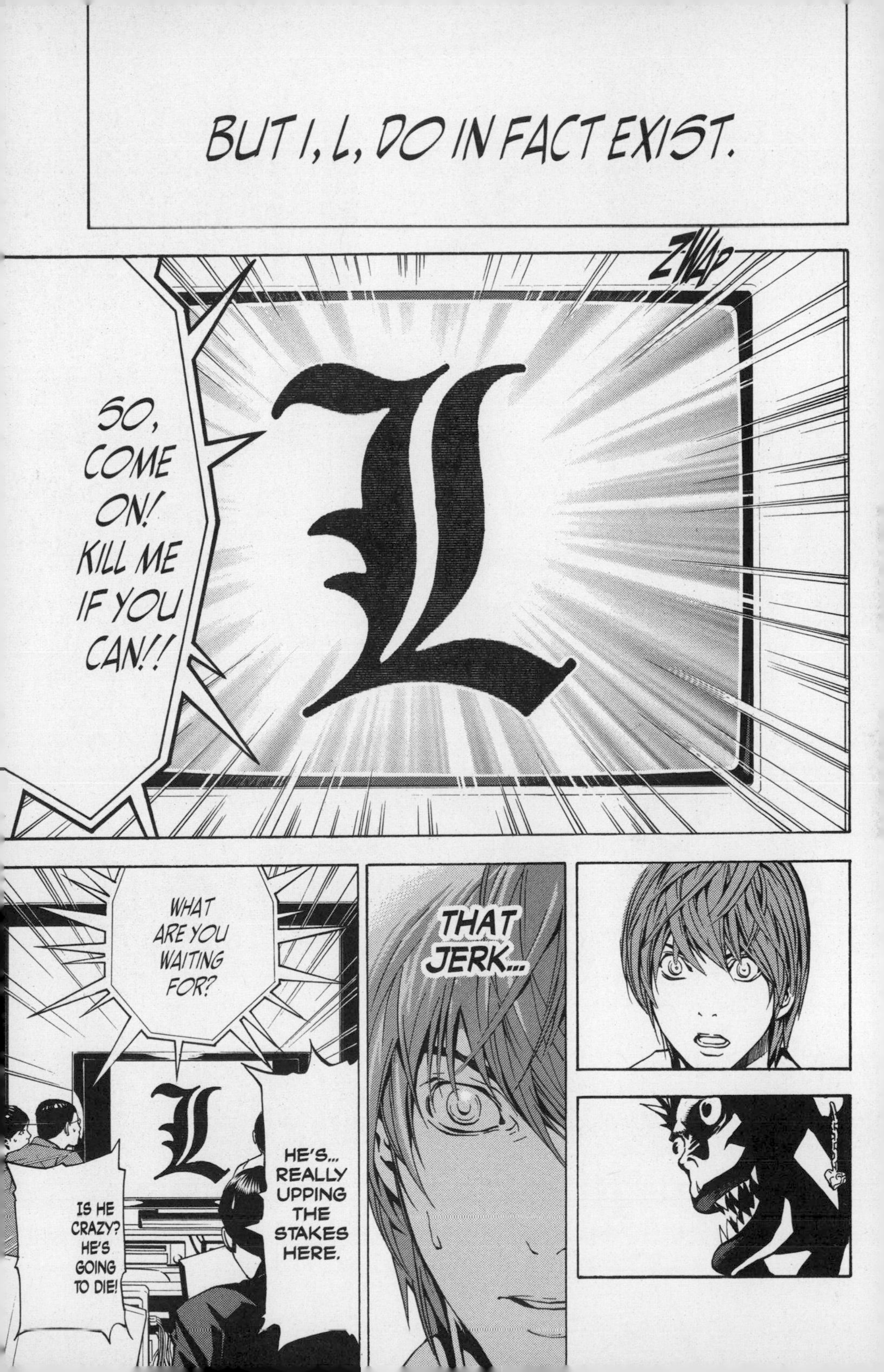
BUT I, L, DO IN FACT EXIST.
ZWAP
SO, COME ON! KILL ME IF YOU CAN!!
THAT JERK...
HE'S... REALLY UPPING THE STAKES HERE.
WHAT ARE YOU WAITING FOR?
IS HE CRAZY? HE'S GOING TO DIE!

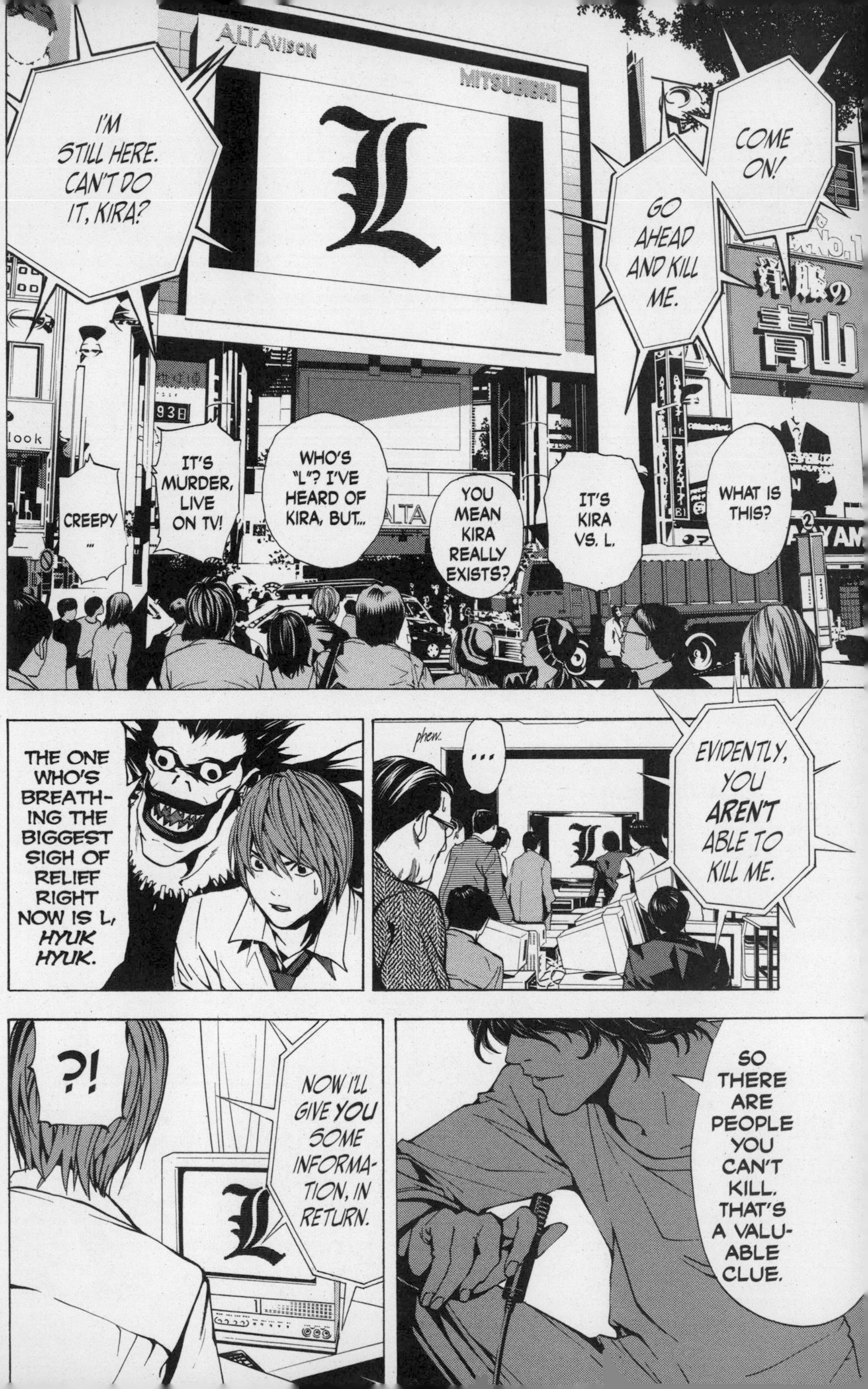
ALTAVISON
MITSUBISHI
COME ON!
GO AHEAD AND KILL ME.
I'M STILL HERE. CAN'T DO IT, KIRA?
WHAT IS THIS?
IT'S KIRA VS. L.
YOU MEAN KIRA REALLY EXISTS?
ALTA
WHO'S "L"? I'VE HEARD OF KIRA, BUT...
IT'S MURDER, LIVE ON TV!
CREEPY...
EVIDENTLY, YOU *AREN'T* ABLE TO KILL ME.
...
phew..
THE ONE WHO'S BREATHING THE BIGGEST SIGH OF RELIEF RIGHT NOW IS L, *HYUK HYUK*.
SO THERE ARE PEOPLE YOU CAN'T KILL. THAT'S A VALUABLE CLUE.
NOW I'LL GIVE *YOU* SOME INFORMATION, IN RETURN.
?!

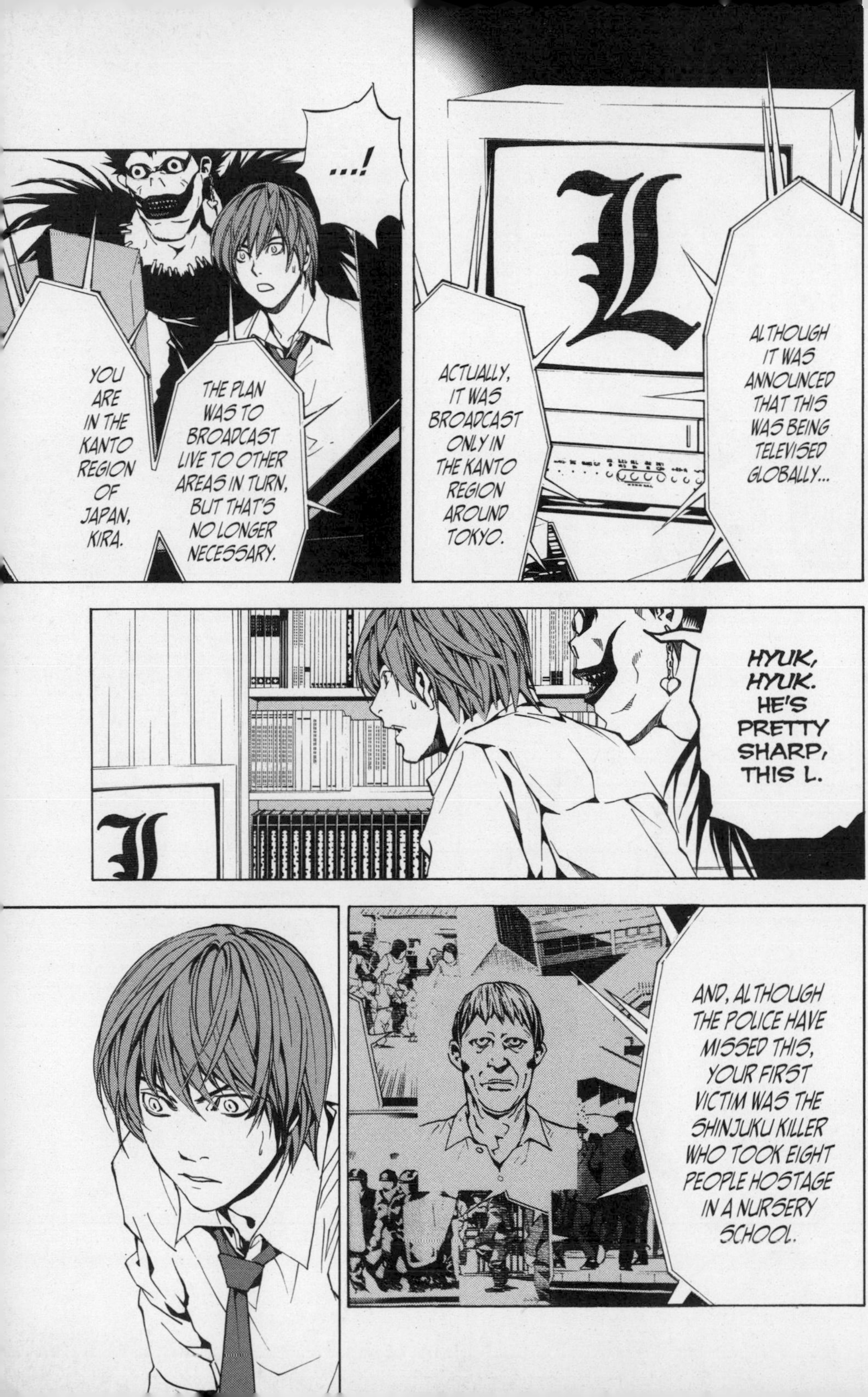
ALTHOUGH IT WAS ANNOUNCED THAT THIS WAS BEING TELEVISED GLOBALLY...
ACTUALLY, IT WAS BROADCAST ONLY IN THE KANTO REGION AROUND TOKYO.
...!
THE PLAN WAS TO BROADCAST LIVE TO OTHER AREAS IN TURN, BUT THAT'S NO LONGER NECESSARY.
YOU ARE IN THE KANTO REGION OF JAPAN, KIRA.
HYUK, HYUK. HE'S PRETTY SHARP, THIS L.
AND, ALTHOUGH THE POLICE HAVE MISSED THIS, YOUR FIRST VICTIM WAS THE SHINJUKU KILLER WHO TOOK EIGHT PEOPLE HOSTAGE IN A NURSERY SCHOOL.

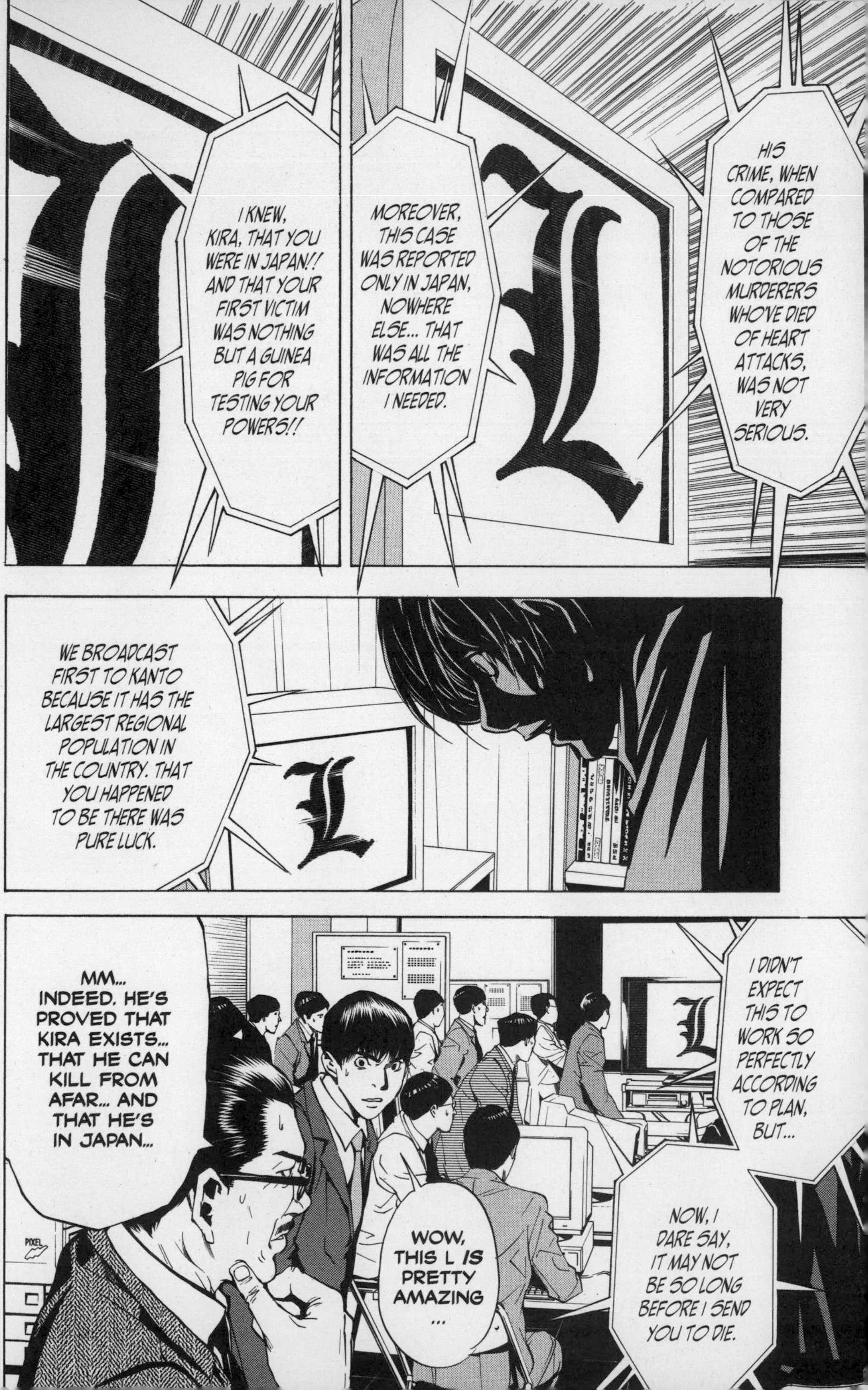
HIS CRIME, WHEN COMPARED TO THOSE OF THE NOTORIOUS MURDERERS WHO'VE DIED OF HEART ATTACKS, WAS NOT VERY SERIOUS.
MOREOVER, THIS CASE WAS REPORTED ONLY IN JAPAN, NOWHERE ELSE... THAT WAS ALL THE INFORMATION I NEEDED.
I KNEW, KIRA, THAT YOU WERE IN JAPAN!! AND THAT YOUR FIRST VICTIM WAS NOTHING BUT A GUINEA PIG FOR TESTING YOUR POWERS!!
WE BROADCAST FIRST TO KANTO BECAUSE IT HAS THE LARGEST REGIONAL POPULATION IN THE COUNTRY. THAT YOU HAPPENED TO BE THERE WAS PURE LUCK.
I DIDN'T EXPECT THIS TO WORK SO PERFECTLY ACCORDING TO PLAN, BUT...
NOW, I DARE SAY, IT MAY NOT BE SO LONG BEFORE I SEND YOU TO DIE.
WOW, THIS L IS PRETTY AMAZING ...
MM... INDEED. HE'S PROVED THAT KIRA EXISTS... THAT HE CAN KILL FROM AFAR... AND THAT HE'S IN JAPAN...

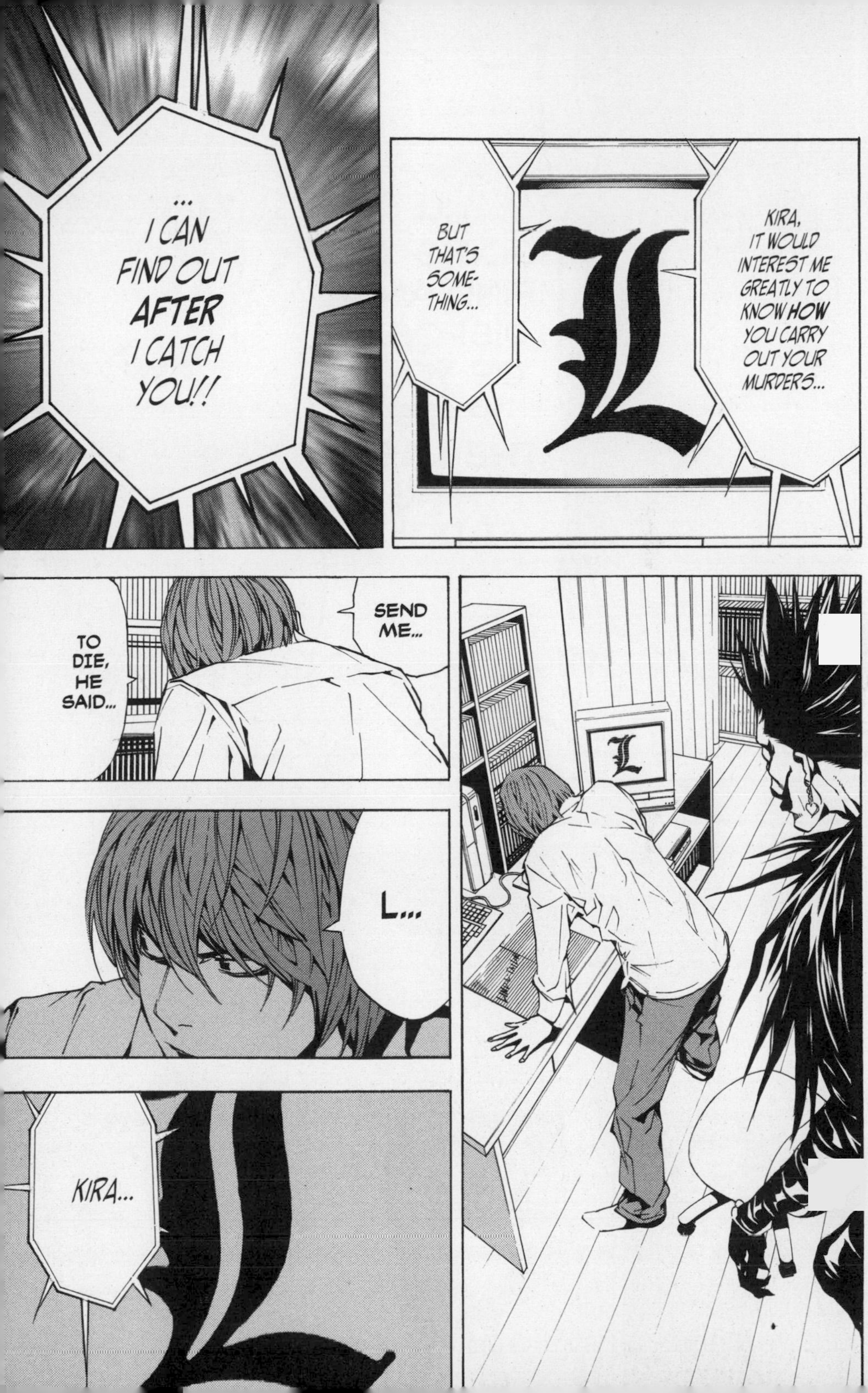
KIRA, IT WOULD INTEREST ME GREATLY TO KNOW HOW YOU CARRY OUT YOUR MURDERS...
BUT THAT'S SOME-THING...
... I CAN FIND OUT AFTER I CATCH YOU!!
SEND ME...
TO DIE, HE SAID...
L...
KIRA...

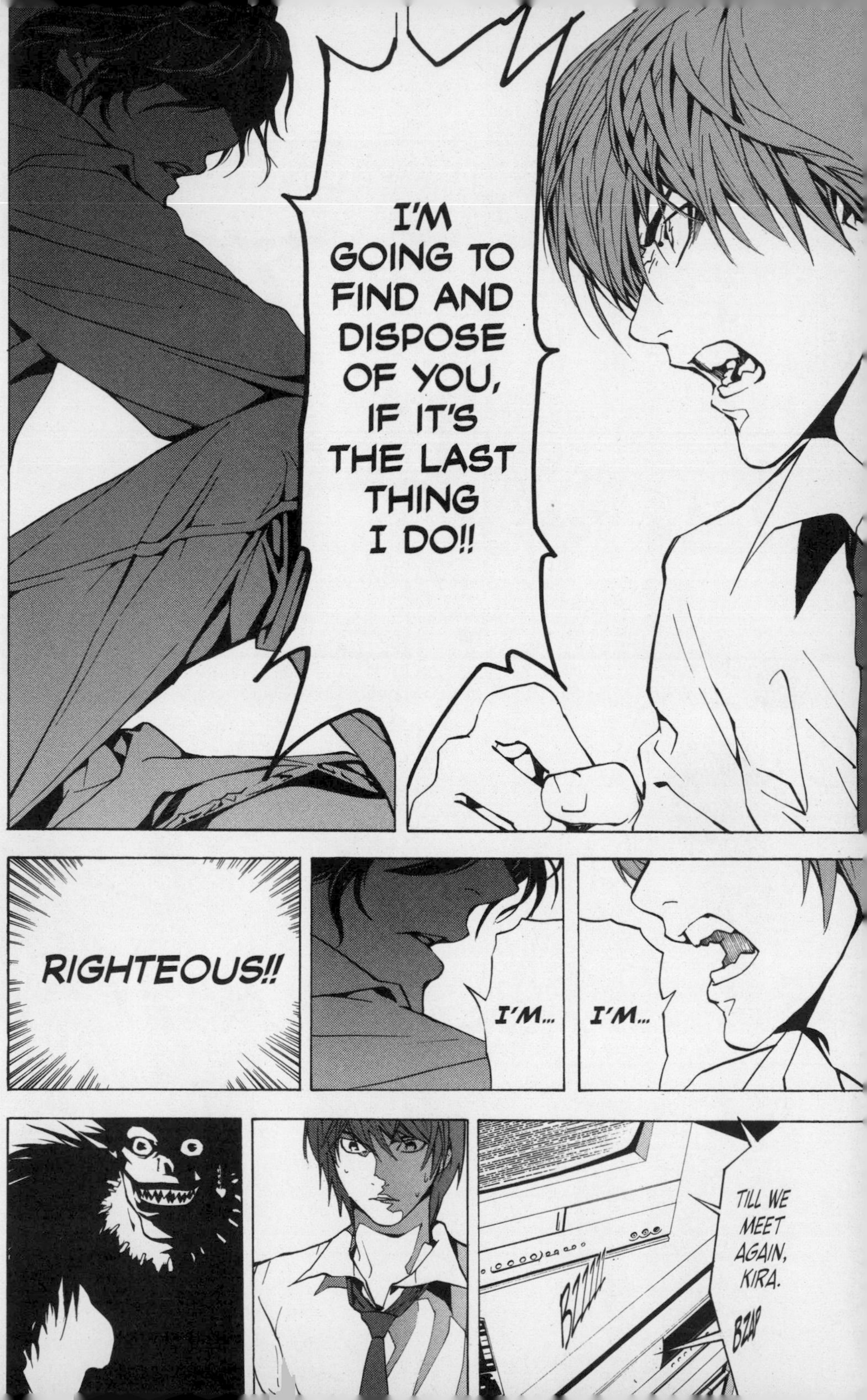
I'M GOING TO FIND AND DISPOSE OF YOU, IF IT'S THE LAST THING I DO!!
I'M...
I'M...
RIGHTEOUS!!
TILL WE MEET AGAIN, KIRA.
BZAP
BZZZZ

READ THIS WAY

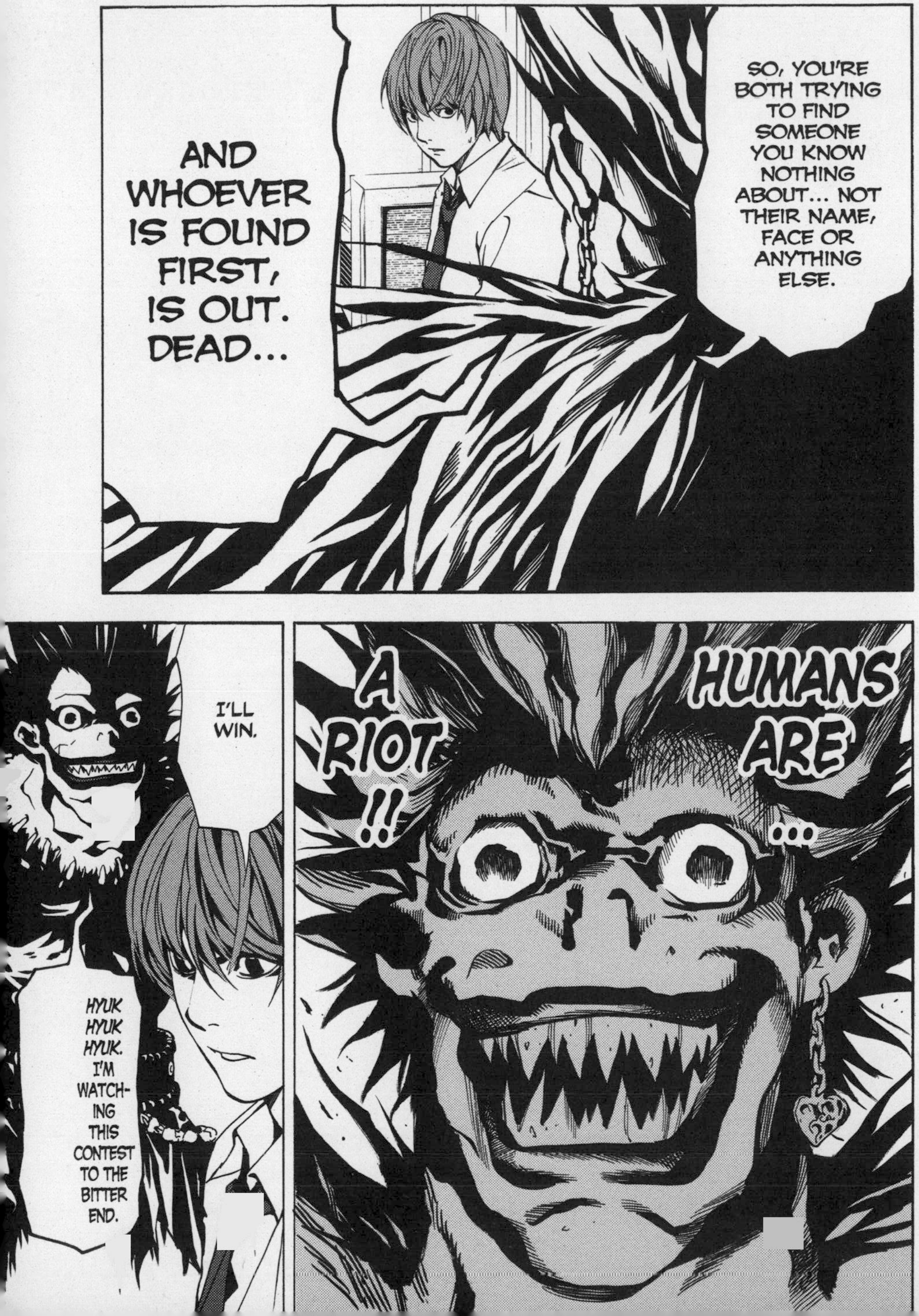
SO, YOU'RE BOTH TRYING TO FIND SOMEONE YOU KNOW NOTHING ABOUT... NOT THEIR NAME, FACE OR ANYTHING ELSE.
AND WHOEVER IS FOUND FIRST, IS OUT. DEAD...
HUMANS ARE...
A RIOT!!
I'LL WIN.
HYUK HYUK HYUK. I'M WATCHING THIS CONTEST TO THE BITTER END.

# DEATH NOTE
## How to use it
### II

- This note shall become the property of the human world, once it touches the ground of (arrives in) the human world.

  このノートは人間界の地に着いた時点から人間界の物となる。


- The owner of the note can recognize the image and voice of its original owner, i.e. a god of death.

  所有者はノートの元の持ち主である死神の姿や声を認知する事ができる。


- The human who uses this note can neither go to Heaven nor Hell.

  このノートを使った人間は天国にも地獄にも行けない。

# chapter 3 Family

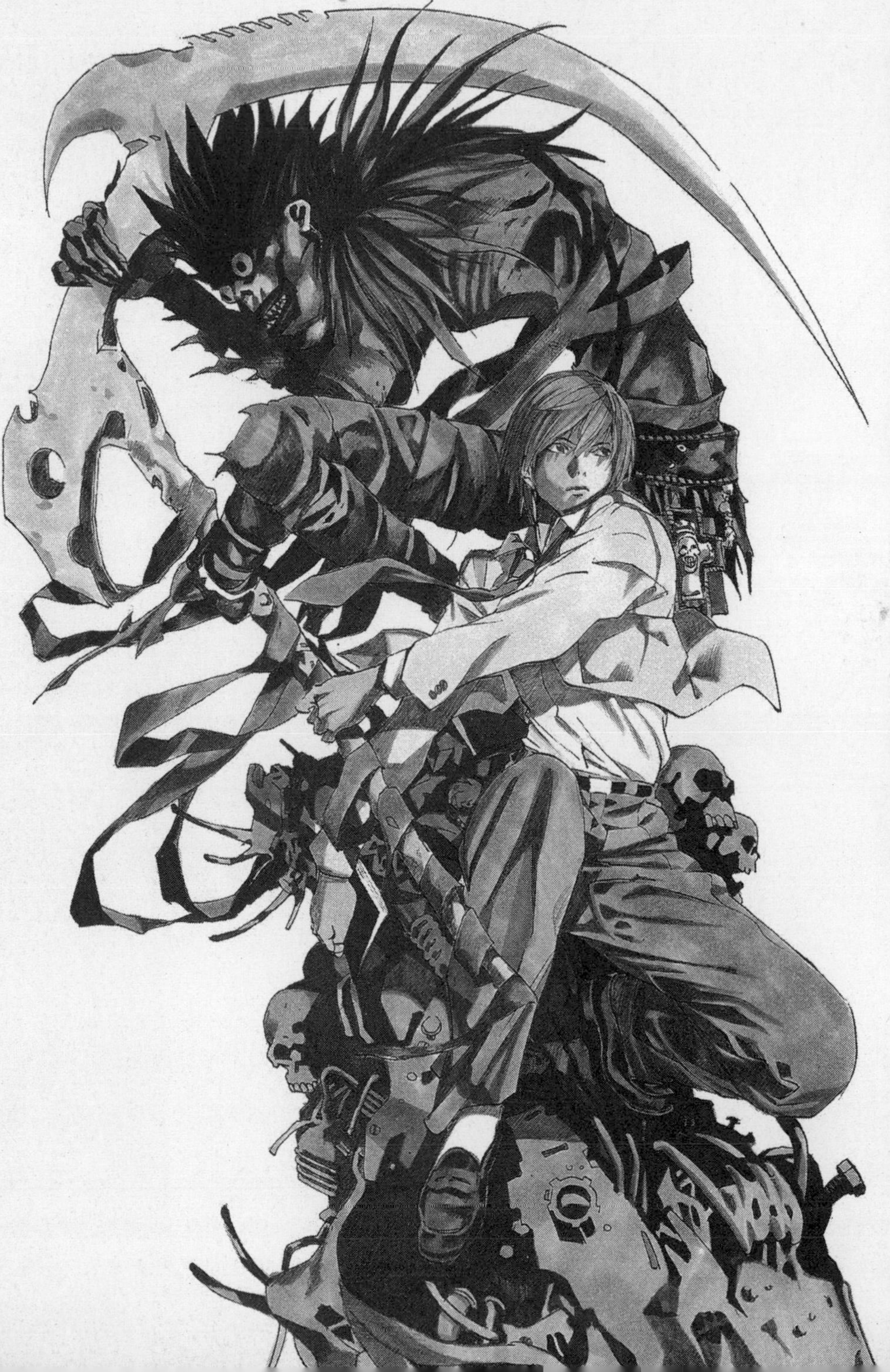

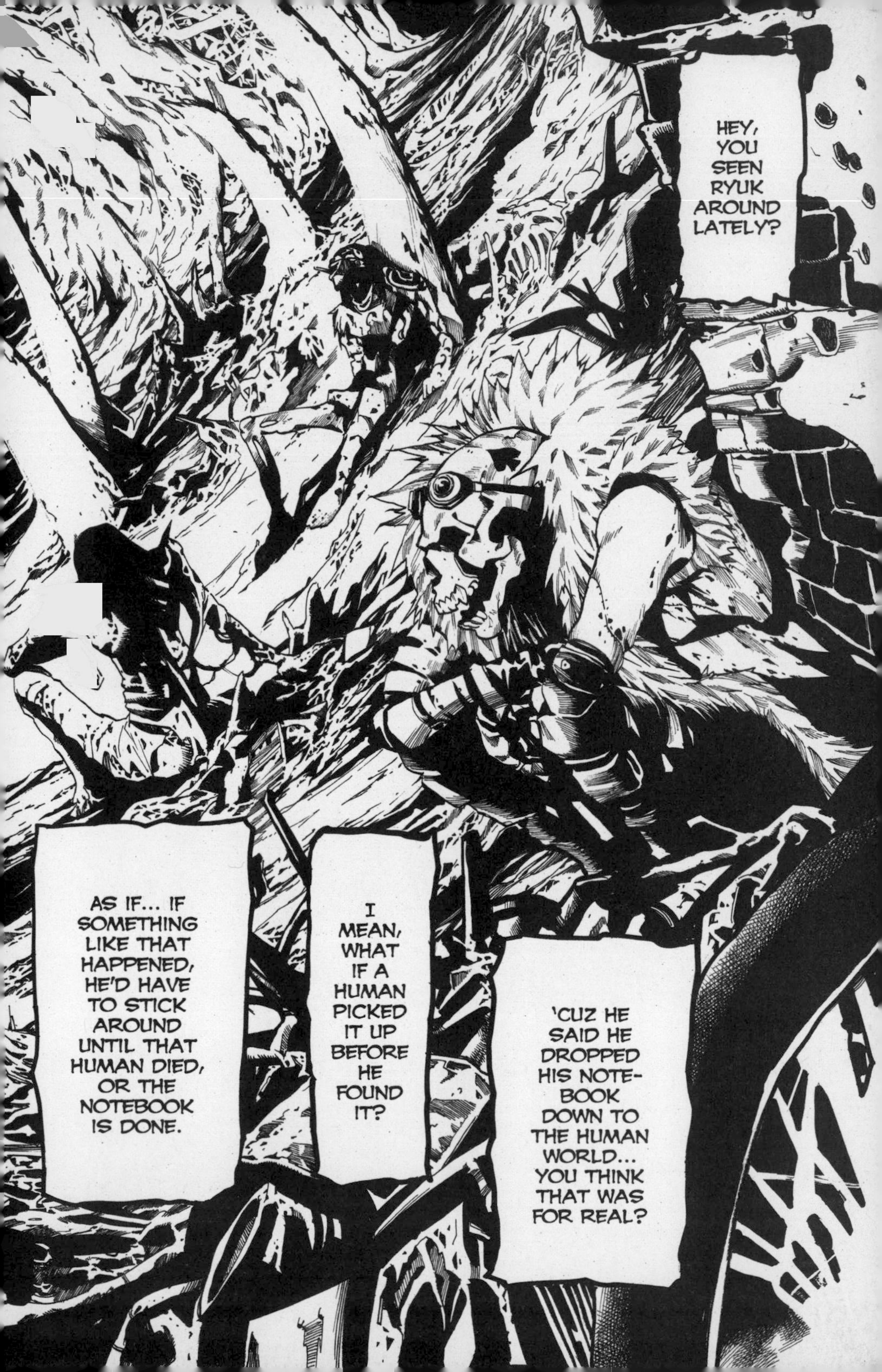
HEY, YOU SEEN RYUK AROUND LATELY?
'CUZ HE SAID HE DROPPED HIS NOTE-BOOK DOWN TO THE HUMAN WORLD... YOU THINK THAT WAS FOR REAL?
I MEAN, WHAT IF A HUMAN PICKED IT UP BEFORE HE FOUND IT?
AS IF... IF SOMETHING LIKE THAT HAPPENED, HE'D HAVE TO STICK AROUND UNTIL THAT HUMAN DIED, OR THE NOTEBOOK IS DONE.

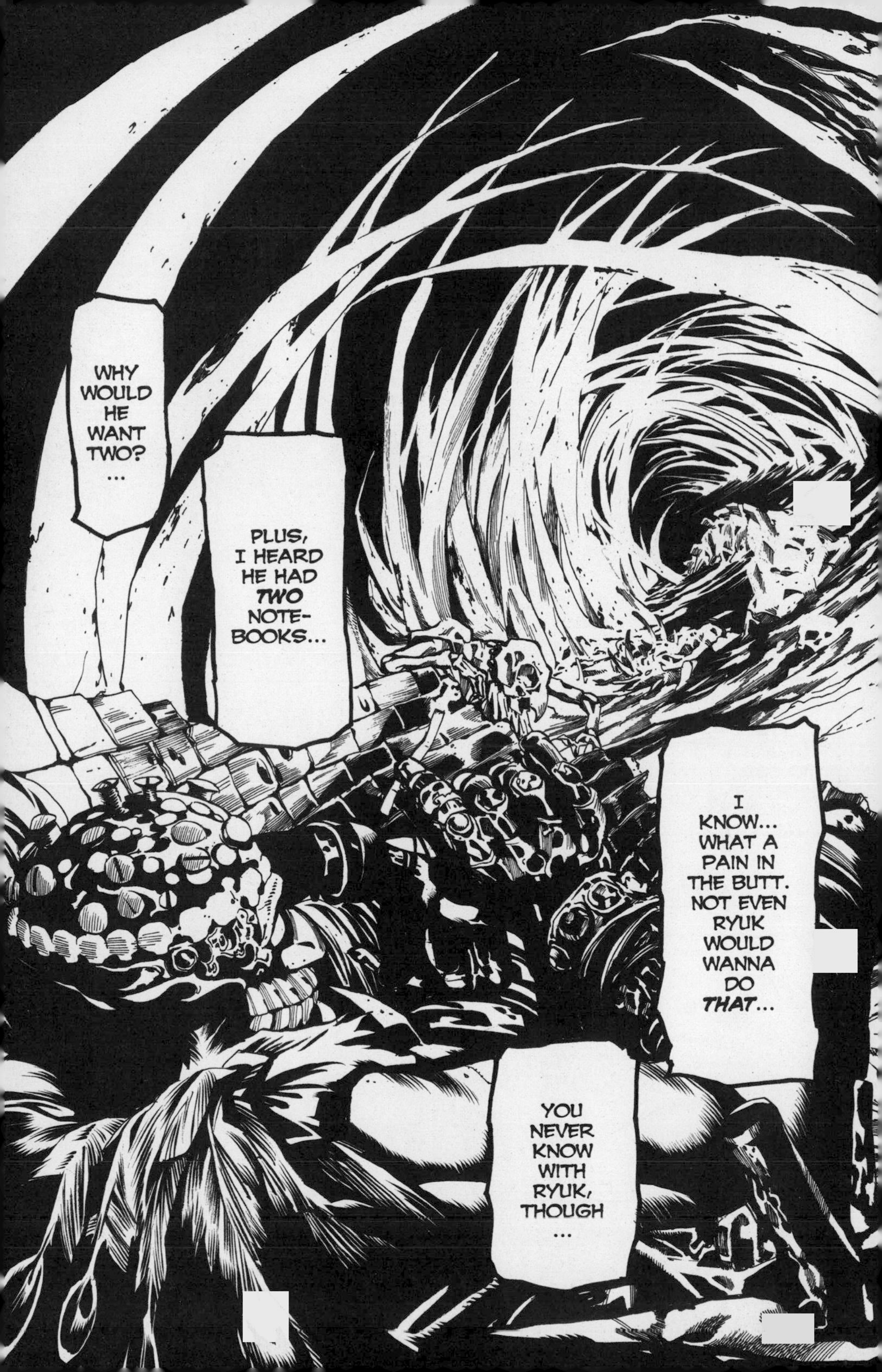
PLUS, I HEARD HE HAD *TWO* NOTE-BOOKS...
WHY WOULD HE WANT TWO? ...
I KNOW... WHAT A PAIN IN THE BUTT. NOT EVEN RYUK WOULD WANNA DO *THAT*...
YOU NEVER KNOW WITH RYUK, THOUGH ...

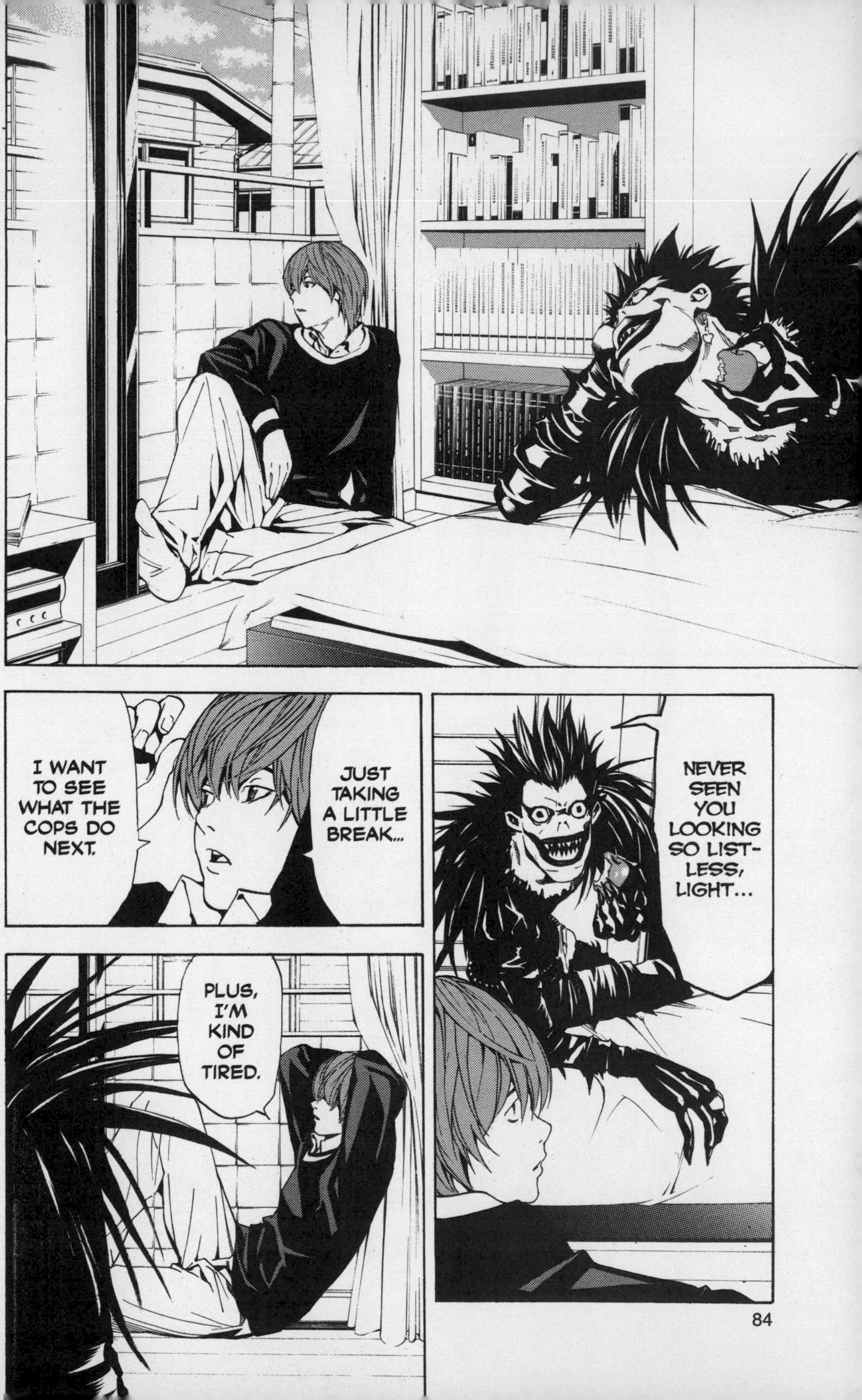
NEVER SEEN YOU LOOKING SO LIST-LESS, LIGHT...
JUST TAKING A LITTLE BREAK...
I WANT TO SEE WHAT THE COPS DO NEXT.
PLUS, I'M KIND OF TIRED.

HA HA.

I GUESS IT MIGHT BE PRETTY INTERESTING IF I WASN'T KIRA.

YOU CAN'T AVOID IT, EVEN IF YOU WANT TO...

TAKE ONE STEP OUT OF THE HOUSE, ALL YOU HEAR ABOUT IS L AND KIRA.

SOME PEOPLE ARE STILL DENYING WE EVEN EXIST...

MEANWHILE, THIS MAGAZINE IS CLAIMING THAT "L AND KIRA WERE INVENTED BY THE POLICE, WHO ARE ELIMINATING CRIMINALS WITHOUT RECOURSE TO LAW."

L VS. KIRA: THE MYSTERY DEEPENS! THE CASE FOR POLICE CONSPIRACY

"SUPER-SLEUTH L, INTERPOL'S SHADOWY MASTERMIND, VS. SUPER-NATURAL KIRA, TELEPATHIC MASS MURDERER."

SEXY ENQUIRER

FLAP

GOTTA GIVE HIS MIND A REST, ONCE IN A WHILE.

IF KIRA PAYS TOO MUCH ATTENTION TO THIS STUFF, IT JUST STRESSES HIM OUT.

TURN ON THE TV OR RADIO, IT'S KIRA VS. L THERE AS WELL.

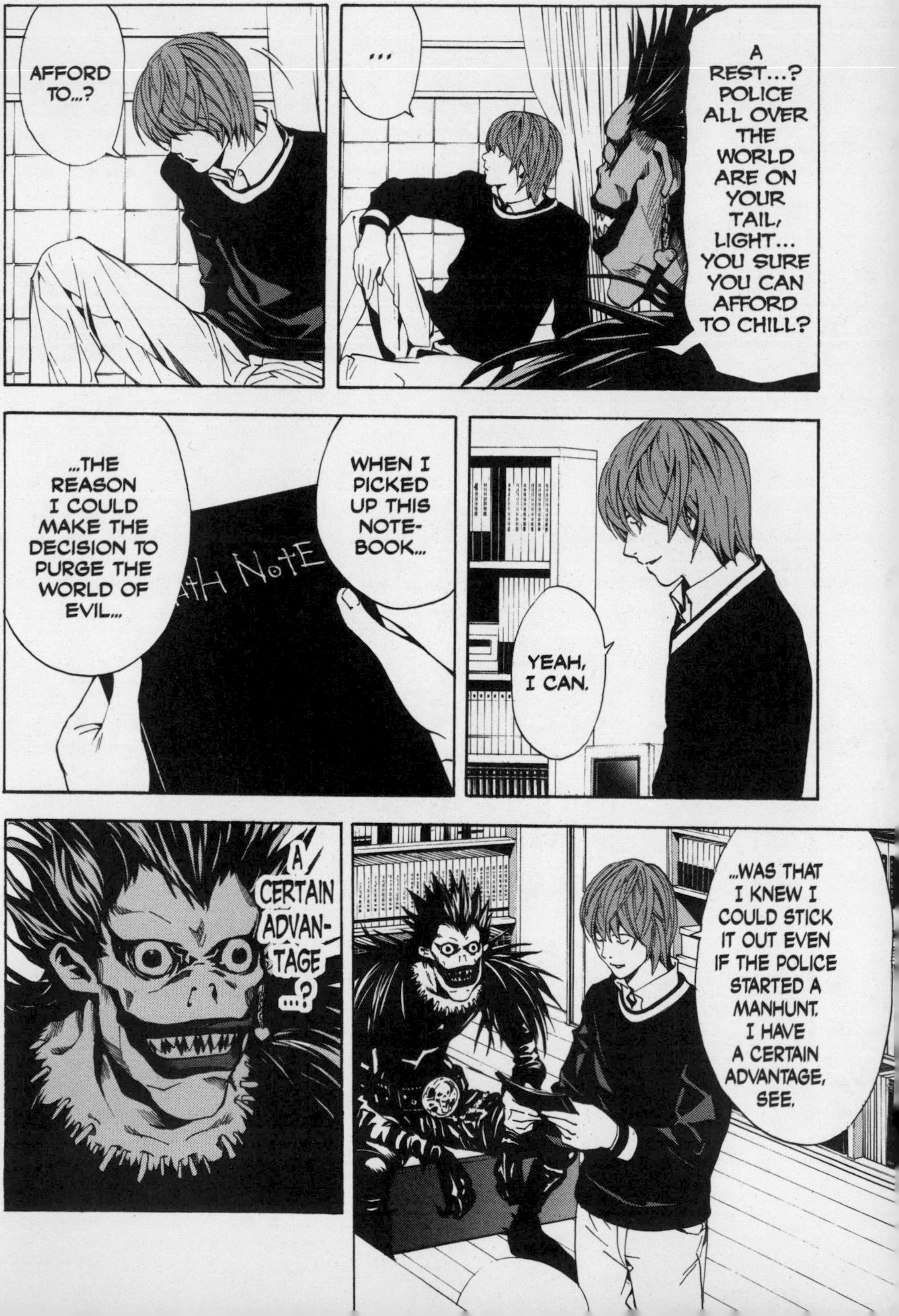
A REST...? POLICE ALL OVER THE WORLD ARE ON YOUR TAIL, LIGHT... YOU SURE YOU CAN AFFORD TO CHILL?
...
AFFORD TO...?
YEAH, I CAN.
WHEN I PICKED UP THIS NOTE-BOOK...
...THE REASON I COULD MAKE THE DECISION TO PURGE THE WORLD OF EVIL...
...WAS THAT I KNEW I COULD STICK IT OUT EVEN IF THE POLICE STARTED A MANHUNT. I HAVE A CERTAIN ADVANTAGE, SEE.
A CERTAIN ADVAN-TAGE ...?

WHY DO YOU HAVE TO LOCK YOUR DOOR, LIGHT?

RATTLE RATTLE RATTLE

KA-CHUNK

I NEED SOME HELP WITH MY HOME-WORK!

WHAT?

OH... HEY, SAYU.

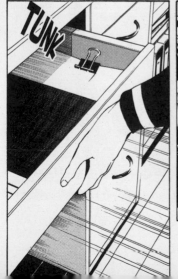

TUNK

OH, OKAY, SURE. HANG ON A SECOND.

ZOOSH

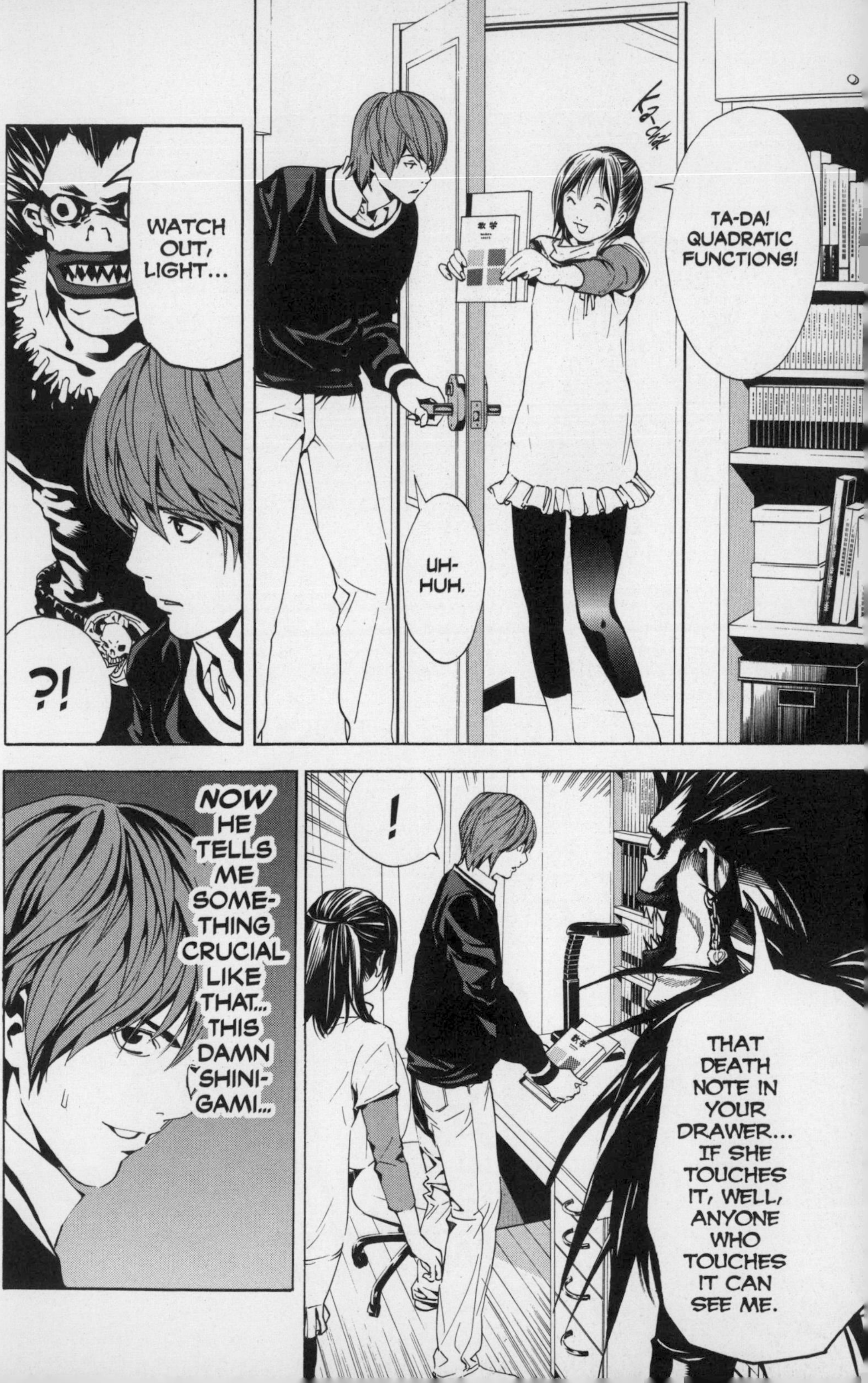
TA-DA! QUADRATIC FUNCTIONS!
UH-HUH.
WATCH OUT, LIGHT...
?!
!
THAT DEATH NOTE IN YOUR DRAWER... IF SHE TOUCHES IT, WELL, ANYONE WHO TOUCHES IT CAN SEE ME.
NOW HE TELLS ME SOMETHING CRUCIAL LIKE THAT... THIS DAMN SHINIGAMI...

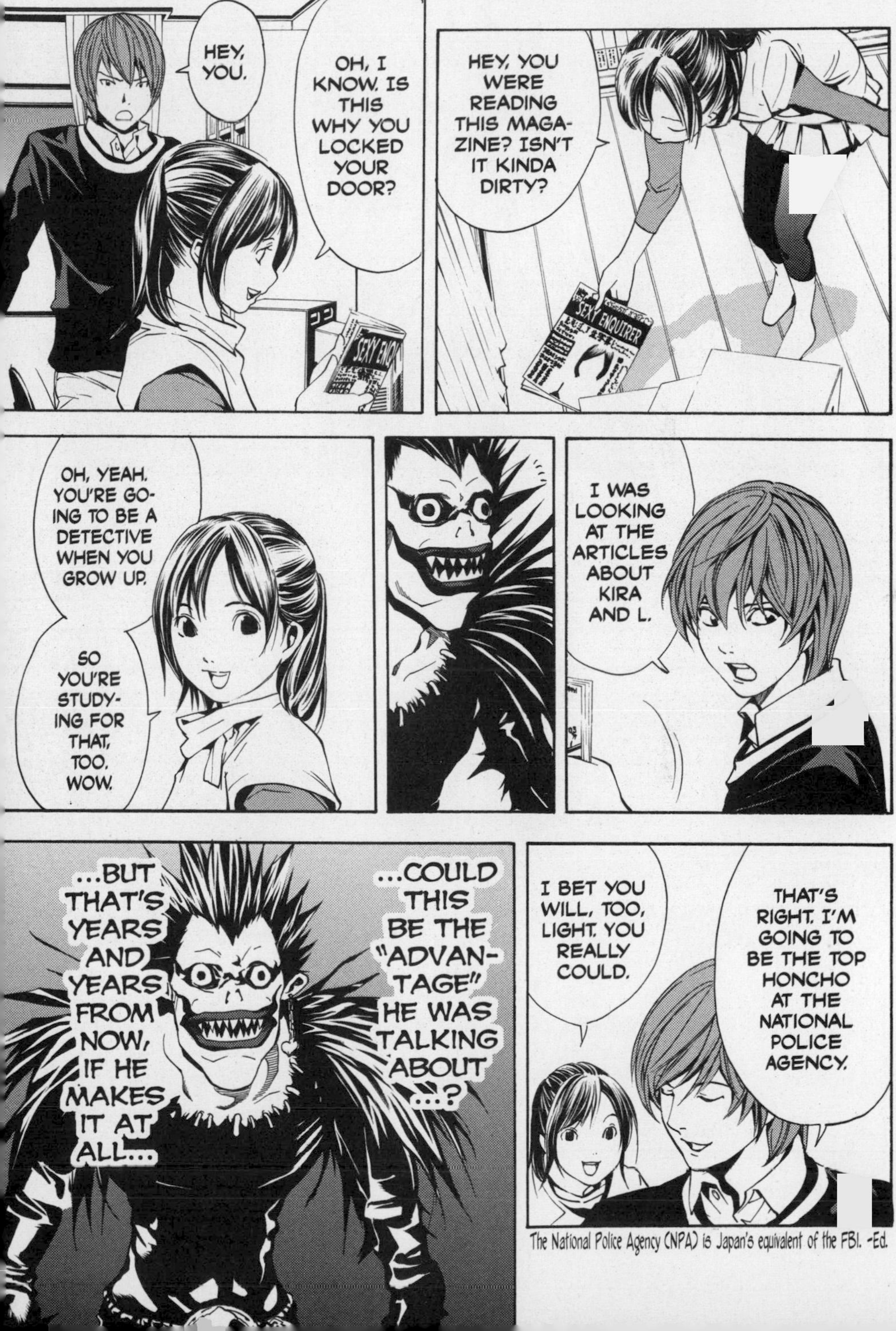
HEY, YOU WERE READING THIS MAGAZINE? ISN'T IT KINDA DIRTY?
SEXY ENQUIRER
OH, I KNOW. IS THIS WHY YOU LOCKED YOUR DOOR?
HEY, YOU.
I WAS LOOKING AT THE ARTICLES ABOUT KIRA AND L.
OH, YEAH. YOU'RE GOING TO BE A DETECTIVE WHEN YOU GROW UP.
SO YOU'RE STUDYING FOR THAT, TOO. WOW.
THAT'S RIGHT. I'M GOING TO BE THE TOP HONCHO AT THE NATIONAL POLICE AGENCY.
I BET YOU WILL, TOO, LIGHT. YOU REALLY COULD.
...COULD THIS BE THE "ADVANTAGE" HE WAS TALKING ABOUT...?
...BUT THAT'S YEARS AND YEARS FROM NOW, IF HE MAKES IT AT ALL...

The National Police Agency (NPA) is Japan's equivalent of the FBI. -Ed.

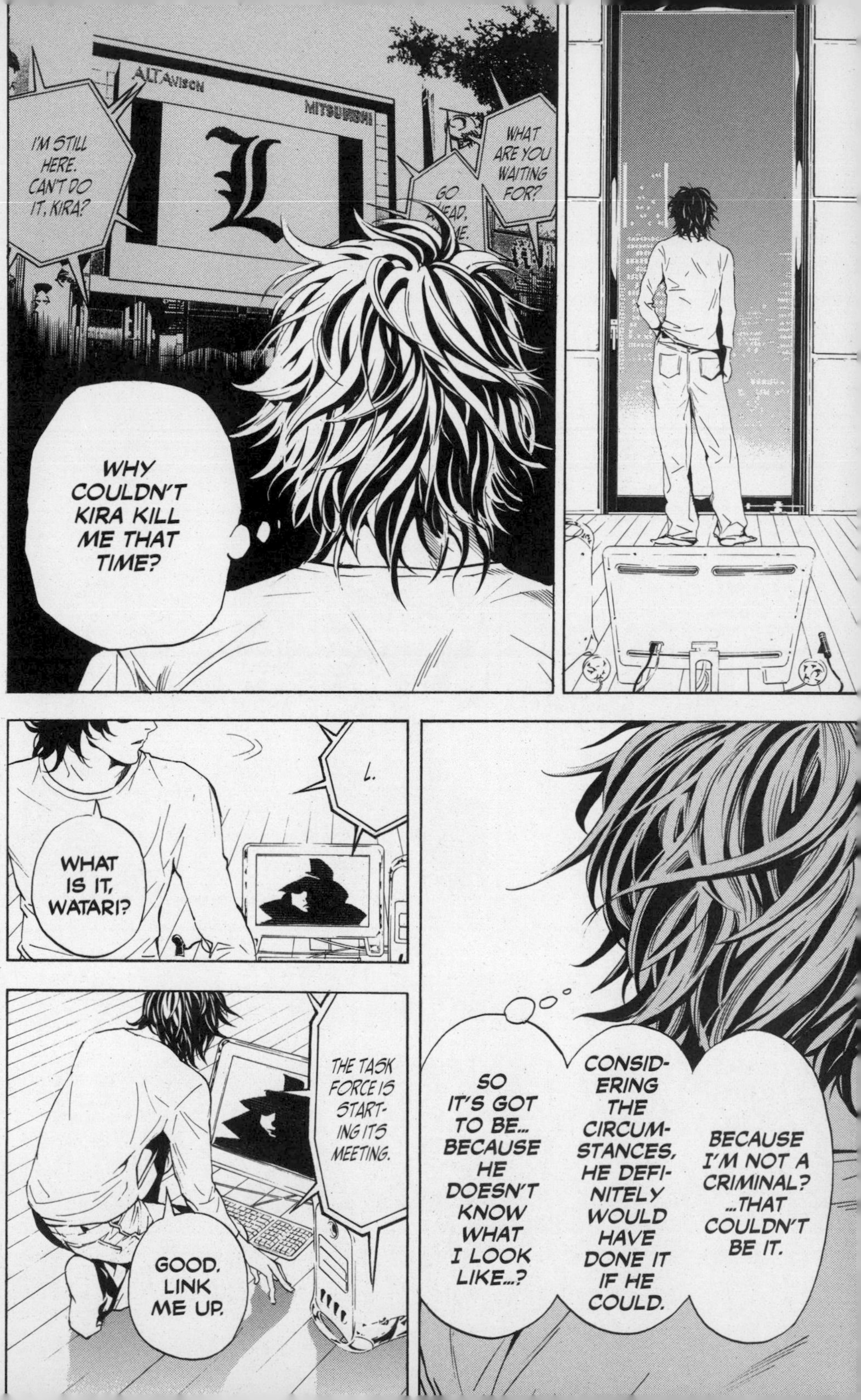
WHAT ARE YOU WAITING FOR?
I'M STILL HERE. CAN'T DO IT, KIRA?
WHY COULDN'T KIRA KILL ME THAT TIME?
BECAUSE I'M NOT A CRIMINAL? ...THAT COULDN'T BE IT.
CONSID-ERING THE CIRCUM-STANCES, HE DEFI-NITELY WOULD HAVE DONE IT IF HE COULD.
SO IT'S GOT TO BE... BECAUSE HE DOESN'T KNOW WHAT I LOOK LIKE...?
L.
WHAT IS IT, WATARI?
THE TASK FORCE IS START-ING ITS MEETING.
GOOD. LINK ME UP.

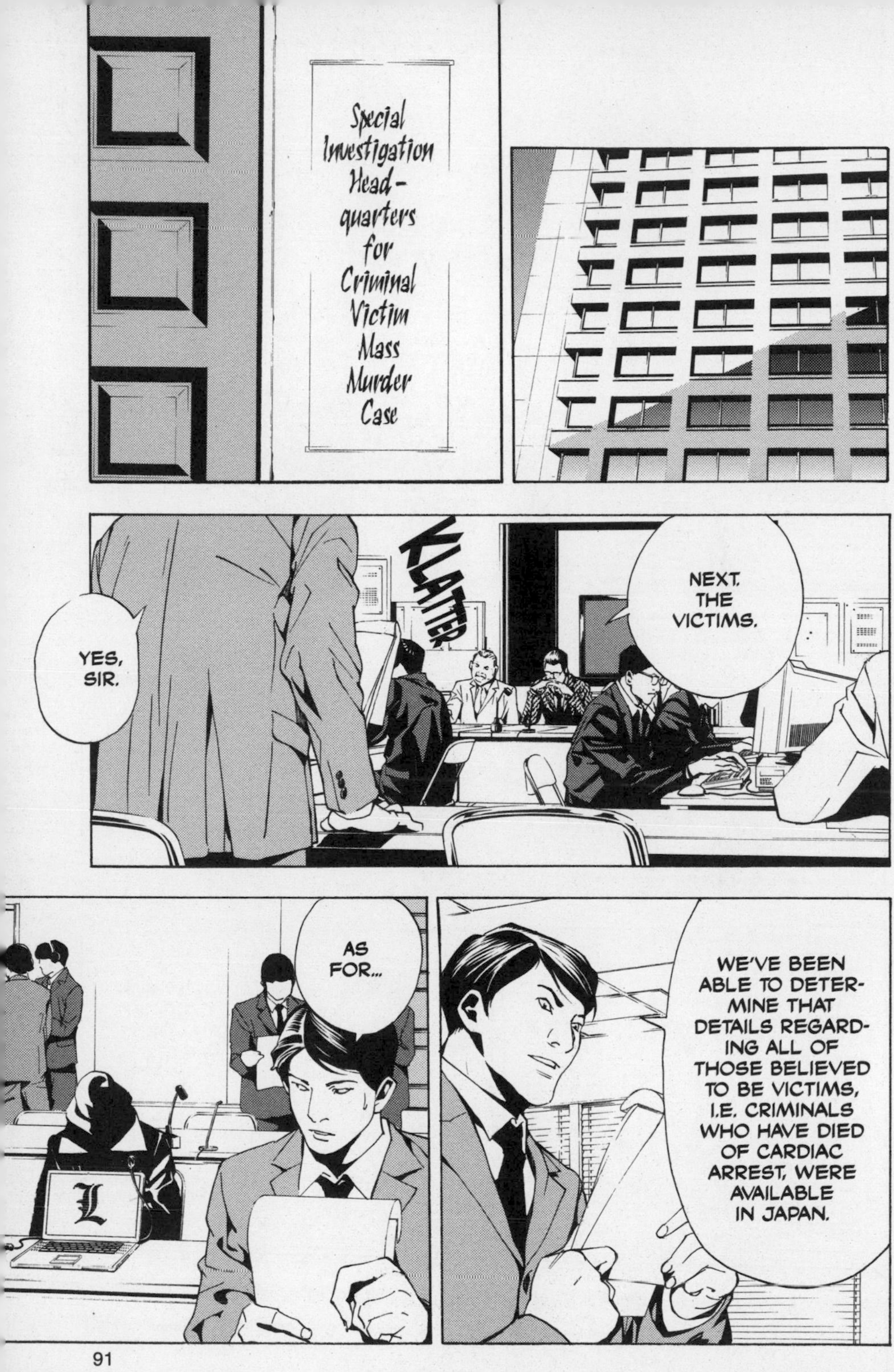
Special Investigation Head-quarters for Criminal Victim Mass Murder Case
NEXT, THE VICTIMS.
KLATTER
YES, SIR.
WE'VE BEEN ABLE TO DETERMINE THAT DETAILS REGARDING ALL OF THOSE BELIEVED TO BE VICTIMS, I.E. CRIMINALS WHO HAVE DIED OF CARDIAC ARREST, WERE AVAILABLE IN JAPAN.
AS FOR...

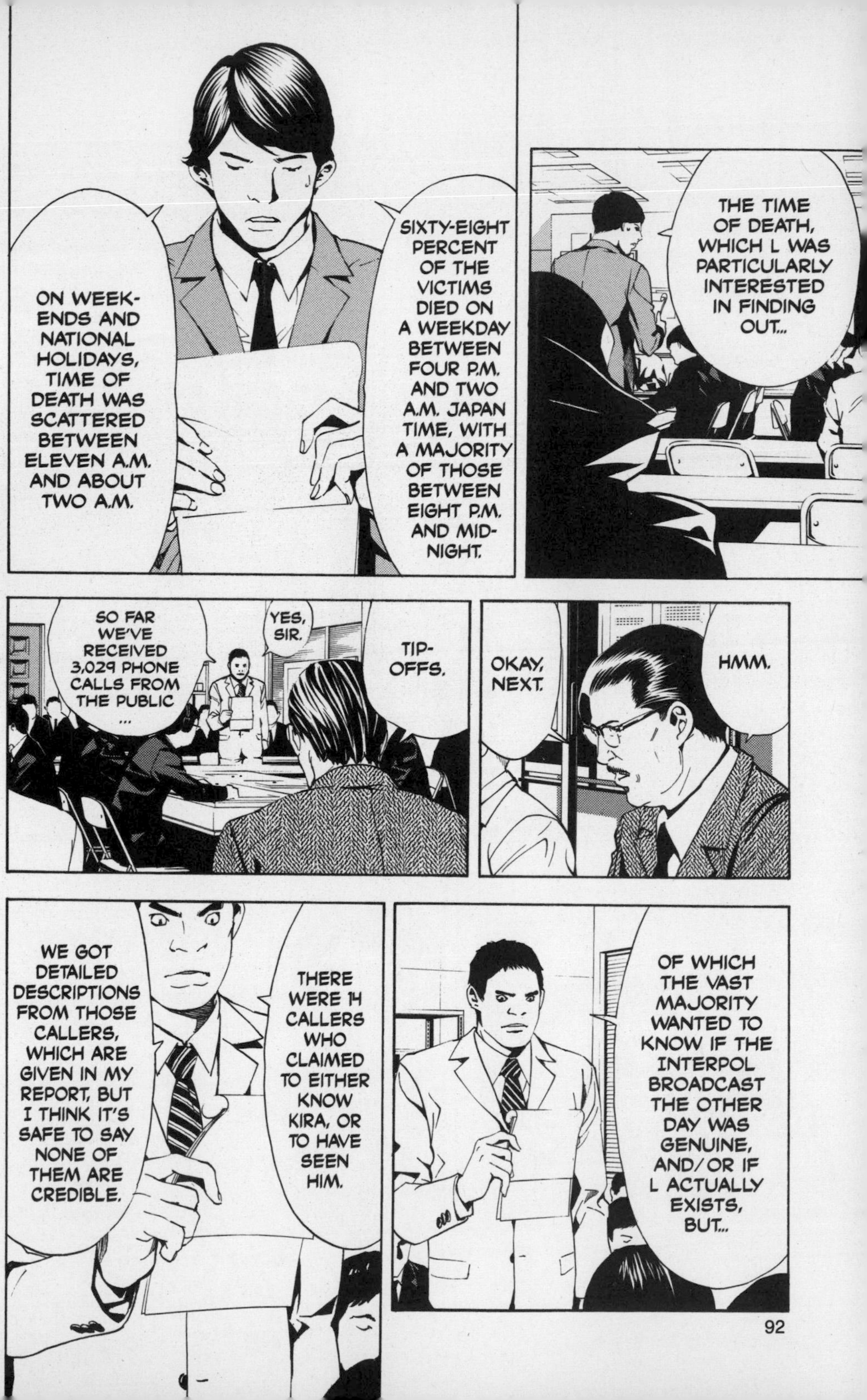
THE TIME OF DEATH, WHICH L WAS PARTICULARLY INTERESTED IN FINDING OUT...
SIXTY-EIGHT PERCENT OF THE VICTIMS DIED ON A WEEKDAY BETWEEN FOUR P.M. AND TWO A.M. JAPAN TIME, WITH A MAJORITY OF THOSE BETWEEN EIGHT P.M. AND MID-NIGHT.
ON WEEK-ENDS AND NATIONAL HOLIDAYS, TIME OF DEATH WAS SCATTERED BETWEEN ELEVEN A.M. AND ABOUT TWO A.M.
HMM.
OKAY, NEXT.
TIP-OFFS.
YES, SIR.
SO FAR WE'VE RECEIVED 3,029 PHONE CALLS FROM THE PUBLIC...
OF WHICH THE VAST MAJORITY WANTED TO KNOW IF THE INTERPOL BROADCAST THE OTHER DAY WAS GENUINE, AND/OR IF L ACTUALLY EXISTS, BUT...
THERE WERE 14 CALLERS WHO CLAIMED TO EITHER KNOW KIRA, OR TO HAVE SEEN HIM.
WE GOT DETAILED DESCRIPTIONS FROM THOSE CALLERS, WHICH ARE GIVEN IN MY REPORT, BUT I THINK IT'S SAFE TO SAY NONE OF THEM ARE CREDIBLE.

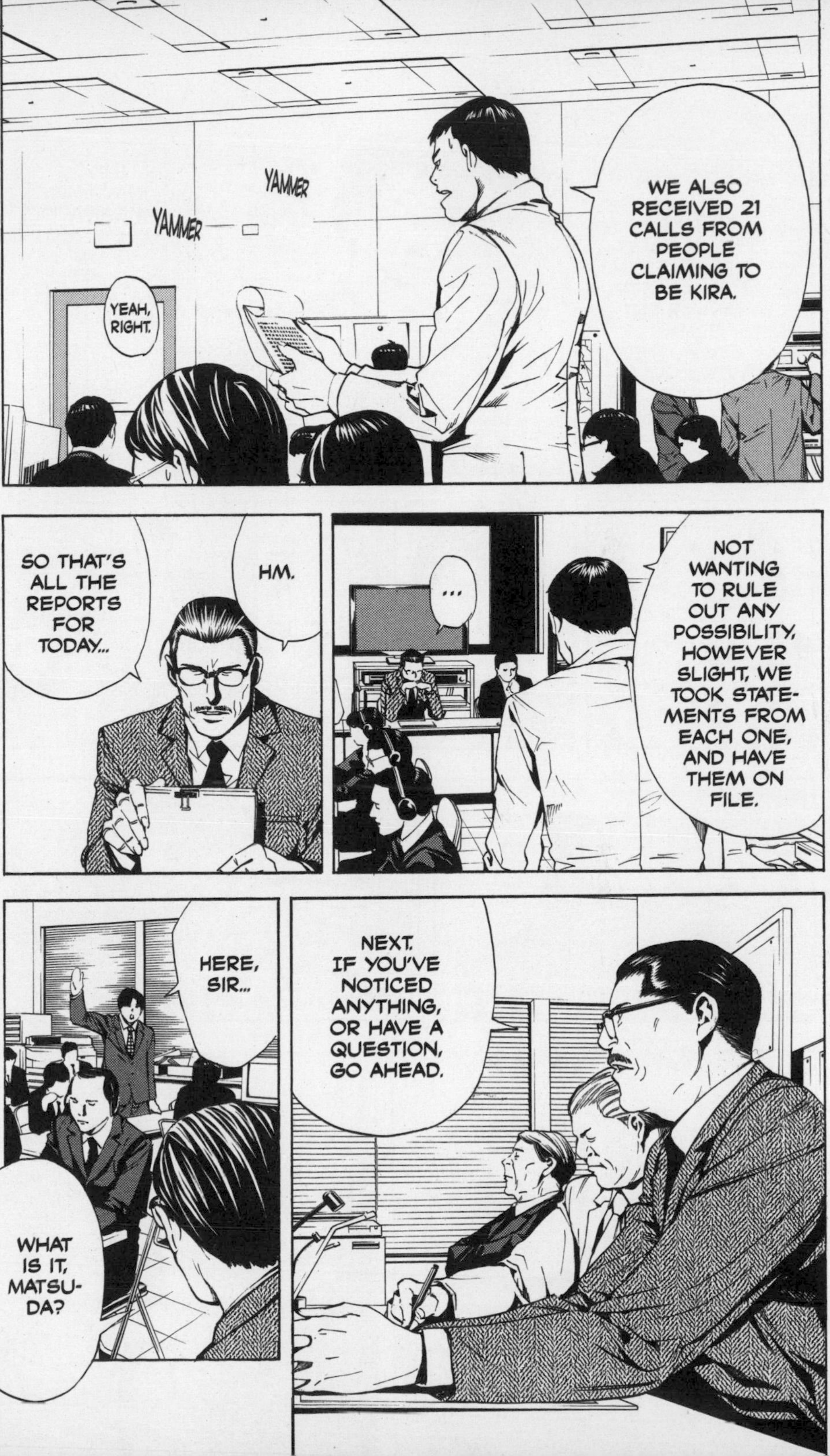
WE ALSO RECEIVED 21 CALLS FROM PEOPLE CLAIMING TO BE KIRA.
YAMMER
YAMMER
YEAH, RIGHT.
NOT WANTING TO RULE OUT ANY POSSIBILITY, HOWEVER SLIGHT, WE TOOK STATEMENTS FROM EACH ONE, AND HAVE THEM ON FILE.
...
HM.
SO THAT'S ALL THE REPORTS FOR TODAY...
NEXT. IF YOU'VE NOTICED ANYTHING, OR HAVE A QUESTION, GO AHEAD.
HERE, SIR...
WHAT IS IT, MATSUDA?

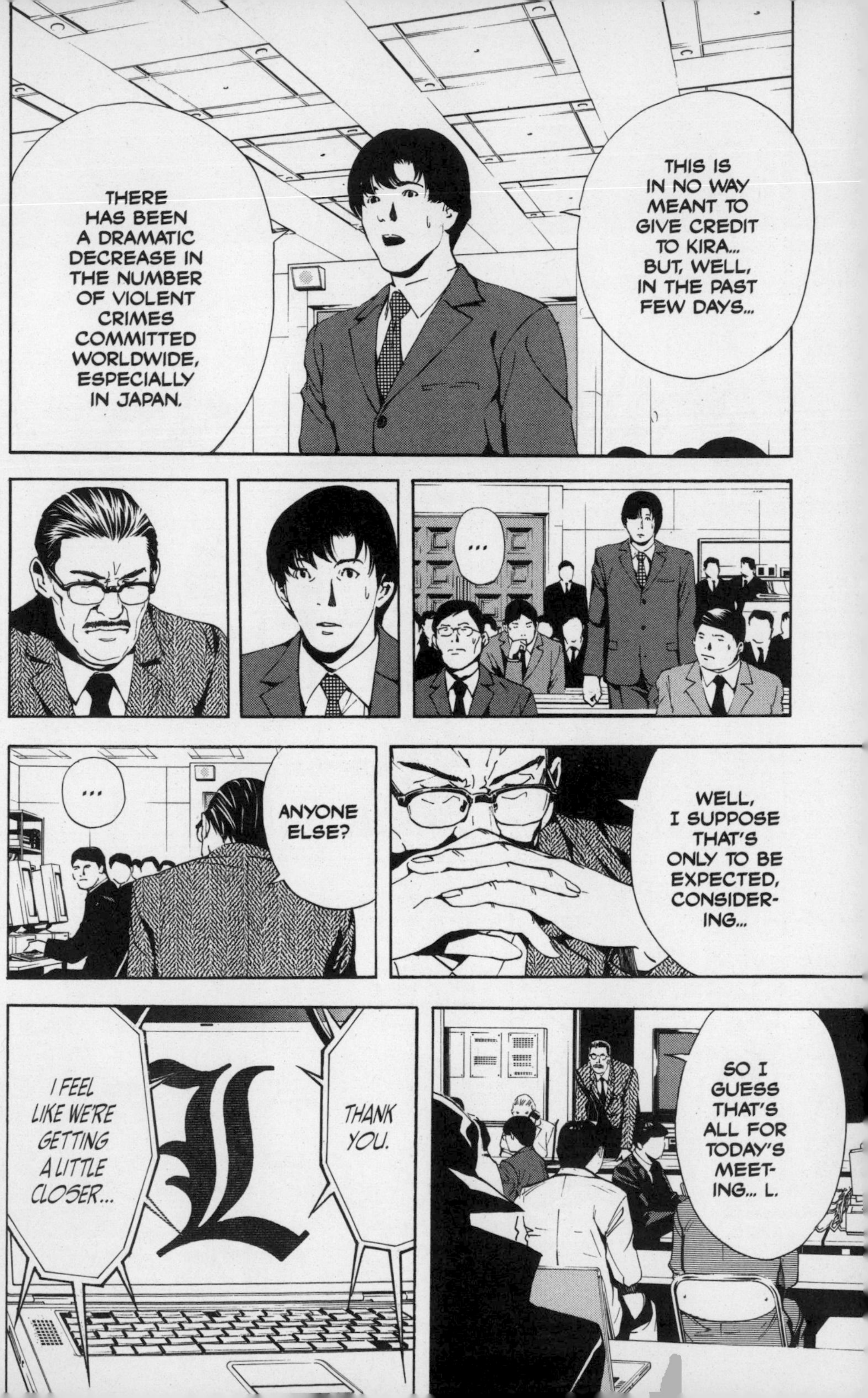
THIS IS IN NO WAY MEANT TO GIVE CREDIT TO KIRA... BUT, WELL, IN THE PAST FEW DAYS...
THERE HAS BEEN A DRAMATIC DECREASE IN THE NUMBER OF VIOLENT CRIMES COMMITTED WORLDWIDE, ESPECIALLY IN JAPAN.
...
WELL, I SUPPOSE THAT'S ONLY TO BE EXPECTED, CONSIDER-ING...
ANYONE ELSE?
...
SO I GUESS THAT'S ALL FOR TODAY'S MEET-ING... L.
THANK YOU.
I FEEL LIKE WE'RE GETTING A LITTLE CLOSER...

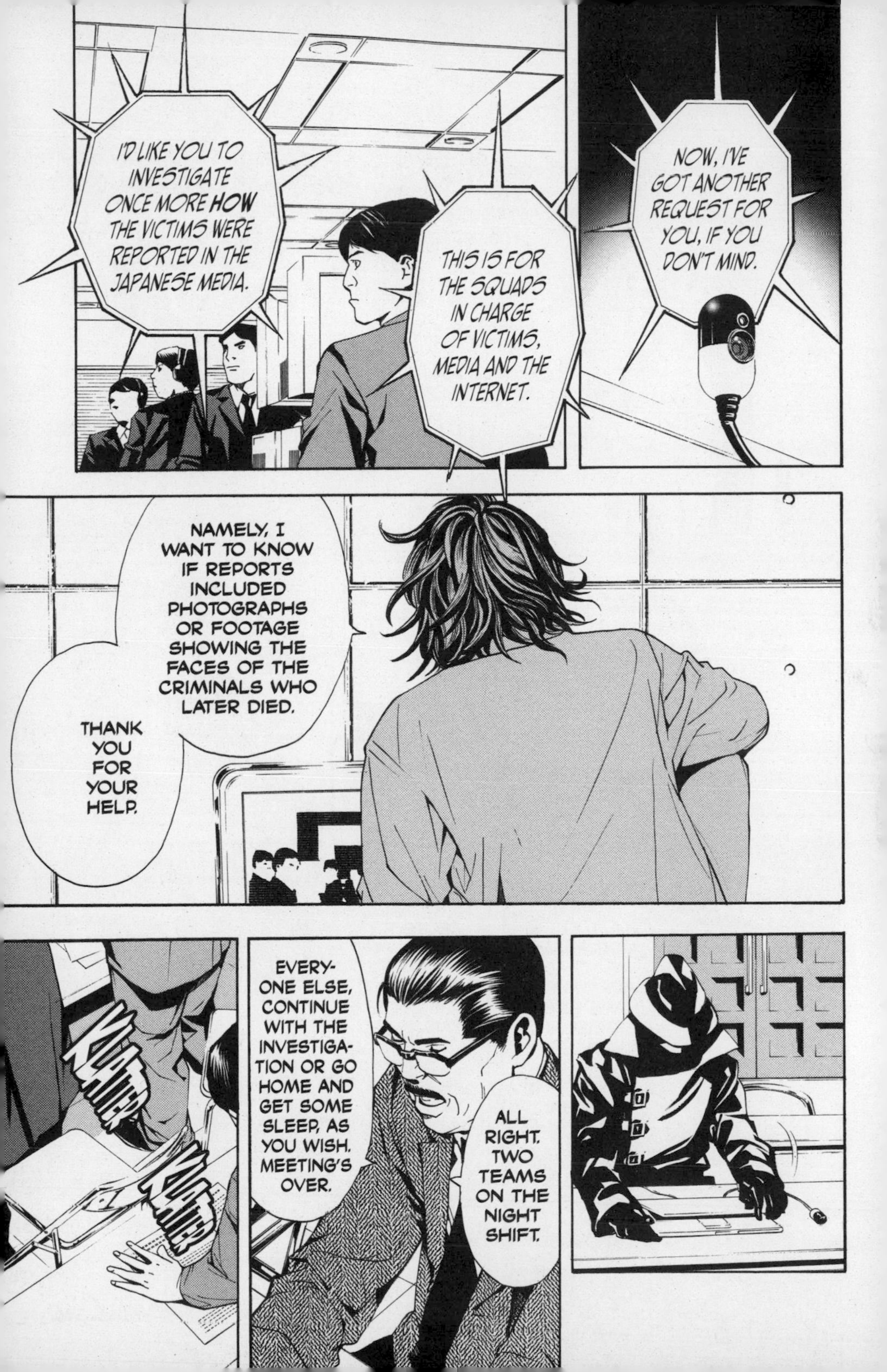
NOW, I'VE GOT ANOTHER REQUEST FOR YOU, IF YOU DON'T MIND.
THIS IS FOR THE SQUADS IN CHARGE OF VICTIMS, MEDIA AND THE INTERNET.
I'D LIKE YOU TO INVESTIGATE ONCE MORE **HOW** THE VICTIMS WERE REPORTED IN THE JAPANESE MEDIA.
NAMELY, I WANT TO KNOW IF REPORTS INCLUDED PHOTOGRAPHS OR FOOTAGE SHOWING THE FACES OF THE CRIMINALS WHO LATER DIED.
THANK YOU FOR YOUR HELP.
ALL RIGHT. TWO TEAMS ON THE NIGHT SHIFT.
EVERY-ONE ELSE, CONTINUE WITH THE INVESTIGA-TION OR GO HOME AND GET SOME SLEEP, AS YOU WISH. MEETING'S OVER.

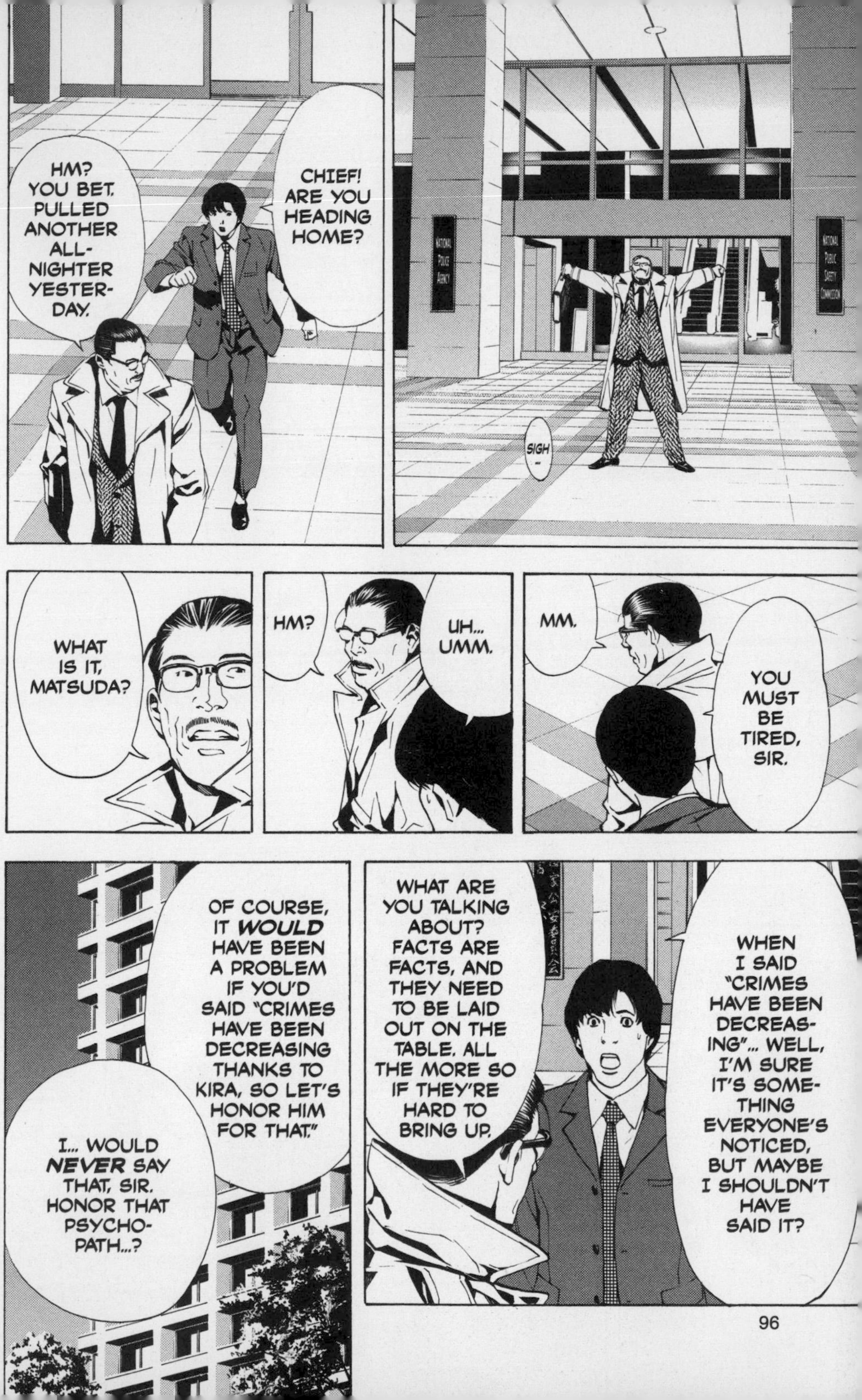
NATIONAL POLICE AGENCY
NATIONAL PUBLIC SAFETY COMMISSION
SIGH...
CHIEF! ARE YOU HEADING HOME?
HM? YOU BET. PULLED ANOTHER ALL-NIGHTER YESTERDAY.
MM.
YOU MUST BE TIRED, SIR.
UH... UMM.
HM?
WHAT IS IT, MATSUDA?
WHEN I SAID "CRIMES HAVE BEEN DECREASING"... WELL, I'M SURE IT'S SOMETHING EVERYONE'S NOTICED, BUT MAYBE I SHOULDN'T HAVE SAID IT?
WHAT ARE YOU TALKING ABOUT? FACTS ARE FACTS, AND THEY NEED TO BE LAID OUT ON THE TABLE. ALL THE MORE SO IF THEY'RE HARD TO BRING UP.
OF COURSE, IT ***WOULD*** HAVE BEEN A PROBLEM IF YOU'D SAID "CRIMES HAVE BEEN DECREASING THANKS TO KIRA, SO LET'S HONOR HIM FOR THAT."
I... WOULD ***NEVER*** SAY THAT, SIR. HONOR THAT PSYCHOPATH...?

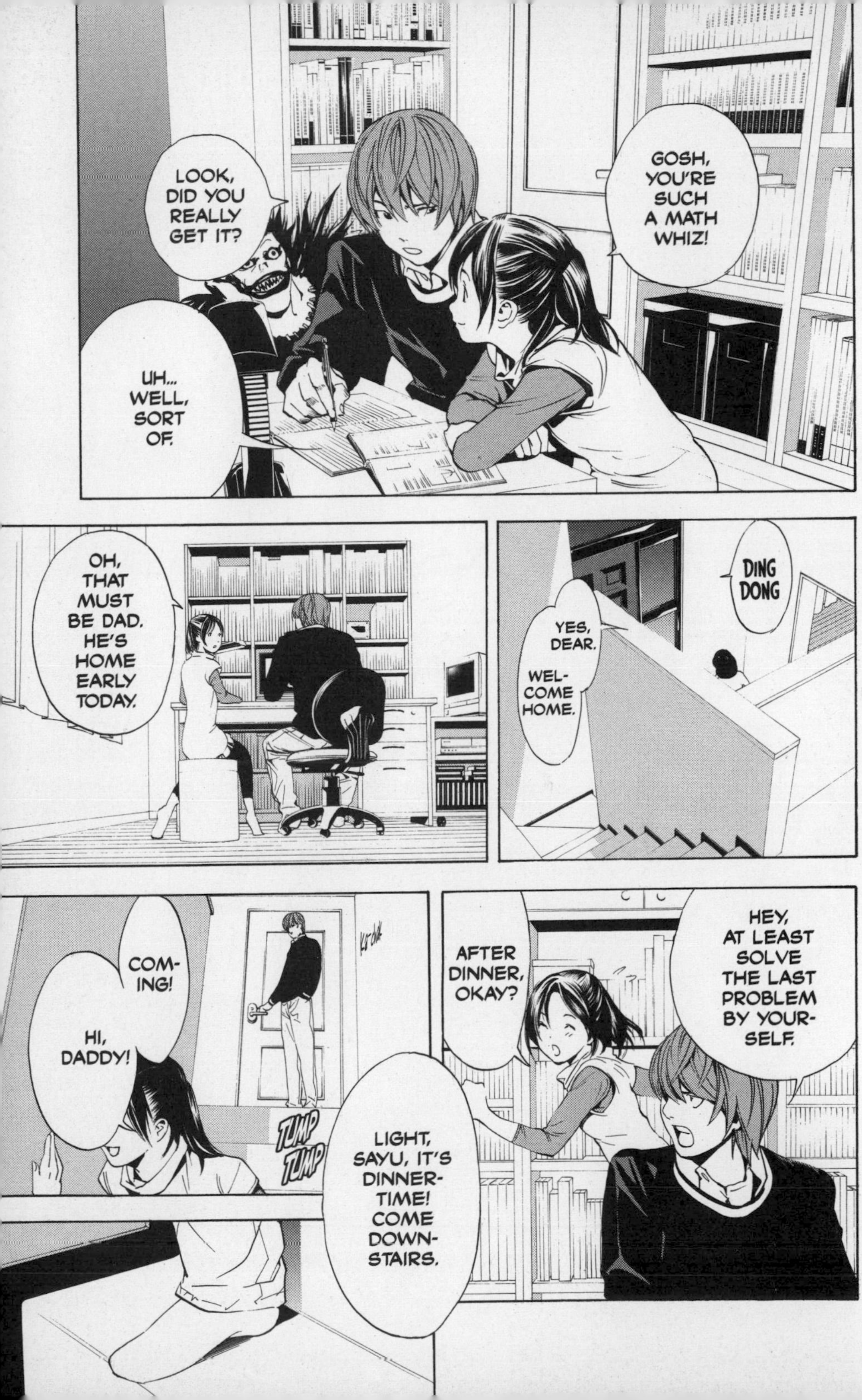
GOSH, YOU'RE SUCH A MATH WHIZ!
LOOK, DID YOU REALLY GET IT?
UH... WELL, SORT OF.
DING DONG
YES, DEAR.
WEL-COME HOME.
OH, THAT MUST BE DAD. HE'S HOME EARLY TODAY.
HEY, AT LEAST SOLVE THE LAST PROBLEM BY YOUR-SELF.
AFTER DINNER, OKAY?
LIGHT, SAYU, IT'S DINNER-TIME! COME DOWN-STAIRS.
COM-ING!
HI, DADDY!
TUMP TUMP

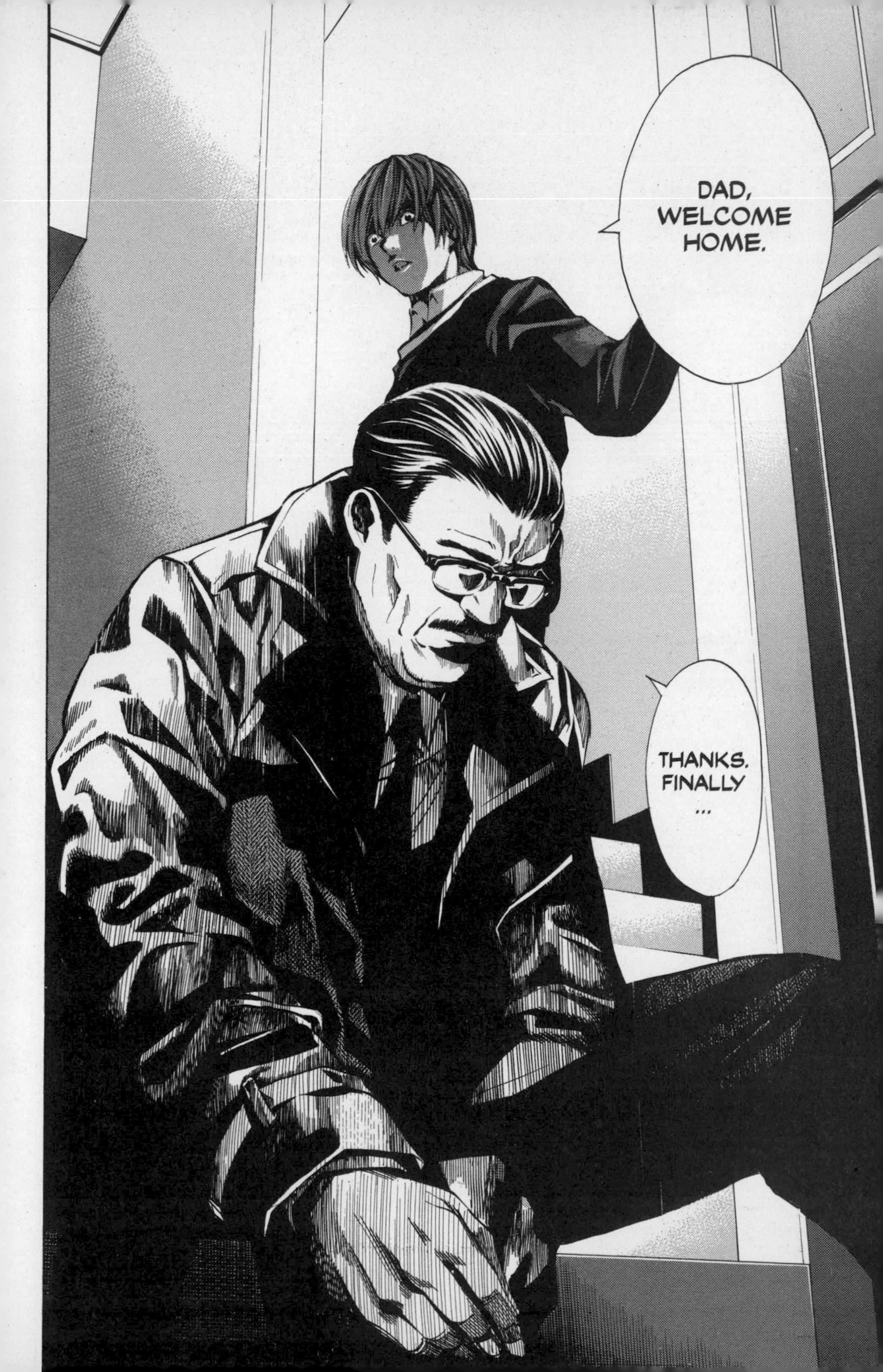
DAD, WELCOME HOME.
THANKS. FINALLY ...

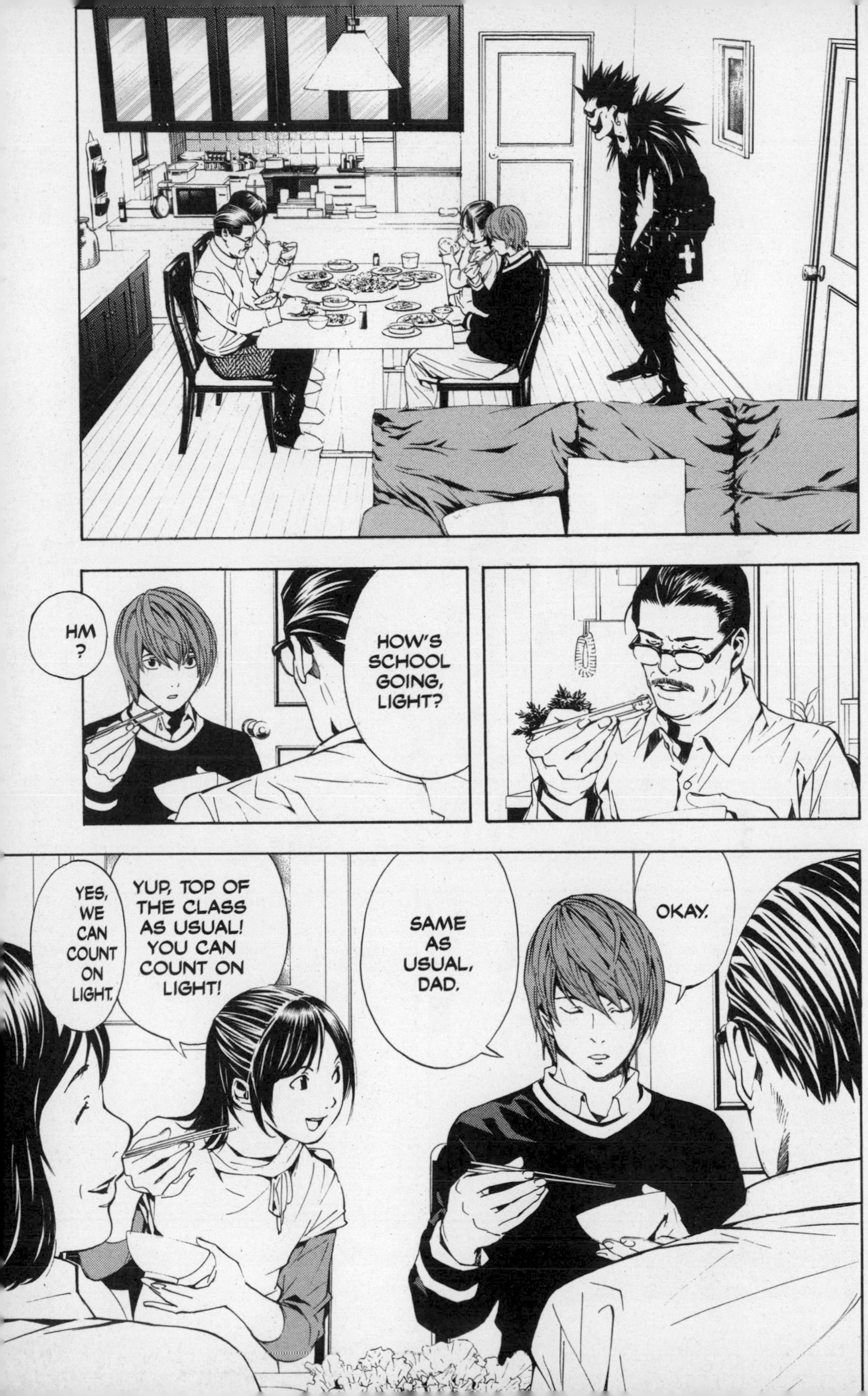
HOW'S SCHOOL GOING, LIGHT?
HM?
OKAY.
SAME AS USUAL, DAD.
YUP, TOP OF THE CLASS AS USUAL! YOU CAN COUNT ON LIGHT!
YES, WE CAN COUNT ON LIGHT.

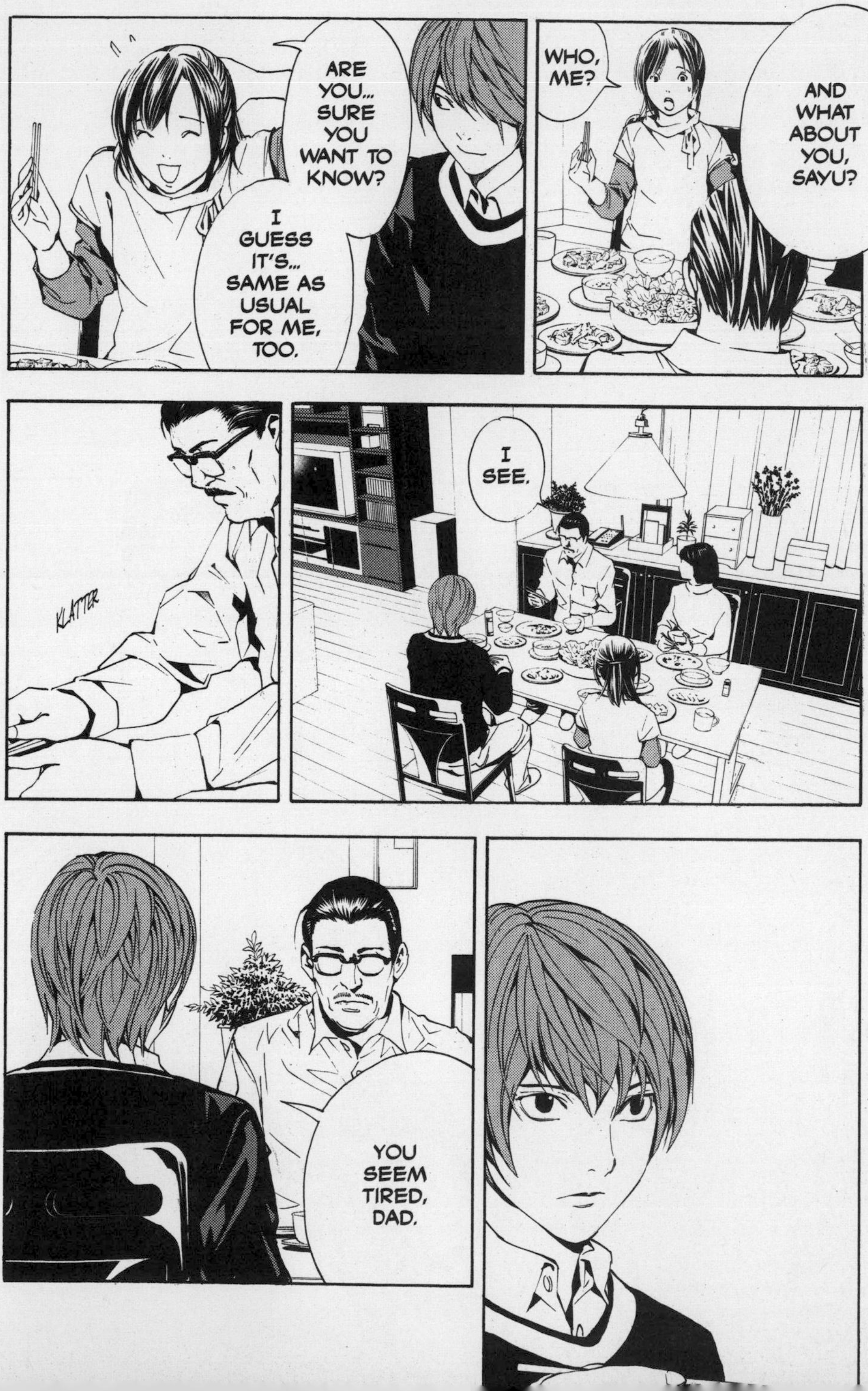
AND WHAT ABOUT YOU, SAYU?
WHO, ME?
ARE YOU... SURE YOU WANT TO KNOW?
I GUESS IT'S... SAME AS USUAL FOR ME, TOO.
I SEE.
KLATTER
YOU SEEM TIRED, DAD.

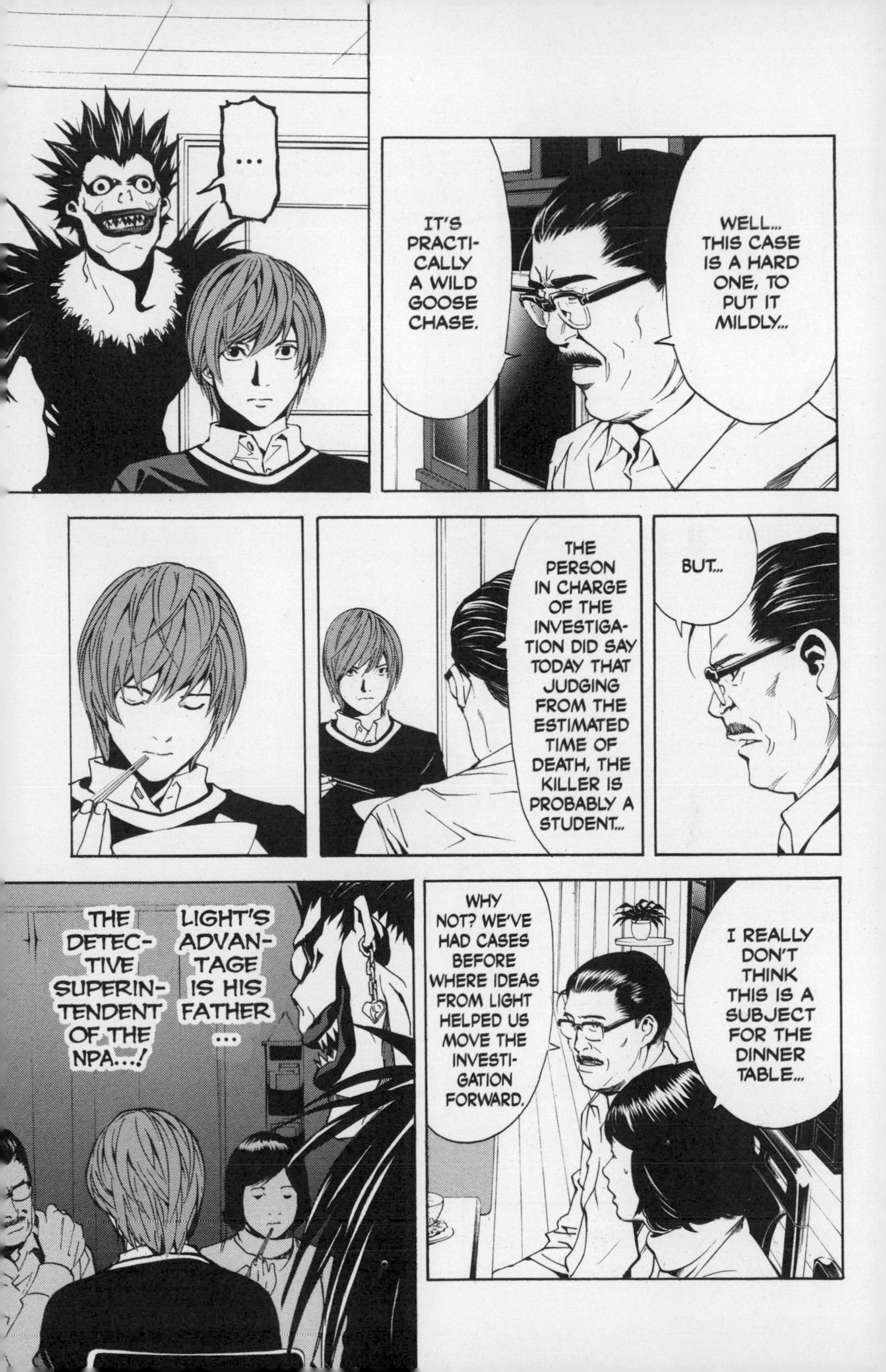
WELL... THIS CASE IS A HARD ONE, TO PUT IT MILDLY...
IT'S PRACTICALLY A WILD GOOSE CHASE.
...
BUT...
THE PERSON IN CHARGE OF THE INVESTIGATION DID SAY TODAY THAT JUDGING FROM THE ESTIMATED TIME OF DEATH, THE KILLER IS PROBABLY A STUDENT...
I REALLY DON'T THINK THIS IS A SUBJECT FOR THE DINNER TABLE...
WHY NOT? WE'VE HAD CASES BEFORE WHERE IDEAS FROM LIGHT HELPED US MOVE THE INVESTIGATION FORWARD.
LIGHT'S ADVANTAGE IS HIS FATHER...
THE DETECTIVE SUPERINTENDENT OF THE NPA...!

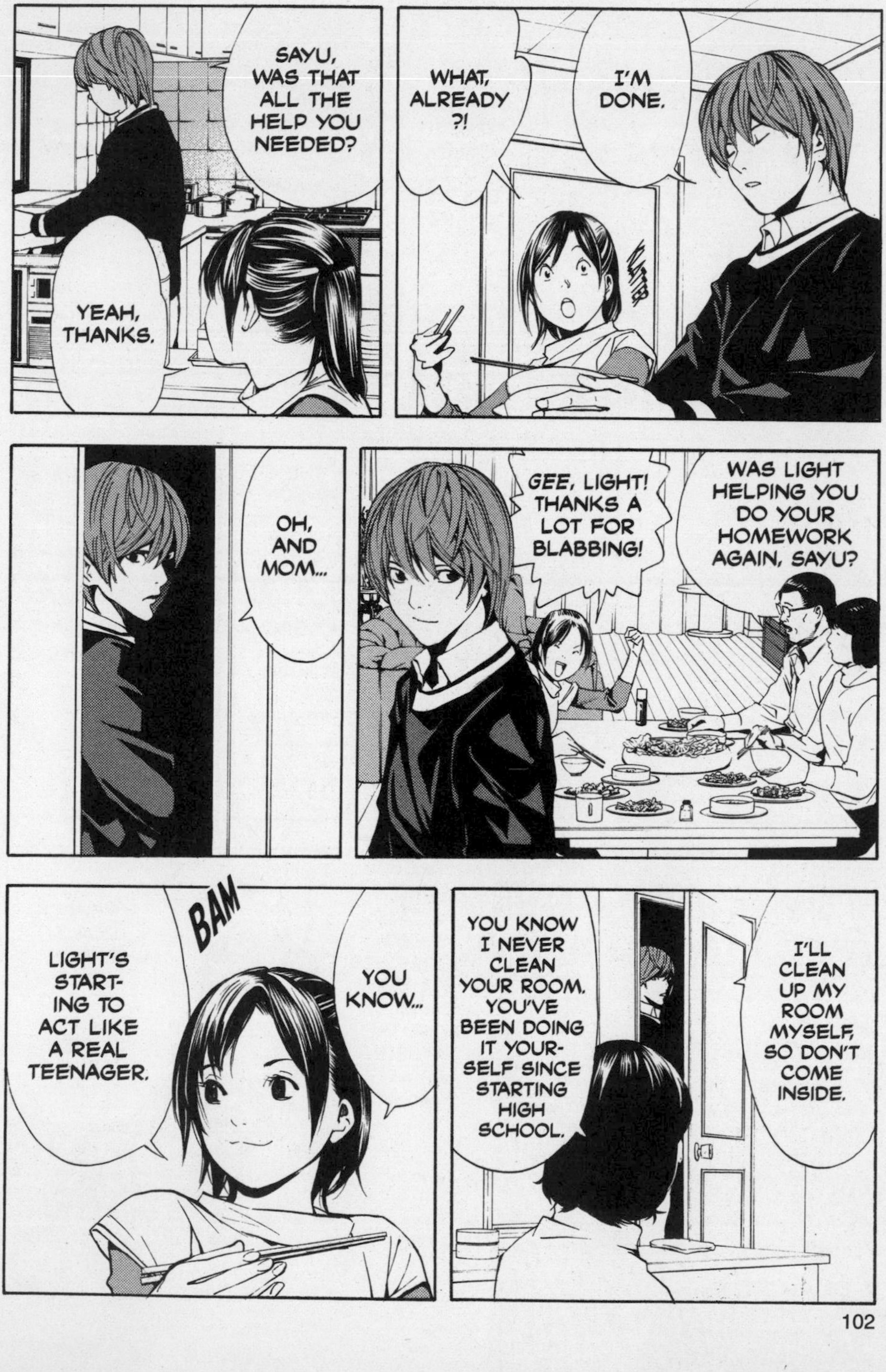
I'M DONE.
WHAT, ALREADY?!
SAYU, WAS THAT ALL THE HELP YOU NEEDED?
YEAH, THANKS.
WAS LIGHT HELPING YOU DO YOUR HOMEWORK AGAIN, SAYU?
GEE, LIGHT! THANKS A LOT FOR BLABBING!
OH, AND MOM...
I'LL CLEAN UP MY ROOM MYSELF, SO DON'T COME INSIDE.
YOU KNOW I NEVER CLEAN YOUR ROOM. YOU'VE BEEN DOING IT YOURSELF SINCE STARTING HIGH SCHOOL.
BAM
YOU KNOW...
LIGHT'S STARTING TO ACT LIKE A REAL TEENAGER.

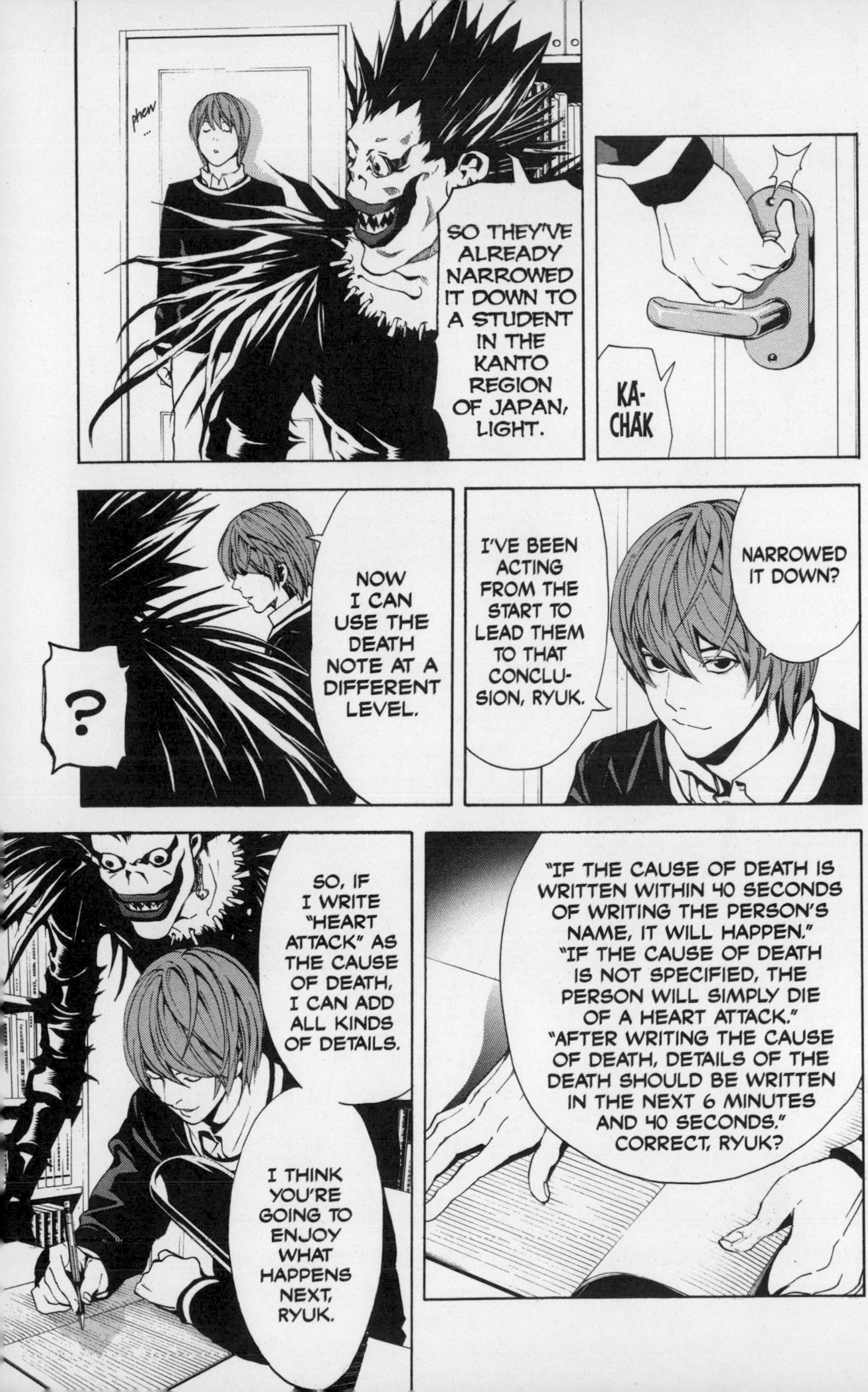
KA-CHAK
phew ...
SO THEY'VE ALREADY NARROWED IT DOWN TO A STUDENT IN THE KANTO REGION OF JAPAN, LIGHT.
NARROWED IT DOWN?
I'VE BEEN ACTING FROM THE START TO LEAD THEM TO THAT CONCLUSION, RYUK.
NOW I CAN USE THE DEATH NOTE AT A DIFFERENT LEVEL.
?
"IF THE CAUSE OF DEATH IS WRITTEN WITHIN 40 SECONDS OF WRITING THE PERSON'S NAME, IT WILL HAPPEN." "IF THE CAUSE OF DEATH IS NOT SPECIFIED, THE PERSON WILL SIMPLY DIE OF A HEART ATTACK." "AFTER WRITING THE CAUSE OF DEATH, DETAILS OF THE DEATH SHOULD BE WRITTEN IN THE NEXT 6 MINUTES AND 40 SECONDS." CORRECT, RYUK?
SO, IF I WRITE "HEART ATTACK" AS THE CAUSE OF DEATH, I CAN ADD ALL KINDS OF DETAILS.
I THINK YOU'RE GOING TO ENJOY WHAT HAPPENS NEXT, RYUK.

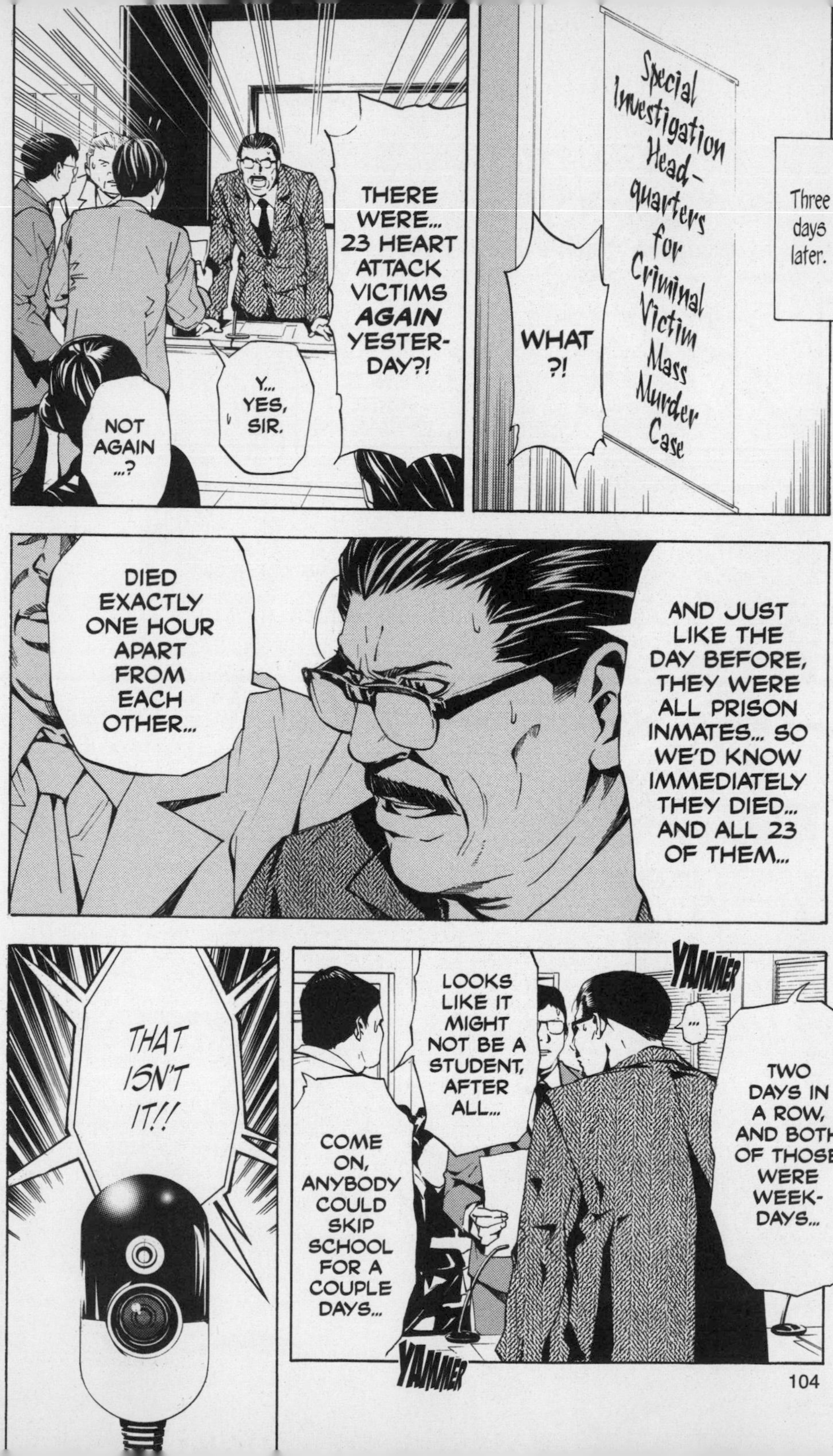
Three days later.
Special Investigation Headquarters for Criminal Victim Mass Murder Case
WHAT ?!
THERE WERE... 23 HEART ATTACK VICTIMS *AGAIN* YESTER-DAY?!
Y... YES, SIR.
NOT AGAIN ...?
AND JUST LIKE THE DAY BEFORE, THEY WERE ALL PRISON INMATES... SO WE'D KNOW IMMEDIATELY THEY DIED... AND ALL 23 OF THEM...
DIED EXACTLY ONE HOUR APART FROM EACH OTHER...
YAMMER
...
TWO DAYS IN A ROW, AND BOTH OF THOSE WERE WEEK-DAYS...
LOOKS LIKE IT MIGHT NOT BE A STUDENT, AFTER ALL...
COME ON, ANYBODY COULD SKIP SCHOOL FOR A COUPLE DAYS...
YAMMER
THAT ISN'T IT!!

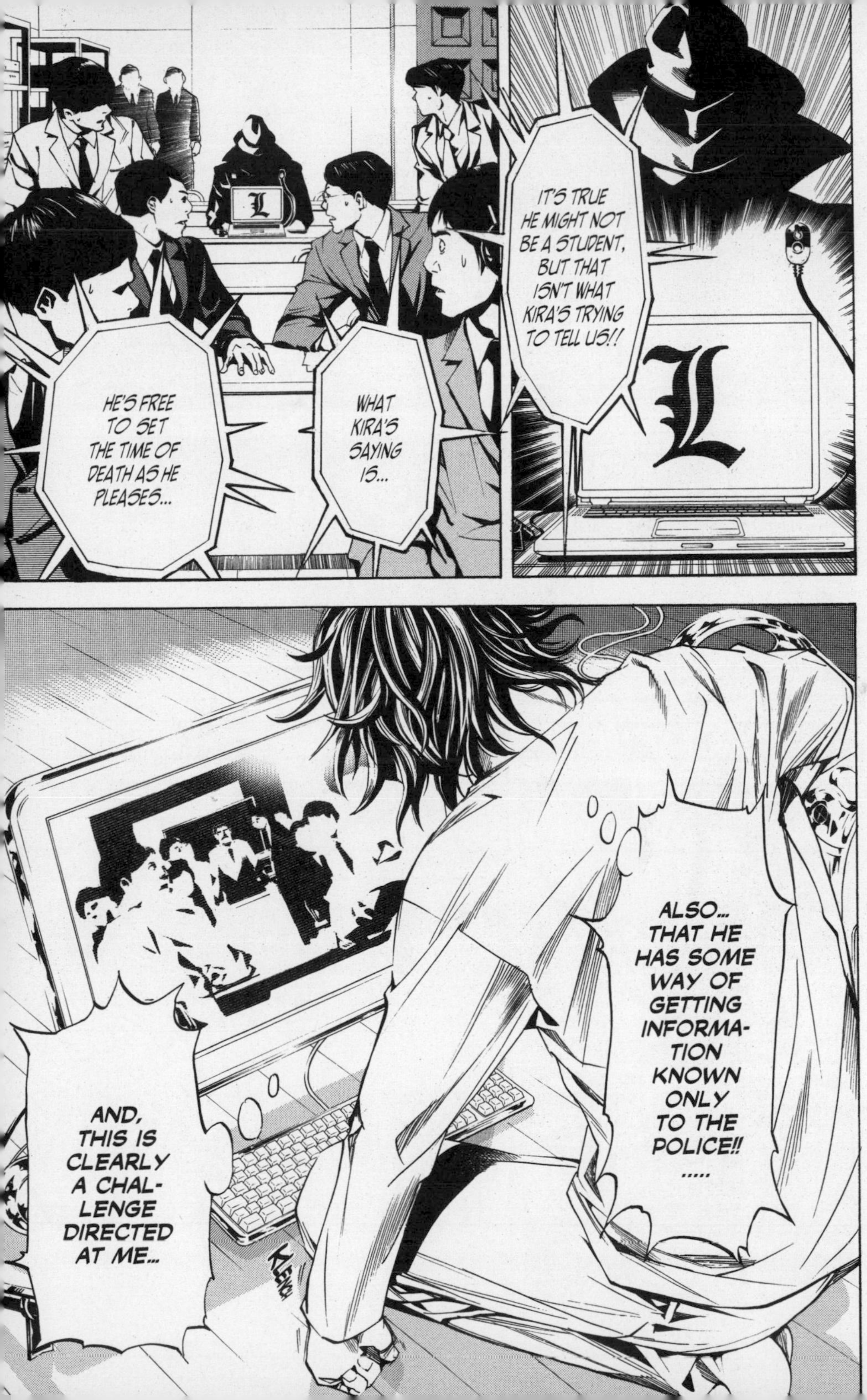

IT'S TRUE HE MIGHT NOT BE A STUDENT, BUT THAT ISN'T WHAT KIRA'S TRYING TO TELL US!!
WHAT KIRA'S SAYING IS...
HE'S FREE TO SET THE TIME OF DEATH AS HE PLEASES...
ALSO... THAT HE HAS SOME WAY OF GETTING INFORMATION KNOWN ONLY TO THE POLICE!! .....
AND, THIS IS CLEARLY A CHALLENGE DIRECTED AT ME...
KLENCH

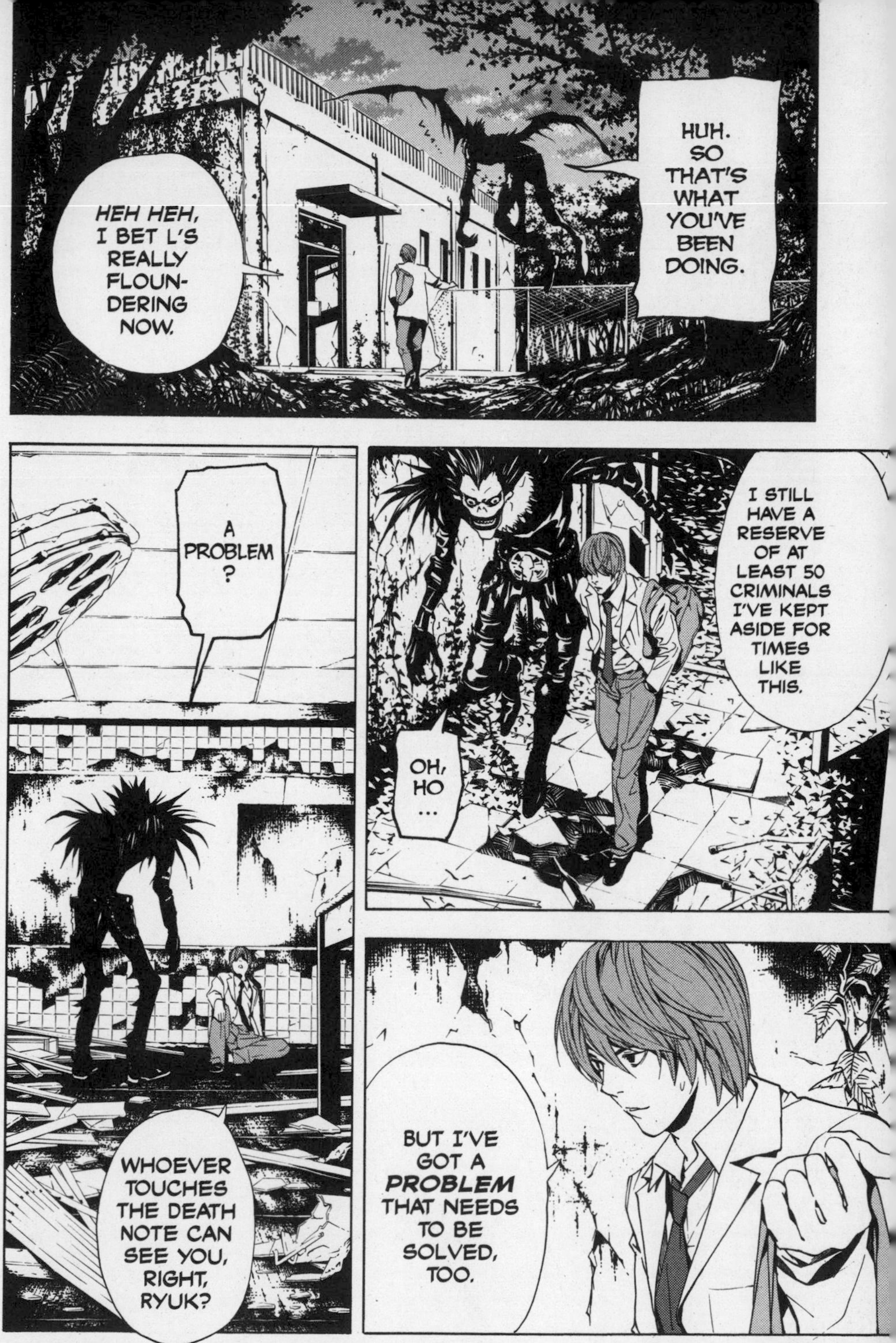
HUH. SO THAT'S WHAT YOU'VE BEEN DOING.
*HEH HEH, I BET L'S REALLY FLOUNDERING NOW.*
I STILL HAVE A RESERVE OF AT LEAST 50 CRIMINALS I'VE KEPT ASIDE FOR TIMES LIKE THIS.
OH, HO ...
BUT I'VE GOT A ***PROBLEM*** THAT NEEDS TO BE SOLVED, TOO.
A PROBLEM?
WHOEVER TOUCHES THE DEATH NOTE CAN SEE YOU, RIGHT, RYUK?

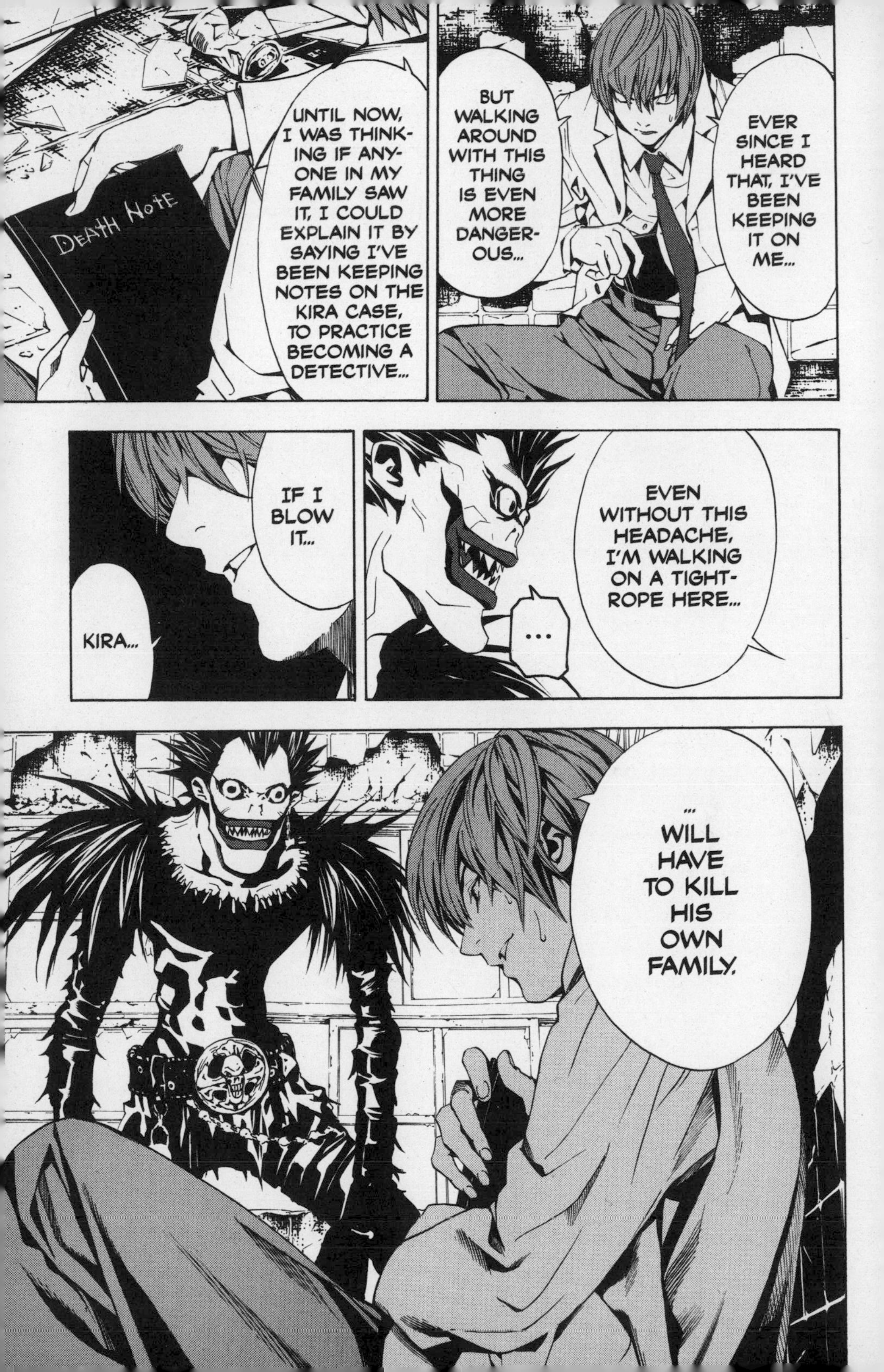
EVER SINCE I HEARD THAT, I'VE BEEN KEEPING IT ON ME...
BUT WALKING AROUND WITH THIS THING IS EVEN MORE DANGEROUS...
UNTIL NOW, I WAS THINKING IF ANYONE IN MY FAMILY SAW IT, I COULD EXPLAIN IT BY SAYING I'VE BEEN KEEPING NOTES ON THE KIRA CASE, TO PRACTICE BECOMING A DETECTIVE...
DEATH NOTE
EVEN WITHOUT THIS HEADACHE, I'M WALKING ON A TIGHTROPE HERE...
...
IF I BLOW IT...
KIRA...
... WILL HAVE TO KILL HIS OWN FAMILY.

# DEATH NOTE
## How to Use It
### III

- If the time of death is written within 40 seconds after writing the cause of death as a heart attack, the time of death can be manipulated, and the time can go into effect within 40 seconds after writing the name.

死因に心臓麻痺と書いた後、40秒以内に死亡時刻を書けば、
心臓麻痺であっても死の時間を操れ、その時刻は名前を書いてからの
40秒以内でも可能である。

- The human who touches the DEATH NOTE can recognize the image and voice of its original owner, a god of death, even if the human is not the owner of the note.

デスノートに触った人間には、そのノートの所有者でなくとも、
元持ち主の死神の姿や声が認知できる。

# chapter 4 Current

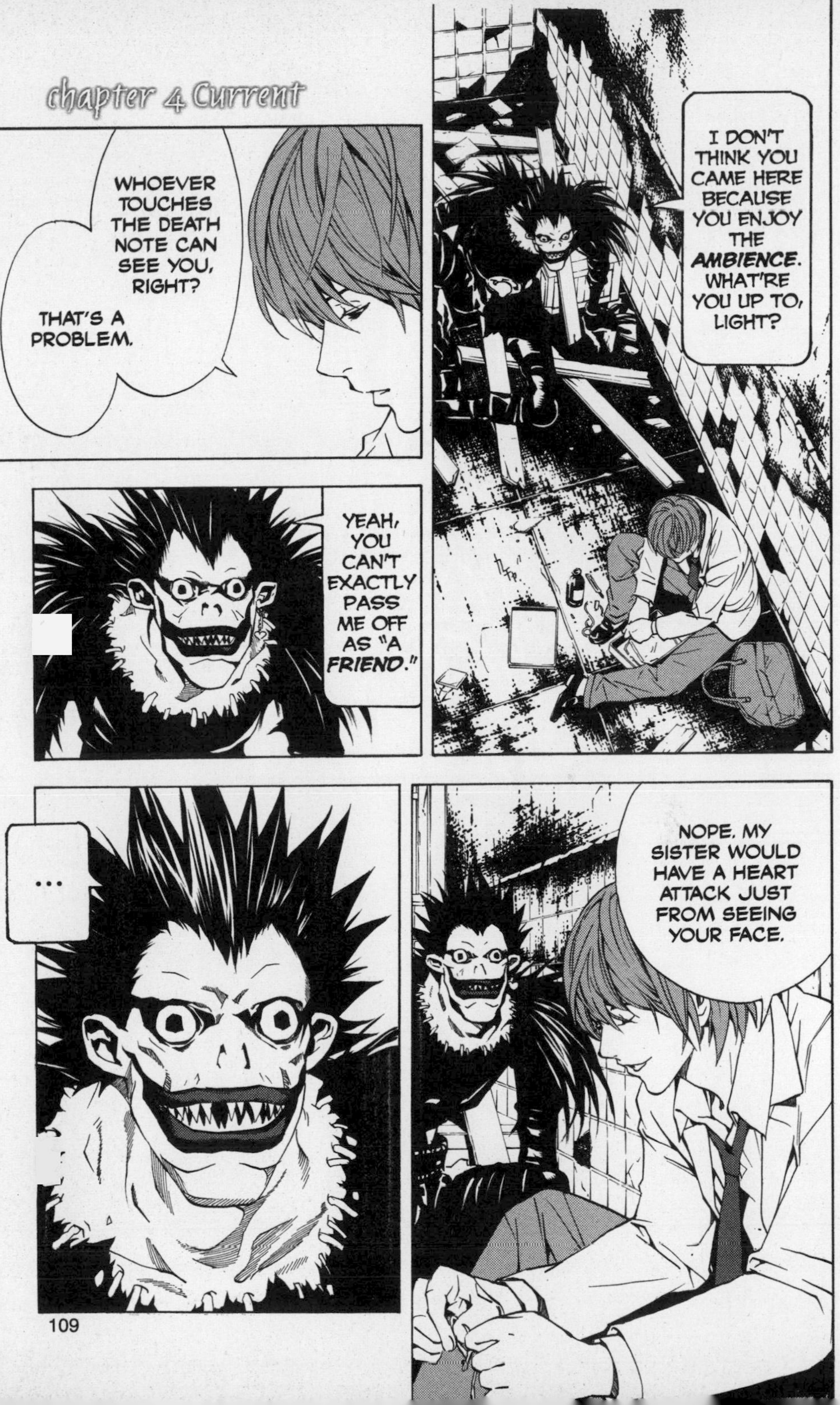

I DON'T THINK YOU CAME HERE BECAUSE YOU ENJOY THE ***AMBIENCE***. WHAT'RE YOU UP TO, LIGHT?
WHOEVER TOUCHES THE DEATH NOTE CAN SEE YOU, RIGHT?
THAT'S A PROBLEM.
YEAH, YOU CAN'T EXACTLY PASS ME OFF AS "A ***FRIEND***."
NOPE. MY SISTER WOULD HAVE A HEART ATTACK JUST FROM SEEING YOUR FACE.
...

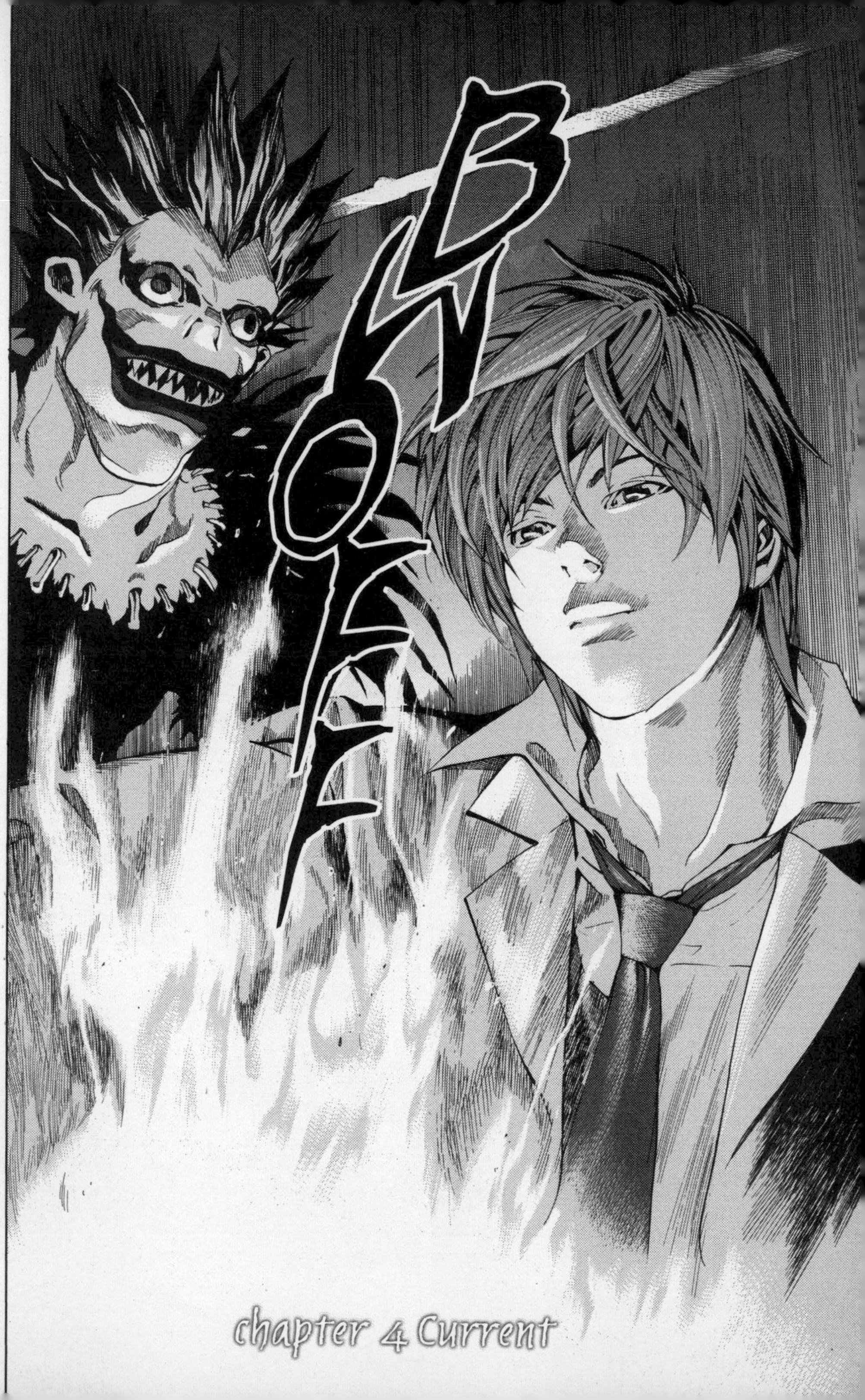
BWOOFF

## chapter 4 Current

READ THIS WAY

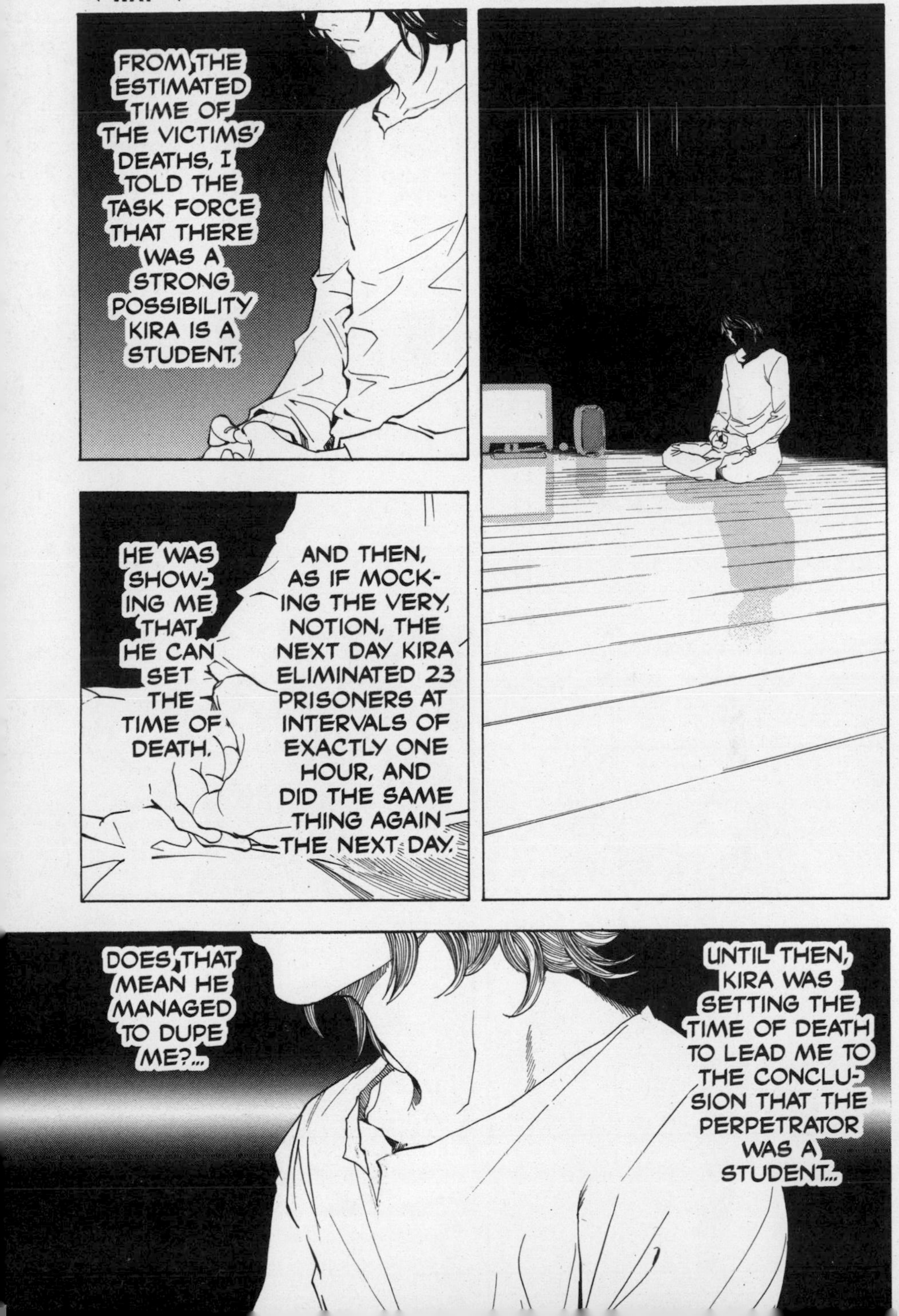
FROM THE ESTIMATED TIME OF THE VICTIMS' DEATHS, I TOLD THE TASK FORCE THAT THERE WAS A STRONG POSSIBILITY KIRA IS A STUDENT.
AND THEN, AS IF MOCKING THE VERY NOTION, THE NEXT DAY KIRA ELIMINATED 23 PRISONERS AT INTERVALS OF EXACTLY ONE HOUR, AND DID THE SAME THING AGAIN THE NEXT DAY.
HE WAS SHOWING ME THAT HE CAN SET THE TIME OF DEATH.
UNTIL THEN, KIRA WAS SETTING THE TIME OF DEATH TO LEAD ME TO THE CONCLUSION THAT THE PERPETRATOR WAS A STUDENT...
DOES THAT MEAN HE MANAGED TO DUPE ME?...

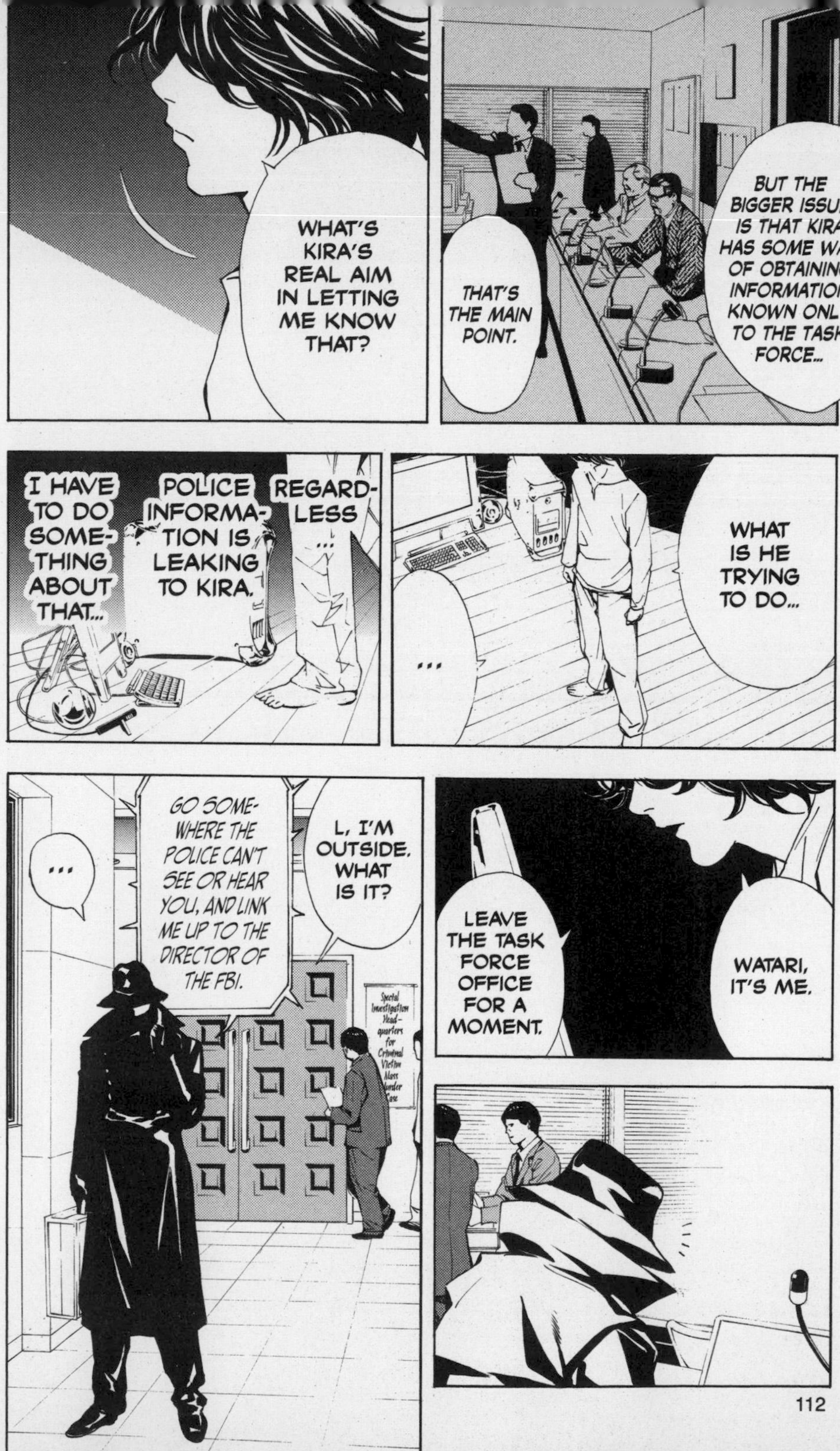
BUT THE BIGGER ISSUE IS THAT KIRA HAS SOME WAY OF OBTAINING INFORMATION KNOWN ONLY TO THE TASK FORCE...
THAT'S THE MAIN POINT.
WHAT'S KIRA'S REAL AIM IN LETTING ME KNOW THAT?
WHAT IS HE TRYING TO DO...
...
REGARDLESS...
POLICE INFORMATION IS LEAKING TO KIRA.
I HAVE TO DO SOMETHING ABOUT THAT...
WATARI, IT'S ME.
LEAVE THE TASK FORCE OFFICE FOR A MOMENT.
L, I'M OUTSIDE. WHAT IS IT?
GO SOMEWHERE THE POLICE CAN'T SEE OR HEAR YOU, AND LINK ME UP TO THE DIRECTOR OF THE FBI.
...
Special Investigation Headquarters for Criminal Victim Mass Murder Case

READ THIS WAY

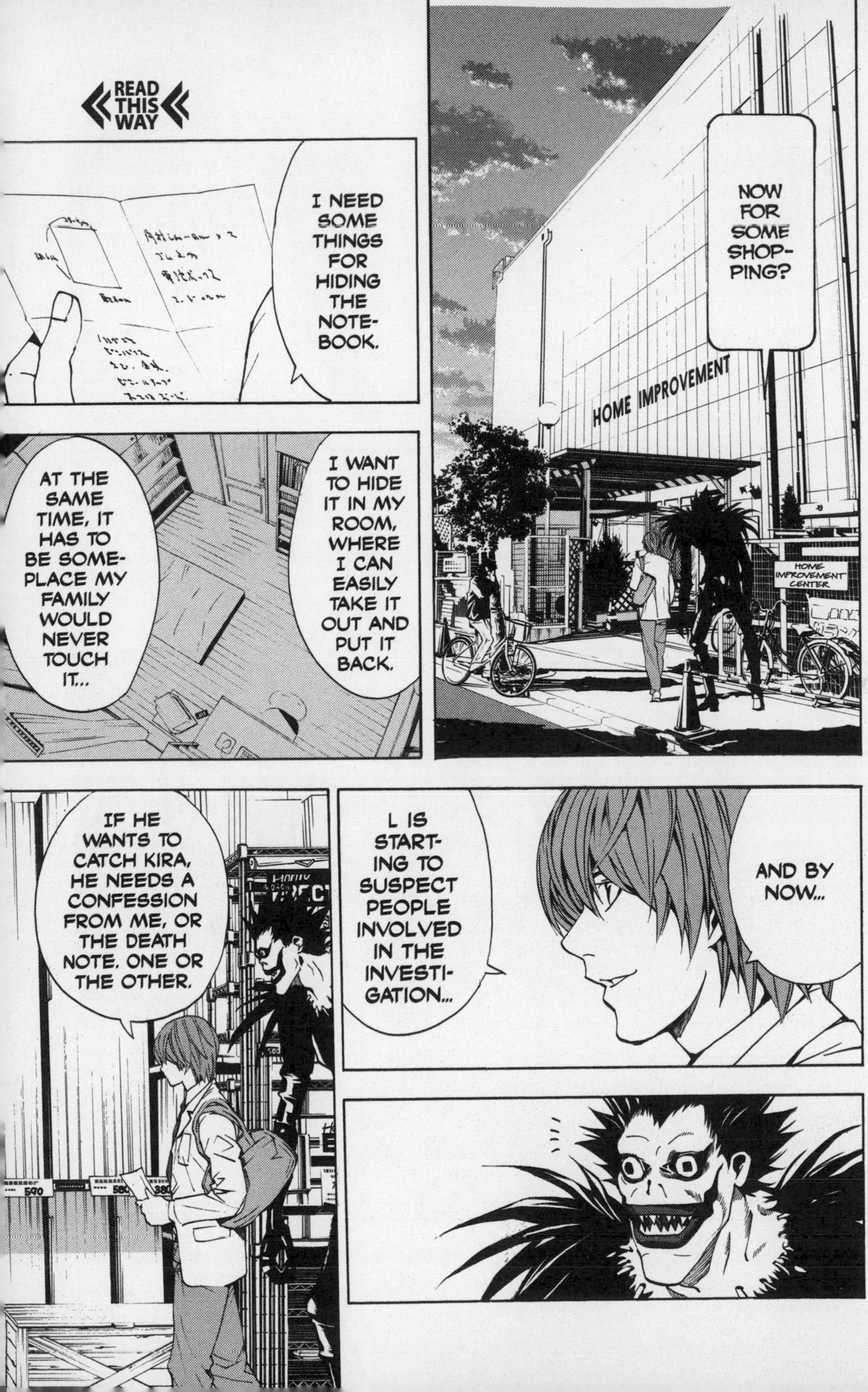
NOW FOR SOME SHOPPING?
HOME IMPROVEMENT
HOME IMPROVEMENT CENTER
I NEED SOME THINGS FOR HIDING THE NOTEBOOK.
I WANT TO HIDE IT IN MY ROOM, WHERE I CAN EASILY TAKE IT OUT AND PUT IT BACK.
AT THE SAME TIME, IT HAS TO BE SOMEPLACE MY FAMILY WOULD NEVER TOUCH IT...
AND BY NOW...
L IS STARTING TO SUSPECT PEOPLE INVOLVED IN THE INVESTIGATION...
IF HE WANTS TO CATCH KIRA, HE NEEDS A CONFESSION FROM ME, OR THE DEATH NOTE. ONE OR THE OTHER.

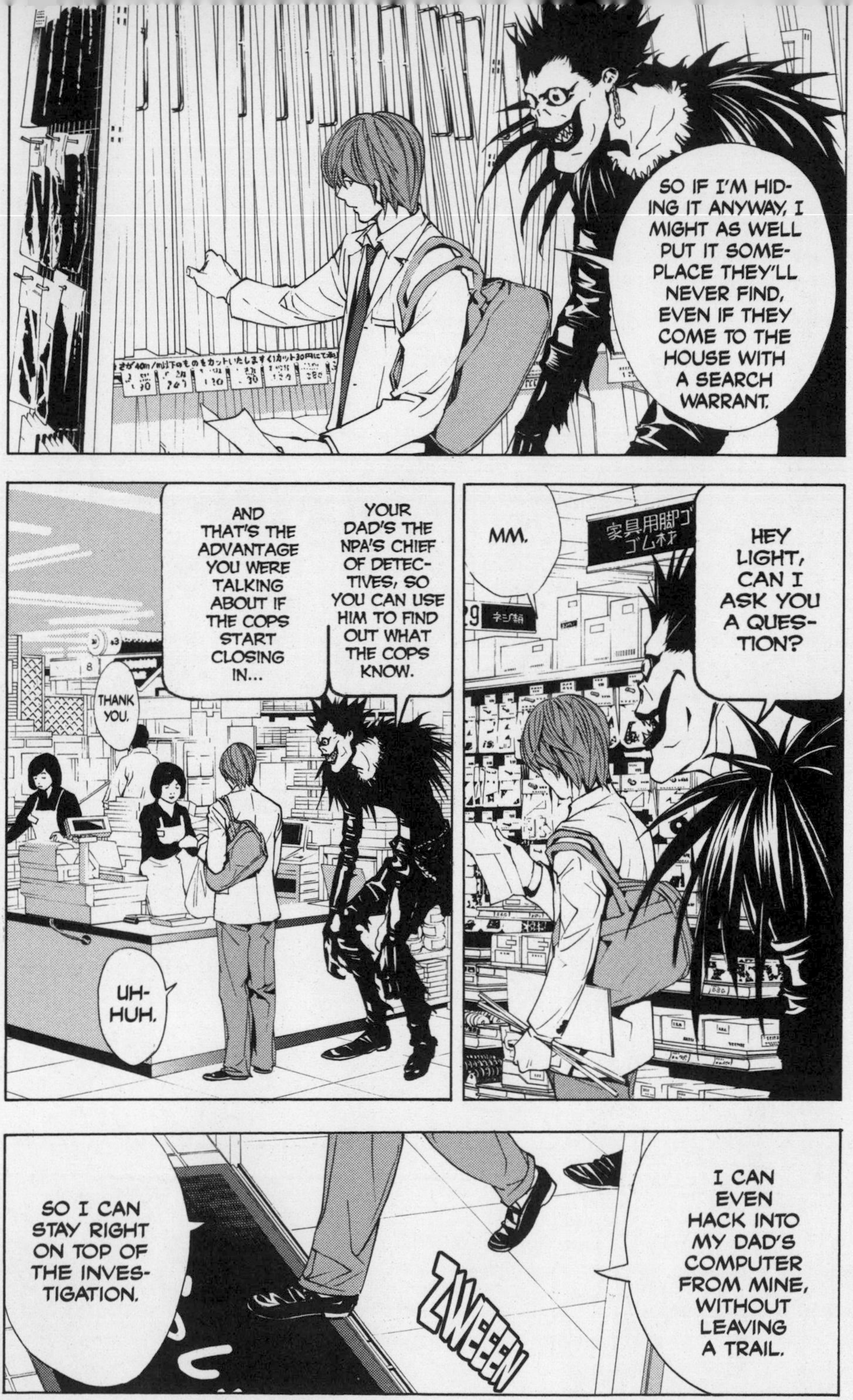
SO IF I'M HIDING IT ANYWAY, I MIGHT AS WELL PUT IT SOMEPLACE THEY'LL NEVER FIND, EVEN IF THEY COME TO THE HOUSE WITH A SEARCH WARRANT.
HEY LIGHT, CAN I ASK YOU A QUESTION?
MM.
YOUR DAD'S THE NPA'S CHIEF OF DETECTIVES, SO YOU CAN USE HIM TO FIND OUT WHAT THE COPS KNOW.
AND THAT'S THE ADVANTAGE YOU WERE TALKING ABOUT IF THE COPS START CLOSING IN...
THANK YOU.
UH-HUH.
I CAN EVEN HACK INTO MY DAD'S COMPUTER FROM MINE, WITHOUT LEAVING A TRAIL.
ZWEEEN
SO I CAN STAY RIGHT ON TOP OF THE INVESTIGATION.

READ THIS WAY

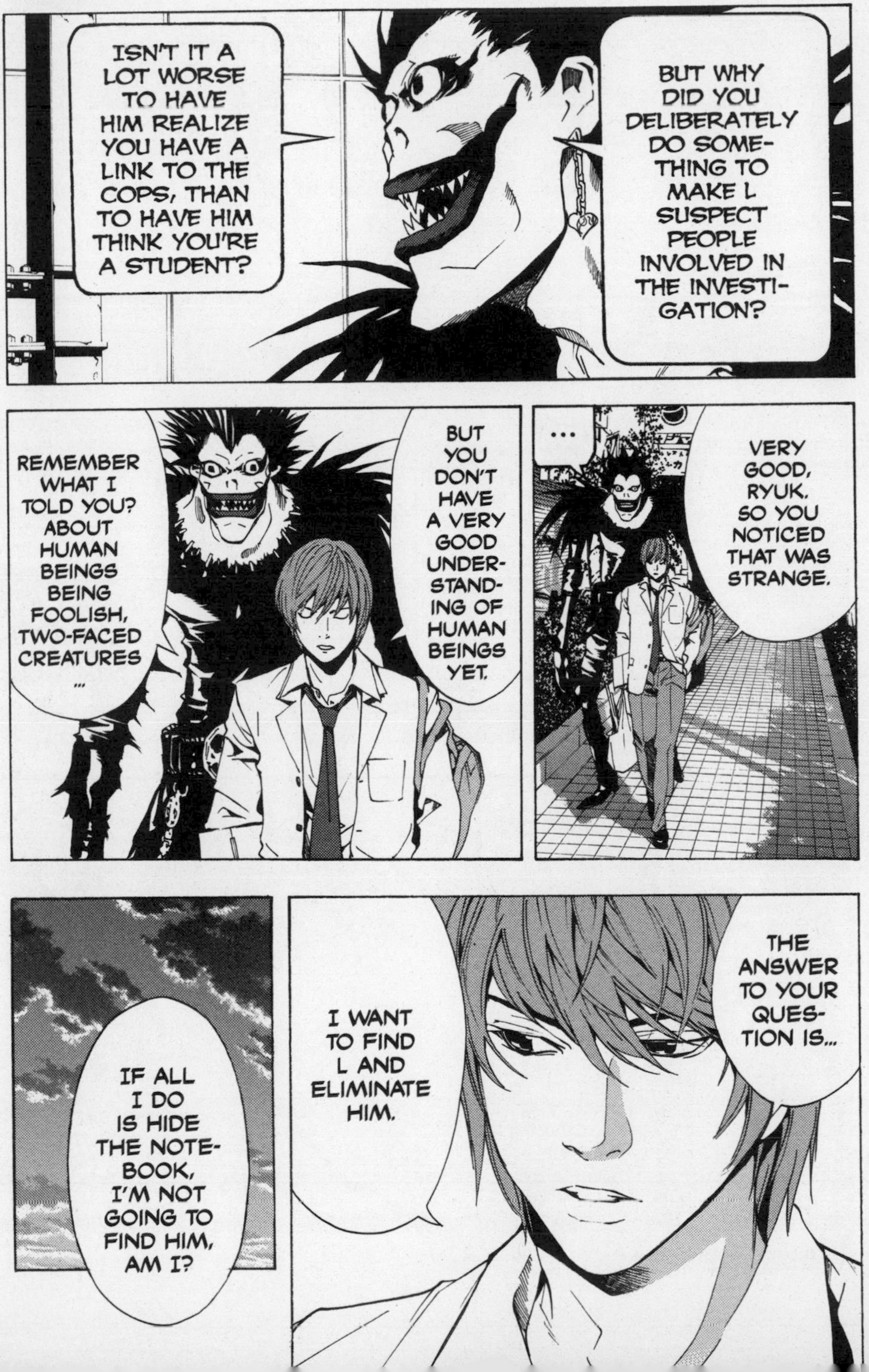
BUT WHY DID YOU DELIBERATELY DO SOME-THING TO MAKE L SUSPECT PEOPLE INVOLVED IN THE INVESTI-GATION?
ISN'T IT A LOT WORSE TO HAVE HIM REALIZE YOU HAVE A LINK TO THE COPS, THAN TO HAVE HIM THINK YOU'RE A STUDENT?
VERY GOOD, RYUK. SO YOU NOTICED THAT WAS STRANGE.
...
BUT YOU DON'T HAVE A VERY GOOD UNDER-STAND-ING OF HUMAN BEINGS YET.
REMEMBER WHAT I TOLD YOU? ABOUT HUMAN BEINGS BEING FOOLISH, TWO-FACED CREATURES ...
THE ANSWER TO YOUR QUES-TION IS...
I WANT TO FIND L AND ELIMINATE HIM.
IF ALL I DO IS HIDE THE NOTE-BOOK, I'M NOT GOING TO FIND HIM, AM I?

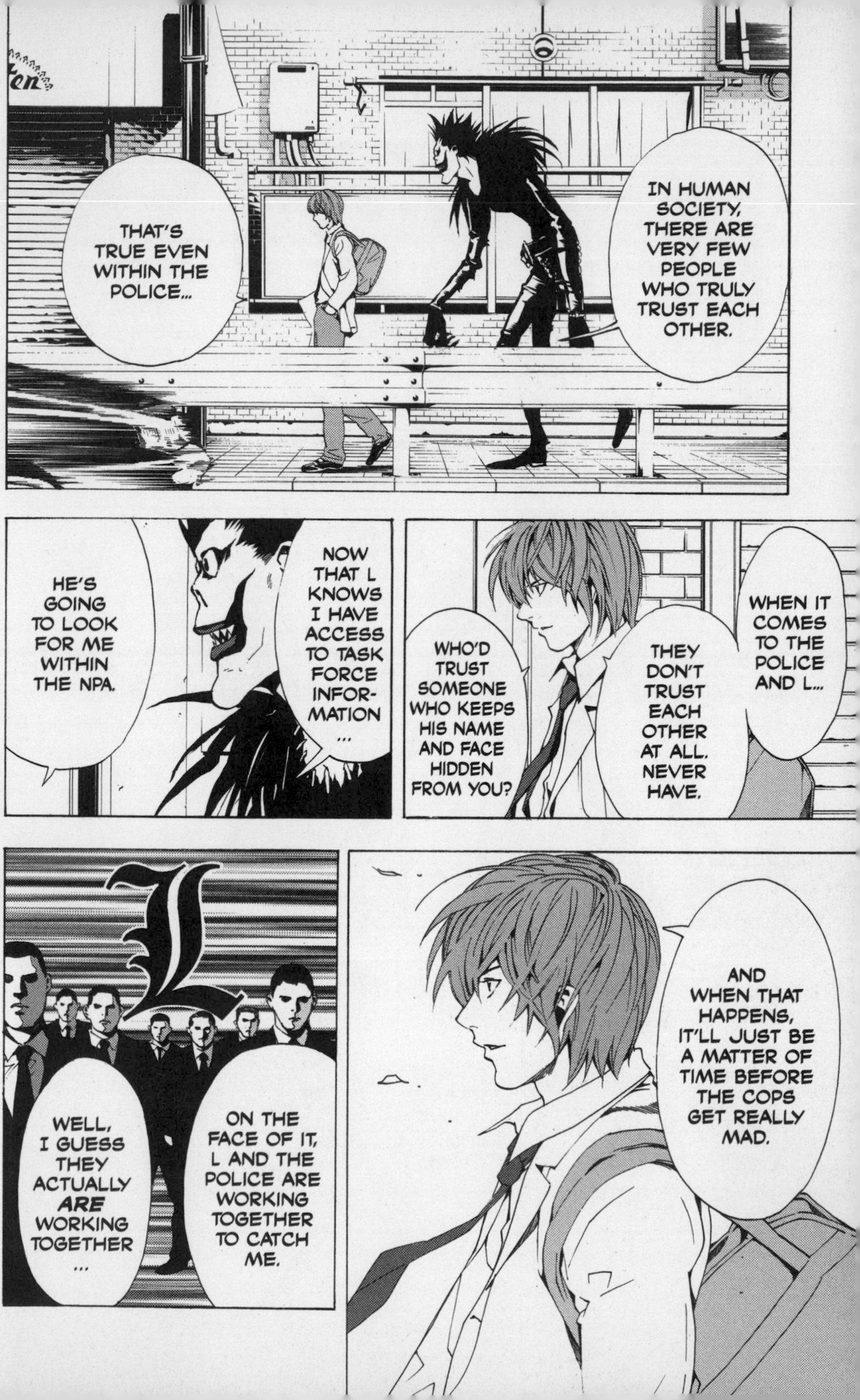
IN HUMAN SOCIETY, THERE ARE VERY FEW PEOPLE WHO TRULY TRUST EACH OTHER.
THAT'S TRUE EVEN WITHIN THE POLICE...
WHEN IT COMES TO THE POLICE AND L...
THEY DON'T TRUST EACH OTHER AT ALL. NEVER HAVE.
WHO'D TRUST SOMEONE WHO KEEPS HIS NAME AND FACE HIDDEN FROM YOU?
NOW THAT L KNOWS I HAVE ACCESS TO TASK FORCE INFOR-MATION...
HE'S GOING TO LOOK FOR ME WITHIN THE NPA.
AND WHEN THAT HAPPENS, IT'LL JUST BE A MATTER OF TIME BEFORE THE COPS GET REALLY MAD.
ON THE FACE OF IT, L AND THE POLICE ARE WORKING TOGETHER TO CATCH ME.
WELL, I GUESS THEY ACTUALLY *ARE* WORKING TOGETHER...

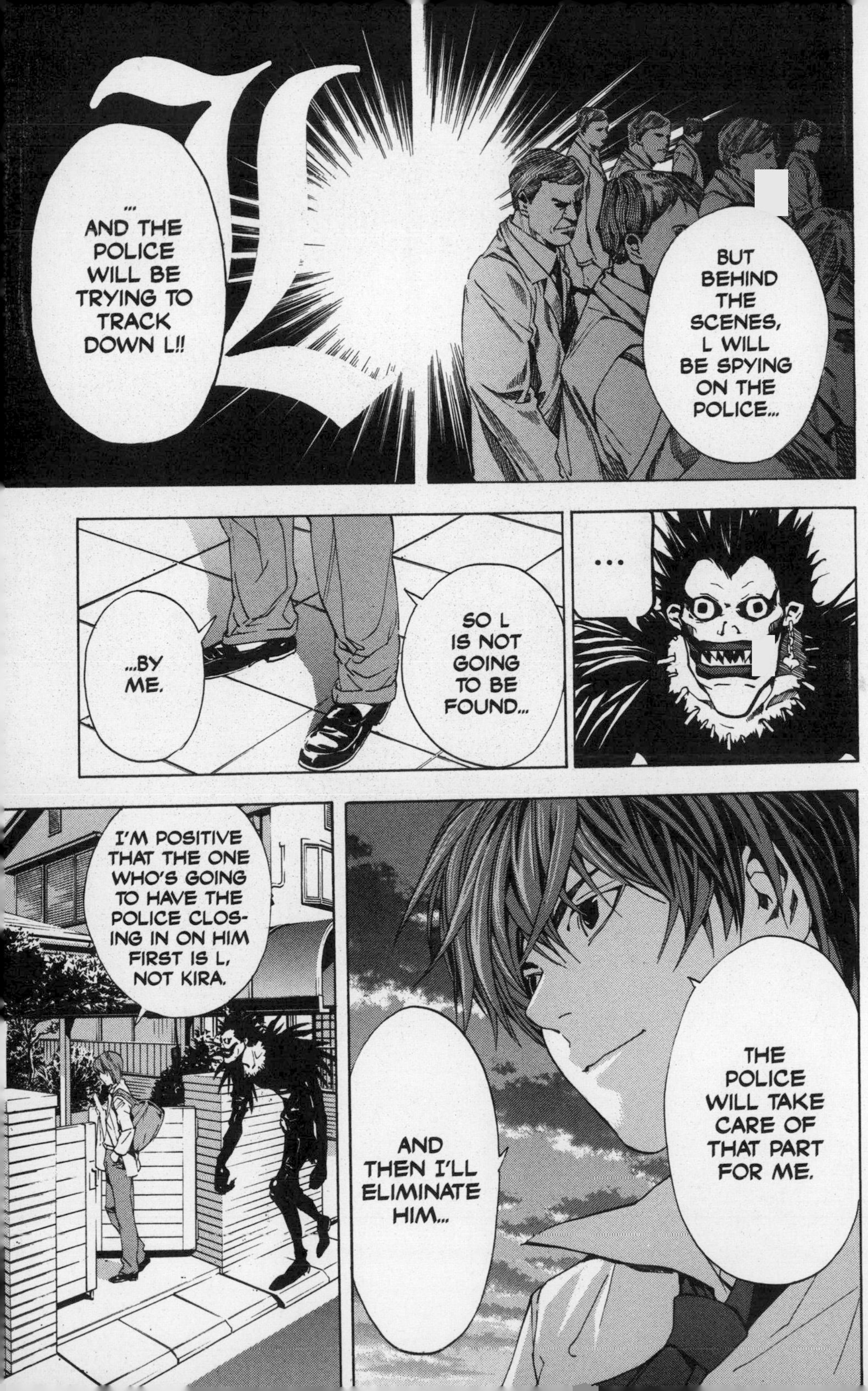
BUT BEHIND THE SCENES, L WILL BE SPYING ON THE POLICE...
...AND THE POLICE WILL BE TRYING TO TRACK DOWN L!!
...
SO L IS NOT GOING TO BE FOUND...
...BY ME.
THE POLICE WILL TAKE CARE OF THAT PART FOR ME.
AND THEN I'LL ELIMINATE HIM...
I'M POSITIVE THAT THE ONE WHO'S GOING TO HAVE THE POLICE CLOS-ING IN ON HIM FIRST IS L, NOT KIRA.

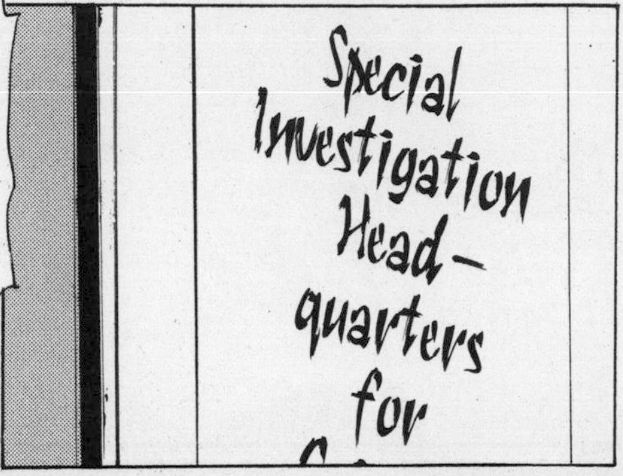
Special Investigation Head-quarters for

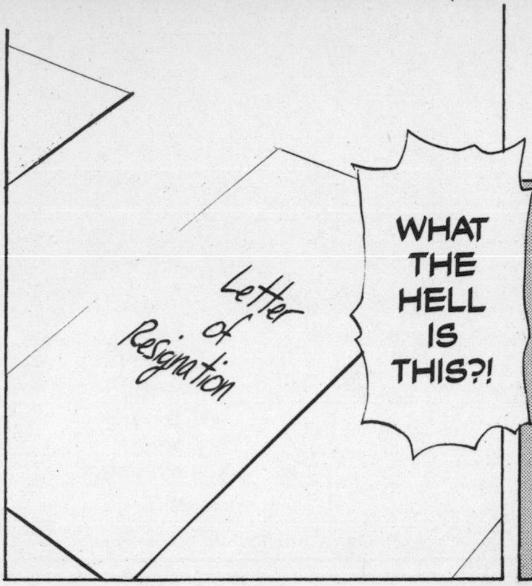
Letter of Resignation
WHAT THE HELL IS THIS?!

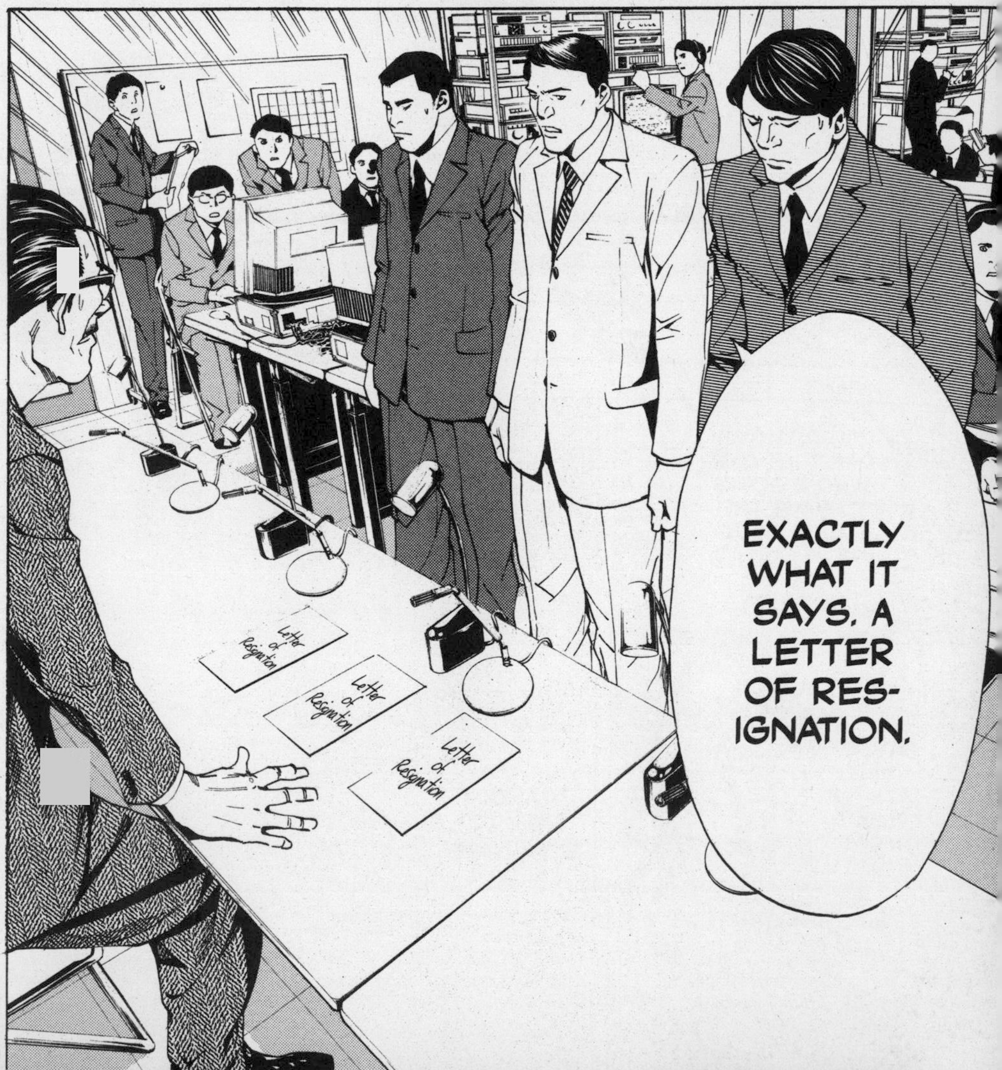
Letter of Resignation
Letter of Resignation
Letter of Resignation
EXACTLY WHAT IT SAYS. A LETTER OF RES-IGNATION.

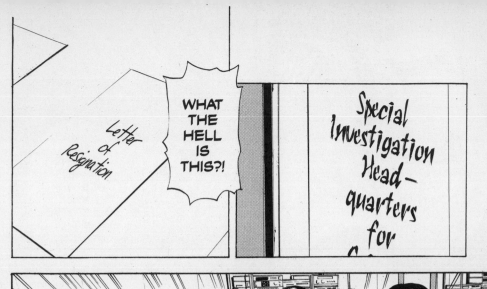

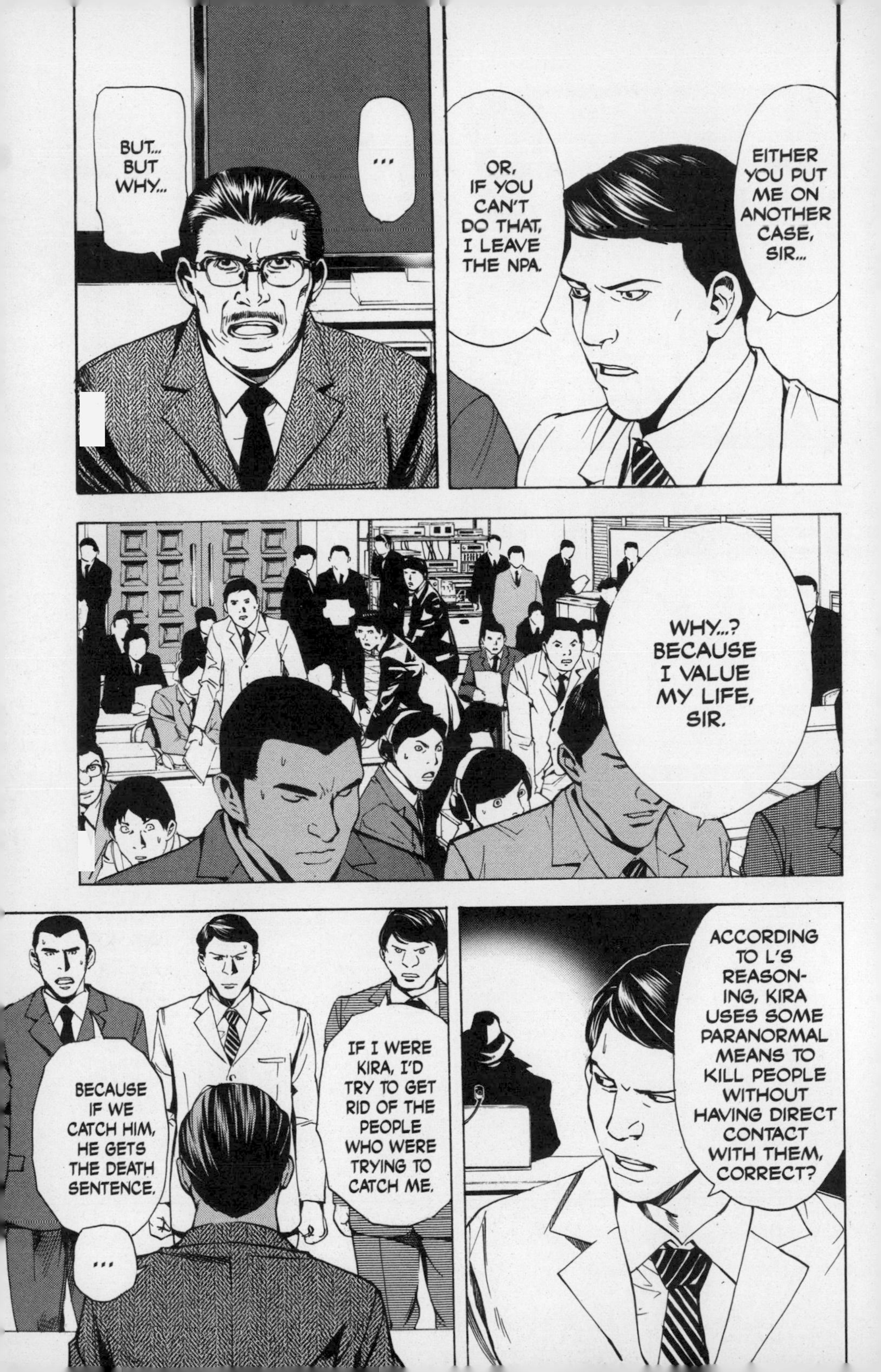
EITHER YOU PUT ME ON ANOTHER CASE, SIR...
OR, IF YOU CAN'T DO THAT, I LEAVE THE NPA.
...
BUT... BUT WHY...
WHY...? BECAUSE I VALUE MY LIFE, SIR.
ACCORDING TO L'S REASON-ING, KIRA USES SOME PARANORMAL MEANS TO KILL PEOPLE WITHOUT HAVING DIRECT CONTACT WITH THEM, CORRECT?
IF I WERE KIRA, I'D TRY TO GET RID OF THE PEOPLE WHO WERE TRYING TO CATCH ME.
BECAUSE IF WE CATCH HIM, HE GETS THE DEATH SENTENCE.
...

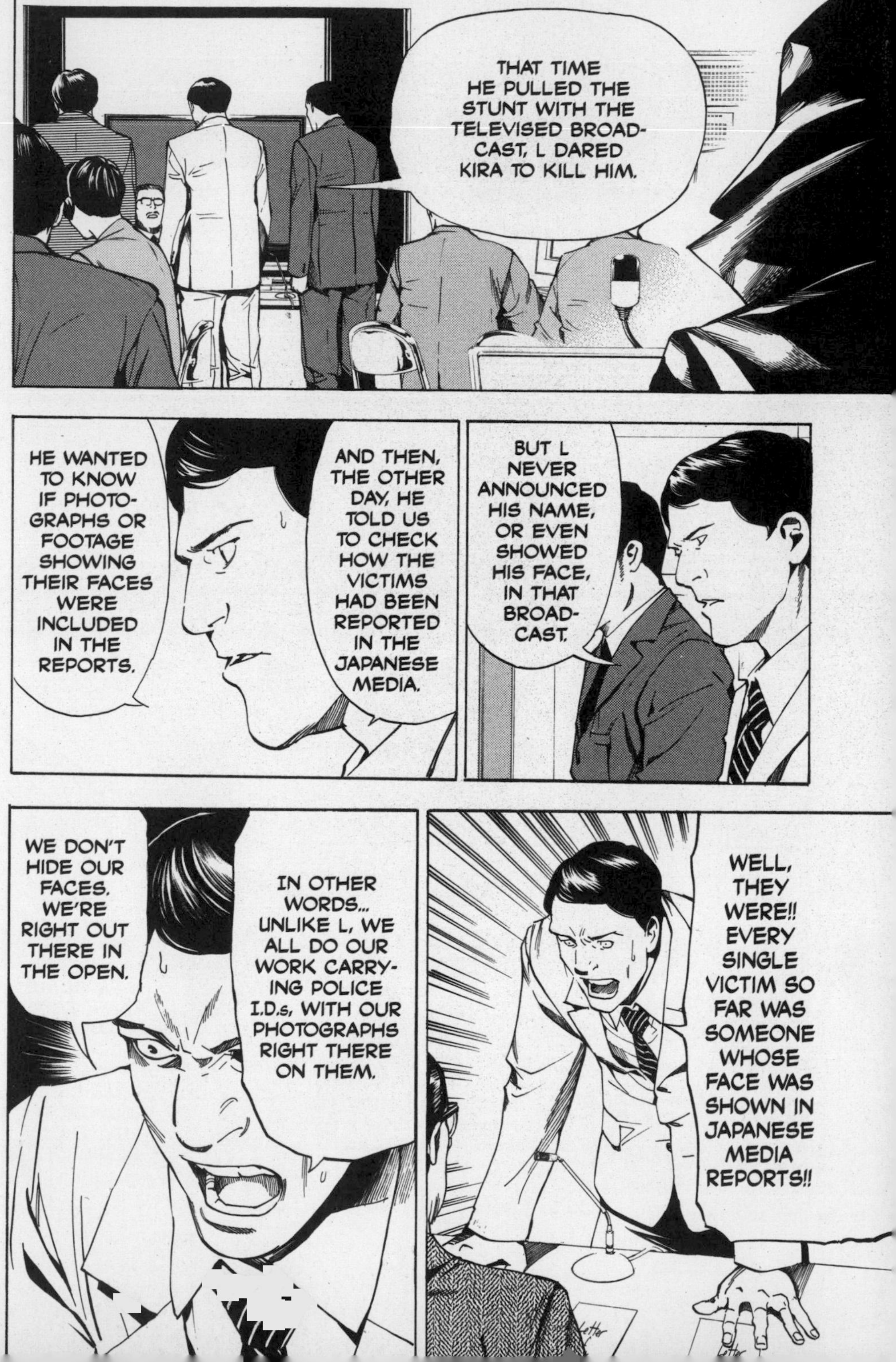
THAT TIME HE PULLED THE STUNT WITH THE TELEVISED BROAD-CAST, L DARED KIRA TO KILL HIM.
BUT L NEVER ANNOUNCED HIS NAME, OR EVEN SHOWED HIS FACE, IN THAT BROAD-CAST.
AND THEN, THE OTHER DAY, HE TOLD US TO CHECK HOW THE VICTIMS HAD BEEN REPORTED IN THE JAPANESE MEDIA.
HE WANTED TO KNOW IF PHOTO-GRAPHS OR FOOTAGE SHOWING THEIR FACES WERE INCLUDED IN THE REPORTS.
WELL, THEY WERE!! EVERY SINGLE VICTIM SO FAR WAS SOMEONE WHOSE FACE WAS SHOWN IN JAPANESE MEDIA REPORTS!!
IN OTHER WORDS... UNLIKE L, WE ALL DO OUR WORK CARRY-ING POLICE I.D.s, WITH OUR PHOTOGRAPHS RIGHT THERE ON THEM.
WE DON'T HIDE OUR FACES. WE'RE RIGHT OUT THERE IN THE OPEN.

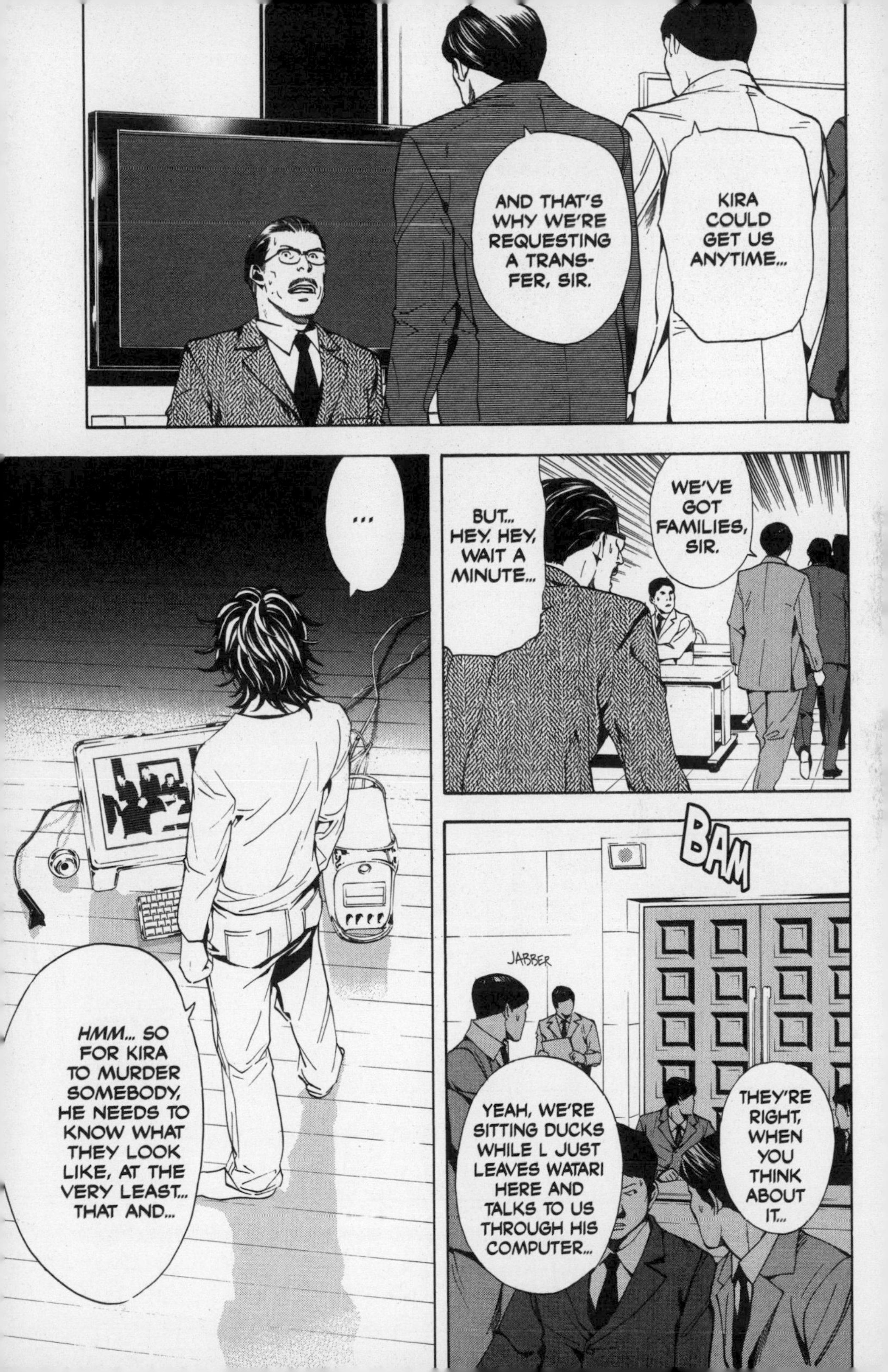
KIRA COULD GET US ANYTIME...
AND THAT'S WHY WE'RE REQUESTING A TRANSFER, SIR.
WE'VE GOT FAMILIES, SIR.
BUT... HEY, HEY, WAIT A MINUTE...
BAM
JABBER
THEY'RE RIGHT, WHEN YOU THINK ABOUT IT...
YEAH, WE'RE SITTING DUCKS WHILE L JUST LEAVES WATARI HERE AND TALKS TO US THROUGH HIS COMPUTER...
...
HMM... SO FOR KIRA TO MURDER SOMEBODY, HE NEEDS TO KNOW WHAT THEY LOOK LIKE, AT THE VERY LEAST... THAT AND...

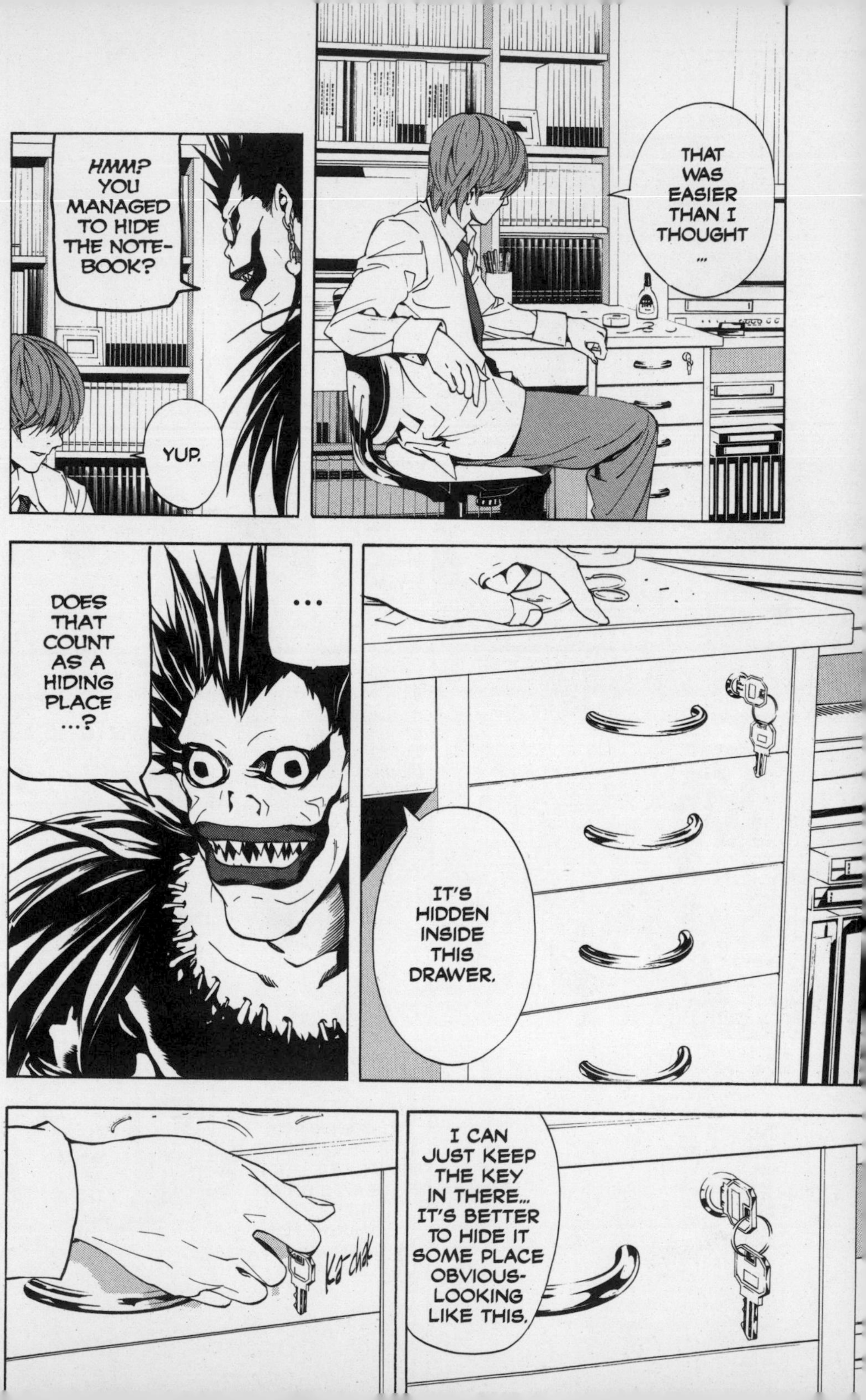
THAT WAS EASIER THAN I THOUGHT ...
HMM? YOU MANAGED TO HIDE THE NOTE-BOOK?
YUP.
IT'S HIDDEN INSIDE THIS DRAWER.
...
DOES THAT COUNT AS A HIDING PLACE ...?
I CAN JUST KEEP THE KEY IN THERE... IT'S BETTER TO HIDE IT SOME PLACE OBVIOUS-LOOKING LIKE THIS.
KA-CHAK

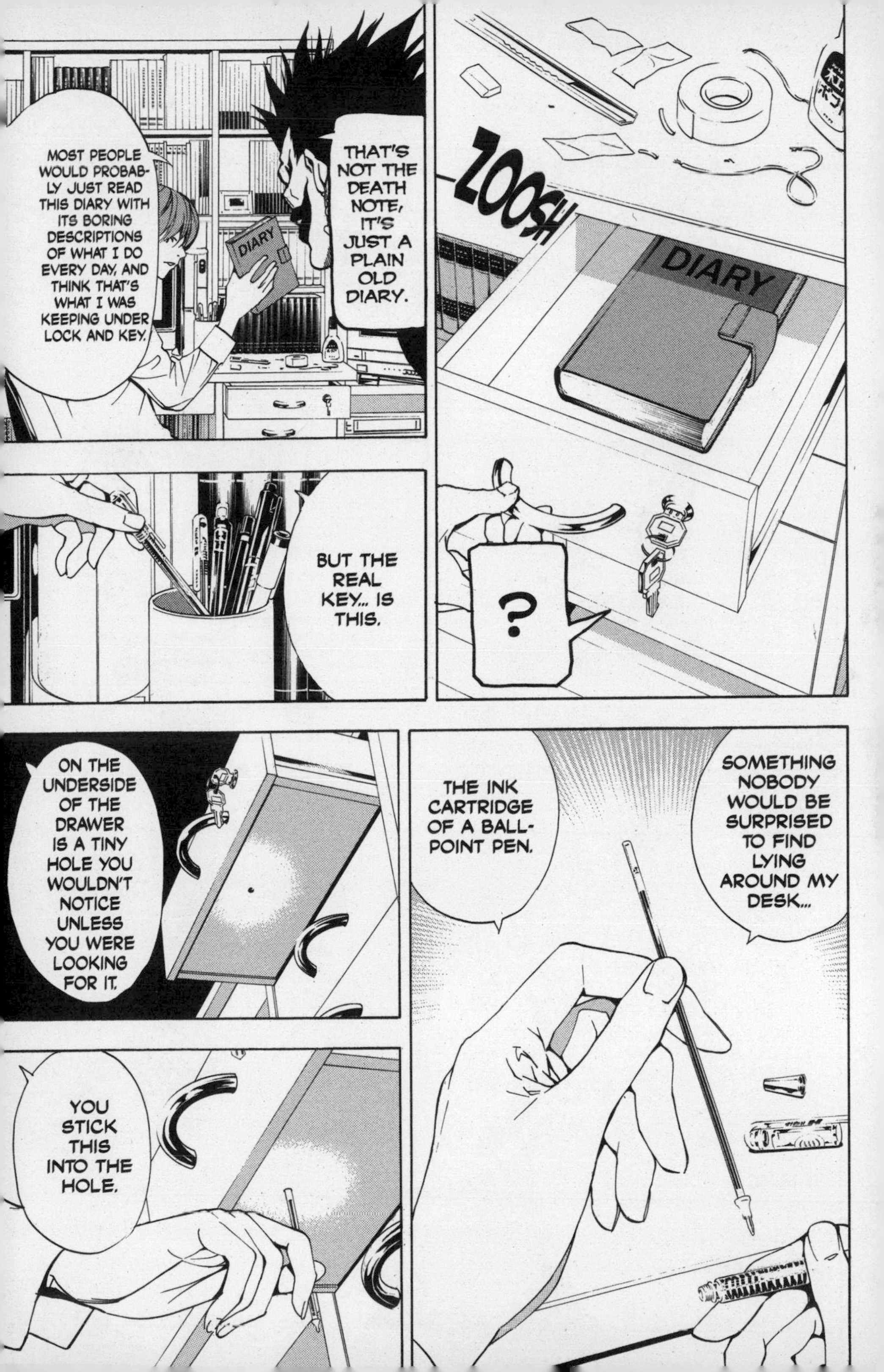
ZOOSH
THAT'S NOT THE DEATH NOTE, IT'S JUST A PLAIN OLD DIARY.
MOST PEOPLE WOULD PROBABLY JUST READ THIS DIARY WITH ITS BORING DESCRIPTIONS OF WHAT I DO EVERY DAY, AND THINK THAT'S WHAT I WAS KEEPING UNDER LOCK AND KEY.
DIARY
DIARY
?
BUT THE REAL KEY... IS THIS.
SOMETHING NOBODY WOULD BE SURPRISED TO FIND LYING AROUND MY DESK...
THE INK CARTRIDGE OF A BALLPOINT PEN.
ON THE UNDERSIDE OF THE DRAWER IS A TINY HOLE YOU WOULDN'T NOTICE UNLESS YOU WERE LOOKING FOR IT.
YOU STICK THIS INTO THE HOLE.

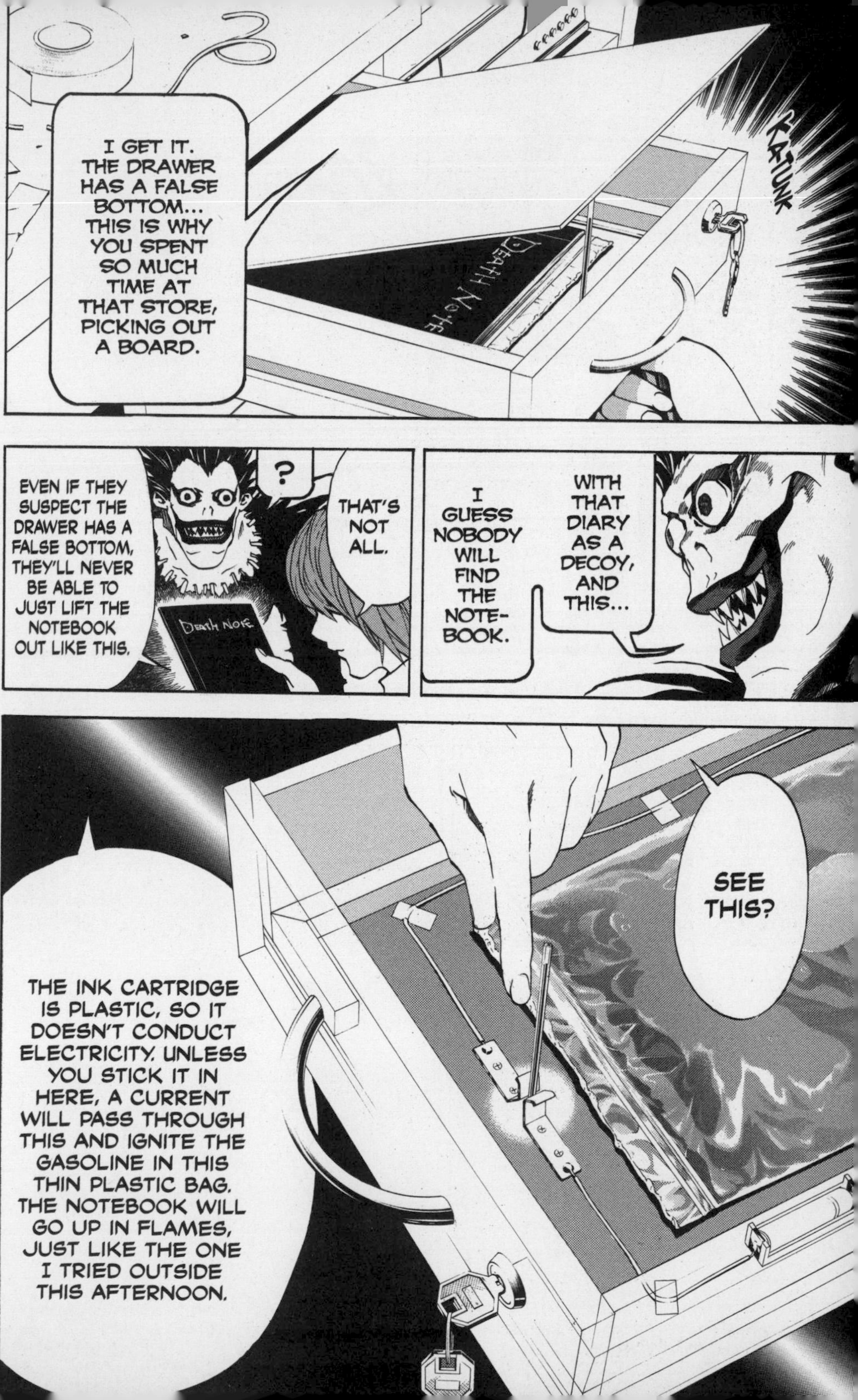
KATUNK
I GET IT. THE DRAWER HAS A FALSE BOTTOM... THIS IS WHY YOU SPENT SO MUCH TIME AT THAT STORE, PICKING OUT A BOARD.
WITH THAT DIARY AS A DECOY, AND THIS...
I GUESS NOBODY WILL FIND THE NOTE-BOOK.
THAT'S NOT ALL.
?
EVEN IF THEY SUSPECT THE DRAWER HAS A FALSE BOTTOM, THEY'LL NEVER BE ABLE TO JUST LIFT THE NOTEBOOK OUT LIKE THIS.
SEE THIS?
THE INK CARTRIDGE IS PLASTIC, SO IT DOESN'T CONDUCT ELECTRICITY. UNLESS YOU STICK IT IN HERE, A CURRENT WILL PASS THROUGH THIS AND IGNITE THE GASOLINE IN THIS THIN PLASTIC BAG. THE NOTEBOOK WILL GO UP IN FLAMES, JUST LIKE THE ONE I TRIED OUTSIDE THIS AFTERNOON.

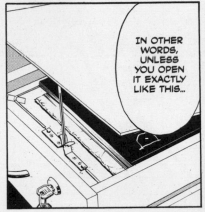

READ THIS WAY
WHEN I CLOSE THE FALSE BOTTOM, THIS RUBBER HERE GOES BETWEEN THE METAL PIECES, SO IT REPLACES THE INK CARTRIDGE AS THE INSULATOR, AND THE CURRENT STAYS INTERRUPTED.
IN OTHER WORDS, UNLESS YOU OPEN IT EXACTLY LIKE THIS...
IF YOU TURN THE DRAWER OVER OR FORCE THE COVER OPEN, THE MOMENT YOU DO THAT...
THE NOTEBOOK GOES UP IN FLAMES AND ALL THE EVIDENCE IS COMPLETELY DESTROYED...
...
IF THEY QUESTION WHY I WENT TO ALL THIS TROUBLE, I JUST HAVE TO SAY THAT WAS MY REAL DIARY AND I DIDN'T WANT ANYONE TO SEE IT. THAT'S THE MOST HUMAN OF REASONS, AND THERE *WILL* BE THE REMAINS OF A NOTEBOOK IN THERE, AFTER ALL.
I'D HEARD THAT WHEN HUMANS GET HOLD OF A DEATH NOTE, FINDING A HIDING PLACE FOR IT BECOMES THEIR NUMBER-ONE HEADACHE.
BUT I BET YOU'RE THE FIRST ONE WHO WENT THIS FAR, LIGHT.

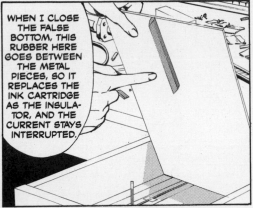

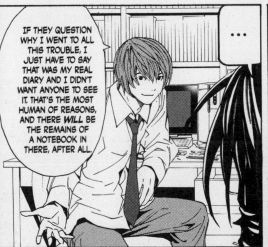

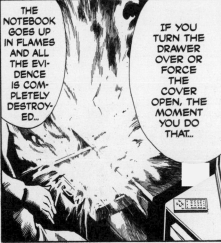

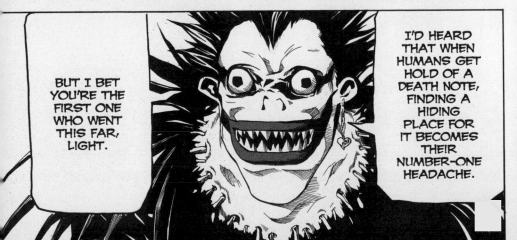

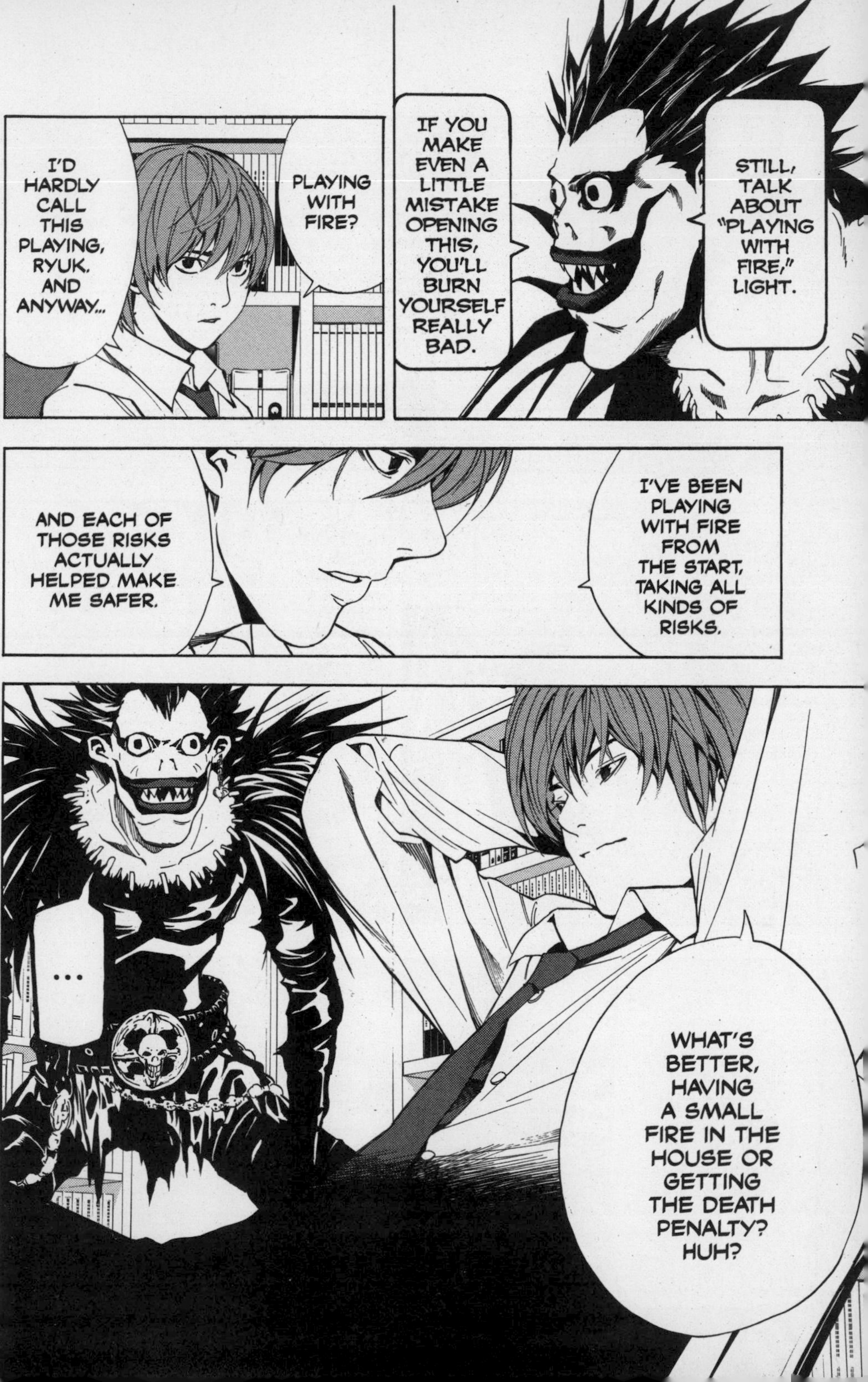
STILL, TALK ABOUT "PLAYING WITH FIRE," LIGHT.
IF YOU MAKE EVEN A LITTLE MISTAKE OPENING THIS, YOU'LL BURN YOURSELF REALLY BAD.
PLAYING WITH FIRE?
I'D HARDLY CALL THIS PLAYING, RYUK. AND ANYWAY...
I'VE BEEN PLAYING WITH FIRE FROM THE START, TAKING ALL KINDS OF RISKS.
AND EACH OF THOSE RISKS ACTUALLY HELPED MAKE ME SAFER.
WHAT'S BETTER, HAVING A SMALL FIRE IN THE HOUSE OR GETTING THE DEATH PENALTY? HUH?
...

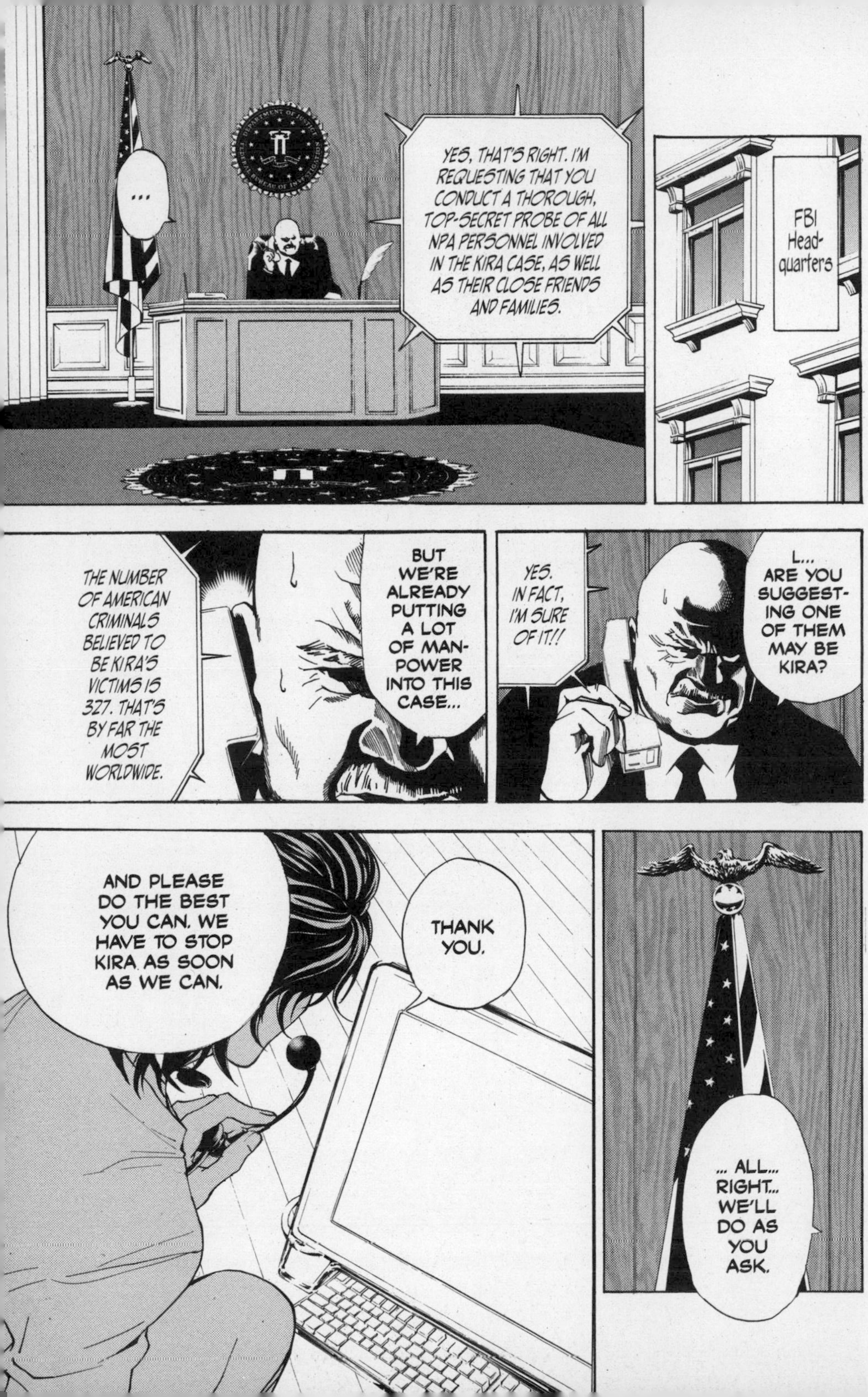
FBI Headquarters
YES, THAT'S RIGHT. I'M REQUESTING THAT YOU CONDUCT A THOROUGH, TOP-SECRET PROBE OF ALL NPA PERSONNEL INVOLVED IN THE KIRA CASE, AS WELL AS THEIR CLOSE FRIENDS AND FAMILIES.
...
L... ARE YOU SUGGESTING ONE OF THEM MAY BE KIRA?
YES. IN FACT, I'M SURE OF IT!!
BUT WE'RE ALREADY PUTTING A LOT OF MANPOWER INTO THIS CASE...
THE NUMBER OF AMERICAN CRIMINALS BELIEVED TO BE KIRA'S VICTIMS IS 327. THAT'S BY FAR THE MOST WORLDWIDE.
... ALL... RIGHT... WE'LL DO AS YOU ASK.
THANK YOU.
AND PLEASE DO THE BEST YOU CAN. WE HAVE TO STOP KIRA AS SOON AS WE CAN.

# DEATH NOTE
## How to use it

### IV

- The person in possession of the DEATH NOTE is possessed by a god of death, its original owner, until they die.

  デスノートを持っている限り、自分が死ぬまで元持ち主である死神が憑いてまわる。

- If a human uses the note, a god of death usually appears in front of him/her within 39 days after he/she uses the note.

  死神は通常、人間がノートを使った39日以内に使った者の前に姿を現す。

- Gods of death, the original owners of the DEATH NOTE, do not do, in principle, anything which will help or prevent the deaths in the note.

  デスノートの元持ち主である死神は、そのノートでの死の手伝いや妨げになる行為は基本的にはしない。

- A god of death has no obligation to completely explain how to use the note or rules which will apply to the human who owns it.

  デスノートの使い方や、それを持つ人間に発生する掟を死神が全て説明する義務はない。

# chapter 5 Eyeballs

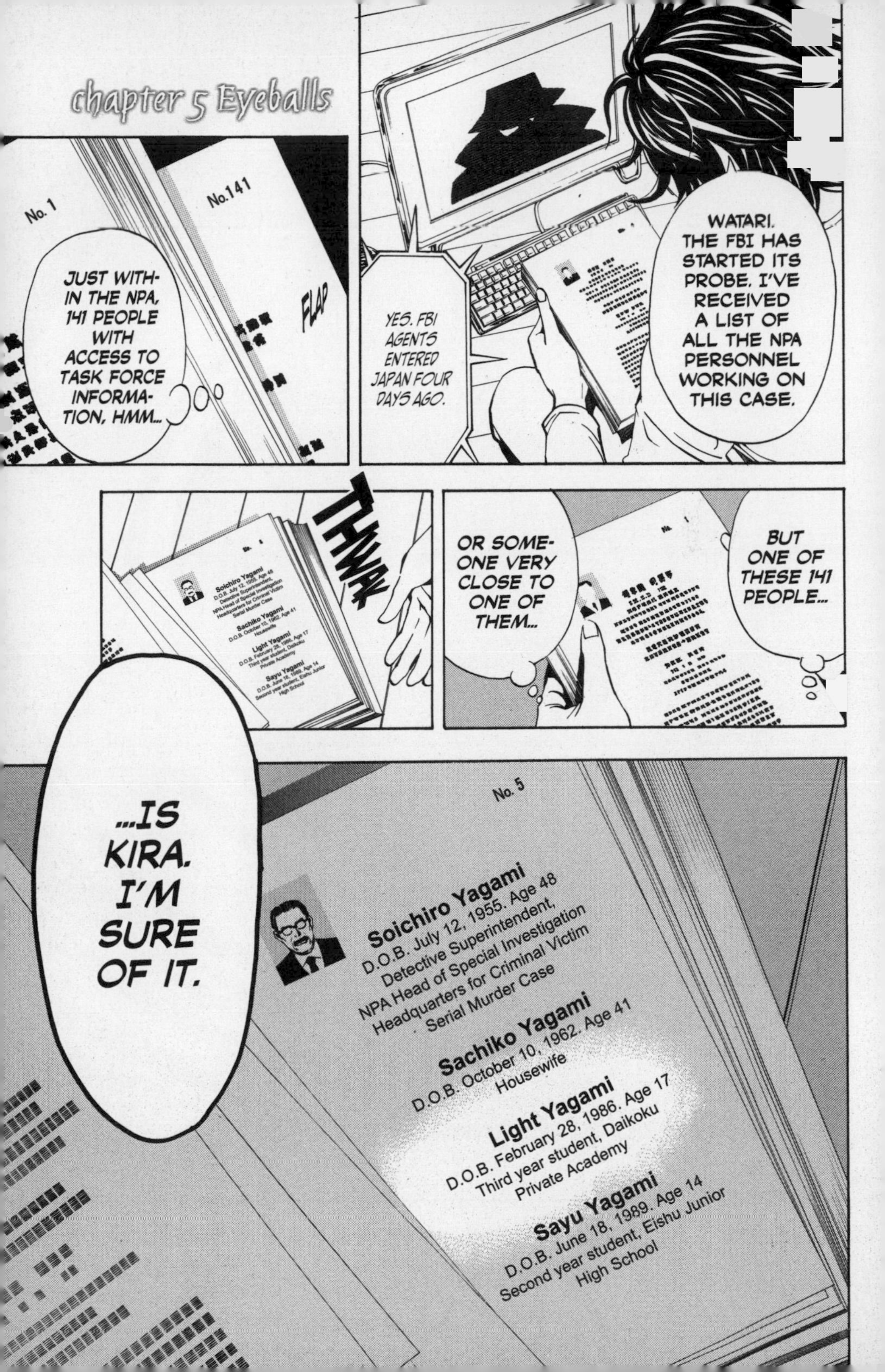
WATARI. THE FBI HAS STARTED ITS PROBE. I'VE RECEIVED A LIST OF ALL THE NPA PERSONNEL WORKING ON THIS CASE.
YES. FBI AGENTS ENTERED JAPAN FOUR DAYS AGO.
No.141
No. 1
JUST WITHIN THE NPA, 141 PEOPLE WITH ACCESS TO TASK FORCE INFORMATION, HMM...
FLAP
BUT ONE OF THESE 141 PEOPLE...
OR SOMEONE VERY CLOSE TO ONE OF THEM...
THWAK
No. 5
Soichiro Yagami
D.O.B. July 12, 1955. Age 48
Detective Superintendent,
NPA Head of Special Investigation
Headquarters for Criminal Victim
Serial Murder Case
Sachiko Yagami
D.O.B. October 10, 1962. Age 41
Housewife
Light Yagami
D.O.B. February 28, 1986. Age 17
Third year student, Daikoku
Private Academy
Sayu Yagami
D.O.B. June 18, 1989. Age 14
Second year student, Eishu Junior
High School
...IS KIRA. I'M SURE OF IT.

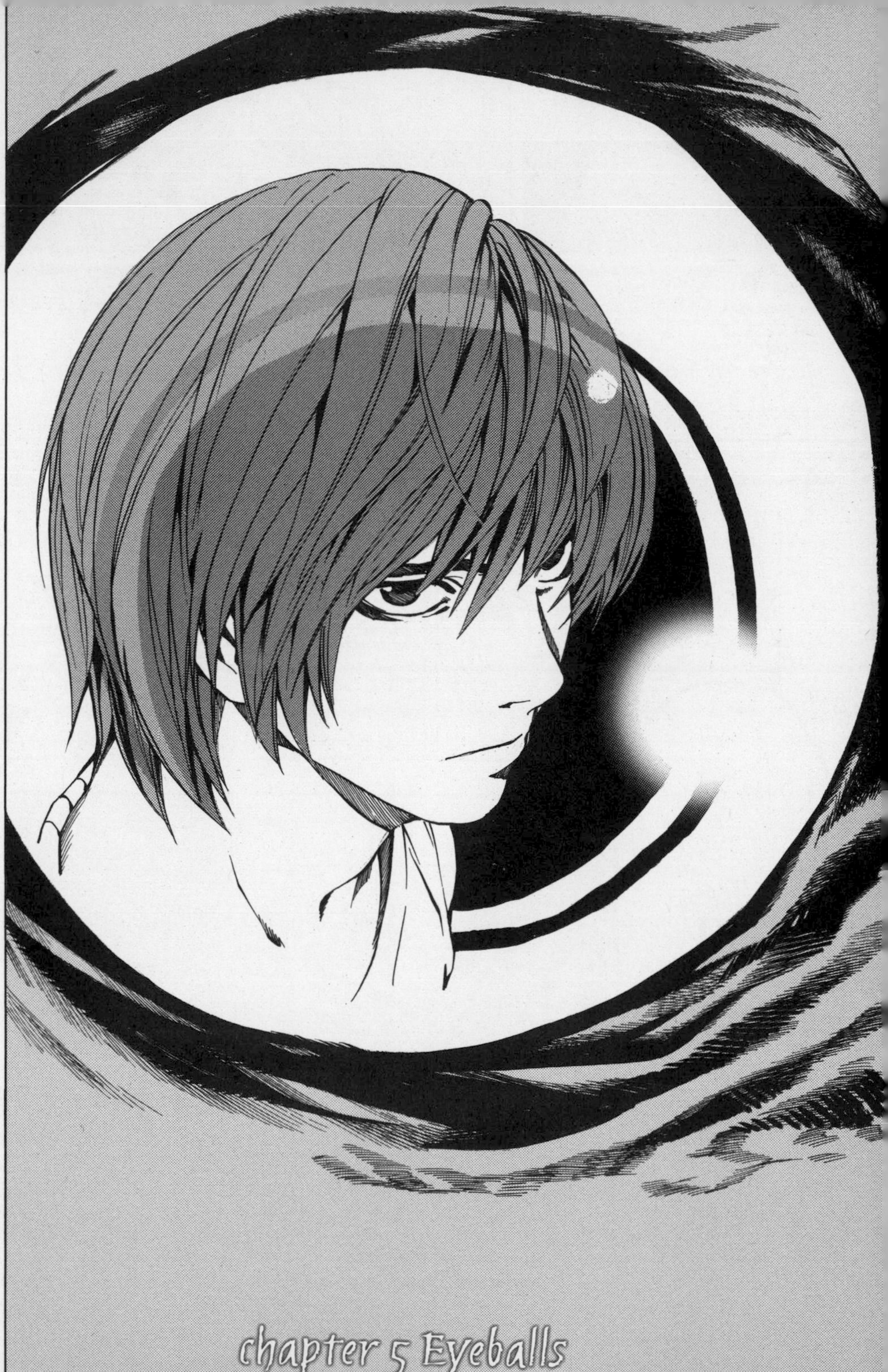

# chapter 5 Eyeballs

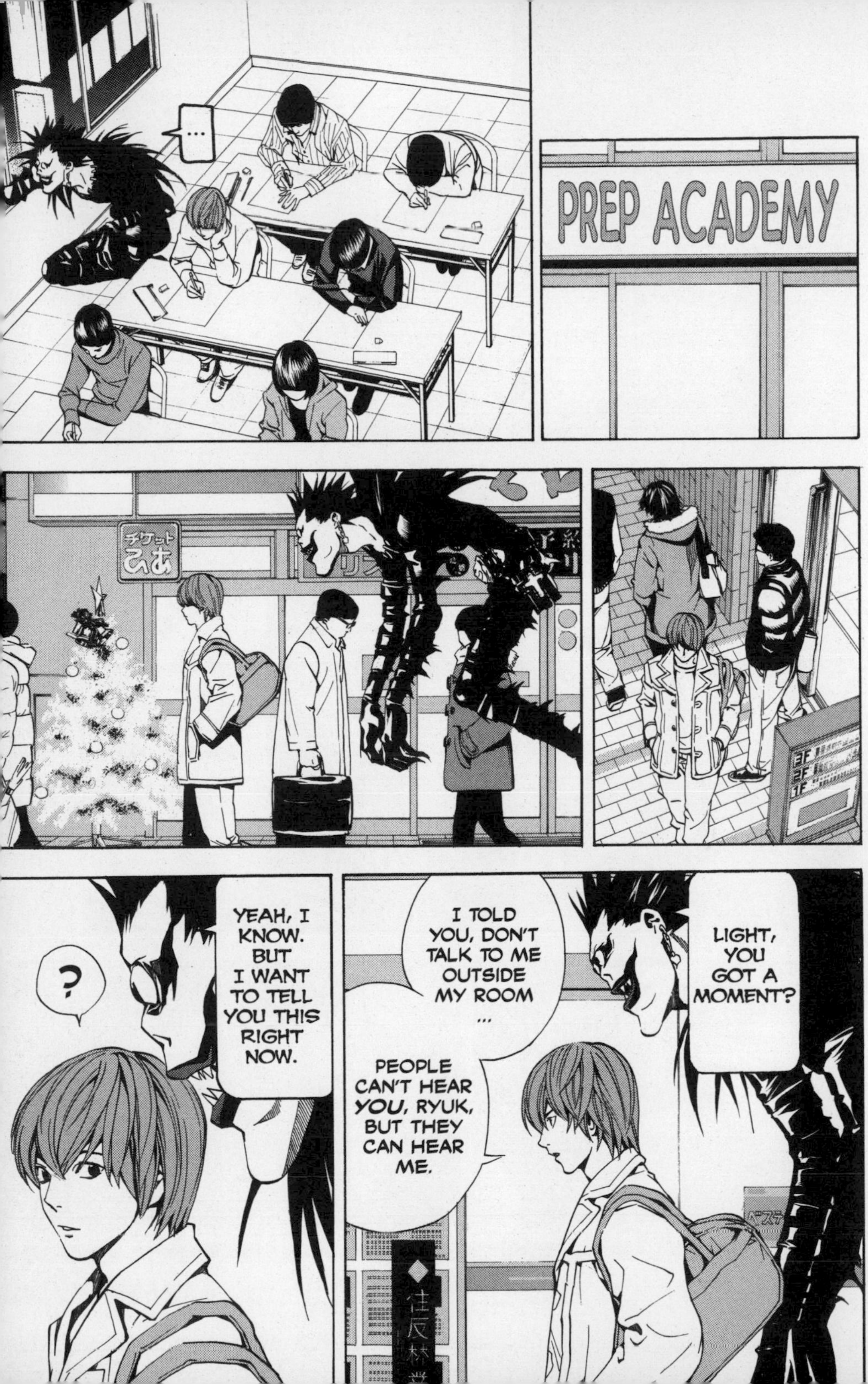
PREP ACADEMY
...
3F
2F
1F
チケットぴあ
LIGHT, YOU GOT A MOMENT?
I TOLD YOU, DON'T TALK TO ME OUTSIDE MY ROOM ...
PEOPLE CAN'T HEAR *YOU*, RYUK, BUT THEY CAN HEAR ME.
YEAH, I KNOW. BUT I WANT TO TELL YOU THIS RIGHT NOW.
?

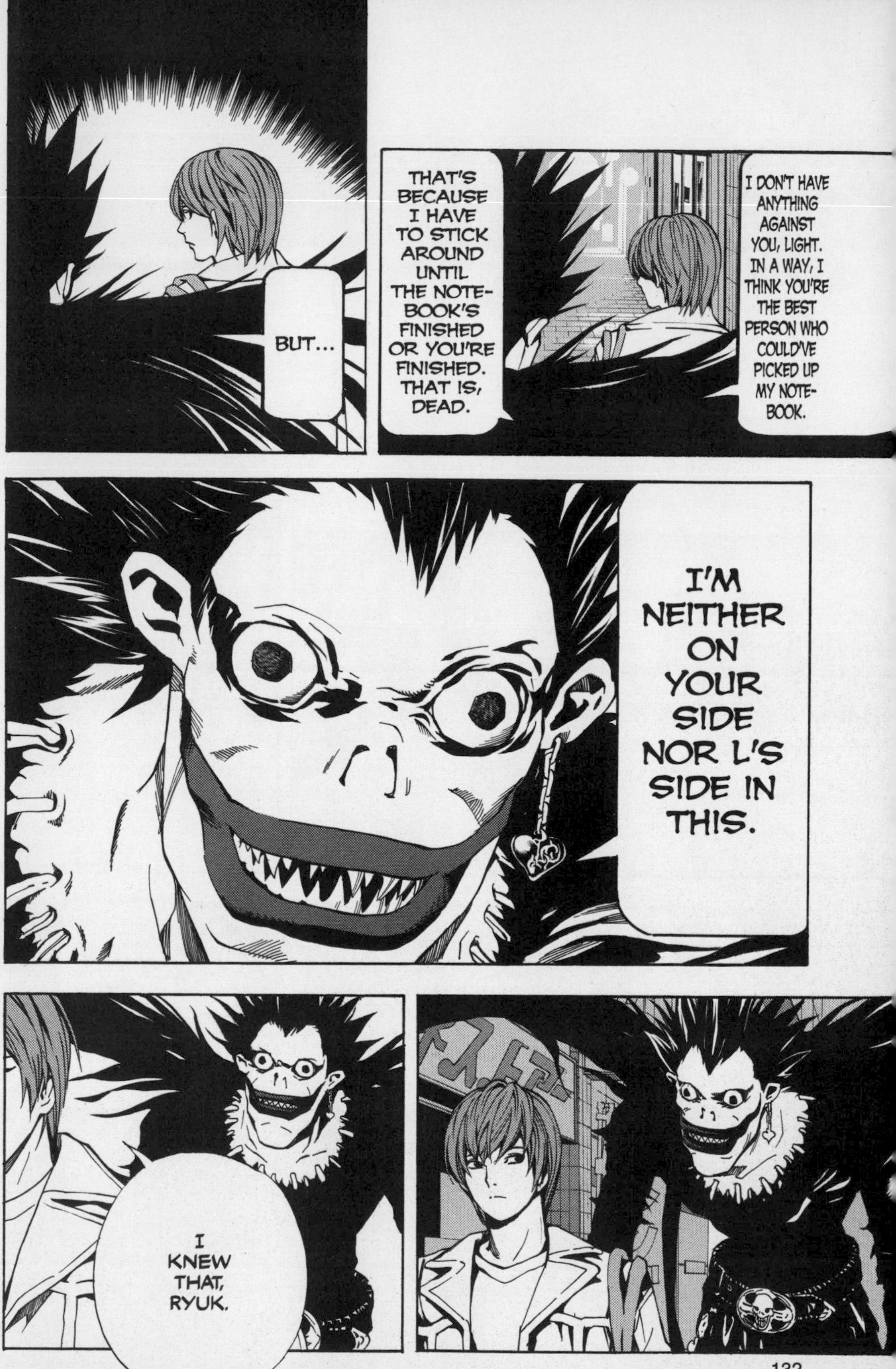
I DON'T HAVE ANYTHING AGAINST YOU, LIGHT. IN A WAY, I THINK YOU'RE THE BEST PERSON WHO COULD'VE PICKED UP MY NOTE-BOOK.
THAT'S BECAUSE I HAVE TO STICK AROUND UNTIL THE NOTE-BOOK'S FINISHED OR YOU'RE FINISHED. THAT IS, DEAD.
BUT...
I'M NEITHER ON YOUR SIDE NOR L'S SIDE IN THIS.
I KNEW THAT, RYUK.

READ THIS WAY

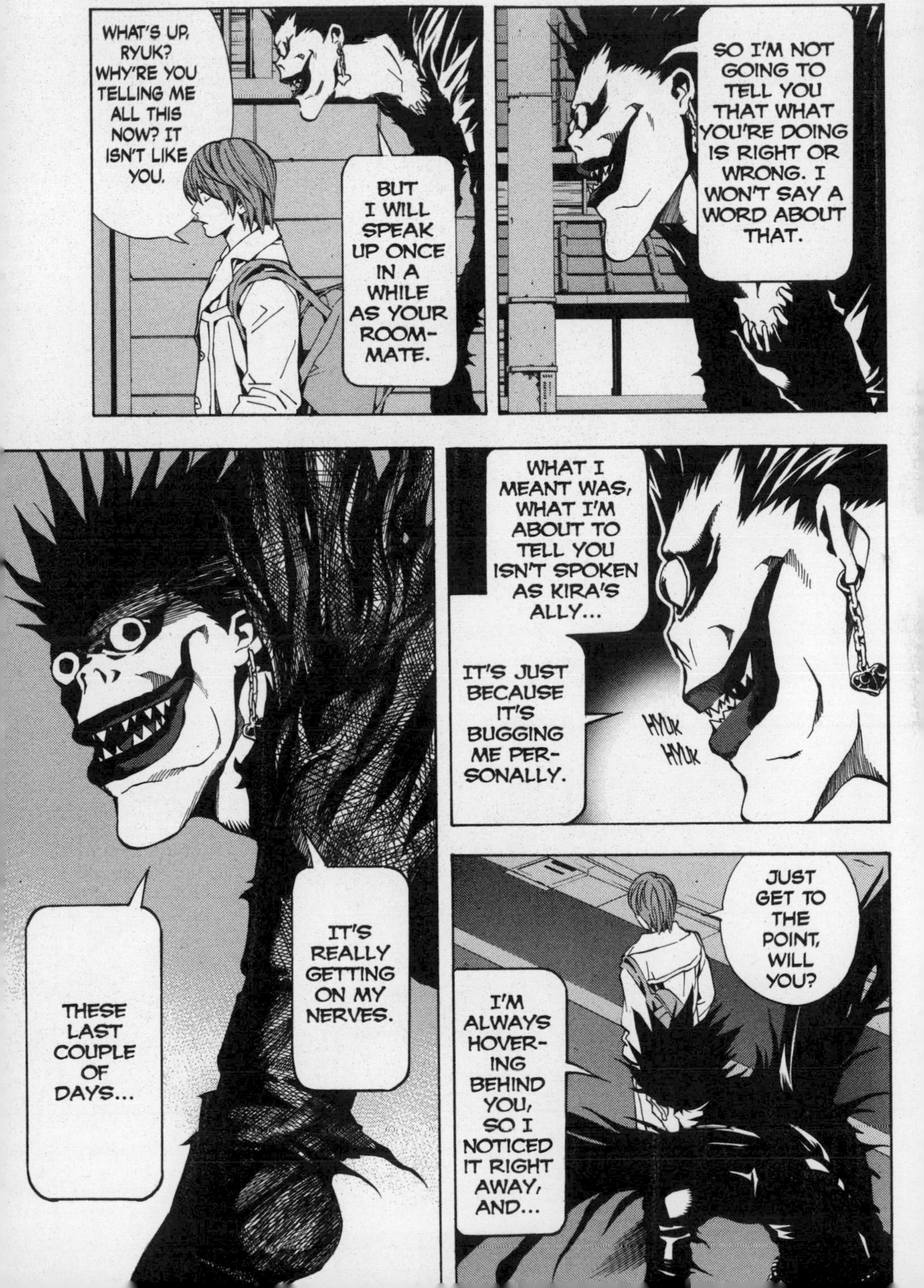
SO I'M NOT GOING TO TELL YOU THAT WHAT YOU'RE DOING IS RIGHT OR WRONG. I WON'T SAY A WORD ABOUT THAT.
BUT I WILL SPEAK UP ONCE IN A WHILE AS YOUR ROOM-MATE.
WHAT'S UP, RYUK? WHY'RE YOU TELLING ME ALL THIS NOW? IT ISN'T LIKE YOU.
WHAT I MEANT WAS, WHAT I'M ABOUT TO TELL YOU ISN'T SPOKEN AS KIRA'S ALLY...
IT'S JUST BECAUSE IT'S BUGGING ME PER-SONALLY.
HYUK HYUK
JUST GET TO THE POINT, WILL YOU?
I'M ALWAYS HOVER-ING BEHIND YOU, SO I NOTICED IT RIGHT AWAY, AND...
IT'S REALLY GETTING ON MY NERVES.
THESE LAST COUPLE OF DAYS...

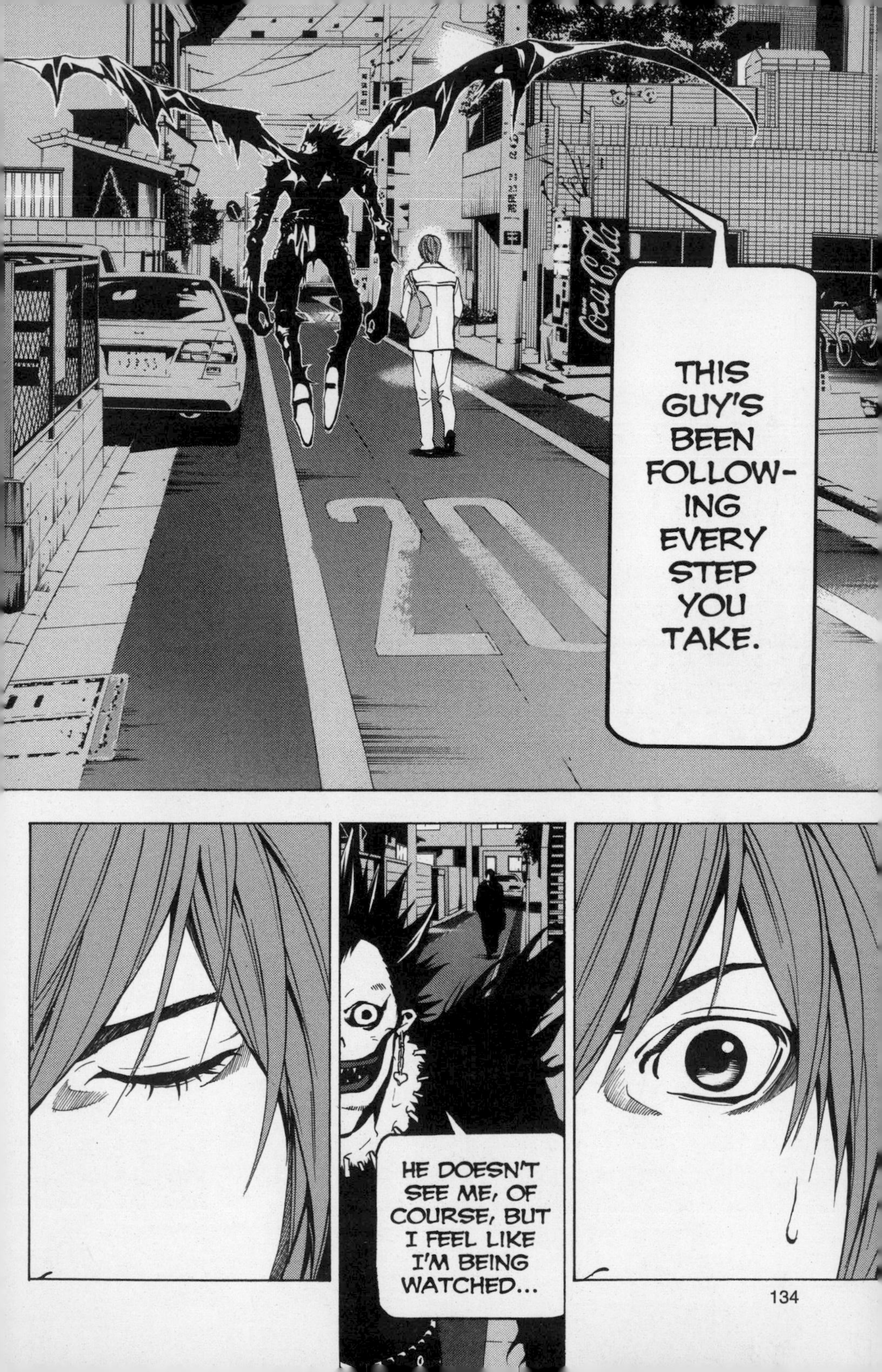
Coca-Cola
THIS GUY'S BEEN FOLLOW-ING EVERY STEP YOU TAKE.
HE DOESN'T SEE ME, OF COURSE, BUT I FEEL LIKE I'M BEING WATCHED...

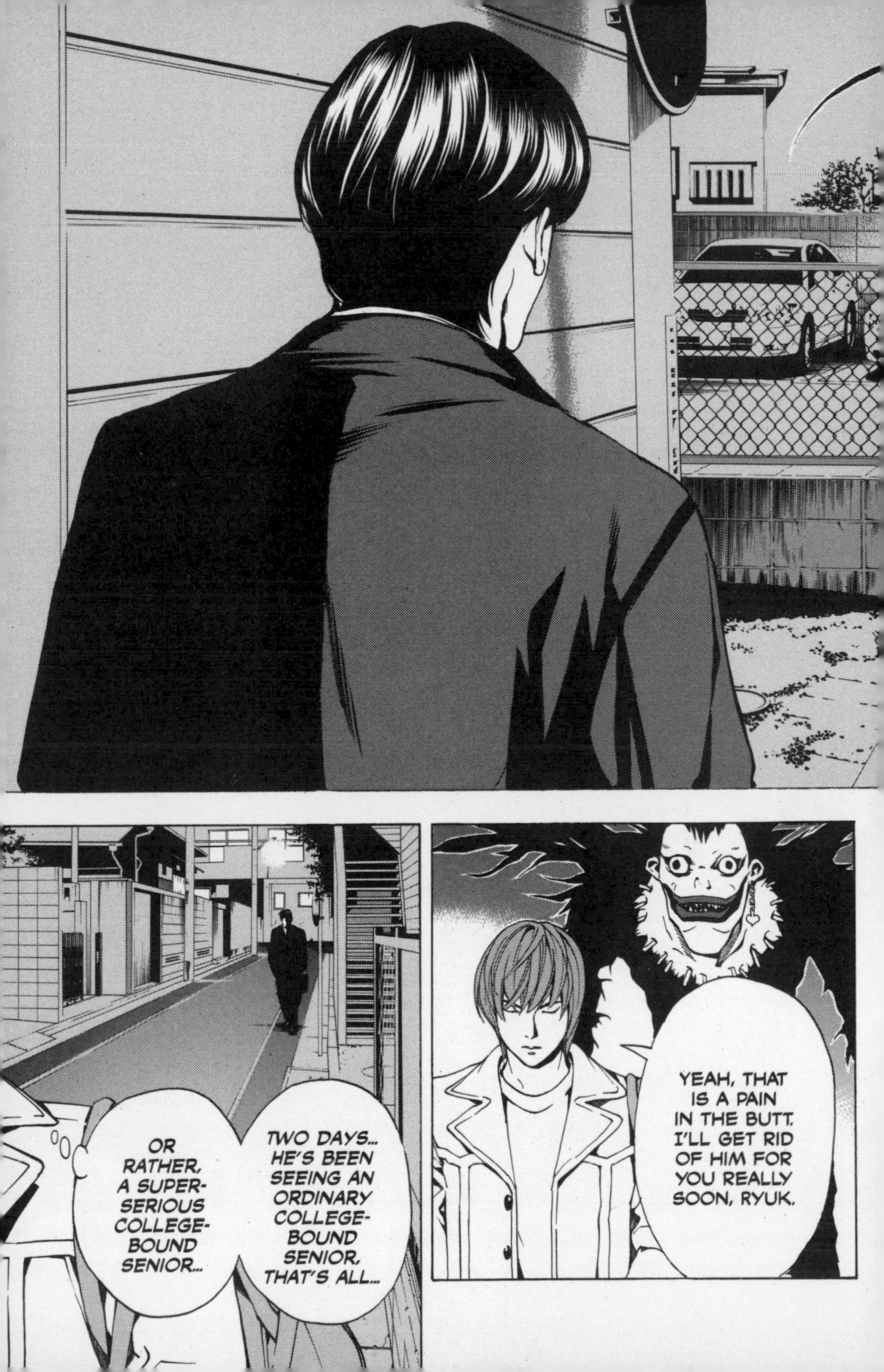
YEAH, THAT IS A PAIN IN THE BUTT. I'LL GET RID OF HIM FOR YOU REALLY SOON, RYUK.
TWO DAYS... HE'S BEEN SEEING AN ORDINARY COLLEGE-BOUND SENIOR, THAT'S ALL...
OR RATHER, A SUPER-SERIOUS COLLEGE-BOUND SENIOR...

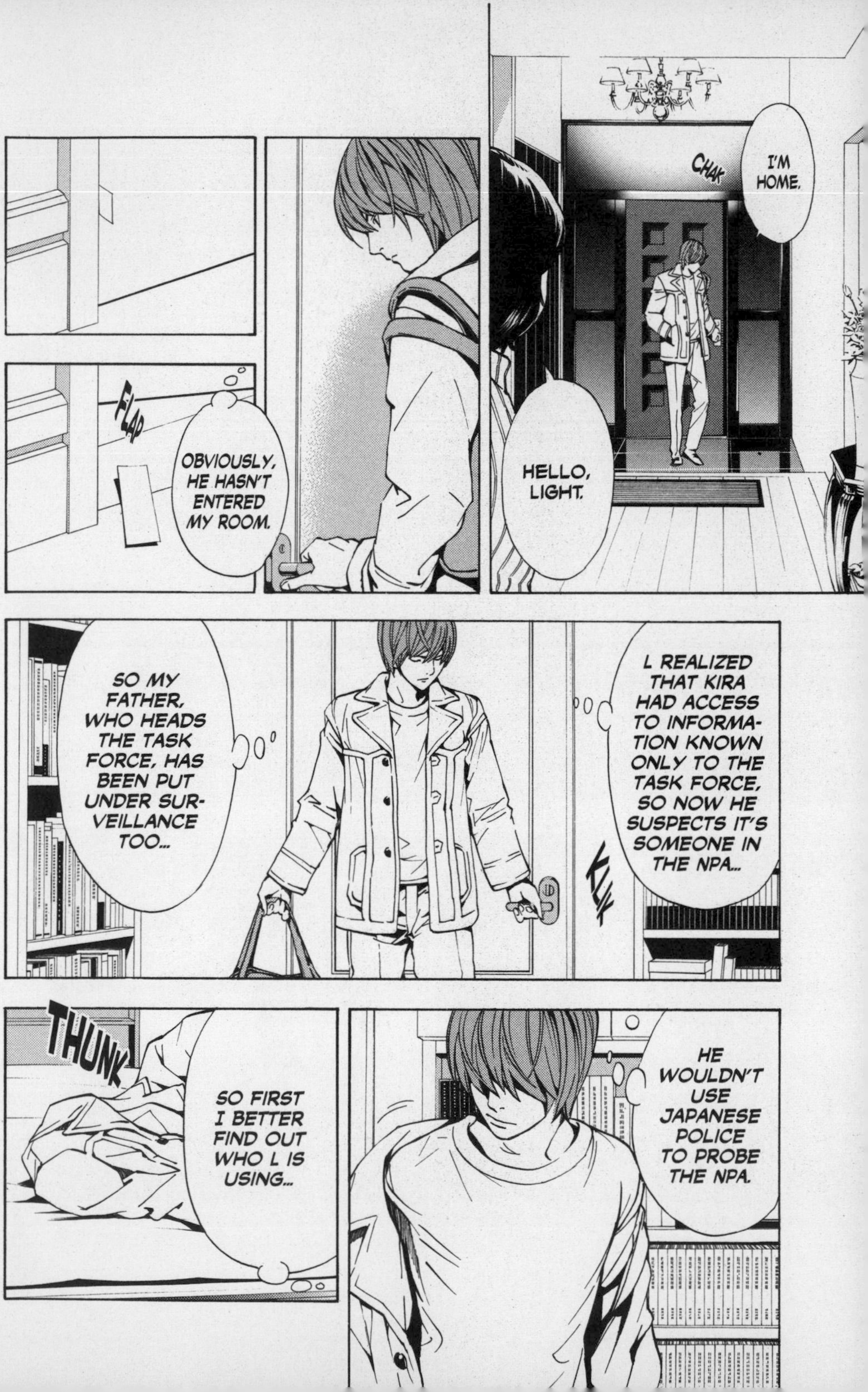
CHAK
I'M HOME.
HELLO, LIGHT.
FLAP
OBVIOUSLY, HE HASN'T ENTERED MY ROOM.
L REALIZED THAT KIRA HAD ACCESS TO INFORMATION KNOWN ONLY TO THE TASK FORCE, SO NOW HE SUSPECTS IT'S SOMEONE IN THE NPA...
KLIK
SO MY FATHER, WHO HEADS THE TASK FORCE, HAS BEEN PUT UNDER SURVEILLANCE TOO...
HE WOULDN'T USE JAPANESE POLICE TO PROBE THE NPA.
THUNK
SO FIRST I BETTER FIND OUT WHO L IS USING...

READ THIS WAY

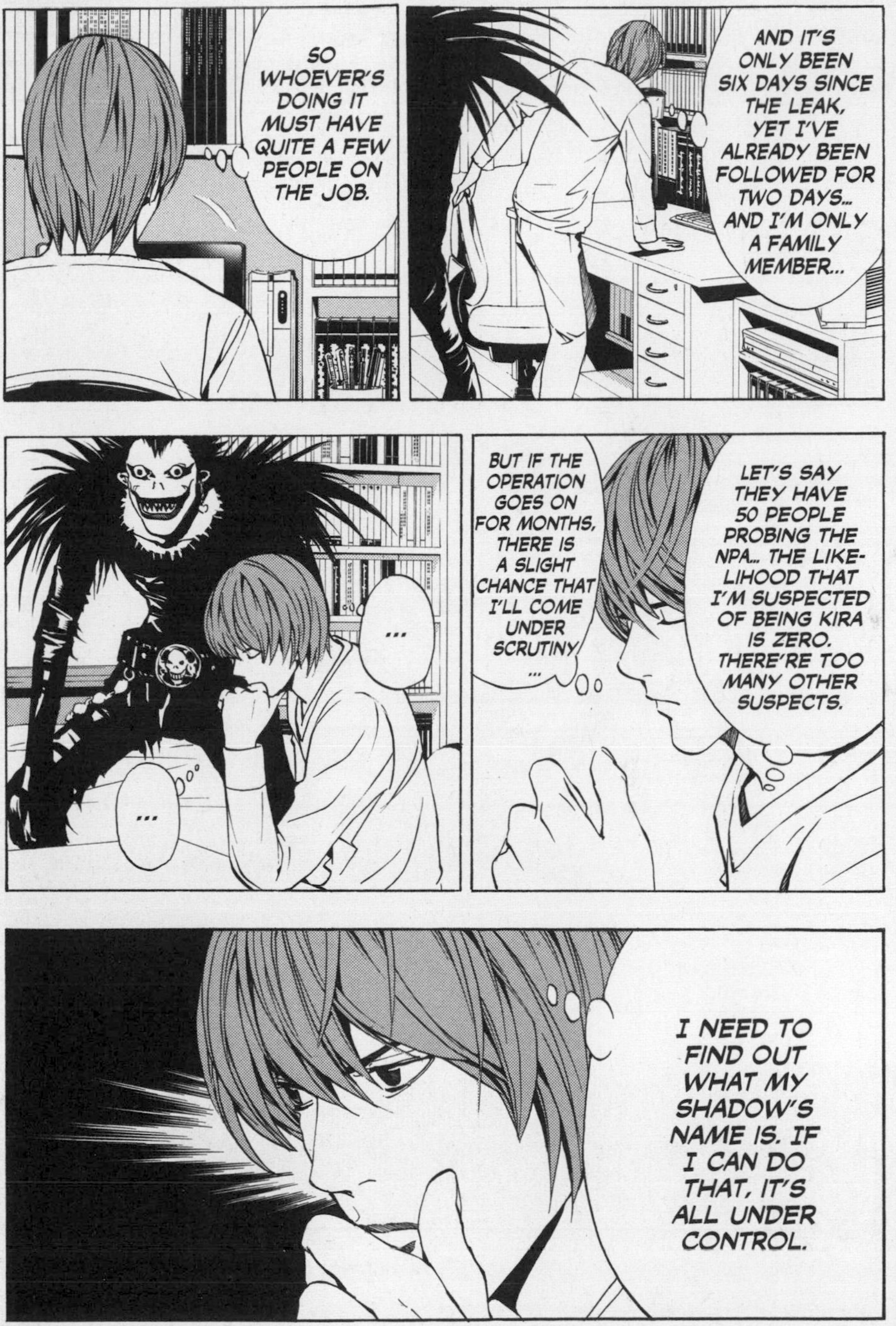
AND IT'S ONLY BEEN SIX DAYS SINCE THE LEAK, YET I'VE ALREADY BEEN FOLLOWED FOR TWO DAYS... AND I'M ONLY A FAMILY MEMBER...
SO WHOEVER'S DOING IT MUST HAVE QUITE A FEW PEOPLE ON THE JOB.
LET'S SAY THEY HAVE 50 PEOPLE PROBING THE NPA... THE LIKE-LIHOOD THAT I'M SUSPECTED OF BEING KIRA IS ZERO. THERE'RE TOO MANY OTHER SUSPECTS.
BUT IF THE OPERATION GOES ON FOR MONTHS, THERE IS A SLIGHT CHANCE THAT I'LL COME UNDER SCRUTINY ...
...
...
I NEED TO FIND OUT WHAT MY SHADOW'S NAME IS. IF I CAN DO THAT, IT'S ALL UNDER CONTROL.

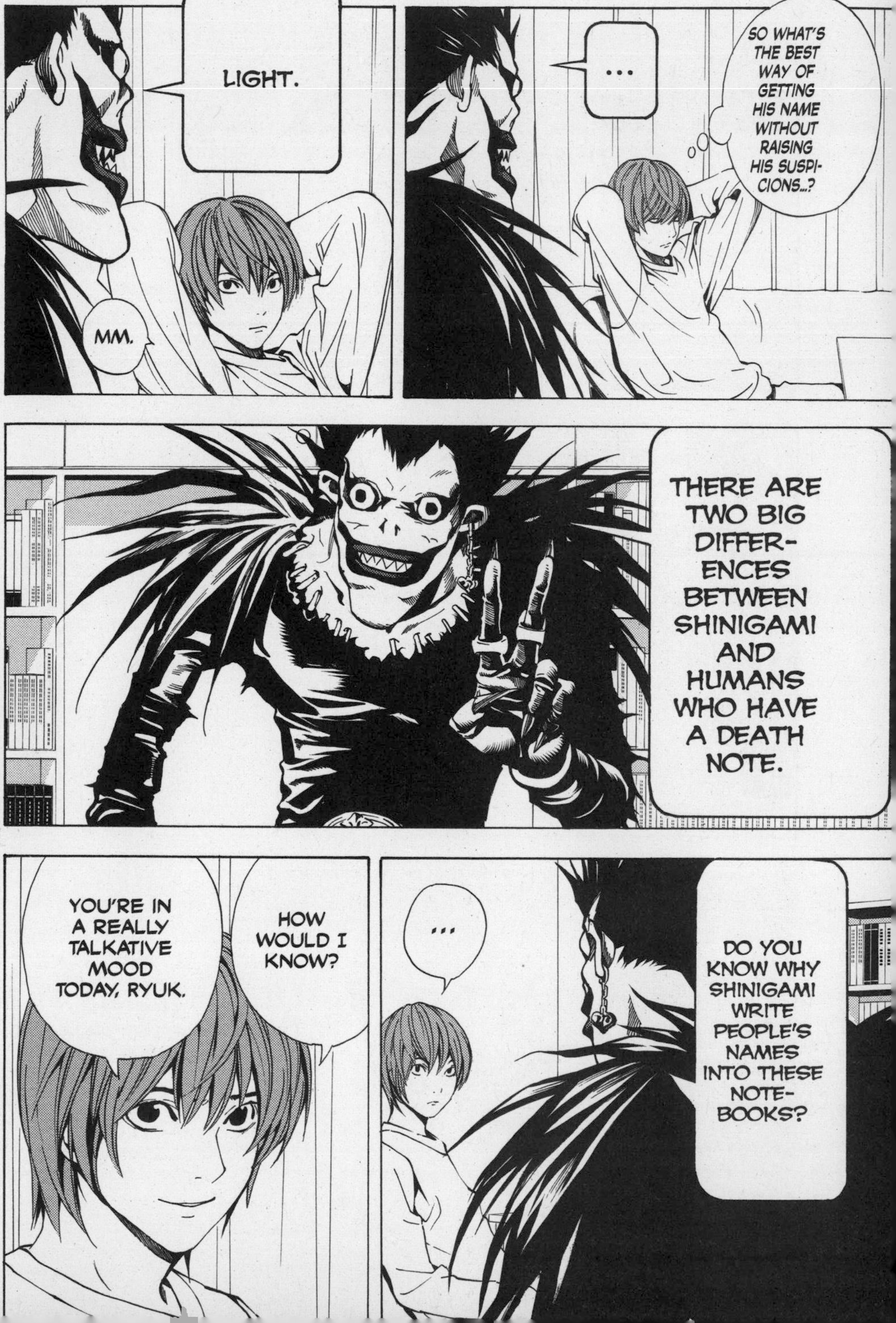
...
SO WHAT'S THE BEST WAY OF GETTING HIS NAME WITHOUT RAISING HIS SUSPICIONS...?
LIGHT.
MM.
THERE ARE TWO BIG DIFFERENCES BETWEEN SHINIGAMI AND HUMANS WHO HAVE A DEATH NOTE.
DO YOU KNOW WHY SHINIGAMI WRITE PEOPLE'S NAMES INTO THESE NOTEBOOKS?
...
HOW WOULD I KNOW?
YOU'RE IN A REALLY TALKATIVE MOOD TODAY, RYUK.

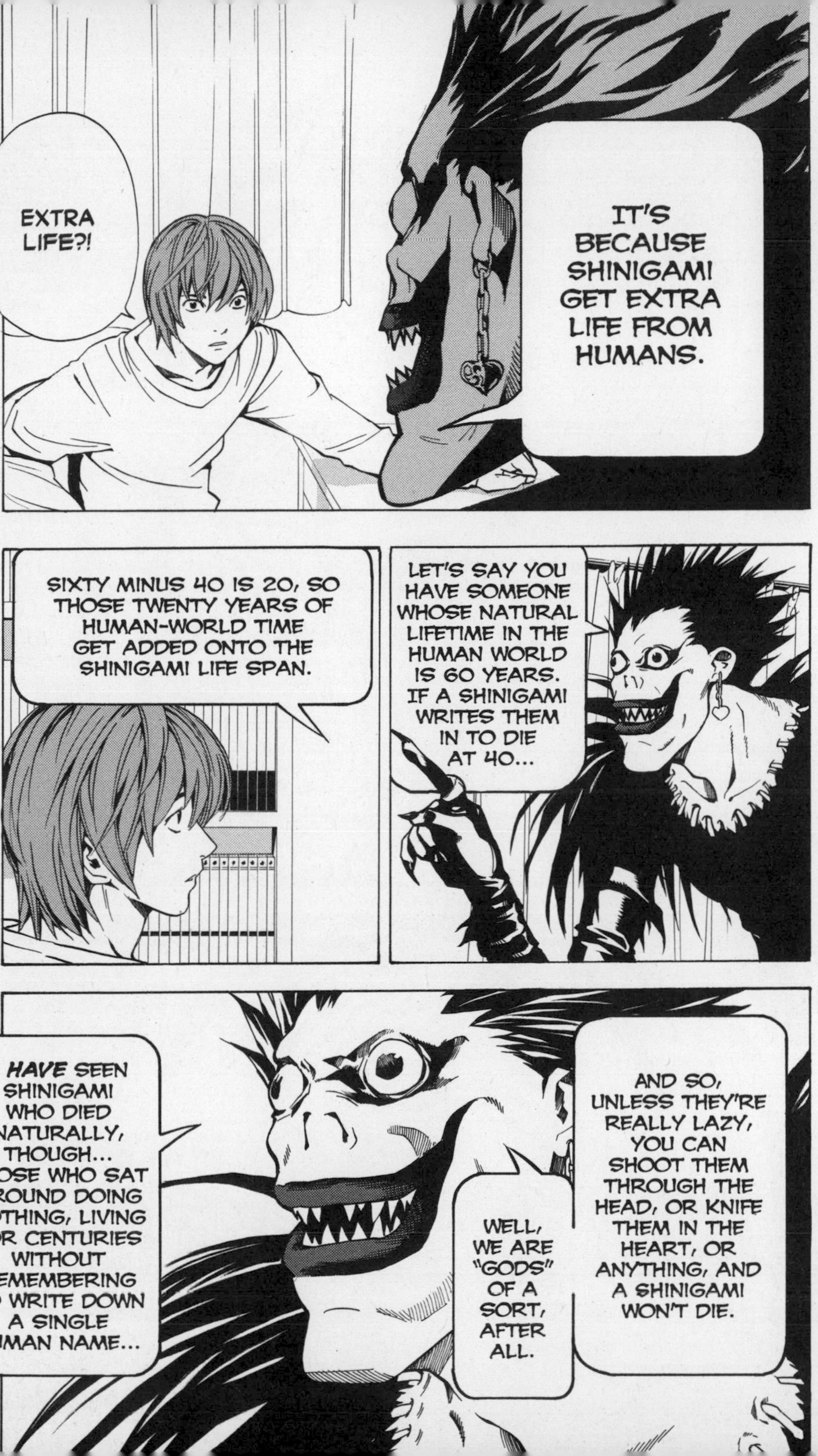
IT'S BECAUSE SHINIGAMI GET EXTRA LIFE FROM HUMANS.
EXTRA LIFE?!
LET'S SAY YOU HAVE SOMEONE WHOSE NATURAL LIFETIME IN THE HUMAN WORLD IS 60 YEARS. IF A SHINIGAMI WRITES THEM IN TO DIE AT 40...
SIXTY MINUS 40 IS 20, SO THOSE TWENTY YEARS OF HUMAN-WORLD TIME GET ADDED ONTO THE SHINIGAMI LIFE SPAN.
AND SO, UNLESS THEY'RE REALLY LAZY, YOU CAN SHOOT THEM THROUGH THE HEAD, OR KNIFE THEM IN THE HEART, OR ANYTHING, AND A SHINIGAMI WON'T DIE.
WELL, WE ARE "GODS" OF A SORT, AFTER ALL.
I *HAVE* SEEN SHINIGAMI WHO DIED NATURALLY, THOUGH... THOSE WHO SAT AROUND DOING NOTHING, LIVING FOR CENTURIES WITHOUT REMEMBERING TO WRITE DOWN A SINGLE HUMAN NAME...

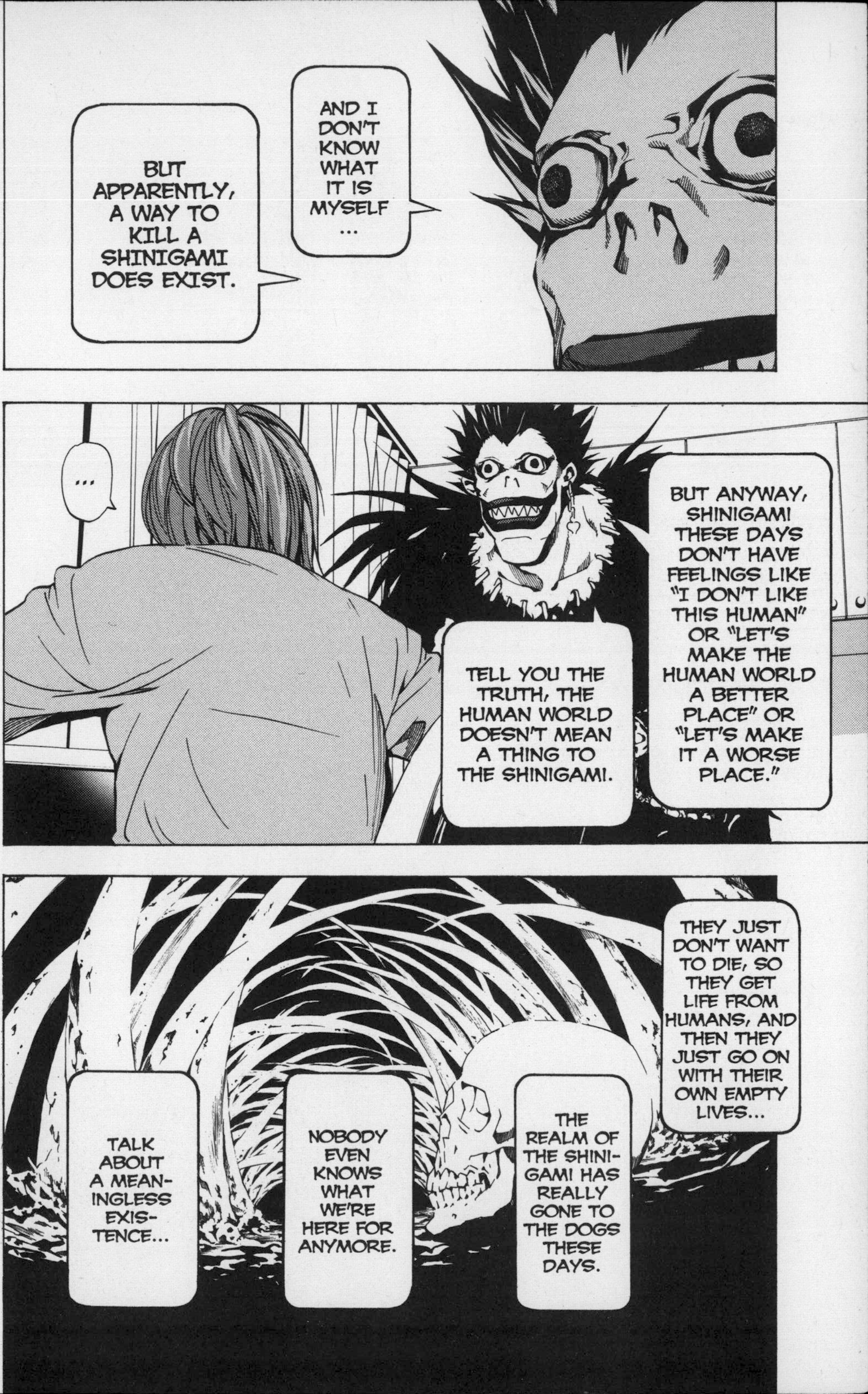
AND I DON'T KNOW WHAT IT IS MYSELF ...
BUT APPARENTLY, A WAY TO KILL A SHINIGAMI DOES EXIST.
BUT ANYWAY, SHINIGAMI THESE DAYS DON'T HAVE FEELINGS LIKE "I DON'T LIKE THIS HUMAN" OR "LET'S MAKE THE HUMAN WORLD A BETTER PLACE" OR "LET'S MAKE IT A WORSE PLACE."
TELL YOU THE TRUTH, THE HUMAN WORLD DOESN'T MEAN A THING TO THE SHINIGAMI.
...
THEY JUST DON'T WANT TO DIE, SO THEY GET LIFE FROM HUMANS, AND THEN THEY JUST GO ON WITH THEIR OWN EMPTY LIVES...
THE REALM OF THE SHINI-GAMI HAS REALLY GONE TO THE DOGS THESE DAYS.
NOBODY EVEN KNOWS WHAT WE'RE HERE FOR ANYMORE.
TALK ABOUT A MEAN-INGLESS EXIS-TENCE...

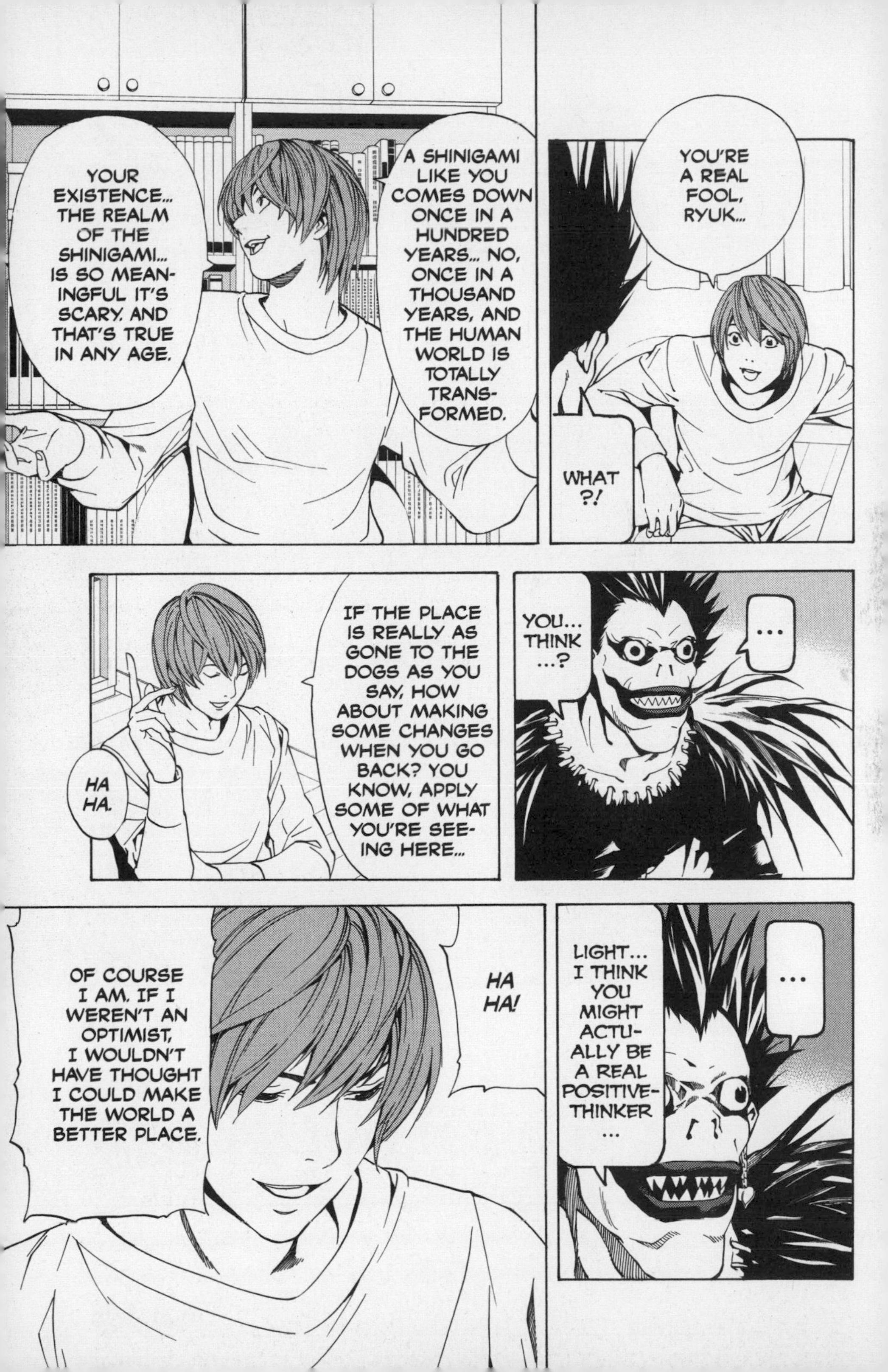
YOU'RE A REAL FOOL, RYUK...
WHAT ?!
A SHINIGAMI LIKE YOU COMES DOWN ONCE IN A HUNDRED YEARS... NO, ONCE IN A THOUSAND YEARS, AND THE HUMAN WORLD IS TOTALLY TRANS-FORMED.
YOUR EXISTENCE... THE REALM OF THE SHINIGAMI... IS SO MEAN-INGFUL IT'S SCARY. AND THAT'S TRUE IN ANY AGE.
...
YOU... THINK ...?
IF THE PLACE IS REALLY AS GONE TO THE DOGS AS YOU SAY, HOW ABOUT MAKING SOME CHANGES WHEN YOU GO BACK? YOU KNOW, APPLY SOME OF WHAT YOU'RE SEE-ING HERE...
HA HA.
...
LIGHT... I THINK YOU MIGHT ACTU-ALLY BE A REAL POSITIVE-THINKER ...
HA HA!
OF COURSE I AM. IF I WEREN'T AN OPTIMIST, I WOULDN'T HAVE THOUGHT I COULD MAKE THE WORLD A BETTER PLACE.

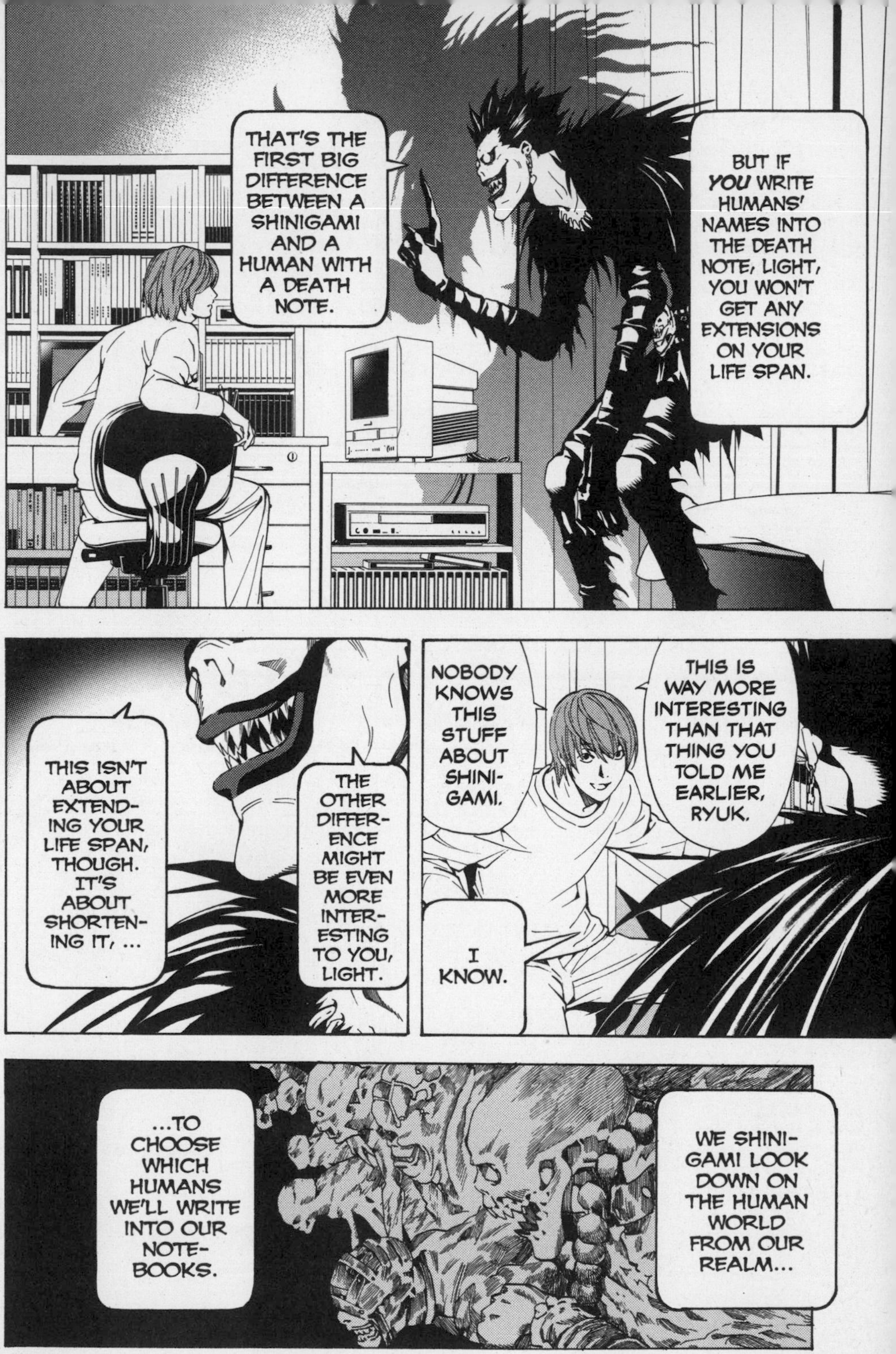
BUT IF *YOU* WRITE HUMANS' NAMES INTO THE DEATH NOTE, LIGHT, YOU WON'T GET ANY EXTENSIONS ON YOUR LIFE SPAN.
THAT'S THE FIRST BIG DIFFERENCE BETWEEN A SHINIGAMI AND A HUMAN WITH A DEATH NOTE.
THIS IS WAY MORE INTERESTING THAN THAT THING YOU TOLD ME EARLIER, RYUK.
NOBODY KNOWS THIS STUFF ABOUT SHINI-GAMI.
I KNOW.
THE OTHER DIFFER-ENCE MIGHT BE EVEN MORE INTER-ESTING TO YOU, LIGHT.
THIS ISN'T ABOUT EXTEND-ING YOUR LIFE SPAN, THOUGH. IT'S ABOUT SHORTEN-ING IT, ...
WE SHINI-GAMI LOOK DOWN ON THE HUMAN WORLD FROM OUR REALM...
...TO CHOOSE WHICH HUMANS WE'LL WRITE INTO OUR NOTE-BOOKS.

READ THIS WAY

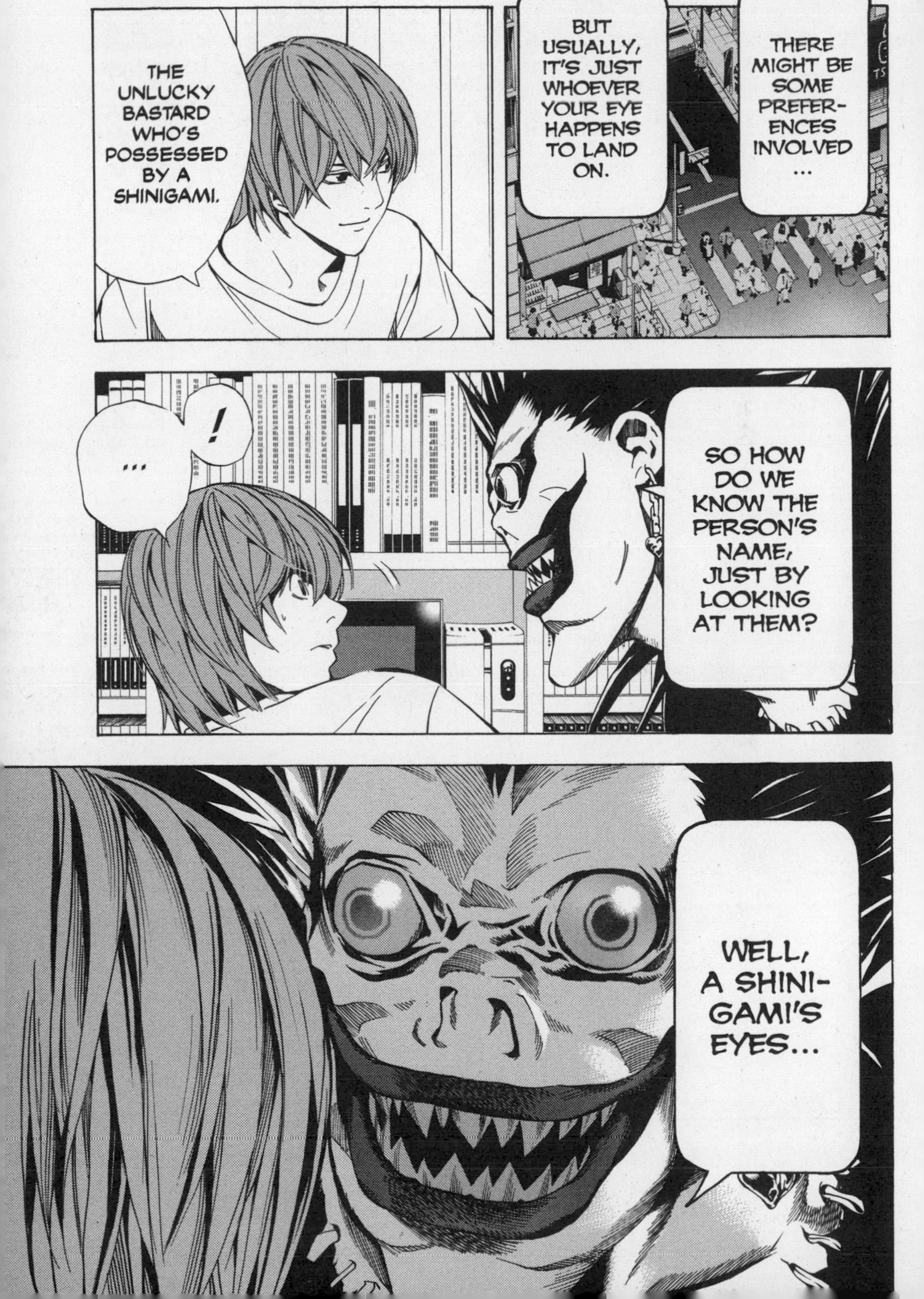
THERE MIGHT BE SOME PREFERENCES INVOLVED ...
BUT USUALLY, IT'S JUST WHOEVER YOUR EYE HAPPENS TO LAND ON.
THE UNLUCKY BASTARD WHO'S POSSESSED BY A SHINIGAMI.
SO HOW DO WE KNOW THE PERSON'S NAME, JUST BY LOOKING AT THEM?
!
...
WELL, A SHINIGAMI'S EYES...

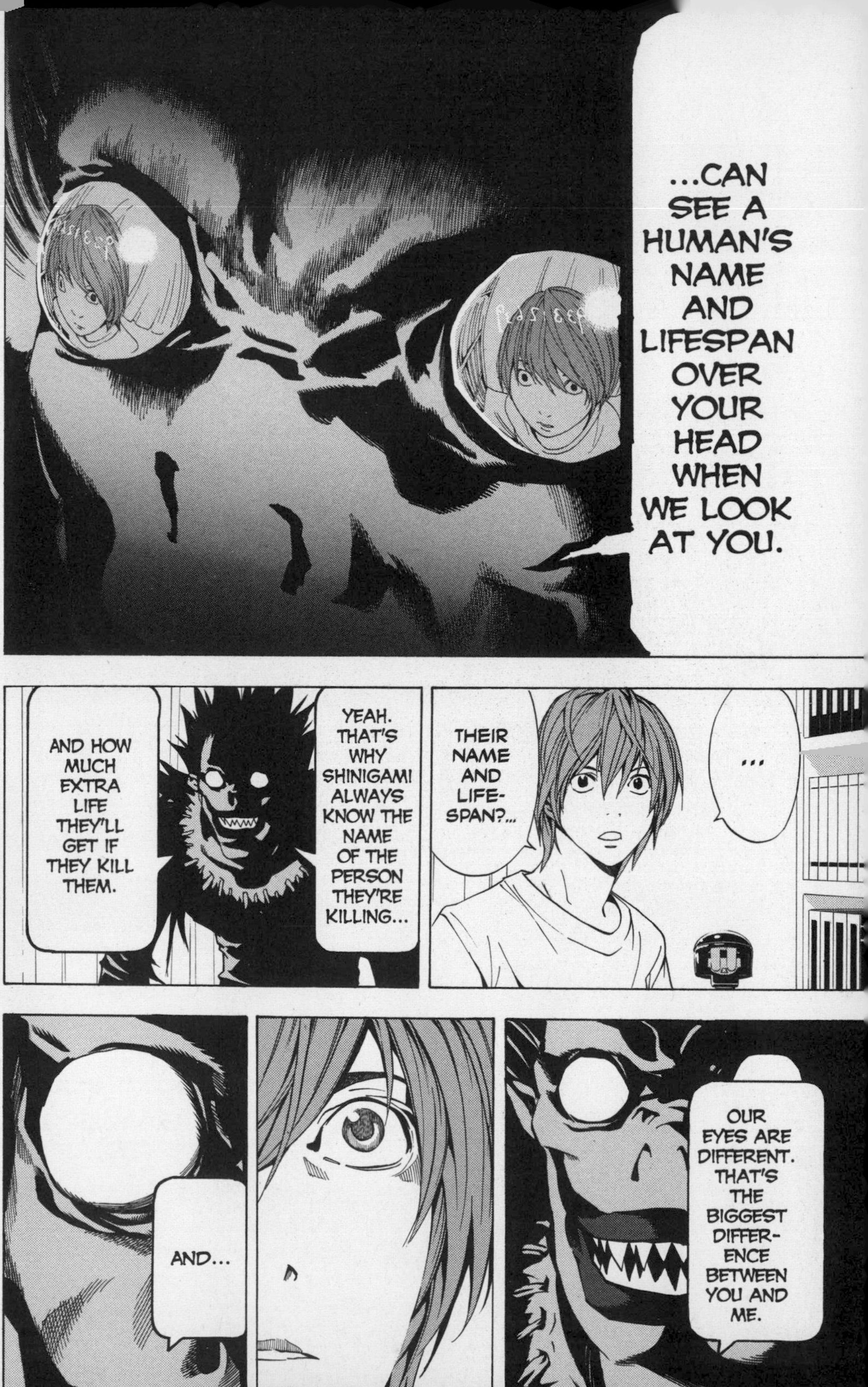
...CAN SEE A HUMAN'S NAME AND LIFESPAN OVER YOUR HEAD WHEN WE LOOK AT YOU.
...
THEIR NAME AND LIFE-SPAN?...
YEAH. THAT'S WHY SHINIGAMI ALWAYS KNOW THE NAME OF THE PERSON THEY'RE KILLING...
AND HOW MUCH EXTRA LIFE THEY'LL GET IF THEY KILL THEM.
OUR EYES ARE DIFFERENT. THAT'S THE BIGGEST DIFFER-ENCE BETWEEN YOU AND ME.
AND...

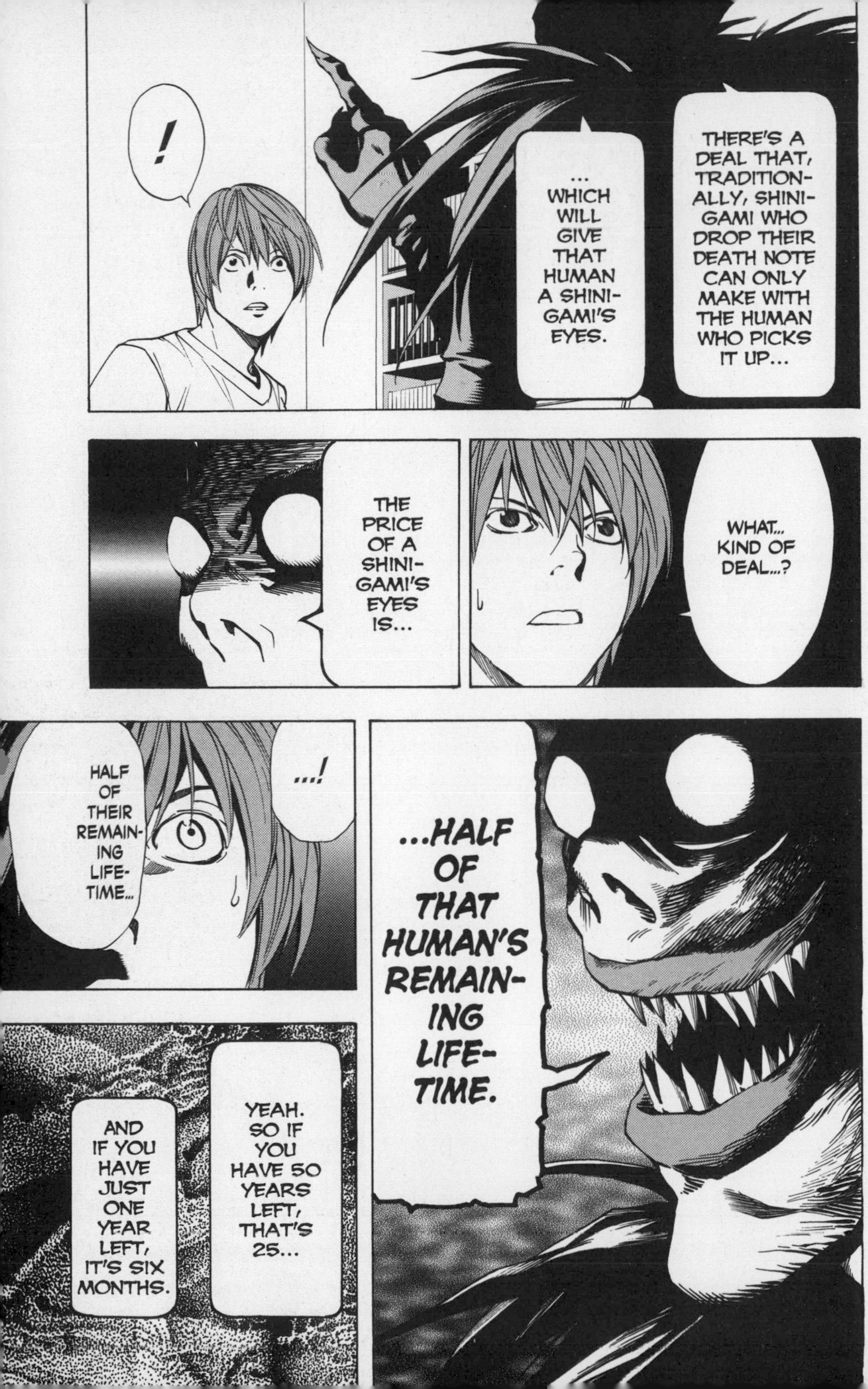
THERE'S A DEAL THAT, TRADITION-ALLY, SHINI-GAMI WHO DROP THEIR DEATH NOTE CAN ONLY MAKE WITH THE HUMAN WHO PICKS IT UP...
... WHICH WILL GIVE THAT HUMAN A SHINI-GAMI'S EYES.
!
WHAT... KIND OF DEAL...?
THE PRICE OF A SHINI-GAMI'S EYES IS...
...HALF OF THAT HUMAN'S REMAIN-ING LIFE-TIME.
...!
HALF OF THEIR REMAIN-ING LIFE-TIME...
YEAH. SO IF YOU HAVE 50 YEARS LEFT, THAT'S 25...
AND IF YOU HAVE JUST ONE YEAR LEFT, IT'S SIX MONTHS.

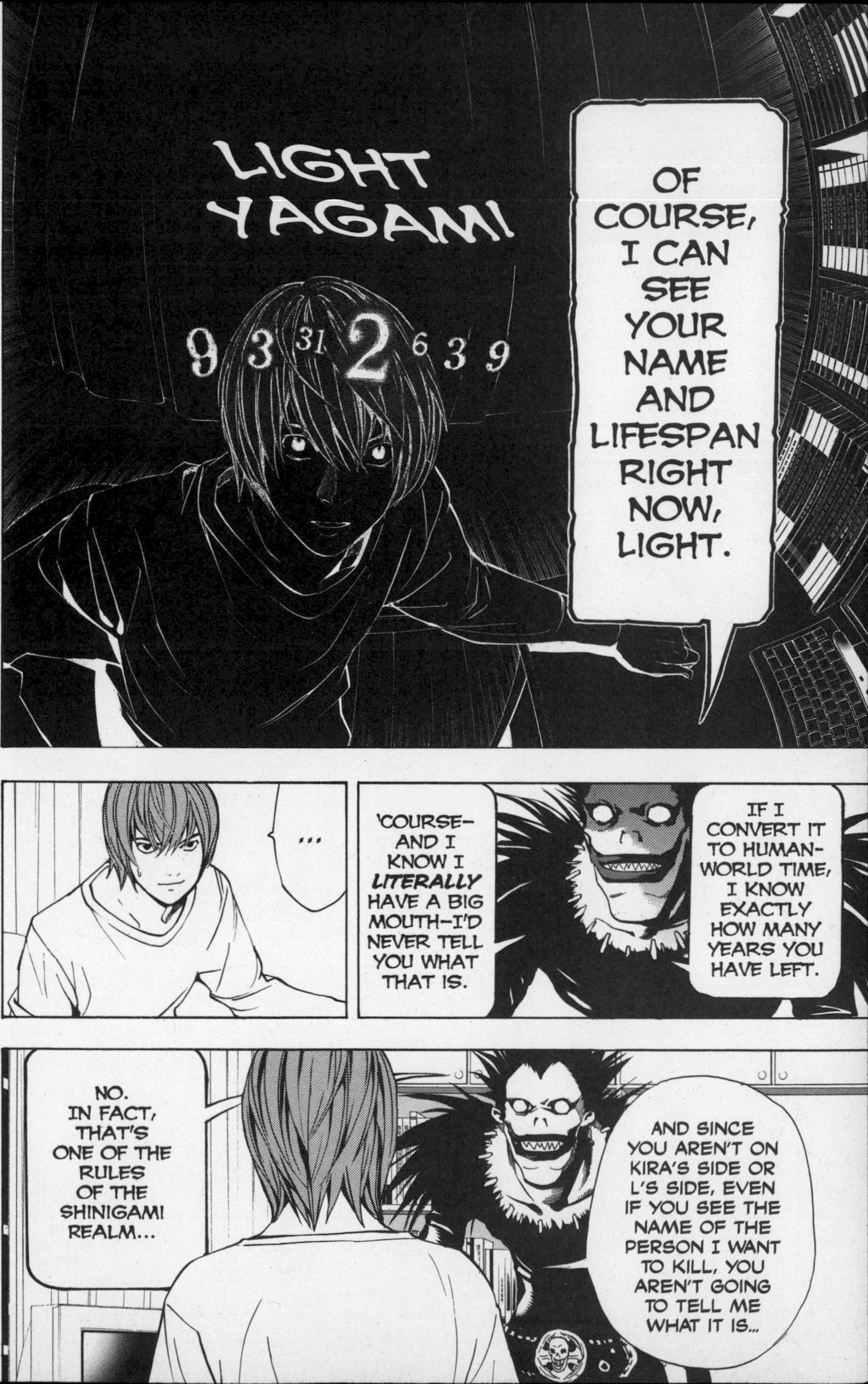
OF COURSE, I CAN SEE YOUR NAME AND LIFESPAN RIGHT NOW, LIGHT.
LIGHT YAGAMI
9 3 31 2 6 3 9
IF I CONVERT IT TO HUMAN-WORLD TIME, I KNOW EXACTLY HOW MANY YEARS YOU HAVE LEFT.
'COURSE-AND I KNOW I *LITERALLY* HAVE A BIG MOUTH-I'D NEVER TELL YOU WHAT THAT IS.
...
AND SINCE YOU AREN'T ON KIRA'S SIDE OR L'S SIDE, EVEN IF YOU SEE THE NAME OF THE PERSON I WANT TO KILL, YOU AREN'T GOING TO TELL ME WHAT IT IS...
NO. IN FACT, THAT'S ONE OF THE RULES OF THE SHINIGAMI REALM...

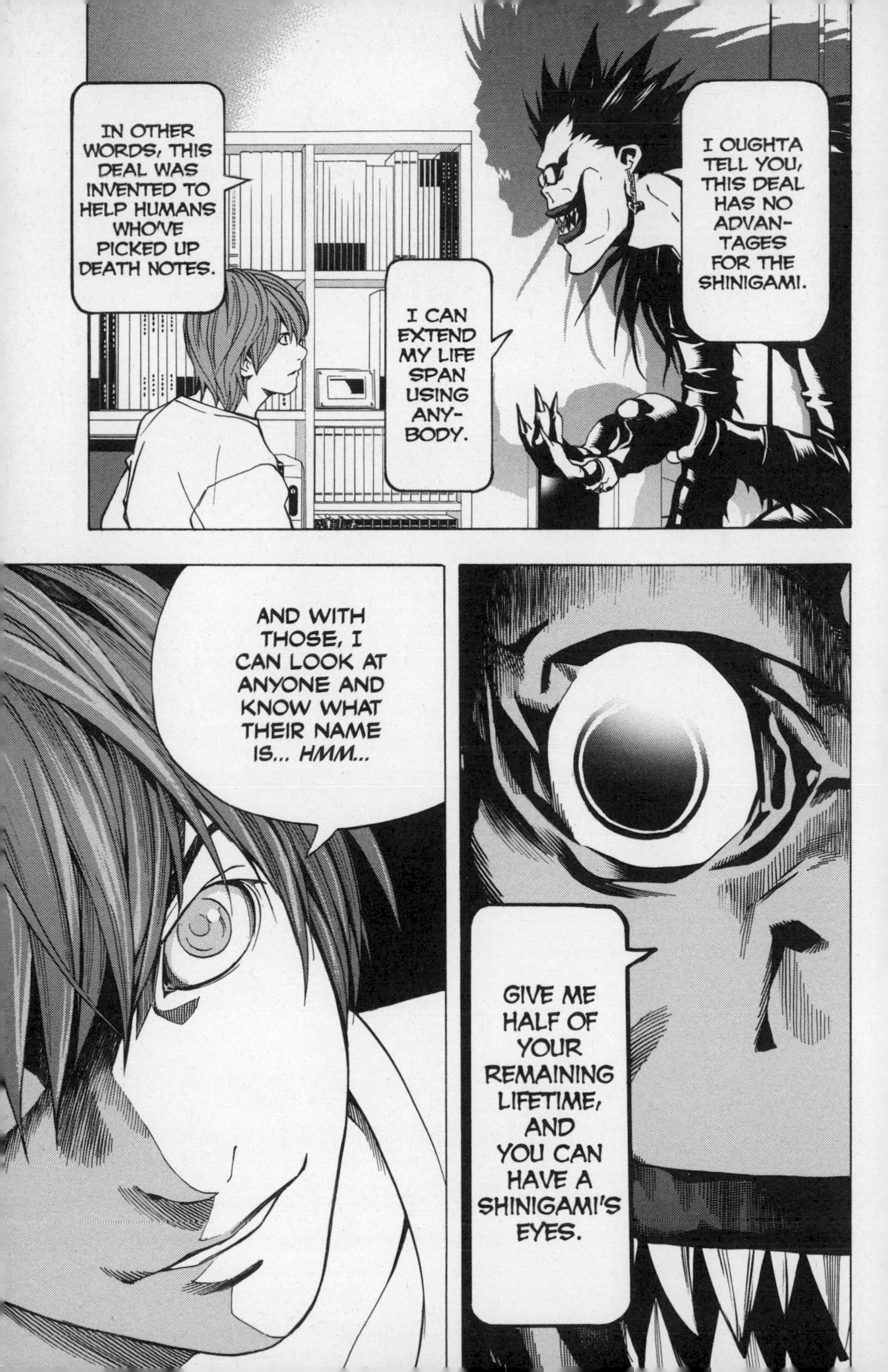
I OUGHTA TELL YOU, THIS DEAL HAS NO ADVANTAGES FOR THE SHINIGAMI.
I CAN EXTEND MY LIFE SPAN USING ANYBODY.
IN OTHER WORDS, THIS DEAL WAS INVENTED TO HELP HUMANS WHO'VE PICKED UP DEATH NOTES.
GIVE ME HALF OF YOUR REMAINING LIFETIME, AND YOU CAN HAVE A SHINIGAMI'S EYES.
AND WITH THOSE, I CAN LOOK AT ANYONE AND KNOW WHAT THEIR NAME IS... *HMM...*

# DEATH NOTE
## How to use it

- A god of death can extend his life by putting human names on the note, but humans cannot.

  死神はデスノートに人間の名前を書く事で自分の寿命を延ばせるが、人間は延ばせない。

- A person can shorten his or her own life by using the note.

  自分で自分の寿命をデスノートによって縮める事はできる。

- The human who becomes the owner of the DEATH NOTE can, in exchange of half of his/her remaining life, get the eyeballs of the god of death which will enable him/her to see a human's name and remaining lifetime when looking through them.

  デスノートの所有者となった人間は、自分の残された寿命の半分と交換に、人間の顔を見るとその人間の名前と寿命の見える死神の眼球をもらう事ができる。

- A god of death cannot be killed even if stabbed in his heart with a knife or shot in the head with a gun. However, there are ways to kill a god of death, which are not generally known to the gods of death.

  死神は心臓をナイフで刺しても頭を銃で撃ち抜いても殺す事はできない。しかし、一介の死神は知らない死神の殺し方は存在する。

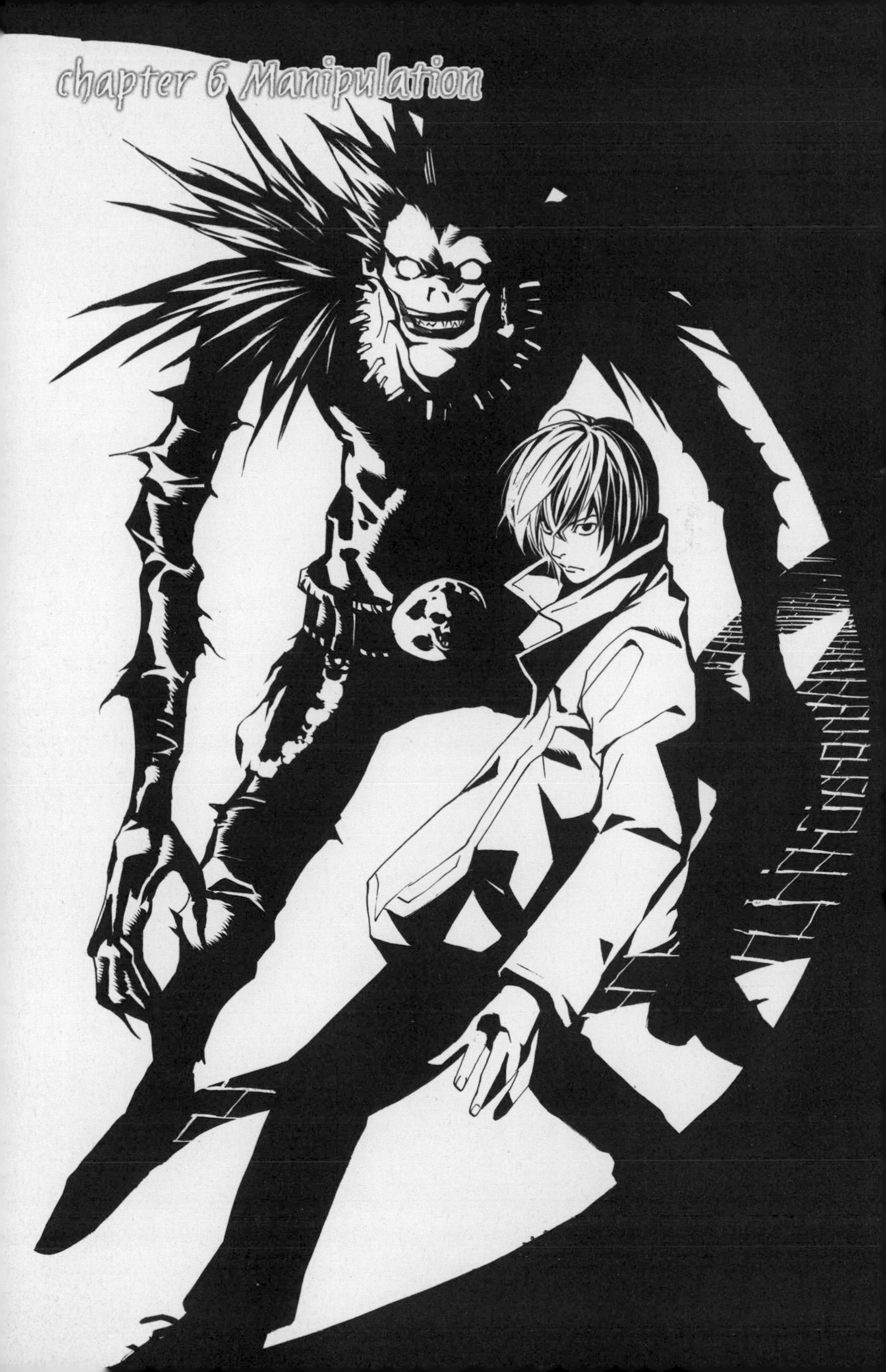
chapter 6 Manipulation

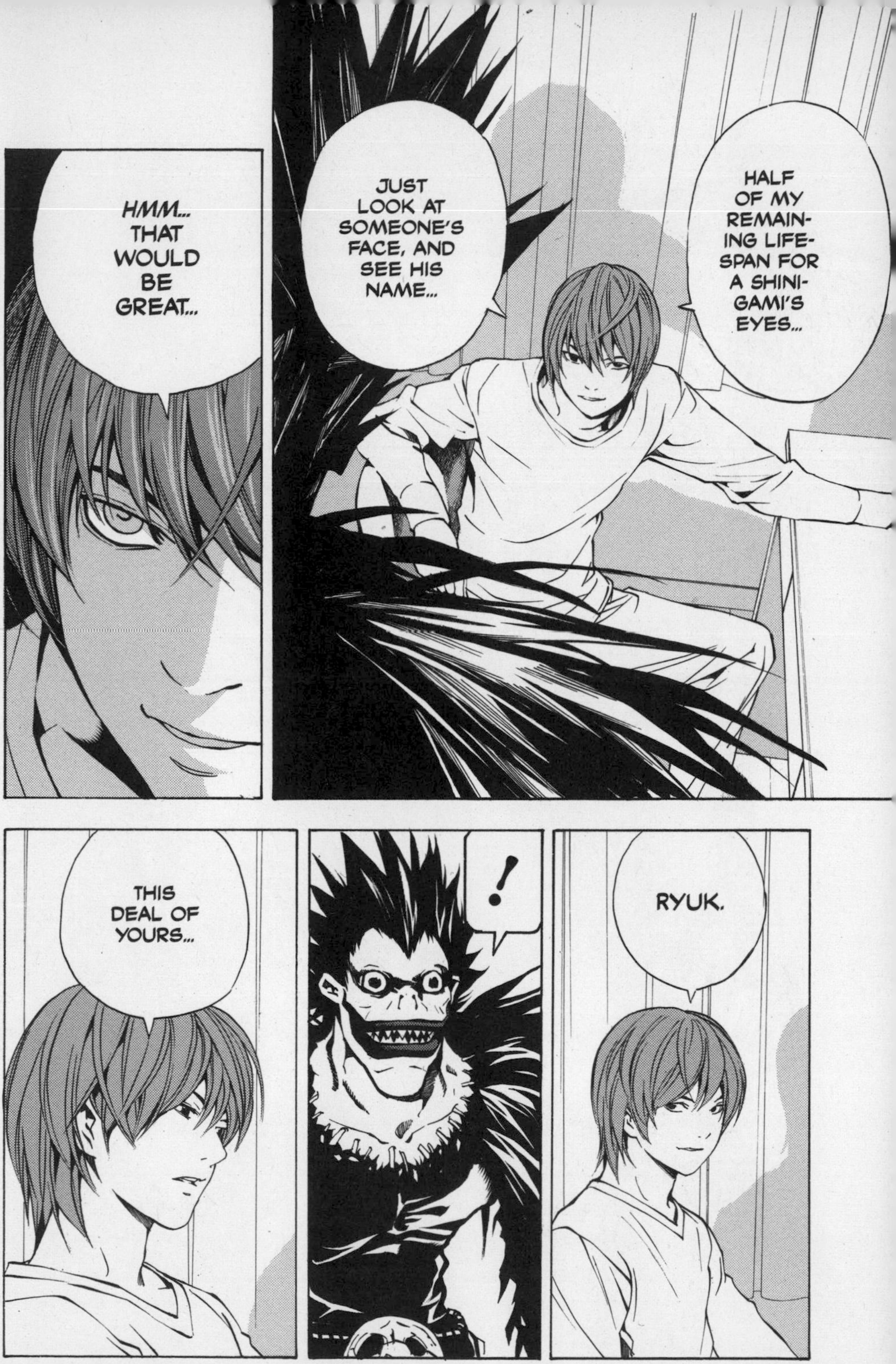
HALF OF MY REMAINING LIFESPAN FOR A SHINIGAMI'S EYES...
JUST LOOK AT SOMEONE'S FACE, AND SEE HIS NAME...
HMM... THAT WOULD BE GREAT...
RYUK.
!
THIS DEAL OF YOURS...

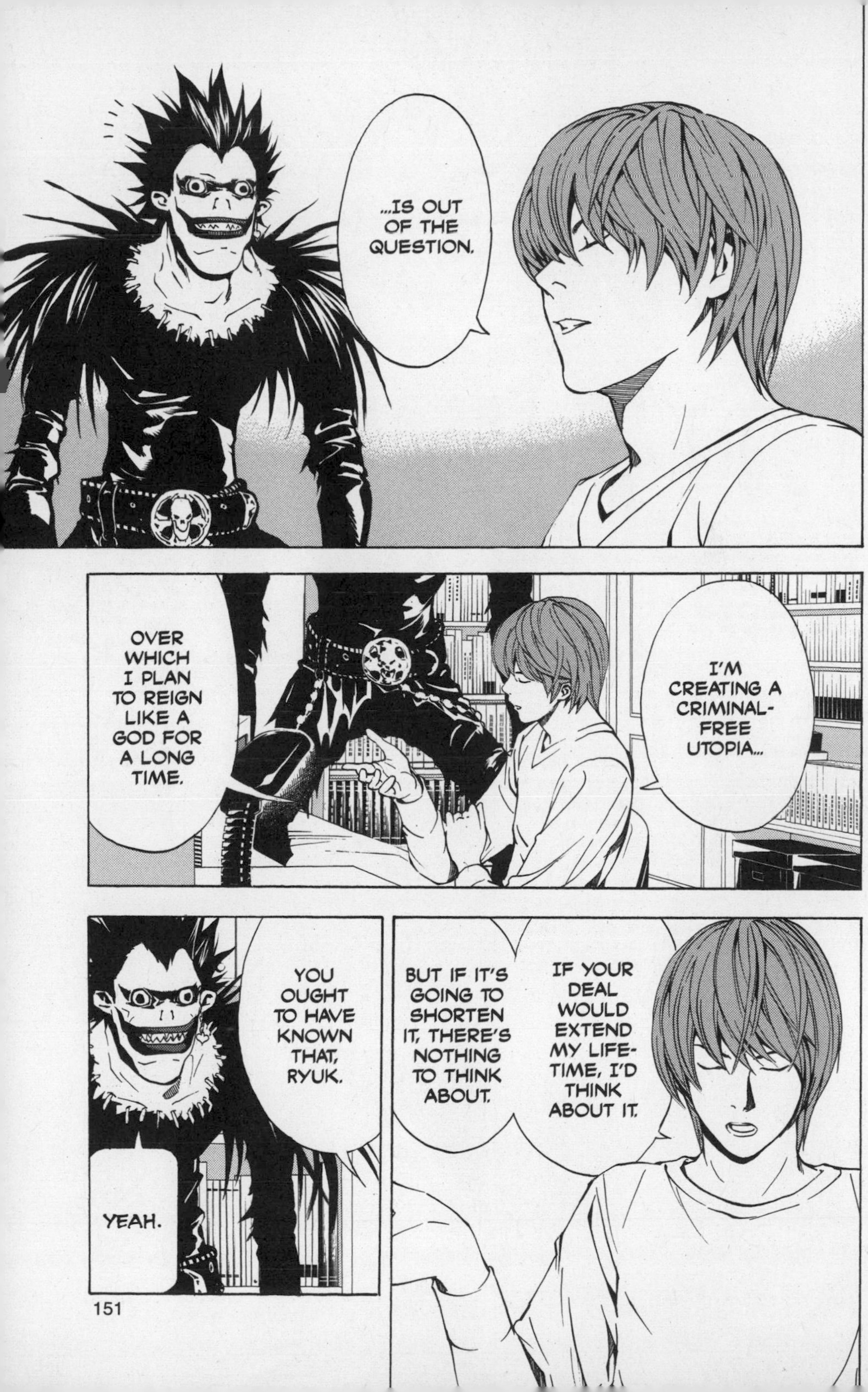
...IS OUT OF THE QUESTION.
I'M CREATING A CRIMINAL-FREE UTOPIA...
OVER WHICH I PLAN TO REIGN LIKE A GOD FOR A LONG TIME.
IF YOUR DEAL WOULD EXTEND MY LIFE-TIME, I'D THINK ABOUT IT.
BUT IF IT'S GOING TO SHORTEN IT, THERE'S NOTHING TO THINK ABOUT.
YOU OUGHT TO HAVE KNOWN THAT, RYUK.
YEAH.

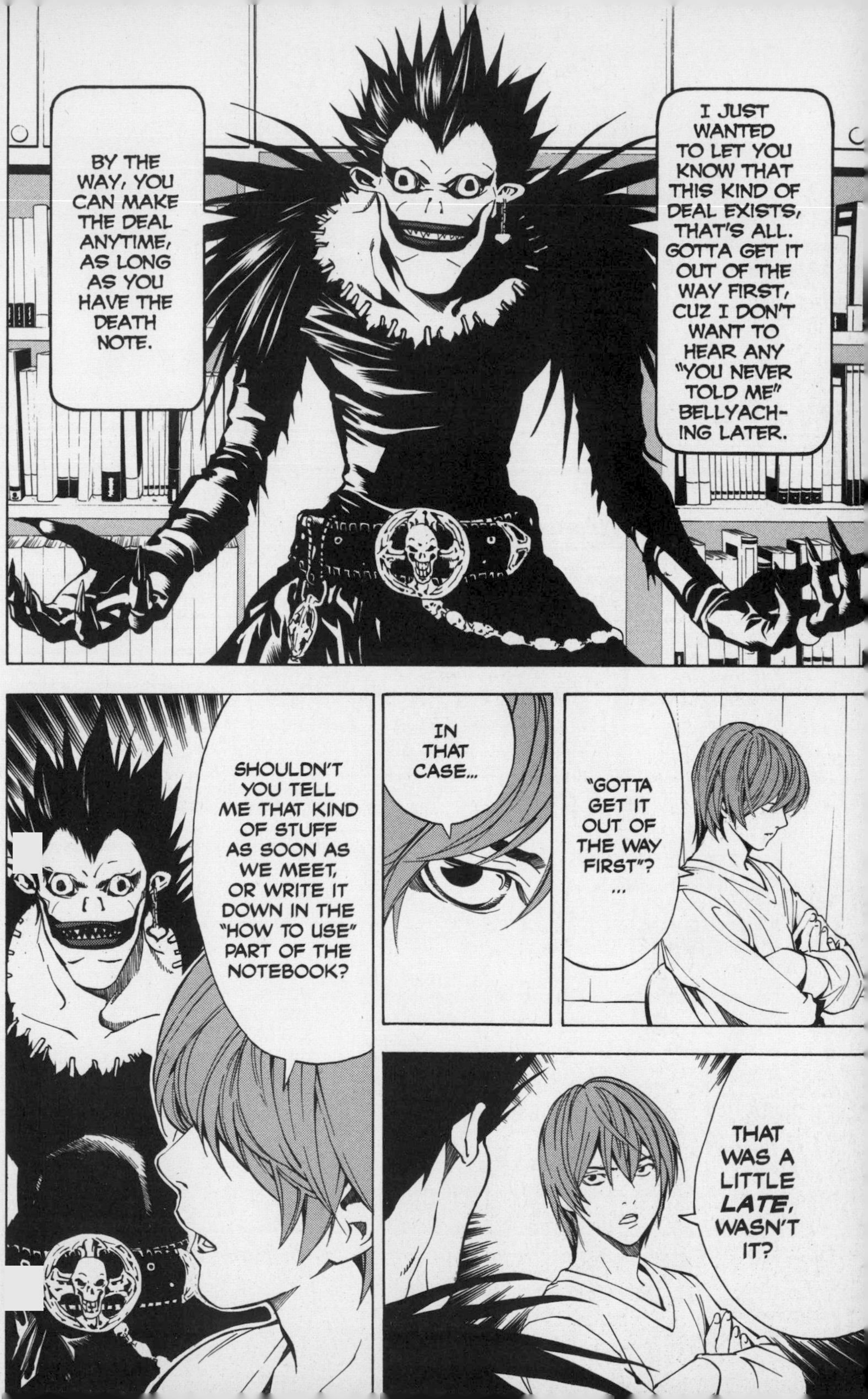
I JUST WANTED TO LET YOU KNOW THAT THIS KIND OF DEAL EXISTS, THAT'S ALL. GOTTA GET IT OUT OF THE WAY FIRST, CUZ I DON'T WANT TO HEAR ANY "YOU NEVER TOLD ME" BELLYACH-ING LATER.
BY THE WAY, YOU CAN MAKE THE DEAL ANYTIME, AS LONG AS YOU HAVE THE DEATH NOTE.
"GOTTA GET IT OUT OF THE WAY FIRST"? ...
IN THAT CASE...
THAT WAS A LITTLE *LATE*, WASN'T IT?
SHOULDN'T YOU TELL ME THAT KIND OF STUFF AS SOON AS WE MEET, OR WRITE IT DOWN IN THE "HOW TO USE" PART OF THE NOTEBOOK?

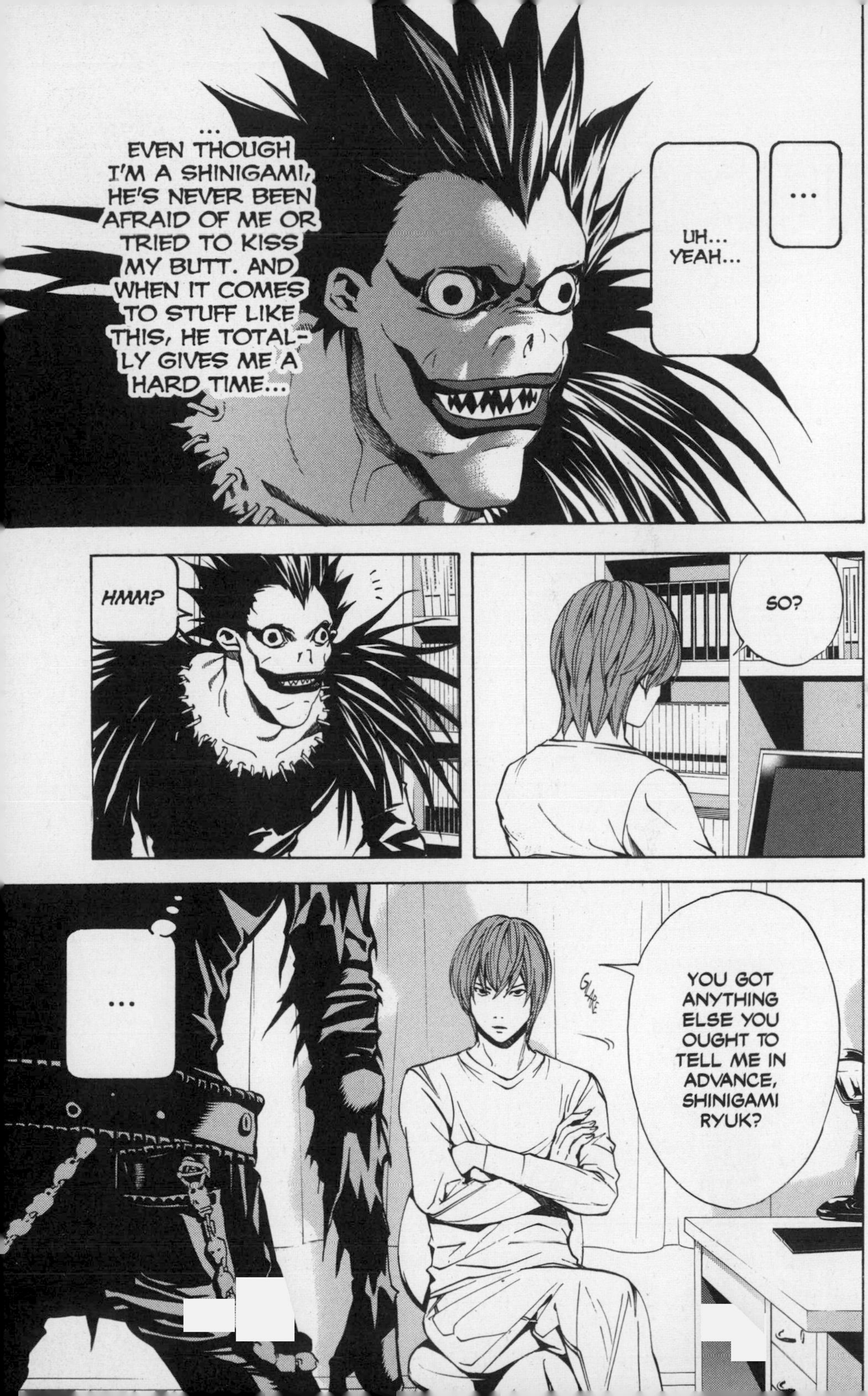
...
UH... YEAH...
... EVEN THOUGH I'M A SHINIGAMI, HE'S NEVER BEEN AFRAID OF ME OR TRIED TO KISS MY BUTT. AND WHEN IT COMES TO STUFF LIKE THIS, HE TOTAL-LY GIVES ME A HARD TIME...
SO?
HMM?
YOU GOT ANYTHING ELSE YOU OUGHT TO TELL ME IN ADVANCE, SHINIGAMI RYUK?
GLARE
...

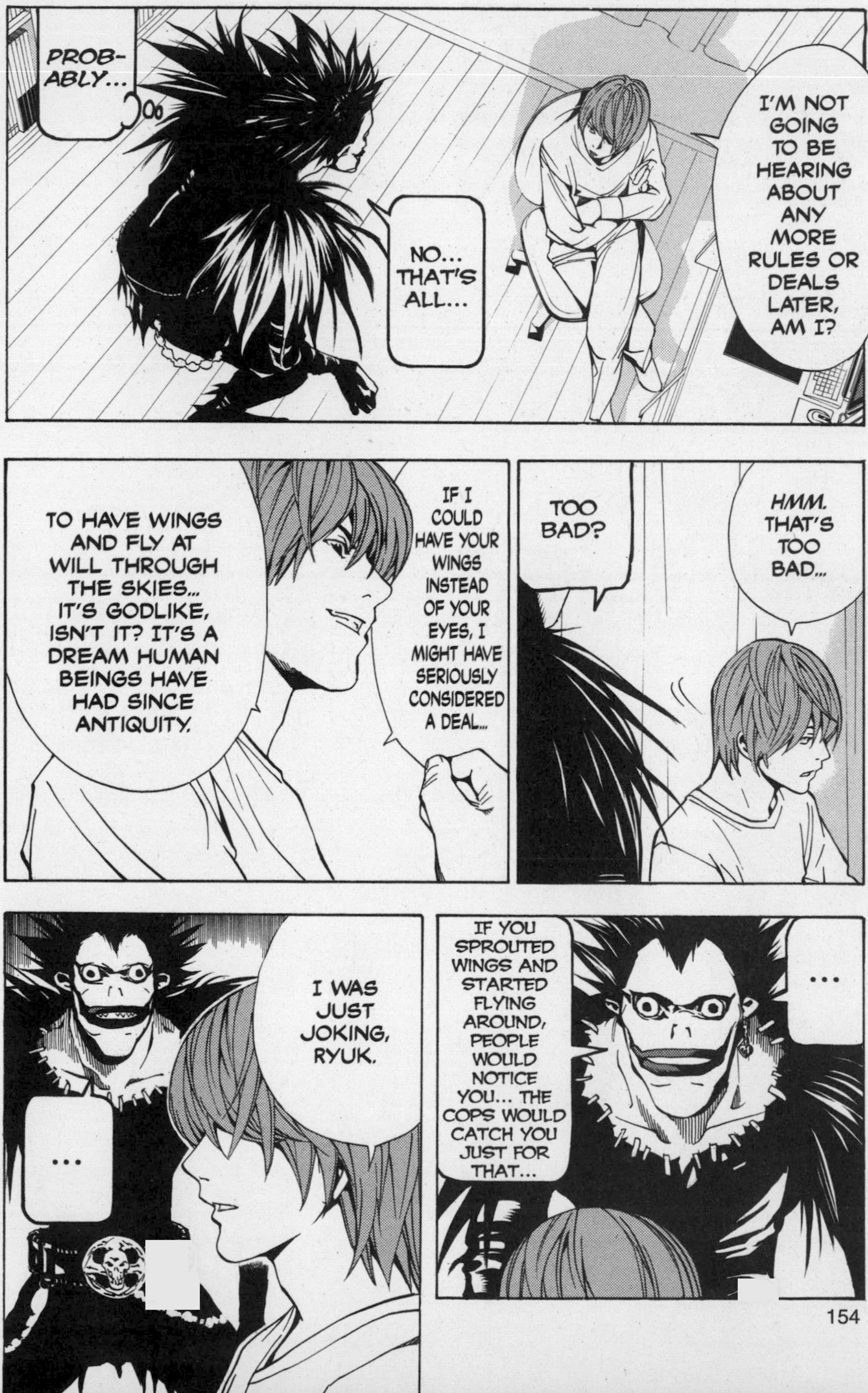
I'M NOT GOING TO BE HEARING ABOUT ANY MORE RULES OR DEALS LATER, AM I?
NO... THAT'S ALL...
PROB-ABLY...
*HMM.* THAT'S TOO BAD...
TOO BAD?
IF I COULD HAVE YOUR WINGS INSTEAD OF YOUR EYES, I MIGHT HAVE SERIOUSLY CONSIDERED A DEAL...
TO HAVE WINGS AND FLY AT WILL THROUGH THE SKIES... IT'S GODLIKE, ISN'T IT? IT'S A DREAM HUMAN BEINGS HAVE HAD SINCE ANTIQUITY.
...
IF YOU SPROUTED WINGS AND STARTED FLYING AROUND, PEOPLE WOULD NOTICE YOU... THE COPS WOULD CATCH YOU JUST FOR THAT...
I WAS JUST JOKING, RYUK.
...

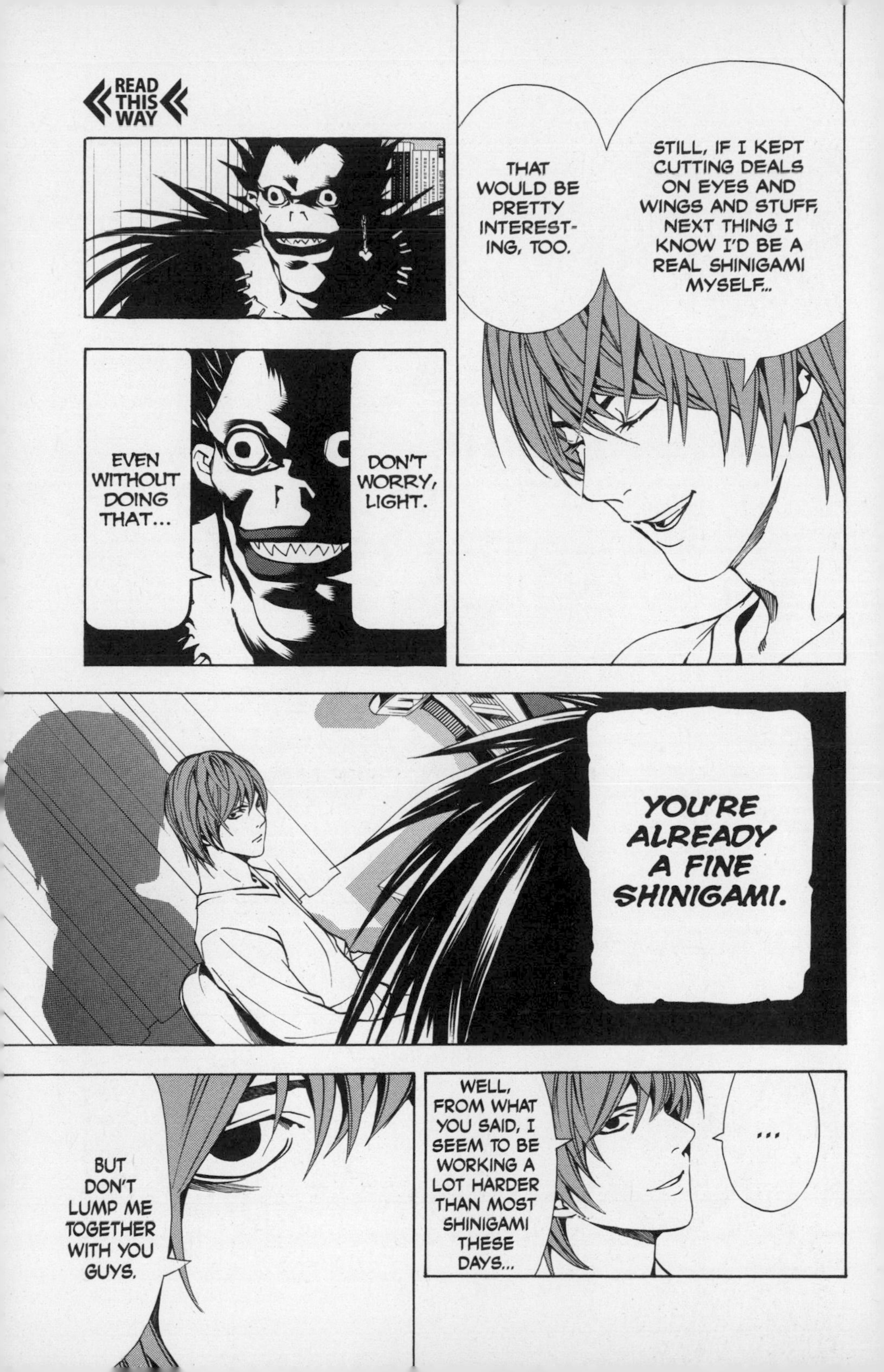
READ THIS WAY
STILL, IF I KEPT CUTTING DEALS ON EYES AND WINGS AND STUFF, NEXT THING I KNOW I'D BE A REAL SHINIGAMI MYSELF...
THAT WOULD BE PRETTY INTEREST-ING, TOO.
DON'T WORRY, LIGHT.
EVEN WITHOUT DOING THAT...
YOU'RE ALREADY A FINE SHINIGAMI.
...
WELL, FROM WHAT YOU SAID, I SEEM TO BE WORKING A LOT HARDER THAN MOST SHINIGAMI THESE DAYS...
BUT DON'T LUMP ME TOGETHER WITH YOU GUYS.

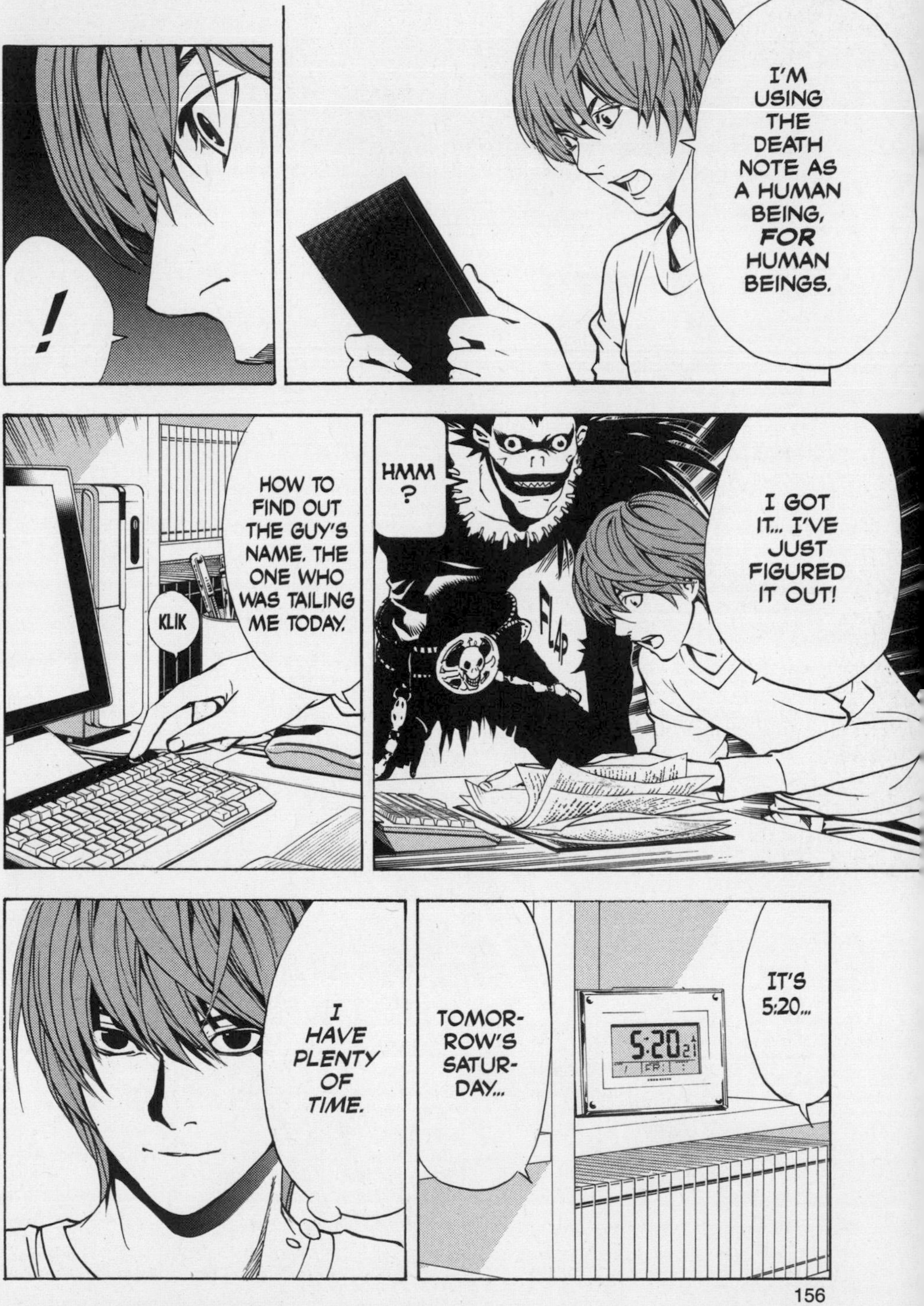
I'M USING THE DEATH NOTE AS A HUMAN BEING, *FOR* HUMAN BEINGS.
!
I GOT IT... I'VE JUST FIGURED IT OUT!
FLAP
HMM ?
HOW TO FIND OUT THE GUY'S NAME. THE ONE WHO WAS TAILING ME TODAY.
KLIK
IT'S 5:20...
TOMORROW'S SATURDAY...
*I HAVE PLENTY OF TIME.*

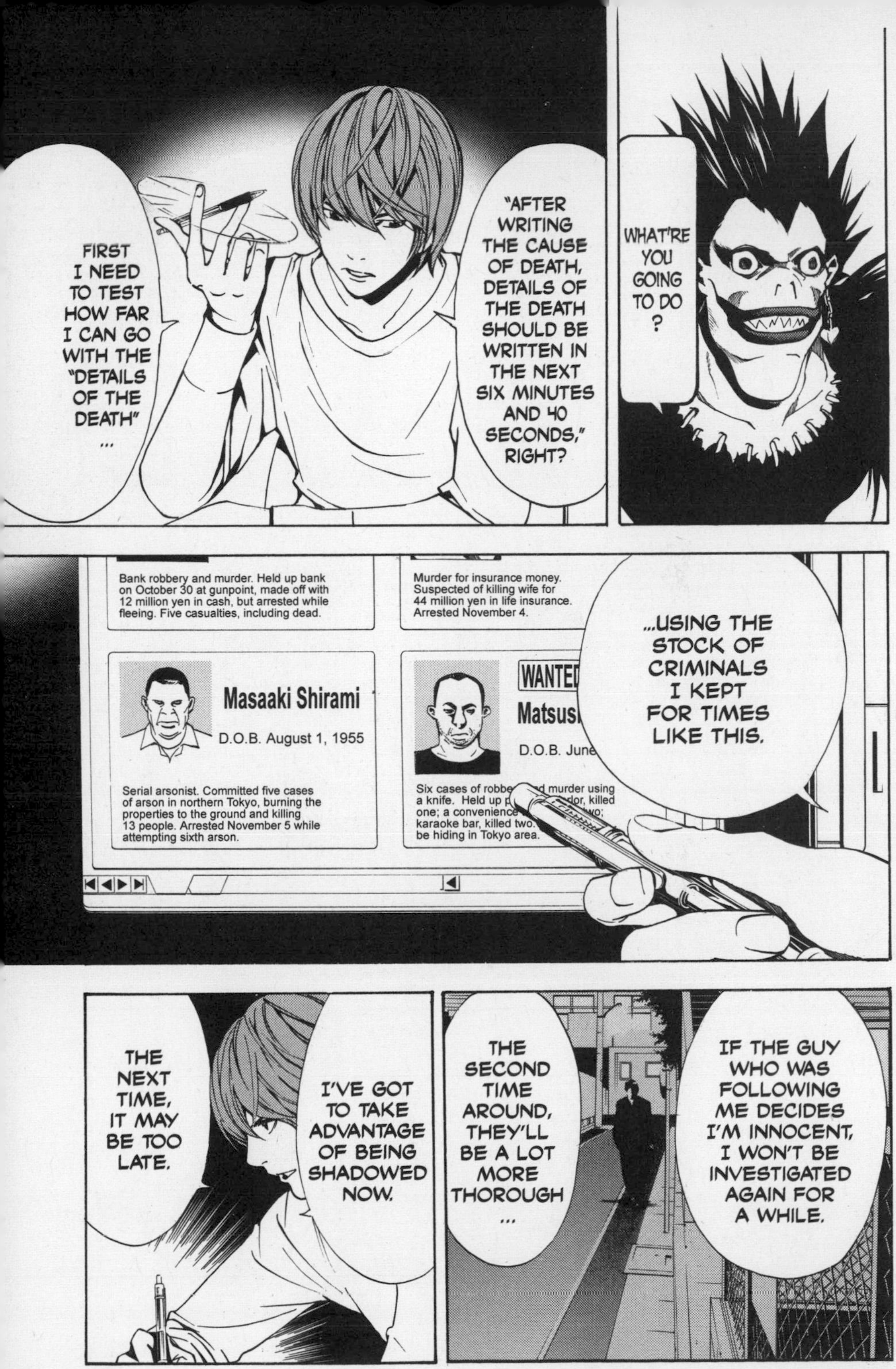
WHAT'RE YOU GOING TO DO?
"AFTER WRITING THE CAUSE OF DEATH, DETAILS OF THE DEATH SHOULD BE WRITTEN IN THE NEXT SIX MINUTES AND 40 SECONDS," RIGHT?
FIRST I NEED TO TEST HOW FAR I CAN GO WITH THE "DETAILS OF THE DEATH"...
...USING THE STOCK OF CRIMINALS I KEPT FOR TIMES LIKE THIS.
Murder for insurance money. Suspected of killing wife for 44 million yen in life insurance. Arrested November 4.
Bank robbery and murder. Held up bank on October 30 at gunpoint, made off with 12 million yen in cash, but arrested while fleeing. Five casualties, including dead.
WANTED
Matsus
D.O.B. June
Masaaki Shirami
D.O.B. August 1, 1955
Serial arsonist. Committed five cases of arson in northern Tokyo, burning the properties to the ground and killing 13 people. Arrested November 5 while attempting sixth arson.
IF THE GUY WHO WAS FOLLOWING ME DECIDES I'M INNOCENT, I WON'T BE INVESTIGATED AGAIN FOR A WHILE.
THE SECOND TIME AROUND, THEY'LL BE A LOT MORE THOROUGH...
I'VE GOT TO TAKE ADVANTAGE OF BEING SHADOWED NOW.
THE NEXT TIME, IT MAY BE TOO LATE.

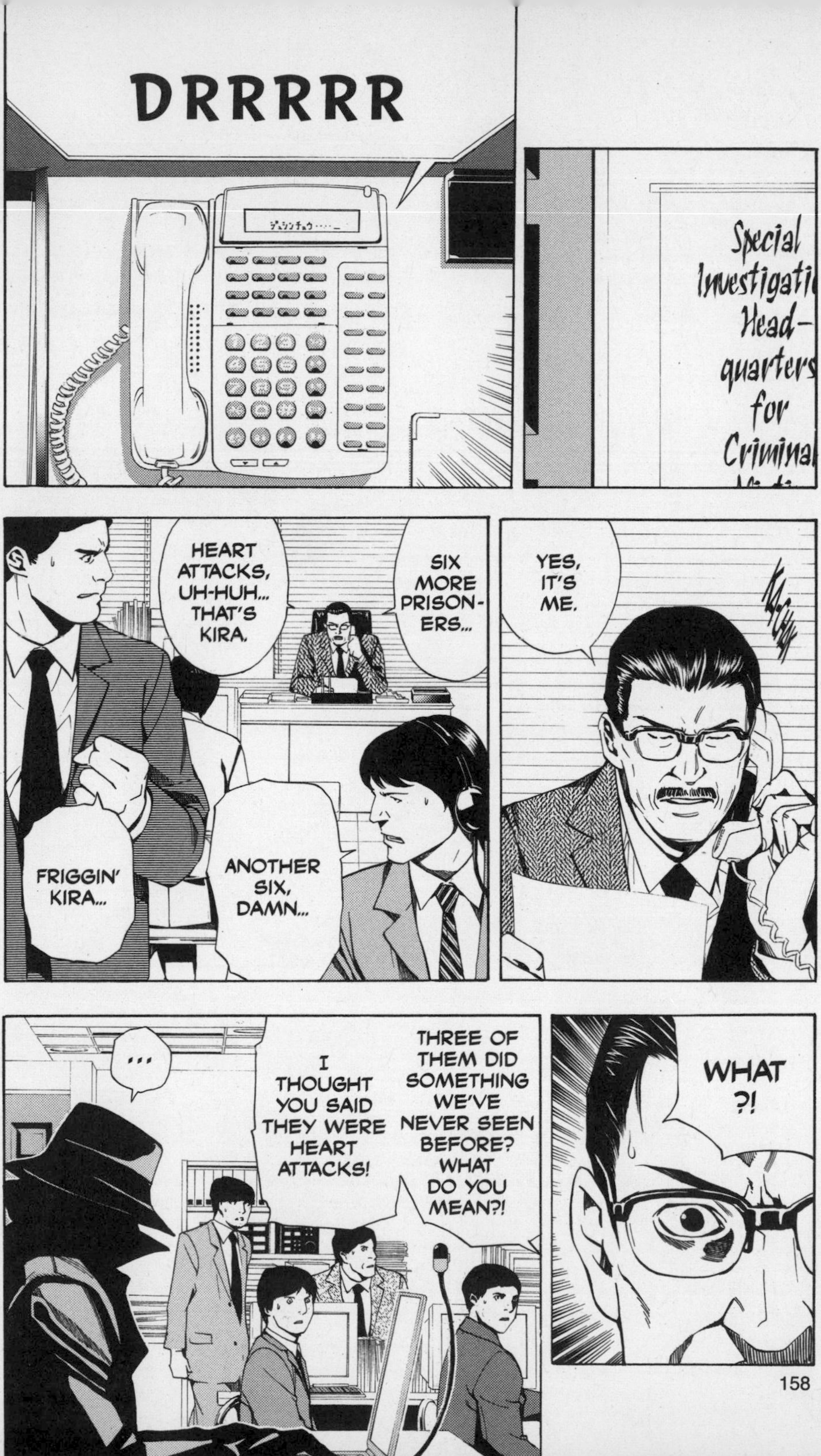
Special
Investigati
Head-
quarters
for
Criminal
DRRRRR
KA-CHUK
YES, IT'S ME.
SIX MORE PRISONERS...
HEART ATTACKS, UH-HUH... THAT'S KIRA.
ANOTHER SIX, DAMN...
FRIGGIN' KIRA...
WHAT ?!
THREE OF THEM DID SOMETHING WE'VE NEVER SEEN BEFORE? WHAT DO YOU MEAN?!
I THOUGHT YOU SAID THEY WERE HEART ATTACKS!
...

READ THIS WAY

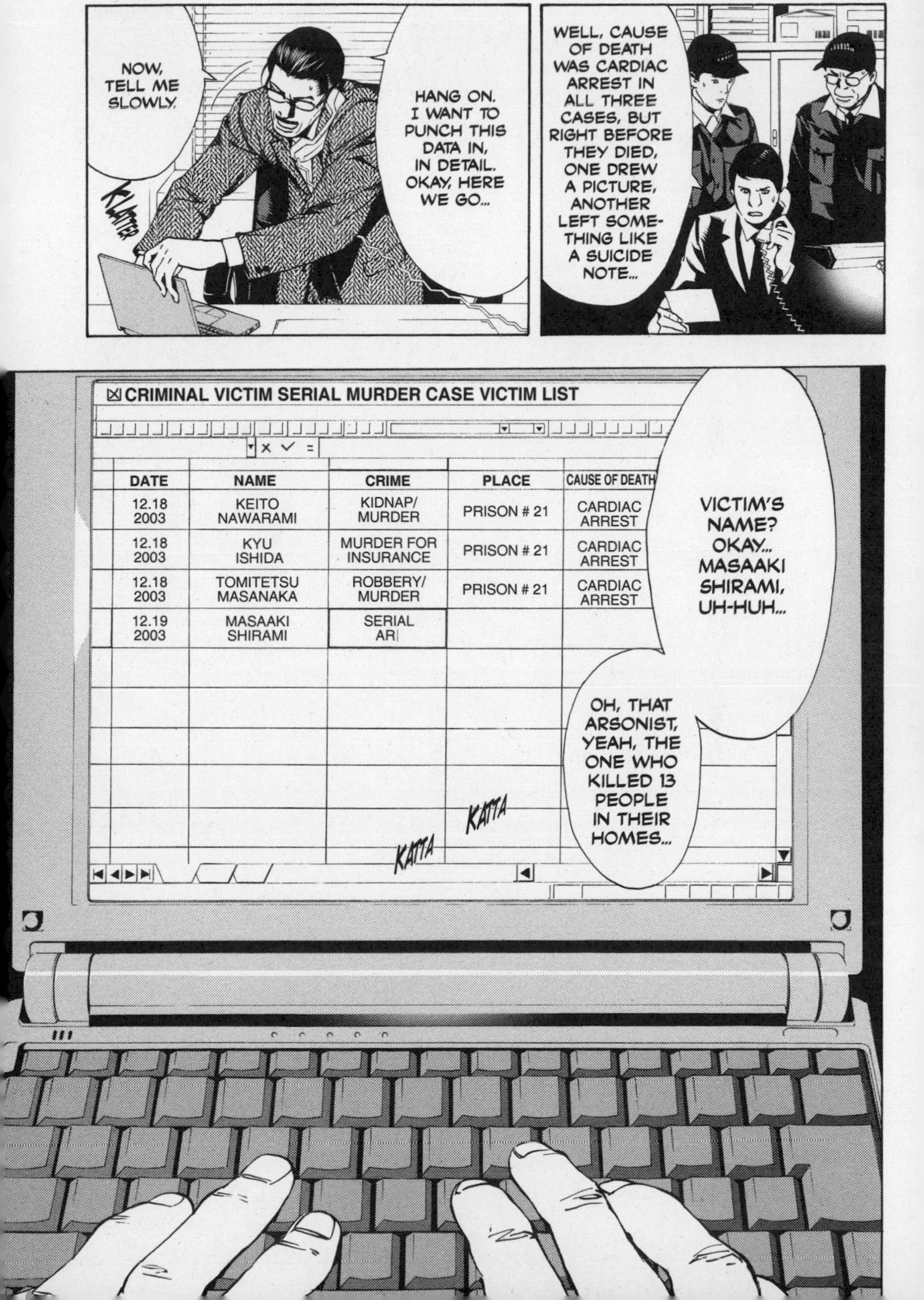
WELL, CAUSE OF DEATH WAS CARDIAC ARREST IN ALL THREE CASES, BUT RIGHT BEFORE THEY DIED, ONE DREW A PICTURE, ANOTHER LEFT SOMETHING LIKE A SUICIDE NOTE...
HANG ON. I WANT TO PUNCH THIS DATA IN, IN DETAIL. OKAY, HERE WE GO...
NOW, TELL ME SLOWLY.
KLUNK
VICTIM'S NAME? OKAY... MASAAKI SHIRAMI, UH-HUH...
OH, THAT ARSONIST, YEAH, THE ONE WHO KILLED 13 PEOPLE IN THEIR HOMES...
CRIMINAL VICTIM SERIAL MURDER CASE VICTIM LIST
DATE | NAME | CRIME | PLACE | CAUSE OF DEATH
12.18 2003 | KEITO NAWARAMI | KIDNAP/ MURDER | PRISON # 21 | CARDIAC ARREST
12.18 2003 | KYU ISHIDA | MURDER FOR INSURANCE | PRISON # 21 | CARDIAC ARREST
12.18 2003 | TOMITETSU MASANAKA | ROBBERY/ MURDER | PRISON # 21 | CARDIAC ARREST
12.19 2003 | MASAAKI SHIRAMI | SERIAL AR
KATTA
KATTA

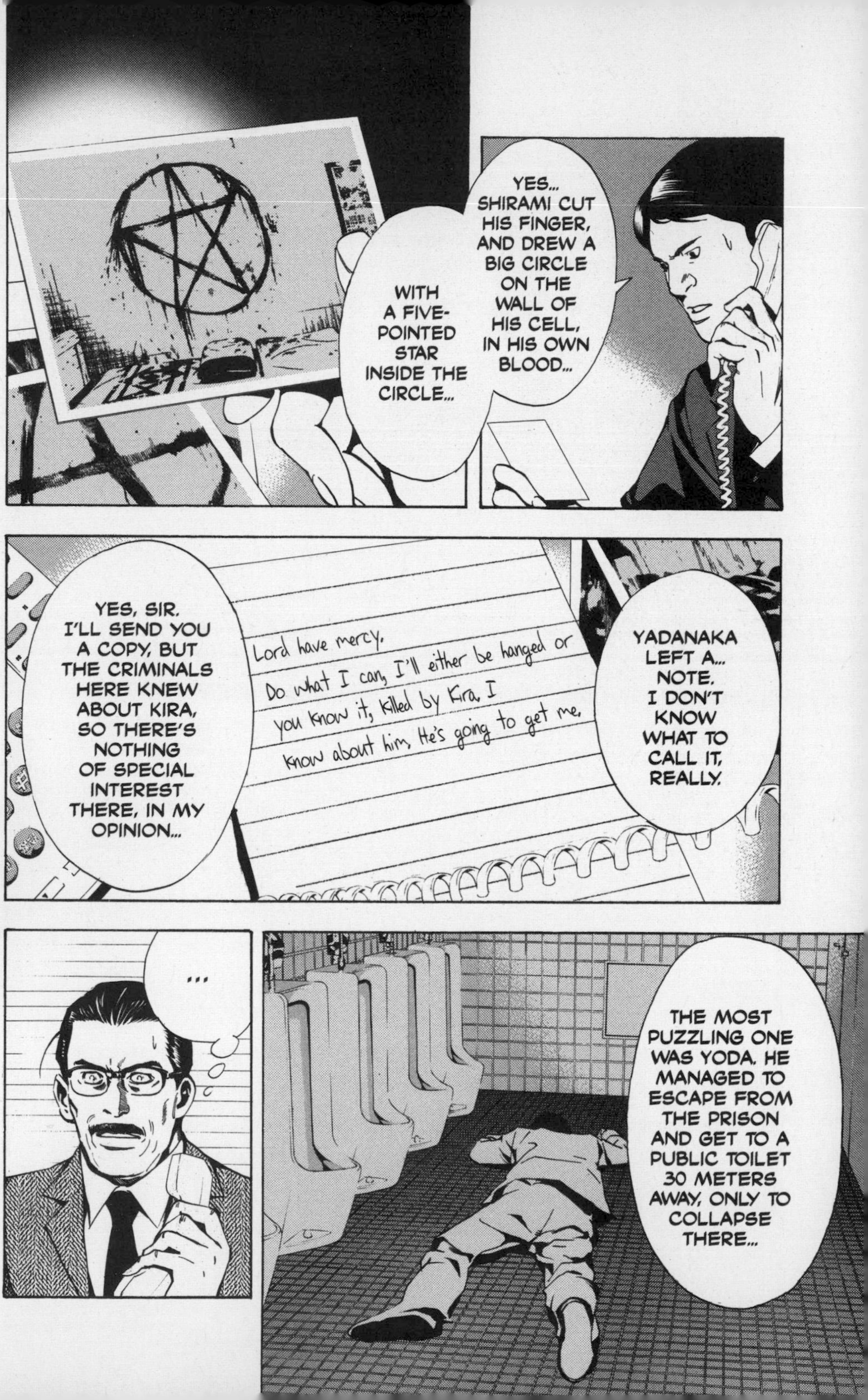
YES... SHIRAMI CUT HIS FINGER, AND DREW A BIG CIRCLE ON THE WALL OF HIS CELL, IN HIS OWN BLOOD...
WITH A FIVE-POINTED STAR INSIDE THE CIRCLE...
YADANAKA LEFT A... NOTE. I DON'T KNOW WHAT TO CALL IT, REALLY.
Lord have mercy.
Do what I can, I'll either be hanged or
you know it, killed by Kira. I
know about him. He's going to get me.
YES, SIR. I'LL SEND YOU A COPY, BUT THE CRIMINALS HERE KNEW ABOUT KIRA, SO THERE'S NOTHING OF SPECIAL INTEREST THERE, IN MY OPINION...
THE MOST PUZZLING ONE WAS YODA. HE MANAGED TO ESCAPE FROM THE PRISON AND GET TO A PUBLIC TOILET 30 METERS AWAY, ONLY TO COLLAPSE THERE...
...

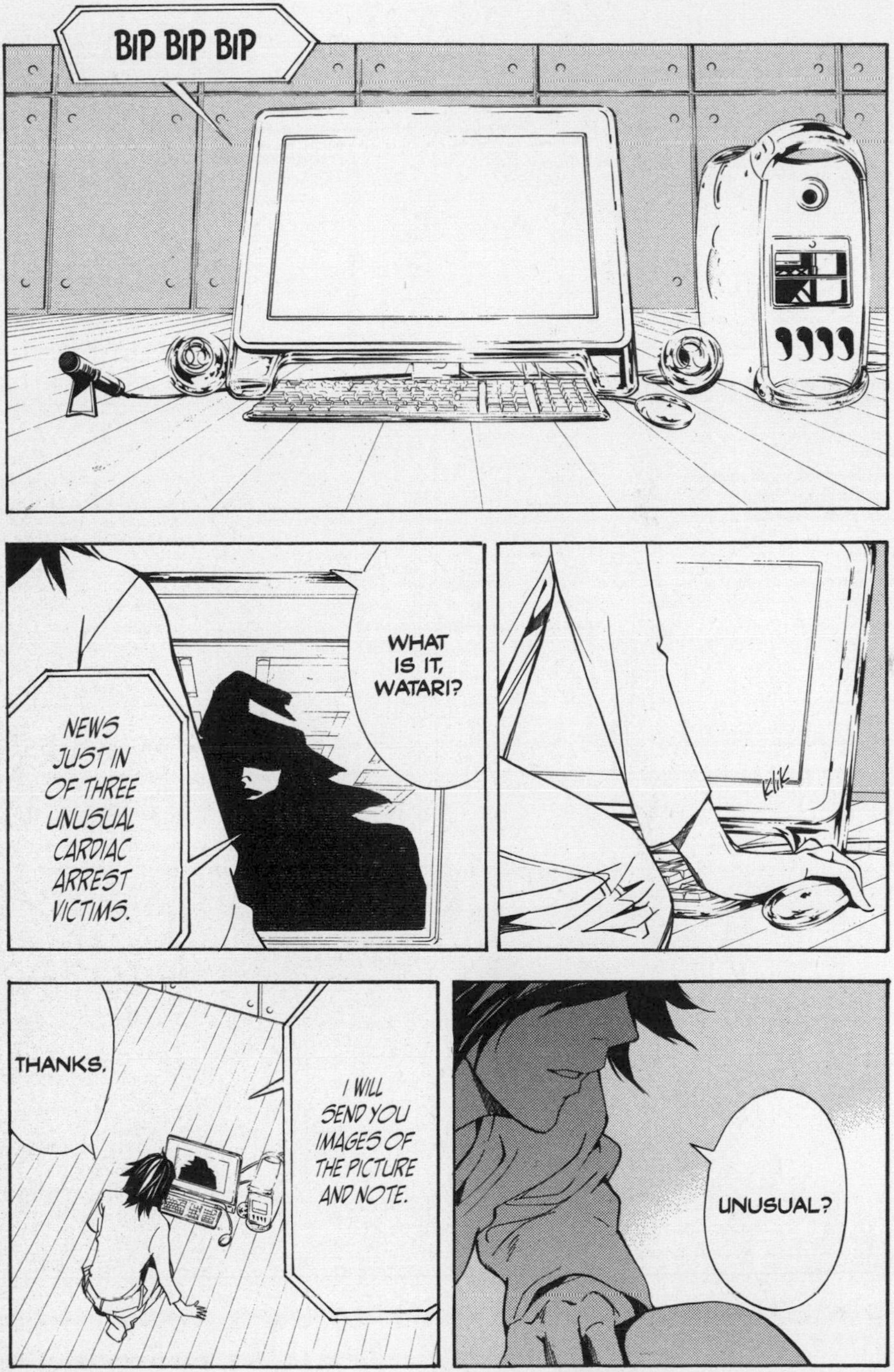
BIP BIP BIP
KLIK
WHAT IS IT, WATARI?
NEWS JUST IN OF THREE UNUSUAL CARDIAC ARREST VICTIMS.
UNUSUAL?
I WILL SEND YOU IMAGES OF THE PICTURE AND NOTE.
THANKS.

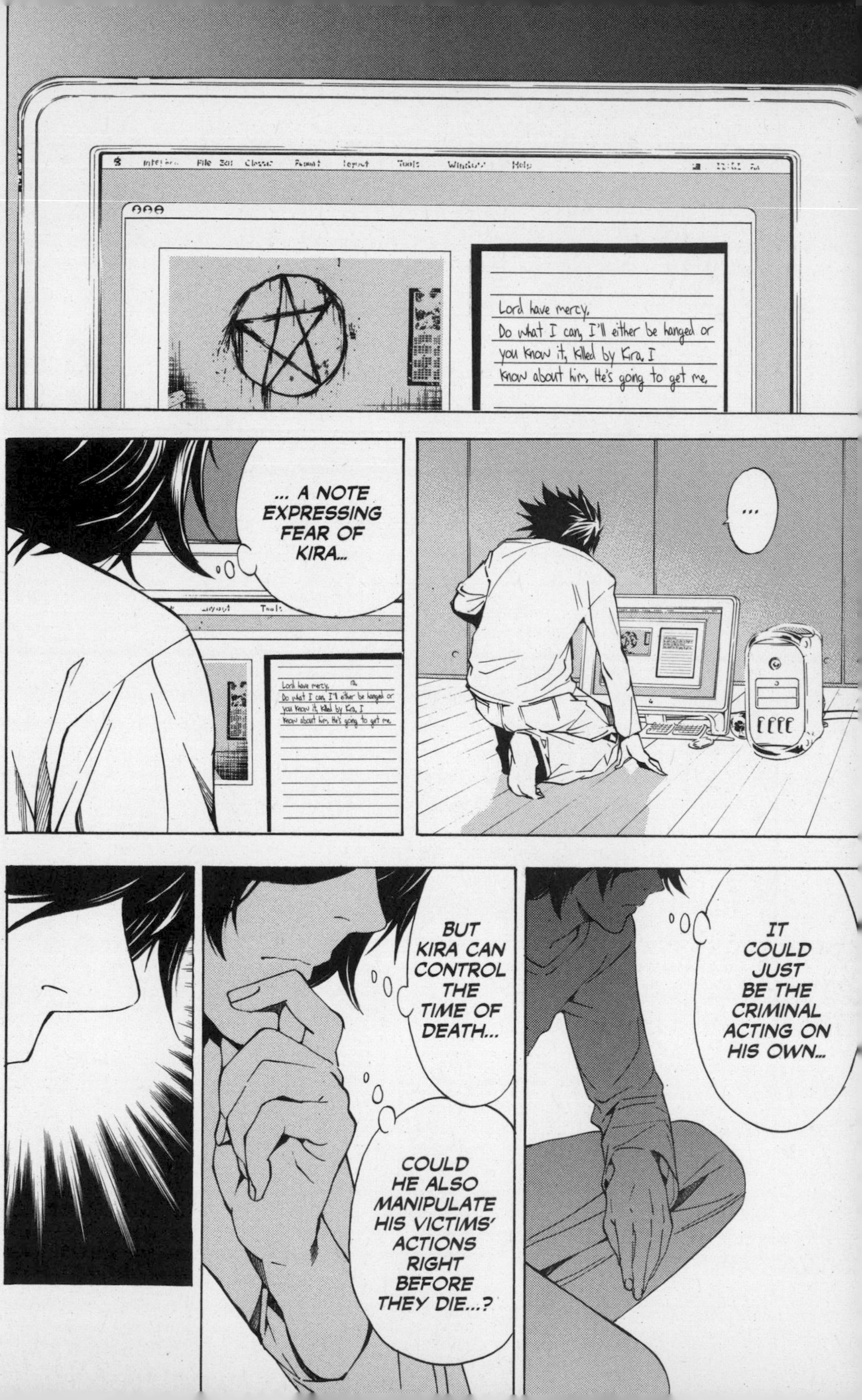
Lord have mercy.
Do what I can, I'll either be hanged or
you know it, killed by Kira. I
know about him. He's going to get me.
...
... A NOTE EXPRESSING FEAR OF KIRA...
IT COULD JUST BE THE CRIMINAL ACTING ON HIS OWN...
BUT KIRA CAN CONTROL THE TIME OF DEATH...
COULD HE ALSO MANIPULATE HIS VICTIMS' ACTIONS RIGHT BEFORE THEY DIE...?

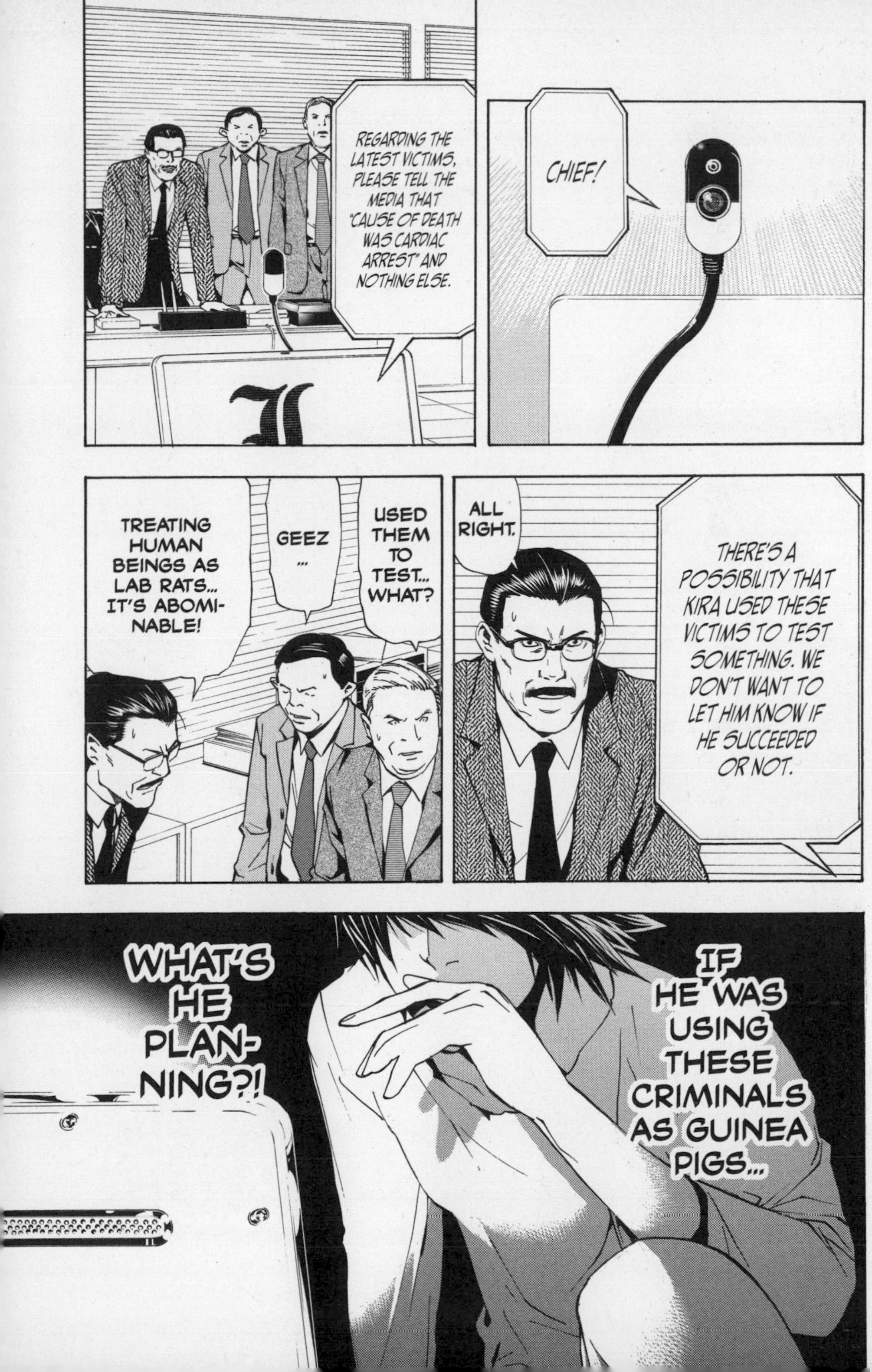
CHIEF!
REGARDING THE LATEST VICTIMS, PLEASE TELL THE MEDIA THAT "CAUSE OF DEATH WAS CARDIAC ARREST" AND NOTHING ELSE.
THERE'S A POSSIBILITY THAT KIRA USED THESE VICTIMS TO TEST SOMETHING. WE DON'T WANT TO LET HIM KNOW IF HE SUCCEEDED OR NOT.
ALL RIGHT.
USED THEM TO TEST... WHAT?
GEEZ ...
TREATING HUMAN BEINGS AS LAB RATS... IT'S ABOMINABLE!
IF HE WAS USING THESE CRIMINALS AS GUINEA PIGS...
WHAT'S HE PLANNING?!

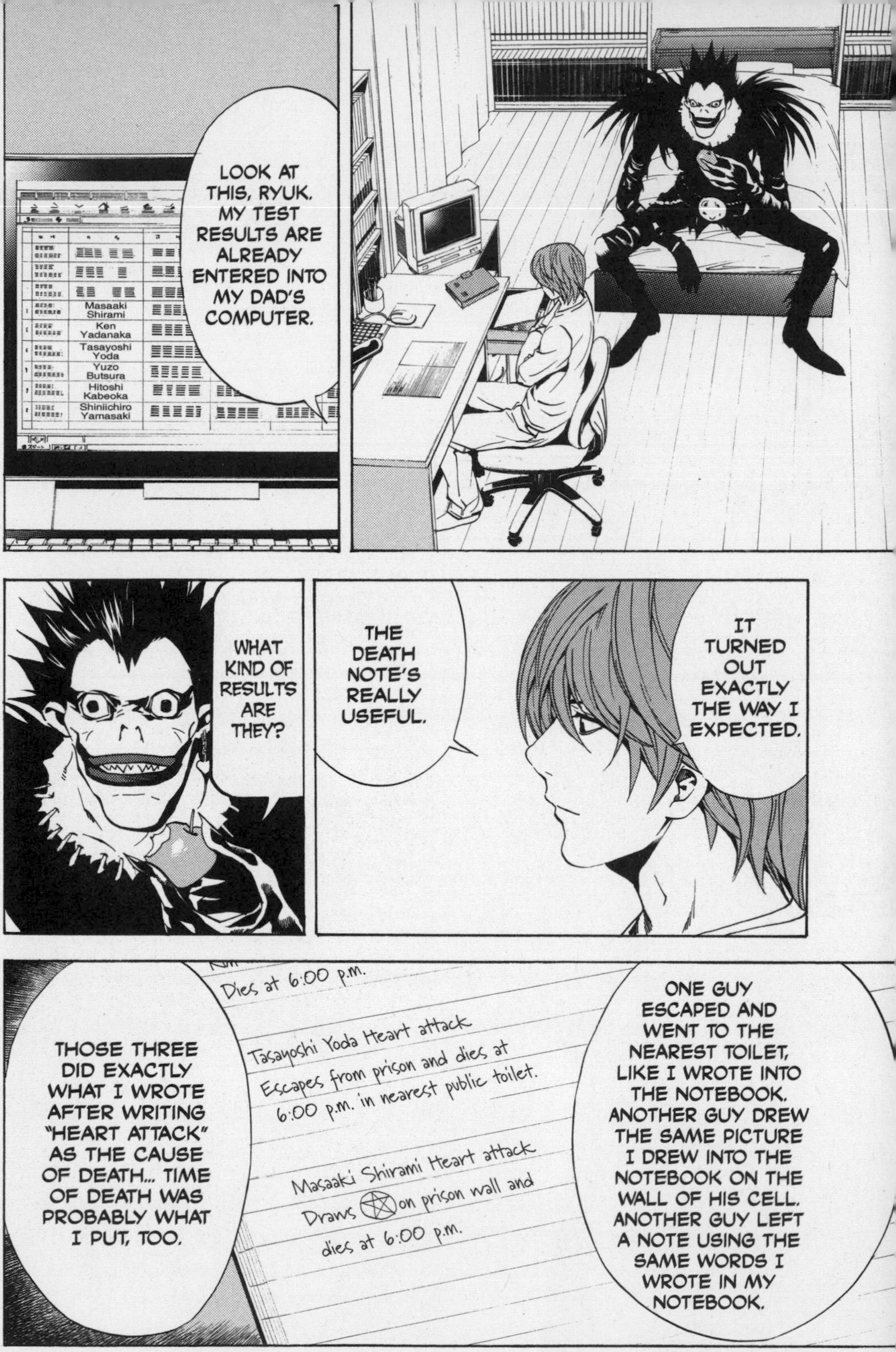
Masaaki Shirami
Ken Yadanaka
Tasayoshi Yoda
Yuzo Butsura
Hitoshi Kabeoka
Shiniichiro Yamasaki
LOOK AT THIS, RYUK. MY TEST RESULTS ARE ALREADY ENTERED INTO MY DAD'S COMPUTER.
IT TURNED OUT EXACTLY THE WAY I EXPECTED.
THE DEATH NOTE'S REALLY USEFUL.
WHAT KIND OF RESULTS ARE THEY?
ONE GUY ESCAPED AND WENT TO THE NEAREST TOILET, LIKE I WROTE INTO THE NOTEBOOK. ANOTHER GUY DREW THE SAME PICTURE I DREW INTO THE NOTEBOOK ON THE WALL OF HIS CELL. ANOTHER GUY LEFT A NOTE USING THE SAME WORDS I WROTE IN MY NOTEBOOK.
Dies at 6:00 p.m.
Tasayoshi Yoda Heart attack
Escapes from prison and dies at 6:00 p.m. in nearest public toilet.
Masaaki Shirami Heart attack
Draws on prison wall and dies at 6:00 p.m.
THOSE THREE DID EXACTLY WHAT I WROTE AFTER WRITING "HEART ATTACK" AS THE CAUSE OF DEATH... TIME OF DEATH WAS PROBABLY WHAT I PUT, TOO.

READ THIS WAY
FOR THE OTHER THREE, I DELIBERATELY WROTE IN PRACTICALLY IMPOSSIBLE DETAILS.
6 : 00
FOR ONE, I WROTE "DIES AT 6:00 P.M. TODAY IN FRONT OF THE EIFFEL TOWER IN FRANCE."
IT'S PHYSICALLY IMPOSSIBLE FOR SOMEONE WHO WAS IN A JAPANESE PRISON AT 5:30 TO DIE IN FRANCE AT 6:00. SO THAT DIDN'T HAPPEN, AND HE JUST DIED OF A HEART ATTACK.
5 : 30
FOR THE NEXT ONE, I WROTE "DRAWS A PERFECT LIKENESS OF L'S FACE ON PRISON WALL"...
BUT YOU CAN'T DRAW SOME-ONE YOU'VE NEVER SEEN.
L
a perfect likeness of L's face
at 6:00 p.m.
Shimichiro Yamasaki
Writes a note saying "I know that L suspects the Japanese police" and dies at 6:00 p.m.
FOR THE LAST ONE, I WROTE "WRITES 'I KNOW THAT L SUSPECTS THE JAPANESE POLICE'."
I THOUGHT THIS ONE MIGHT WORK, BUT SINCE IT DIDN'T, IT MEANS THAT HE COULDN'T WRITE SOME-THING THAT HE HIMSELF DIDN'T KNOW OR THINK.
BUT... ACTIONS THAT AREN'T UNNATURAL FOR THAT PERSON CAN BE WRITTEN INTO HOW THEY DIE, AND THEY'LL DO THEM.
IN OTHER WORDS, EVEN WITH THE DEATH NOTE, YOU CAN'T DO SOMETHING THAT ISN'T POSSIBLE.

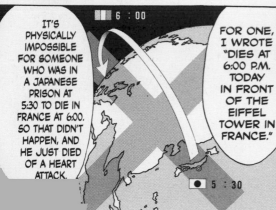

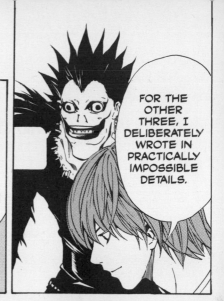

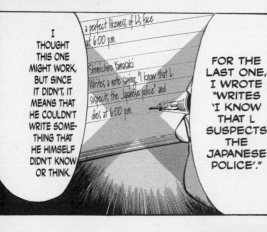

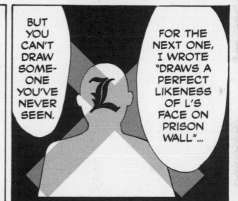

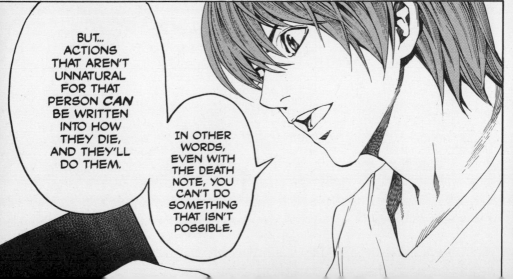

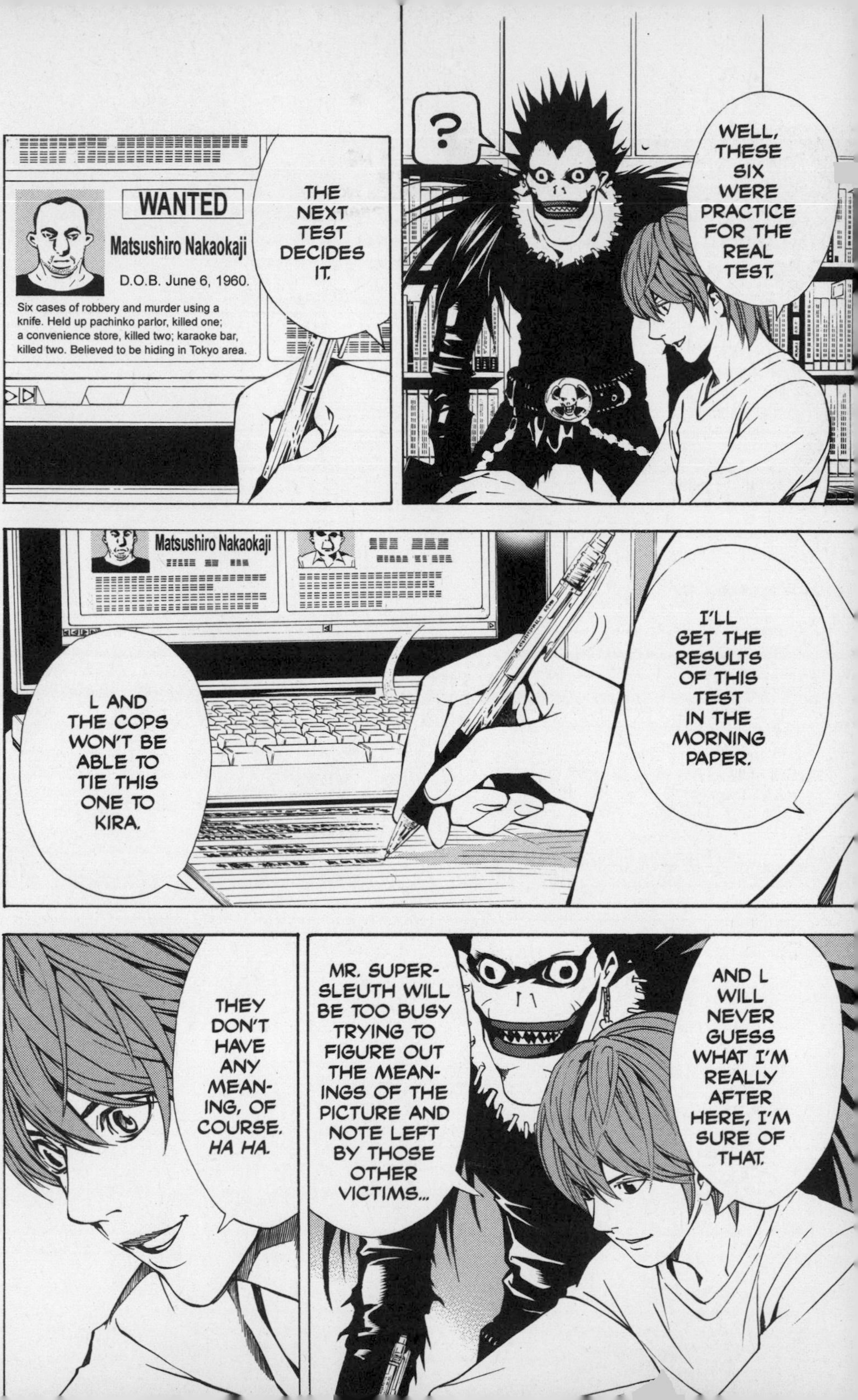
WELL, THESE SIX WERE PRACTICE FOR THE REAL TEST.
?
THE NEXT TEST DECIDES IT.
WANTED
Matsushiro Nakaokaji
D.O.B. June 6, 1960.
Six cases of robbery and murder using a knife. Held up pachinko parlor, killed one; a convenience store, killed two; karaoke bar, killed two. Believed to be hiding in Tokyo area.
Matsushiro Nakaokaji
I'LL GET THE RESULTS OF THIS TEST IN THE MORNING PAPER.
L AND THE COPS WON'T BE ABLE TO TIE THIS ONE TO KIRA.
AND L WILL NEVER GUESS WHAT I'M REALLY AFTER HERE, I'M SURE OF THAT.
MR. SUPER-SLEUTH WILL BE TOO BUSY TRYING TO FIGURE OUT THE MEANINGS OF THE PICTURE AND NOTE LEFT BY THOSE OTHER VICTIMS...
THEY DON'T HAVE ANY MEANING, OF COURSE. HA HA.

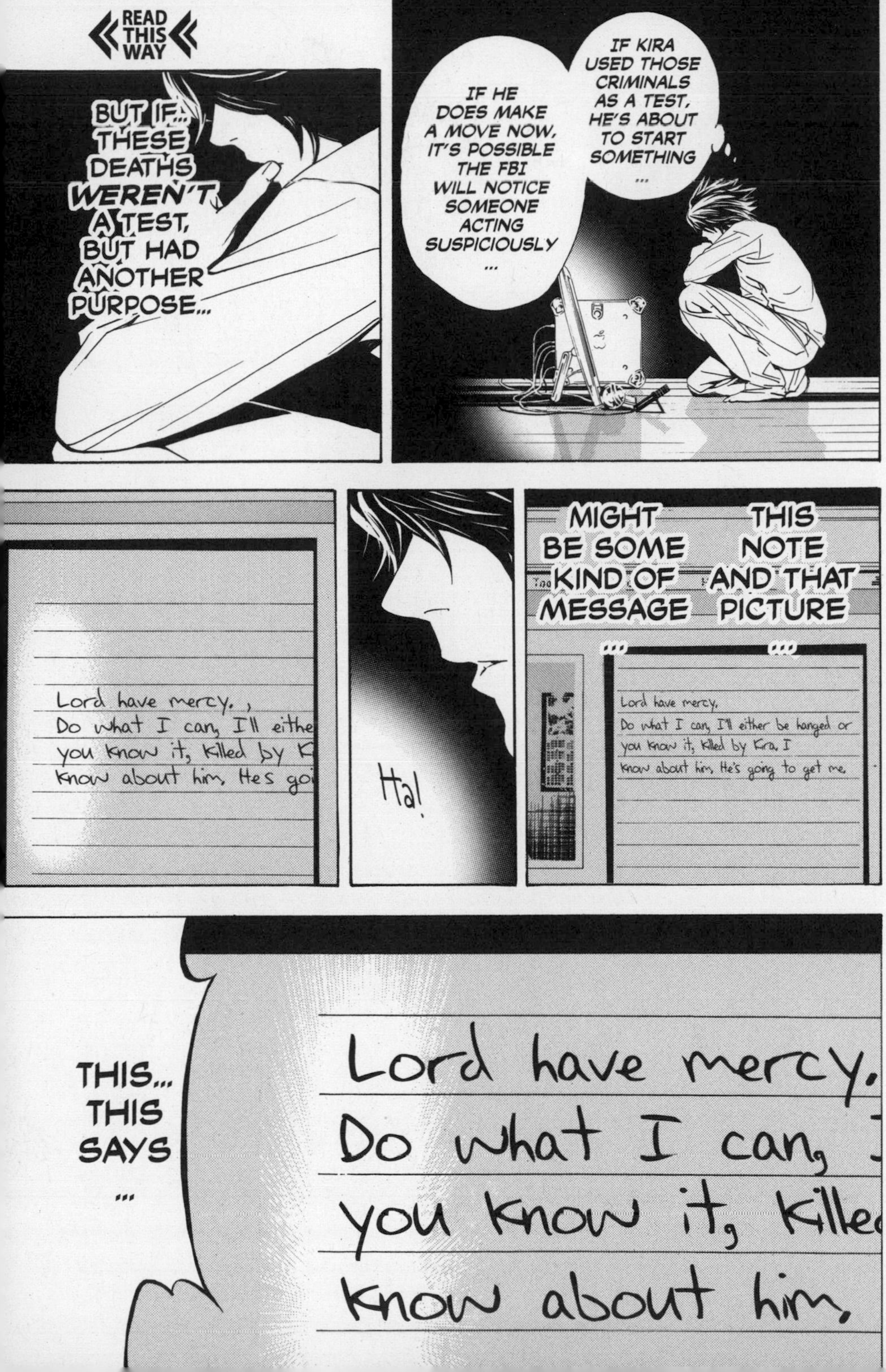
READ THIS WAY
IF KIRA USED THOSE CRIMINALS AS A TEST, HE'S ABOUT TO START SOMETHING...
IF HE DOES MAKE A MOVE NOW, IT'S POSSIBLE THE FBI WILL NOTICE SOMEONE ACTING SUSPICIOUSLY...
BUT IF... THESE DEATHS *WEREN'T* A TEST, BUT HAD ANOTHER PURPOSE...
THIS NOTE AND THAT PICTURE...
MIGHT BE SOME KIND OF MESSAGE...
Lord have mercy.
Do what I can, I'll either be hanged or
you know it, Killed by Kira. I
know about him. He's going to get me.
Ha!
Lord have mercy.,
Do what I can, I'll eithe
you know it, Killed by
know about him. He's goi
THIS... THIS SAYS...
Lord have mercy.
Do what I can,
you know it,
know about him.

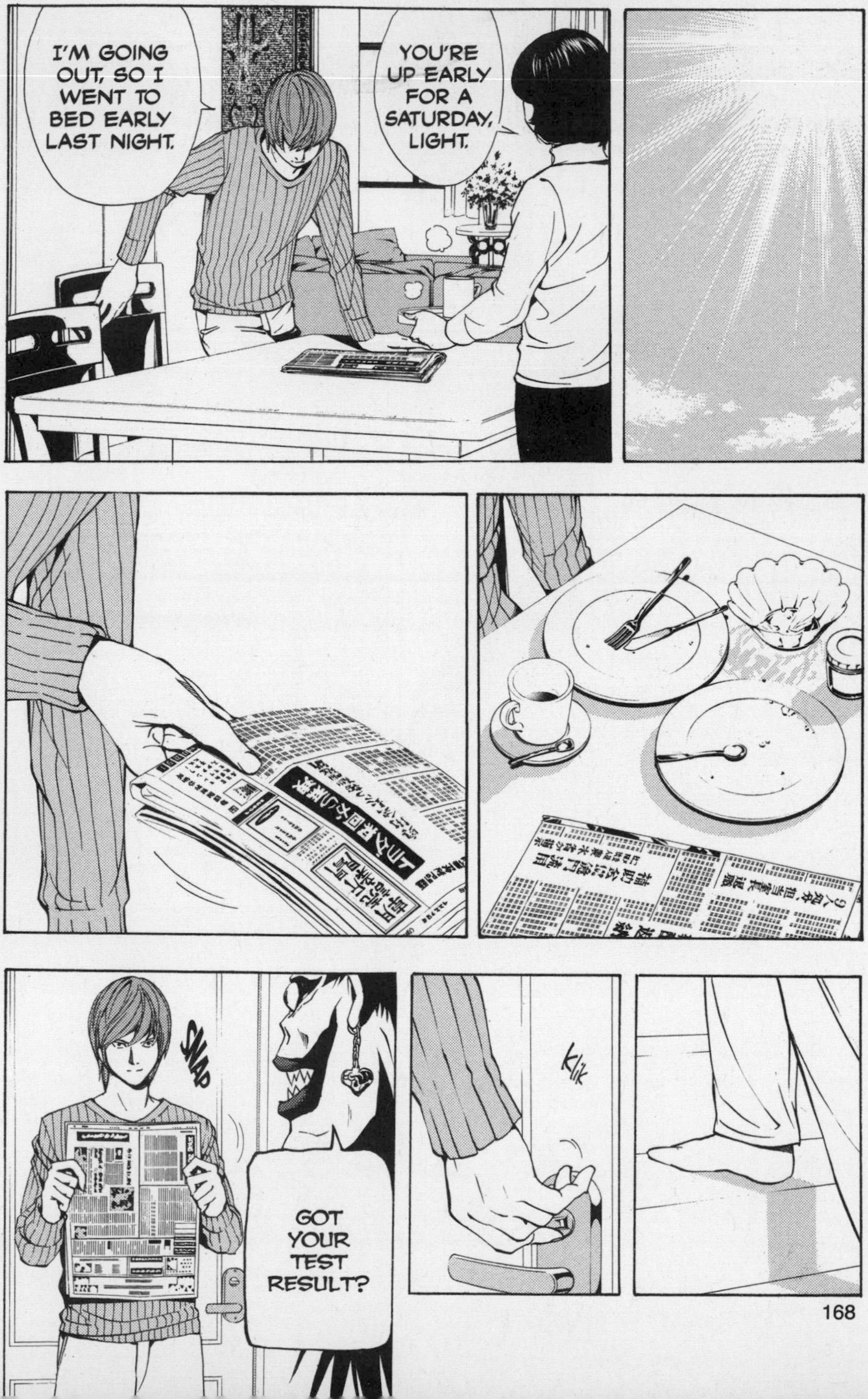
YOU'RE UP EARLY FOR A SATURDAY, LIGHT.
I'M GOING OUT, SO I WENT TO BED EARLY LAST NIGHT.
KLIK
SNAP
GOT YOUR TEST RESULT?

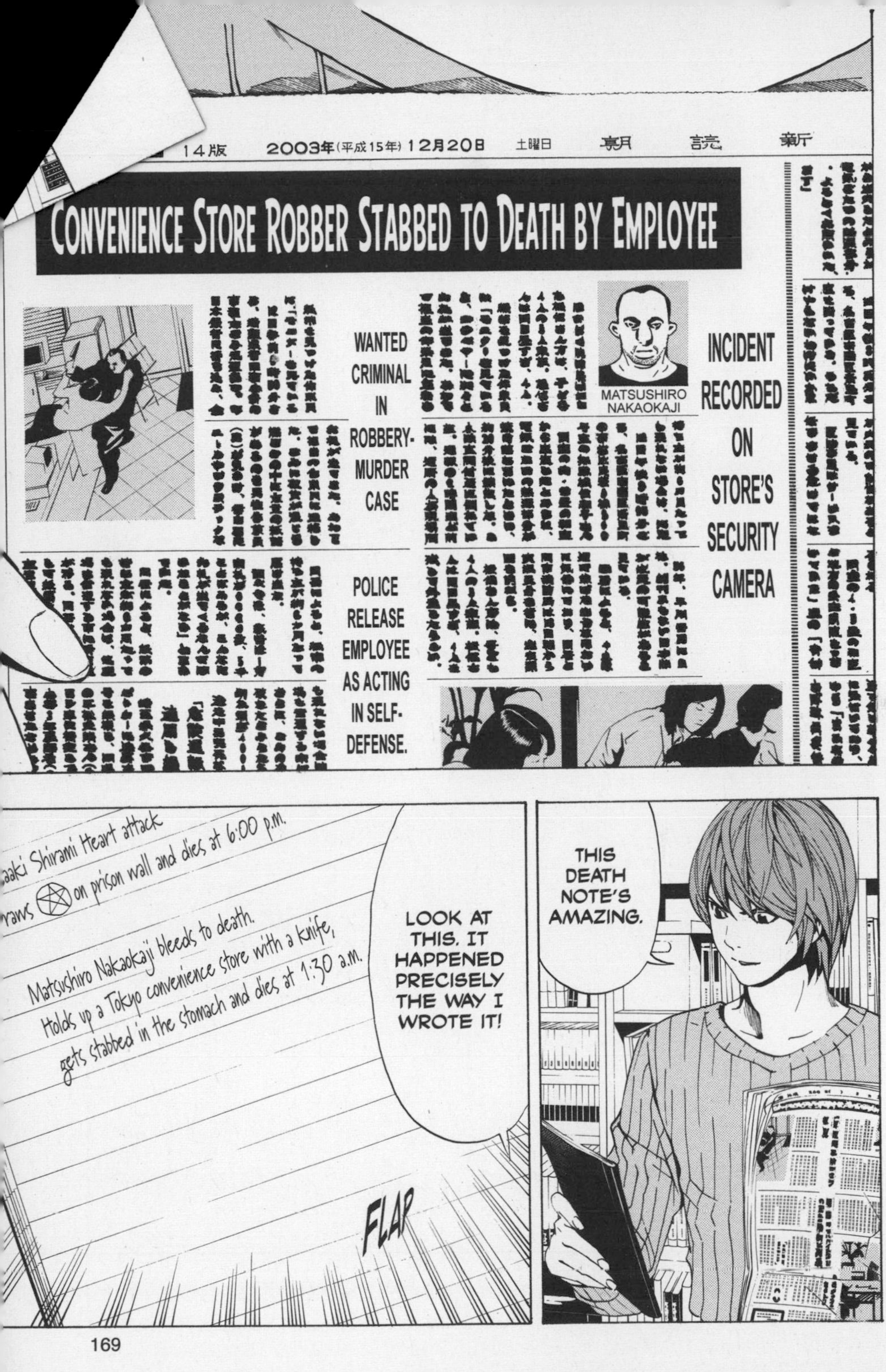
14版 2003年(平成15年)12月20日 土曜日
CONVENIENCE STORE ROBBER STABBED TO DEATH BY EMPLOYEE
INCIDENT RECORDED ON STORE'S SECURITY CAMERA
MATSUSHIRO NAKAOKAJI
WANTED CRIMINAL IN ROBBERY-MURDER CASE
POLICE RELEASE EMPLOYEE AS ACTING IN SELF-DEFENSE.
THIS DEATH NOTE'S AMAZING.
LOOK AT THIS. IT HAPPENED PRECISELY THE WAY I WROTE IT!
aaki Shirami Heart attack
raws on prison wall and dies at 6:00 p.m.
Matsushiro Nakaokaji bleeds to death.
Holds up a Tokyo convenience store with a knife,
gets stabbed in the stomach and dies at 1:30 a.m.
FLAP

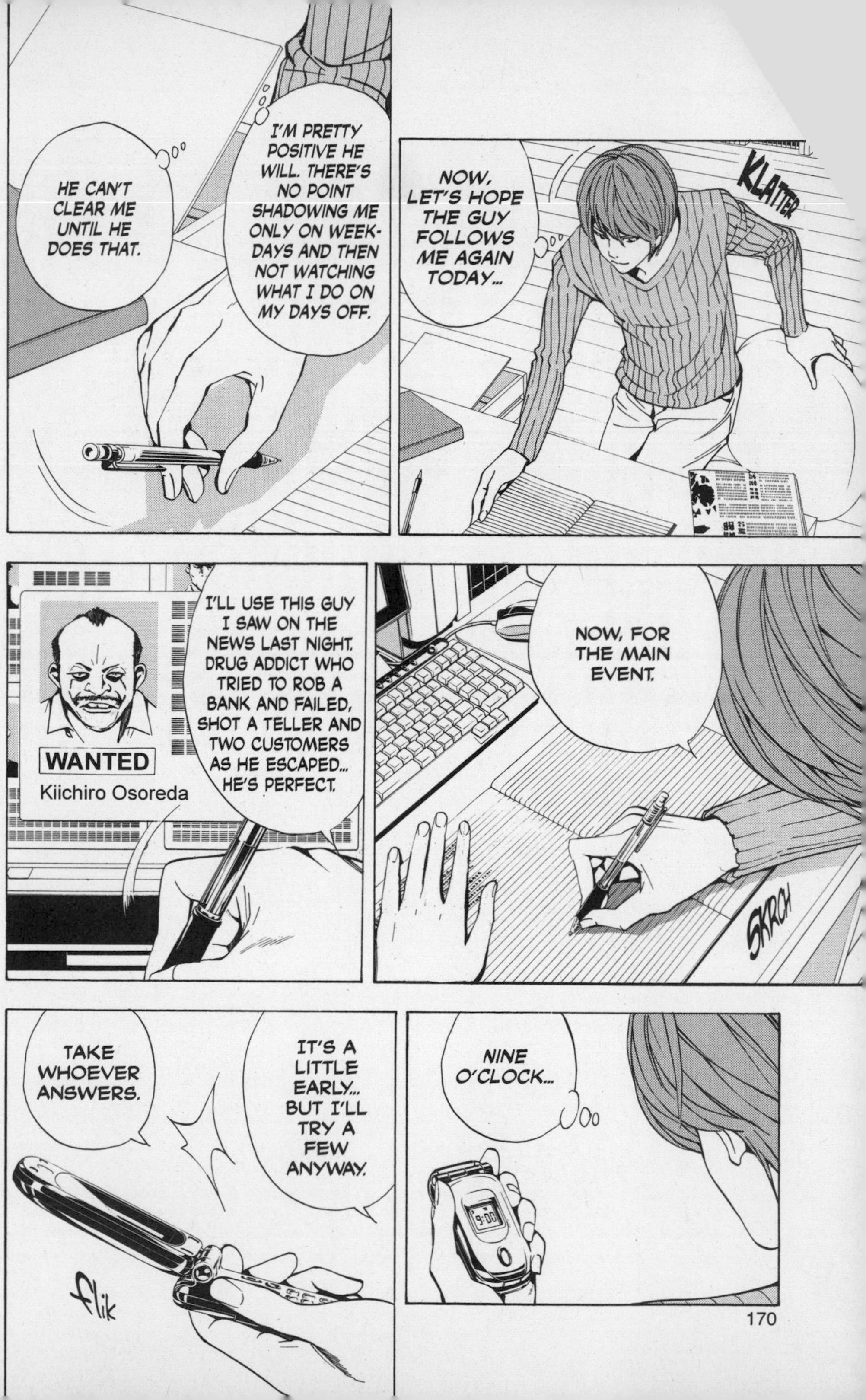
KLATTER
NOW, LET'S HOPE THE GUY FOLLOWS ME AGAIN TODAY...
I'M PRETTY POSITIVE HE WILL. THERE'S NO POINT SHADOWING ME ONLY ON WEEK-DAYS AND THEN NOT WATCHING WHAT I DO ON MY DAYS OFF.
HE CAN'T CLEAR ME UNTIL HE DOES THAT.
NOW, FOR THE MAIN EVENT.
SKRCH
I'LL USE THIS GUY I SAW ON THE NEWS LAST NIGHT. DRUG ADDICT WHO TRIED TO ROB A BANK AND FAILED, SHOT A TELLER AND TWO CUSTOMERS AS HE ESCAPED... HE'S PERFECT.
WANTED
Kiichiro Osoreda
NINE O'CLOCK...
9:00
IT'S A LITTLE EARLY... BUT I'LL TRY A FEW ANYWAY.
TAKE WHOEVER ANSWERS.
flik

THIS MIGHT SURPRISE YOU, BUT I'M PRETTY POPULAR WITH THE LADIES, RYUK.

TRY A FEW ...?

GIRLS.

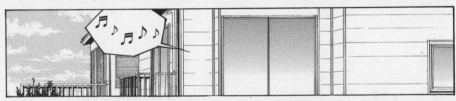

♪♪♪♪

UH, YEAH... HI...

NGH?! LIGHT?

♪♪♪♪

# DEATH NOTE
## How to Use It
### VI

° The conditions for death will not be realized unless it is physically possible for that human or it is reasonably assumed to be carried out by that human.

書き入れる死の状況は、その人間が物理的に可能な事、その人間がやってもおかしくない範囲の行動でなければ実現しない。

° The specific scope of the condition for death is not known to the gods of death, either. So, you must examine and find out.

死の状況で可能になる事の詳細な範囲は死神にもわからないので、自分で検証し明らかにしていくしかない。

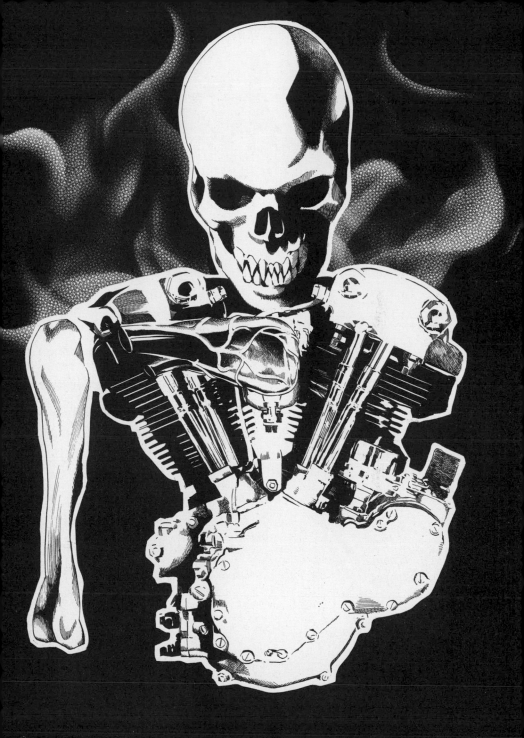

chapter 7 Target

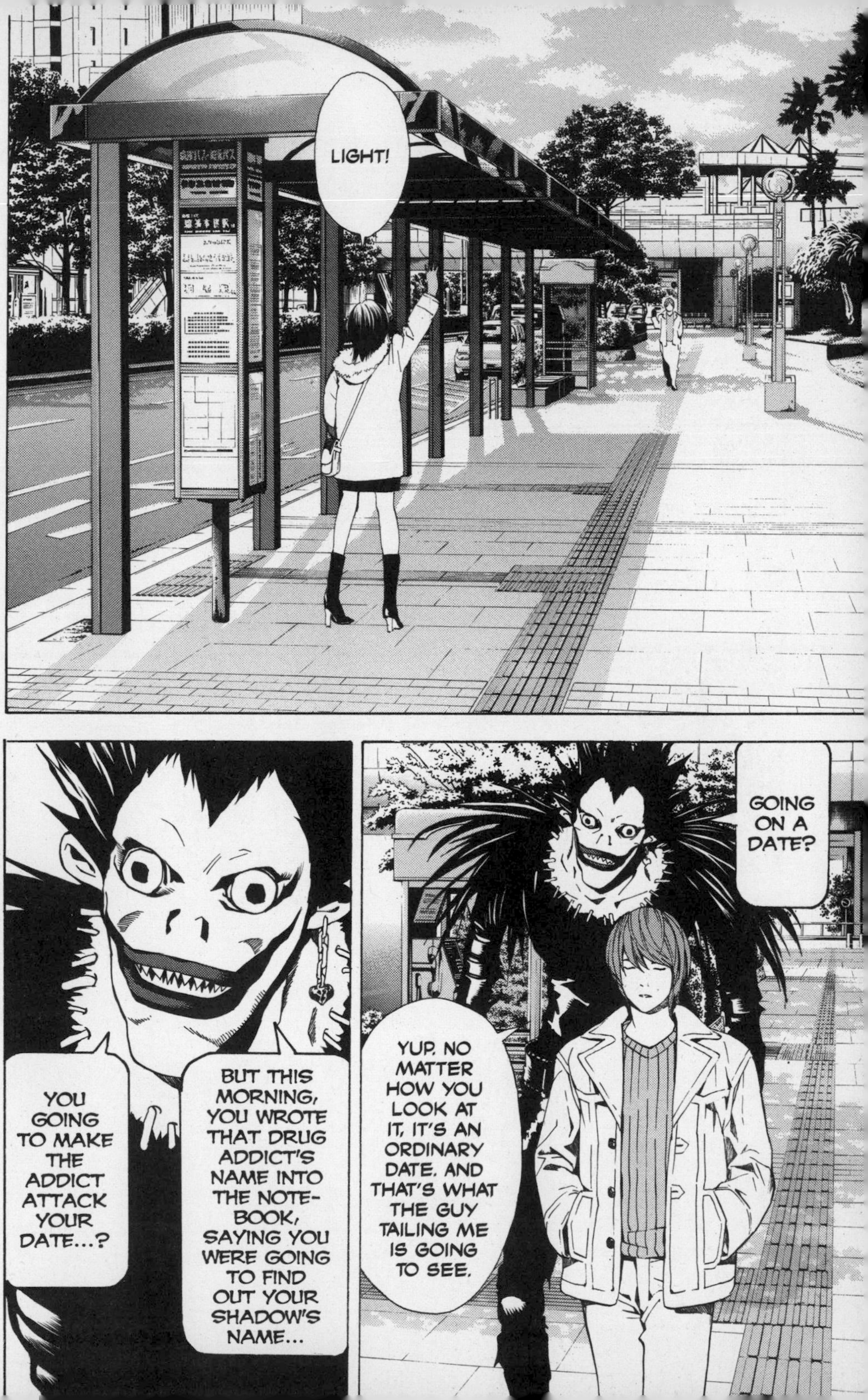
LIGHT!
GOING ON A DATE?
YUP. NO MATTER HOW YOU LOOK AT IT, IT'S AN ORDINARY DATE. AND THAT'S WHAT THE GUY TAILING ME IS GOING TO SEE.
BUT THIS MORNING, YOU WROTE THAT DRUG ADDICT'S NAME INTO THE NOTE-BOOK, SAYING YOU WERE GOING TO FIND OUT YOUR SHADOW'S NAME...
YOU GOING TO MAKE THE ADDICT ATTACK YOUR DATE...?

READ THIS WAY

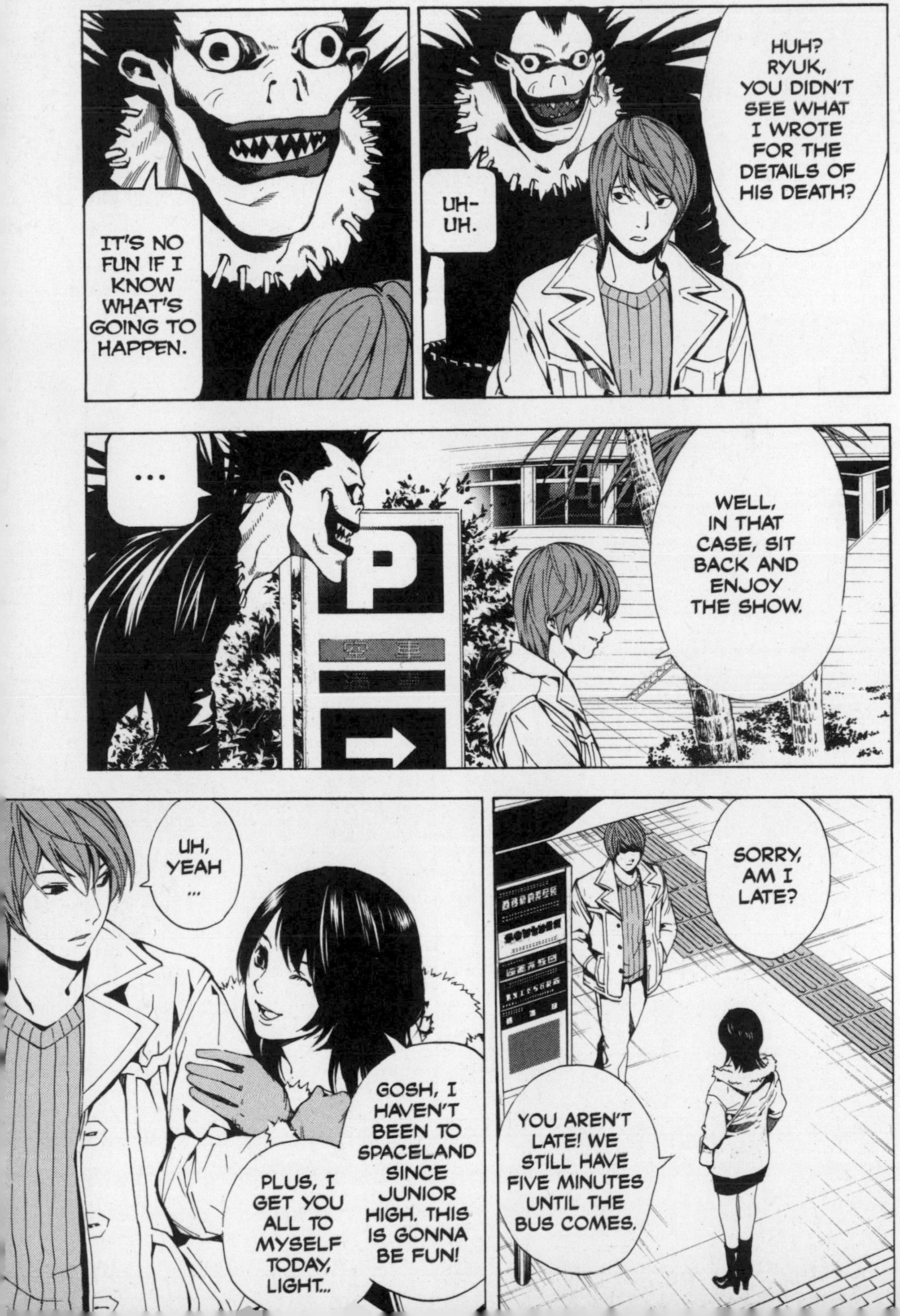
HUH? RYUK, YOU DIDN'T SEE WHAT I WROTE FOR THE DETAILS OF HIS DEATH?
UH-UH.
IT'S NO FUN IF I KNOW WHAT'S GOING TO HAPPEN.
WELL, IN THAT CASE, SIT BACK AND ENJOY THE SHOW.
...
P
SORRY, AM I LATE?
YOU AREN'T LATE! WE STILL HAVE FIVE MINUTES UNTIL THE BUS COMES.
GOSH, I HAVEN'T BEEN TO SPACELAND SINCE JUNIOR HIGH. THIS IS GONNA BE FUN!
PLUS, I GET YOU ALL TO MYSELF TODAY, LIGHT...
UH, YEAH ...

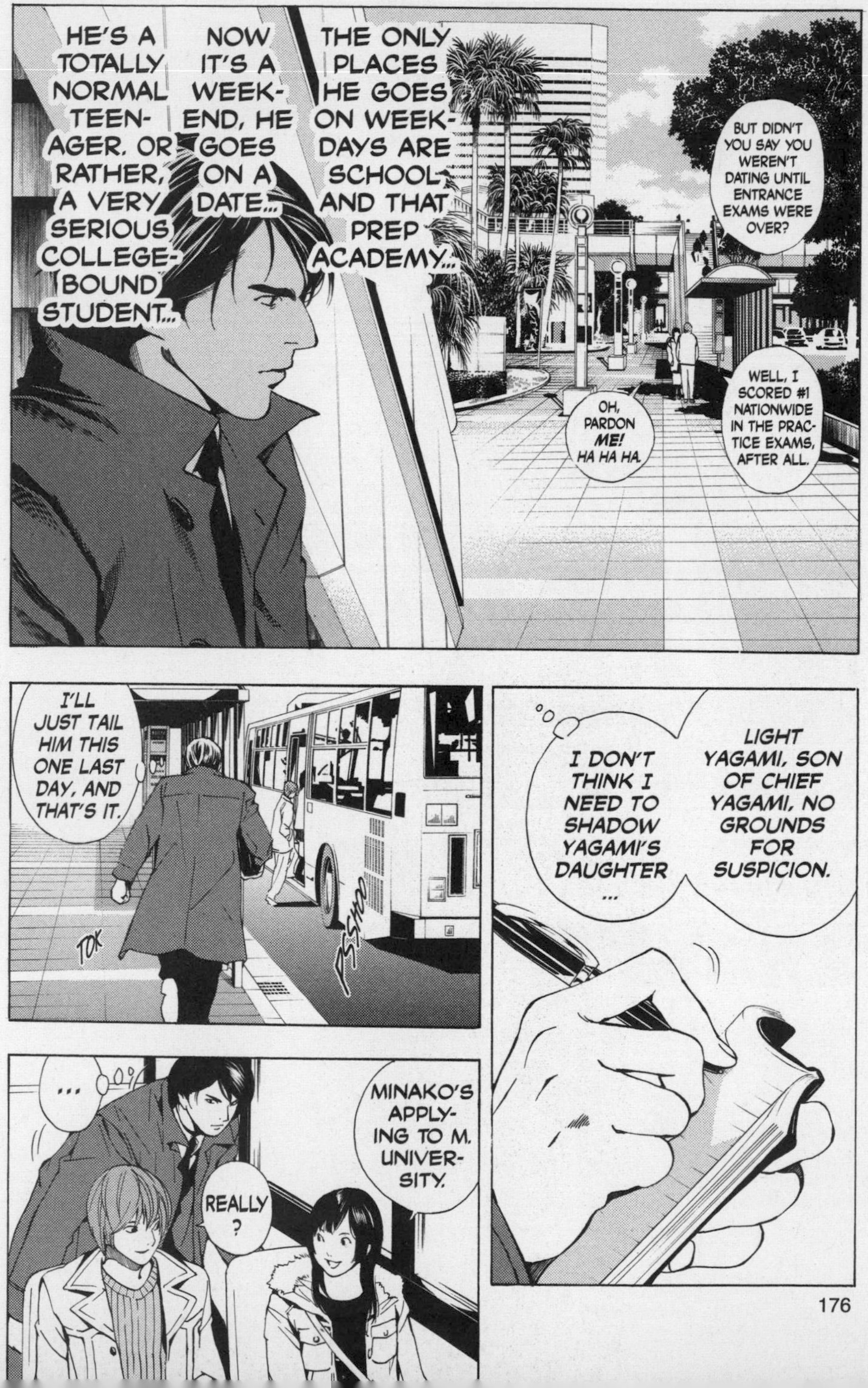
BUT DIDN'T YOU SAY YOU WEREN'T DATING UNTIL ENTRANCE EXAMS WERE OVER?
WELL, I SCORED #1 NATIONWIDE IN THE PRACTICE EXAMS, AFTER ALL.
OH, PARDON ME! HA HA HA.
THE ONLY PLACES HE GOES ON WEEKDAYS ARE SCHOOL AND THAT PREP ACADEMY...
NOW IT'S A WEEKEND, HE GOES ON A DATE...
HE'S A TOTALLY NORMAL TEENAGER. OR RATHER, A VERY SERIOUS COLLEGE-BOUND STUDENT...
LIGHT YAGAMI, SON OF CHIEF YAGAMI, NO GROUNDS FOR SUSPICION.
I DON'T THINK I NEED TO SHADOW YAGAMI'S DAUGHTER ...
I'LL JUST TAIL HIM THIS ONE LAST DAY, AND THAT'S IT.
TOK
PSSHOO
MINAKO'S APPLYING TO M. UNIVERSITY.
REALLY?
...

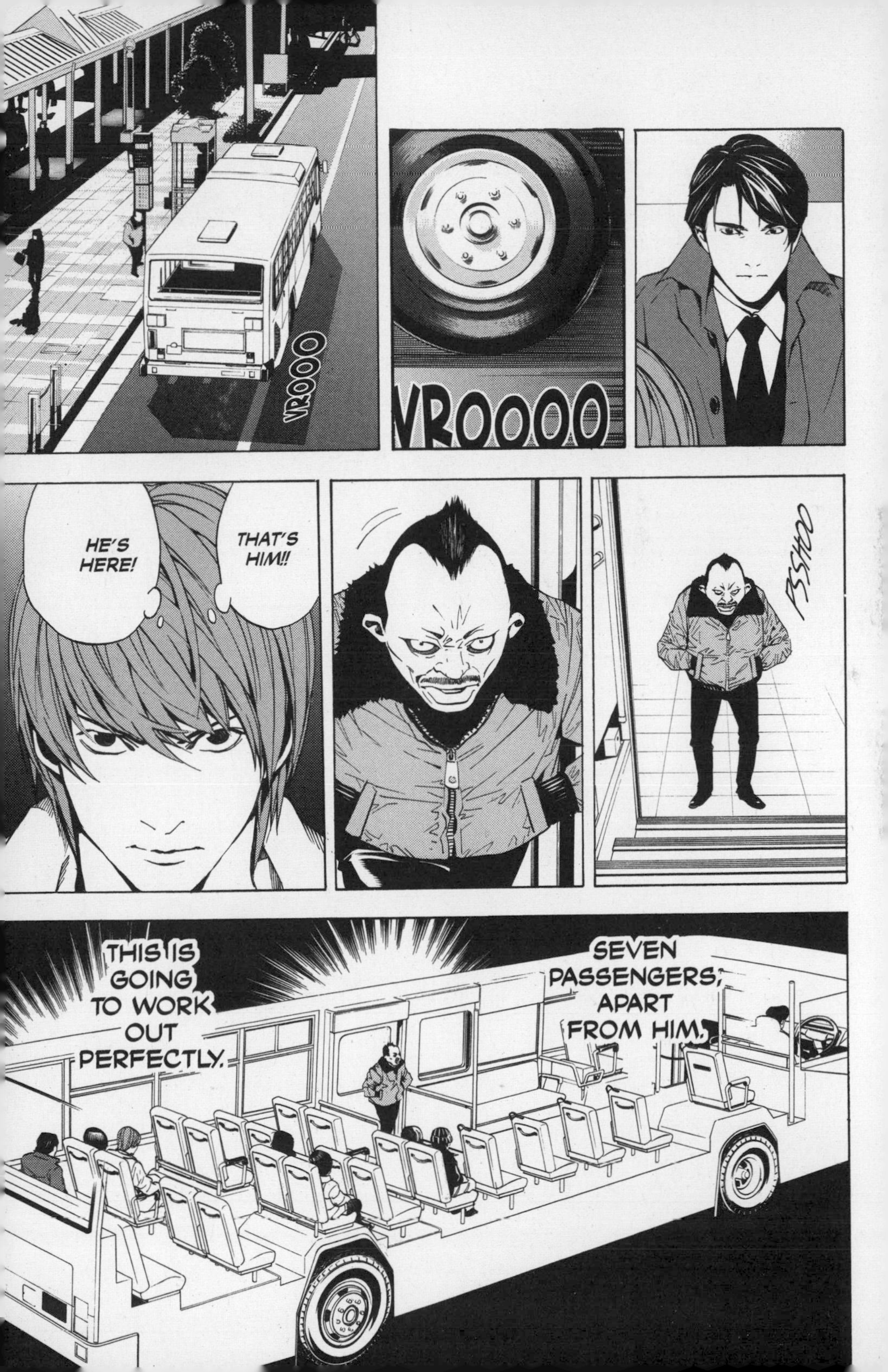
VROOOO
VROOOO
PSSHOO
THAT'S HIM!!
HE'S HERE!
SEVEN PASSENGERS, APART FROM HIM.
THIS IS GOING TO WORK OUT PERFECTLY.

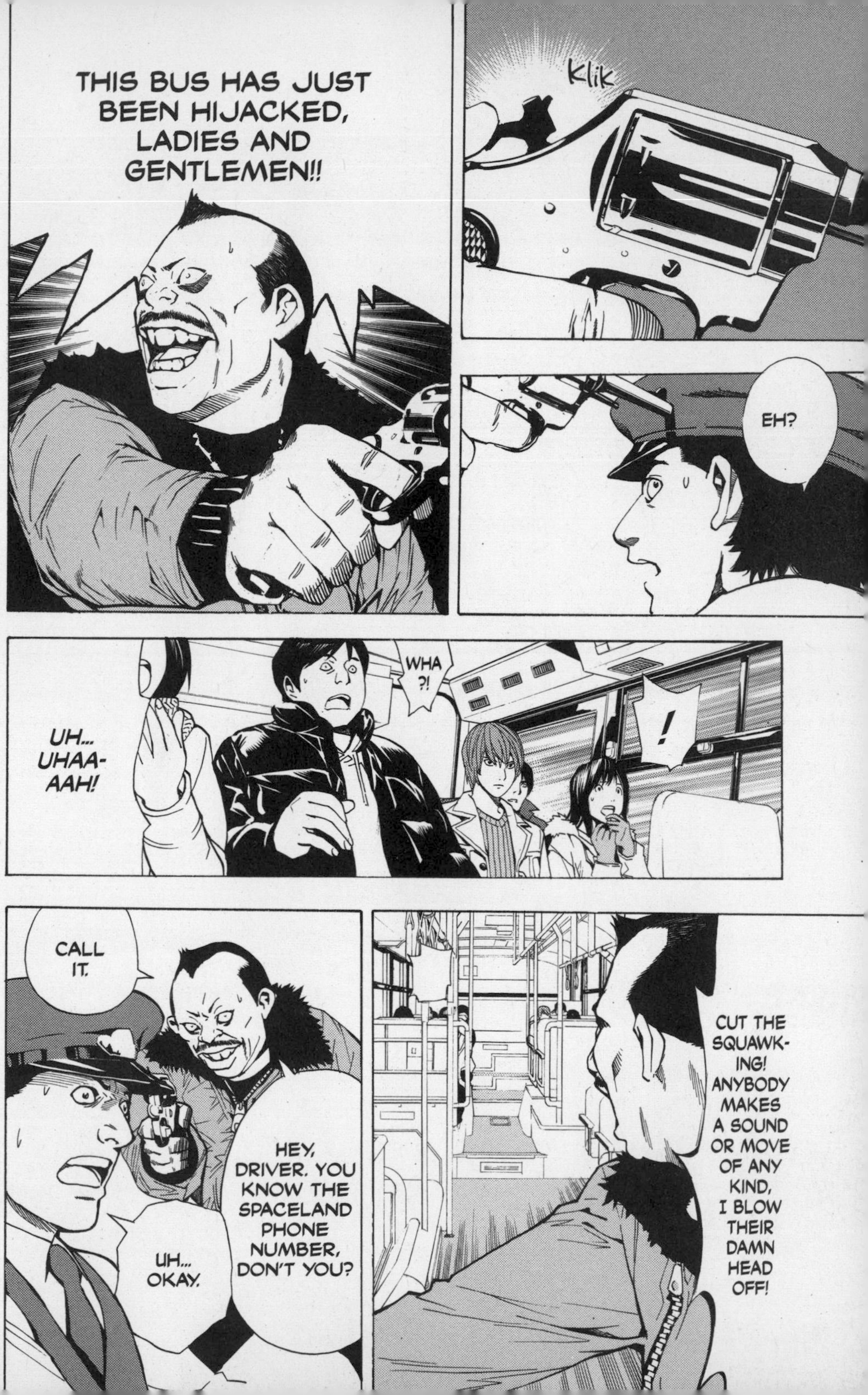
Klik
EH?
THIS BUS HAS JUST BEEN HIJACKED, LADIES AND GENTLEMEN!!
!
WHA ?!
UH... UHAA-AAH!
CUT THE SQUAWK-ING! ANYBODY MAKES A SOUND OR MOVE OF ANY KIND, I BLOW THEIR DAMN HEAD OFF!
HEY, DRIVER. YOU KNOW THE SPACELAND PHONE NUMBER, DON'T YOU?
UH... OKAY.
CALL IT.

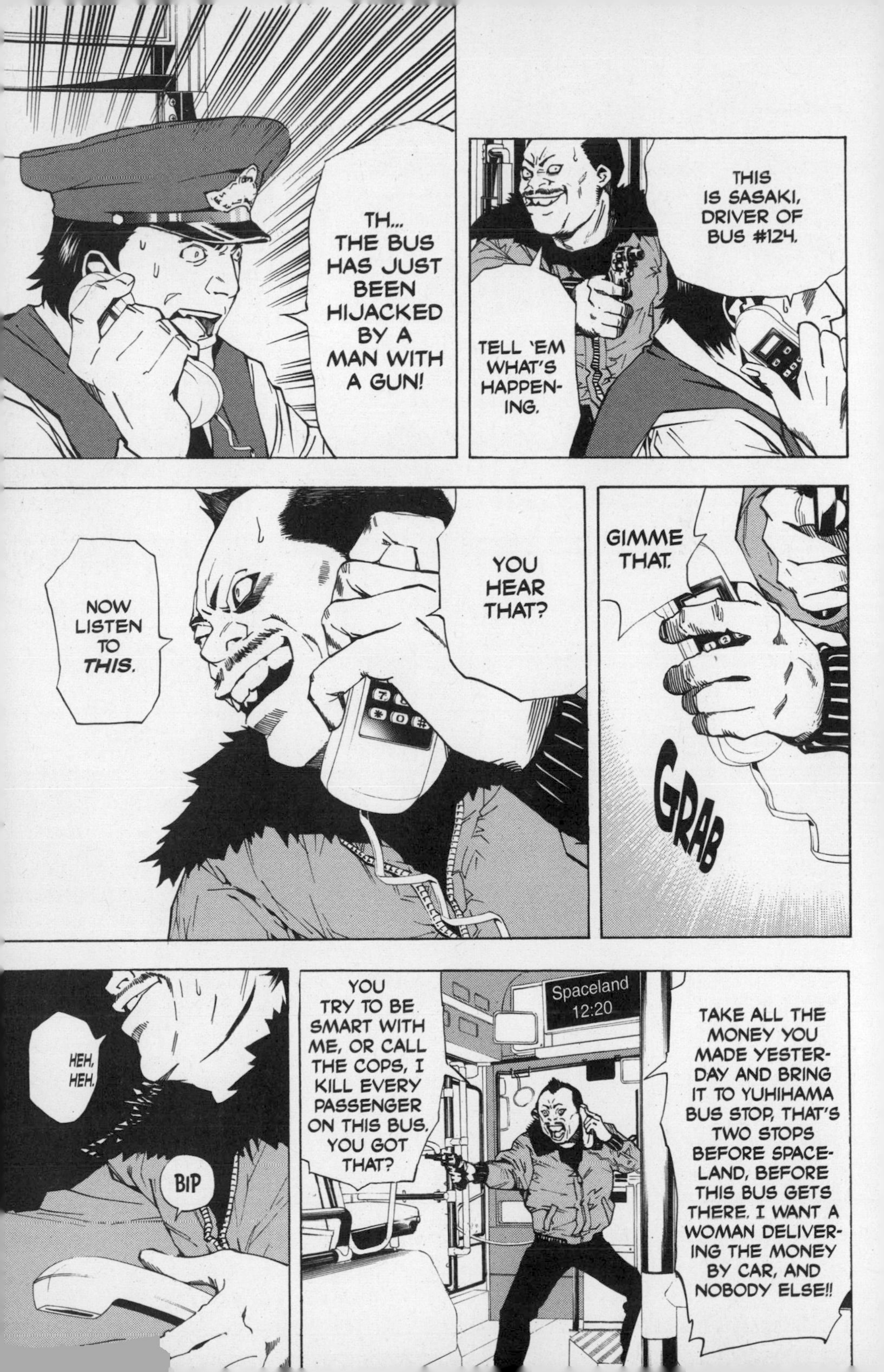
THIS IS SASAKI, DRIVER OF BUS #124.
TELL 'EM WHAT'S HAPPEN- ING.
TH... THE BUS HAS JUST BEEN HIJACKED BY A MAN WITH A GUN!
GIMME THAT.
GRAB
YOU HEAR THAT?
NOW LISTEN TO *THIS.*
Spaceland 12:20
TAKE ALL THE MONEY YOU MADE YESTER- DAY AND BRING IT TO YUHIHAMA BUS STOP, THAT'S TWO STOPS BEFORE SPACE- LAND, BEFORE THIS BUS GETS THERE. I WANT A WOMAN DELIVER- ING THE MONEY BY CAR, AND NOBODY ELSE!!
YOU TRY TO BE SMART WITH ME, OR CALL THE COPS, I KILL EVERY PASSENGER ON THIS BUS. YOU GOT THAT?
HEH, HEH.
BIP

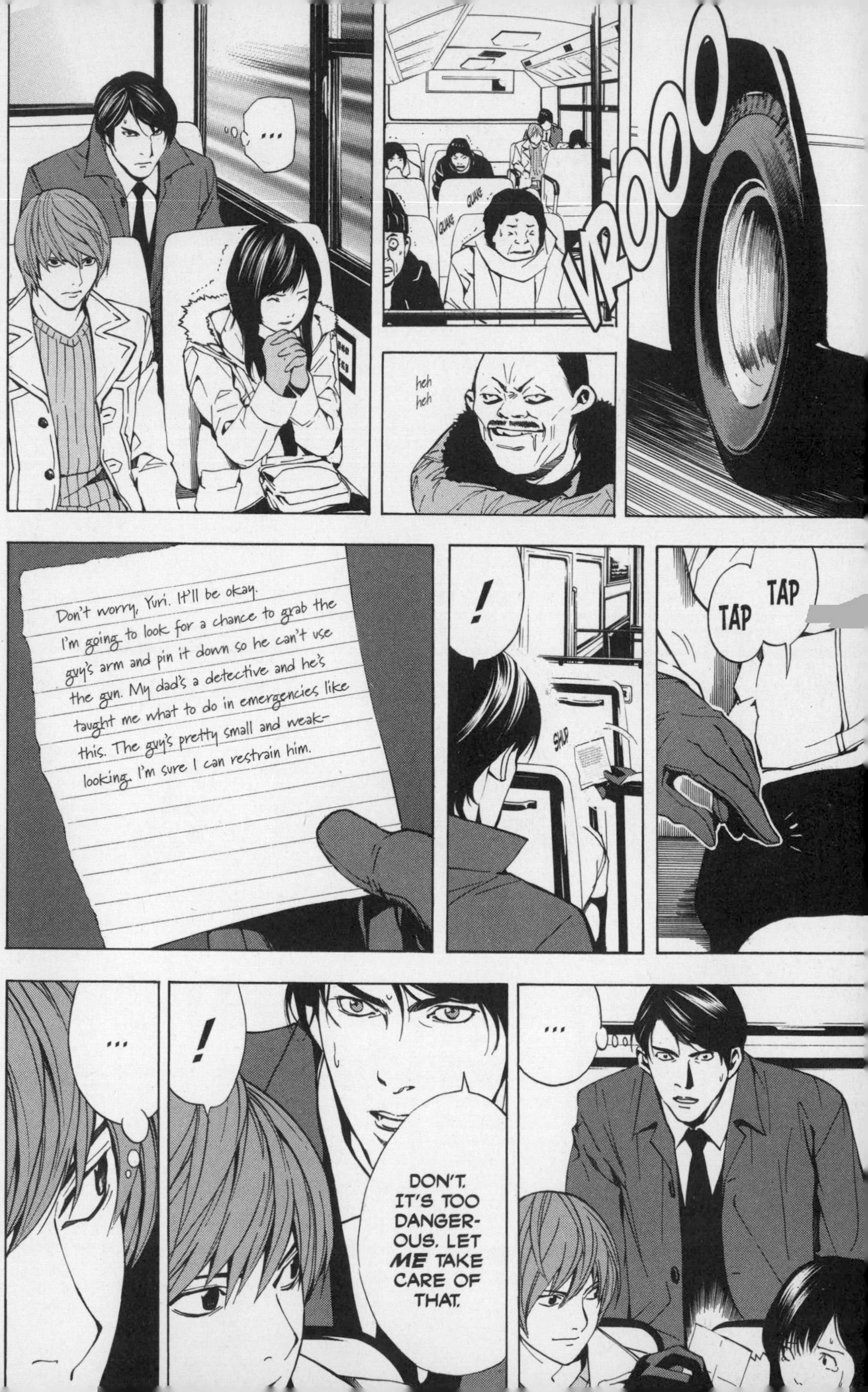
VROOOO
QUAKE
QUAKE
heh heh
...
TAP
TAP
SHUP
!
Don't worry, Yuri. It'll be okay.
I'm going to look for a chance to grab the guy's arm and pin it down so he can't use the gun. My dad's a detective and he's taught me what to do in emergencies like this. The guy's pretty small and weak-looking. I'm sure I can restrain him.
...
!
DON'T. IT'S TOO DANGER-OUS. LET *ME* TAKE CARE OF THAT.
...

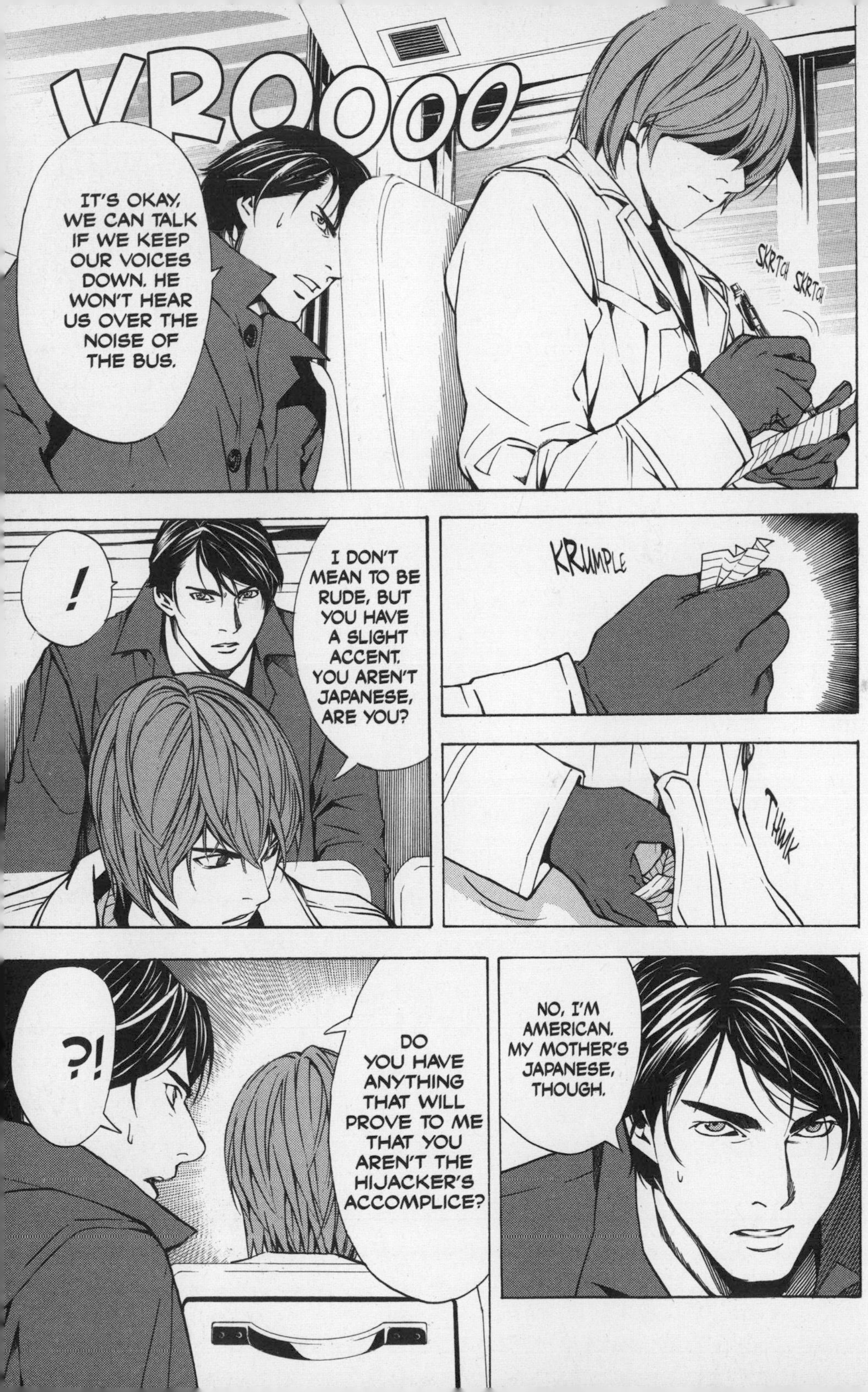
VROOOO
SKRTCH SKRTCH
IT'S OKAY, WE CAN TALK IF WE KEEP OUR VOICES DOWN. HE WON'T HEAR US OVER THE NOISE OF THE BUS.
KRUMPLE
THUNK
I DON'T MEAN TO BE RUDE, BUT YOU HAVE A SLIGHT ACCENT. YOU AREN'T JAPANESE, ARE YOU?
!
NO, I'M AMERICAN. MY MOTHER'S JAPANESE, THOUGH.
DO YOU HAVE ANYTHING THAT WILL PROVE TO ME THAT YOU AREN'T THE HIJACKER'S ACCOMPLICE?
?!

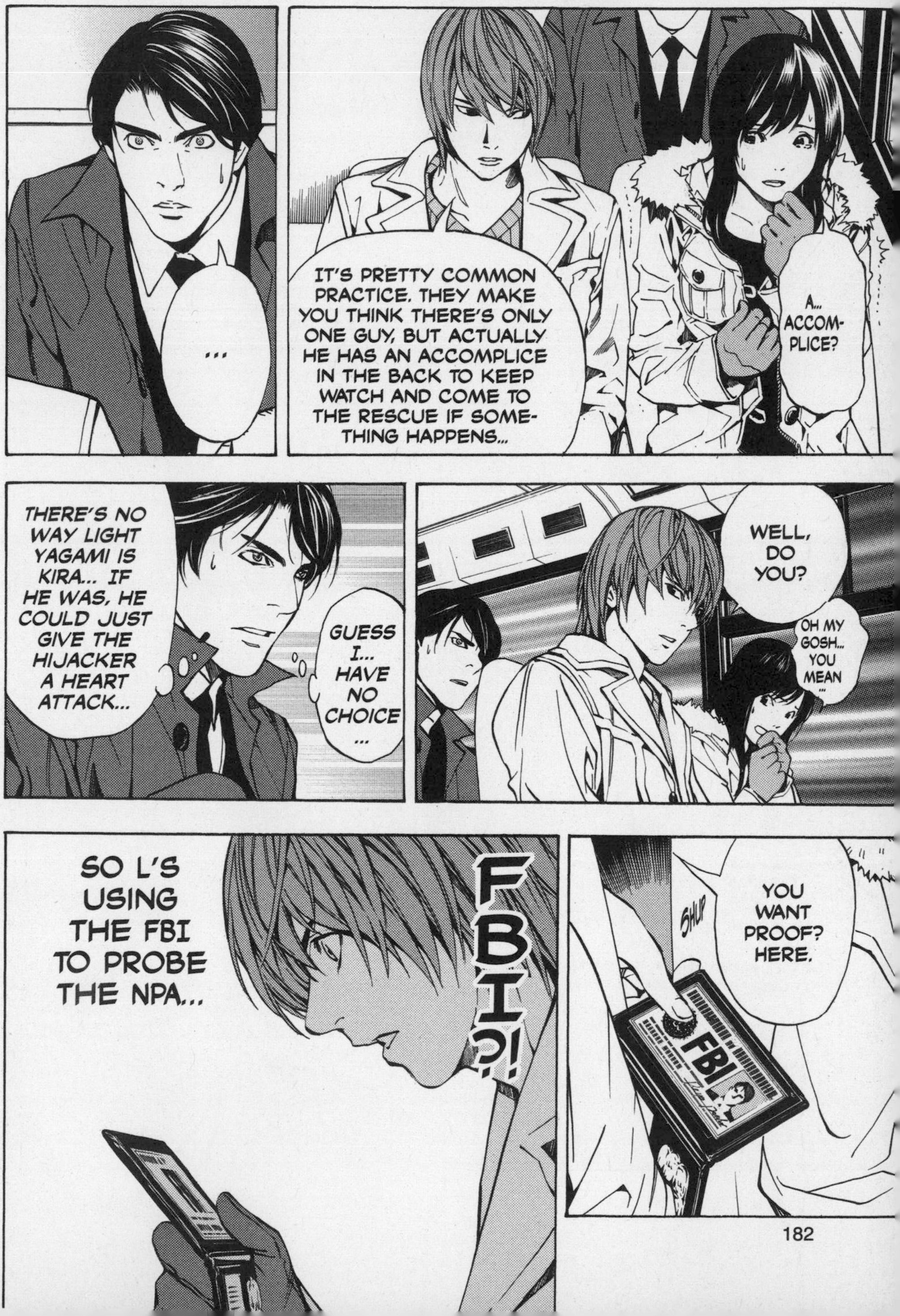
A... ACCOMPLICE?
IT'S PRETTY COMMON PRACTICE. THEY MAKE YOU THINK THERE'S ONLY ONE GUY, BUT ACTUALLY HE HAS AN ACCOMPLICE IN THE BACK TO KEEP WATCH AND COME TO THE RESCUE IF SOMETHING HAPPENS...
...
WELL, DO YOU?
OH MY GOSH... YOU MEAN ...
THERE'S NO WAY LIGHT YAGAMI IS KIRA... IF HE WAS, HE COULD JUST GIVE THE HIJACKER A HEART ATTACK...
GUESS I... HAVE NO CHOICE ...
YOU WANT PROOF? HERE.
SHUP
FBI
FBI?!
SO L'S USING THE FBI TO PROBE THE NPA...

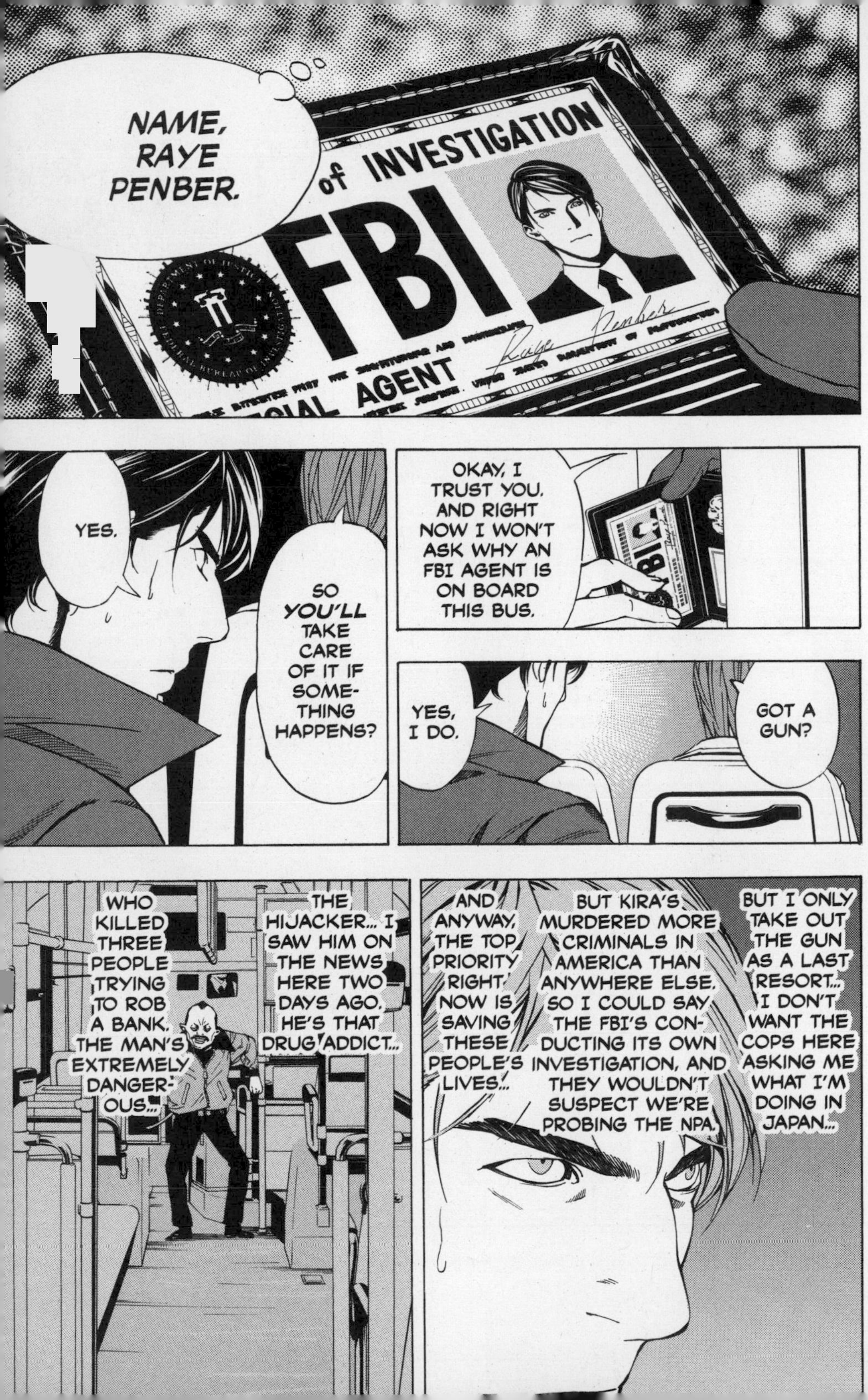
NAME, RAYE PENBER.
of INVESTIGATION
FBI
OKAY, I TRUST YOU. AND RIGHT NOW I WON'T ASK WHY AN FBI AGENT IS ON BOARD THIS BUS.
GOT A GUN?
YES, I DO.
SO *YOU'LL* TAKE CARE OF IT IF SOME-THING HAPPENS?
YES.
BUT I ONLY TAKE OUT THE GUN AS A LAST RESORT... I DON'T WANT THE COPS HERE ASKING ME WHAT I'M DOING IN JAPAN...
BUT KIRA'S MURDERED MORE CRIMINALS IN AMERICA THAN ANYWHERE ELSE, SO I COULD SAY THE FBI'S CON-DUCTING ITS OWN INVESTIGATION, AND THEY WOULDN'T SUSPECT WE'RE PROBING THE NPA.
AND ANYWAY, THE TOP PRIORITY RIGHT NOW IS SAVING THESE PEOPLE'S LIVES...
THE HIJACKER... I SAW HIM ON THE NEWS HERE TWO DAYS AGO. HE'S THAT DRUG ADDICT...
WHO KILLED THREE PEOPLE TRYING TO ROB A BANK. THE MAN'S EXTREMELY DANGER-OUS...

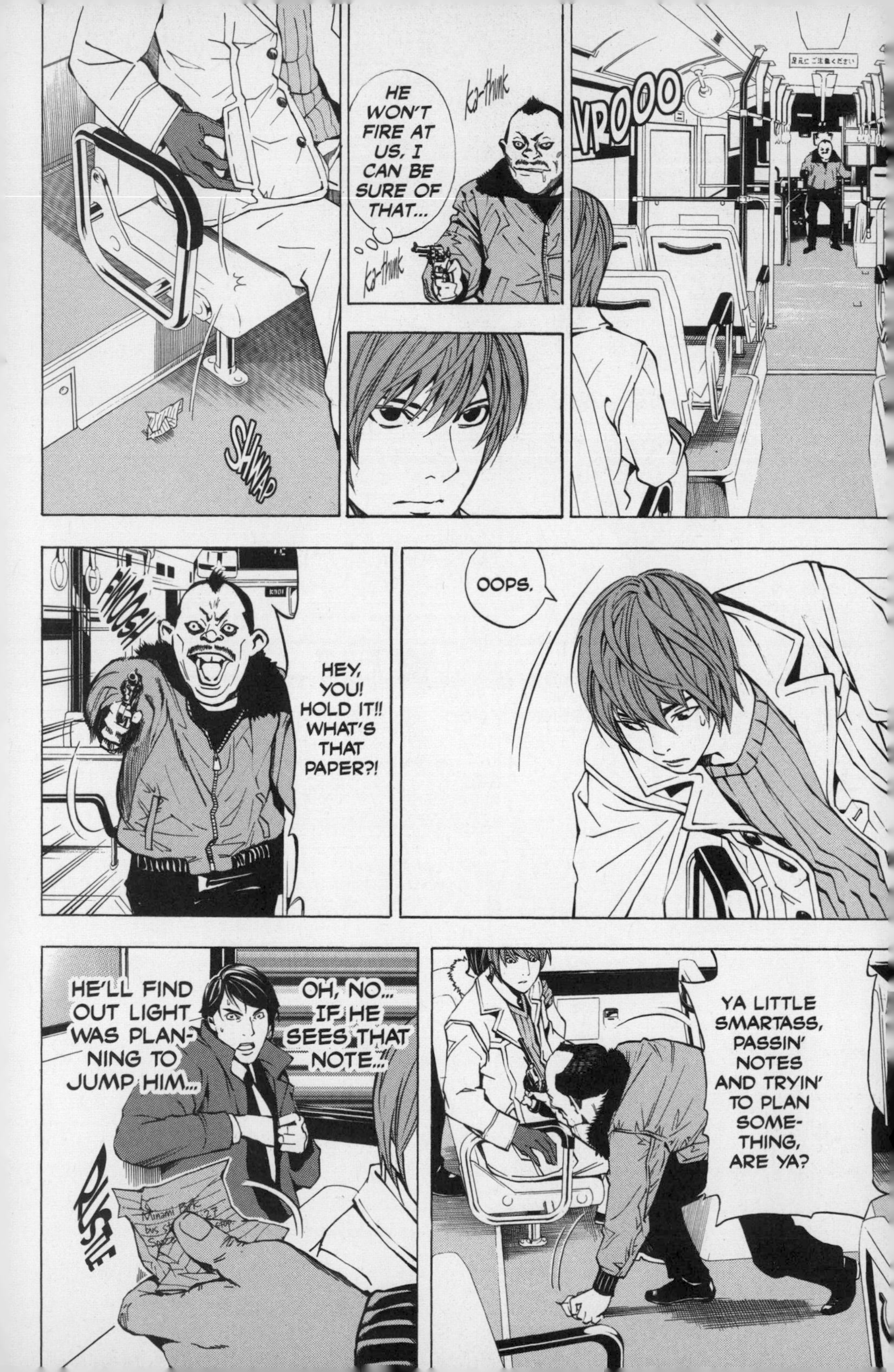
VROOO
HE WON'T FIRE AT US, I CAN BE SURE OF THAT...
ka-thunk
ka-thunk
SHWAP
OOPS.
FWOOSH
HEY, YOU! HOLD IT!! WHAT'S THAT PAPER?!
YA LITTLE SMARTASS, PASSIN' NOTES AND TRYIN' TO PLAN SOME-THING, ARE YA?
OH, NO... IF HE SEES THAT NOTE...
HE'LL FIND OUT LIGHT WAS PLAN-NING TO JUMP HIM...
RUSTLE

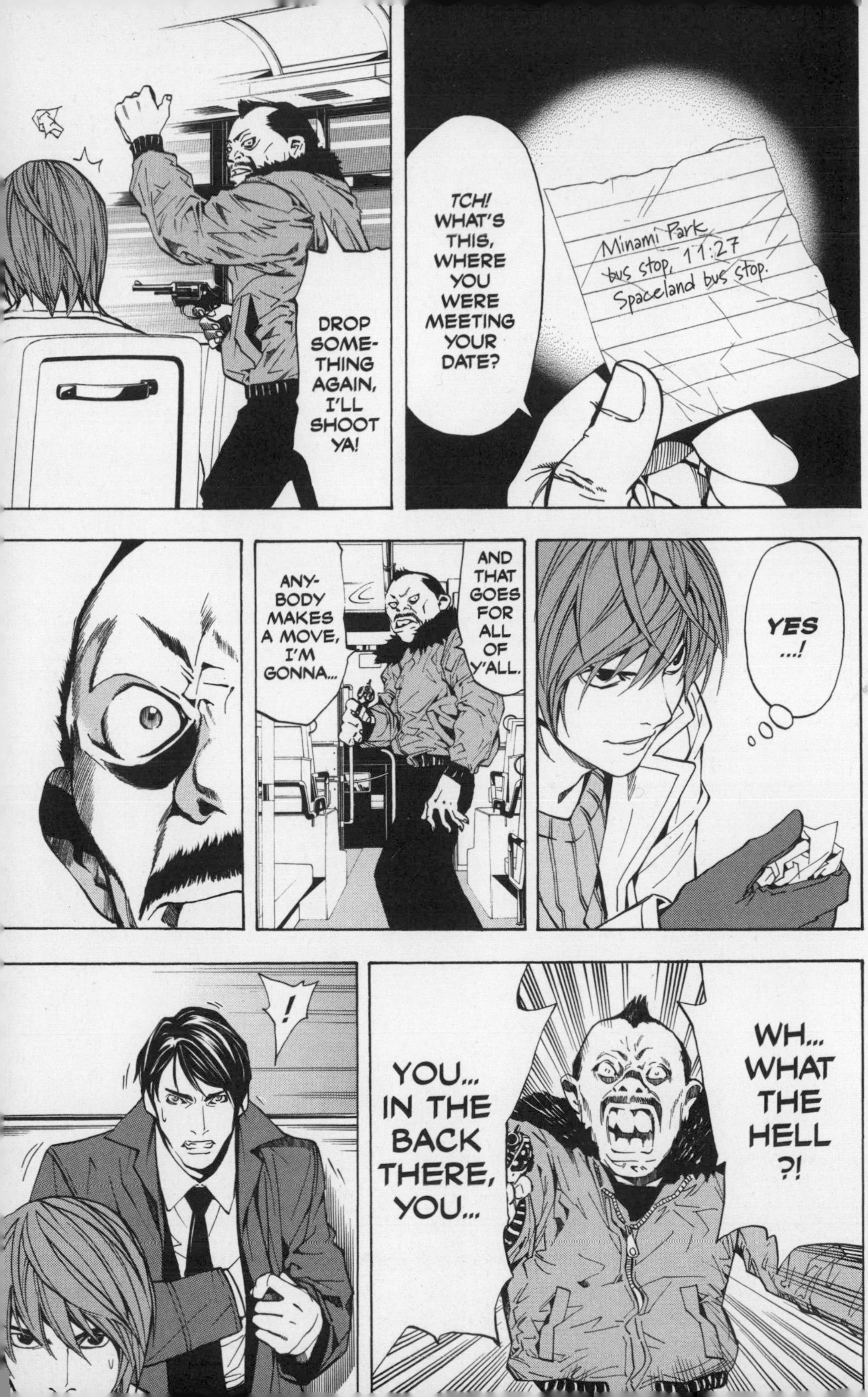
Minami Park bus stop, 11:27 Spaceland bus stop.
TCH! WHAT'S THIS, WHERE YOU WERE MEETING YOUR DATE?
DROP SOME-THING AGAIN, I'LL SHOOT YA!
YES ...!
AND THAT GOES FOR ALL OF Y'ALL.
ANY-BODY MAKES A MOVE, I'M GONNA...
WH... WHAT THE HELL ?!
YOU... IN THE BACK THERE, YOU...
!

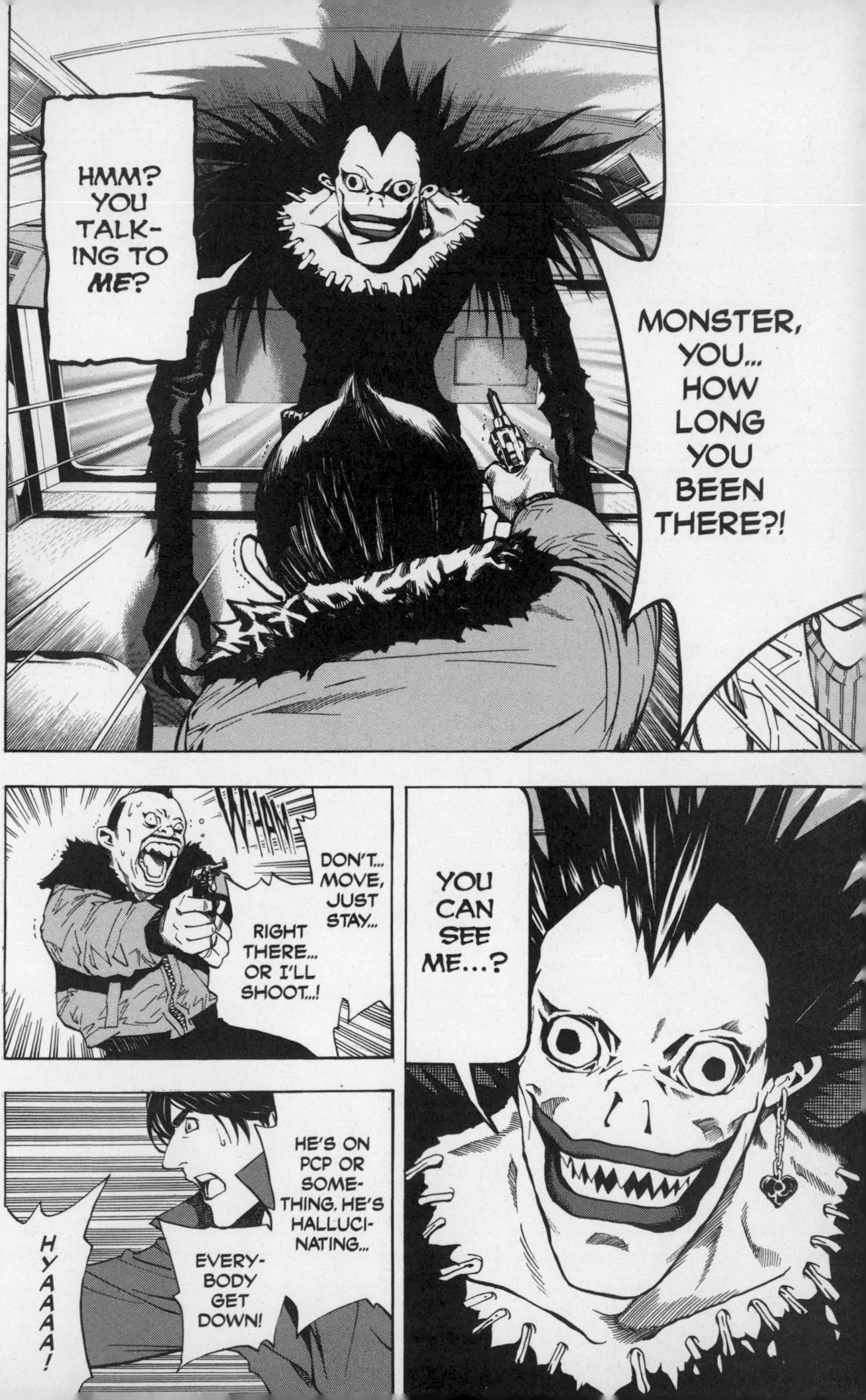
MONSTER, YOU... HOW LONG YOU BEEN THERE?!
HMM? YOU TALKING-ING TO *ME*?
YOU CAN SEE ME...?
WHAM
DON'T... MOVE, JUST STAY...
RIGHT THERE... OR I'LL SHOOT...!
HYAAAAA!
HE'S ON PCP OR SOME-THING. HE'S HALLUCI-NATING...
EVERY-BODY GET DOWN!

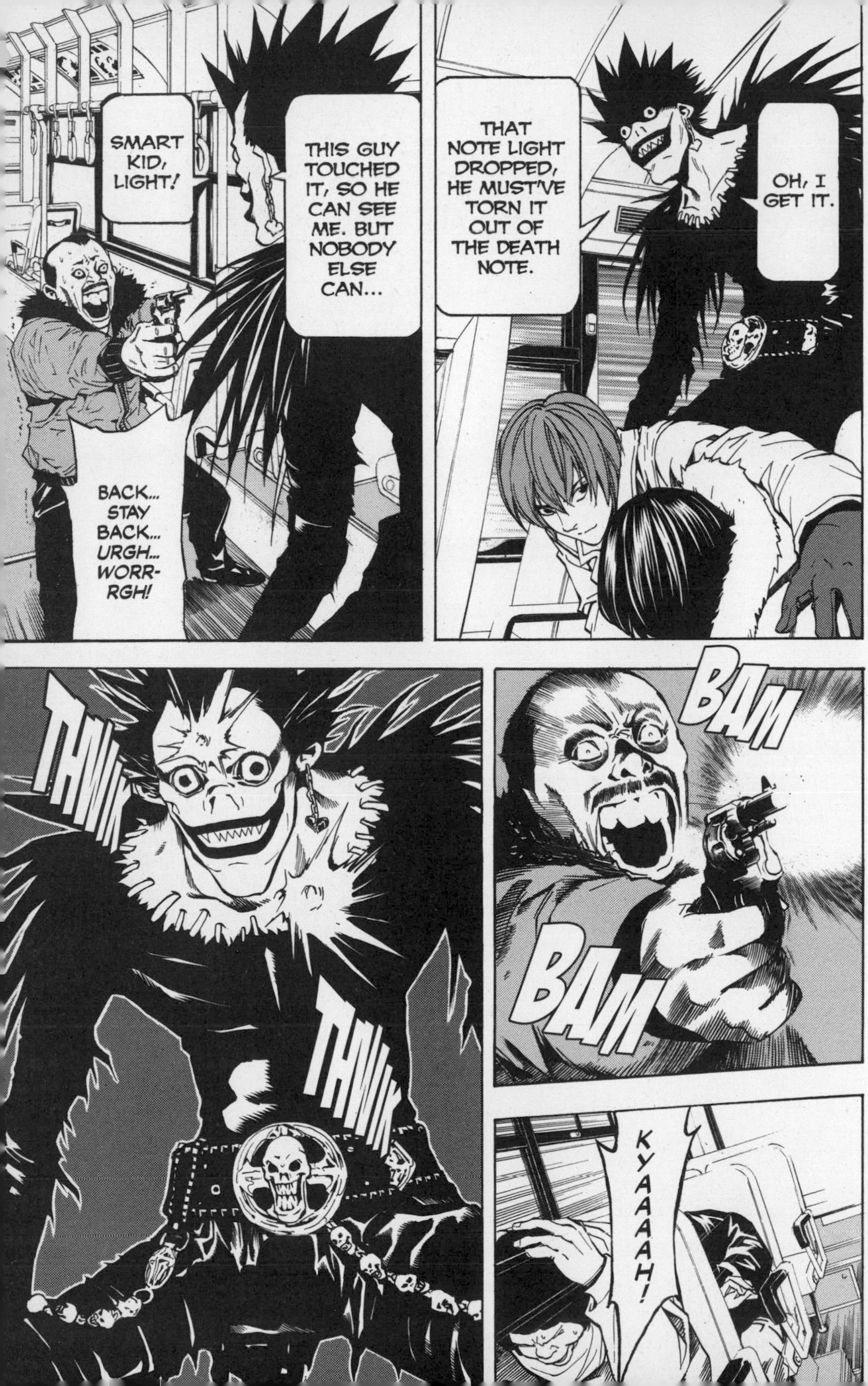
OH, I GET IT.
THAT NOTE LIGHT DROPPED, HE MUST'VE TORN IT OUT OF THE DEATH NOTE.
THIS GUY TOUCHED IT, SO HE CAN SEE ME. BUT NOBODY ELSE CAN...
SMART KID, LIGHT!
BACK... STAY BACK... URGH... WORRRGH!
BAM
BAM
KYAAAAH!
THWIK
THWIK

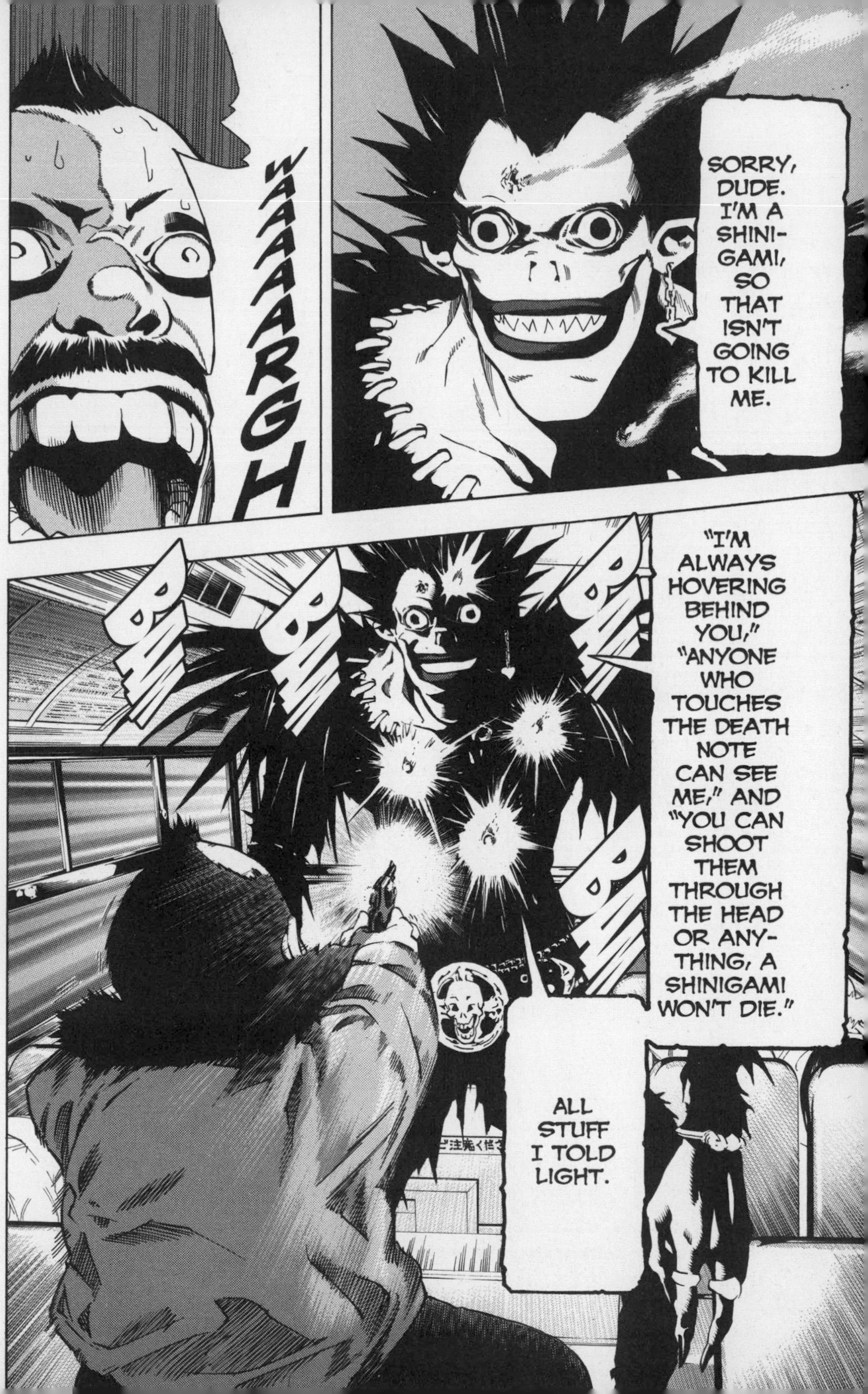
SORRY, DUDE. I'M A SHINI-GAMI, SO THAT ISN'T GOING TO KILL ME.
WAAAAARGH
"I'M ALWAYS HOVERING BEHIND YOU," "ANYONE WHO TOUCHES THE DEATH NOTE CAN SEE ME," AND "YOU CAN SHOOT THEM THROUGH THE HEAD OR ANY-THING, A SHINIGAMI WON'T DIE."
BLAM
BLAM
BLAM
BLAM
ALL STUFF I TOLD LIGHT.

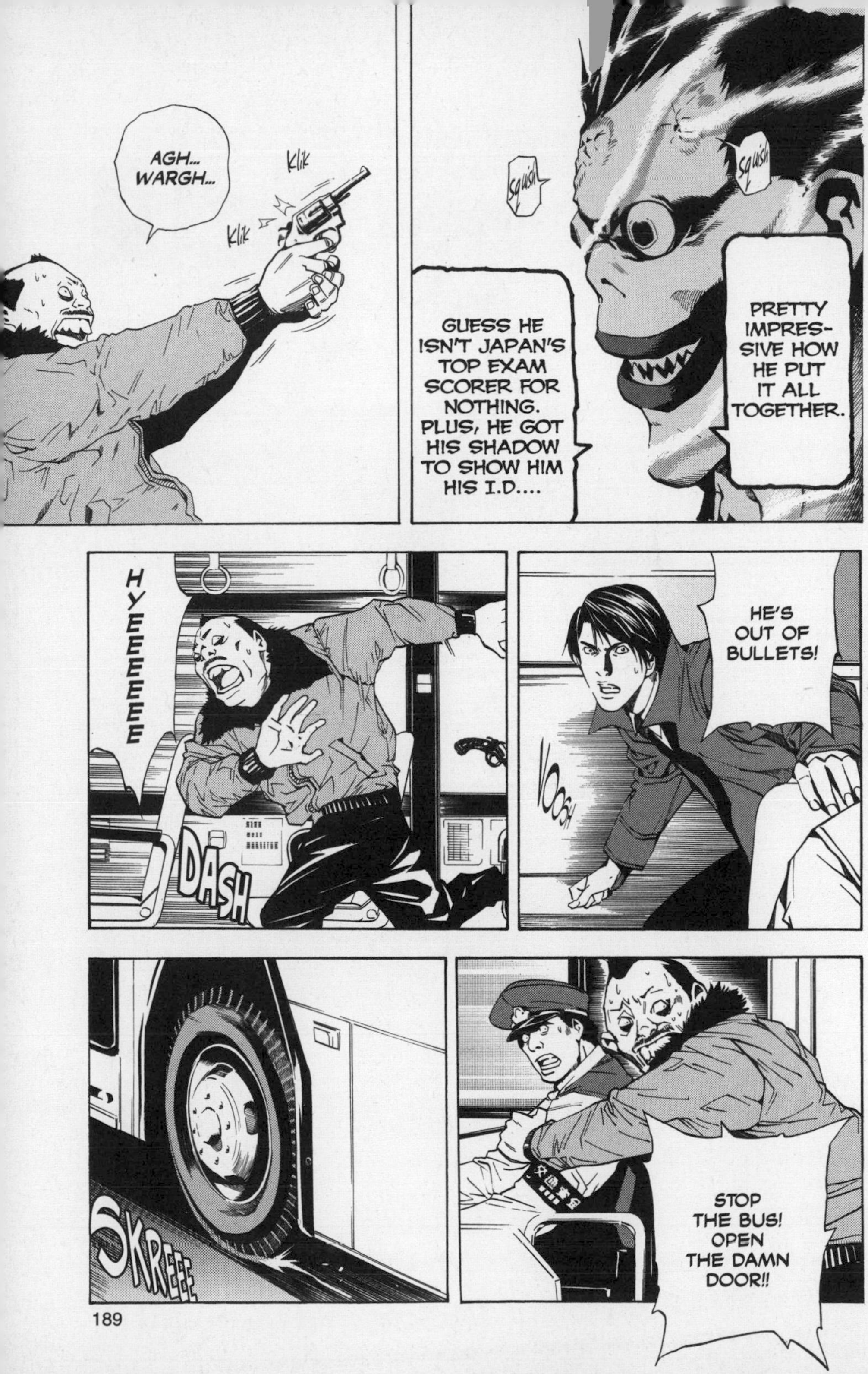
squish
squish
PRETTY IMPRESSIVE HOW HE PUT IT ALL TOGETHER.
GUESS HE ISN'T JAPAN'S TOP EXAM SCORER FOR NOTHING. PLUS, HE GOT HIS SHADOW TO SHOW HIM HIS I.D....
AGH... WARGH...
Klik
Klik
HE'S OUT OF BULLETS!
VOOSH
HYEEEEEEE
DASH
STOP THE BUS! OPEN THE DAMN DOOR!!
SKREEEE

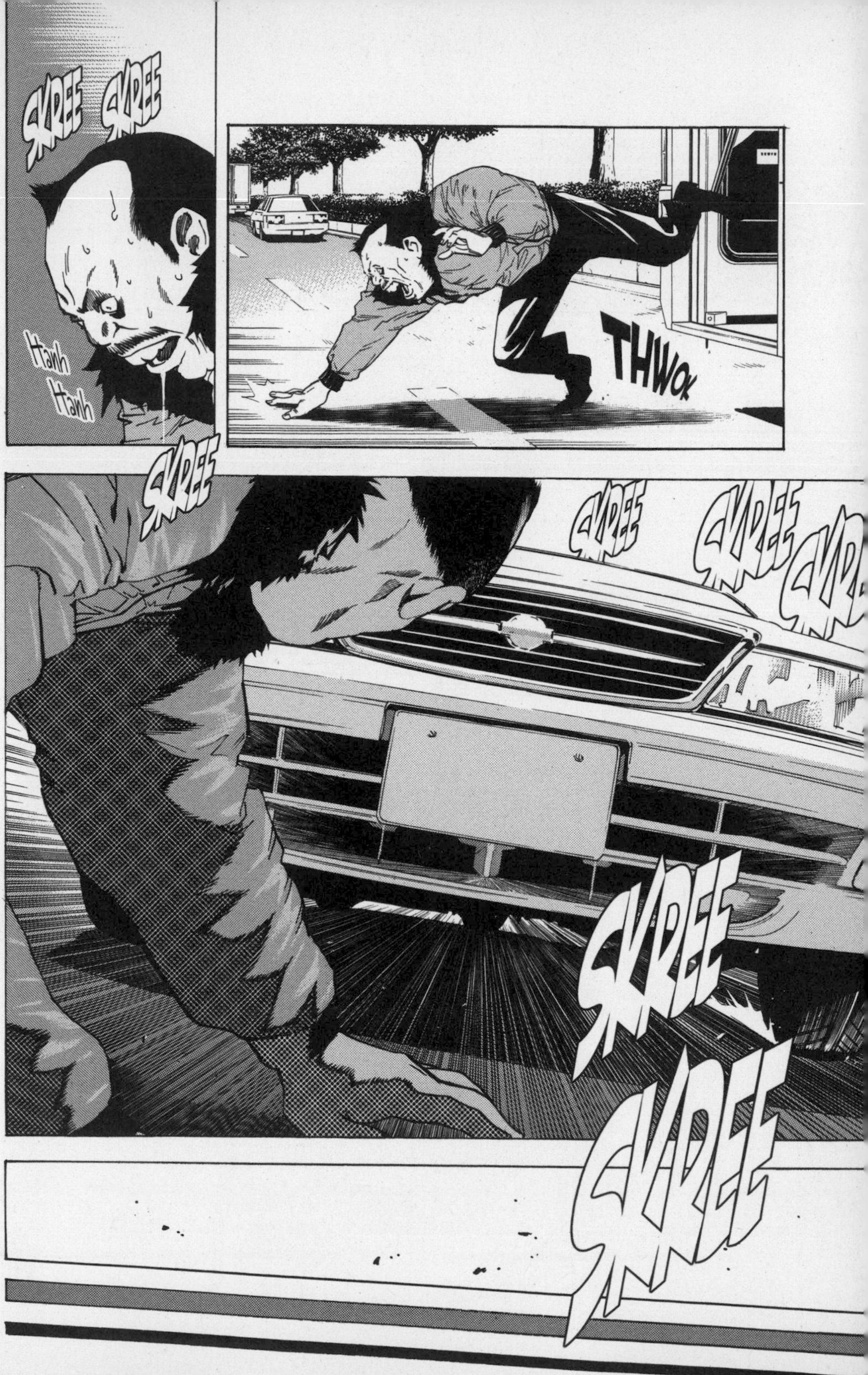
THWOK
SKREE SKREE
Hanh Hanh
SKREE
SKREE SKREE SKREE
SKREE
SKREE

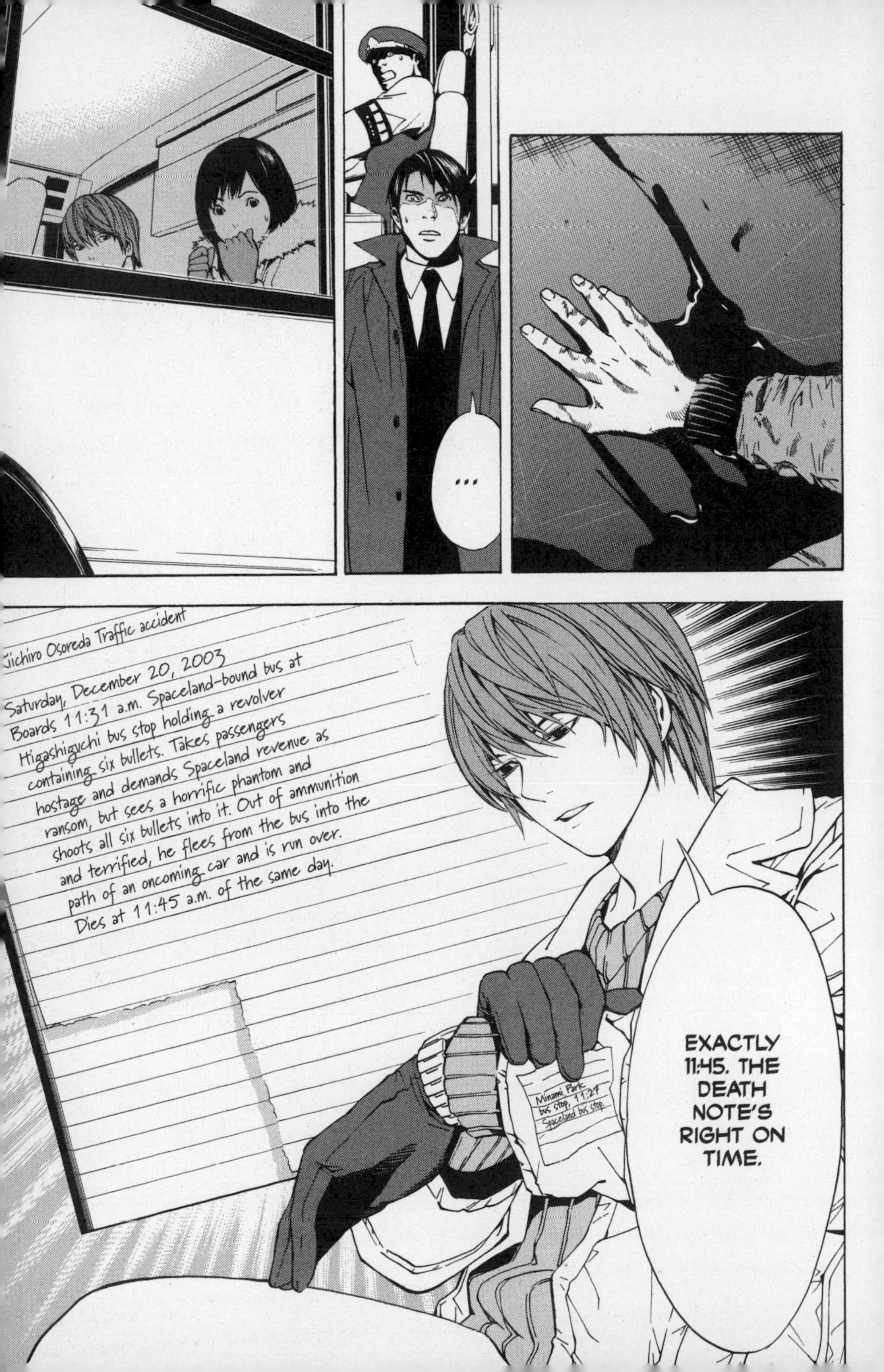
...
Kiichiro Osoreda Traffic accident
Saturday, December 20, 2003
Boards 11:31 a.m. Spaceland-bound bus at Higashiguchi bus stop holding a revolver containing six bullets. Takes passengers hostage and demands Spaceland revenue as ransom, but sees a horrific phantom and shoots all six bullets into it. Out of ammunition and terrified, he flees from the bus into the path of an oncoming car and is run over. Dies at 11:45 a.m. of the same day.
Minami Park bus stop, 11:27 Spaceland bus stop.
EXACTLY 11:45. THE DEATH NOTE'S RIGHT ON TIME.

# DEATH NOTE
## How to use it

### VII

○ One page taken from the DEATH NOTE, or even a fragment of the page, contains the full effects of the note.

デスノートから切り取った1ページやその切れ端でも全て、
デスノートの特性が有効である。

○ The instrument to write with can be anything, ((e.g. cosmetics, blood, etc)) as long as it can write directly onto the note and remains as legible letters.

文字として残る物であれば、書く道具はノートに直に書き込みさえすれば
何でもよい。化粧品や血でも構わない。

○ Even the original owners of the DEATH NOTE, gods of death, do not know much about the note.

デスノートについて、わからない事は元持ち主の死神でも沢山ある。

I hear that the comic version of *Death Note* will first
hit Japanese bookstores on April 2, 2004.

Snowmelt flows into streams
And below the dancing petals of cherry blossoms
Stirred up by the spring wind
First graders, brightly colored with their shiny leather backpacks,
Hold hands and step out toward hope on the green.

-Tsugumi Ohba

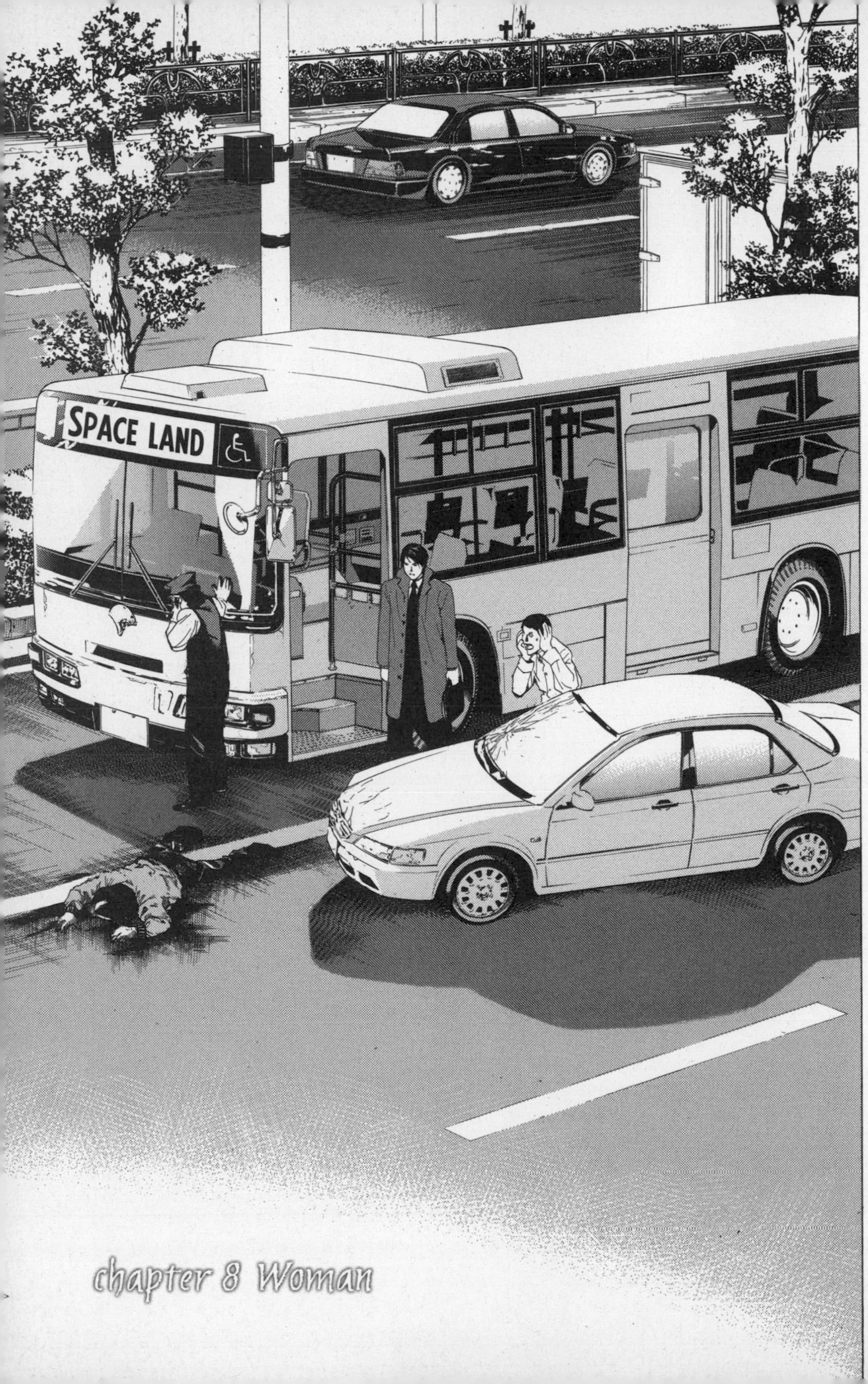
SPACE LAND

# chapter 8 Woman

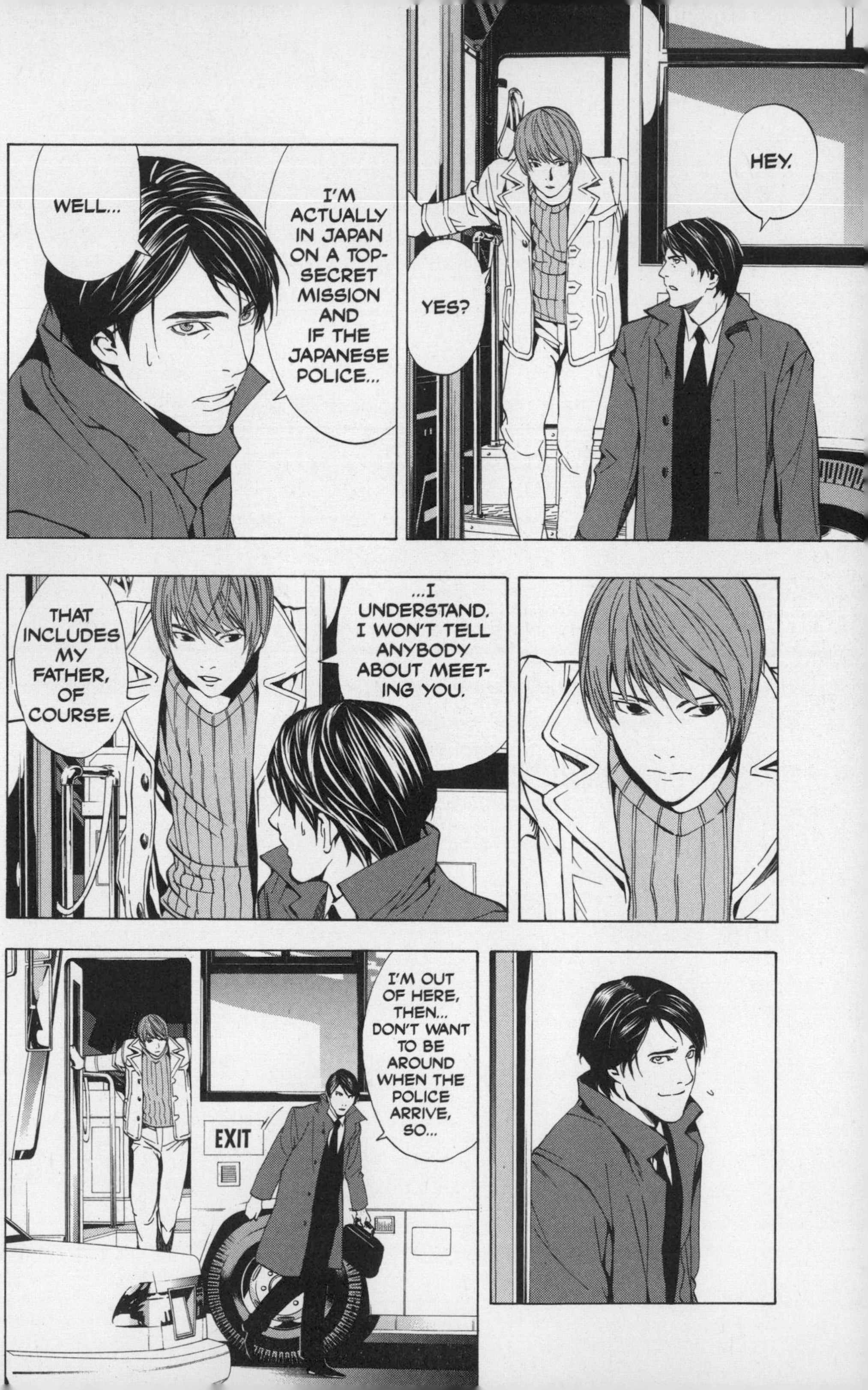
HEY.
YES?
I'M ACTUALLY IN JAPAN ON A TOP-SECRET MISSION AND IF THE JAPANESE POLICE...
WELL...
...I UNDERSTAND. I WON'T TELL ANYBODY ABOUT MEET-ING YOU.
THAT INCLUDES MY FATHER, OF COURSE.
I'M OUT OF HERE, THEN... DON'T WANT TO BE AROUND WHEN THE POLICE ARRIVE, SO...
EXIT

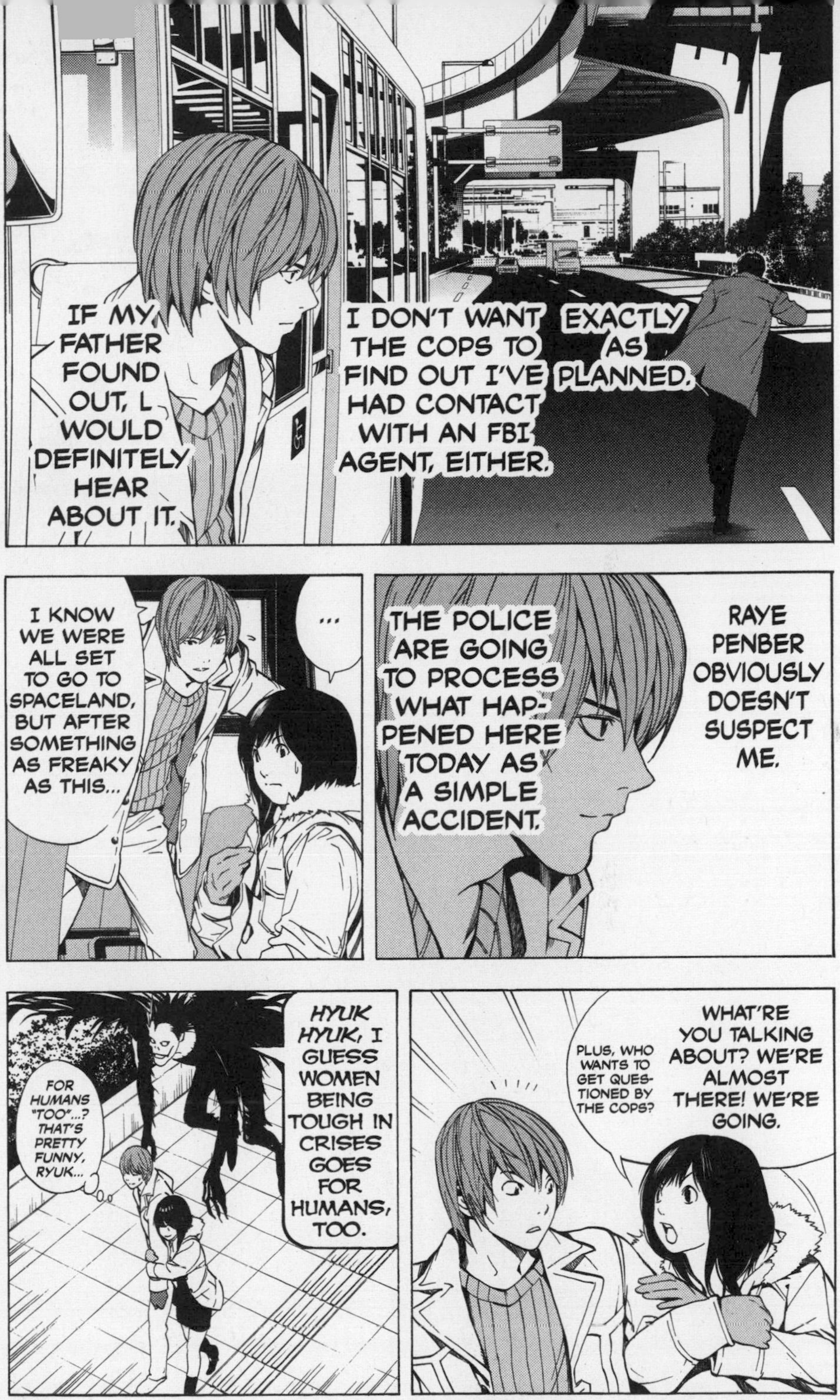
EXACTLY AS PLANNED.
I DON'T WANT THE COPS TO FIND OUT I'VE HAD CONTACT WITH AN FBI AGENT, EITHER.
IF MY FATHER FOUND OUT, L WOULD DEFINITELY HEAR ABOUT IT.
RAYE PENBER OBVIOUSLY DOESN'T SUSPECT ME.
THE POLICE ARE GOING TO PROCESS WHAT HAP-PENED HERE TODAY AS A SIMPLE ACCIDENT.
...
I KNOW WE WERE ALL SET TO GO TO SPACELAND, BUT AFTER SOMETHING AS FREAKY AS THIS...
WHAT'RE YOU TALKING ABOUT? WE'RE ALMOST THERE! WE'RE GOING.
PLUS, WHO WANTS TO GET QUES-TIONED BY THE COPS?
*HYUK HYUK*, I GUESS WOMEN BEING TOUGH IN CRISES GOES FOR HUMANS, TOO.
FOR HUMANS "TOO"...? THAT'S PRETTY FUNNY, RYUK...

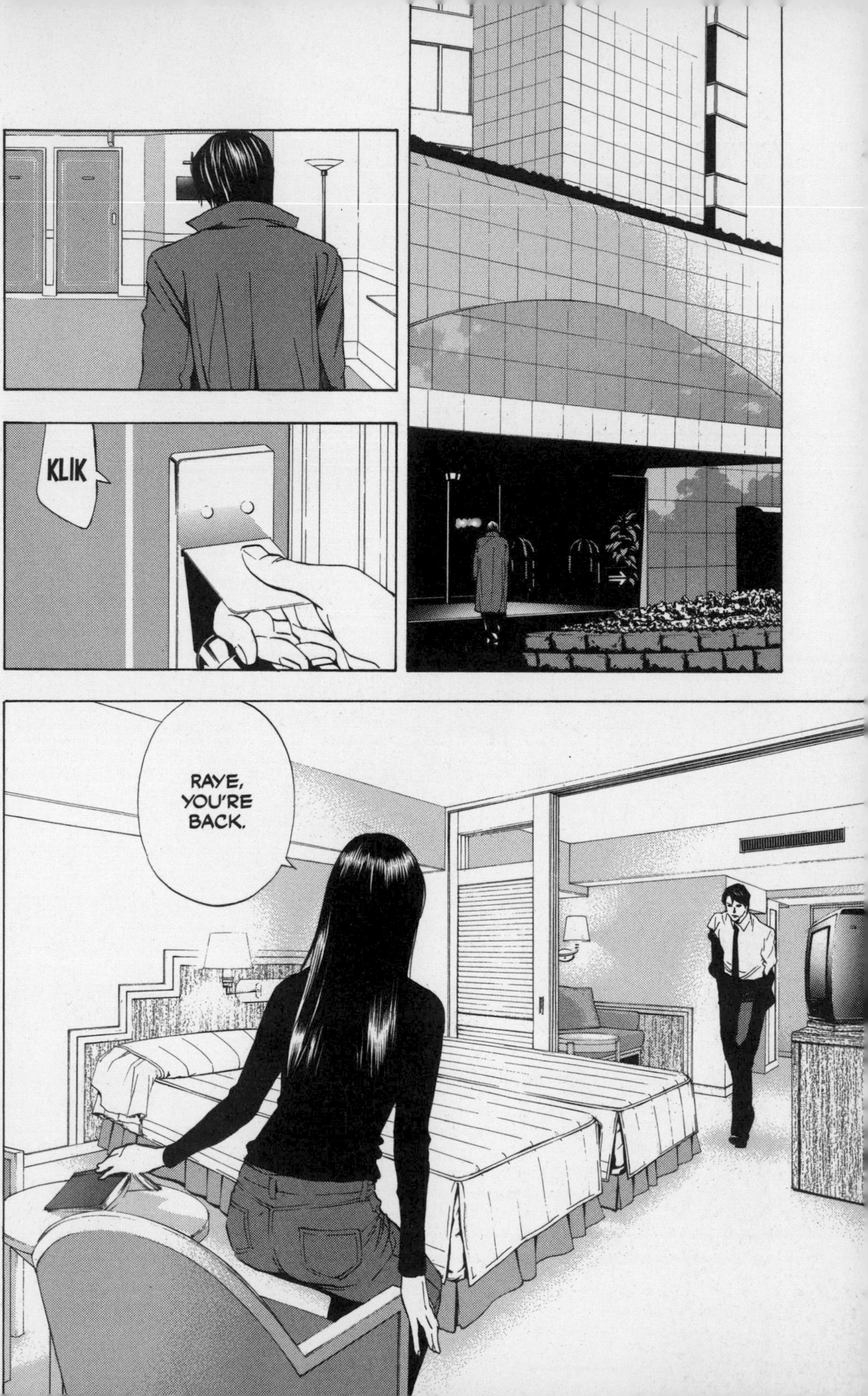
KLIK
RAYE, YOU'RE BACK.

READ THIS WAY

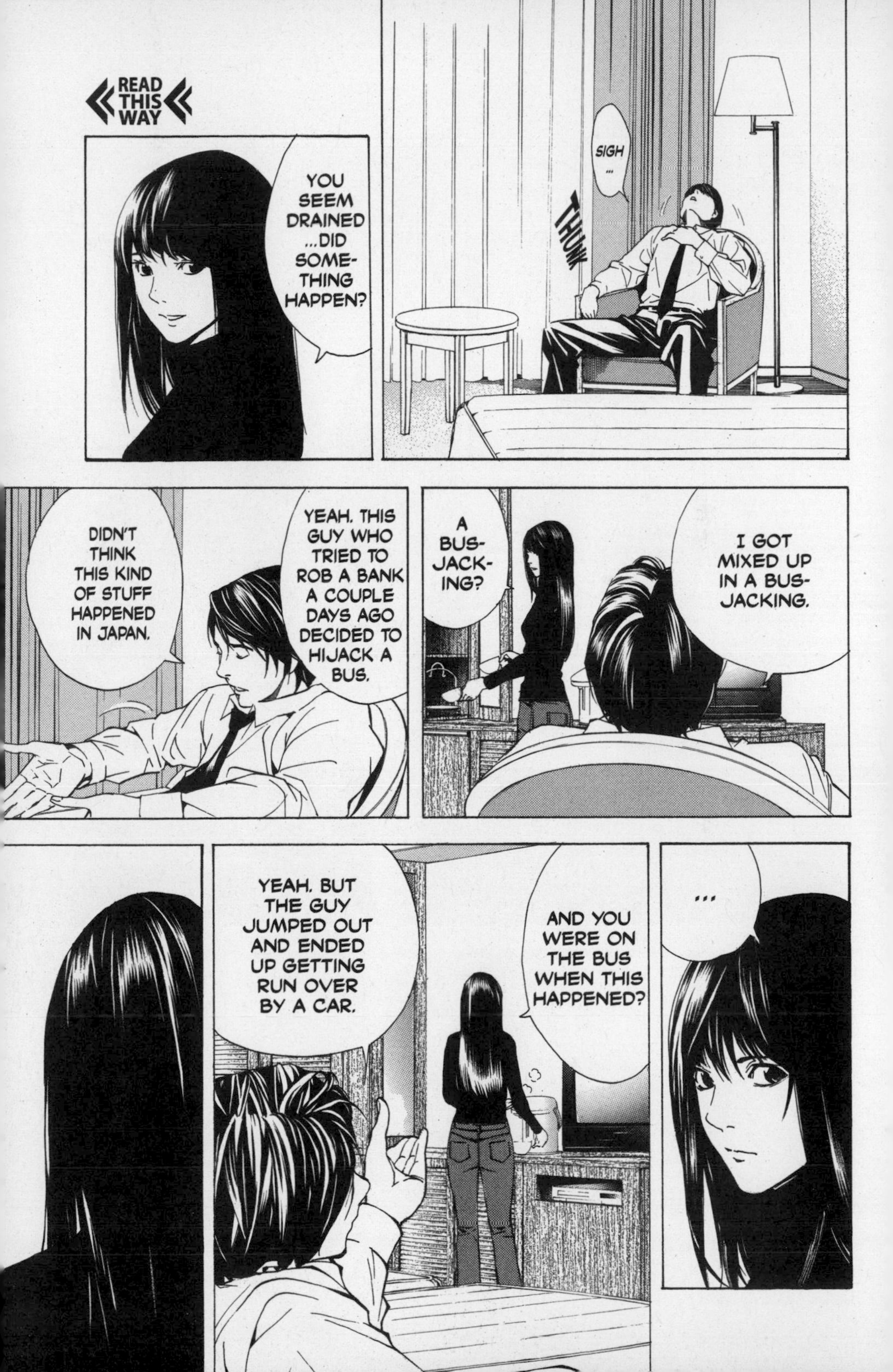
THUNK
SIGH ...
YOU SEEM DRAINED ...DID SOMETHING HAPPEN?
I GOT MIXED UP IN A BUS-JACKING.
A BUS-JACKING?
YEAH. THIS GUY WHO TRIED TO ROB A BANK A COUPLE DAYS AGO DECIDED TO HIJACK A BUS.
DIDN'T THINK THIS KIND OF STUFF HAPPENED IN JAPAN.
...
AND YOU WERE ON THE BUS WHEN THIS HAPPENED?
YEAH. BUT THE GUY JUMPED OUT AND ENDED UP GETTING RUN OVER BY A CAR.

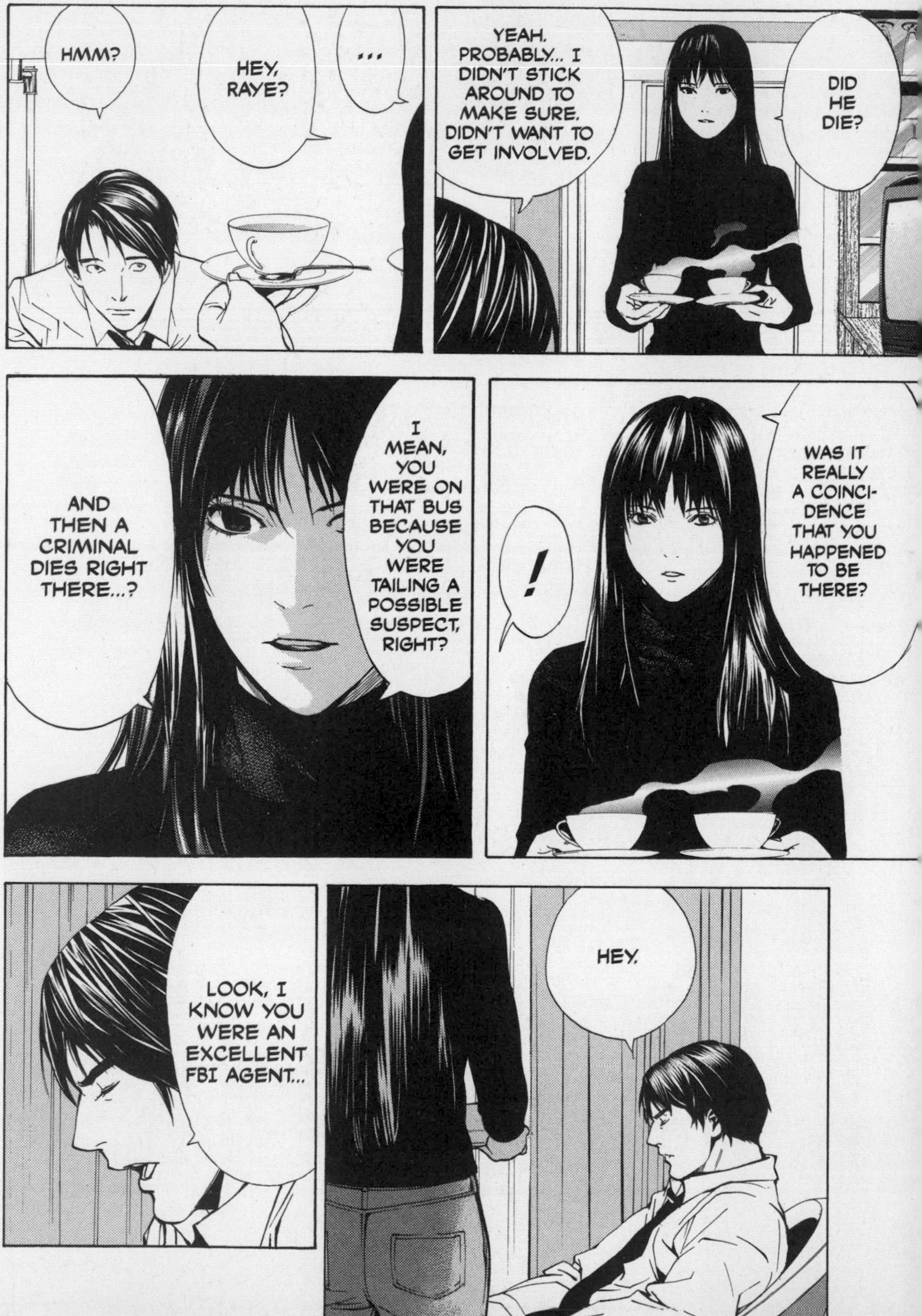
DID HE DIE?
YEAH. PROBABLY... I DIDN'T STICK AROUND TO MAKE SURE. DIDN'T WANT TO GET INVOLVED.
...
HEY, RAYE?
HMM?
WAS IT REALLY A COINCIDENCE THAT YOU HAPPENED TO BE THERE?
!
I MEAN, YOU WERE ON THAT BUS BECAUSE YOU WERE TAILING A POSSIBLE SUSPECT, RIGHT?
AND THEN A CRIMINAL DIES RIGHT THERE...?
HEY.
LOOK, I KNOW YOU WERE AN EXCELLENT FBI AGENT...

READ THIS WAY

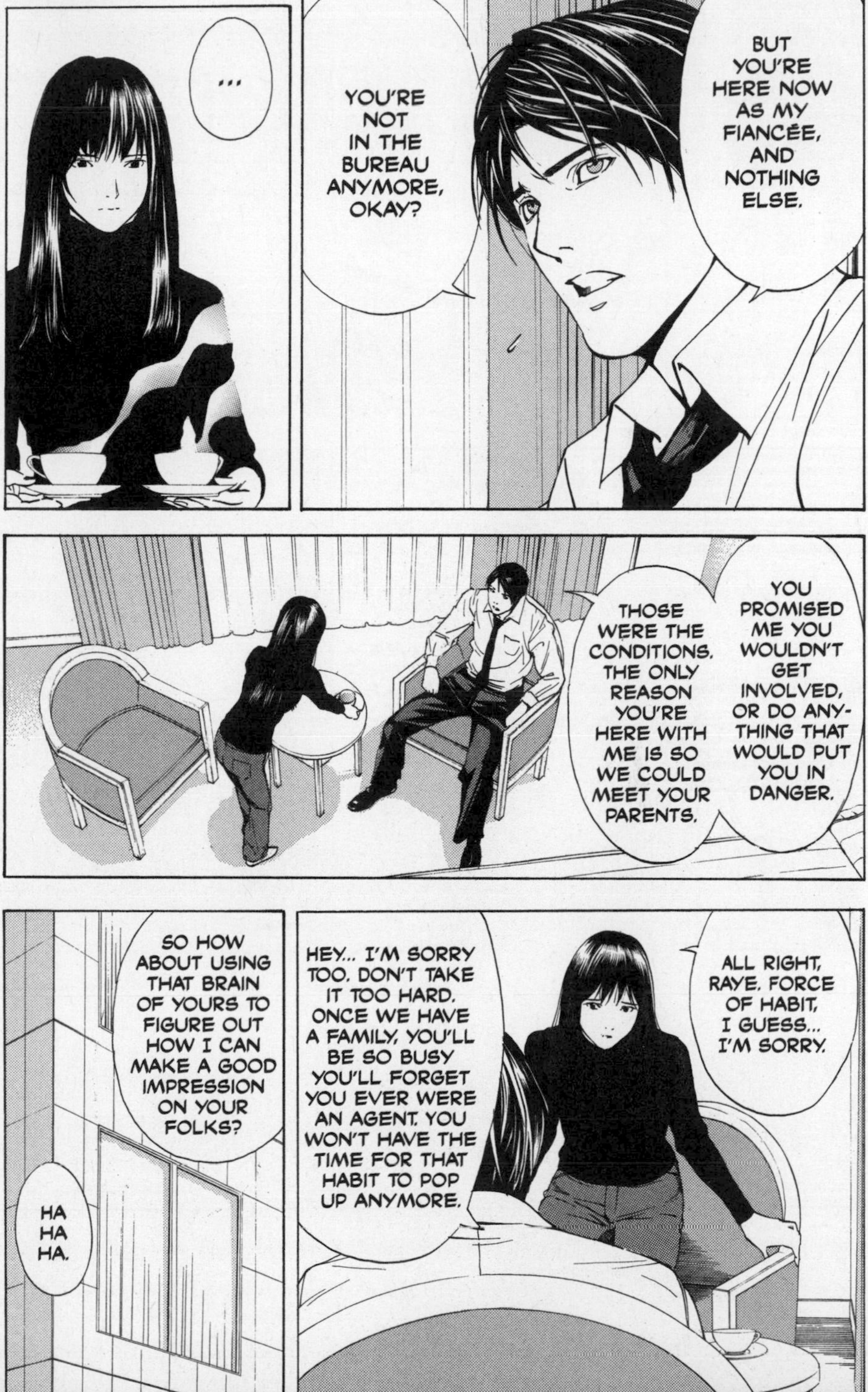
BUT YOU'RE HERE NOW AS MY FIANCÉE, AND NOTHING ELSE.
YOU'RE NOT IN THE BUREAU ANYMORE, OKAY?
...
YOU PROMISED ME YOU WOULDN'T GET INVOLVED, OR DO ANY-THING THAT WOULD PUT YOU IN DANGER.
THOSE WERE THE CONDITIONS. THE ONLY REASON YOU'RE HERE WITH ME IS SO WE COULD MEET YOUR PARENTS.
ALL RIGHT, RAYE. FORCE OF HABIT, I GUESS... I'M SORRY.
HEY... I'M SORRY TOO. DON'T TAKE IT TOO HARD. ONCE WE HAVE A FAMILY, YOU'LL BE SO BUSY YOU'LL FORGET YOU EVER WERE AN AGENT. YOU WON'T HAVE THE TIME FOR THAT HABIT TO POP UP ANYMORE.
SO HOW ABOUT USING THAT BRAIN OF YOURS TO FIGURE OUT HOW I CAN MAKE A GOOD IMPRESSION ON YOUR FOLKS?
HA HA HA.

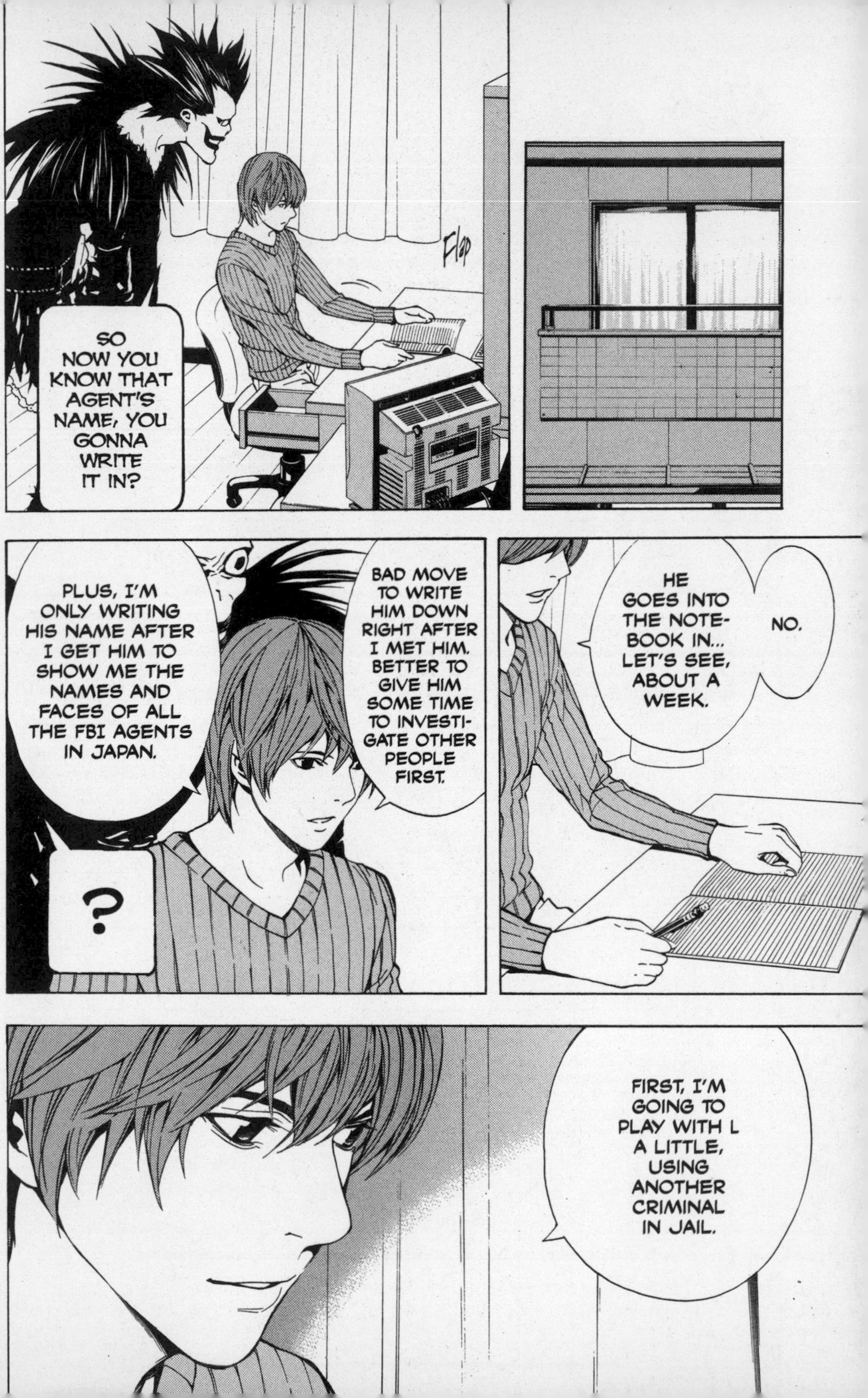
Flap
SO NOW YOU KNOW THAT AGENT'S NAME, YOU GONNA WRITE IT IN?
NO.
HE GOES INTO THE NOTE-BOOK IN... LET'S SEE, ABOUT A WEEK.
BAD MOVE TO WRITE HIM DOWN RIGHT AFTER I MET HIM. BETTER TO GIVE HIM SOME TIME TO INVESTI-GATE OTHER PEOPLE FIRST.
PLUS, I'M ONLY WRITING HIS NAME AFTER I GET HIM TO SHOW ME THE NAMES AND FACES OF ALL THE FBI AGENTS IN JAPAN.
?
FIRST, I'M GOING TO PLAY WITH L A LITTLE, USING ANOTHER CRIMINAL IN JAIL.

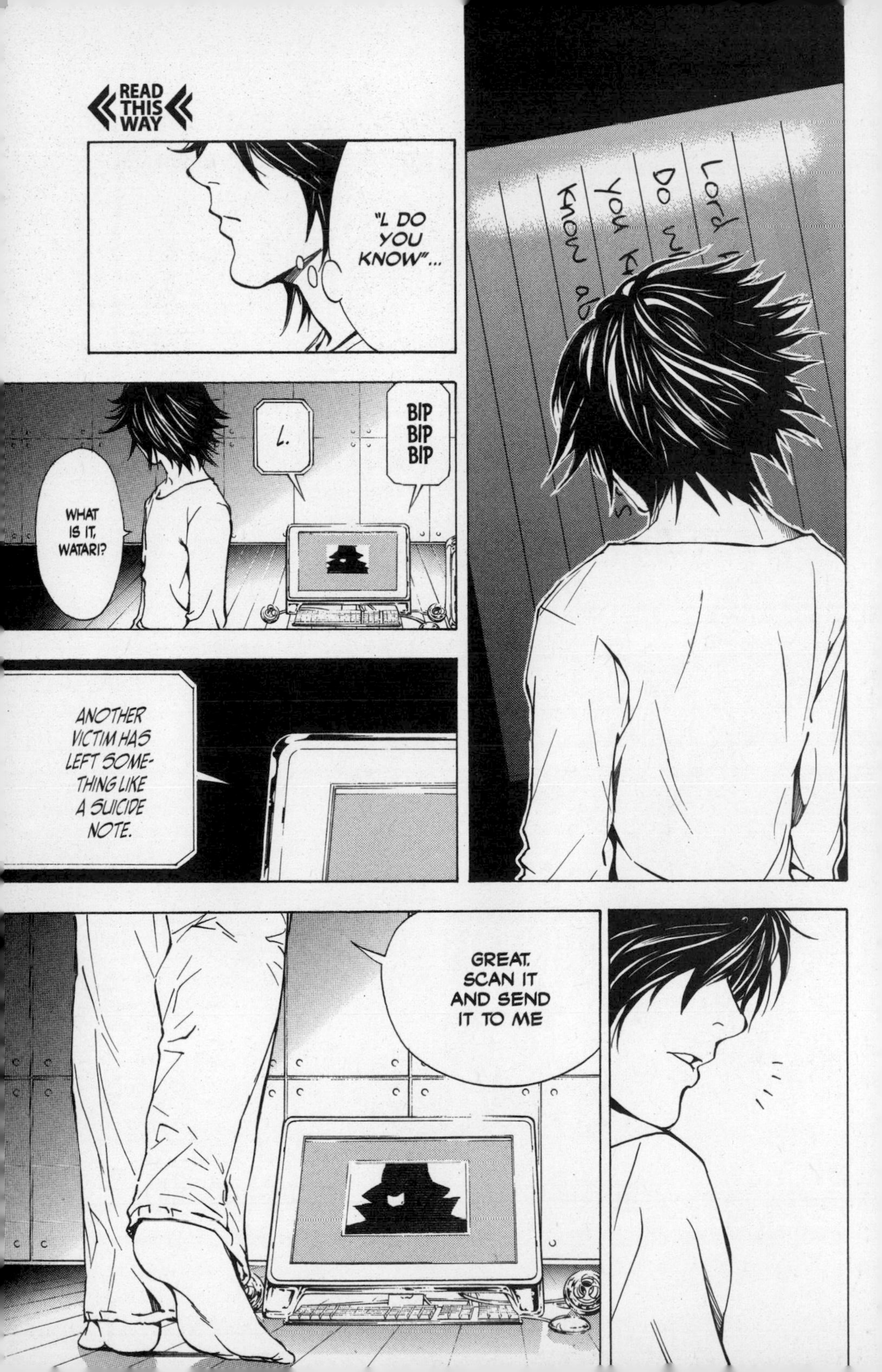
READ THIS WAY
"L DO YOU KNOW"...
BIP BIP BIP
L.
WHAT IS IT, WATARI?
ANOTHER VICTIM HAS LEFT SOME-THING LIKE A SUICIDE NOTE.
GREAT. SCAN IT AND SEND IT TO ME

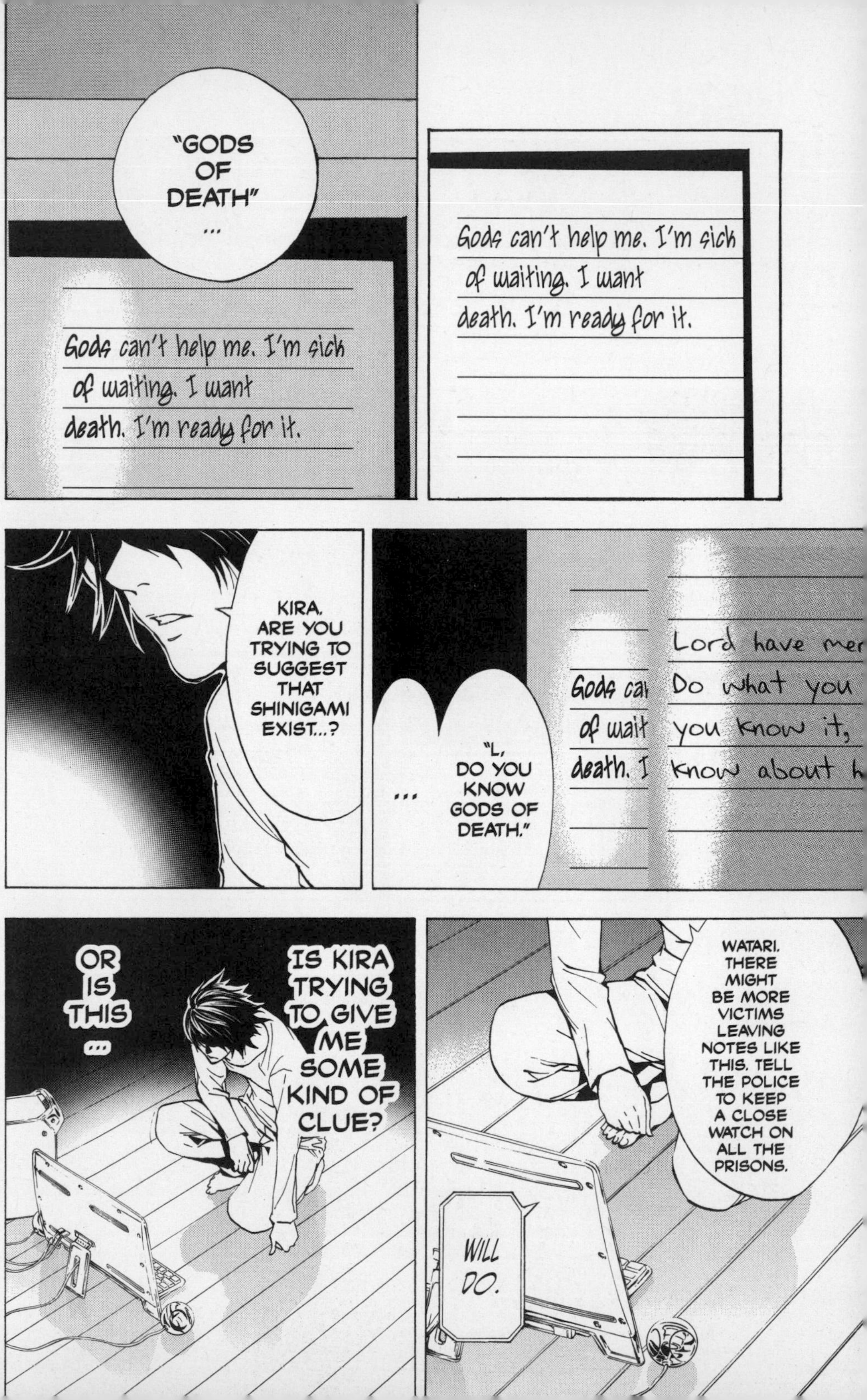
Gods can't help me. I'm sick of waiting. I want death. I'm ready for it.
"GODS OF DEATH" ...
Gods can't help me. I'm sick of waiting. I want death. I'm ready for it.
"L, DO YOU KNOW GODS OF DEATH."
...
KIRA. ARE YOU TRYING TO SUGGEST THAT SHINIGAMI EXIST...?
WATARI. THERE MIGHT BE MORE VICTIMS LEAVING NOTES LIKE THIS. TELL THE POLICE TO KEEP A CLOSE WATCH ON ALL THE PRISONS.
WILL DO.
IS KIRA TRYING TO GIVE ME SOME KIND OF CLUE?
OR IS THIS ...

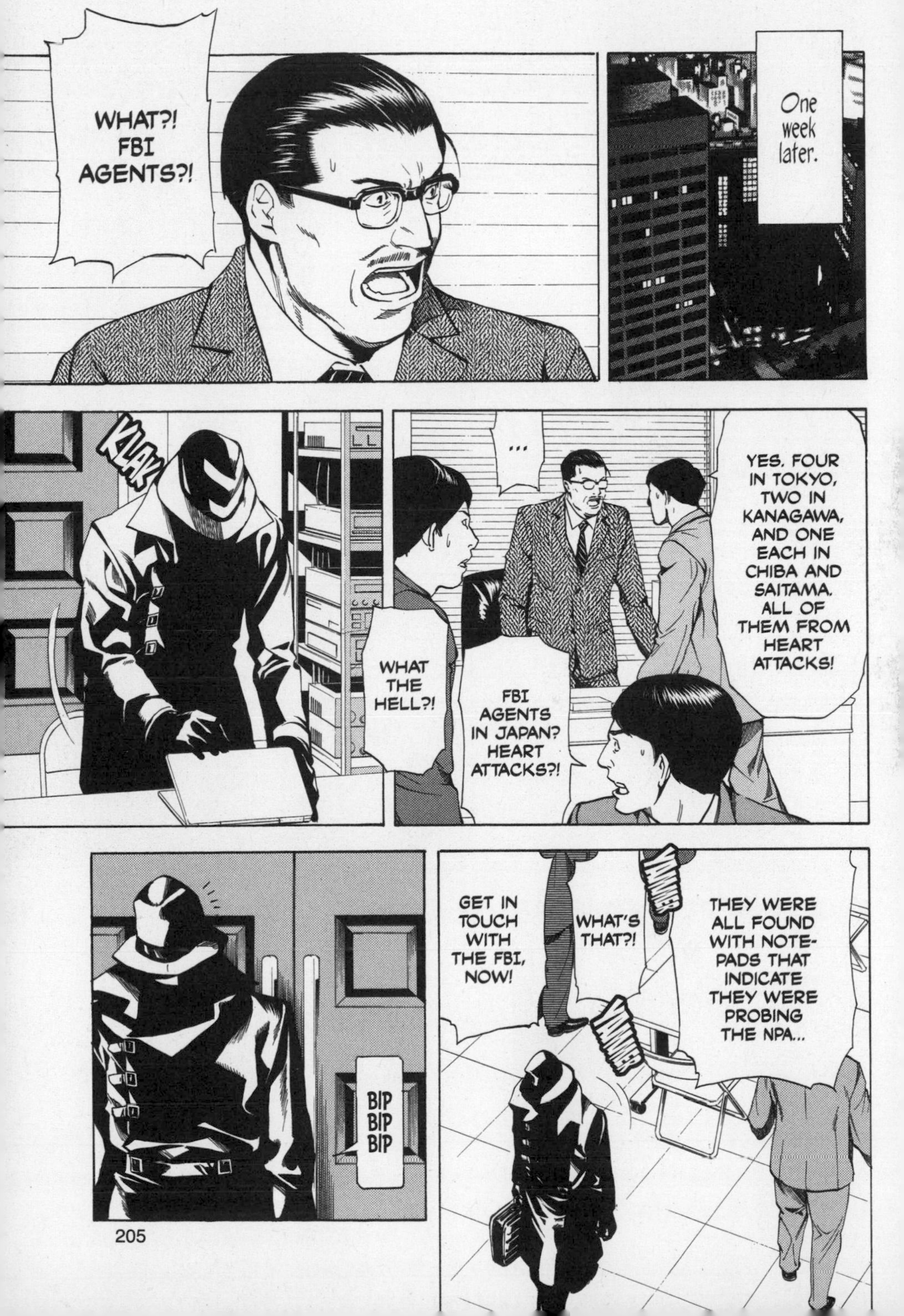
One week later.
WHAT?! FBI AGENTS?!
YES. FOUR IN TOKYO, TWO IN KANAGAWA, AND ONE EACH IN CHIBA AND SAITAMA. ALL OF THEM FROM HEART ATTACKS!
...
FBI AGENTS IN JAPAN? HEART ATTACKS?!
WHAT THE HELL?!
KLAK
THEY WERE ALL FOUND WITH NOTE-PADS THAT INDICATE THEY WERE PROBING THE NPA...
WHAT'S THAT?!
GET IN TOUCH WITH THE FBI, NOW!
BIP BIP BIP

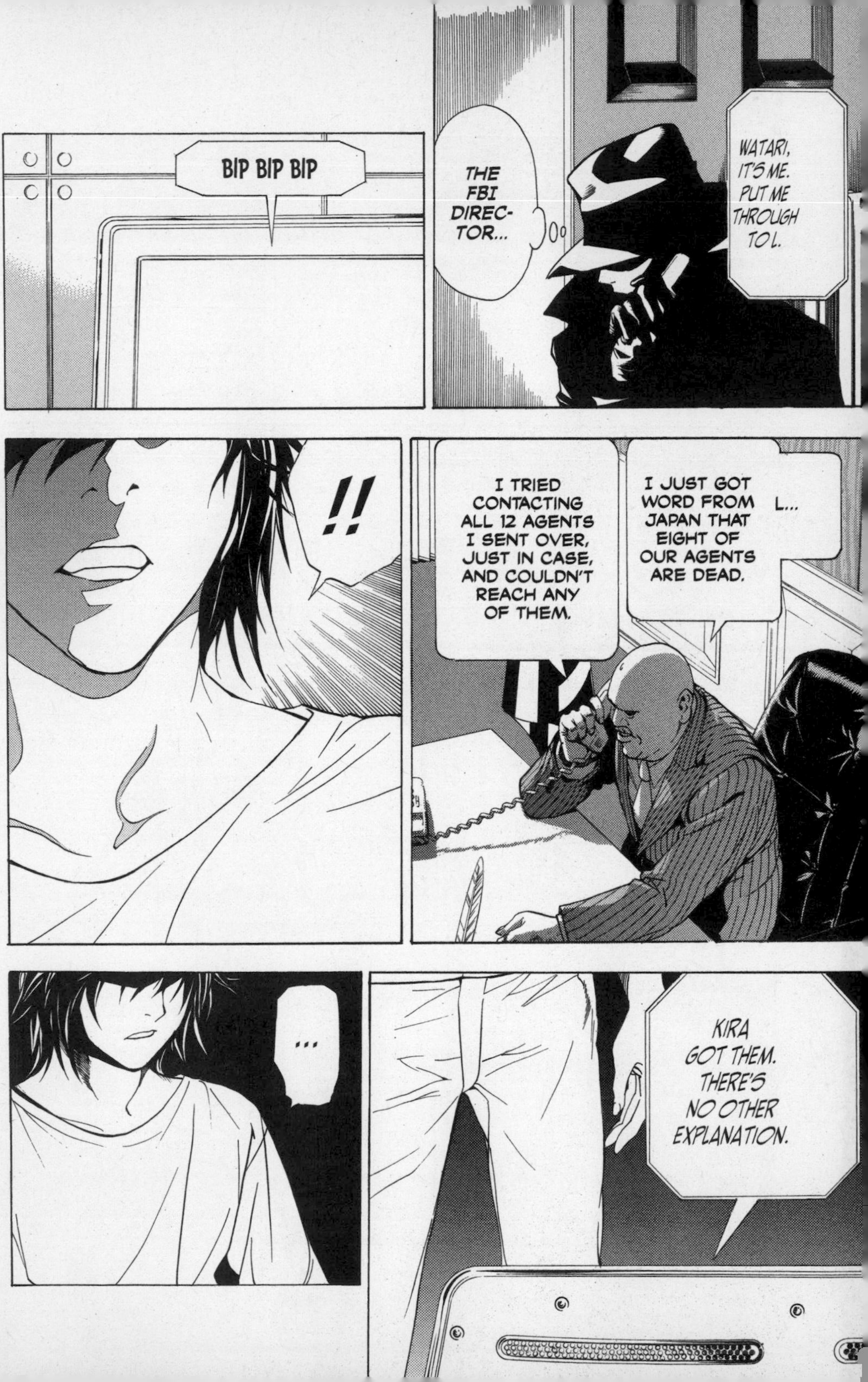
WATARI, IT'S ME. PUT ME THROUGH TO L.
THE FBI DIRECTOR...
BIP BIP BIP
L...
I JUST GOT WORD FROM JAPAN THAT EIGHT OF OUR AGENTS ARE DEAD.
I TRIED CONTACTING ALL 12 AGENTS I SENT OVER, JUST IN CASE, AND COULDN'T REACH ANY OF THEM.
!!
KIRA GOT THEM. THERE'S NO OTHER EXPLANATION.
...

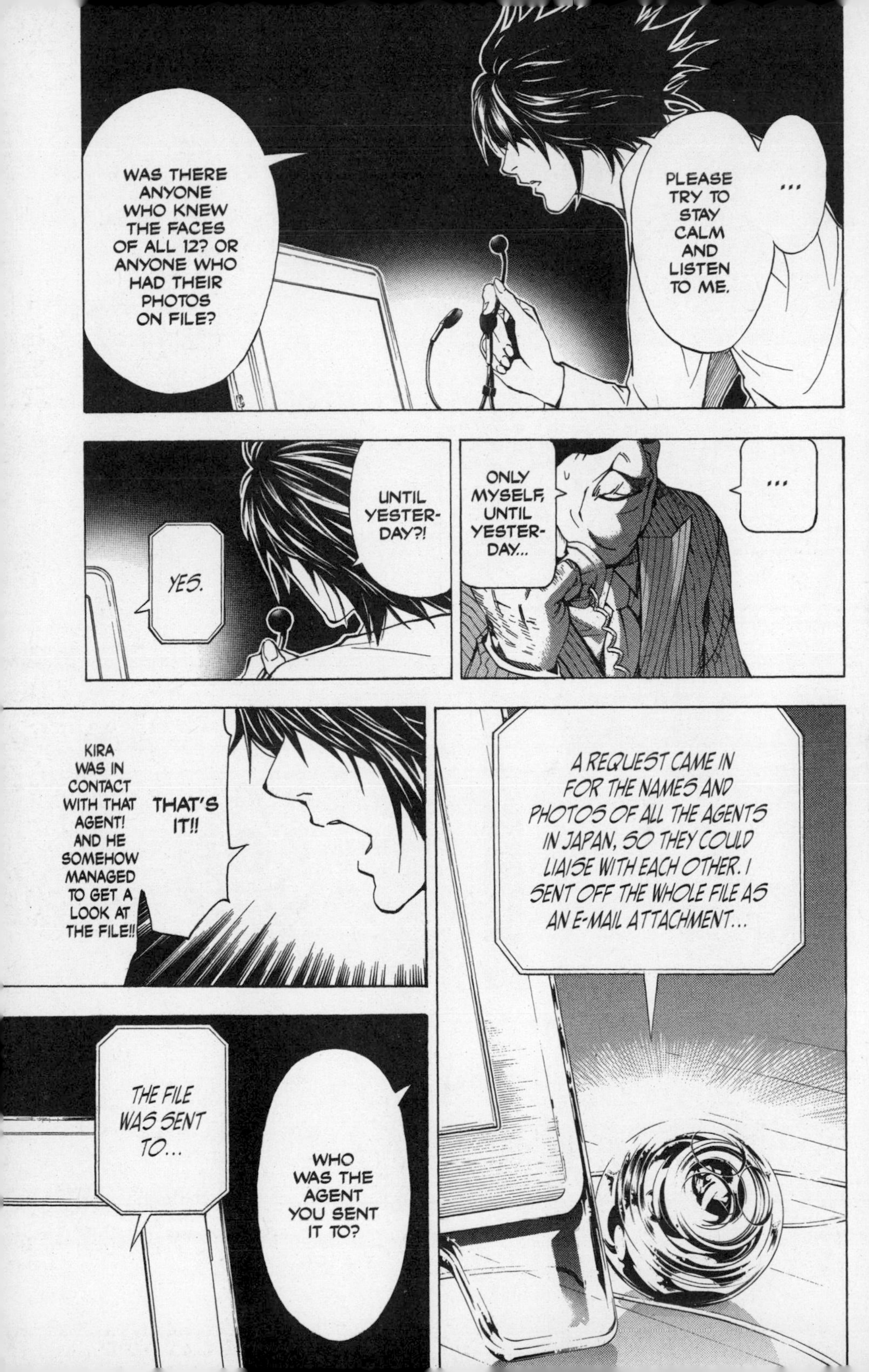
...
PLEASE TRY TO STAY CALM AND LISTEN TO ME.
WAS THERE ANYONE WHO KNEW THE FACES OF ALL 12? OR ANYONE WHO HAD THEIR PHOTOS ON FILE?
...
ONLY MYSELF, UNTIL YESTERDAY...
UNTIL YESTERDAY?!
YES.
A REQUEST CAME IN FOR THE NAMES AND PHOTOS OF ALL THE AGENTS IN JAPAN, SO THEY COULD LIAISE WITH EACH OTHER. I SENT OFF THE WHOLE FILE AS AN E-MAIL ATTACHMENT...
THAT'S IT!!
KIRA WAS IN CONTACT WITH THAT AGENT! AND HE SOMEHOW MANAGED TO GET A LOOK AT THE FILE!!
WHO WAS THE AGENT YOU SENT IT TO?
THE FILE WAS SENT TO...

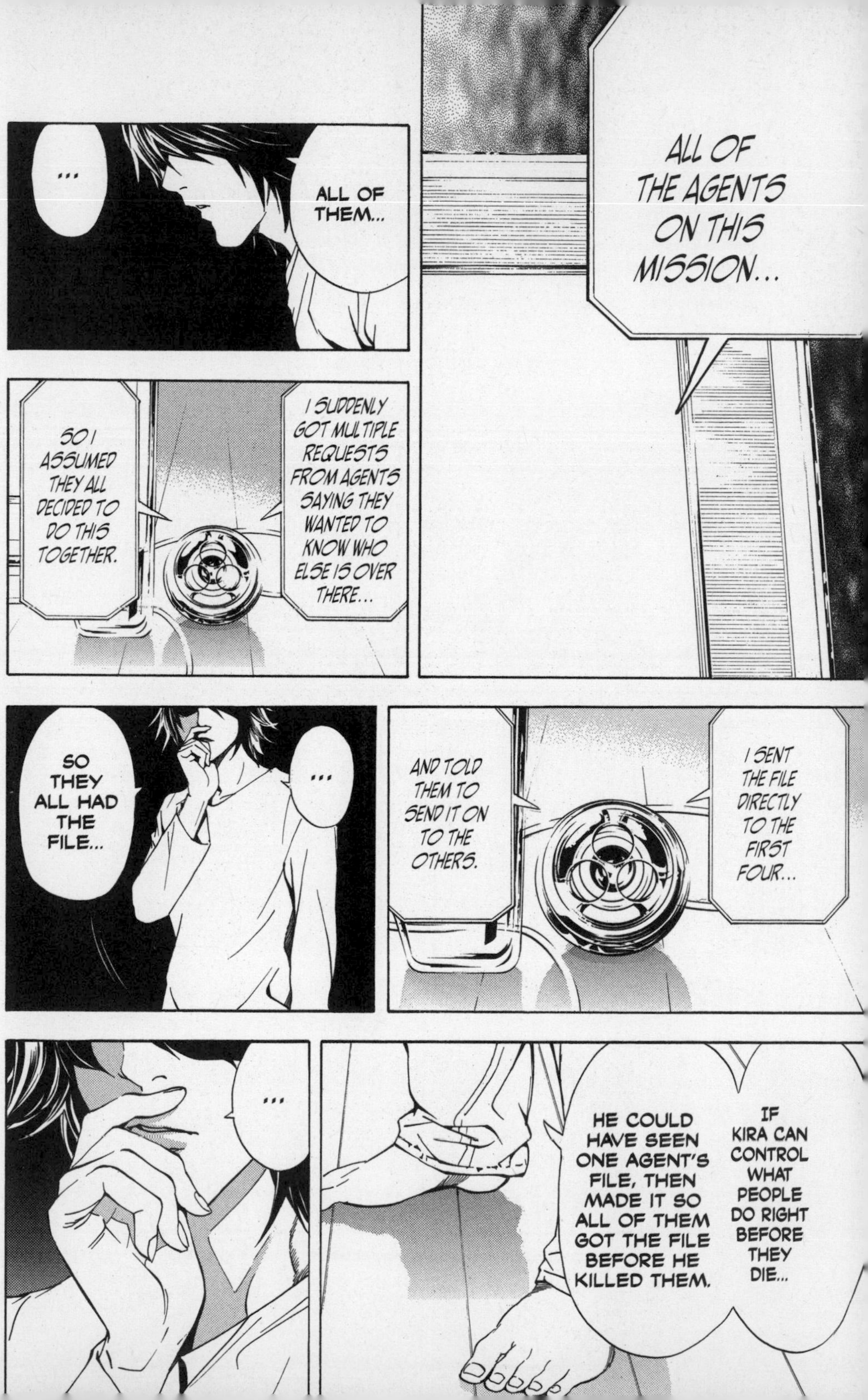
ALL OF THE AGENTS ON THIS MISSION...
ALL OF THEM...
...
I SUDDENLY GOT MULTIPLE REQUESTS FROM AGENTS SAYING THEY WANTED TO KNOW WHO ELSE IS OVER THERE...
SO I ASSUMED THEY ALL DECIDED TO DO THIS TOGETHER.
I SENT THE FILE DIRECTLY TO THE FIRST FOUR...
AND TOLD THEM TO SEND IT ON TO THE OTHERS.
...
SO THEY ALL HAD THE FILE...
IF KIRA CAN CONTROL WHAT PEOPLE DO RIGHT BEFORE THEY DIE...
HE COULD HAVE SEEN ONE AGENT'S FILE, THEN MADE IT SO ALL OF THEM GOT THE FILE BEFORE HE KILLED THEM.
...

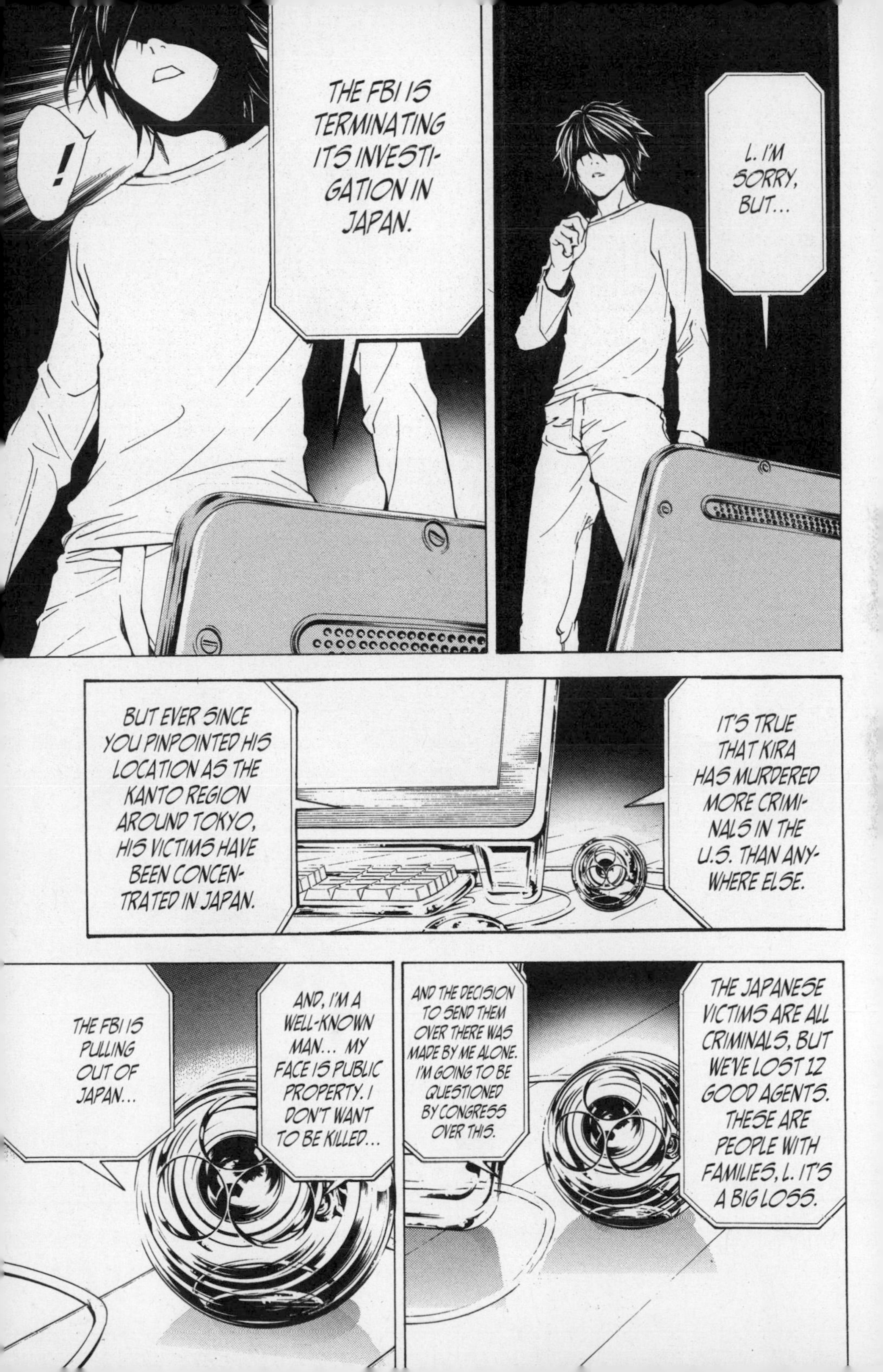
L. I'M SORRY, BUT...
THE FBI IS TERMINATING ITS INVESTIGATION IN JAPAN.
!
IT'S TRUE THAT KIRA HAS MURDERED MORE CRIMINALS IN THE U.S. THAN ANYWHERE ELSE.
BUT EVER SINCE YOU PINPOINTED HIS LOCATION AS THE KANTO REGION AROUND TOKYO, HIS VICTIMS HAVE BEEN CONCENTRATED IN JAPAN.
THE JAPANESE VICTIMS ARE ALL CRIMINALS, BUT WE'VE LOST 12 GOOD AGENTS. THESE ARE PEOPLE WITH FAMILIES, L. IT'S A BIG LOSS.
AND THE DECISION TO SEND THEM OVER THERE WAS MADE BY ME ALONE. I'M GOING TO BE QUESTIONED BY CONGRESS OVER THIS.
AND, I'M A WELL-KNOWN MAN... MY FACE IS PUBLIC PROPERTY. I DON'T WANT TO BE KILLED...
THE FBI IS PULLING OUT OF JAPAN...

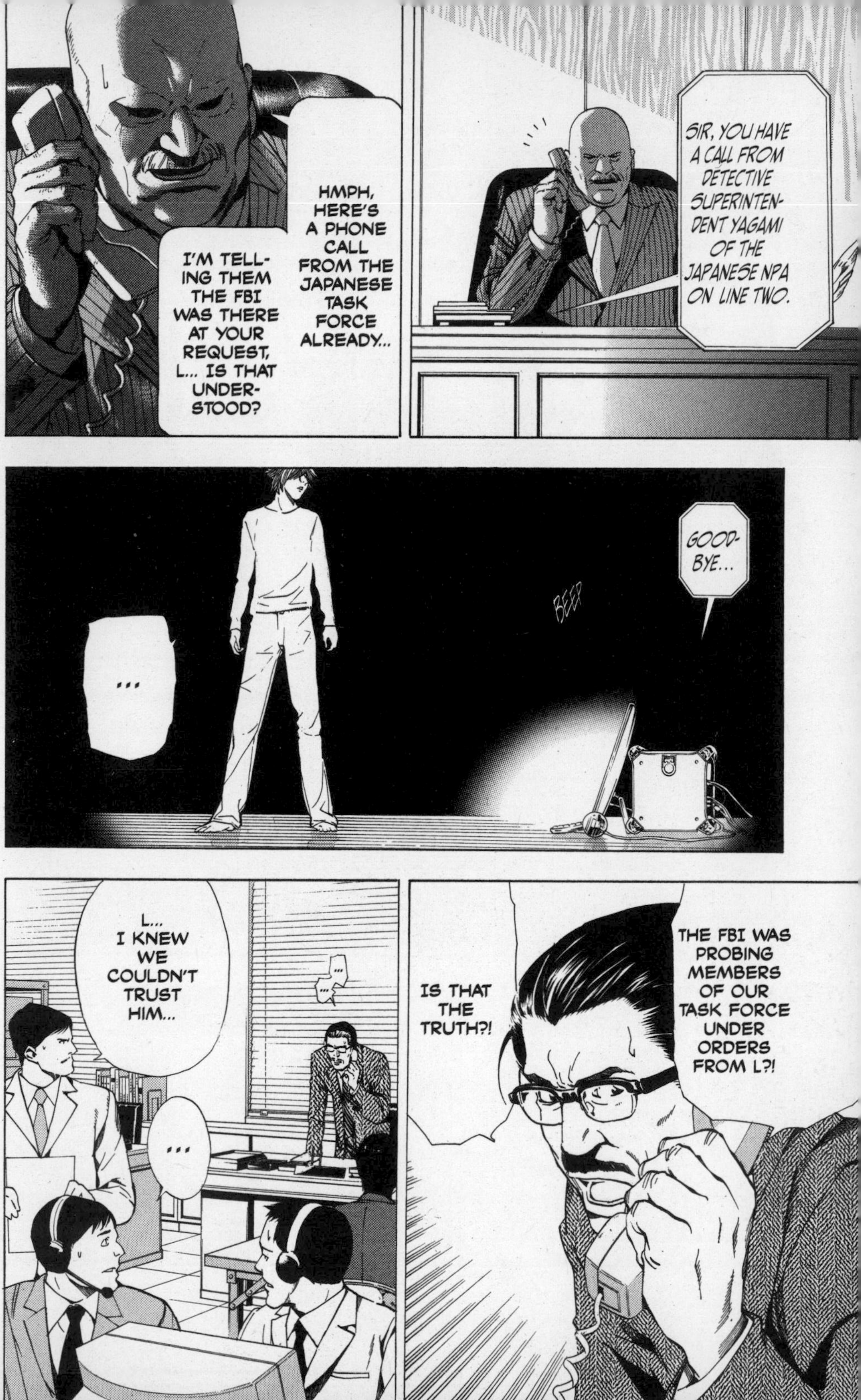
SIR, YOU HAVE A CALL FROM DETECTIVE SUPERINTEN-DENT YAGAMI OF THE JAPANESE NPA ON LINE TWO.
HMPH, HERE'S A PHONE CALL FROM THE JAPANESE TASK FORCE ALREADY...
I'M TELL-ING THEM THE FBI WAS THERE AT YOUR REQUEST, L... IS THAT UNDER-STOOD?
GOOD-BYE...
BEEP
...
THE FBI WAS PROBING MEMBERS OF OUR TASK FORCE UNDER ORDERS FROM L?!
IS THAT THE TRUTH?!
L... I KNEW WE COULDN'T TRUST HIM...
...
...
...

READ THIS WAY

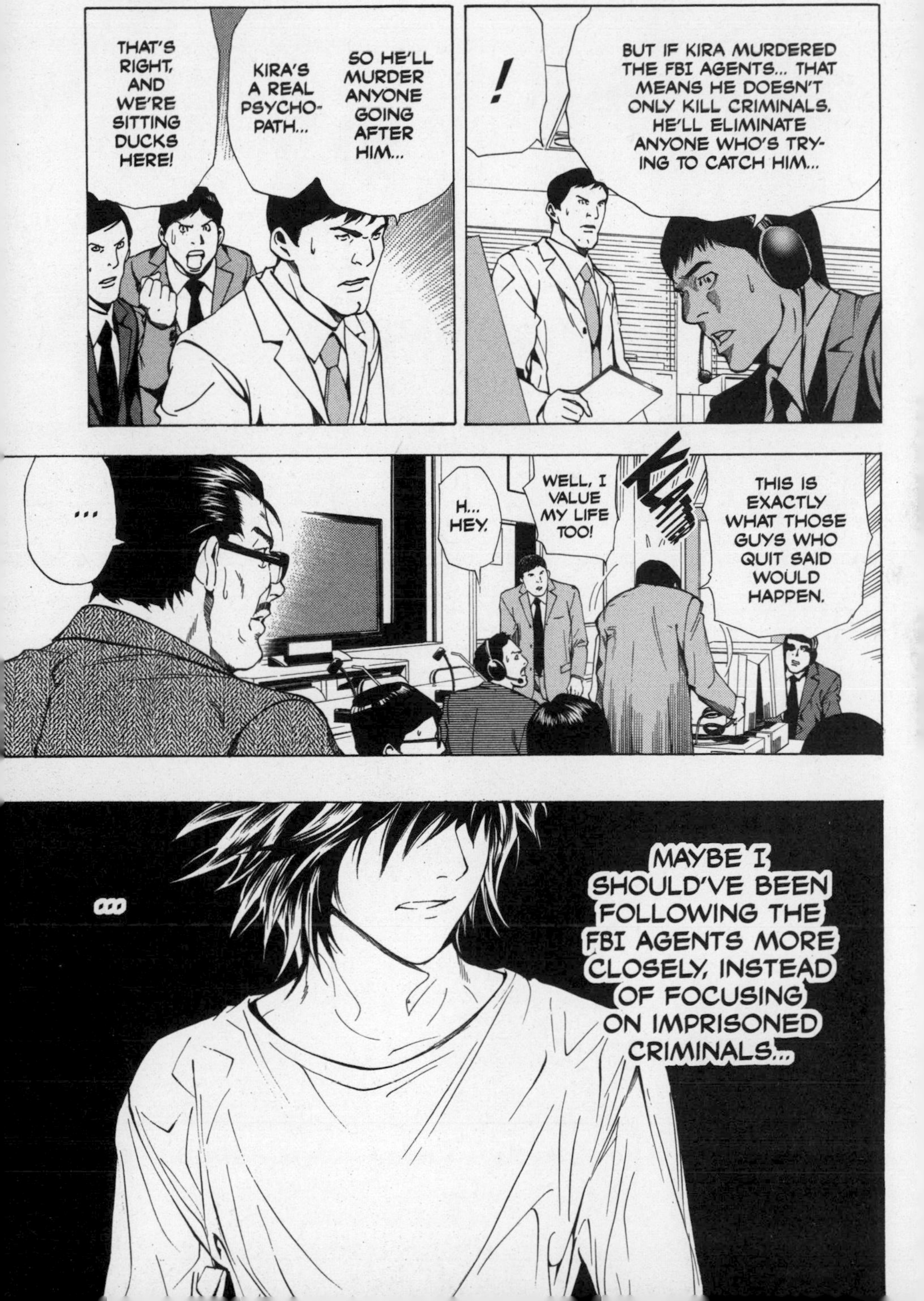
BUT IF KIRA MURDERED THE FBI AGENTS... THAT MEANS HE DOESN'T ONLY KILL CRIMINALS. HE'LL ELIMINATE ANYONE WHO'S TRYING TO CATCH HIM...
!
SO HE'LL MURDER ANYONE GOING AFTER HIM...
KIRA'S A REAL PSYCHOPATH...
THAT'S RIGHT, AND WE'RE SITTING DUCKS HERE!
THIS IS EXACTLY WHAT THOSE GUYS WHO QUIT SAID WOULD HAPPEN.
WELL, I VALUE MY LIFE TOO!
H... HEY.
...
MAYBE I SHOULD'VE BEEN FOLLOWING THE FBI AGENTS MORE CLOSELY, INSTEAD OF FOCUSING ON IMPRISONED CRIMINALS...
...

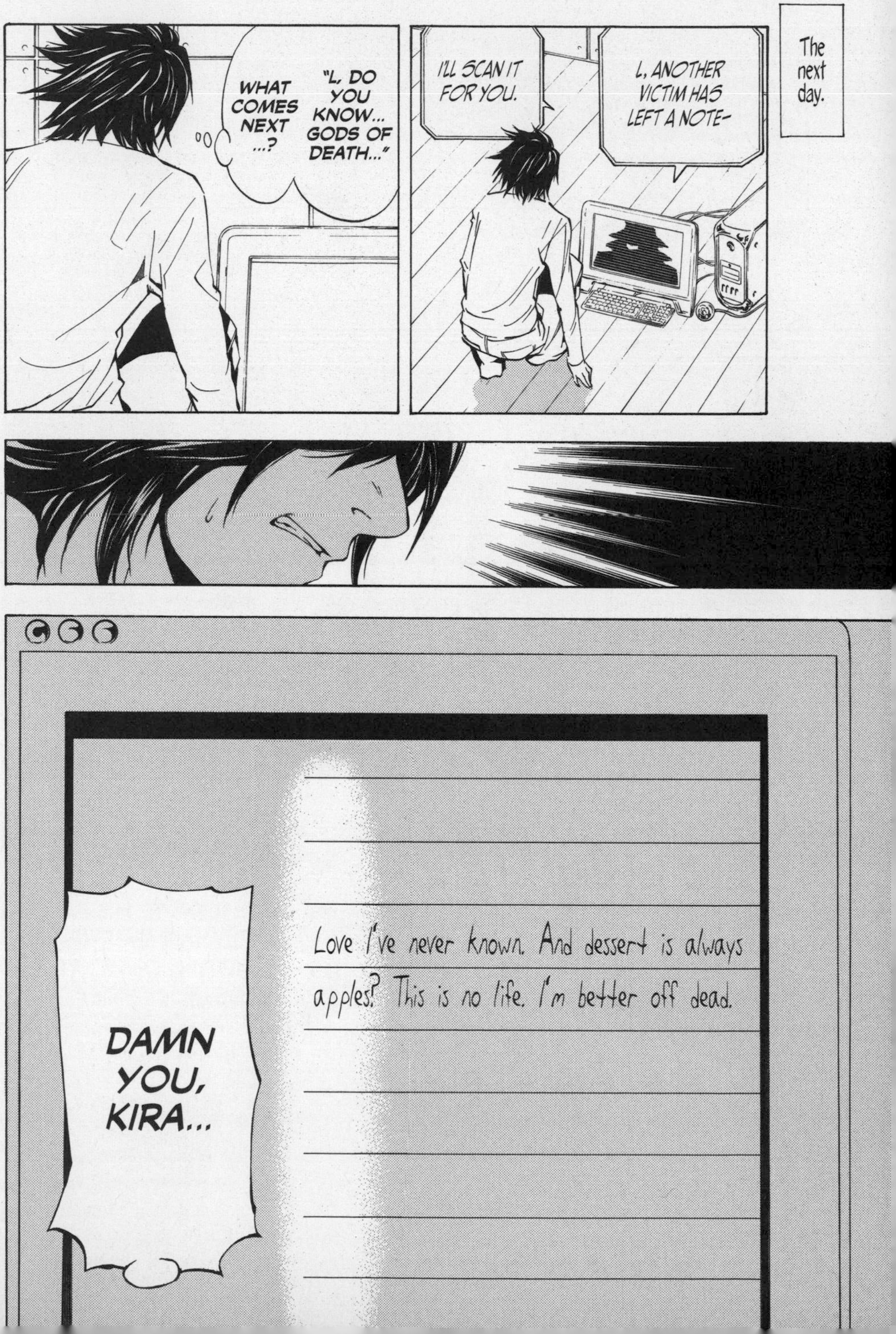

The next day.
L, ANOTHER VICTIM HAS LEFT A NOTE-
I'LL SCAN IT FOR YOU.
"L, DO YOU KNOW... GODS OF DEATH..."
WHAT COMES NEXT ...?
Love I've never known. And dessert is always apples? This is no life. I'm better off dead.
DAMN YOU, KIRA...

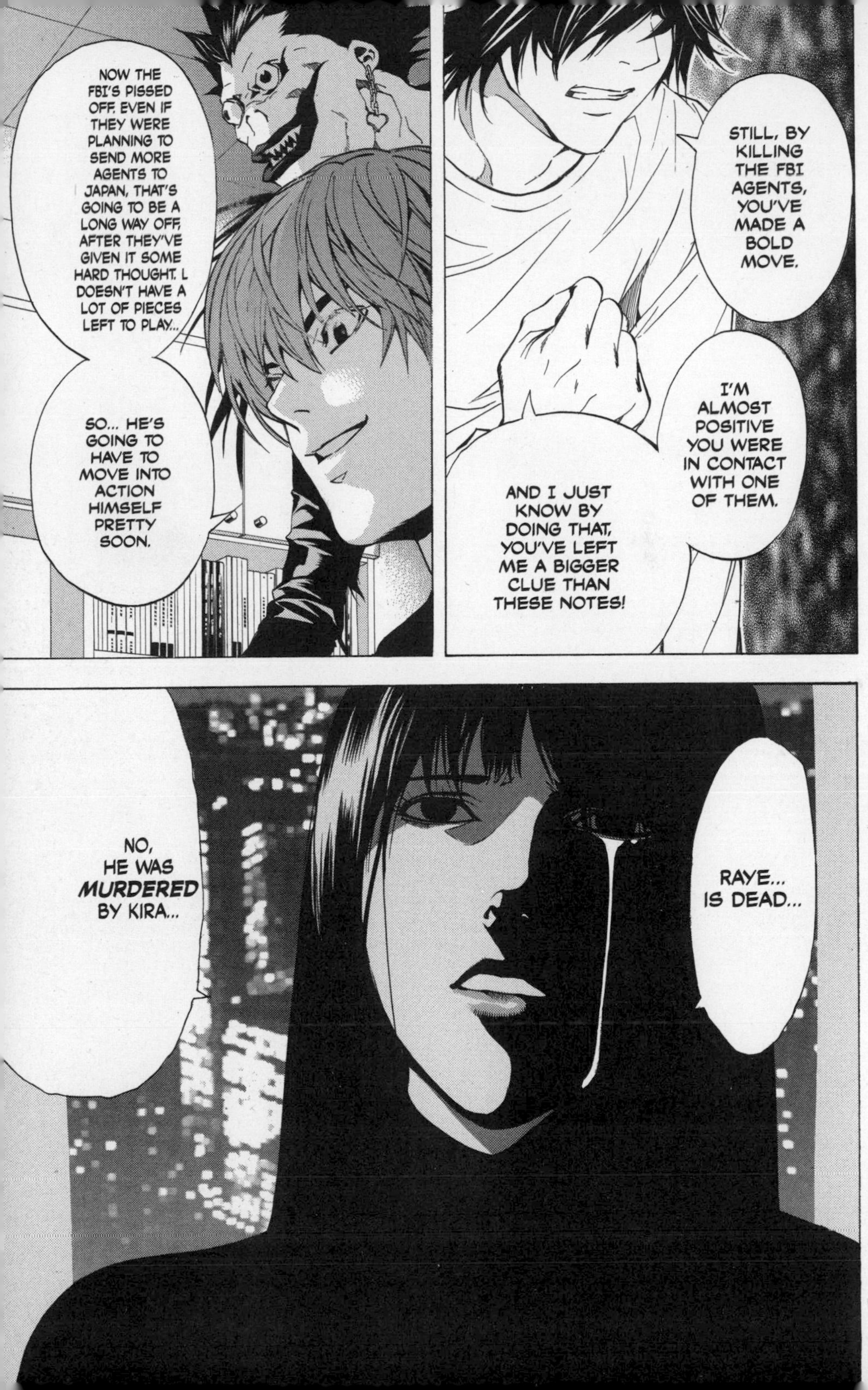
STILL, BY KILLING THE FBI AGENTS, YOU'VE MADE A BOLD MOVE.
I'M ALMOST POSITIVE YOU WERE IN CONTACT WITH ONE OF THEM.
AND I JUST KNOW BY DOING THAT, YOU'VE LEFT ME A BIGGER CLUE THAN THESE NOTES!
NOW THE FBI'S PISSED OFF. EVEN IF THEY WERE PLANNING TO SEND MORE AGENTS TO JAPAN, THAT'S GOING TO BE A LONG WAY OFF, AFTER THEY'VE GIVEN IT SOME HARD THOUGHT. L DOESN'T HAVE A LOT OF PIECES LEFT TO PLAY...
SO... HE'S GOING TO HAVE TO MOVE INTO ACTION HIMSELF PRETTY SOON.
RAYE... IS DEAD...
NO, HE WAS ***MURDERED*** BY KIRA...

# chapter 9 Slots

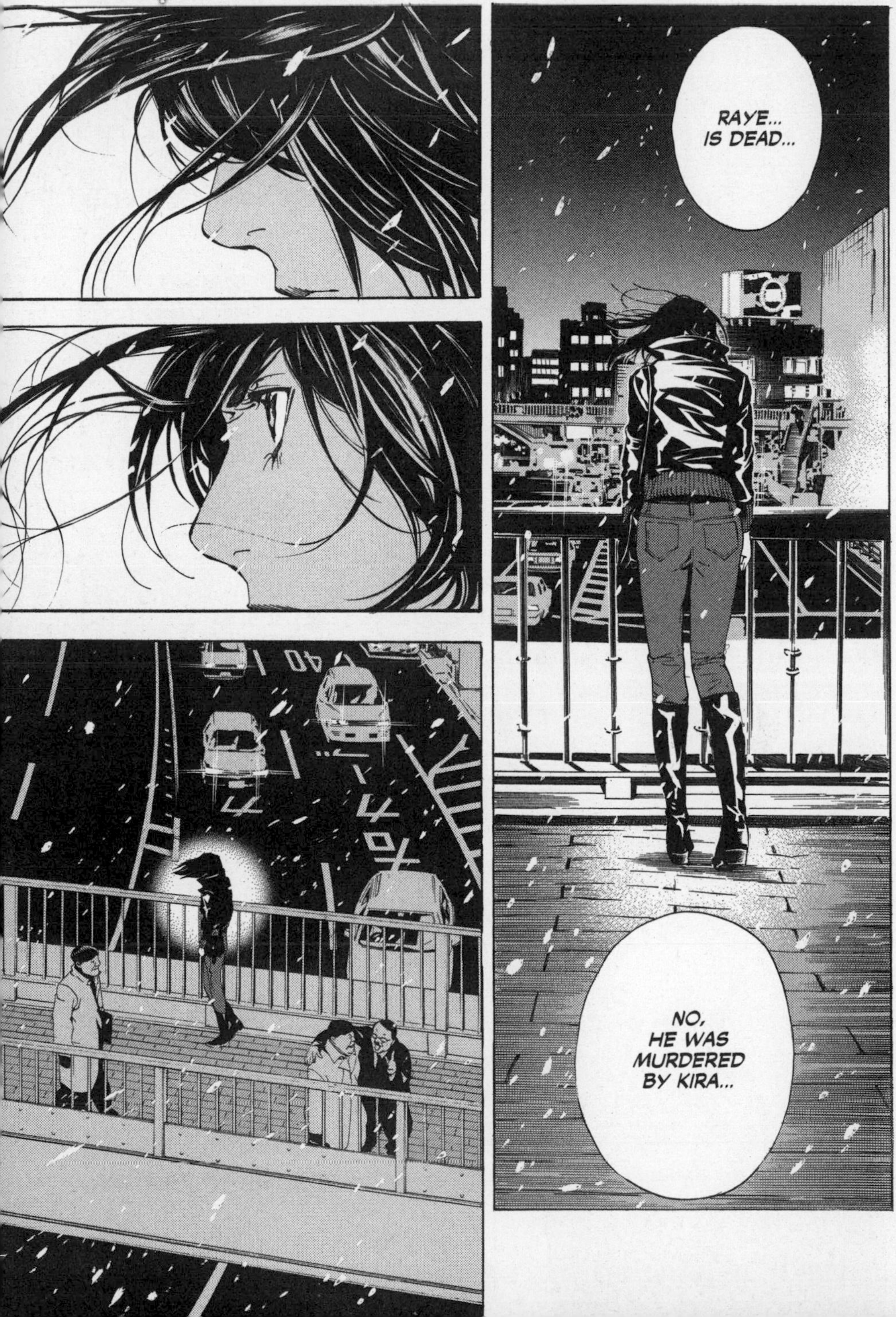
RAYE... IS DEAD...
NO, HE WAS MURDERED BY KIRA...

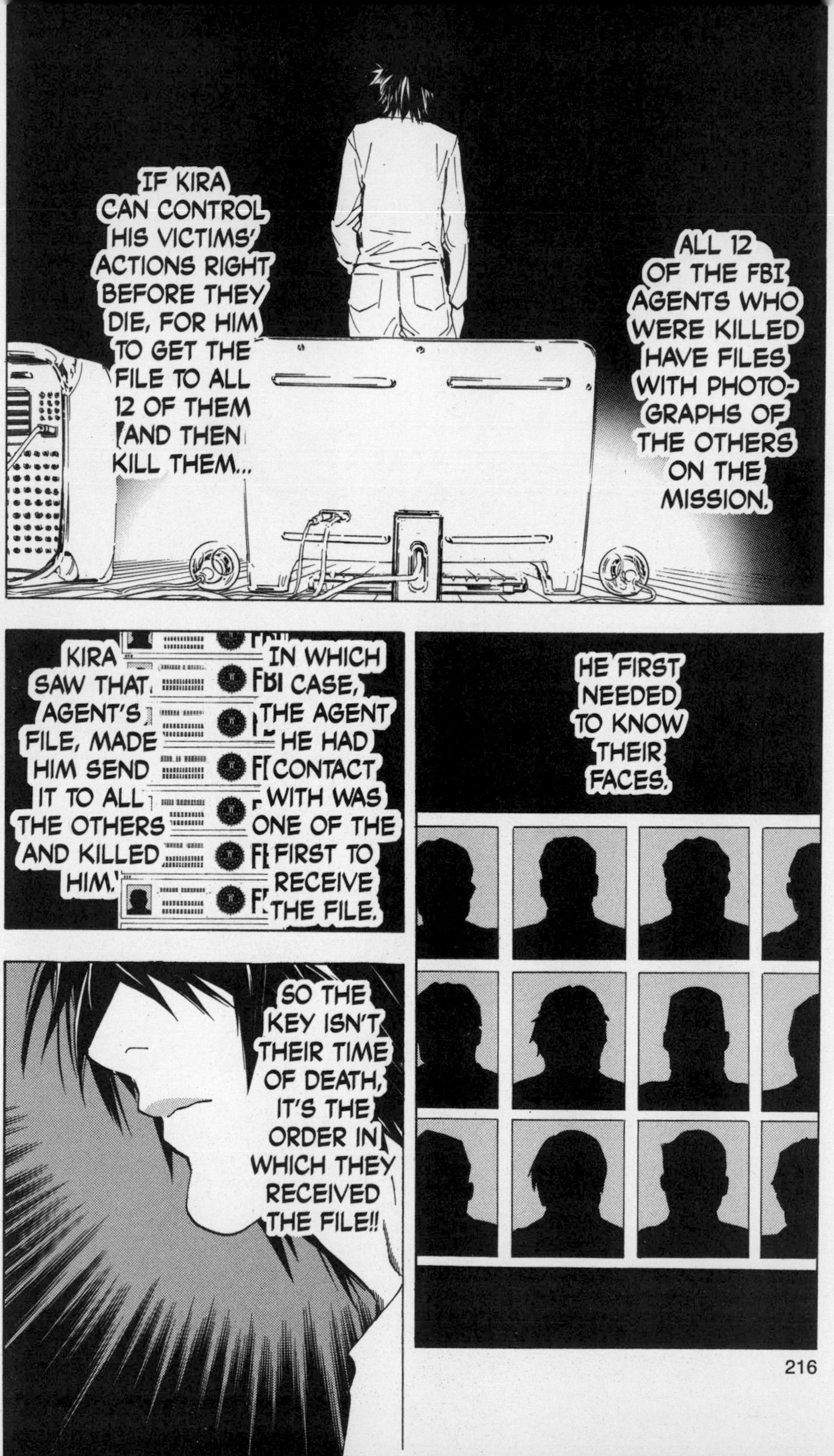
ALL 12 OF THE FBI AGENTS WHO WERE KILLED HAVE FILES WITH PHOTOGRAPHS OF THE OTHERS ON THE MISSION.
IF KIRA CAN CONTROL HIS VICTIMS' ACTIONS RIGHT BEFORE THEY DIE, FOR HIM TO GET THE FILE TO ALL 12 OF THEM AND THEN KILL THEM...
HE FIRST NEEDED TO KNOW THEIR FACES.
IN WHICH CASE, THE AGENT HE HAD CONTACT WITH WAS ONE OF THE FIRST TO RECEIVE THE FILE.
KIRA SAW THAT AGENT'S FILE, MADE HIM SEND IT TO ALL THE OTHERS AND KILLED HIM.
SO THE KEY ISN'T THEIR TIME OF DEATH, IT'S THE ORDER IN WHICH THEY RECEIVED THE FILE!!

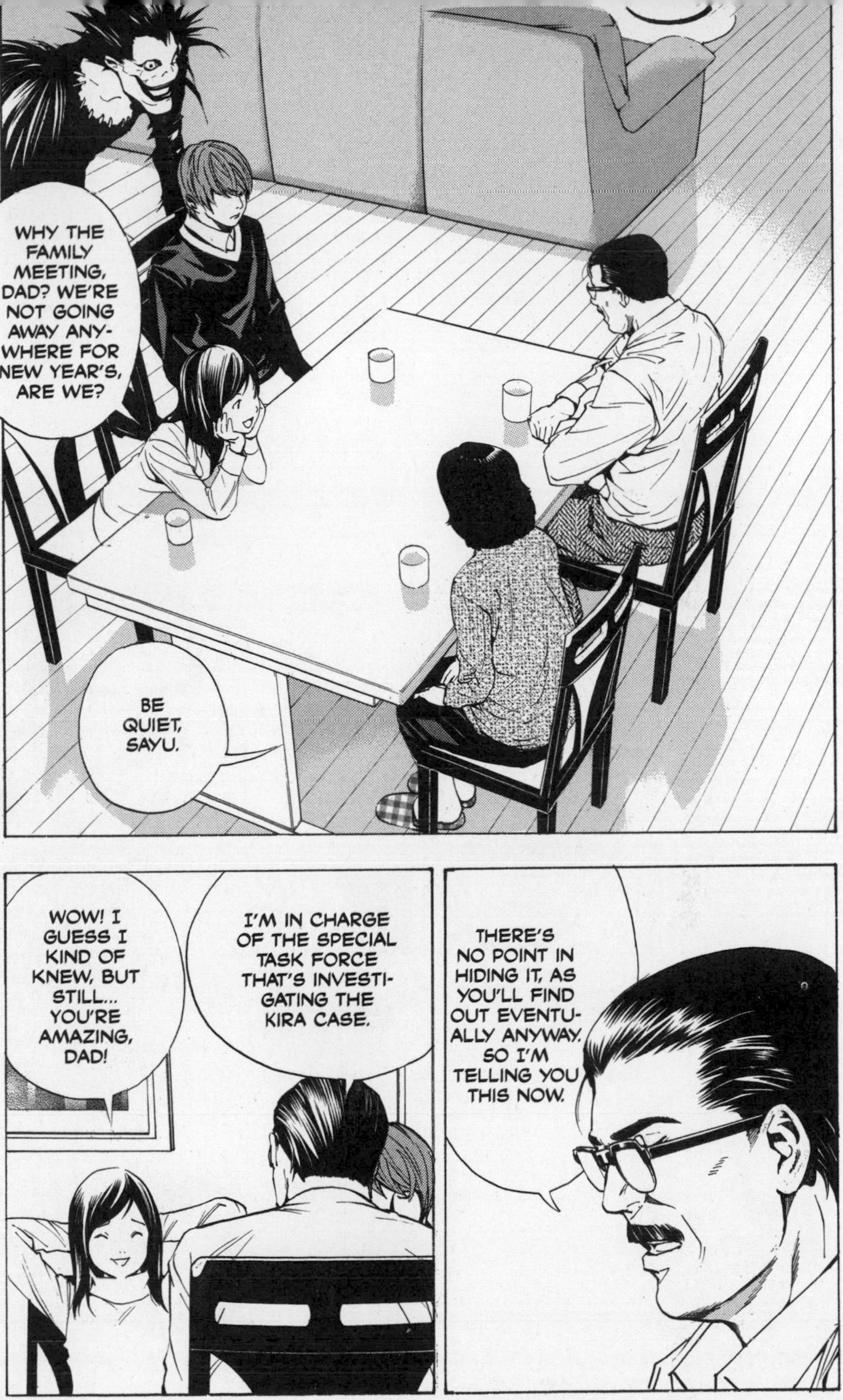
WHY THE FAMILY MEETING, DAD? WE'RE NOT GOING AWAY ANY-WHERE FOR NEW YEAR'S, ARE WE?
BE QUIET, SAYU.
THERE'S NO POINT IN HIDING IT, AS YOU'LL FIND OUT EVENTU-ALLY ANYWAY. SO I'M TELLING YOU THIS NOW.
I'M IN CHARGE OF THE SPECIAL TASK FORCE THAT'S INVESTI-GATING THE KIRA CASE.
WOW! I GUESS I KIND OF KNEW, BUT STILL... YOU'RE AMAZING, DAD!

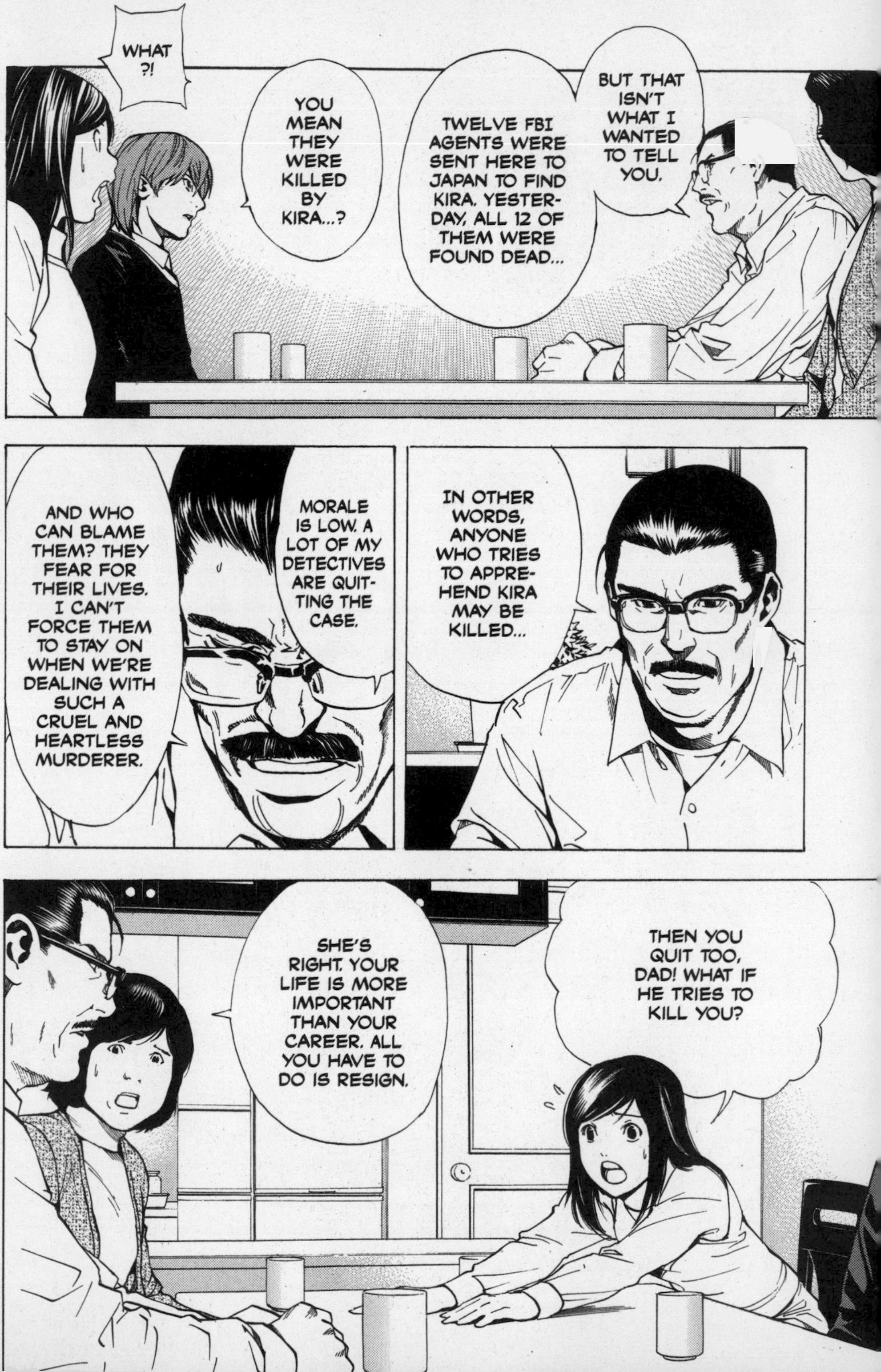
BUT THAT ISN'T WHAT I WANTED TO TELL YOU.
TWELVE FBI AGENTS WERE SENT HERE TO JAPAN TO FIND KIRA. YESTERDAY, ALL 12 OF THEM WERE FOUND DEAD...
YOU MEAN THEY WERE KILLED BY KIRA...?
WHAT?!
IN OTHER WORDS, ANYONE WHO TRIES TO APPREHEND KIRA MAY BE KILLED...
MORALE IS LOW. A LOT OF MY DETECTIVES ARE QUITTING THE CASE.
AND WHO CAN BLAME THEM? THEY FEAR FOR THEIR LIVES. I CAN'T FORCE THEM TO STAY ON WHEN WE'RE DEALING WITH SUCH A CRUEL AND HEARTLESS MURDERER.
THEN YOU QUIT TOO, DAD! WHAT IF HE TRIES TO KILL YOU?
SHE'S RIGHT. YOUR LIFE IS MORE IMPORTANT THAN YOUR CAREER. ALL YOU HAVE TO DO IS RESIGN.

READ THIS WAY

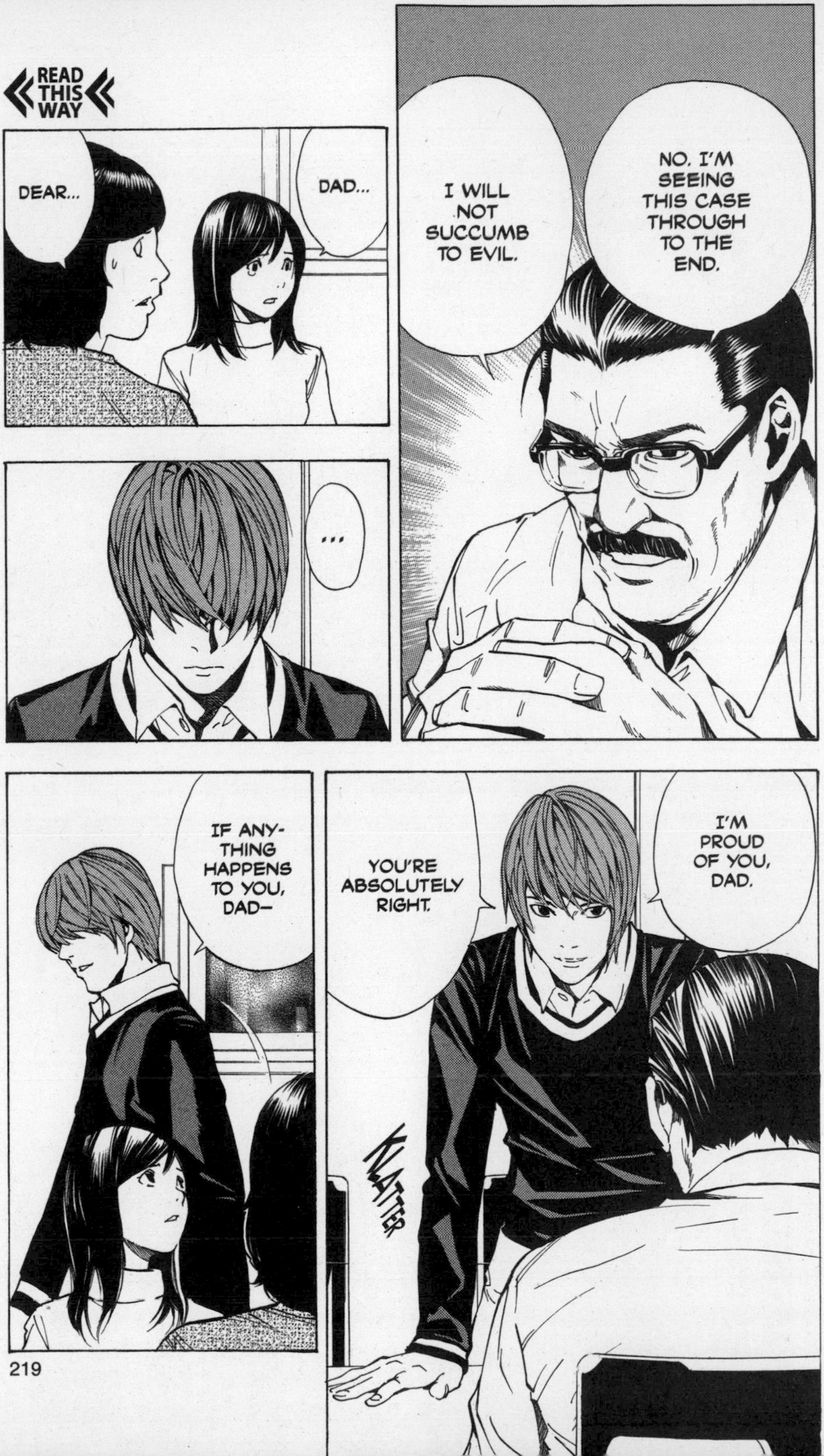
NO, I'M SEEING THIS CASE THROUGH TO THE END.
I WILL NOT SUCCUMB TO EVIL.
DAD...
DEAR...
...
I'M PROUD OF YOU, DAD.
YOU'RE ABSOLUTELY RIGHT.
KLATTER
IF ANY-THING HAPPENS TO YOU, DAD—

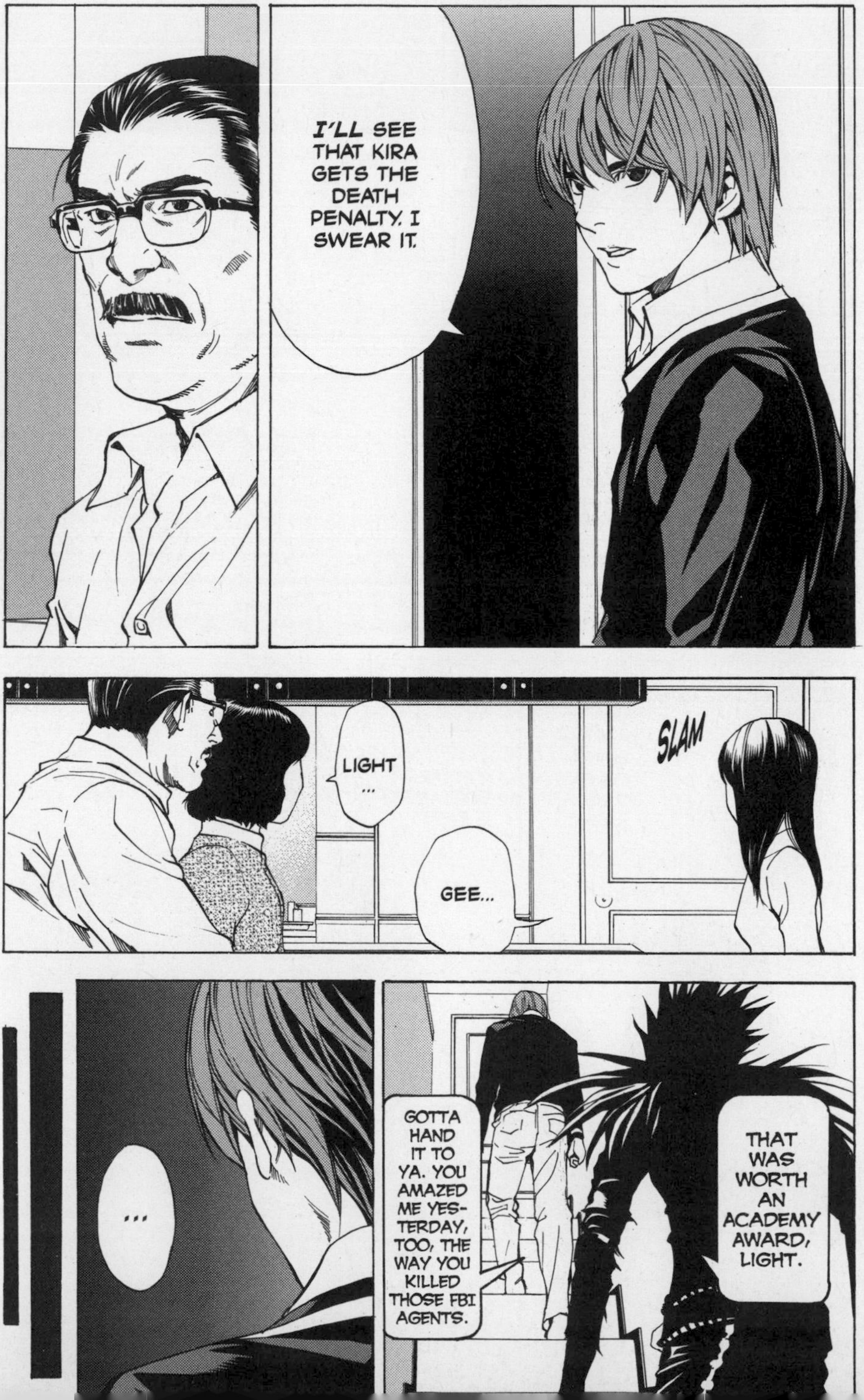
I'LL SEE THAT KIRA GETS THE DEATH PENALTY. I SWEAR IT.
SLAM
LIGHT ...
GEE...
THAT WAS WORTH AN ACADEMY AWARD, LIGHT.
GOTTA HAND IT TO YA. YOU AMAZED ME YES-TERDAY, TOO, THE WAY YOU KILLED THOSE FBI AGENTS.
...

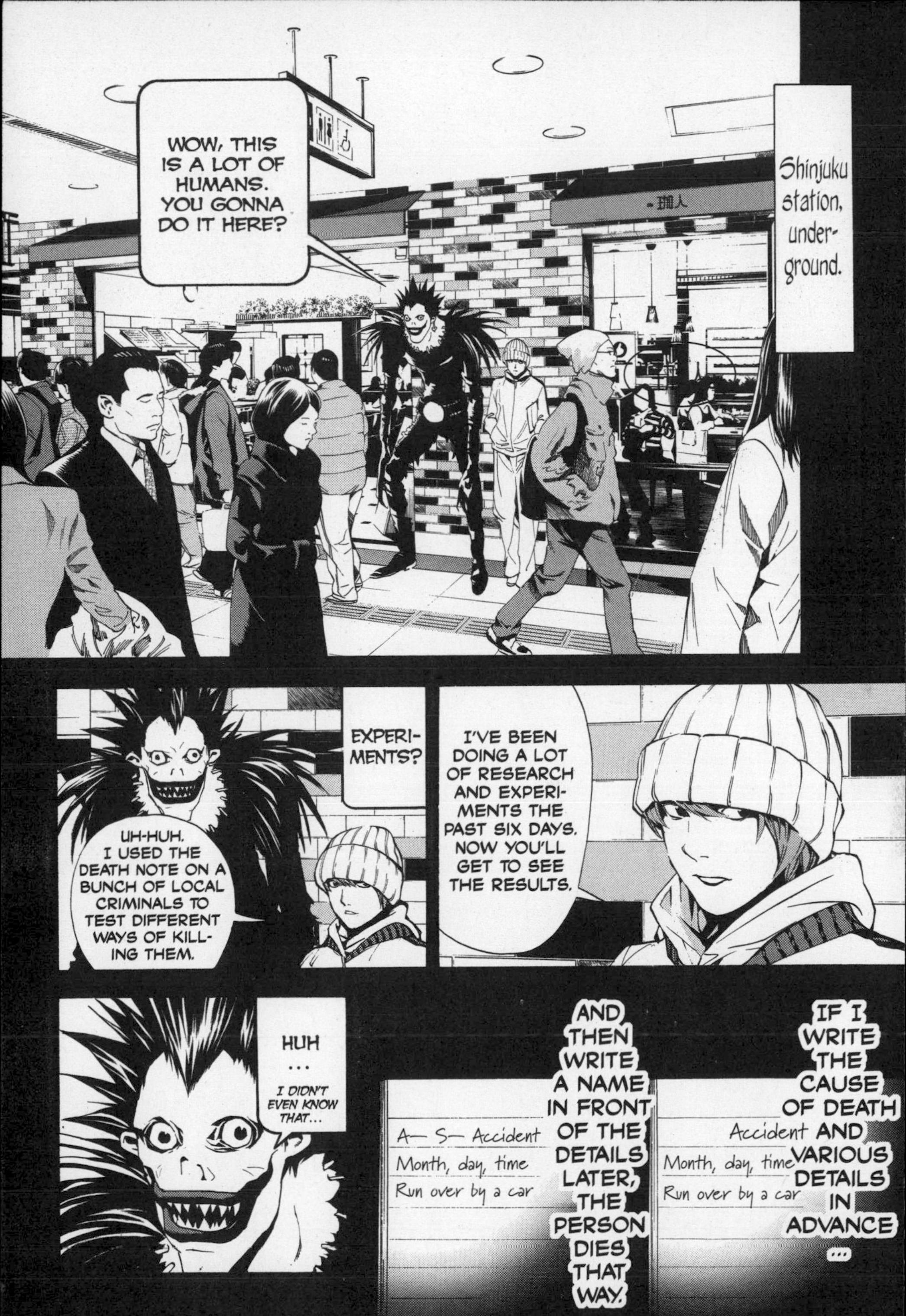
Shinjuku station, under-ground.
WOW, THIS IS A LOT OF HUMANS. YOU GONNA DO IT HERE?
I'VE BEEN DOING A LOT OF RESEARCH AND EXPERI-MENTS THE PAST SIX DAYS. NOW YOU'LL GET TO SEE THE RESULTS.
EXPERI-MENTS?
UH-HUH. I USED THE DEATH NOTE ON A BUNCH OF LOCAL CRIMINALS TO TEST DIFFERENT WAYS OF KILL-ING THEM.
IF I WRITE THE CAUSE OF DEATH AND VARIOUS DETAILS IN ADVANCE ...
Accident
Month, day, time
Run over by a car
A— S— Accident
Month, day, time
Run over by a car
AND THEN WRITE A NAME IN FRONT OF THE DETAILS LATER, THE PERSON DIES THAT WAY.
HUH ...
I DIDN'T EVEN KNOW THAT...

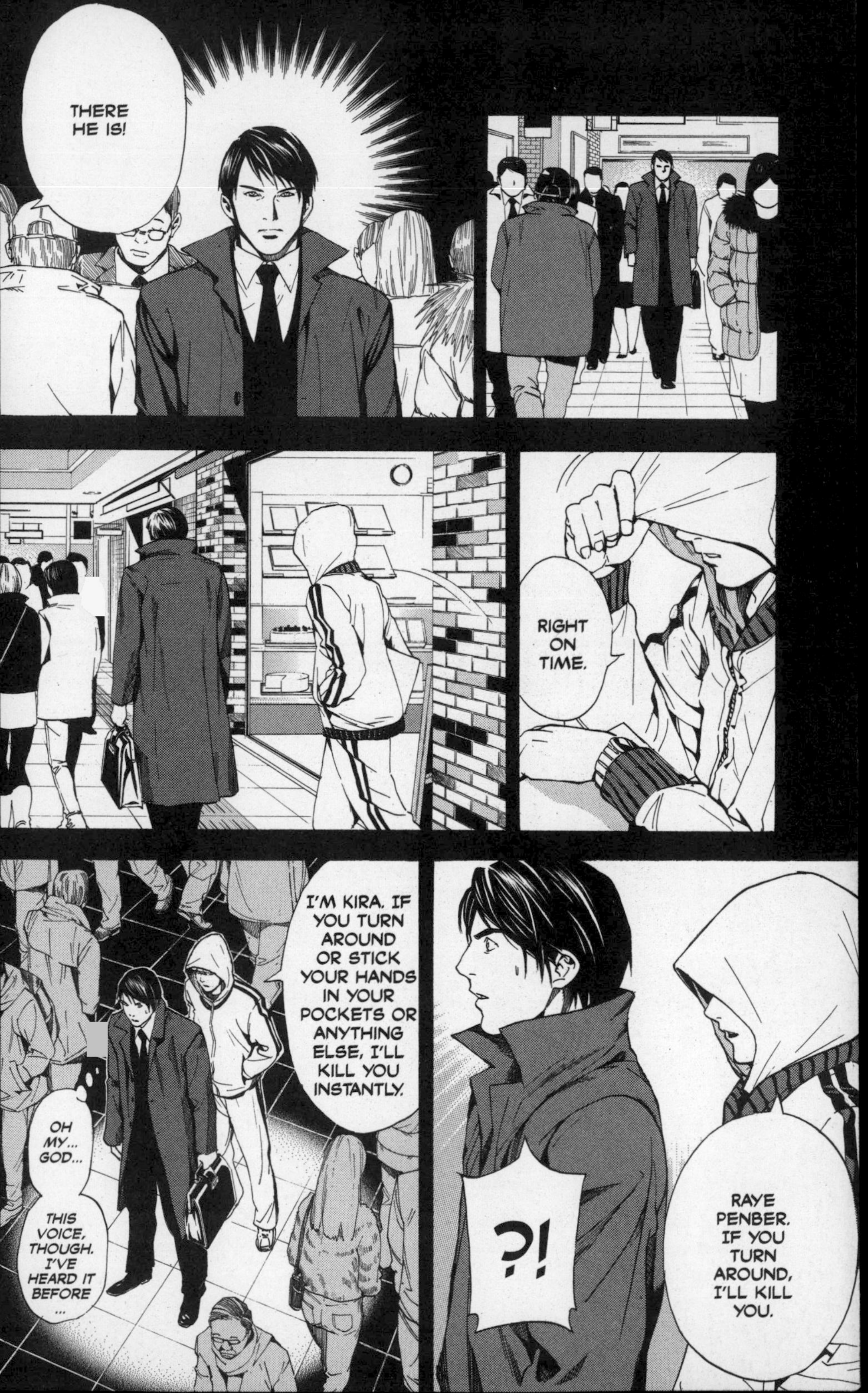
THERE HE IS!
RIGHT ON TIME.
RAYE PENBER. IF YOU TURN AROUND, I'LL KILL YOU.
?!
I'M KIRA. IF YOU TURN AROUND OR STICK YOUR HANDS IN YOUR POCKETS OR ANYTHING ELSE, I'LL KILL YOU INSTANTLY.
OH MY... GOD...
THIS VOICE, THOUGH. I'VE HEARD IT BEFORE ...

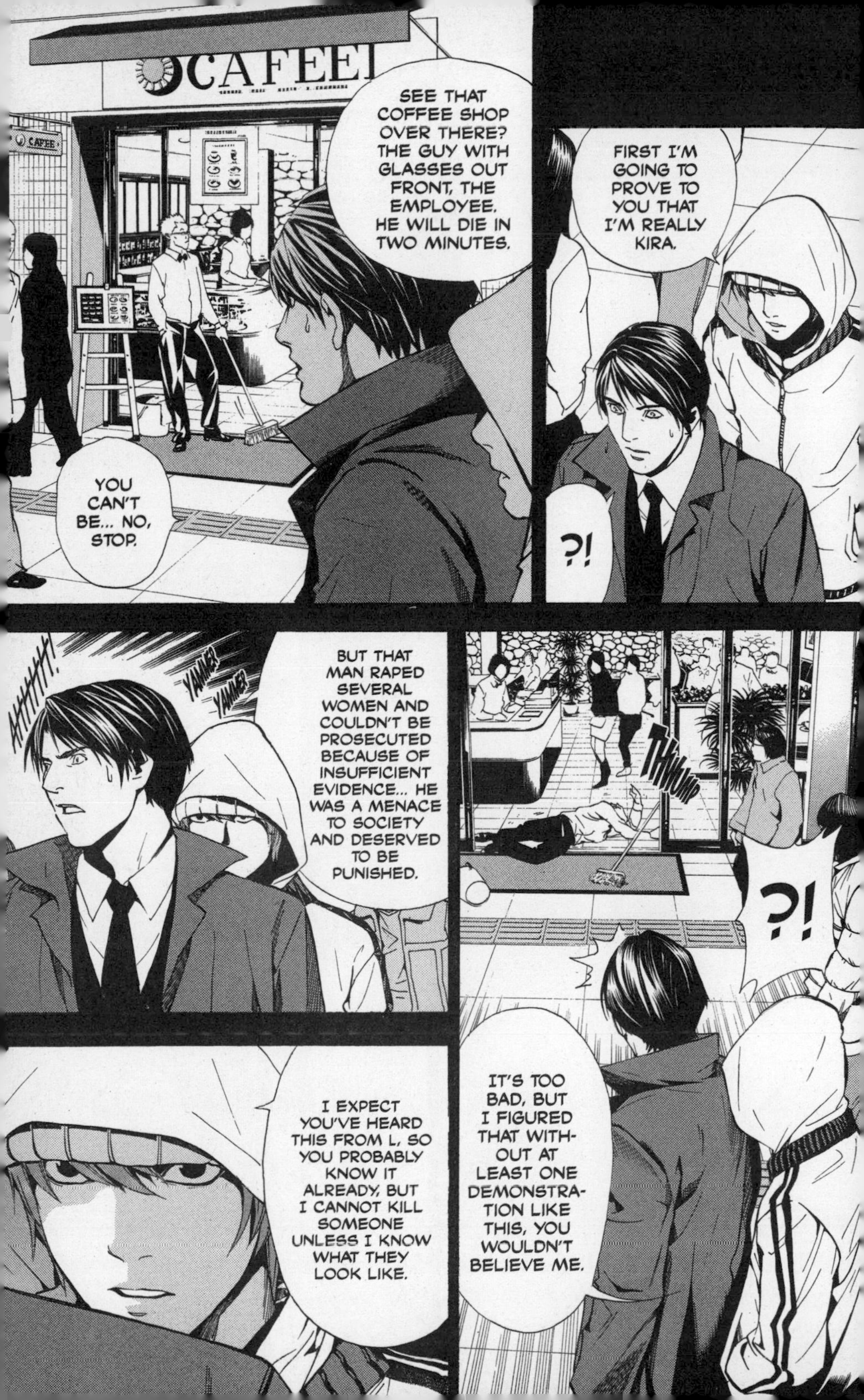
FIRST I'M GOING TO PROVE TO YOU THAT I'M REALLY KIRA.
?!
SEE THAT COFFEE SHOP OVER THERE? THE GUY WITH GLASSES OUT FRONT, THE EMPLOYEE. HE WILL DIE IN TWO MINUTES.
YOU CAN'T BE... NO, STOP.
THWUMP
?!
AHHHHH!
YAMMER YAMMER
BUT THAT MAN RAPED SEVERAL WOMEN AND COULDN'T BE PROSECUTED BECAUSE OF INSUFFICIENT EVIDENCE... HE WAS A MENACE TO SOCIETY AND DESERVED TO BE PUNISHED.
IT'S TOO BAD, BUT I FIGURED THAT WITH-OUT AT LEAST ONE DEMONSTRA-TION LIKE THIS, YOU WOULDN'T BELIEVE ME.
I EXPECT YOU'VE HEARD THIS FROM L, SO YOU PROBABLY KNOW IT ALREADY, BUT I CANNOT KILL SOMEONE UNLESS I KNOW WHAT THEY LOOK LIKE.

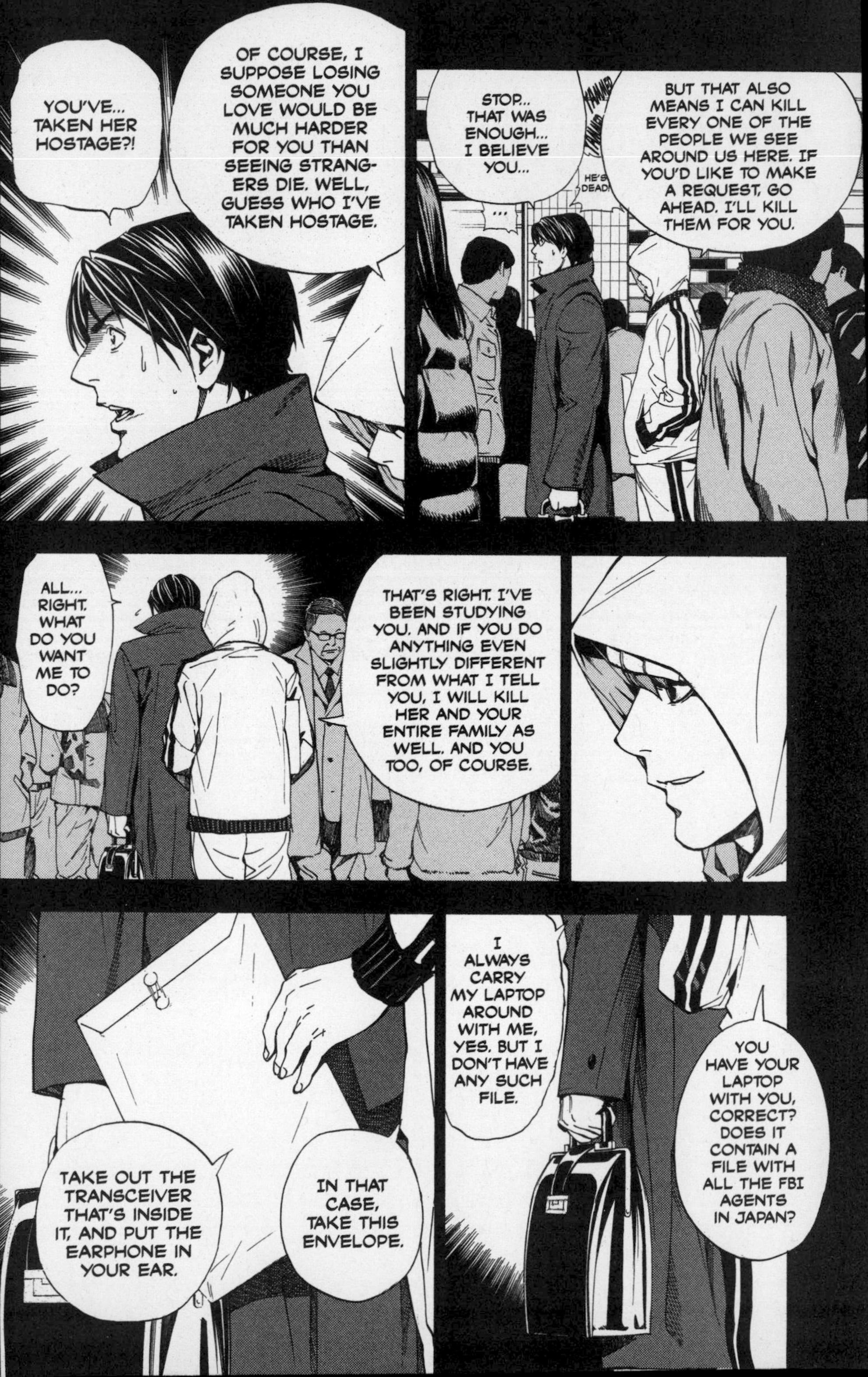
BUT THAT ALSO MEANS I CAN KILL EVERY ONE OF THE PEOPLE WE SEE AROUND US HERE. IF YOU'D LIKE TO MAKE A REQUEST, GO AHEAD. I'LL KILL THEM FOR YOU.
STOP... THAT WAS ENOUGH... I BELIEVE YOU...
HE'S DEAD!
...
OF COURSE, I SUPPOSE LOSING SOMEONE YOU LOVE WOULD BE MUCH HARDER FOR YOU THAN SEEING STRANGERS DIE. WELL, GUESS WHO I'VE TAKEN HOSTAGE.
YOU'VE... TAKEN HER HOSTAGE?!
THAT'S RIGHT. I'VE BEEN STUDYING YOU. AND IF YOU DO ANYTHING EVEN SLIGHTLY DIFFERENT FROM WHAT I TELL YOU, I WILL KILL HER AND YOUR ENTIRE FAMILY AS WELL. AND YOU TOO, OF COURSE.
ALL... RIGHT. WHAT DO YOU WANT ME TO DO?
YOU HAVE YOUR LAPTOP WITH YOU, CORRECT? DOES IT CONTAIN A FILE WITH ALL THE FBI AGENTS IN JAPAN?
I ALWAYS CARRY MY LAPTOP AROUND WITH ME, YES. BUT I DON'T HAVE ANY SUCH FILE.
IN THAT CASE, TAKE THIS ENVELOPE.
TAKE OUT THE TRANSCEIVER THAT'S INSIDE IT, AND PUT THE EARPHONE IN YOUR EAR.

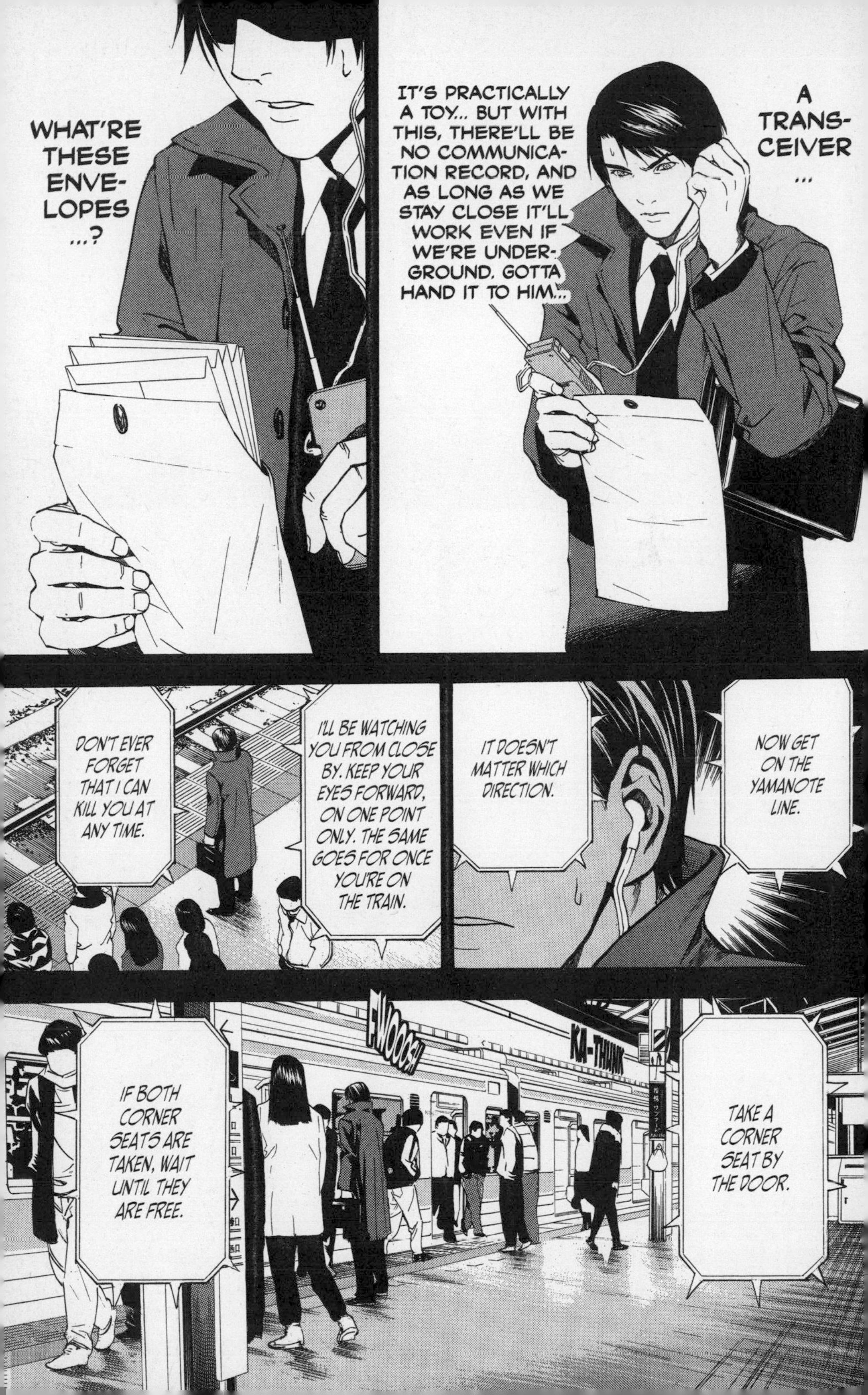
A TRANSCEIVER...
IT'S PRACTICALLY A TOY... BUT WITH THIS, THERE'LL BE NO COMMUNICATION RECORD, AND AS LONG AS WE STAY CLOSE IT'LL WORK EVEN IF WE'RE UNDERGROUND. GOTTA HAND IT TO HIM...
WHAT'RE THESE ENVELOPES...?
NOW GET ON THE YAMANOTE LINE.
IT DOESN'T MATTER WHICH DIRECTION.
I'LL BE WATCHING YOU FROM CLOSE BY. KEEP YOUR EYES FORWARD, ON ONE POINT ONLY. THE SAME GOES FOR ONCE YOU'RE ON THE TRAIN.
DON'T EVER FORGET THAT I CAN KILL YOU AT ANY TIME.
TAKE A CORNER SEAT BY THE DOOR.
KA-THUNK
FWOOOSH
IF BOTH CORNER SEATS ARE TAKEN, WAIT UNTIL THEY ARE FREE.

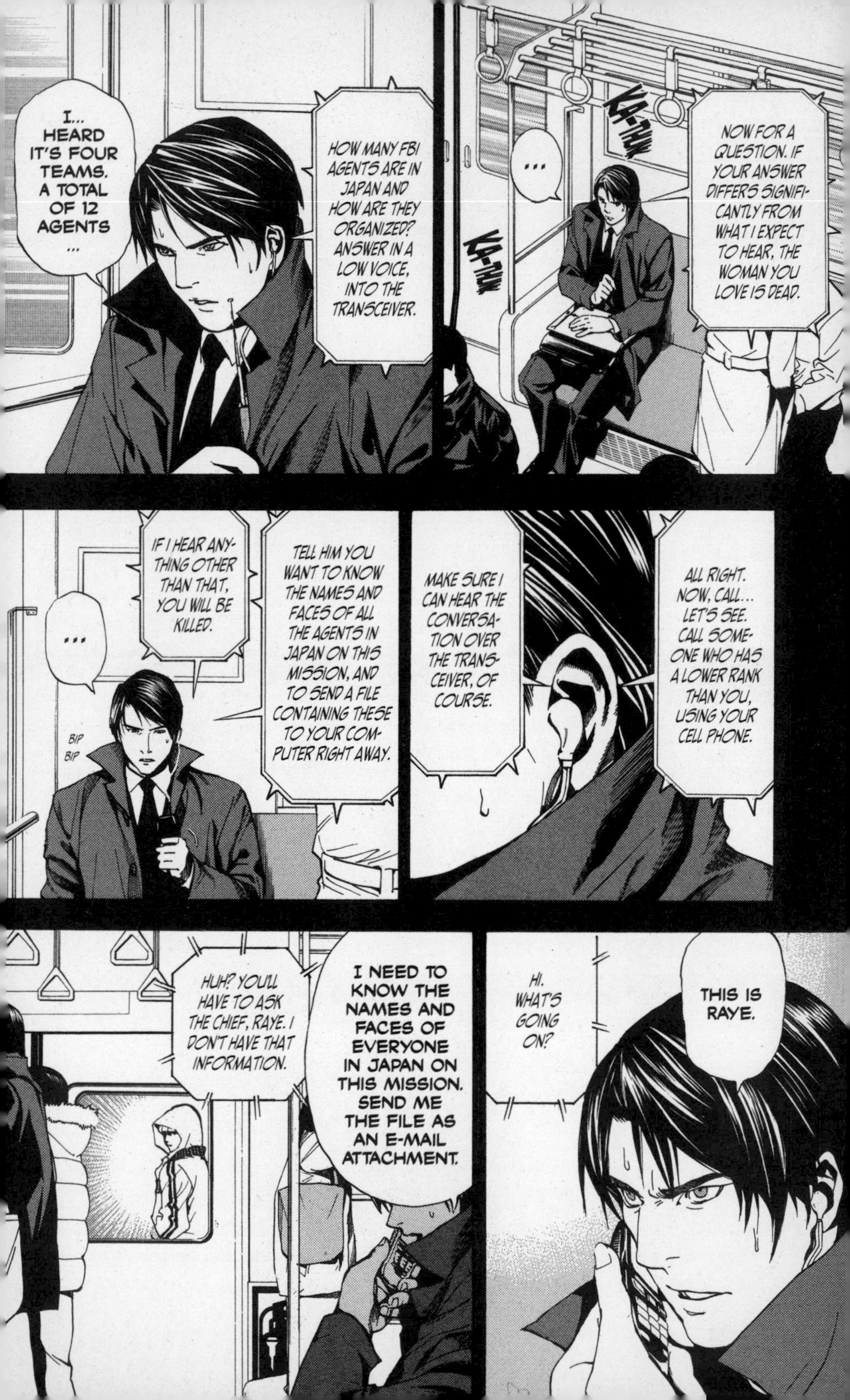
NOW FOR A QUESTION. IF YOUR ANSWER DIFFERS SIGNIFICANTLY FROM WHAT I EXPECT TO HEAR, THE WOMAN YOU LOVE IS DEAD.
KA-TUNK
...
KA-TUNK
HOW MANY FBI AGENTS ARE IN JAPAN AND HOW ARE THEY ORGANIZED? ANSWER IN A LOW VOICE, INTO THE TRANSCEIVER.
I... HEARD IT'S FOUR TEAMS. A TOTAL OF 12 AGENTS ...
ALL RIGHT. NOW, CALL... LET'S SEE. CALL SOMEONE WHO HAS A LOWER RANK THAN YOU, USING YOUR CELL PHONE.
MAKE SURE I CAN HEAR THE CONVERSATION OVER THE TRANSCEIVER, OF COURSE.
TELL HIM YOU WANT TO KNOW THE NAMES AND FACES OF ALL THE AGENTS IN JAPAN ON THIS MISSION, AND TO SEND A FILE CONTAINING THESE TO YOUR COMPUTER RIGHT AWAY.
IF I HEAR ANYTHING OTHER THAN THAT, YOU WILL BE KILLED.
...
BIP BIP
THIS IS RAYE.
HI. WHAT'S GOING ON?
I NEED TO KNOW THE NAMES AND FACES OF EVERYONE IN JAPAN ON THIS MISSION. SEND ME THE FILE AS AN E-MAIL ATTACHMENT.
HUH? YOU'LL HAVE TO ASK THE CHIEF, RAYE. I DON'T HAVE THAT INFORMATION.

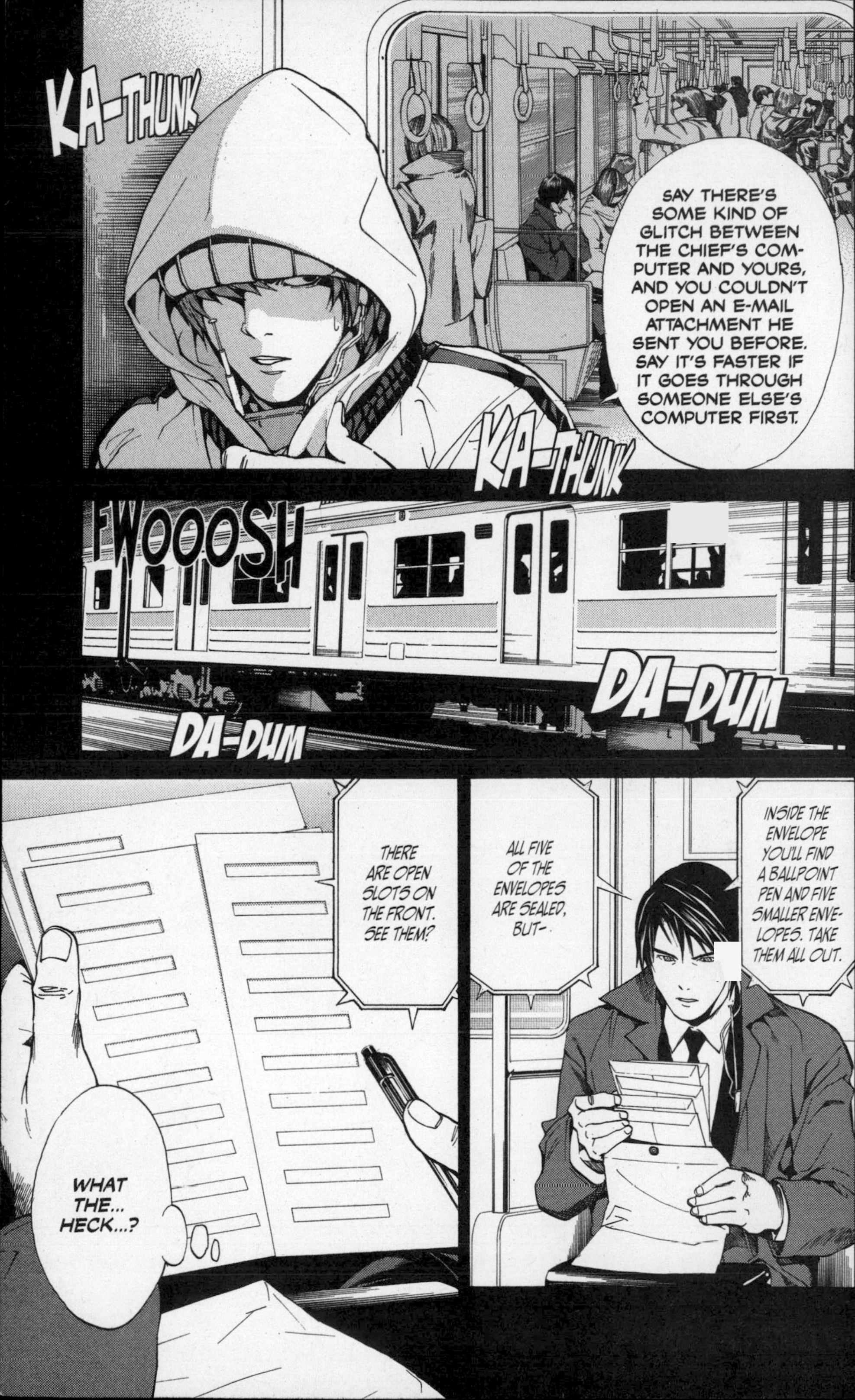

SAY THERE'S SOME KIND OF GLITCH BETWEEN THE CHIEF'S COM-PUTER AND YOURS, AND YOU COULDN'T OPEN AN E-MAIL ATTACHMENT HE SENT YOU BEFORE. SAY IT'S FASTER IF IT GOES THROUGH SOMEONE ELSE'S COMPUTER FIRST.
KA-THUNK
KA-THUNK
FWOOOSH
DA-DUM
DA-DUM
INSIDE THE ENVELOPE YOU'LL FIND A BALLPOINT PEN AND FIVE SMALLER ENVE-LOPES. TAKE THEM ALL OUT.
ALL FIVE OF THE ENVELOPES ARE SEALED, BUT-
THERE ARE OPEN SLOTS ON THE FRONT. SEE THEM?
WHAT THE... HECK...?

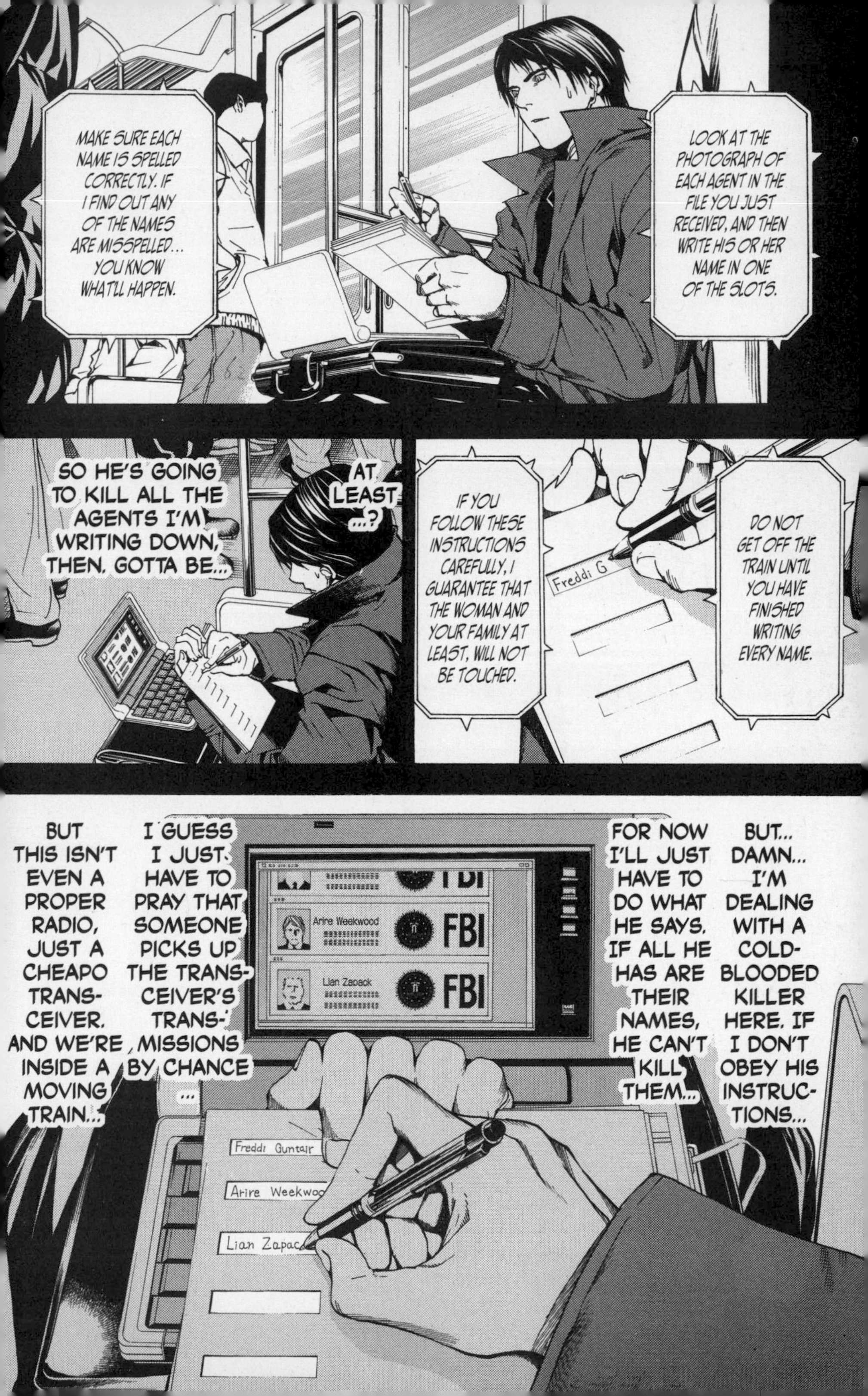
LOOK AT THE PHOTOGRAPH OF EACH AGENT IN THE FILE YOU JUST RECEIVED, AND THEN WRITE HIS OR HER NAME IN ONE OF THE SLOTS.
MAKE SURE EACH NAME IS SPELLED CORRECTLY. IF I FIND OUT ANY OF THE NAMES ARE MISSPELLED... YOU KNOW WHAT'LL HAPPEN.
DO NOT GET OFF THE TRAIN UNTIL YOU HAVE FINISHED WRITING EVERY NAME.
IF YOU FOLLOW THESE INSTRUCTIONS CAREFULLY, I GUARANTEE THAT THE WOMAN AND YOUR FAMILY AT LEAST, WILL NOT BE TOUCHED.
AT LEAST ...?
SO HE'S GOING TO KILL ALL THE AGENTS I'M WRITING DOWN, THEN. GOTTA BE...
BUT... DAMN... I'M DEALING WITH A COLD-BLOODED KILLER HERE. IF I DON'T OBEY HIS INSTRUCTIONS...
FOR NOW I'LL JUST HAVE TO DO WHAT HE SAYS. IF ALL HE HAS ARE THEIR NAMES, HE CAN'T KILL THEM...
I GUESS I JUST HAVE TO PRAY THAT SOMEONE PICKS UP THE TRANSCEIVER'S TRANSMISSIONS BY CHANCE...
BUT THIS ISN'T EVEN A PROPER RADIO, JUST A CHEAPO TRANSCEIVER. AND WE'RE INSIDE A MOVING TRAIN...
Arire Weekwood
FBI
Lian Zapack
FBI

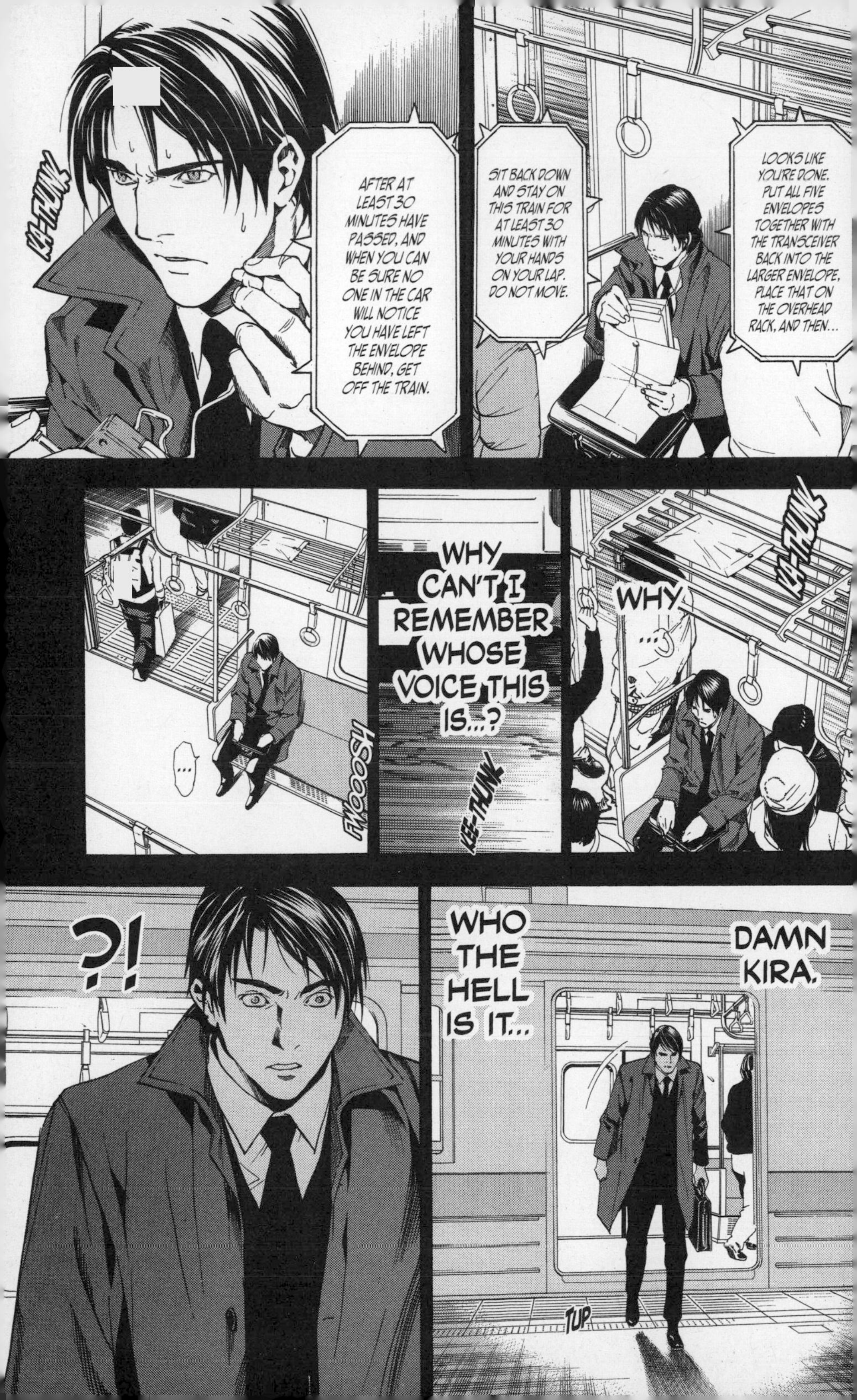
LOOKS LIKE YOU'RE DONE. PUT ALL FIVE ENVELOPES TOGETHER WITH THE TRANSCEIVER BACK INTO THE LARGER ENVELOPE, PLACE THAT ON THE OVERHEAD RACK, AND THEN...
SIT BACK DOWN AND STAY ON THIS TRAIN FOR AT LEAST 30 MINUTES WITH YOUR HANDS ON YOUR LAP. DO NOT MOVE.
AFTER AT LEAST 30 MINUTES HAVE PASSED, AND WHEN YOU CAN BE SURE NO ONE IN THE CAR WILL NOTICE YOU HAVE LEFT THE ENVELOPE BEHIND, GET OFF THE TRAIN.
KA-THUNK
KA-THUNK
WHY ...
WHY CAN'T I REMEMBER WHOSE VOICE THIS IS...?
KEE-THUNK
...
FWOOOSH
DAMN KIRA.
WHO THE HELL IS IT...
TUP
?!

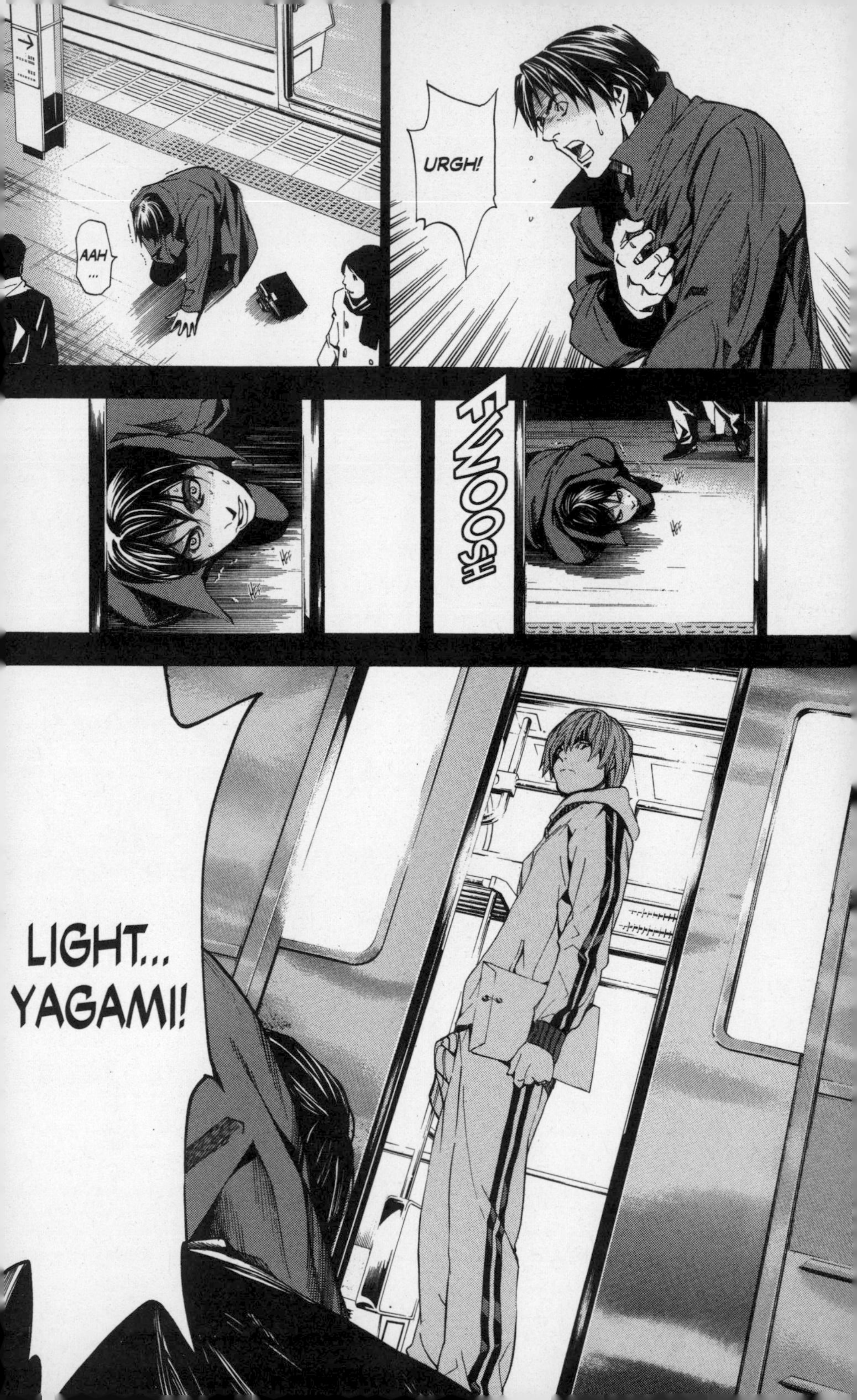
URGH!
AAH ...
HFF
HFF
FWOOSH
HFF
HFF
LIGHT... YAGAMI!

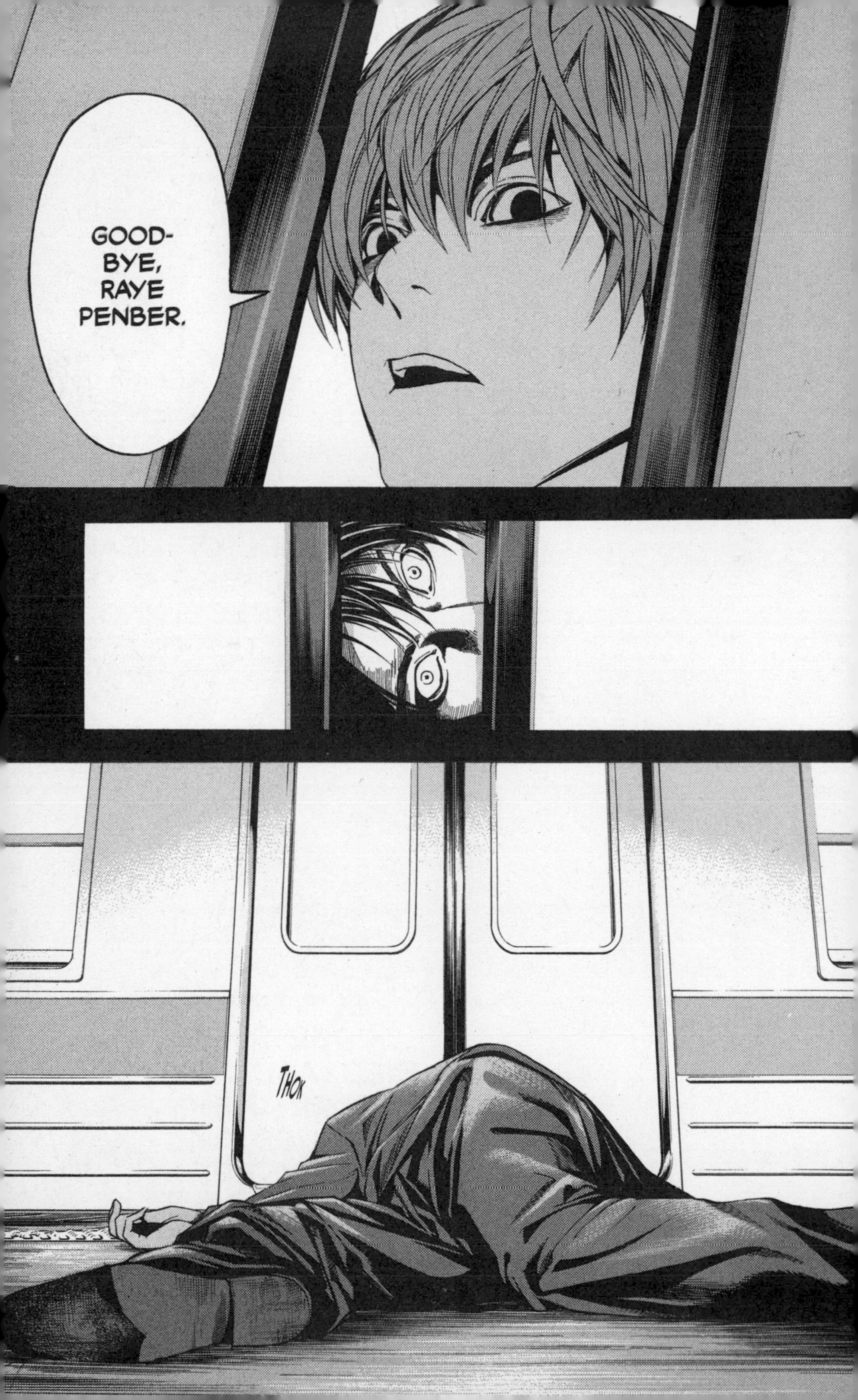
GOOD-BYE, RAYE PENBER.
THOK

Yonegoro Nusumi Heart attack
Dies at 3:05 p.m. on December 27, 2003

Raye Penber Heart attack
Passes in front of the "CAFEEL"
coffee shop in Shinjuku station under-
ground at 3:00 p.m. on December 27,
2003, carrying his laptop computer,
and boards a train on the Yamanote
line. Dies three seconds after getting
off the train.

December 27, 2003 after
ontaining the names and photos
in Japan on the Kira case.
ttack on December 27, 2003
00 p.m. on December 27, the
obtaining a file containing the
he FBI agents in Japan on the Kira case.

| Freddi Guntair | Heart attack<br>Dies at 4:00 p.m. on December 27, 2003 after<br>obtaining a file containing the names and photos<br>of all the FBI agents in Japan on the Kira case. |
| Arire Weeknvood | Heart attack<br>Dies at 3:00 p.m. on December 27, 2003 after<br>obtaining a file containing the names and photos<br>of all the FBI agents in Japan on the Kira case. |
| Lian Zapack | Heart attack<br>Dies at 5:00 p.m. on December 27, 2003 after<br>obtaining a file containing the names and photos<br>of all the FBI agents in Japan on the Kira case. |
| Toors Denote | Heart attack<br>Dies at 3:00 p.m. on December 27, 2003 after<br>obtaining a file containing the names and photos<br>of all the FBI agents in Japan on the Kira case. |
| Ale Funderrem | Heart attack<br>Dies at 4:00 p.m. on December 27, 2003 a<br>obtaining a file containing the names and photos<br>of all the FBI agents in Japan on the Kira case. |
| Bess Skelletd | Heart attack<br>Dies at 5:00 p.m. on December 27, 2003 after |

NOW ALL THE FBI AGENTS HAVE ACTED THE SAME WAY... AND DIED OF HEART ATTACKS AFTER RECEIVING THE FILE.

BUT THE ORDER THEY DIED, AND THE ORDER THEY RECEIVED THE FILES, WERE TOTALLY RANDOM.

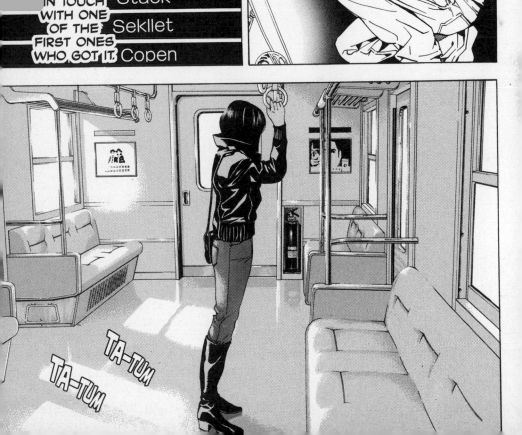

| NAME | FILE | DEATH |
|---|---|---|
| Haley Belle | 1 | 5 |
| Raye Penber | 2 | 9 |
| Lian Zapack | 3 | 11 |
| Arire Weekwood | 4 | 2 |

THANK YOU, DIRECTOR. WITH YOUR COMPUTER RECORDS AND INFORMATION FROM THE NPA, I'VE BEEN ABLE TO WORK OUT THE ORDER THEY RECEIVED THE FILES, AND THE ORDER THEY WERE KILLED.

Haley Belle
Penber
apack
eekwood
nderrem
Guntair
Staek
Sekllet
Copen

BUT IF MY DEDUCTION IS CORRECT, THE ORDER IN WHICH THESE AGENTS RECEIVED THE FILE IS AN IMPORTANT CLUE. YOU WERE IN TOUCH WITH ONE OF THE FIRST ONES WHO GOT IT.

KIRA, I'M SURE YOU CONTROLLED THIS AS MUCH AS YOU COULD.

TA-TUM

TA-TUM

# DEATH NOTE
## How to use it
### VIII

○ You may also write the cause and/or details of death prior to filling in the name of the individual. Be sure to insert the name in front of the written cause of death.

You have about 19 days (according to the human calendar) in order to fill in a name.

死因や死の状況を先に書き、
後から名前をその文字の前に書き込んでも有効となる。
その際、名前を書くまでの有効期間は人間界単位で約１９日間。

○ Even if you do not actually possess the DEATH NOTE, the effect will be the same if you can recognize the person and his/her name to place in the blank.

デスノートの所有者以外でも、顔と名前の認識を持って名前を書き込めば、
所有者が使う時と同じ効果がある。

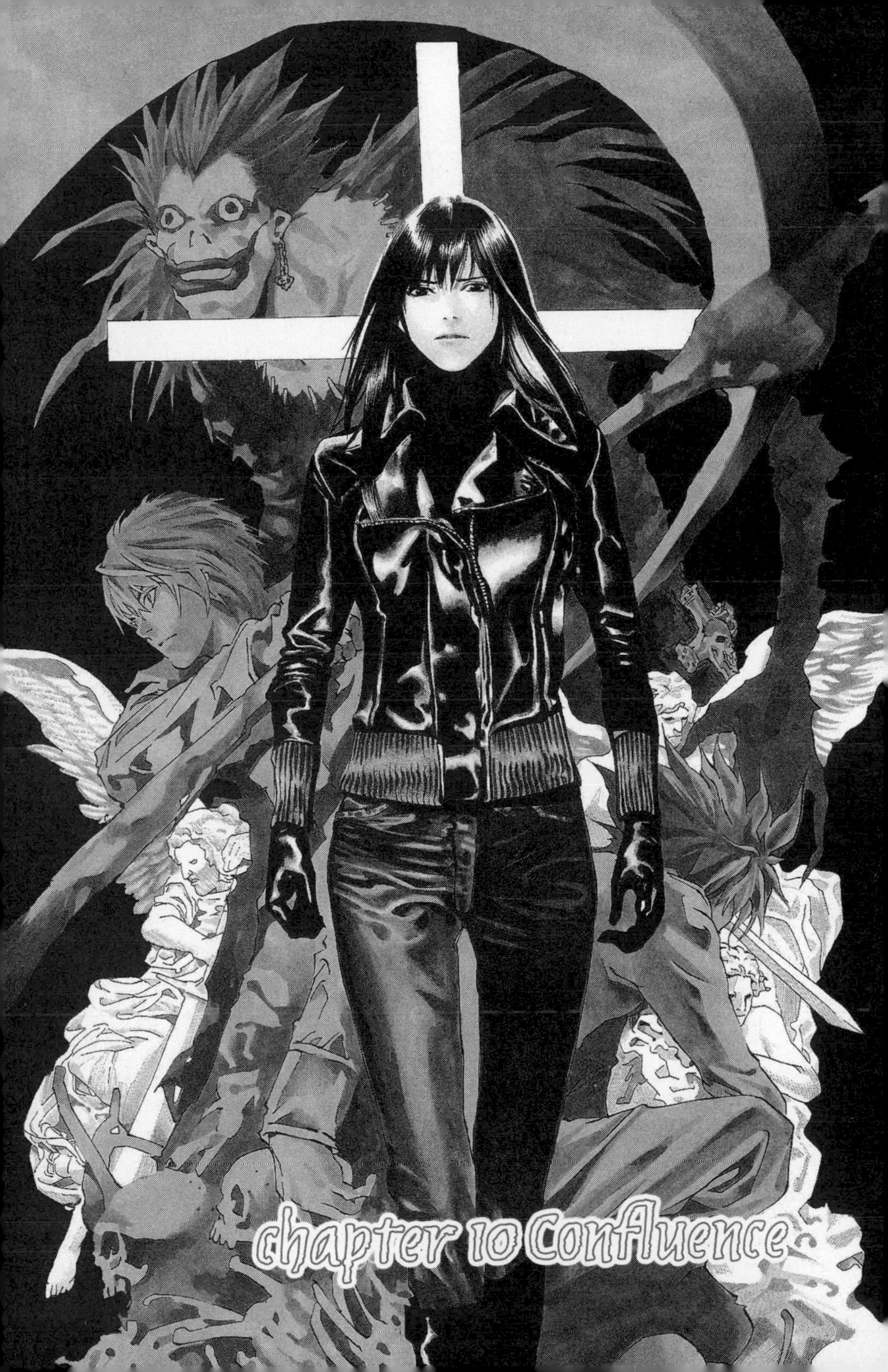
chapter 10 Confluence

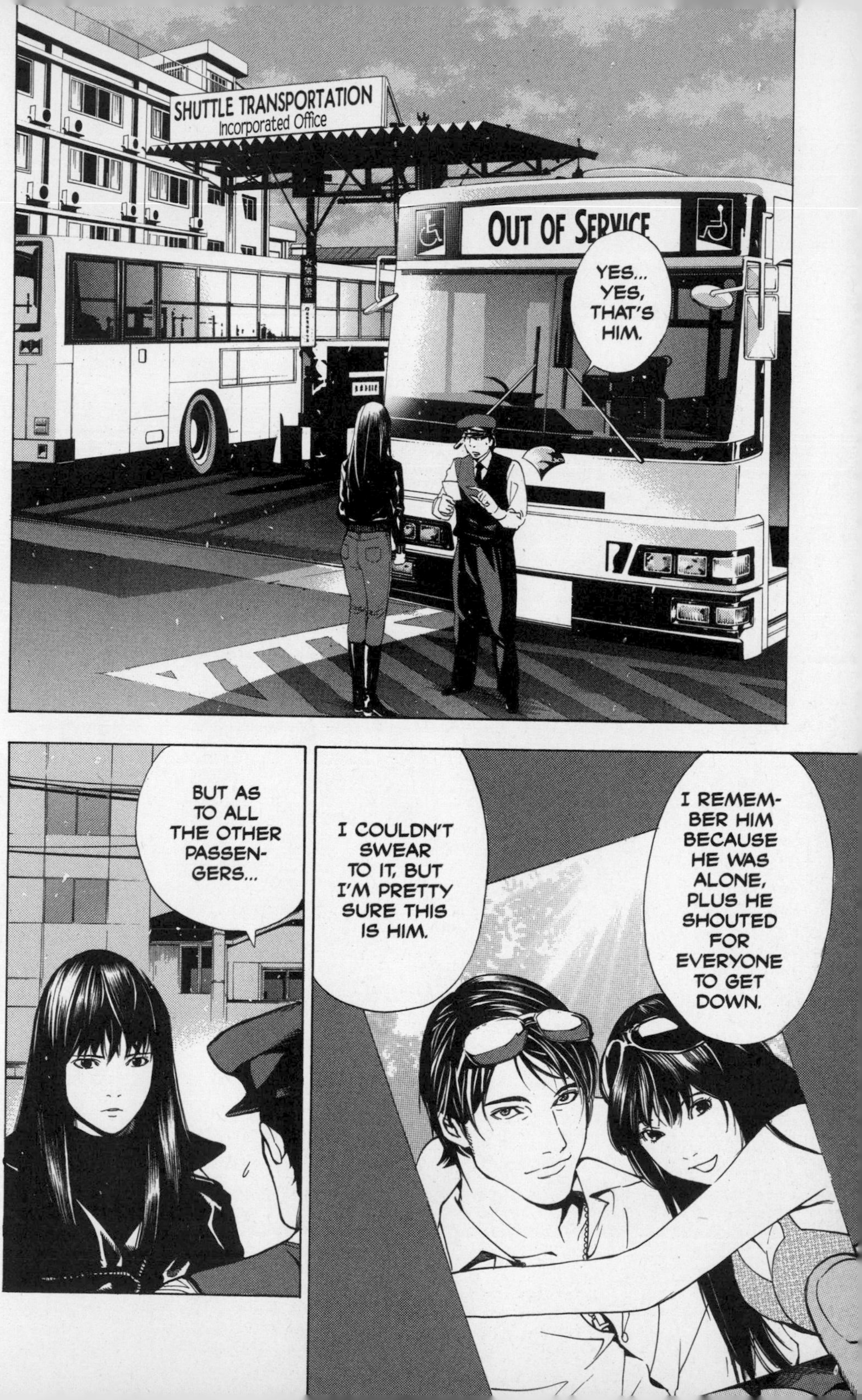
SHUTTLE TRANSPORTATION
Incorporated Office
OUT OF SERVICE
YES... YES, THAT'S HIM.
I REMEMBER HIM BECAUSE HE WAS ALONE, PLUS HE SHOUTED FOR EVERYONE TO GET DOWN.
I COULDN'T SWEAR TO IT, BUT I'M PRETTY SURE THIS IS HIM.
BUT AS TO ALL THE OTHER PASSENGERS...

READ THIS WAY

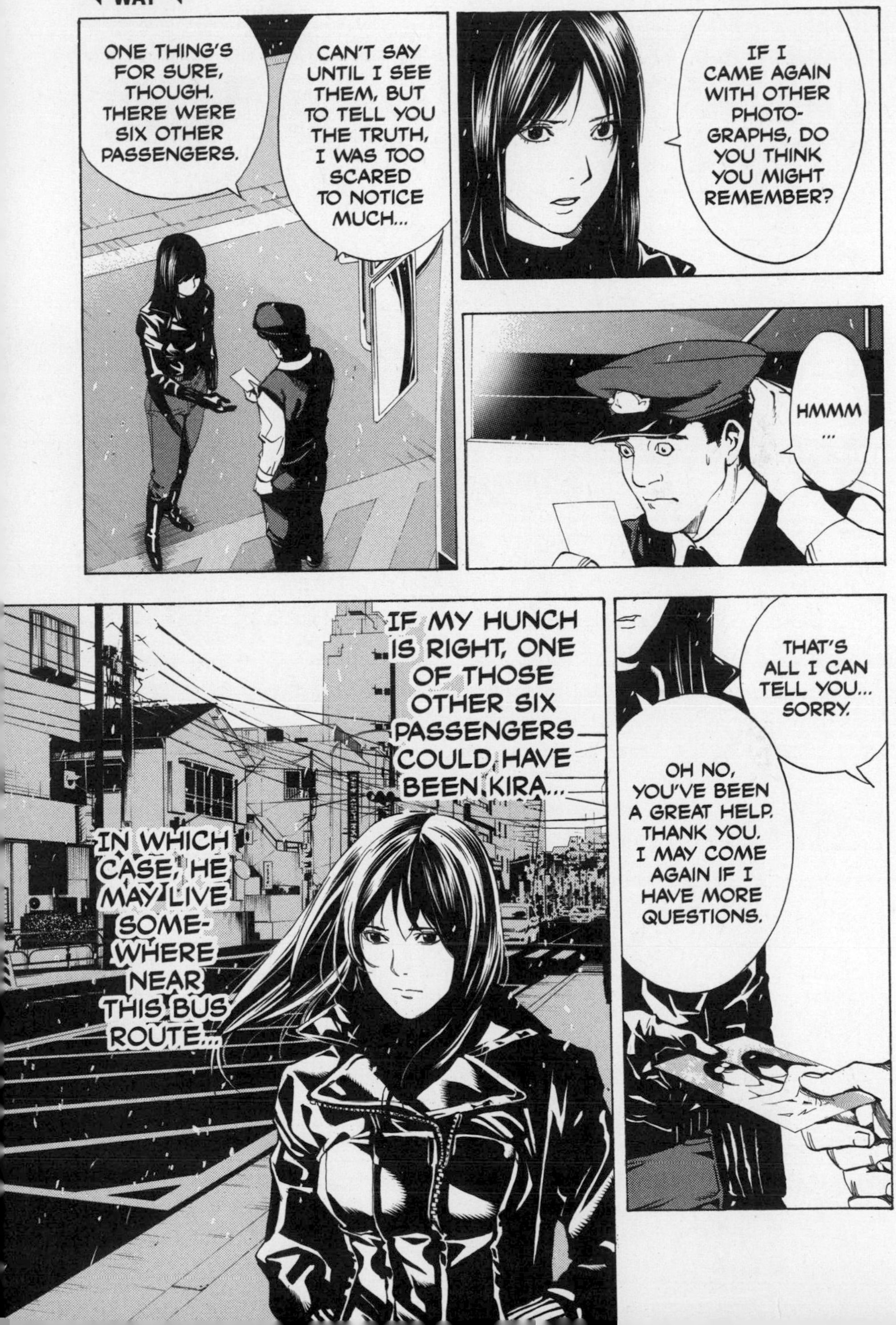
IF I CAME AGAIN WITH OTHER PHOTO-GRAPHS, DO YOU THINK YOU MIGHT REMEMBER?
HMMM ...
CAN'T SAY UNTIL I SEE THEM, BUT TO TELL YOU THE TRUTH, I WAS TOO SCARED TO NOTICE MUCH...
ONE THING'S FOR SURE, THOUGH. THERE WERE SIX OTHER PASSENGERS.
THAT'S ALL I CAN TELL YOU... SORRY.
OH NO, YOU'VE BEEN A GREAT HELP. THANK YOU. I MAY COME AGAIN IF I HAVE MORE QUESTIONS.
IF MY HUNCH IS RIGHT, ONE OF THOSE OTHER SIX PASSENGERS COULD HAVE BEEN KIRA...
IN WHICH CASE, HE MAY LIVE SOME-WHERE NEAR THIS BUS ROUTE...

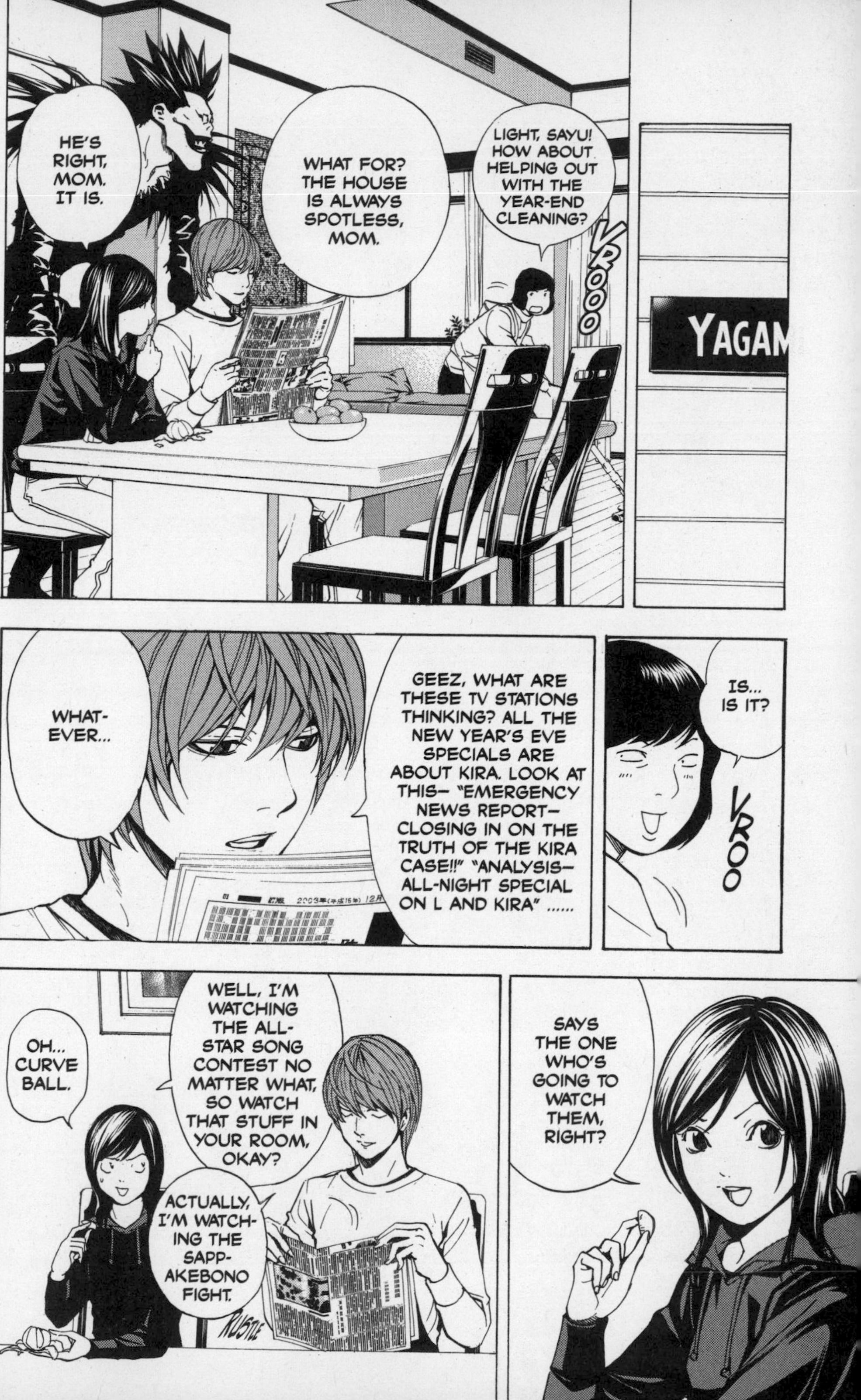
YAGAM
LIGHT, SAYU! HOW ABOUT HELPING OUT WITH THE YEAR-END CLEANING?
VROOOO
WHAT FOR? THE HOUSE IS ALWAYS SPOTLESS, MOM.
HE'S RIGHT, MOM. IT IS.
IS... IS IT?
VROO
GEEZ, WHAT ARE THESE TV STATIONS THINKING? ALL THE NEW YEAR'S EVE SPECIALS ARE ABOUT KIRA. LOOK AT THIS— "EMERGENCY NEWS REPORT— CLOSING IN ON THE TRUTH OF THE KIRA CASE!!" "ANALYSIS— ALL-NIGHT SPECIAL ON L AND KIRA" ......
WHAT-EVER...
SAYS THE ONE WHO'S GOING TO WATCH THEM, RIGHT?
WELL, I'M WATCHING THE ALL-STAR SONG CONTEST NO MATTER WHAT, SO WATCH THAT STUFF IN YOUR ROOM, OKAY?
ACTUALLY, I'M WATCHING THE SAPP-AKEBONO FIGHT.
OH... CURVE BALL.
RUSTLE

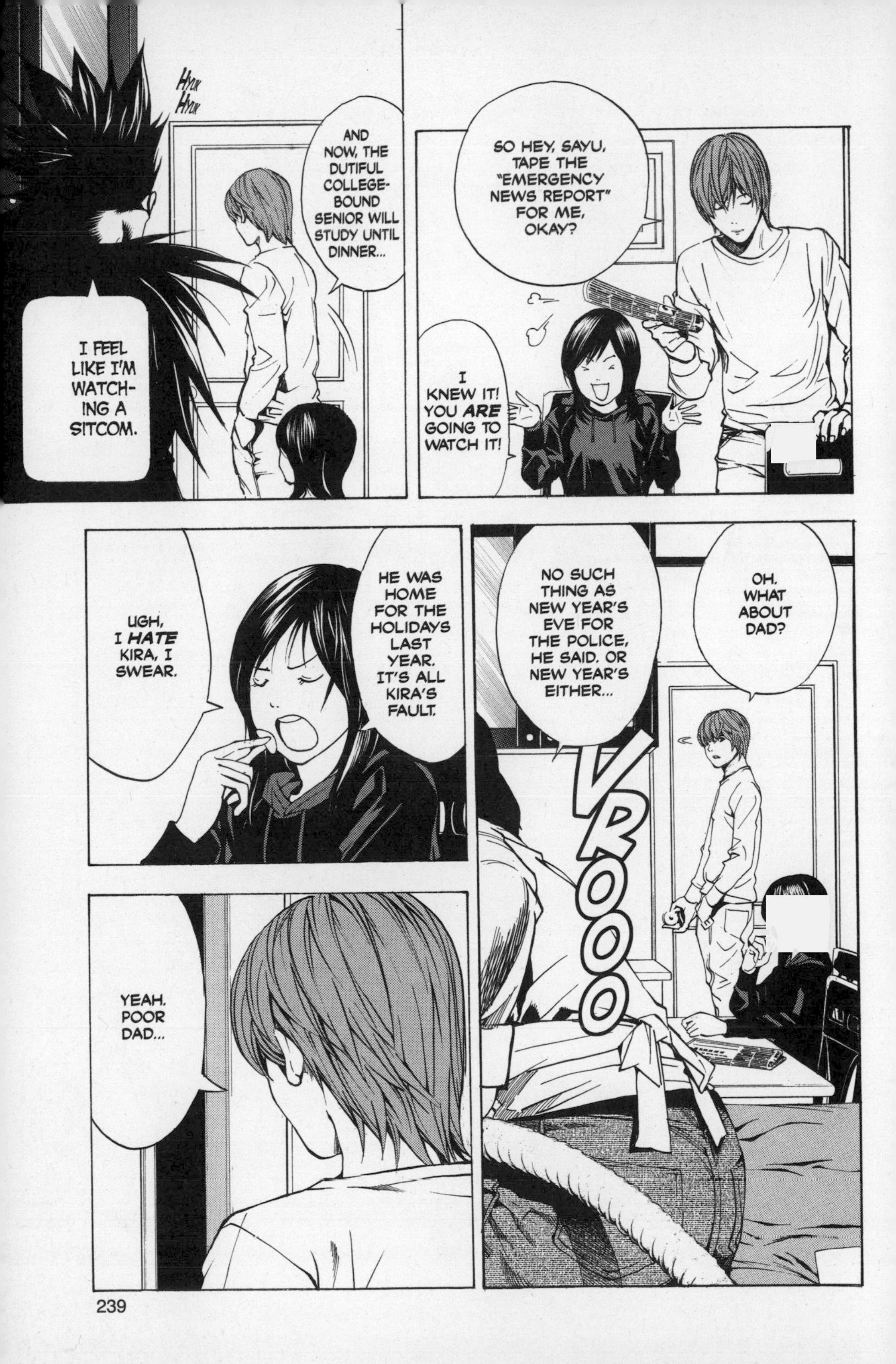
SO HEY, SAYU, TAPE THE "EMERGENCY NEWS REPORT" FOR ME, OKAY?
I KNEW IT! YOU *ARE* GOING TO WATCH IT!
AND NOW, THE DUTIFUL COLLEGE-BOUND SENIOR WILL STUDY UNTIL DINNER...
HYUK HYUK
I FEEL LIKE I'M WATCHING A SITCOM.
OH. WHAT ABOUT DAD?
NO SUCH THING AS NEW YEAR'S EVE FOR THE POLICE, HE SAID. OR NEW YEAR'S EITHER...
VROOO
HE WAS HOME FOR THE HOLIDAYS LAST YEAR. IT'S ALL KIRA'S FAULT.
UGH, I *HATE* KIRA, I SWEAR.
YEAH. POOR DAD...

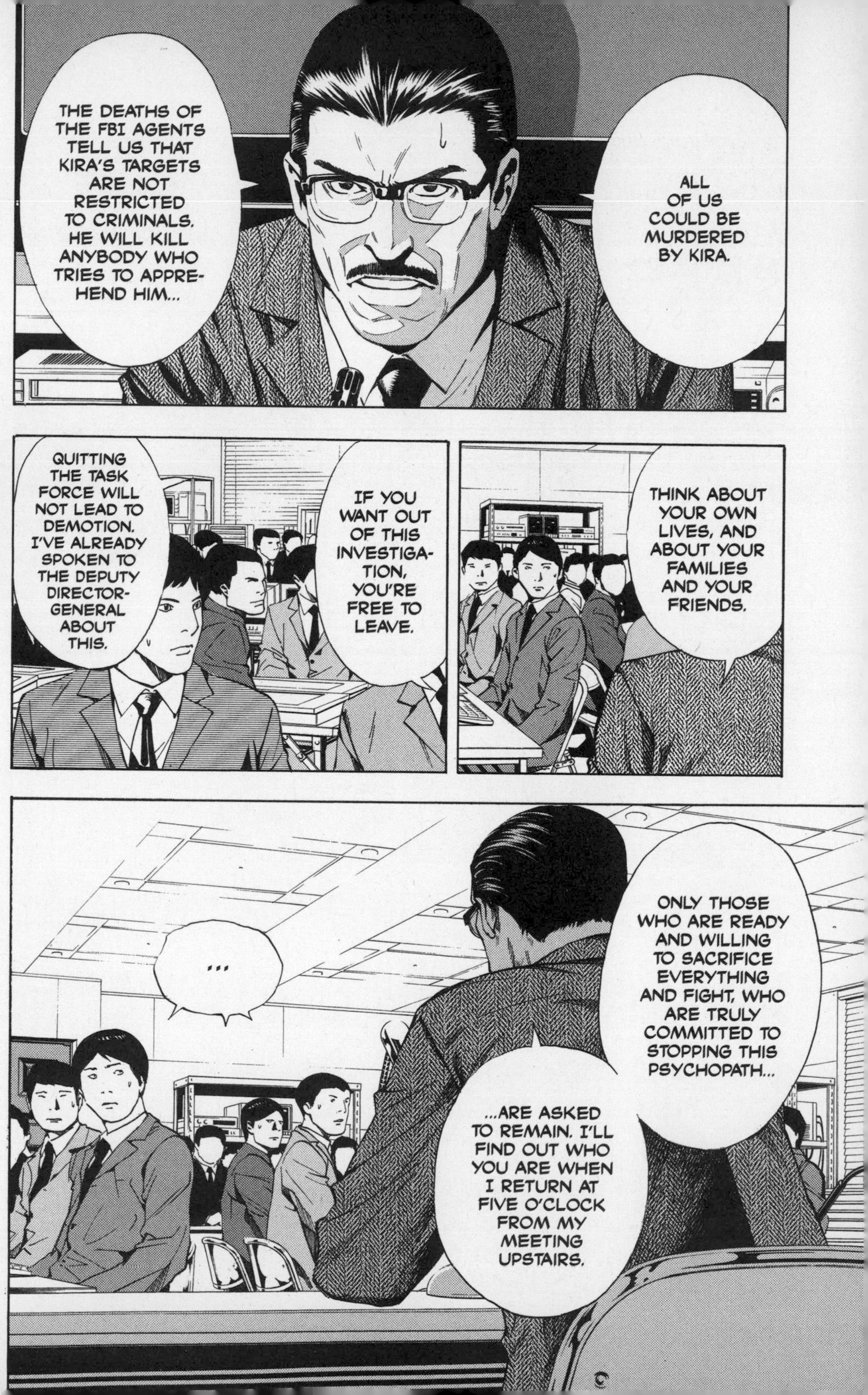
ALL OF US COULD BE MURDERED BY KIRA.
THE DEATHS OF THE FBI AGENTS TELL US THAT KIRA'S TARGETS ARE NOT RESTRICTED TO CRIMINALS. HE WILL KILL ANYBODY WHO TRIES TO APPRE-HEND HIM...
THINK ABOUT YOUR OWN LIVES, AND ABOUT YOUR FAMILIES AND YOUR FRIENDS.
IF YOU WANT OUT OF THIS INVESTIGA-TION, YOU'RE FREE TO LEAVE.
QUITTING THE TASK FORCE WILL NOT LEAD TO DEMOTION. I'VE ALREADY SPOKEN TO THE DEPUTY DIRECTOR-GENERAL ABOUT THIS.
ONLY THOSE WHO ARE READY AND WILLING TO SACRIFICE EVERYTHING AND FIGHT, WHO ARE TRULY COMMITTED TO STOPPING THIS PSYCHOPATH...
...ARE ASKED TO REMAIN. I'LL FIND OUT WHO YOU ARE WHEN I RETURN AT FIVE O'CLOCK FROM MY MEETING UPSTAIRS.
...

READ THIS WAY

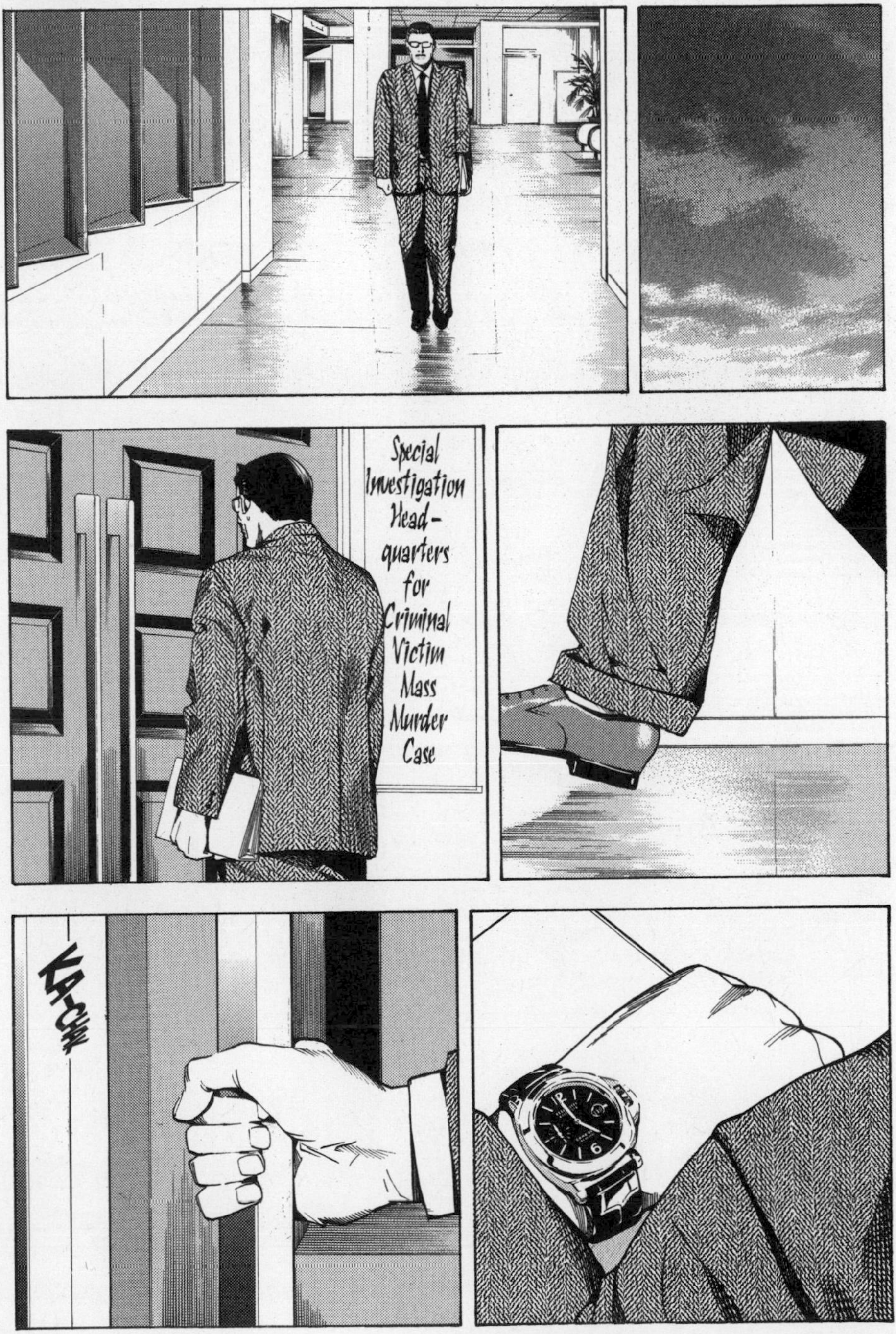
Special Investigation Head-quarters for Criminal Victim Mass Murder Case
KA-CHK

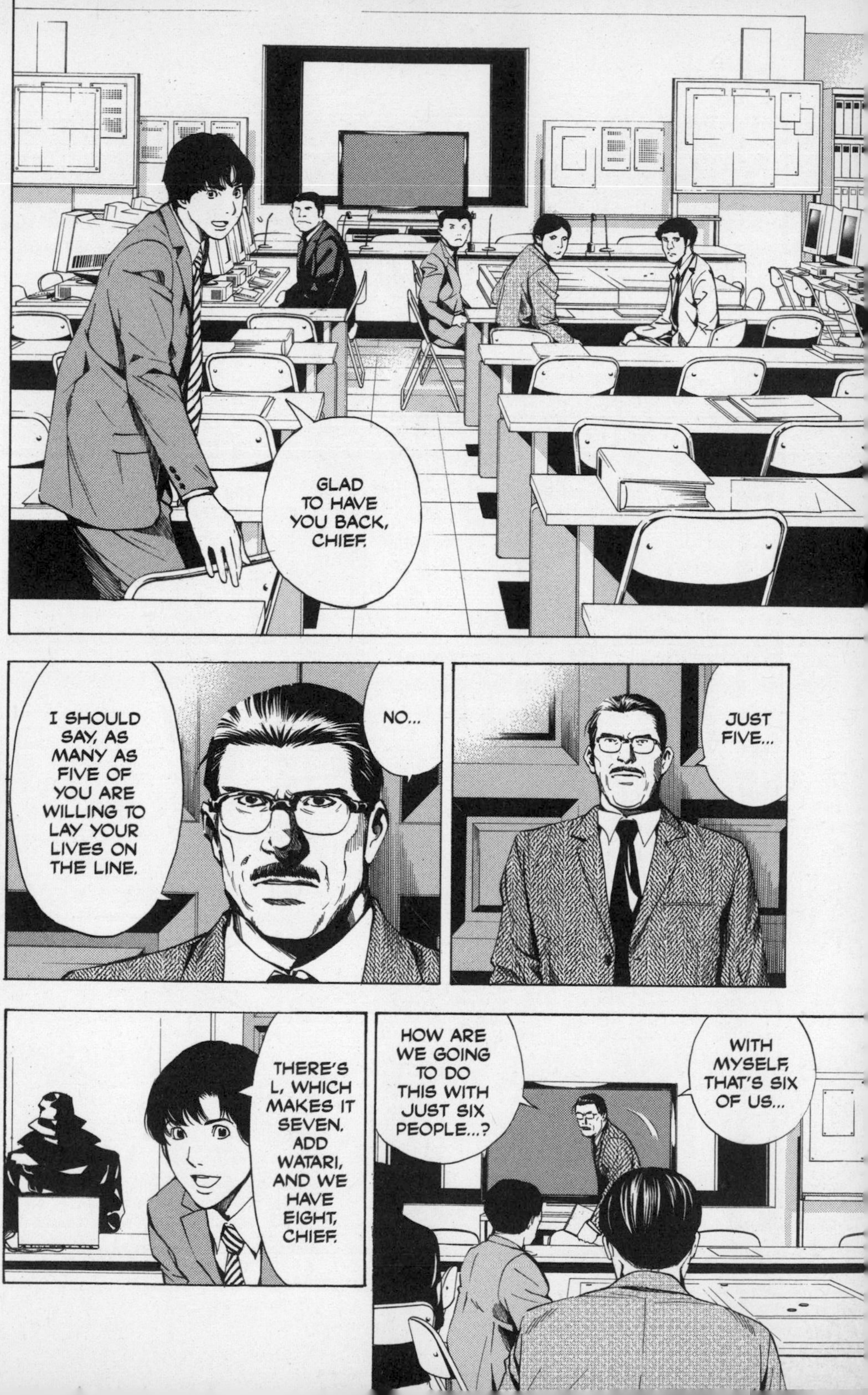
GLAD TO HAVE YOU BACK, CHIEF.
JUST FIVE...
NO...
I SHOULD SAY, AS MANY AS FIVE OF YOU ARE WILLING TO LAY YOUR LIVES ON THE LINE.
WITH MYSELF, THAT'S SIX OF US...
HOW ARE WE GOING TO DO THIS WITH JUST SIX PEOPLE...?
THERE'S L, WHICH MAKES IT SEVEN. ADD WATARI, AND WE HAVE EIGHT, CHIEF.

READ THIS WAY

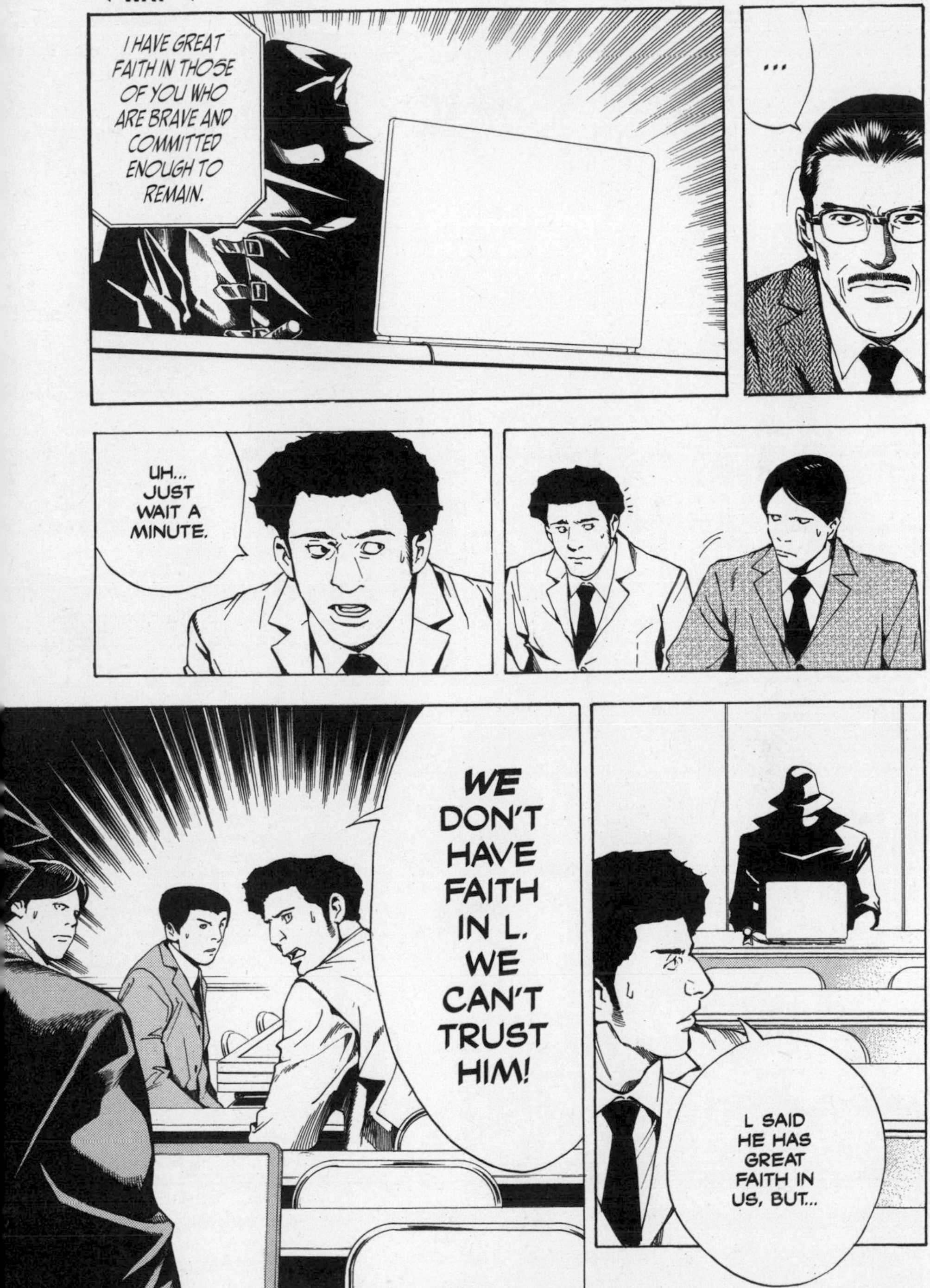
...
I HAVE GREAT FAITH IN THOSE OF YOU WHO ARE BRAVE AND COMMITTED ENOUGH TO REMAIN.
UH... JUST WAIT A MINUTE.
L SAID HE HAS GREAT FAITH IN US, BUT...
WE DON'T HAVE FAITH IN L. WE CAN'T TRUST HIM!

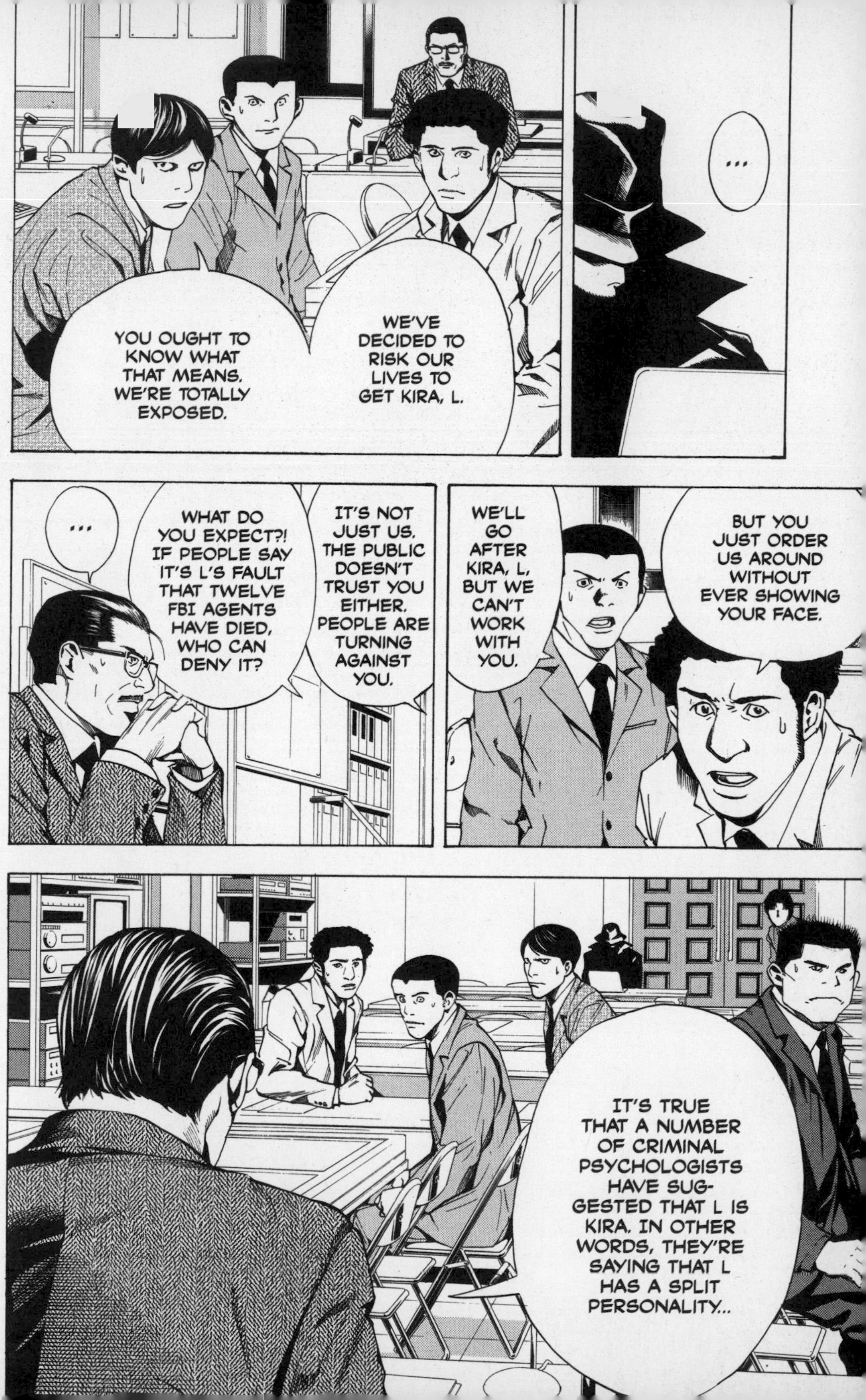
...
WE'VE DECIDED TO RISK OUR LIVES TO GET KIRA, L.
YOU OUGHT TO KNOW WHAT THAT MEANS. WE'RE TOTALLY EXPOSED.
BUT YOU JUST ORDER US AROUND WITHOUT EVER SHOWING YOUR FACE.
WE'LL GO AFTER KIRA, L, BUT WE CAN'T WORK WITH YOU.
IT'S NOT JUST US. THE PUBLIC DOESN'T TRUST YOU EITHER. PEOPLE ARE TURNING AGAINST YOU.
WHAT DO YOU EXPECT?! IF PEOPLE SAY IT'S L'S FAULT THAT TWELVE FBI AGENTS HAVE DIED, WHO CAN DENY IT?
...
IT'S TRUE THAT A NUMBER OF CRIMINAL PSYCHOLOGISTS HAVE SUG-GESTED THAT L IS KIRA. IN OTHER WORDS, THEY'RE SAYING THAT L HAS A SPLIT PERSONALITY...

READ THIS WAY

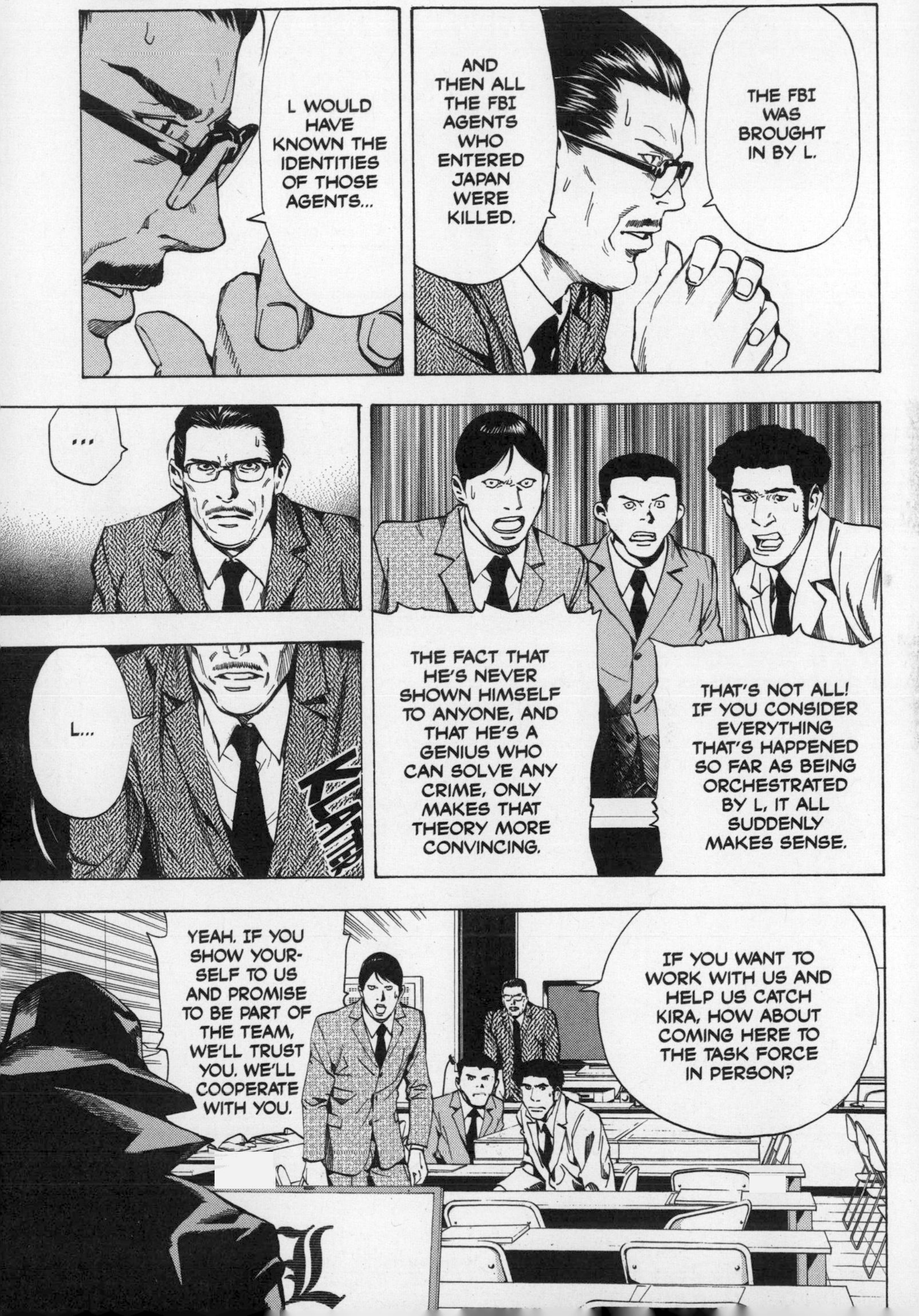
THE FBI WAS BROUGHT IN BY L.
AND THEN ALL THE FBI AGENTS WHO ENTERED JAPAN WERE KILLED.
L WOULD HAVE KNOWN THE IDENTITIES OF THOSE AGENTS...
THAT'S NOT ALL! IF YOU CONSIDER EVERYTHING THAT'S HAPPENED SO FAR AS BEING ORCHESTRATED BY L, IT ALL SUDDENLY MAKES SENSE.
THE FACT THAT HE'S NEVER SHOWN HIMSELF TO ANYONE, AND THAT HE'S A GENIUS WHO CAN SOLVE ANY CRIME, ONLY MAKES THAT THEORY MORE CONVINCING.
...
L...
KLATTER
IF YOU WANT TO WORK WITH US AND HELP US CATCH KIRA, HOW ABOUT COMING HERE TO THE TASK FORCE IN PERSON?
YEAH. IF YOU SHOW YOURSELF TO US AND PROMISE TO BE PART OF THE TEAM, WE'LL TRUST YOU. WE'LL COOPERATE WITH YOU.

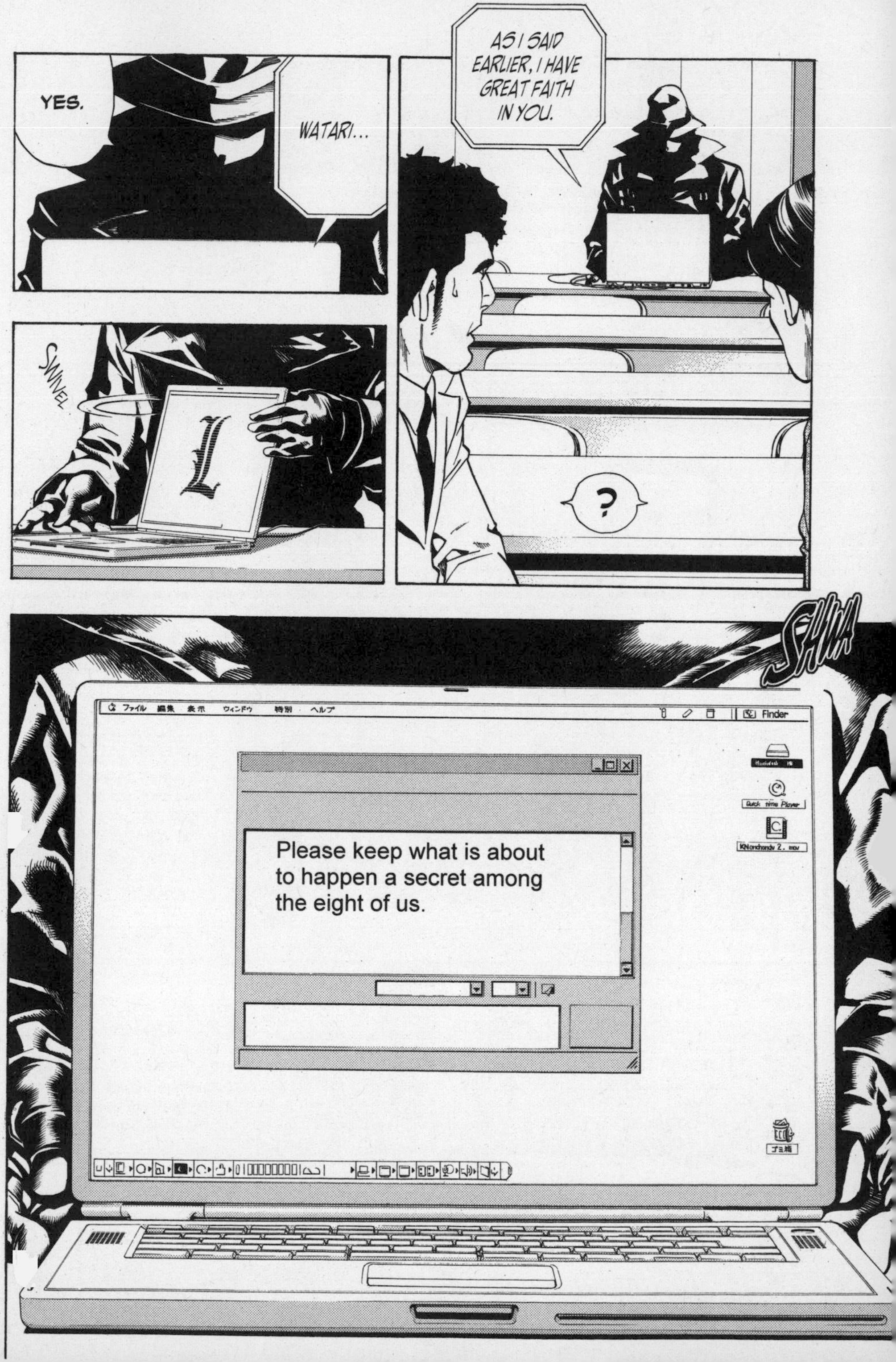
AS I SAID EARLIER, I HAVE GREAT FAITH IN YOU.
?
WATARI...
YES.
SWIVEL
SHAA
ファイル 編集 表示 ウィンドウ 特別 ヘルプ
Finder
Please keep what is about to happen a secret among the eight of us.

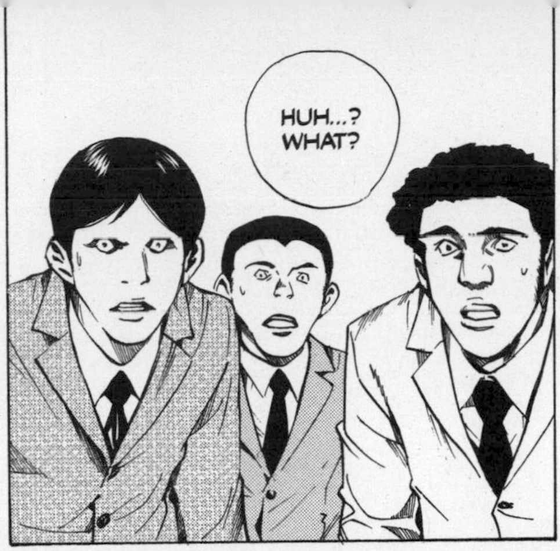
HUH...? WHAT?
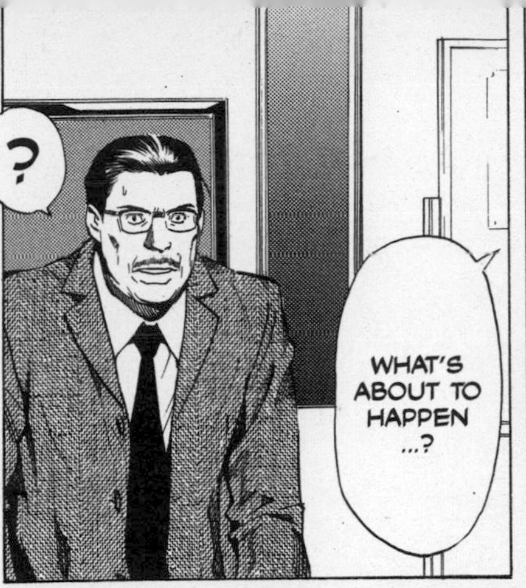
?
WHAT'S ABOUT TO HAPPEN ...?
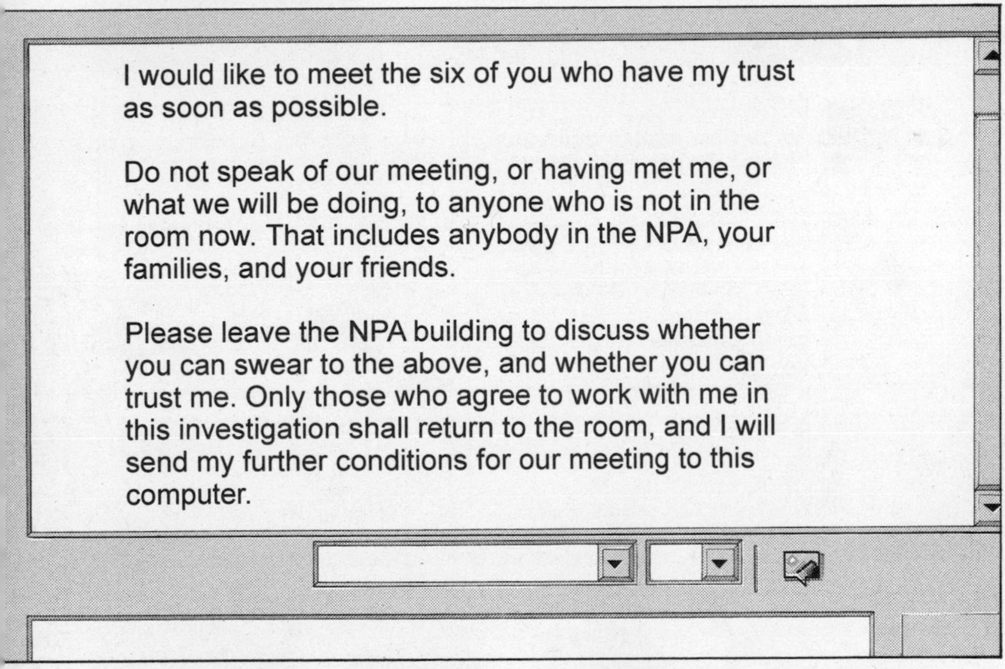
I would like to meet the six of you who have my trust as soon as possible.
Do not speak of our meeting, or having met me, or what we will be doing, to anyone who is not in the room now. That includes anybody in the NPA, your families, and your friends.
Please leave the NPA building to discuss whether you can swear to the above, and whether you can trust me. Only those who agree to work with me in this investigation shall return to the room, and I will send my further conditions for our meeting to this computer.
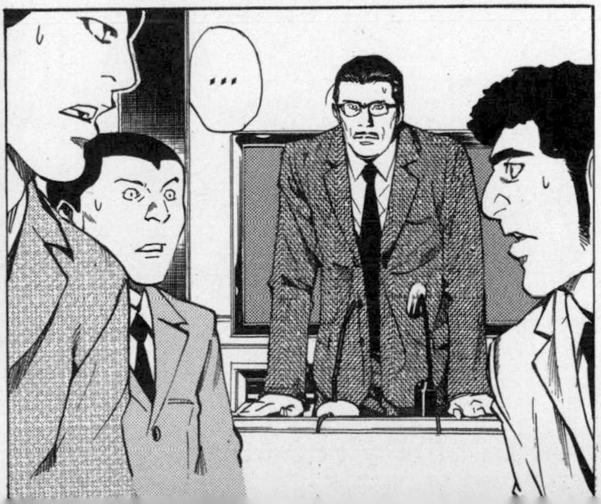
...
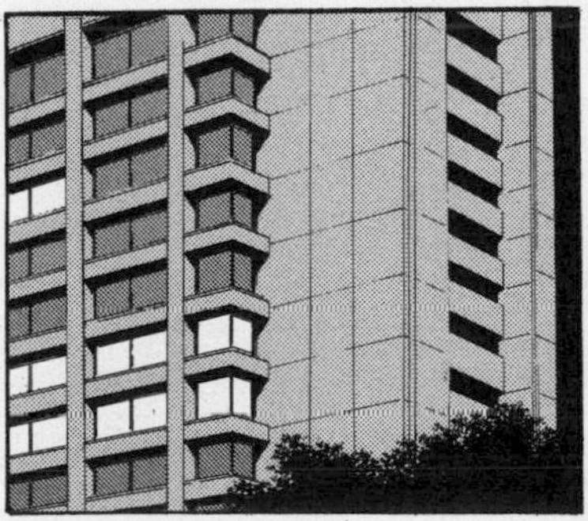

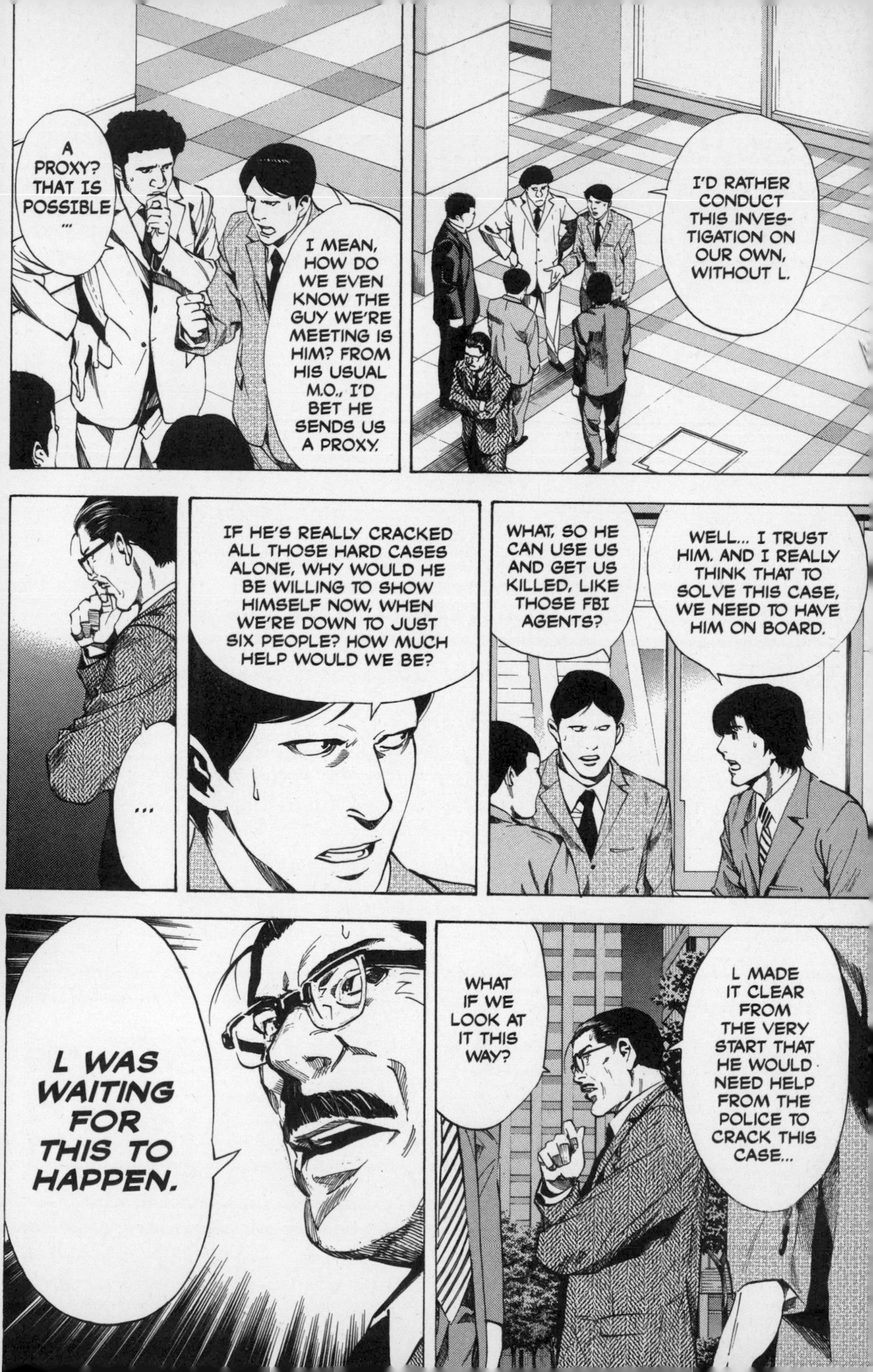
I'D RATHER CONDUCT THIS INVESTIGATION ON OUR OWN, WITHOUT L.
I MEAN, HOW DO WE EVEN KNOW THE GUY WE'RE MEETING IS HIM? FROM HIS USUAL M.O., I'D BET HE SENDS US A PROXY.
A PROXY? THAT IS POSSIBLE...
WELL... I TRUST HIM. AND I REALLY THINK THAT TO SOLVE THIS CASE, WE NEED TO HAVE HIM ON BOARD.
WHAT, SO HE CAN USE US AND GET US KILLED, LIKE THOSE FBI AGENTS?
IF HE'S REALLY CRACKED ALL THOSE HARD CASES ALONE, WHY WOULD HE BE WILLING TO SHOW HIMSELF NOW, WHEN WE'RE DOWN TO JUST SIX PEOPLE? HOW MUCH HELP WOULD WE BE?
...
WHAT IF WE LOOK AT IT THIS WAY?
L MADE IT CLEAR FROM THE VERY START THAT HE WOULD NEED HELP FROM THE POLICE TO CRACK THIS CASE...
L WAS WAITING FOR THIS TO HAPPEN.

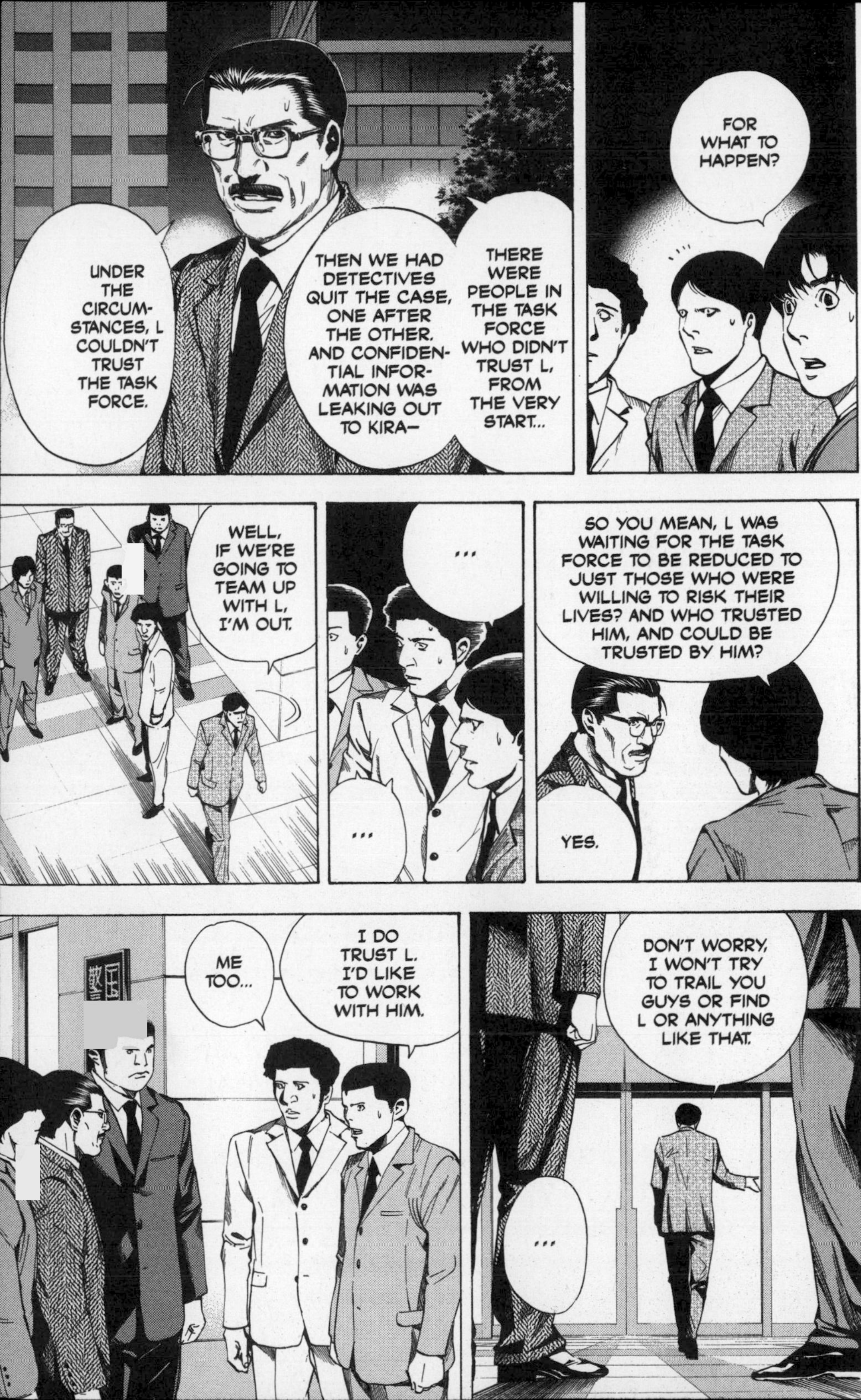
FOR WHAT TO HAPPEN?
THERE WERE PEOPLE IN THE TASK FORCE WHO DIDN'T TRUST L, FROM THE VERY START...
THEN WE HAD DETECTIVES QUIT THE CASE, ONE AFTER THE OTHER. AND CONFIDENTIAL INFORMATION WAS LEAKING OUT TO KIRA—
UNDER THE CIRCUMSTANCES, L COULDN'T TRUST THE TASK FORCE.
SO YOU MEAN, L WAS WAITING FOR THE TASK FORCE TO BE REDUCED TO JUST THOSE WHO WERE WILLING TO RISK THEIR LIVES? AND WHO TRUSTED HIM, AND COULD BE TRUSTED BY HIM?
YES.
...
...
WELL, IF WE'RE GOING TO TEAM UP WITH L, I'M OUT.
DON'T WORRY, I WON'T TRY TO TRAIL YOU GUYS OR FIND L OR ANYTHING LIKE THAT.
...
I DO TRUST L. I'D LIKE TO WORK WITH HIM.
ME TOO...

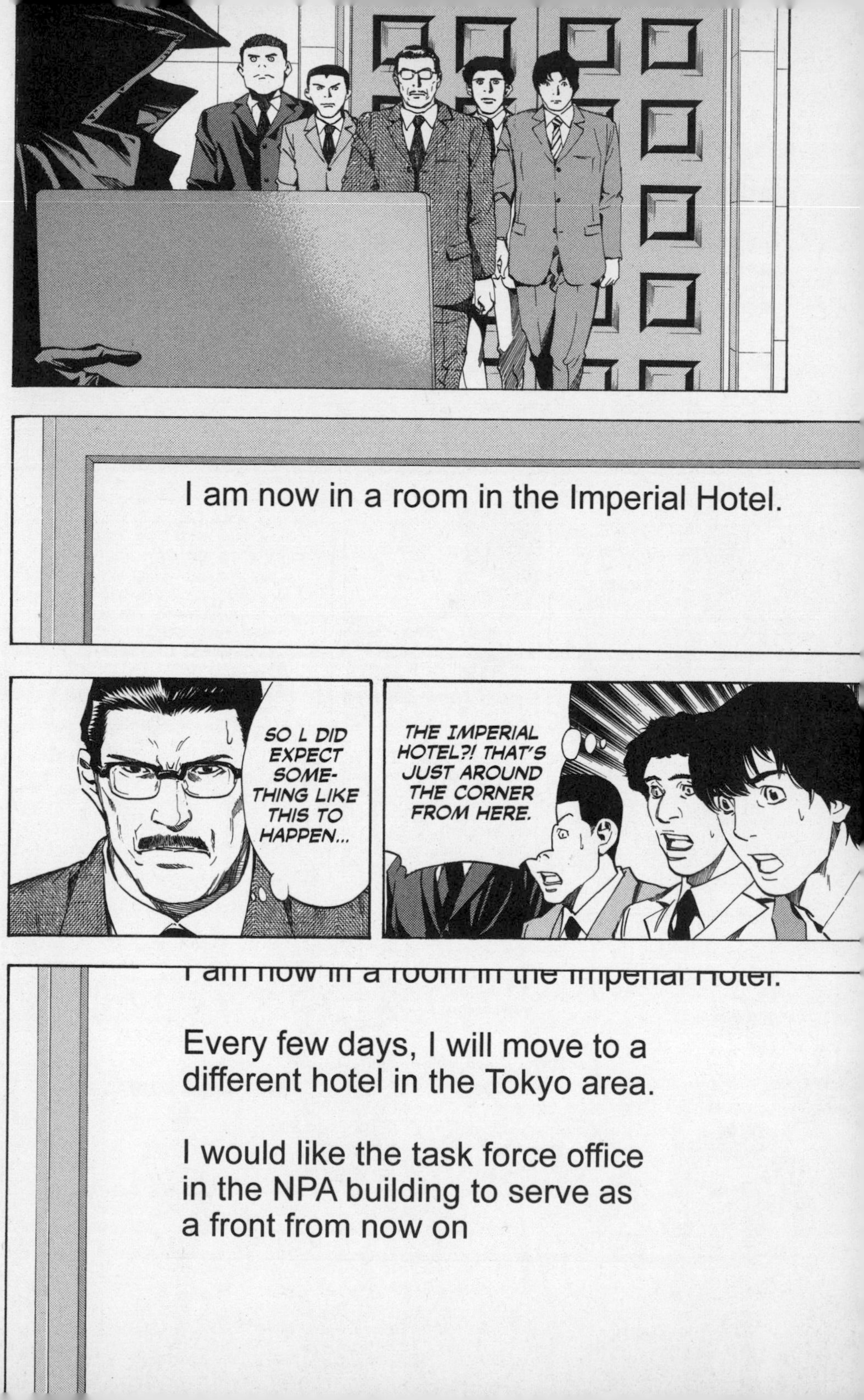
I am now in a room in the Imperial Hotel.
THE IMPERIAL HOTEL?! THAT'S JUST AROUND THE CORNER FROM HERE.
SO L DID EXPECT SOME-THING LIKE THIS TO HAPPEN...
I am now in a room in the Imperial Hotel.
Every few days, I will move to a different hotel in the Tokyo area.
I would like the task force office in the NPA building to serve as a front from now on

with my hotel room serving as the de facto center of the investigation.

Of course, this is a defensive measure to prevent Kira from learning what I look like, and I realize this means I will have an unfair advantage over all of you in that regard.

However, this is as far I am able to go at this point in order to gain your trust and work with you on this investigation.

If you are able to cooperate with me on these terms, please split into two teams and come to my room by midnight, that is by the year 2004, leaving at least a 30-minute interval between the two teams. Watari will hand you a memo with my room number.

I'll be waiting.

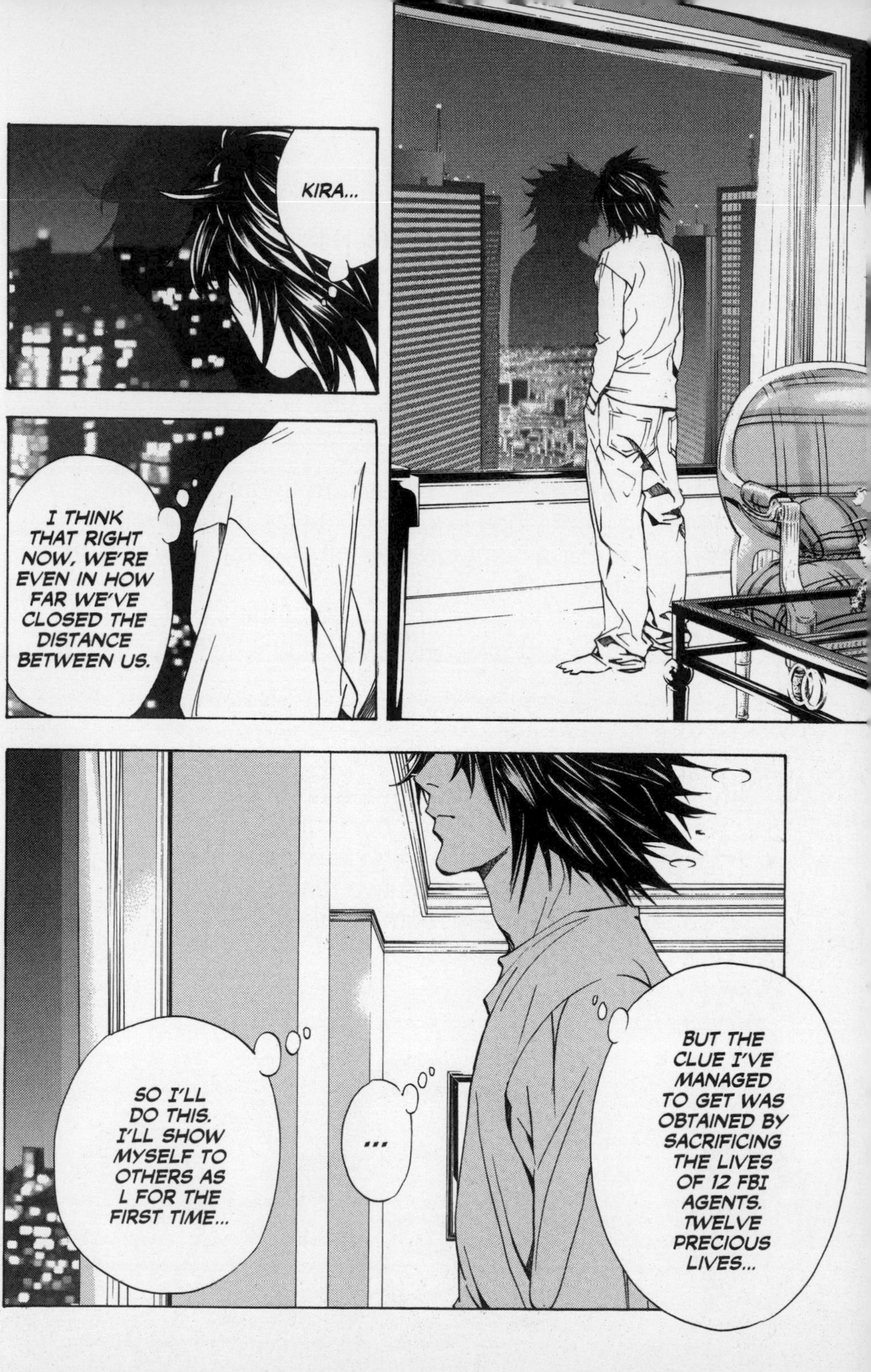
KIRA...
I THINK THAT RIGHT NOW, WE'RE EVEN IN HOW FAR WE'VE CLOSED THE DISTANCE BETWEEN US.
BUT THE CLUE I'VE MANAGED TO GET WAS OBTAINED BY SACRIFICING THE LIVES OF 12 FBI AGENTS. TWELVE PRECIOUS LIVES...
...
SO I'LL DO THIS. I'LL SHOW MYSELF TO OTHERS AS L FOR THE FIRST TIME...

READ THIS WAY

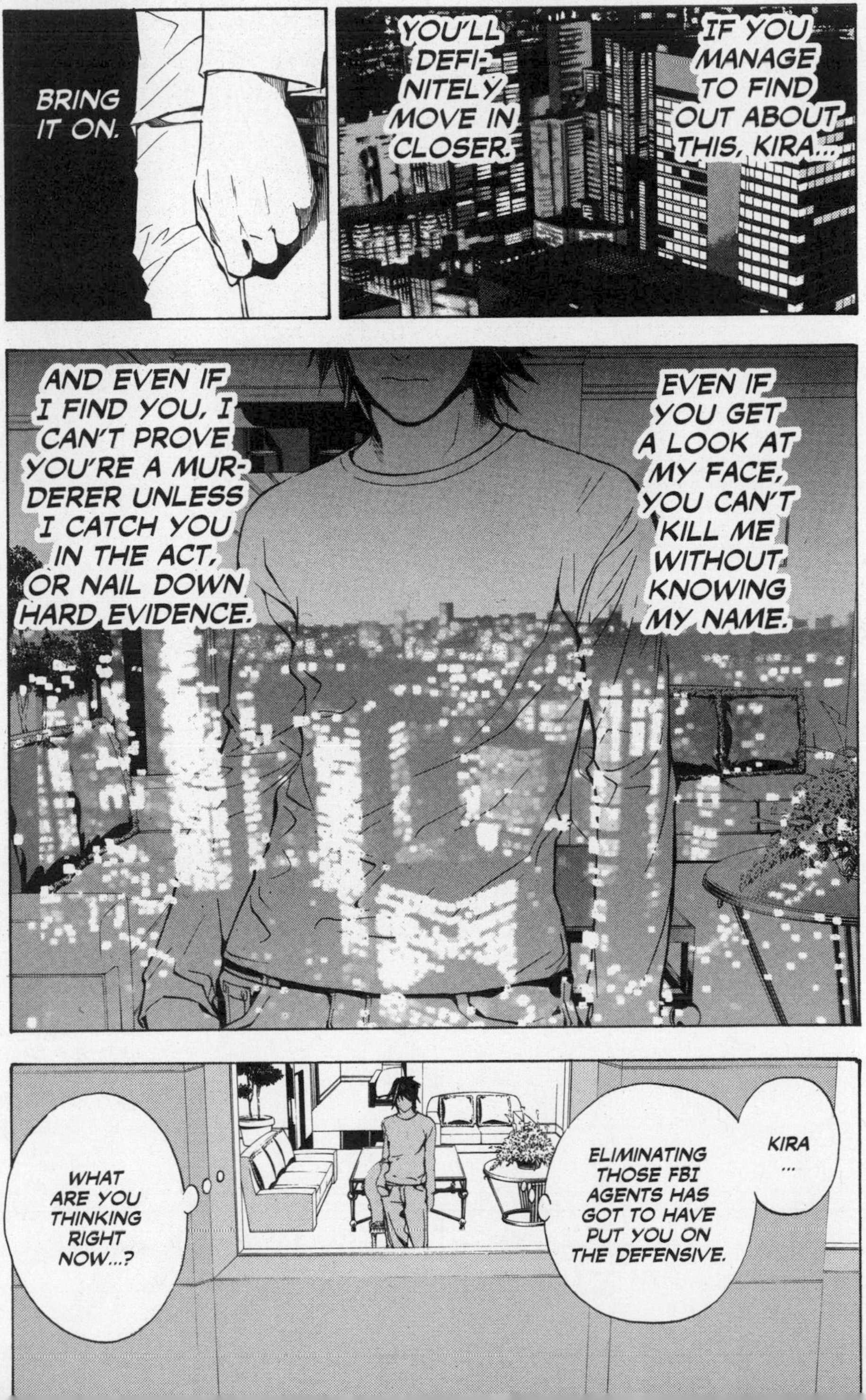

IF YOU MANAGE TO FIND OUT ABOUT THIS, KIRA...
YOU'LL DEFI-NITELY MOVE IN CLOSER.
BRING IT ON.
EVEN IF YOU GET A LOOK AT MY FACE, YOU CAN'T KILL ME WITHOUT KNOWING MY NAME.
AND EVEN IF I FIND YOU, I CAN'T PROVE YOU'RE A MUR-DERER UNLESS I CATCH YOU IN THE ACT, OR NAIL DOWN HARD EVIDENCE.
KIRA ...
ELIMINATING THOSE FBI AGENTS HAS GOT TO HAVE PUT YOU ON THE DEFENSIVE.
WHAT ARE YOU THINKING RIGHT NOW...?

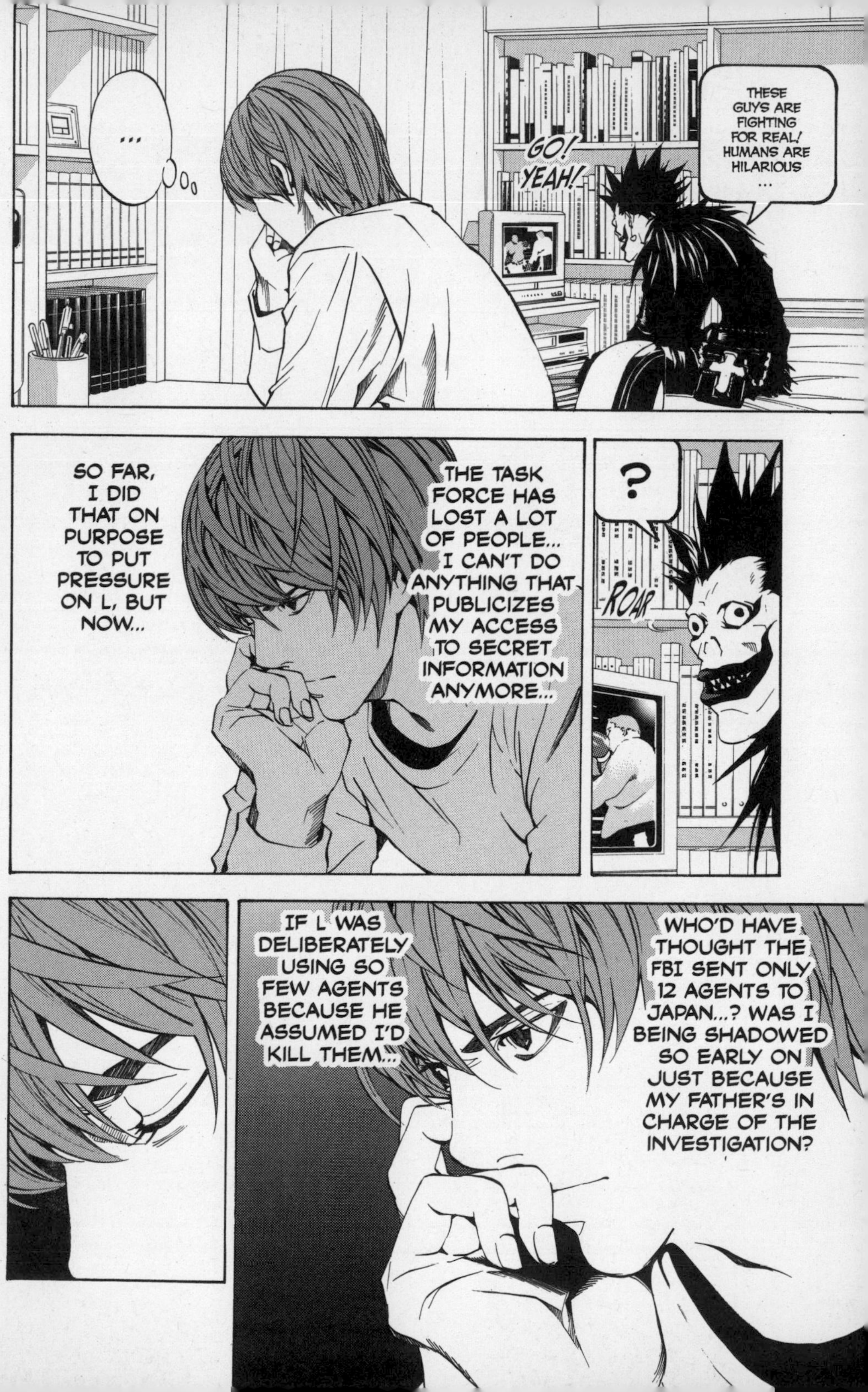
THESE GUYS ARE FIGHTING FOR REAL! HUMANS ARE HILARIOUS ...
GO! YEAH!
...
?
ROAR
THE TASK FORCE HAS LOST A LOT OF PEOPLE... I CAN'T DO ANYTHING THAT PUBLICIZES MY ACCESS TO SECRET INFORMATION ANYMORE...
SO FAR, I DID THAT ON PURPOSE TO PUT PRESSURE ON L, BUT NOW...
WHO'D HAVE THOUGHT THE FBI SENT ONLY 12 AGENTS TO JAPAN...? WAS I BEING SHADOWED SO EARLY ON JUST BECAUSE MY FATHER'S IN CHARGE OF THE INVESTIGATION?
IF L WAS DELIBERATELY USING SO FEW AGENTS BECAUSE HE ASSUMED I'D KILL THEM...

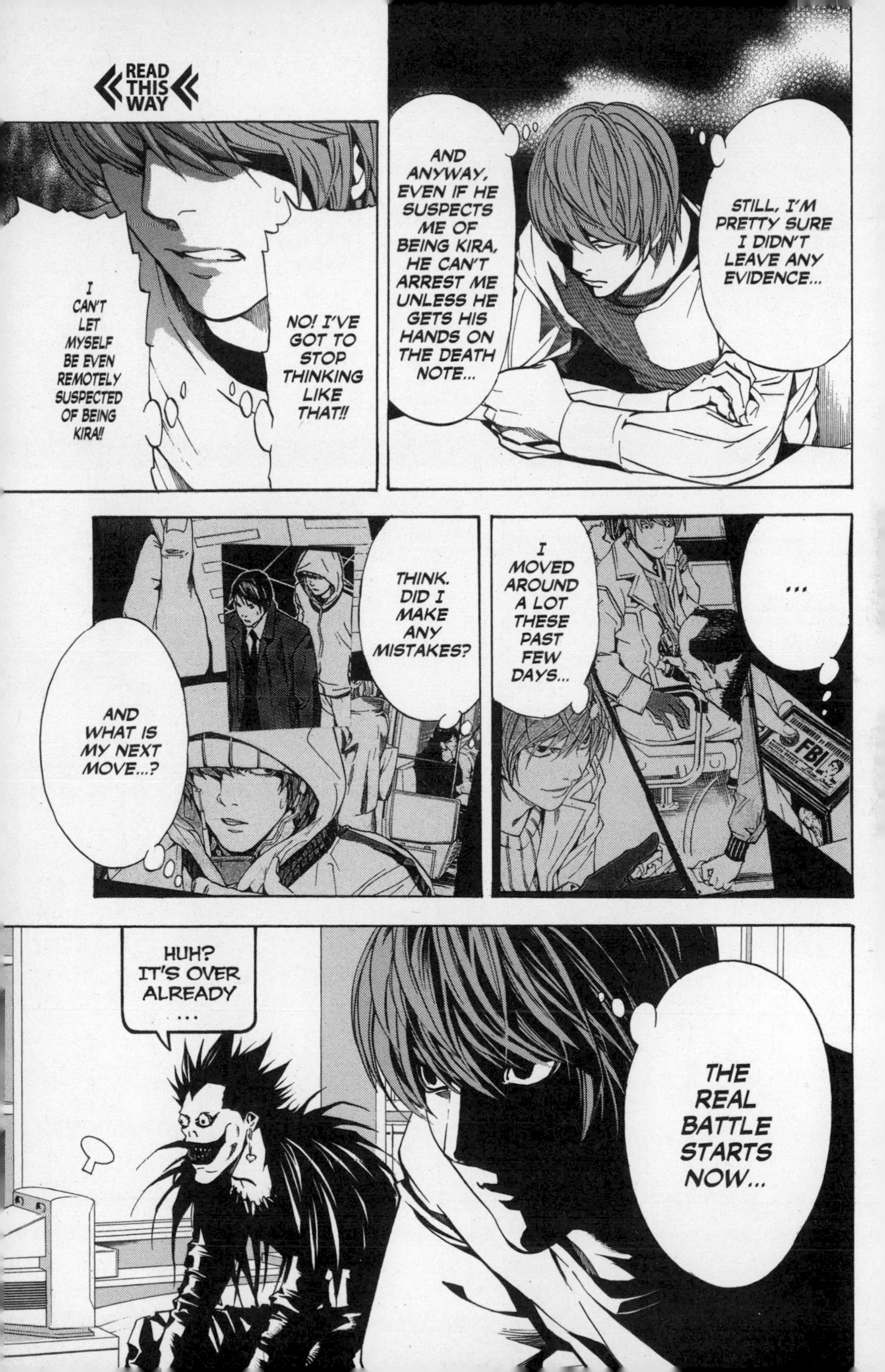
READ THIS WAY
STILL, I'M PRETTY SURE I DIDN'T LEAVE ANY EVIDENCE...
AND ANYWAY, EVEN IF HE SUSPECTS ME OF BEING KIRA, HE CAN'T ARREST ME UNLESS HE GETS HIS HANDS ON THE DEATH NOTE...
NO! I'VE GOT TO STOP THINKING LIKE THAT!!
I CAN'T LET MYSELF BE EVEN REMOTELY SUSPECTED OF BEING KIRA!!
...
I MOVED AROUND A LOT THESE PAST FEW DAYS...
THINK. DID I MAKE ANY MISTAKES?
AND WHAT IS MY NEXT MOVE...?
FBI
THE REAL BATTLE STARTS NOW...
HUH? IT'S OVER ALREADY...

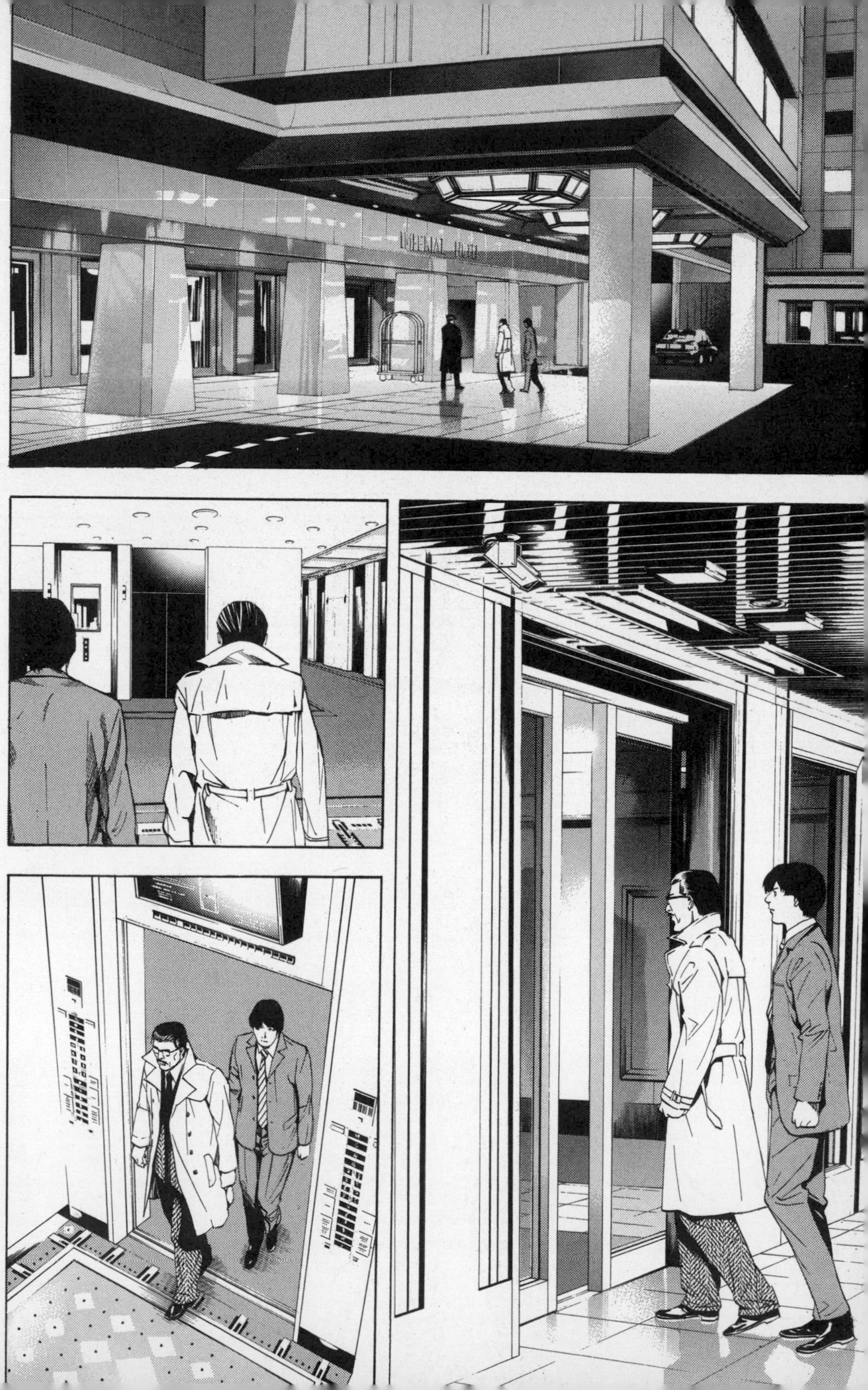

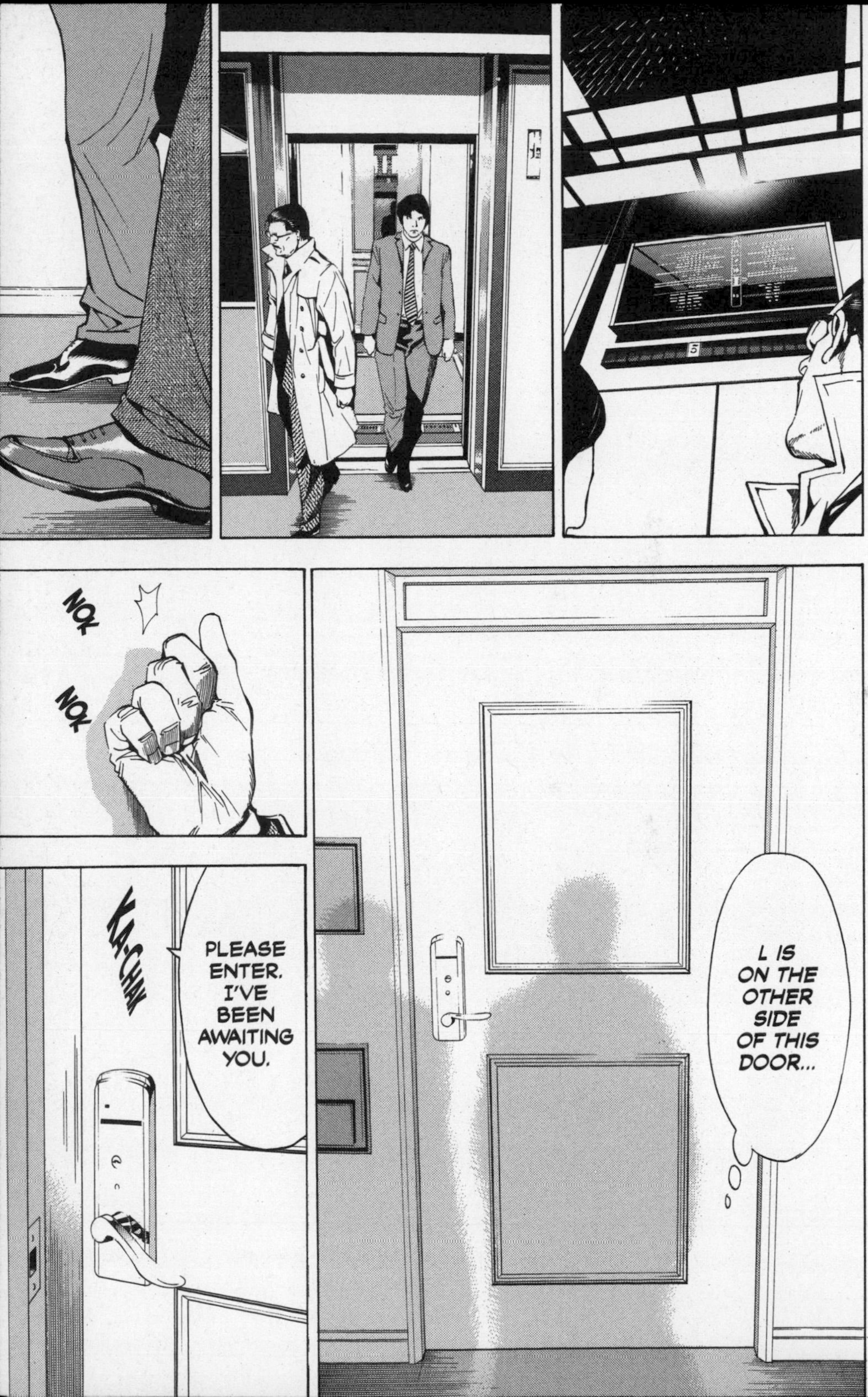
L IS ON THE OTHER SIDE OF THIS DOOR...
NOK
NOK
PLEASE ENTER. I'VE BEEN AWAITING YOU.
KA-CHAK

# chapter 11 One

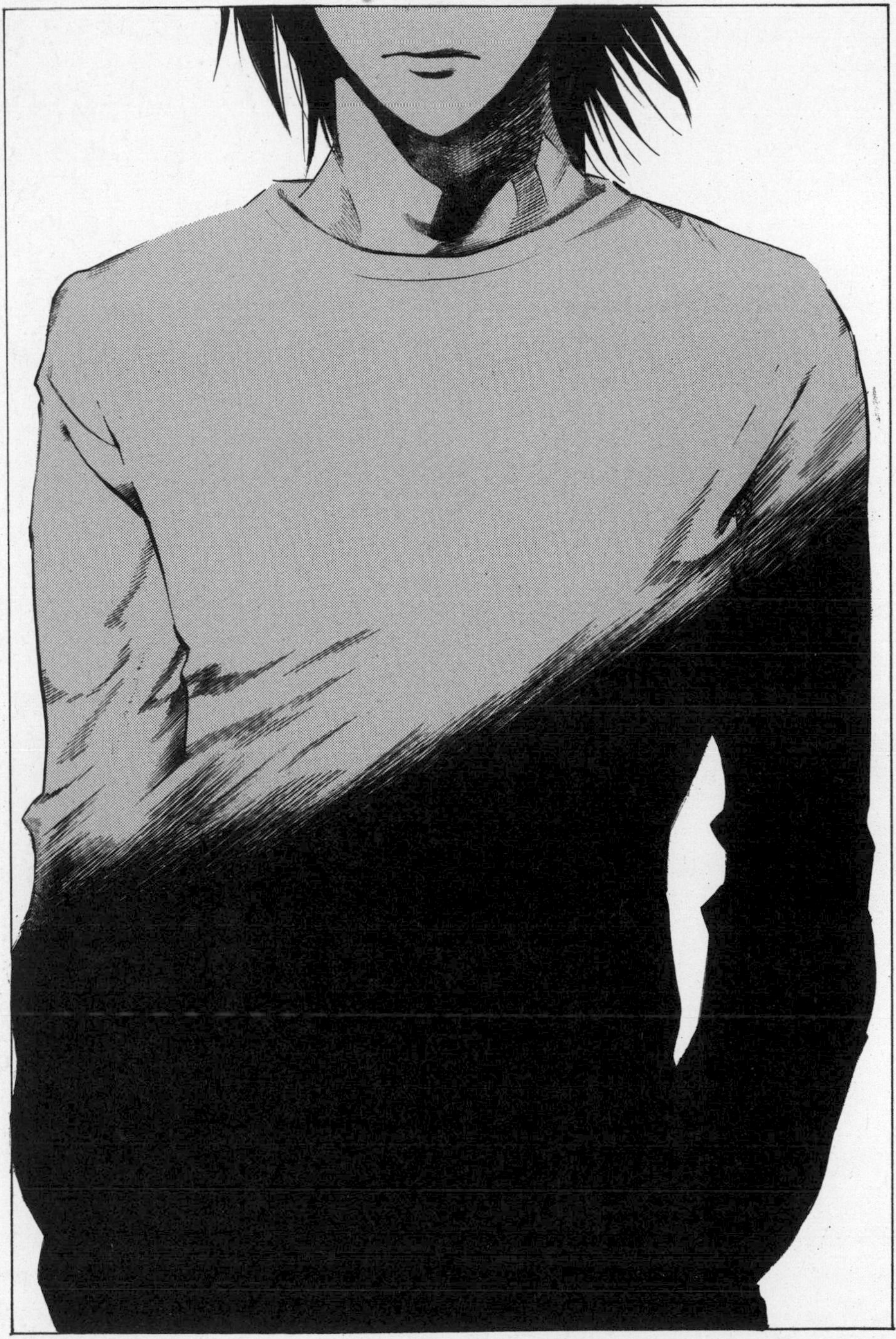

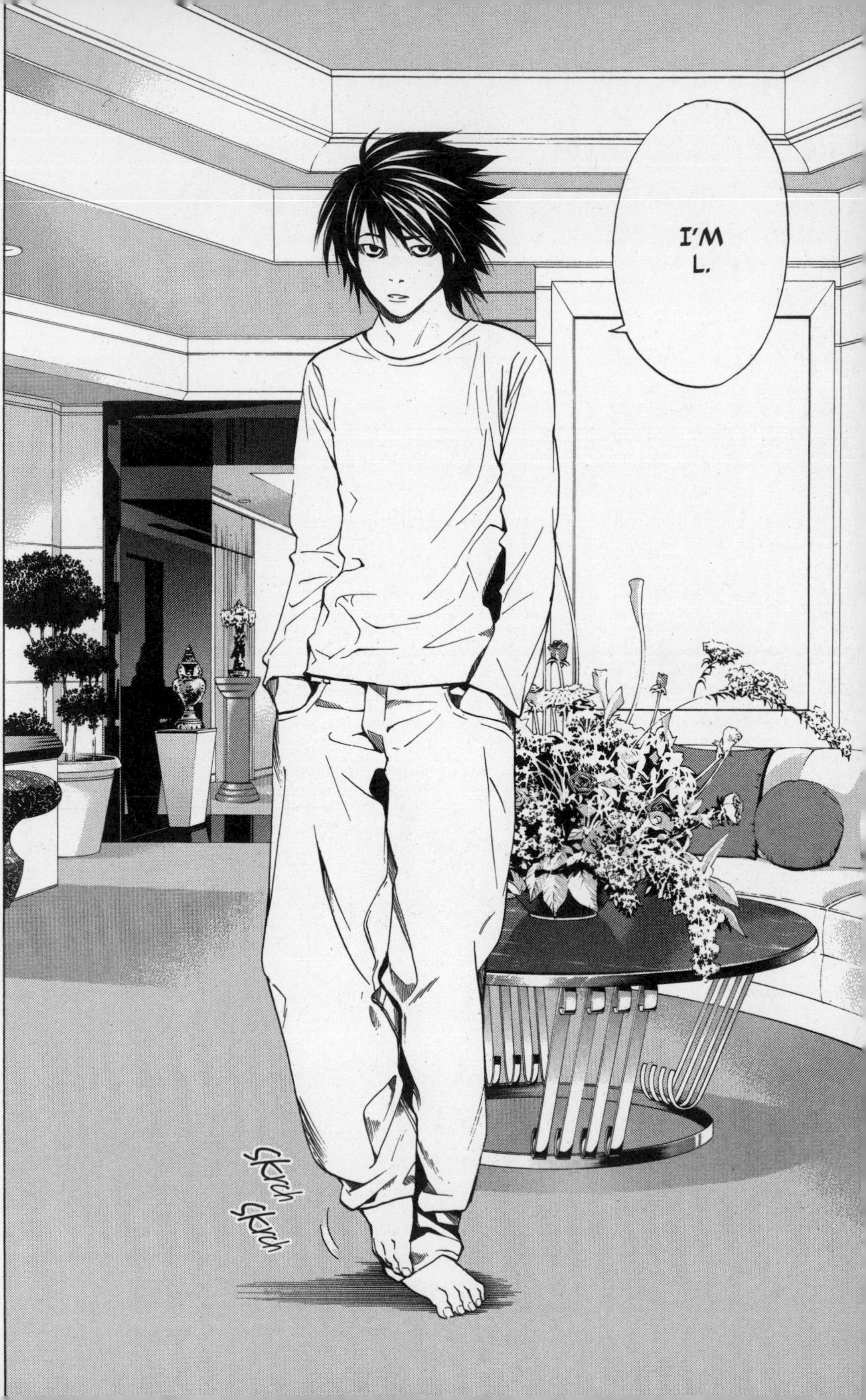
I'M L.
SKRCH SKRCH

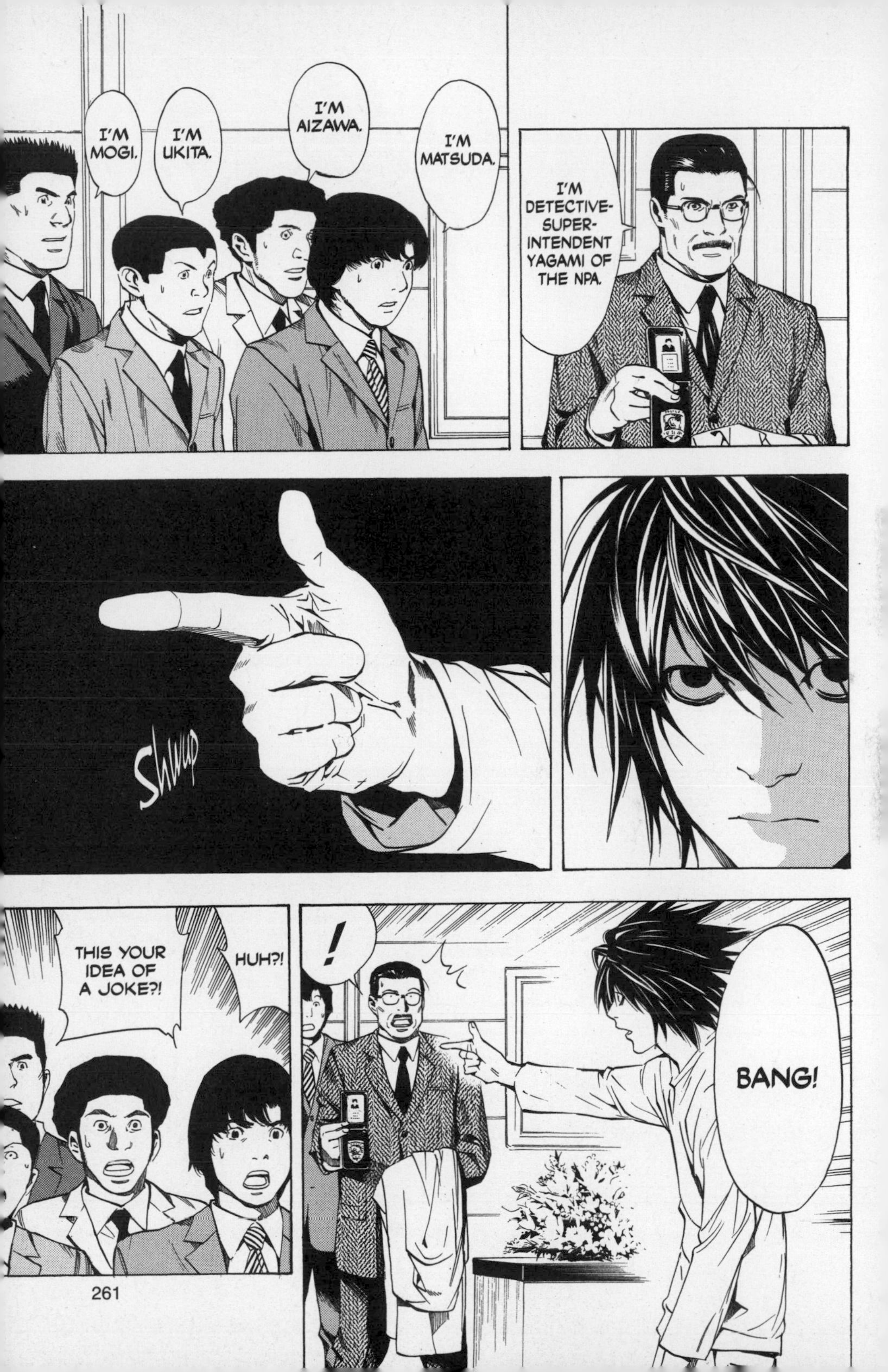
I'M DETECTIVE-SUPER-INTENDENT YAGAMI OF THE NPA.
I'M MATSUDA.
I'M AIZAWA.
I'M UKITA.
I'M MOGI.
Shwup
!
BANG!
HUH?!
THIS YOUR IDEA OF A JOKE?!

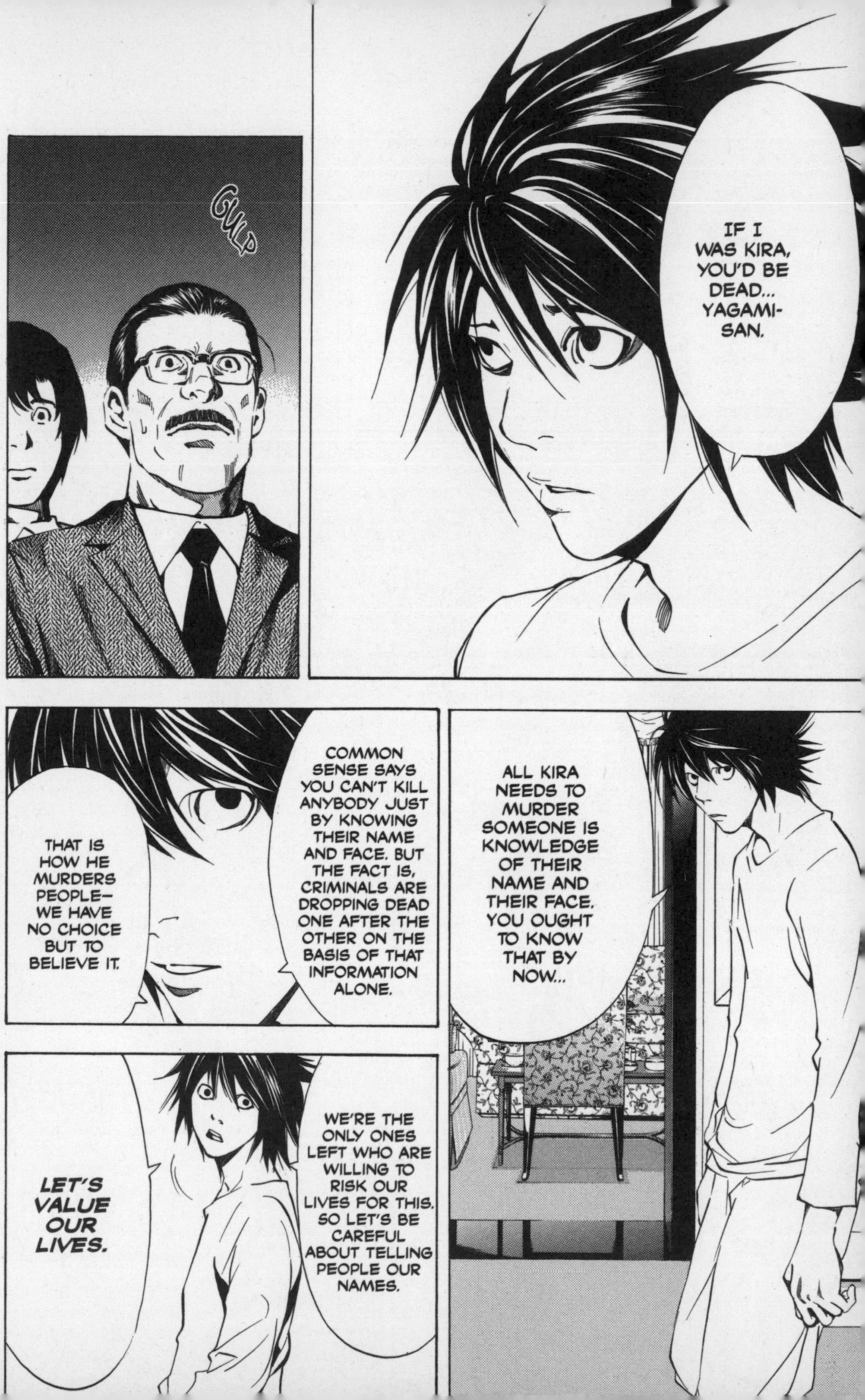
IF I WAS KIRA, YOU'D BE DEAD... YAGAMI-SAN.
GULP
ALL KIRA NEEDS TO MURDER SOMEONE IS KNOWLEDGE OF THEIR NAME AND THEIR FACE. YOU OUGHT TO KNOW THAT BY NOW...
COMMON SENSE SAYS YOU CAN'T KILL ANYBODY JUST BY KNOWING THEIR NAME AND FACE. BUT THE FACT IS, CRIMINALS ARE DROPPING DEAD ONE AFTER THE OTHER ON THE BASIS OF THAT INFORMATION ALONE.
THAT IS HOW HE MURDERS PEOPLE—WE HAVE NO CHOICE BUT TO BELIEVE IT.
WE'RE THE ONLY ONES LEFT WHO ARE WILLING TO RISK OUR LIVES FOR THIS, SO LET'S BE CAREFUL ABOUT TELLING PEOPLE OUR NAMES.
LET'S VALUE OUR LIVES.

READ THIS WAY

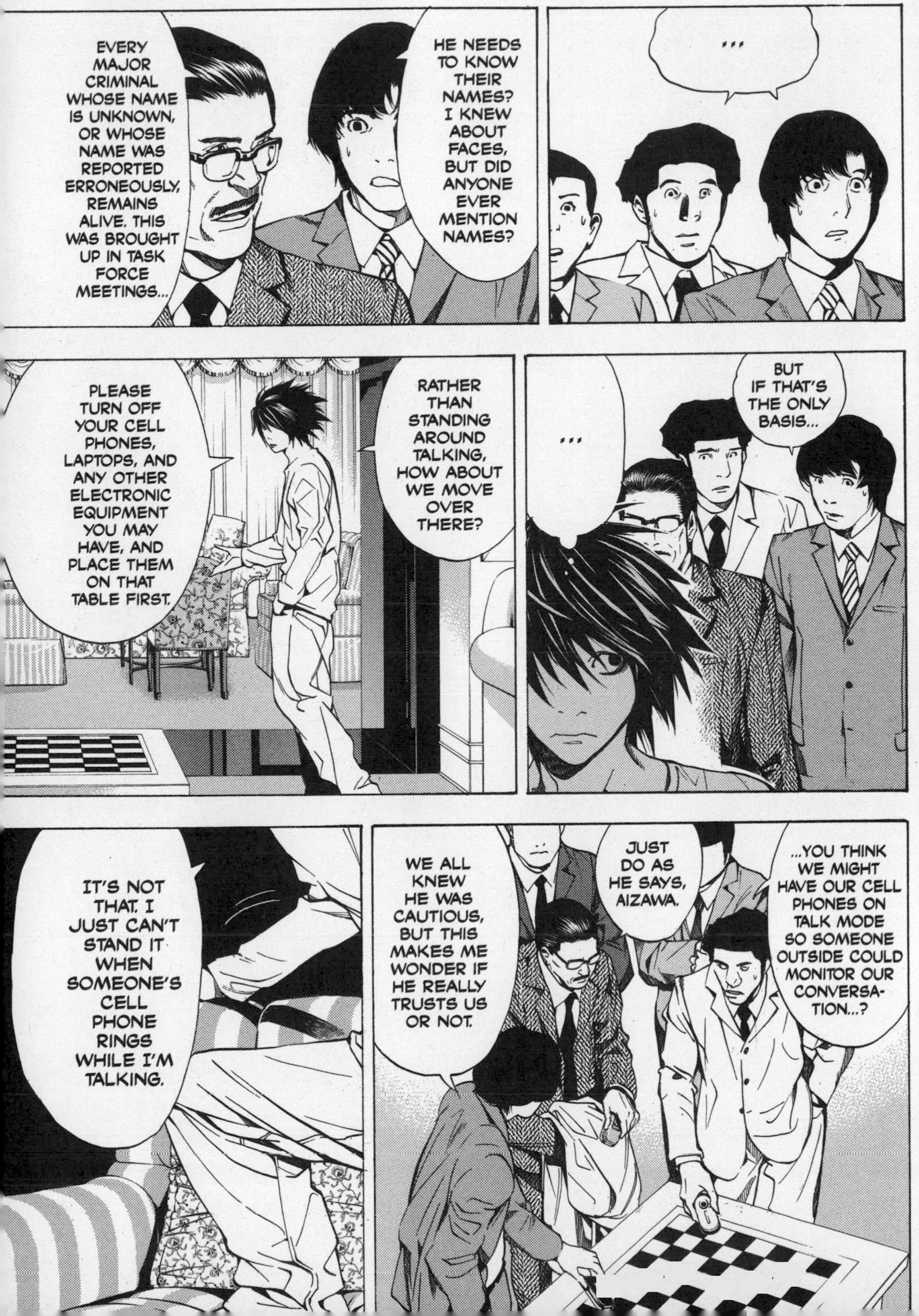
...
HE NEEDS TO KNOW THEIR NAMES? I KNEW ABOUT FACES, BUT DID ANYONE EVER MENTION NAMES?
EVERY MAJOR CRIMINAL WHOSE NAME IS UNKNOWN, OR WHOSE NAME WAS REPORTED ERRONEOUSLY, REMAINS ALIVE. THIS WAS BROUGHT UP IN TASK FORCE MEETINGS...
BUT IF THAT'S THE ONLY BASIS...
...
RATHER THAN STANDING AROUND TALKING, HOW ABOUT WE MOVE OVER THERE?
PLEASE TURN OFF YOUR CELL PHONES, LAPTOPS, AND ANY OTHER ELECTRONIC EQUIPMENT YOU MAY HAVE, AND PLACE THEM ON THAT TABLE FIRST.
...YOU THINK WE MIGHT HAVE OUR CELL PHONES ON TALK MODE SO SOMEONE OUTSIDE COULD MONITOR OUR CONVERSATION...?
JUST DO AS HE SAYS, AIZAWA.
WE ALL KNEW HE WAS CAUTIOUS, BUT THIS MAKES ME WONDER IF HE REALLY TRUSTS US OR NOT.
IT'S NOT THAT. I JUST CAN'T STAND IT WHEN SOMEONE'S CELL PHONE RINGS WHILE I'M TALKING.

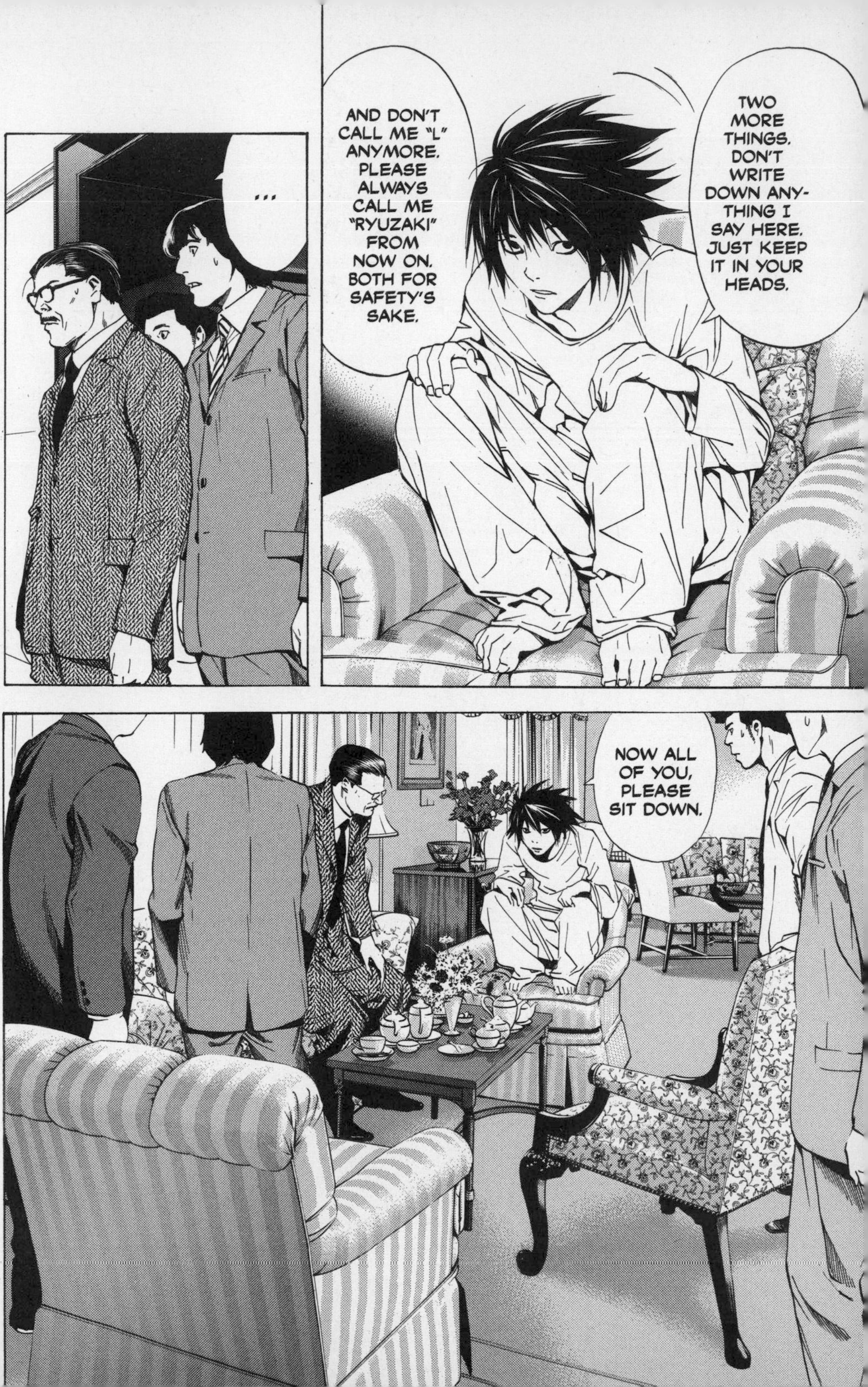
TWO MORE THINGS. DON'T WRITE DOWN ANY-THING I SAY HERE. JUST KEEP IT IN YOUR HEADS.
AND DON'T CALL ME "L" ANYMORE. PLEASE ALWAYS CALL ME "RYUZAKI" FROM NOW ON. BOTH FOR SAFETY'S SAKE.
...
NOW ALL OF YOU, PLEASE SIT DOWN.

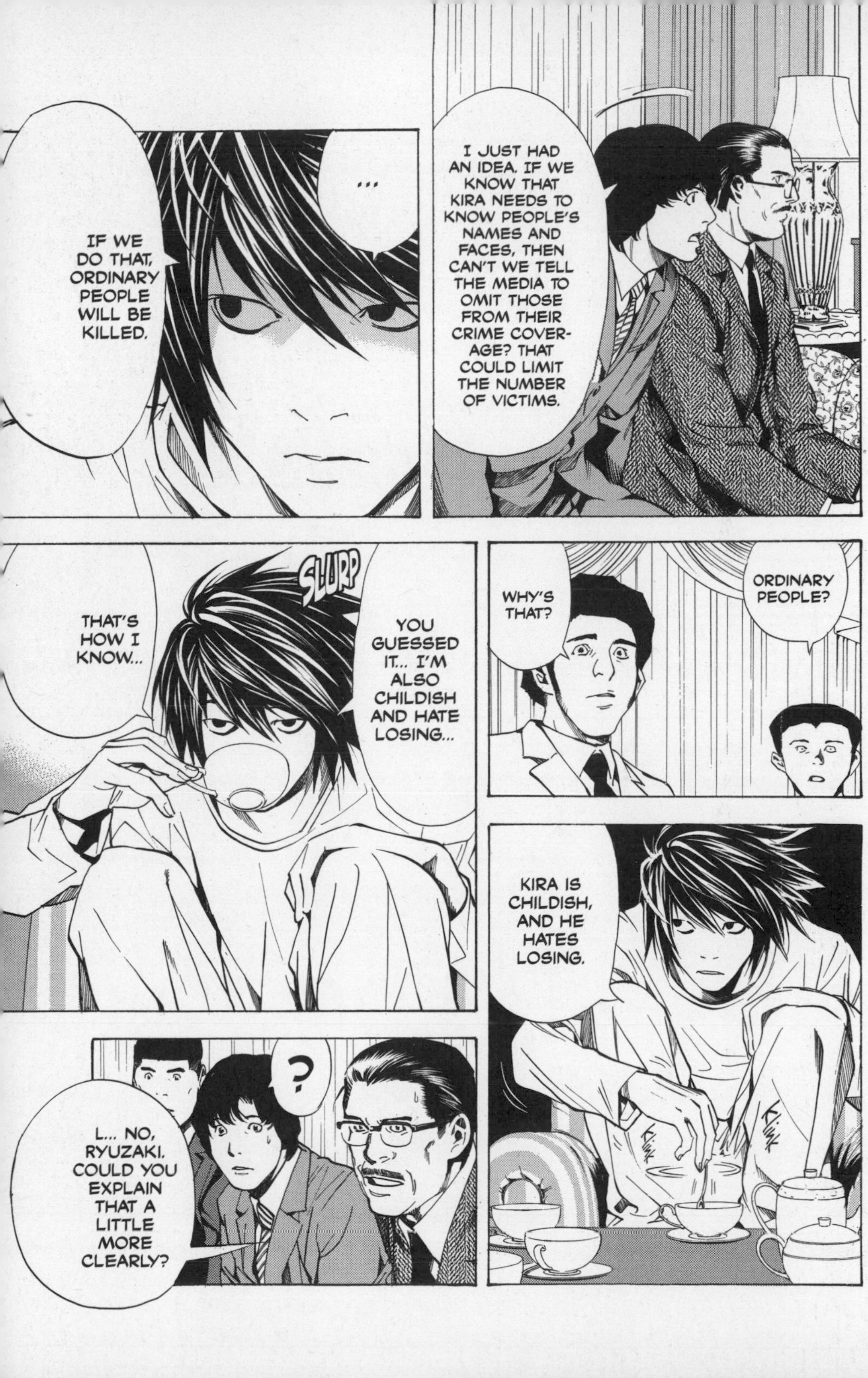
I JUST HAD AN IDEA. IF WE KNOW THAT KIRA NEEDS TO KNOW PEOPLE'S NAMES AND FACES, THEN CAN'T WE TELL THE MEDIA TO OMIT THOSE FROM THEIR CRIME COVERAGE? THAT COULD LIMIT THE NUMBER OF VICTIMS.
...
IF WE DO THAT, ORDINARY PEOPLE WILL BE KILLED.
ORDINARY PEOPLE?
WHY'S THAT?
KIRA IS CHILDISH, AND HE HATES LOSING.
KLINK
KLINK
SLURP
YOU GUESSED IT... I'M ALSO CHILDISH AND HATE LOSING...
THAT'S HOW I KNOW...
?
L... NO, RYUZAKI. COULD YOU EXPLAIN THAT A LITTLE MORE CLEARLY?

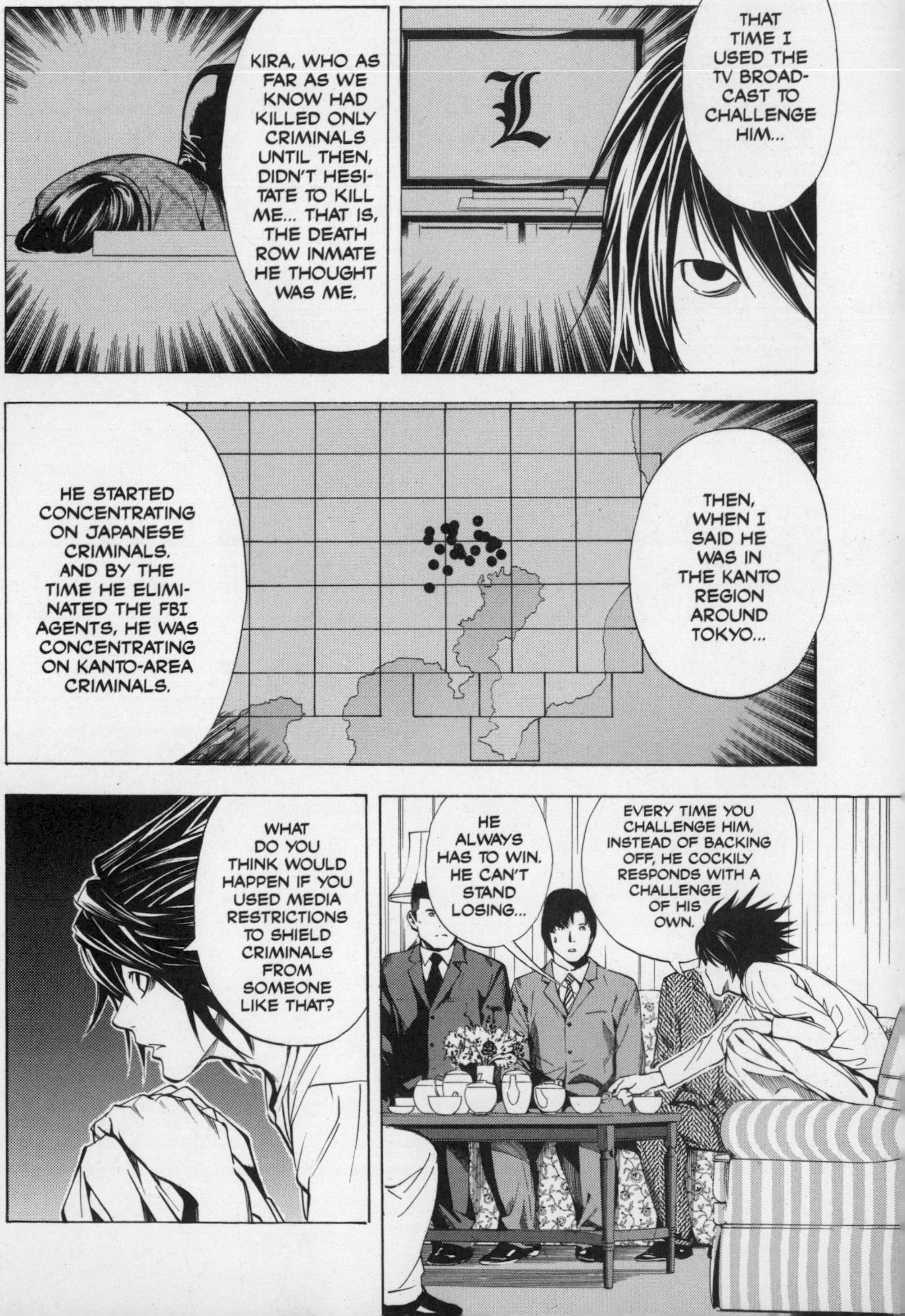
THAT TIME I USED THE TV BROAD-CAST TO CHALLENGE HIM...
KIRA, WHO AS FAR AS WE KNOW HAD KILLED ONLY CRIMINALS UNTIL THEN, DIDN'T HESI-TATE TO KILL ME... THAT IS, THE DEATH ROW INMATE HE THOUGHT WAS ME.
THEN, WHEN I SAID HE WAS IN THE KANTO REGION AROUND TOKYO...
HE STARTED CONCENTRATING ON JAPANESE CRIMINALS. AND BY THE TIME HE ELIMI-NATED THE FBI AGENTS, HE WAS CONCENTRATING ON KANTO-AREA CRIMINALS.
EVERY TIME YOU CHALLENGE HIM, INSTEAD OF BACKING OFF, HE COCKILY RESPONDS WITH A CHALLENGE OF HIS OWN.
HE ALWAYS HAS TO WIN. HE CAN'T STAND LOSING...
WHAT DO YOU THINK WOULD HAPPEN IF YOU USED MEDIA RESTRICTIONS TO SHIELD CRIMINALS FROM SOMEONE LIKE THAT?

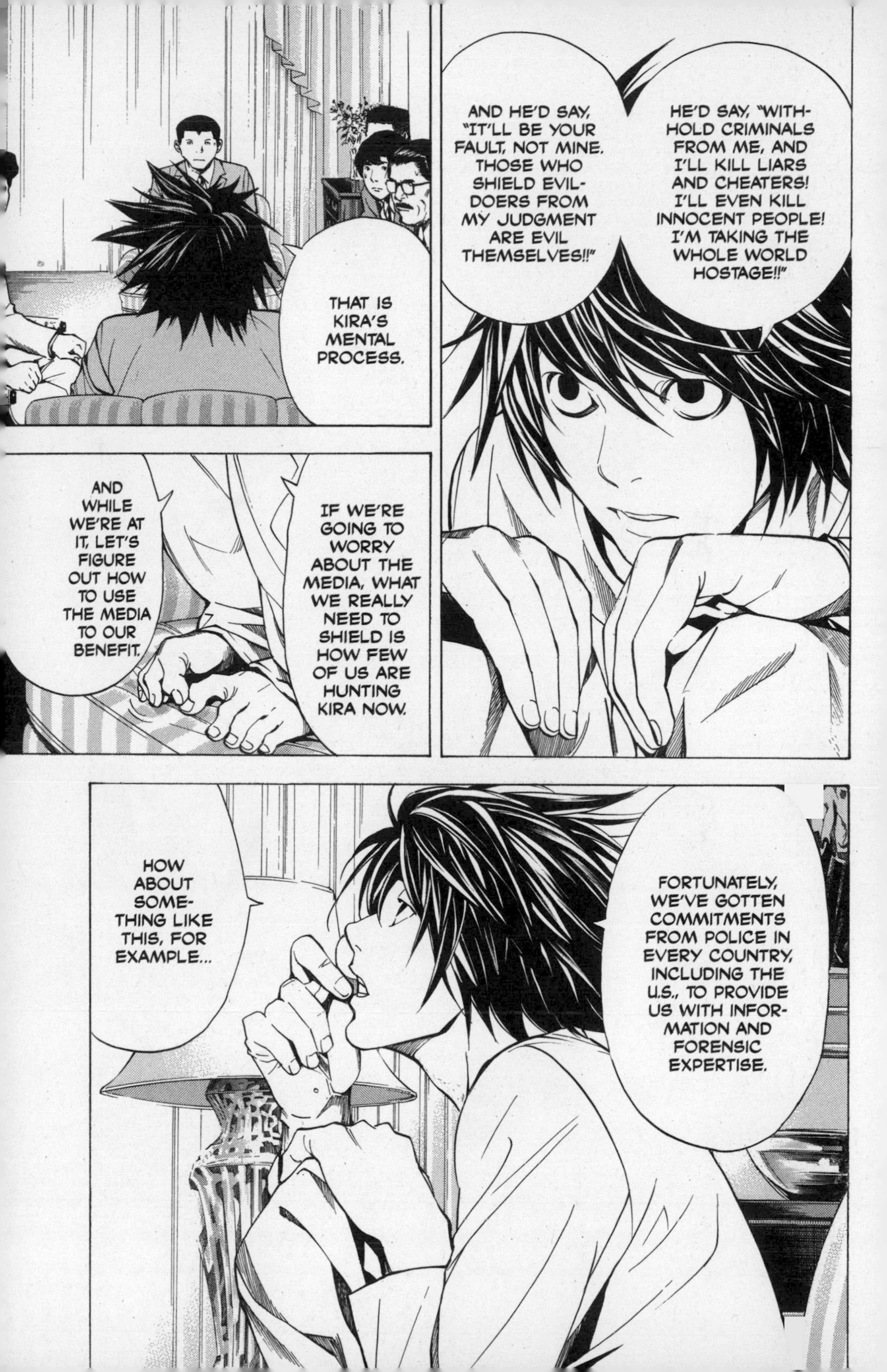
HE'D SAY, "WITHHOLD CRIMINALS FROM ME, AND I'LL KILL LIARS AND CHEATERS! I'LL EVEN KILL INNOCENT PEOPLE! I'M TAKING THE WHOLE WORLD HOSTAGE!!"
AND HE'D SAY, "IT'LL BE YOUR FAULT, NOT MINE. THOSE WHO SHIELD EVILDOERS FROM MY JUDGMENT ARE EVIL THEMSELVES!!"
THAT IS KIRA'S MENTAL PROCESS.
IF WE'RE GOING TO WORRY ABOUT THE MEDIA, WHAT WE REALLY NEED TO SHIELD IS HOW FEW OF US ARE HUNTING KIRA NOW.
AND WHILE WE'RE AT IT, LET'S FIGURE OUT HOW TO USE THE MEDIA TO OUR BENEFIT.
FORTUNATELY, WE'VE GOTTEN COMMITMENTS FROM POLICE IN EVERY COUNTRY, INCLUDING THE U.S., TO PROVIDE US WITH INFORMATION AND FORENSIC EXPERTISE.
HOW ABOUT SOMETHING LIKE THIS, FOR EXAMPLE...

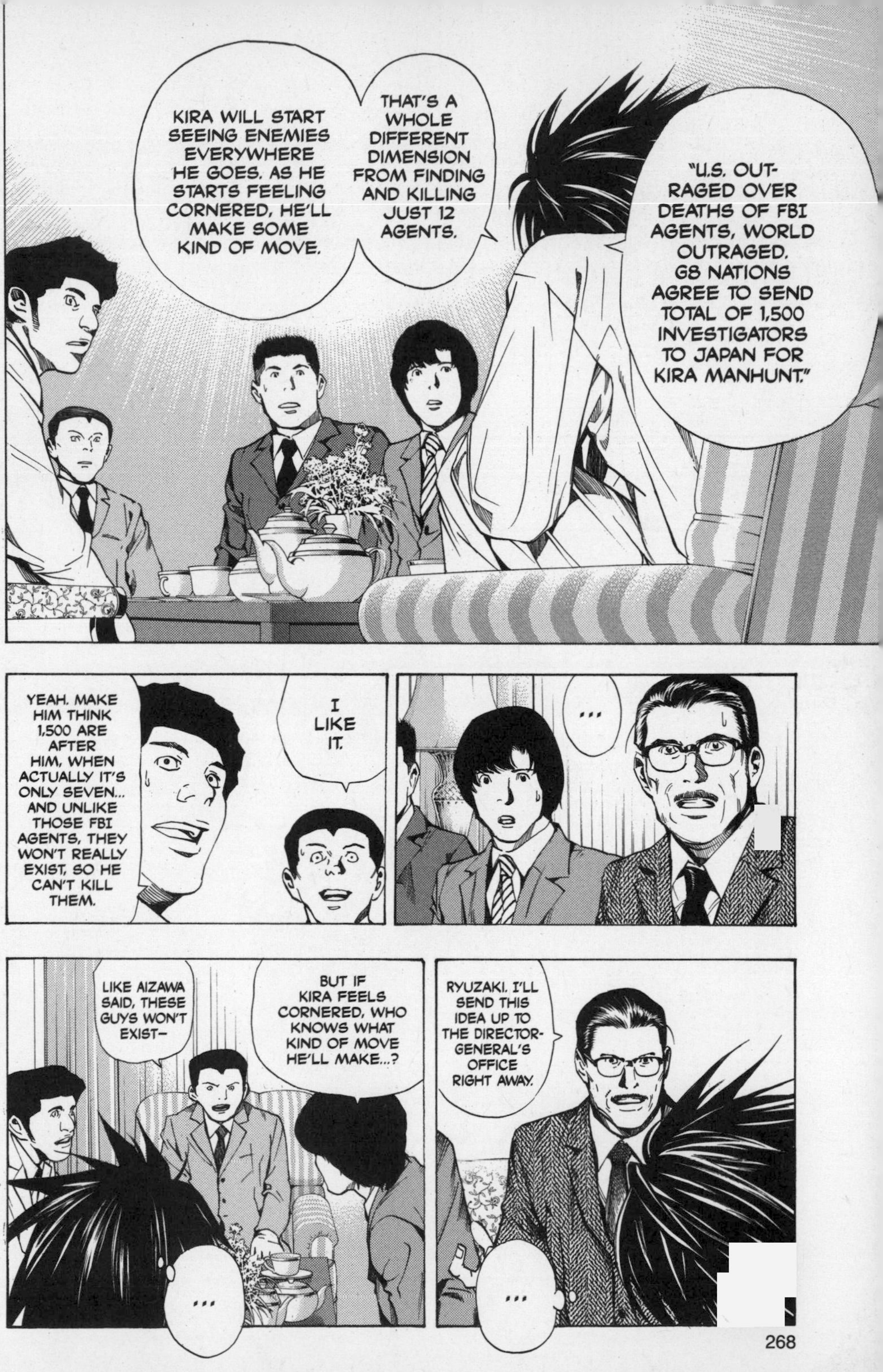
"U.S. OUT-RAGED OVER DEATHS OF FBI AGENTS, WORLD OUTRAGED. G8 NATIONS AGREE TO SEND TOTAL OF 1,500 INVESTIGATORS TO JAPAN FOR KIRA MANHUNT."
THAT'S A WHOLE DIFFERENT DIMENSION FROM FINDING AND KILLING JUST 12 AGENTS.
KIRA WILL START SEEING ENEMIES EVERYWHERE HE GOES. AS HE STARTS FEELING CORNERED, HE'LL MAKE SOME KIND OF MOVE.
...
I LIKE IT.
YEAH. MAKE HIM THINK 1,500 ARE AFTER HIM, WHEN ACTUALLY IT'S ONLY SEVEN... AND UNLIKE THOSE FBI AGENTS, THEY WON'T REALLY EXIST, SO HE CAN'T KILL THEM.
RYUZAKI. I'LL SEND THIS IDEA UP TO THE DIRECTOR-GENERAL'S OFFICE RIGHT AWAY.
...
BUT IF KIRA FEELS CORNERED, WHO KNOWS WHAT KIND OF MOVE HE'LL MAKE...?
LIKE AIZAWA SAID, THESE GUYS WON'T EXIST–
...

READ THIS WAY

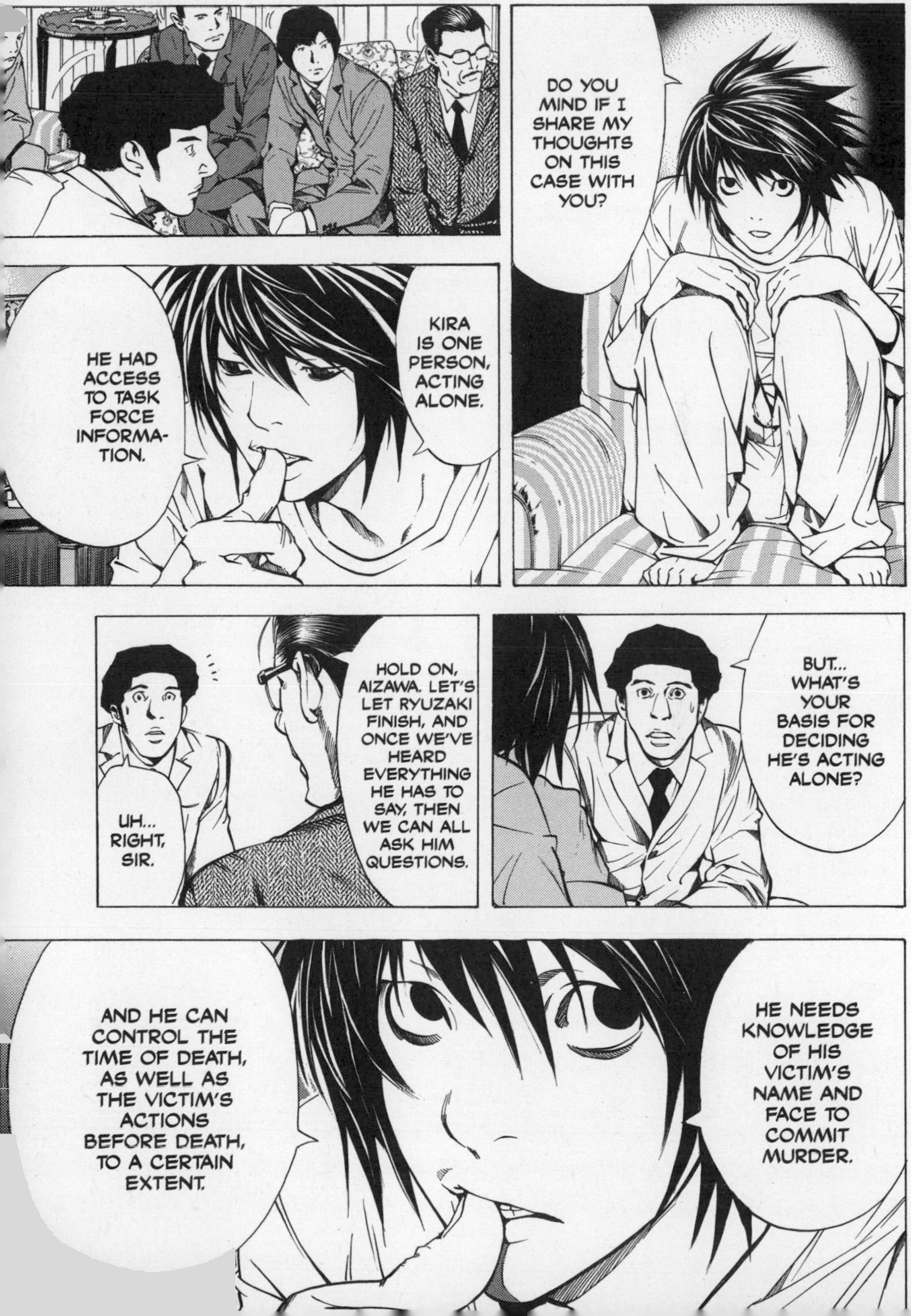
DO YOU MIND IF I SHARE MY THOUGHTS ON THIS CASE WITH YOU?
KIRA IS ONE PERSON, ACTING ALONE.
HE HAD ACCESS TO TASK FORCE INFORMATION.
BUT... WHAT'S YOUR BASIS FOR DECIDING HE'S ACTING ALONE?
HOLD ON, AIZAWA. LET'S LET RYUZAKI FINISH, AND ONCE WE'VE HEARD EVERYTHING HE HAS TO SAY, THEN WE CAN ALL ASK HIM QUESTIONS.
UH... RIGHT, SIR.
HE NEEDS KNOWLEDGE OF HIS VICTIM'S NAME AND FACE TO COMMIT MURDER.
AND HE CAN CONTROL THE TIME OF DEATH, AS WELL AS THE VICTIM'S ACTIONS BEFORE DEATH, TO A CERTAIN EXTENT.

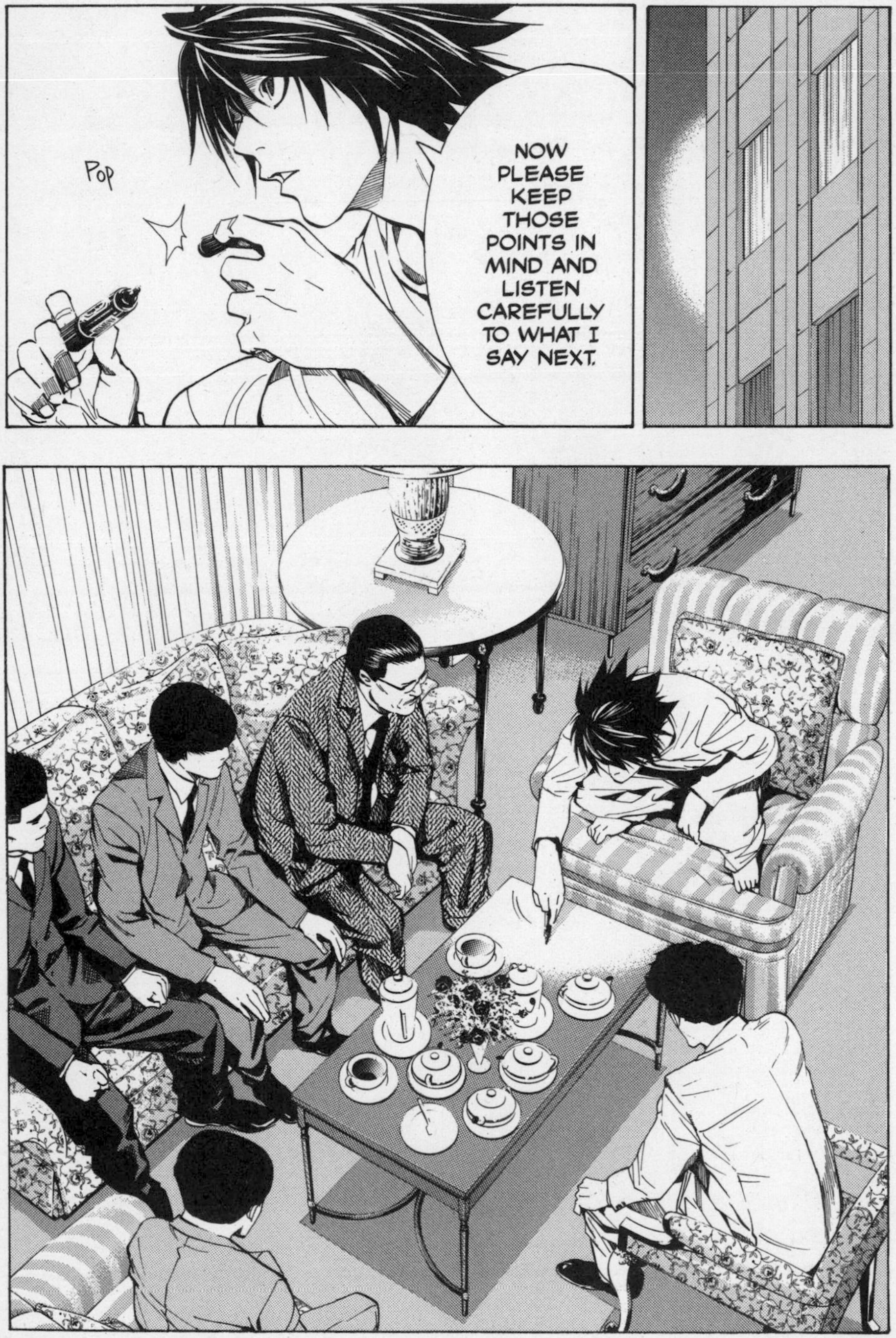
NOW PLEASE KEEP THOSE POINTS IN MIND AND LISTEN CAREFULLY TO WHAT I SAY NEXT.
Pop

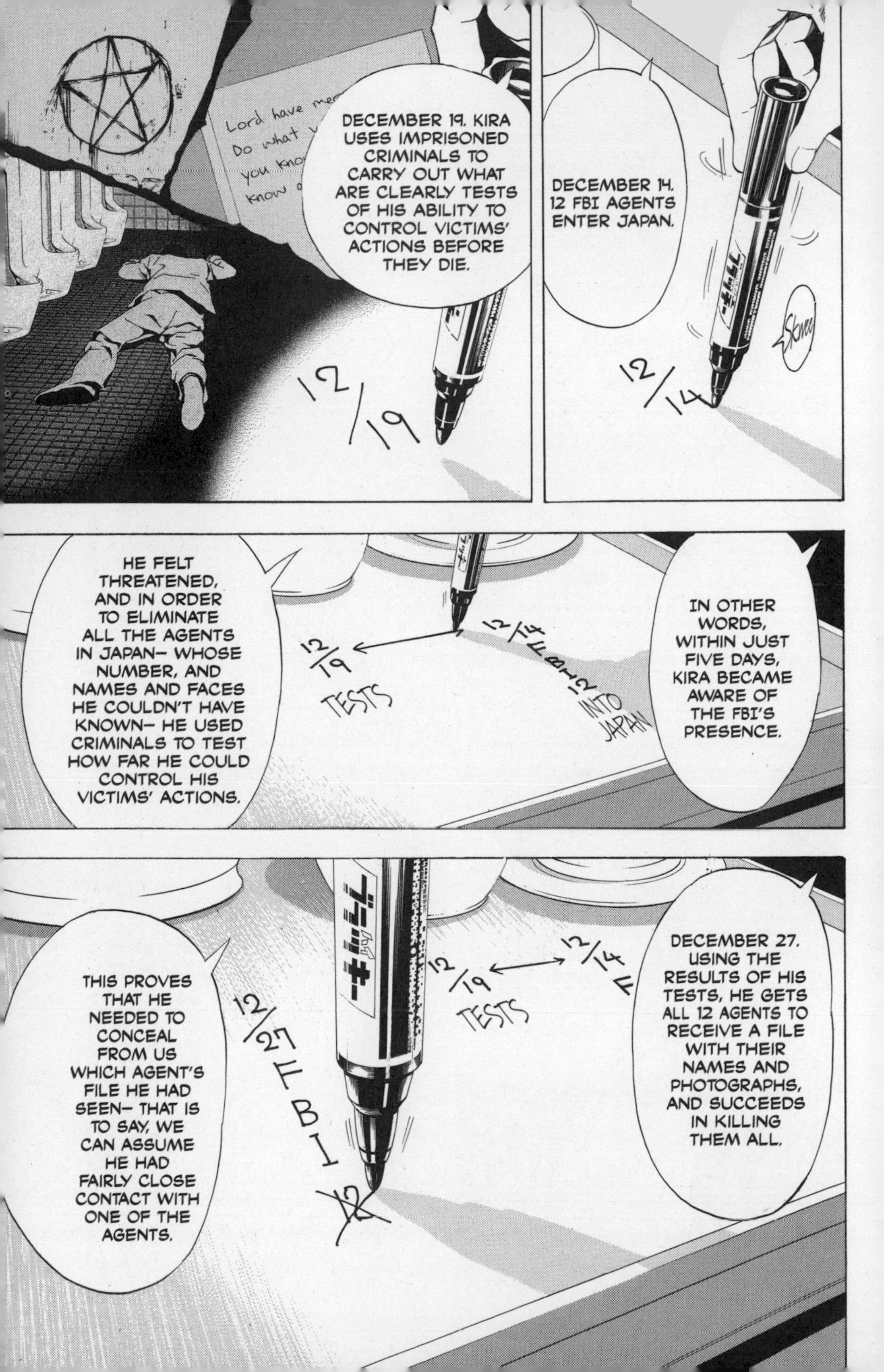
DECEMBER 14. 12 FBI AGENTS ENTER JAPAN.
Skwee
12/14
DECEMBER 19. KIRA USES IMPRISONED CRIMINALS TO CARRY OUT WHAT ARE CLEARLY TESTS OF HIS ABILITY TO CONTROL VICTIMS' ACTIONS BEFORE THEY DIE.
12/19
IN OTHER WORDS, WITHIN JUST FIVE DAYS, KIRA BECAME AWARE OF THE FBI'S PRESENCE.
12/14
INTO JAPAN
12/19
TESTS
HE FELT THREATENED, AND IN ORDER TO ELIMINATE ALL THE AGENTS IN JAPAN– WHOSE NUMBER, AND NAMES AND FACES HE COULDN'T HAVE KNOWN– HE USED CRIMINALS TO TEST HOW FAR HE COULD CONTROL HIS VICTIMS' ACTIONS.
DECEMBER 27. USING THE RESULTS OF HIS TESTS, HE GETS ALL 12 AGENTS TO RECEIVE A FILE WITH THEIR NAMES AND PHOTOGRAPHS, AND SUCCEEDS IN KILLING THEM ALL.
12/14
F
12/19
TESTS
12/27
FBI
12
THIS PROVES THAT HE NEEDED TO CONCEAL FROM US WHICH AGENT'S FILE HE HAD SEEN– THAT IS TO SAY, WE CAN ASSUME HE HAD FAIRLY CLOSE CONTACT WITH ONE OF THE AGENTS.

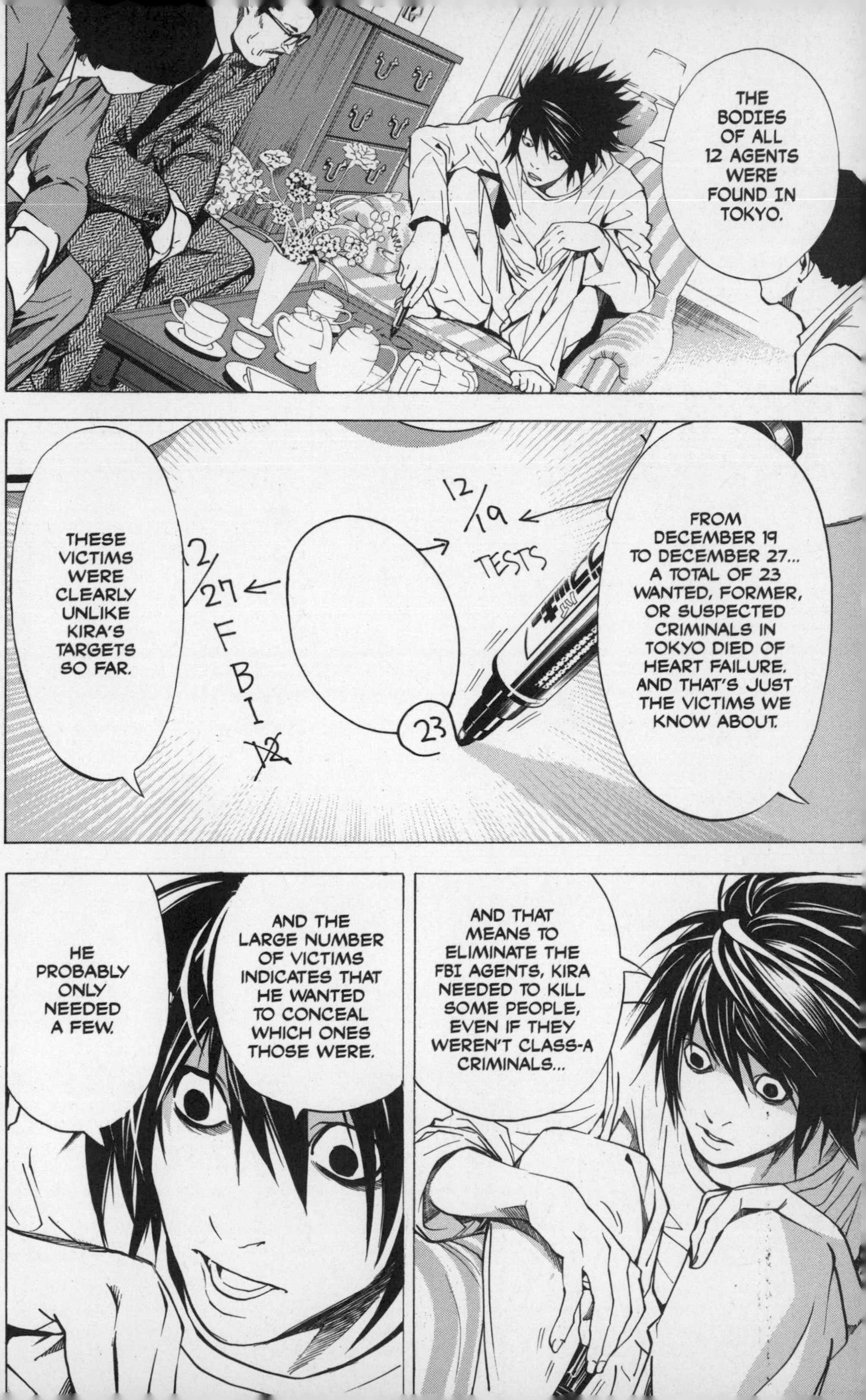
THE BODIES OF ALL 12 AGENTS WERE FOUND IN TOKYO.
FROM DECEMBER 19 TO DECEMBER 27... A TOTAL OF 23 WANTED, FORMER, OR SUSPECTED CRIMINALS IN TOKYO DIED OF HEART FAILURE. AND THAT'S JUST THE VICTIMS WE KNOW ABOUT.
12/19
TESTS
23
12/27
FBI
12
THESE VICTIMS WERE CLEARLY UNLIKE KIRA'S TARGETS SO FAR.
AND THAT MEANS TO ELIMINATE THE FBI AGENTS, KIRA NEEDED TO KILL SOME PEOPLE, EVEN IF THEY WEREN'T CLASS-A CRIMINALS...
AND THE LARGE NUMBER OF VICTIMS INDICATES THAT HE WANTED TO CONCEAL WHICH ONES THOSE WERE.
HE PROBABLY ONLY NEEDED A FEW.

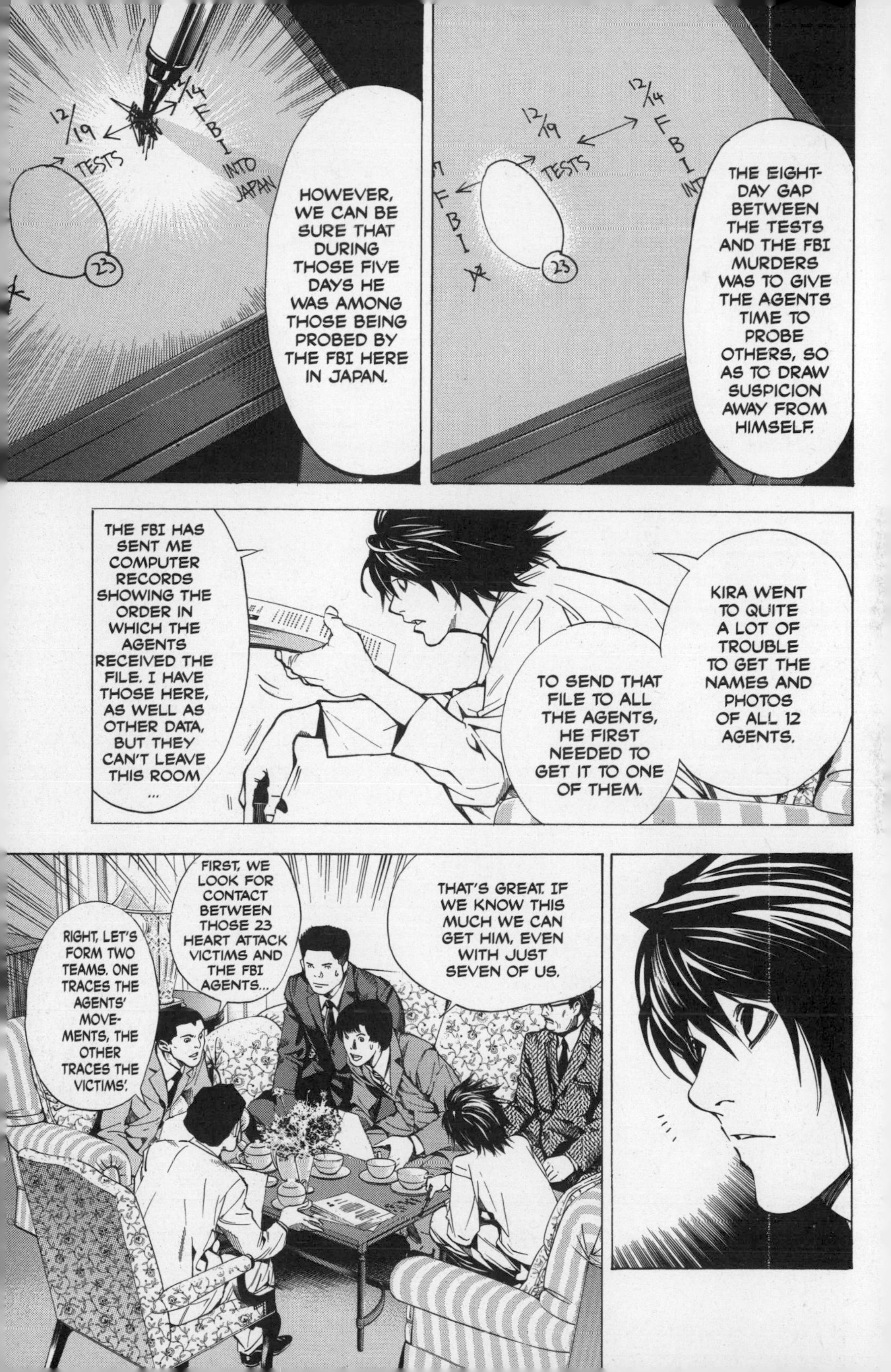
THE EIGHT-DAY GAP BETWEEN THE TESTS AND THE FBI MURDERS WAS TO GIVE THE AGENTS TIME TO PROBE OTHERS, SO AS TO DRAW SUSPICION AWAY FROM HIMSELF.
12/14
FBI
12/19
TESTS
23
HOWEVER, WE CAN BE SURE THAT DURING THOSE FIVE DAYS HE WAS AMONG THOSE BEING PROBED BY THE FBI HERE IN JAPAN.
12/14
FBI INTO JAPAN
12/19
TESTS
23
KIRA WENT TO QUITE A LOT OF TROUBLE TO GET THE NAMES AND PHOTOS OF ALL 12 AGENTS.
TO SEND THAT FILE TO ALL THE AGENTS, HE FIRST NEEDED TO GET IT TO ONE OF THEM.
THE FBI HAS SENT ME COMPUTER RECORDS SHOWING THE ORDER IN WHICH THE AGENTS RECEIVED THE FILE. I HAVE THOSE HERE, AS WELL AS OTHER DATA, BUT THEY CAN'T LEAVE THIS ROOM ...
THAT'S GREAT. IF WE KNOW THIS MUCH WE CAN GET HIM, EVEN WITH JUST SEVEN OF US.
FIRST, WE LOOK FOR CONTACT BETWEEN THOSE 23 HEART ATTACK VICTIMS AND THE FBI AGENTS...
RIGHT, LET'S FORM TWO TEAMS. ONE TRACES THE AGENTS' MOVE-MENTS, THE OTHER TRACES THE VICTIMS'.

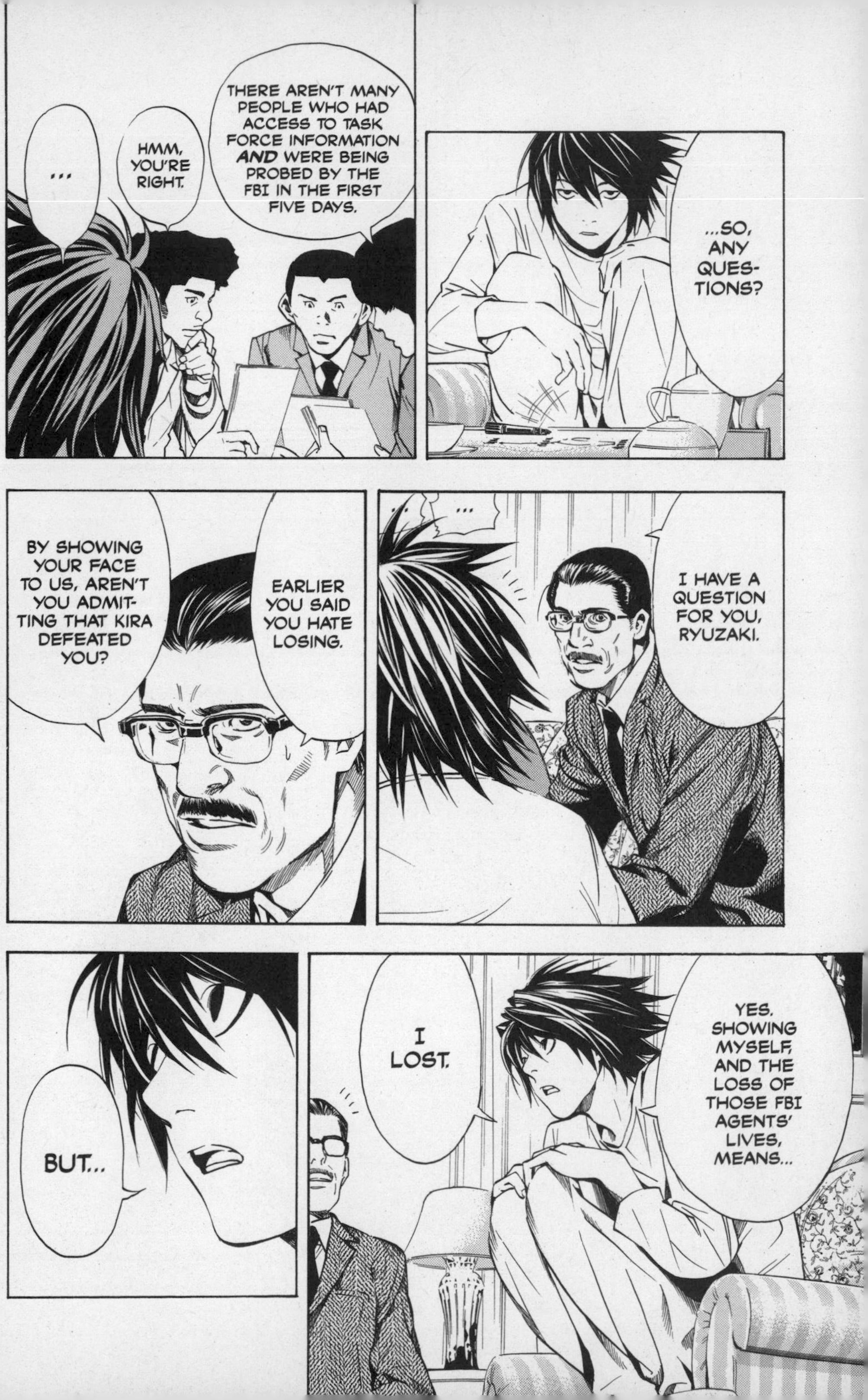
...SO, ANY QUES- TIONS?
THERE AREN'T MANY PEOPLE WHO HAD ACCESS TO TASK FORCE INFORMATION *AND* WERE BEING PROBED BY THE FBI IN THE FIRST FIVE DAYS.
HMM, YOU'RE RIGHT.
...
I HAVE A QUESTION FOR YOU, RYUZAKI.
...
...
EARLIER YOU SAID YOU HATE LOSING.
BY SHOWING YOUR FACE TO US, AREN'T YOU ADMIT- TING THAT KIRA DEFEATED YOU?
YES. SHOWING MYSELF, AND THE LOSS OF THOSE FBI AGENTS' LIVES, MEANS...
I LOST.
BUT...

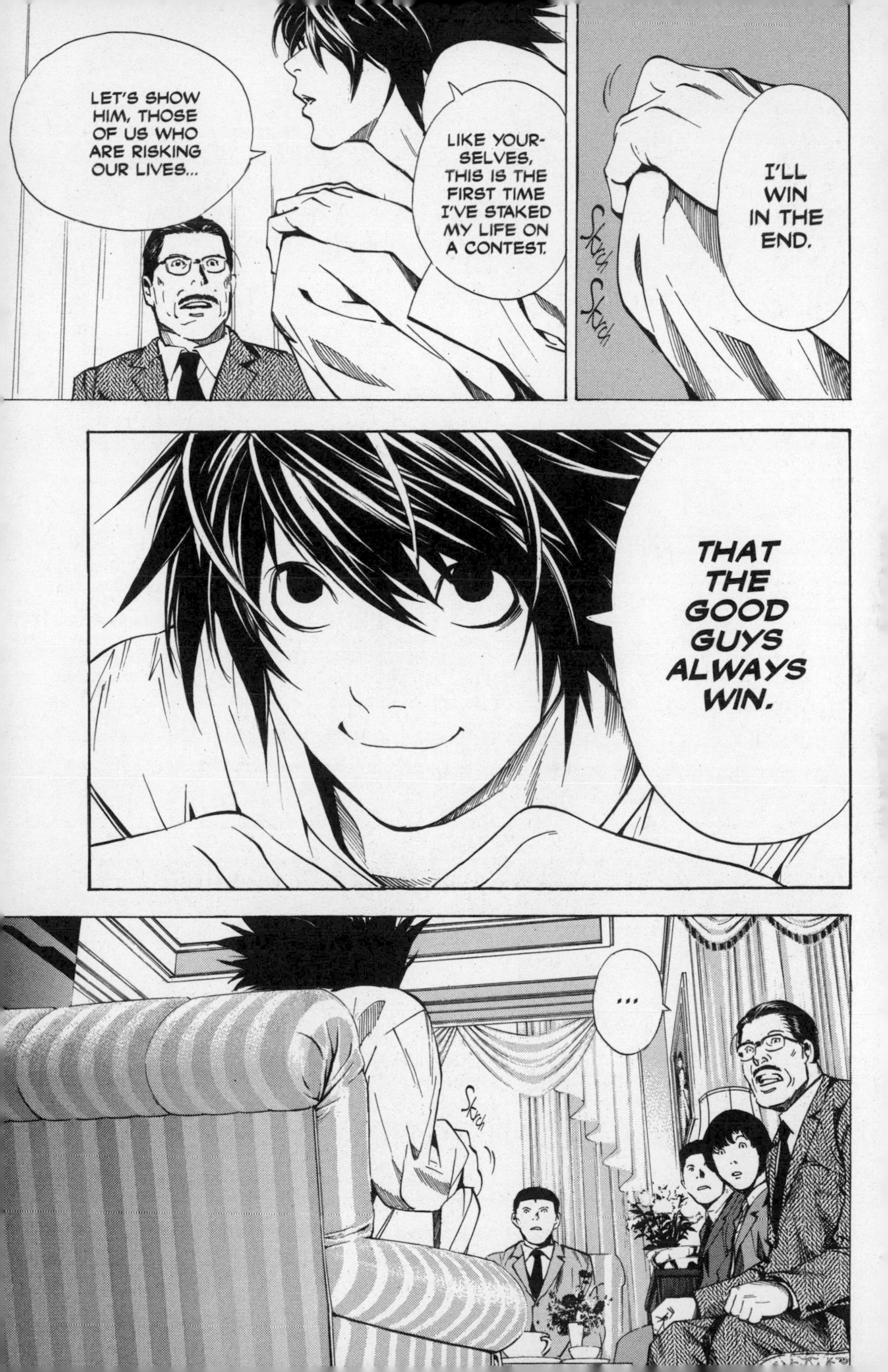
Skrch Skrch
I'LL WIN IN THE END.
LIKE YOUR-SELVES, THIS IS THE FIRST TIME I'VE STAKED MY LIFE ON A CONTEST.
LET'S SHOW HIM, THOSE OF US WHO ARE RISKING OUR LIVES...
THAT THE GOOD GUYS ALWAYS WIN.
...
Skrch

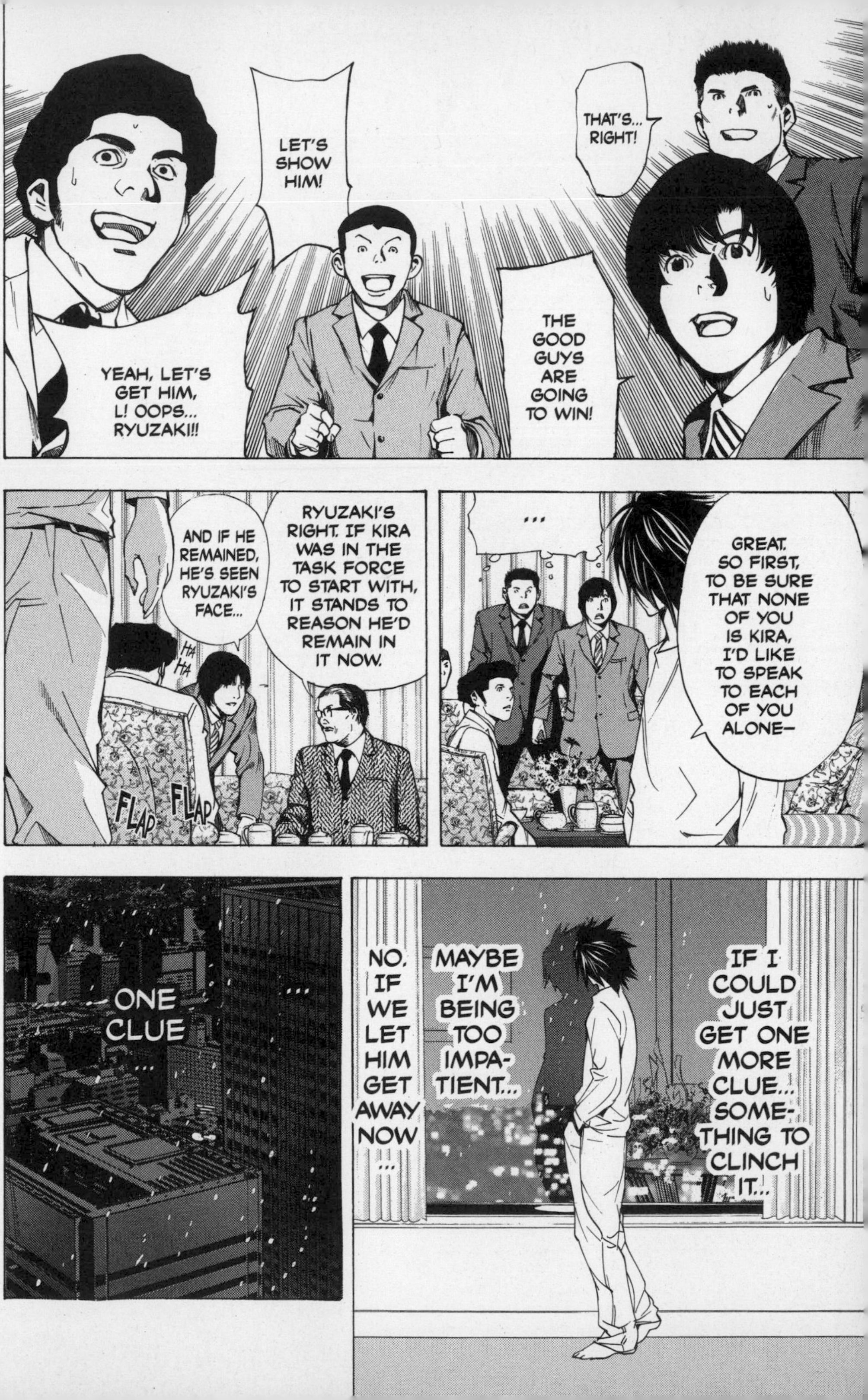
THAT'S... RIGHT!
LET'S SHOW HIM!
THE GOOD GUYS ARE GOING TO WIN!
YEAH, LET'S GET HIM, L! OOPS... RYUZAKI!!
GREAT. SO FIRST, TO BE SURE THAT NONE OF YOU IS KIRA, I'D LIKE TO SPEAK TO EACH OF YOU ALONE—
...
RYUZAKI'S RIGHT. IF KIRA WAS IN THE TASK FORCE TO START WITH, IT STANDS TO REASON HE'D REMAIN IN IT NOW.
AND IF HE REMAINED, HE'S SEEN RYUZAKI'S FACE...
HA HA
FLAP FLAP
IF I COULD JUST GET ONE MORE CLUE... SOMETHING TO CLINCH IT...
MAYBE I'M BEING TOO IMPATIENT...
NO. IF WE LET HIM GET AWAY NOW...
...
ONE CLUE...

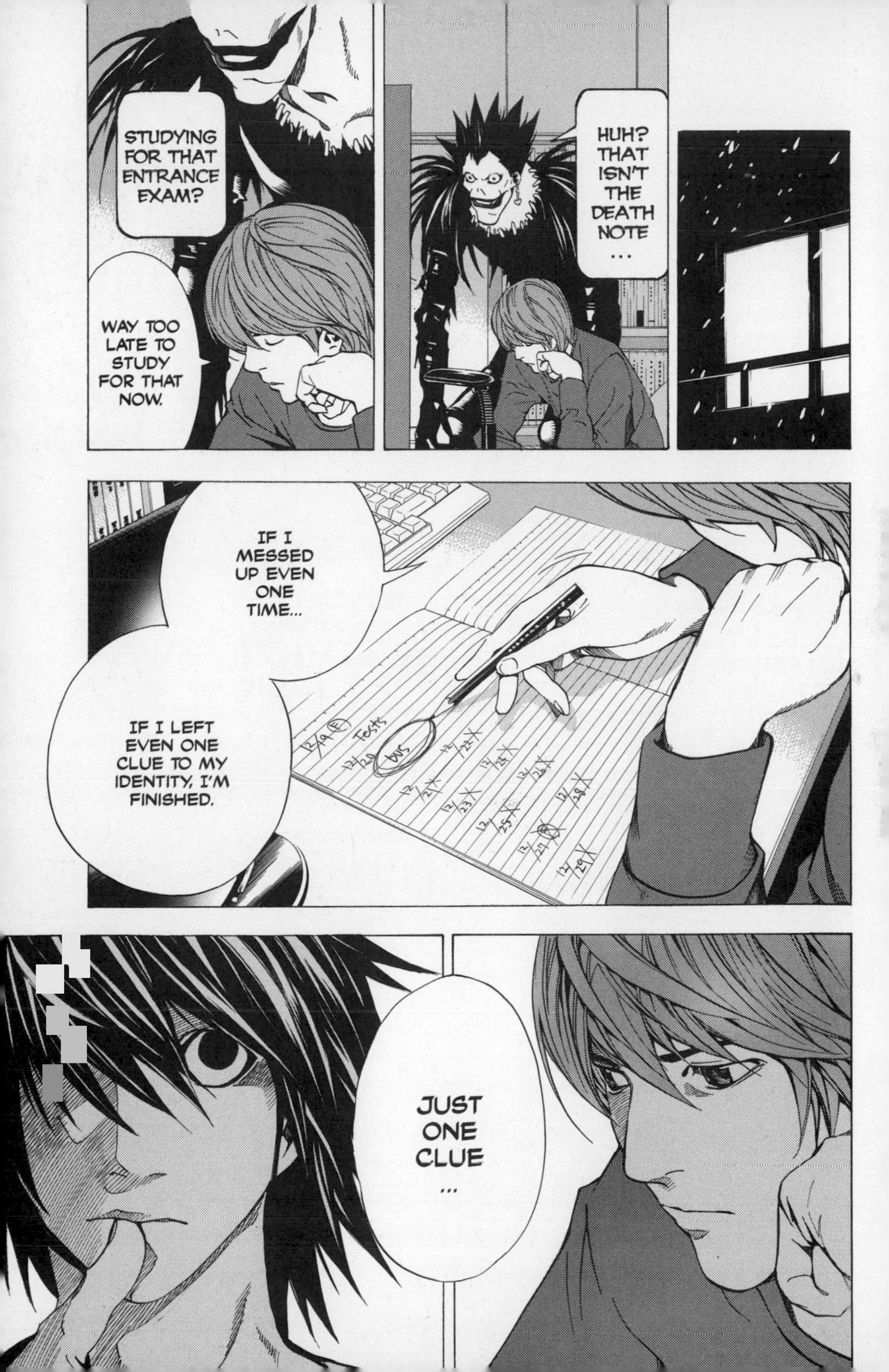
HUH? THAT ISN'T THE DEATH NOTE ...
STUDYING FOR THAT ENTRANCE EXAM?
WAY TOO LATE TO STUDY FOR THAT NOW.
IF I MESSED UP EVEN ONE TIME...
IF I LEFT EVEN ONE CLUE TO MY IDENTITY, I'M FINISHED.
JUST ONE CLUE ...

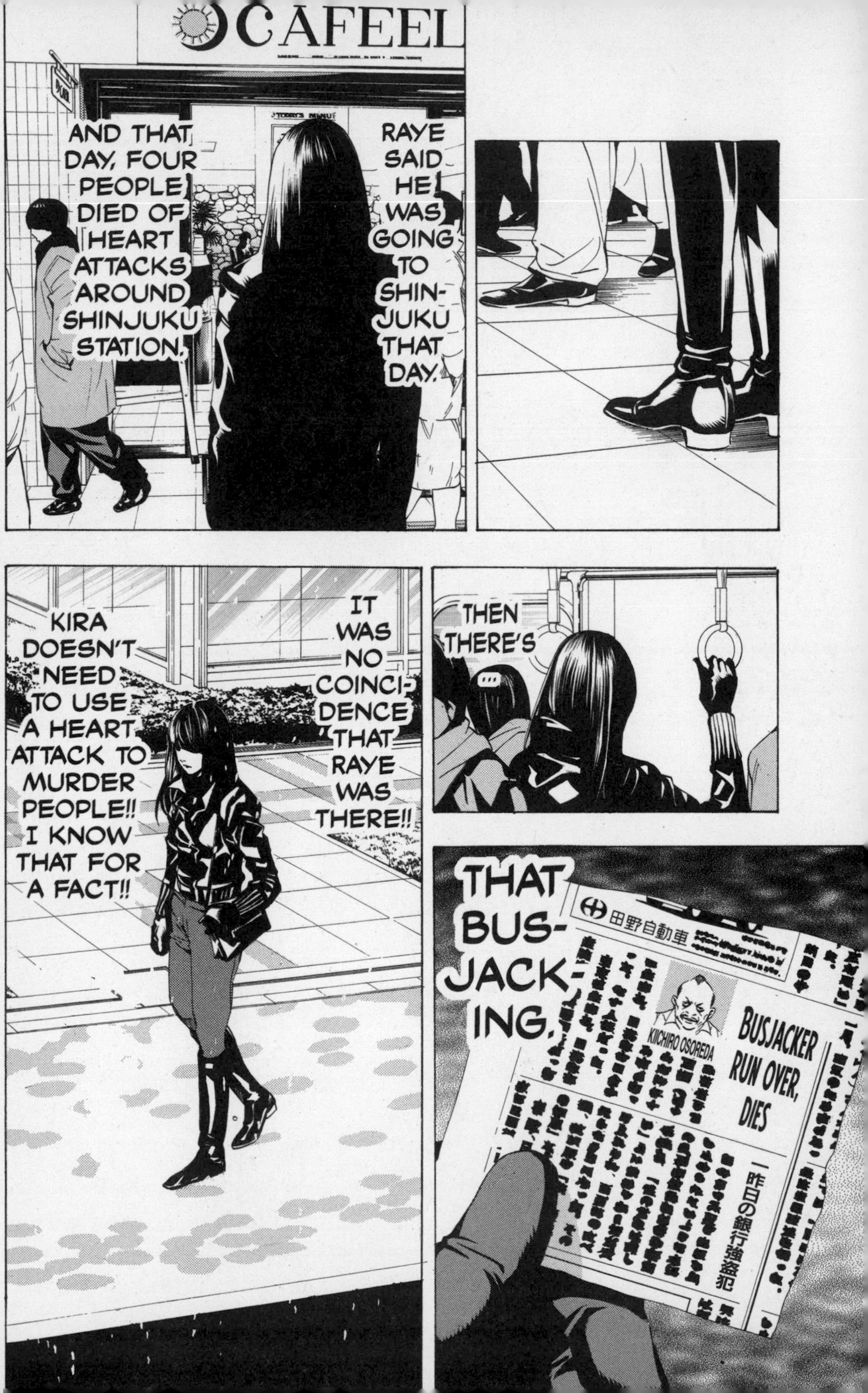
CAFEEL
RAYE SAID HE WAS GOING TO SHINJUKU THAT DAY.
AND THAT DAY, FOUR PEOPLE DIED OF HEART ATTACKS AROUND SHINJUKU STATION.
THEN THERE'S
...
THAT BUS-JACKING.
田野自動車
BUSJACKER RUN OVER, DIES
KIICHIRO OSOREDA
一昨日の銀行強盗犯
IT WAS NO COINCIDENCE THAT RAYE WAS THERE!!
KIRA DOESN'T NEED TO USE A HEART ATTACK TO MURDER PEOPLE!! I KNOW THAT FOR A FACT!!

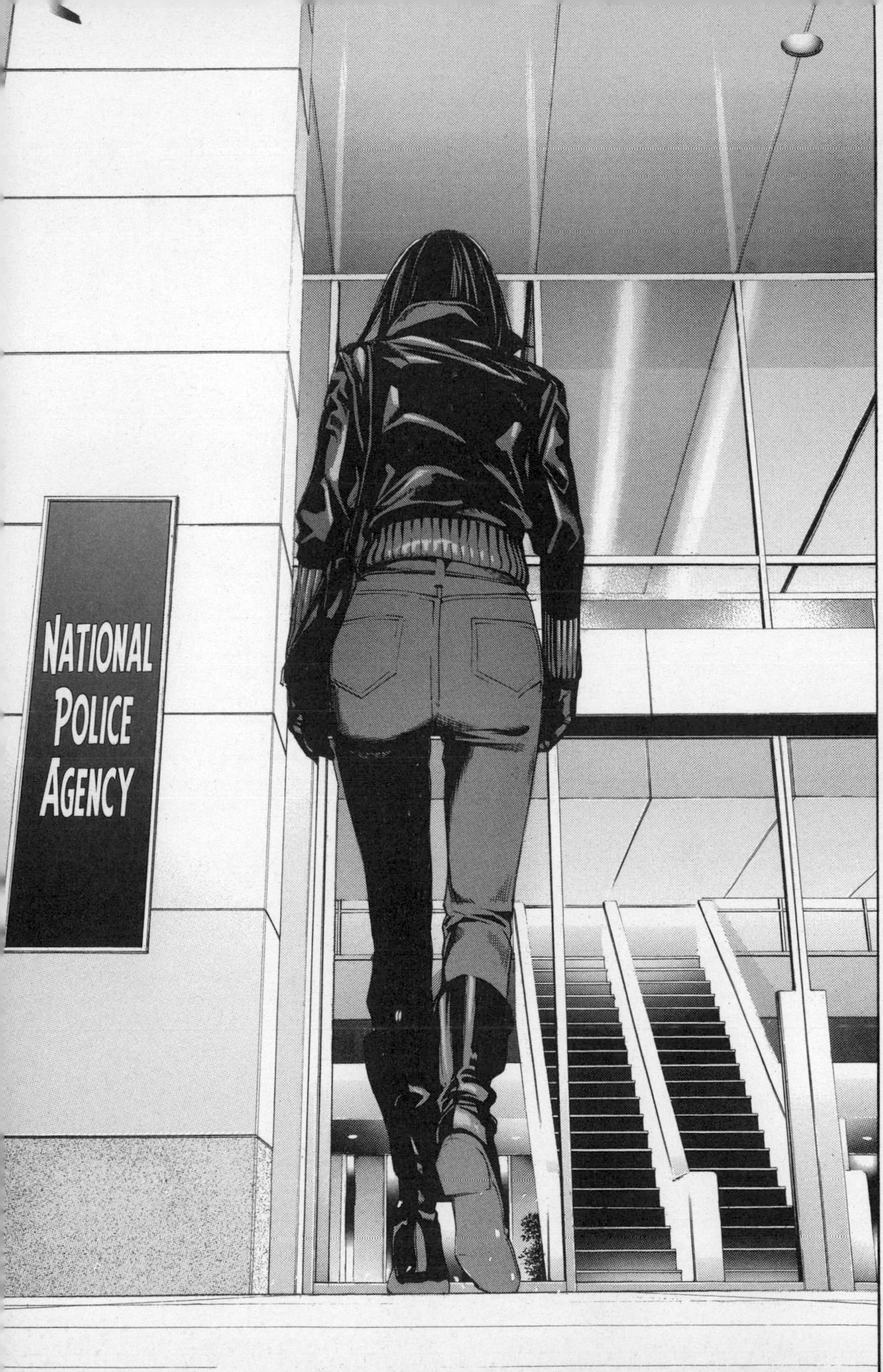
NATIONAL
POLICE
AGENCY

I KNOW THAT FOR A FACT.

KIRA DOESN'T NEED TO USE A HEART ATTACK TO MURDER PEOPLE.

NATIONAL POLICE AGENCY

# chapter 12 God

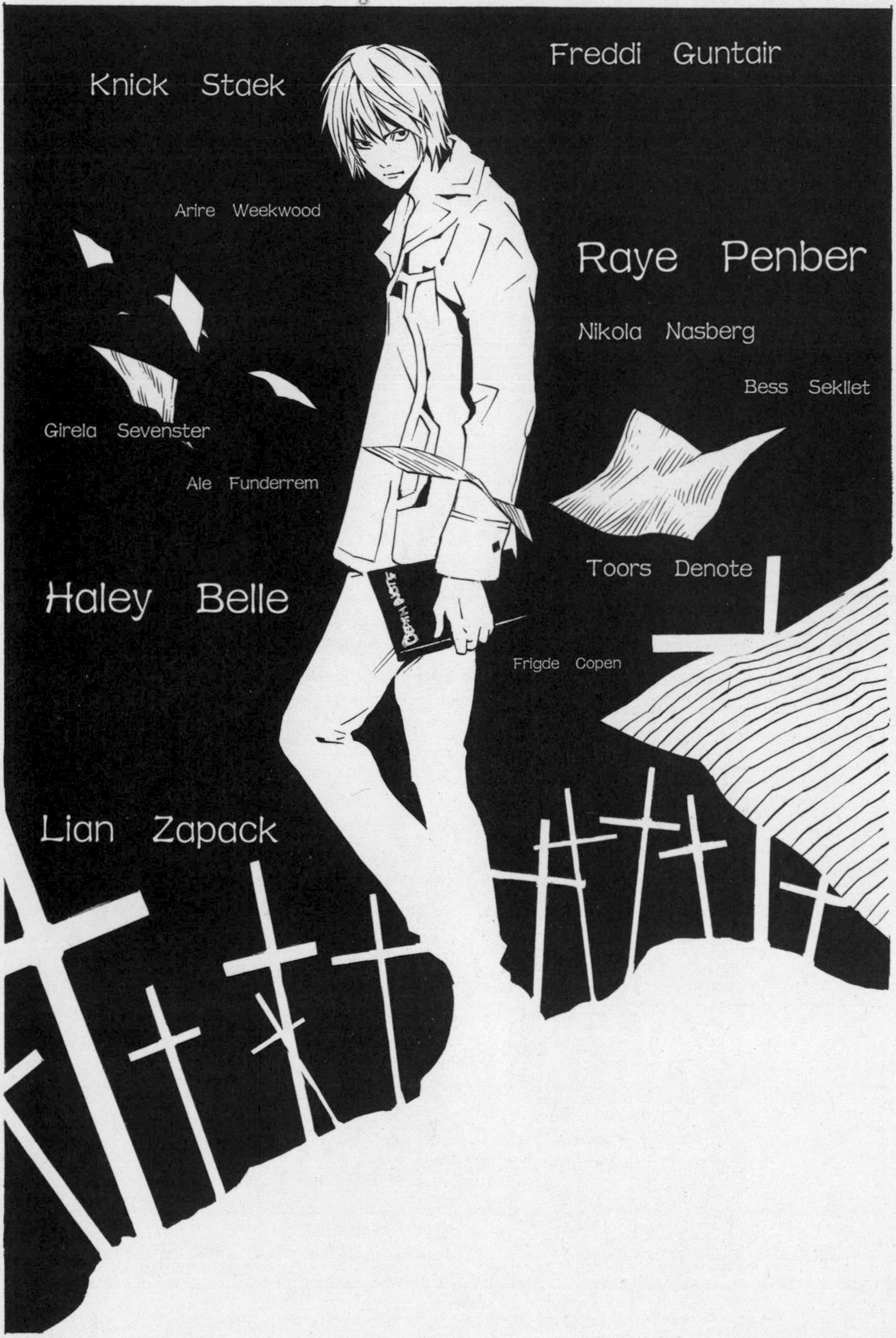
Freddi Guntair
Knick Staek
Arire Weekwood
Raye Penber
Nikola Nasberg
Bess Sekllet
Girela Sevenster
Ale Funderrem
Toors Denote
Haley Belle
Frigde Copen
Lian Zapack

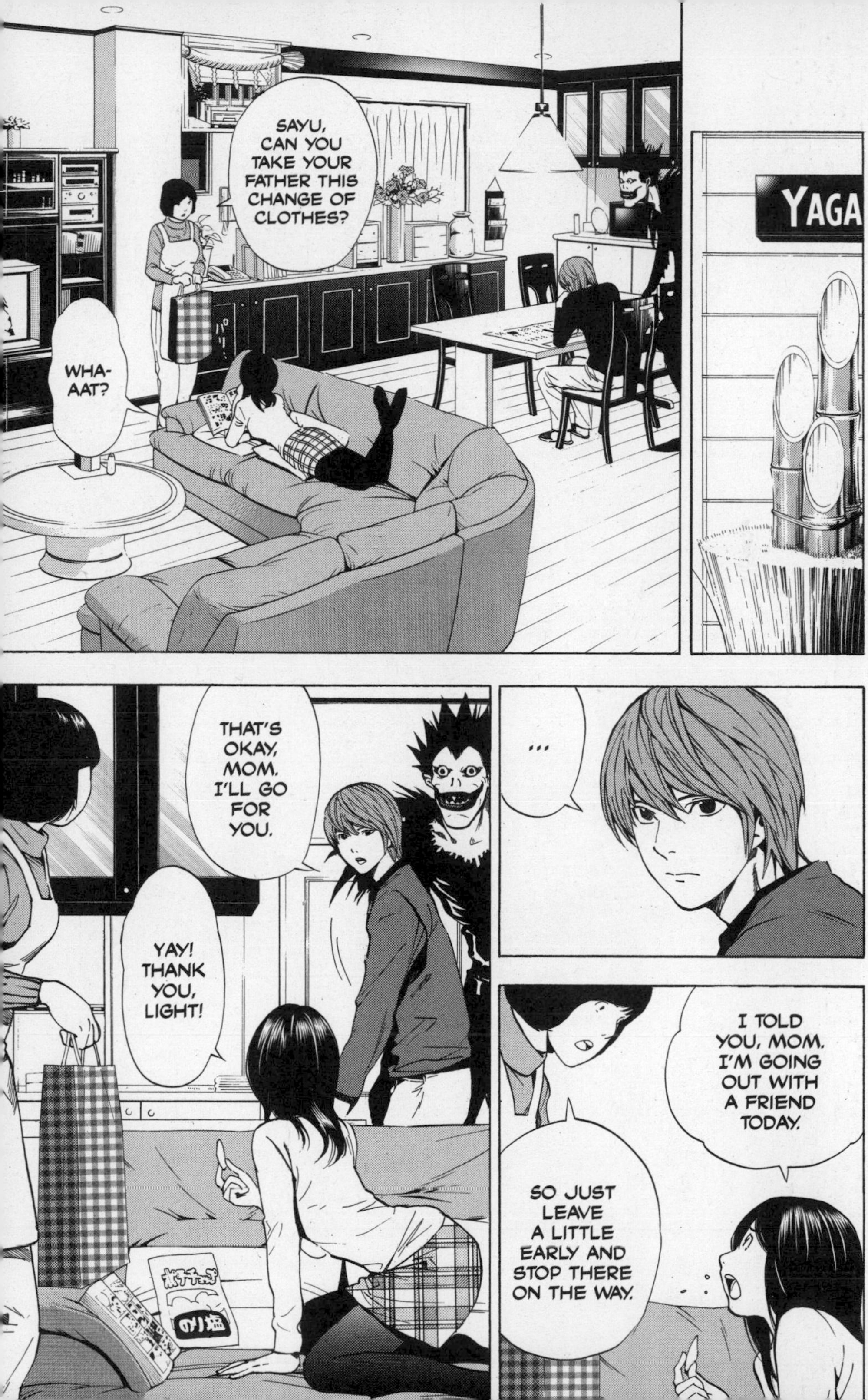
YAGA
SAYU, CAN YOU TAKE YOUR FATHER THIS CHANGE OF CLOTHES?
WHA-AAT?
...
I TOLD YOU, MOM. I'M GOING OUT WITH A FRIEND TODAY.
SO JUST LEAVE A LITTLE EARLY AND STOP THERE ON THE WAY.
THAT'S OKAY, MOM. I'LL GO FOR YOU.
YAY! THANK YOU, LIGHT!

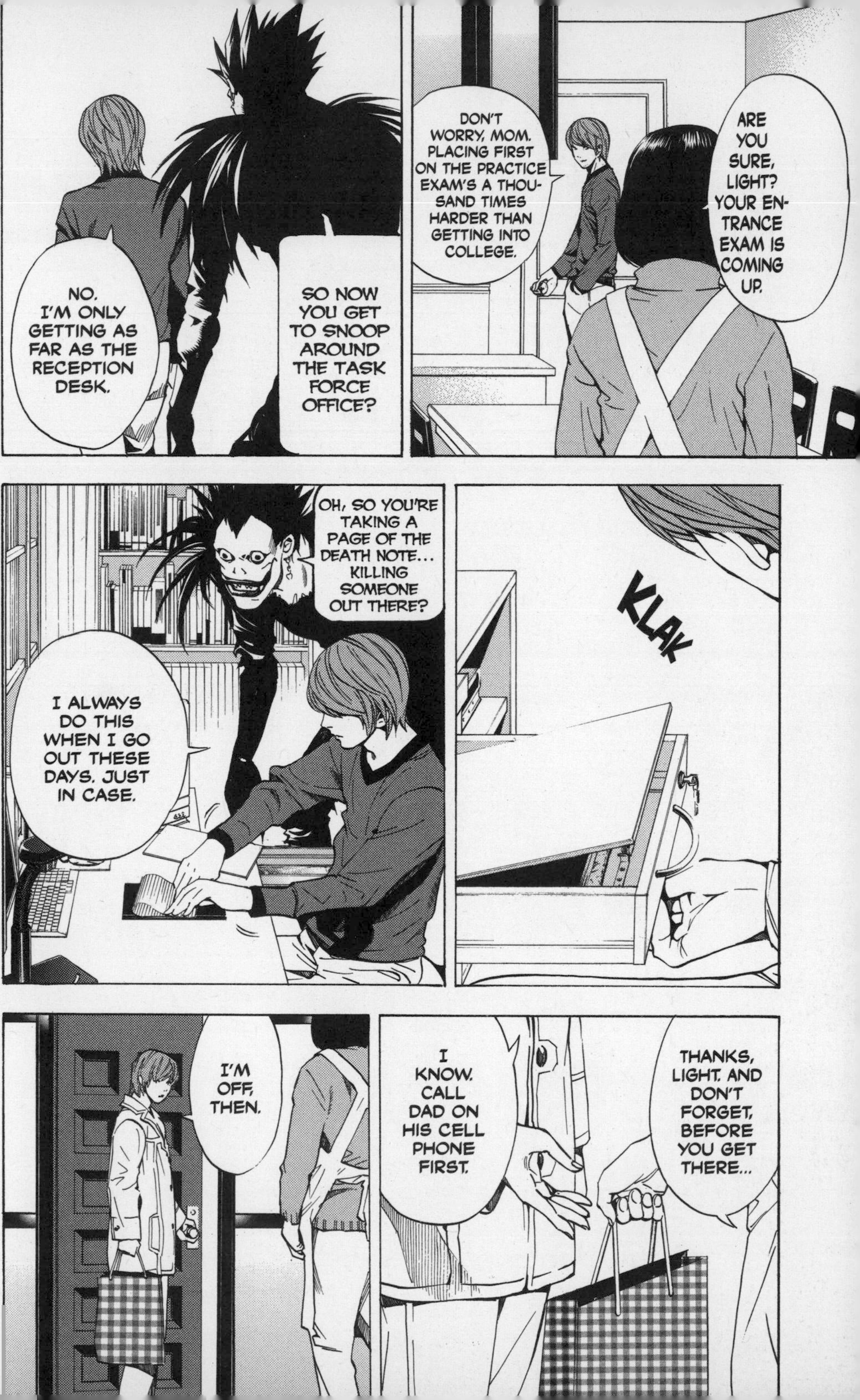
ARE YOU SURE, LIGHT? YOUR ENTRANCE EXAM IS COMING UP.
DON'T WORRY, MOM. PLACING FIRST ON THE PRACTICE EXAM'S A THOUSAND TIMES HARDER THAN GETTING INTO COLLEGE.
SO NOW YOU GET TO SNOOP AROUND THE TASK FORCE OFFICE?
NO. I'M ONLY GETTING AS FAR AS THE RECEPTION DESK.
KLAK
OH, SO YOU'RE TAKING A PAGE OF THE DEATH NOTE… KILLING SOMEONE OUT THERE?
I ALWAYS DO THIS WHEN I GO OUT THESE DAYS. JUST IN CASE.
THANKS, LIGHT. AND DON'T FORGET, BEFORE YOU GET THERE…
I KNOW. CALL DAD ON HIS CELL PHONE FIRST.
I'M OFF, THEN.

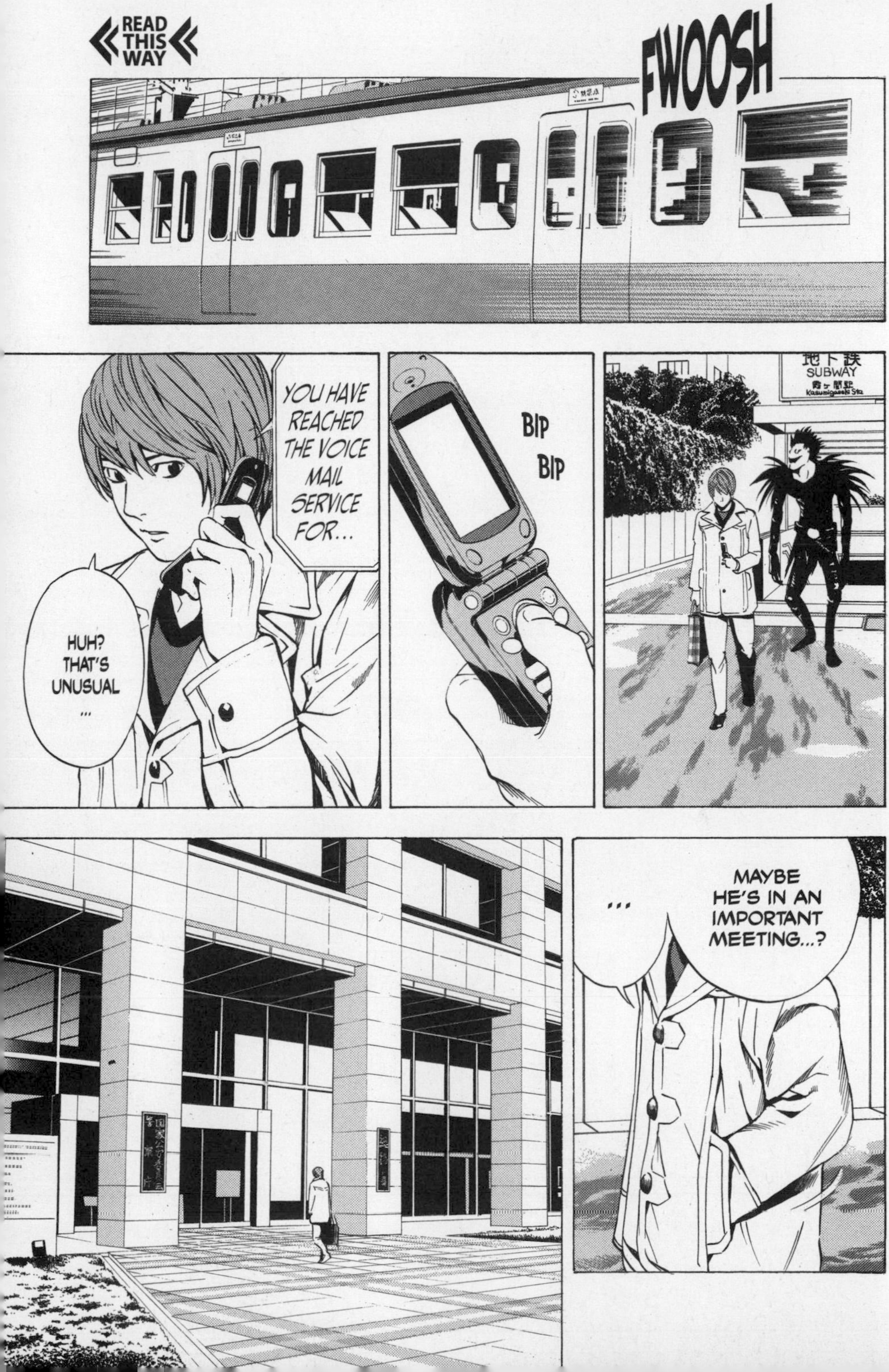
READ THIS WAY
FWOOSH
地下鉄
SUBWAY
BIP
BIP
YOU HAVE REACHED THE VOICE MAIL SERVICE FOR...
HUH? THAT'S UNUSUAL ...
MAYBE HE'S IN AN IMPORTANT MEETING...?
...

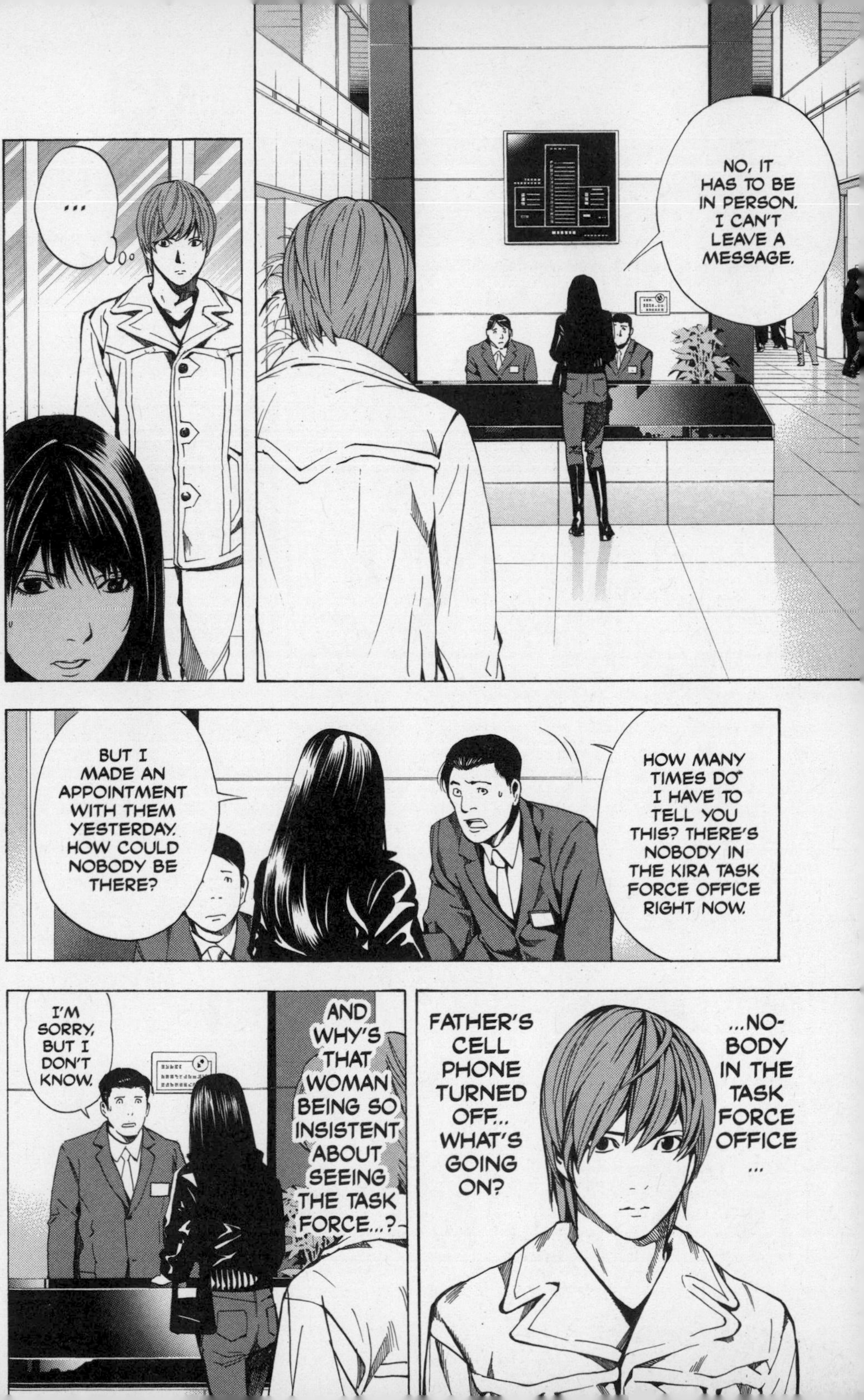
NO, IT HAS TO BE IN PERSON. I CAN'T LEAVE A MESSAGE.
...
HOW MANY TIMES DO I HAVE TO TELL YOU THIS? THERE'S NOBODY IN THE KIRA TASK FORCE OFFICE RIGHT NOW.
BUT I MADE AN APPOINTMENT WITH THEM YESTERDAY. HOW COULD NOBODY BE THERE?
...NO-BODY IN THE TASK FORCE OFFICE ...
FATHER'S CELL PHONE TURNED OFF... WHAT'S GOING ON?
AND WHY'S THAT WOMAN BEING SO INSISTENT ABOUT SEEING THE TASK FORCE...?
I'M SORRY, BUT I DON'T KNOW.

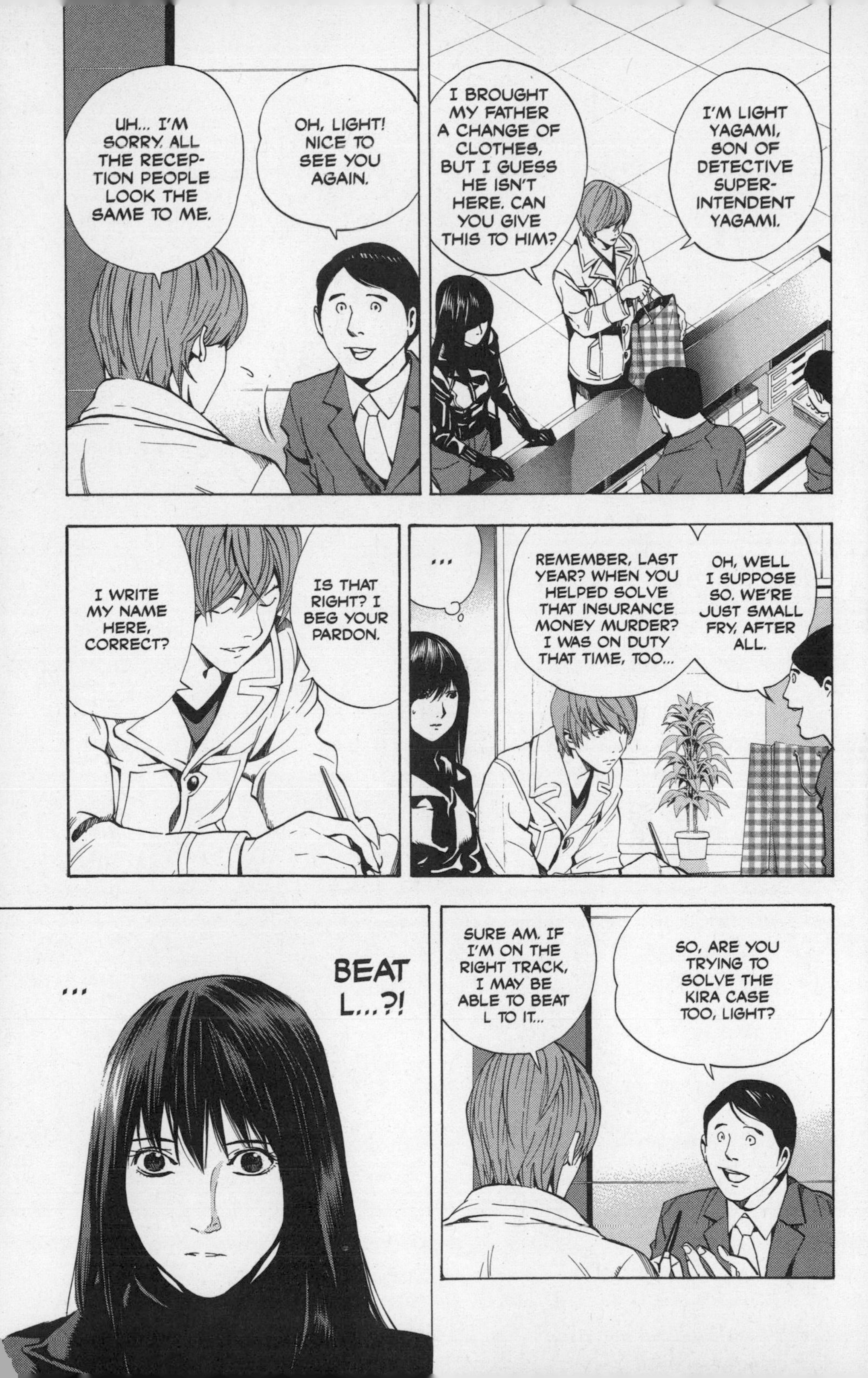
I'M LIGHT YAGAMI, SON OF DETECTIVE SUPER-INTENDENT YAGAMI.
I BROUGHT MY FATHER A CHANGE OF CLOTHES, BUT I GUESS HE ISN'T HERE. CAN YOU GIVE THIS TO HIM?
OH, LIGHT! NICE TO SEE YOU AGAIN.
UH... I'M SORRY. ALL THE RECEP-TION PEOPLE LOOK THE SAME TO ME.
OH, WELL I SUPPOSE SO. WE'RE JUST SMALL FRY, AFTER ALL.
REMEMBER, LAST YEAR? WHEN YOU HELPED SOLVE THAT INSURANCE MONEY MURDER? I WAS ON DUTY THAT TIME, TOO...
...
IS THAT RIGHT? I BEG YOUR PARDON.
I WRITE MY NAME HERE, CORRECT?
SO, ARE YOU TRYING TO SOLVE THE KIRA CASE TOO, LIGHT?
SURE AM. IF I'M ON THE RIGHT TRACK, I MAY BE ABLE TO BEAT L TO IT...
BEAT L...?!
...

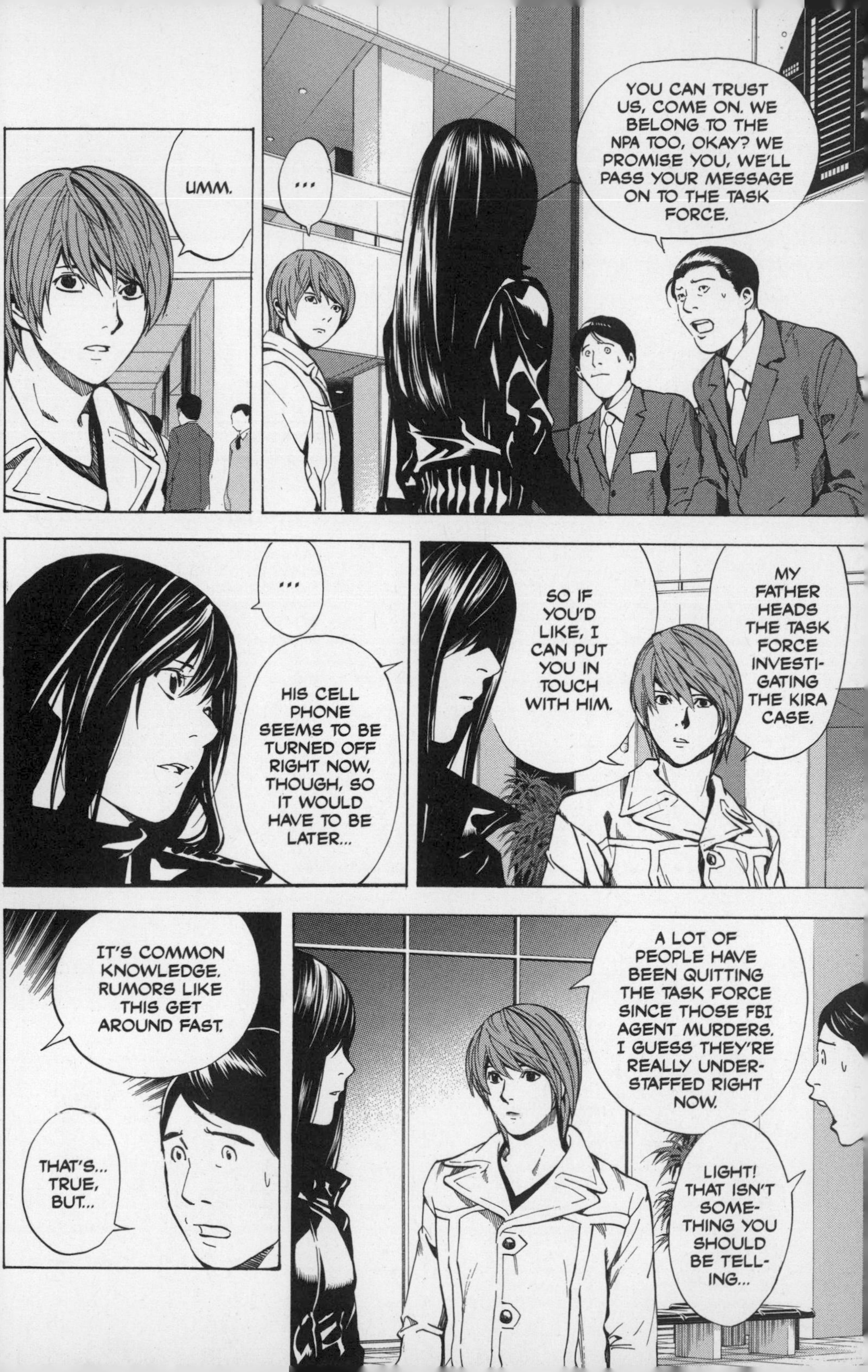
YOU CAN TRUST US, COME ON. WE BELONG TO THE NPA TOO, OKAY? WE PROMISE YOU, WE'LL PASS YOUR MESSAGE ON TO THE TASK FORCE.
...
UMM.
MY FATHER HEADS THE TASK FORCE INVESTI-GATING THE KIRA CASE.
SO IF YOU'D LIKE, I CAN PUT YOU IN TOUCH WITH HIM.
...
HIS CELL PHONE SEEMS TO BE TURNED OFF RIGHT NOW, THOUGH, SO IT WOULD HAVE TO BE LATER...
A LOT OF PEOPLE HAVE BEEN QUITTING THE TASK FORCE SINCE THOSE FBI AGENT MURDERS. I GUESS THEY'RE REALLY UNDER-STAFFED RIGHT NOW.
LIGHT! THAT ISN'T SOME-THING YOU SHOULD BE TELL-ING...
IT'S COMMON KNOWLEDGE. RUMORS LIKE THIS GET AROUND FAST.
THAT'S... TRUE, BUT...

READ THIS WAY

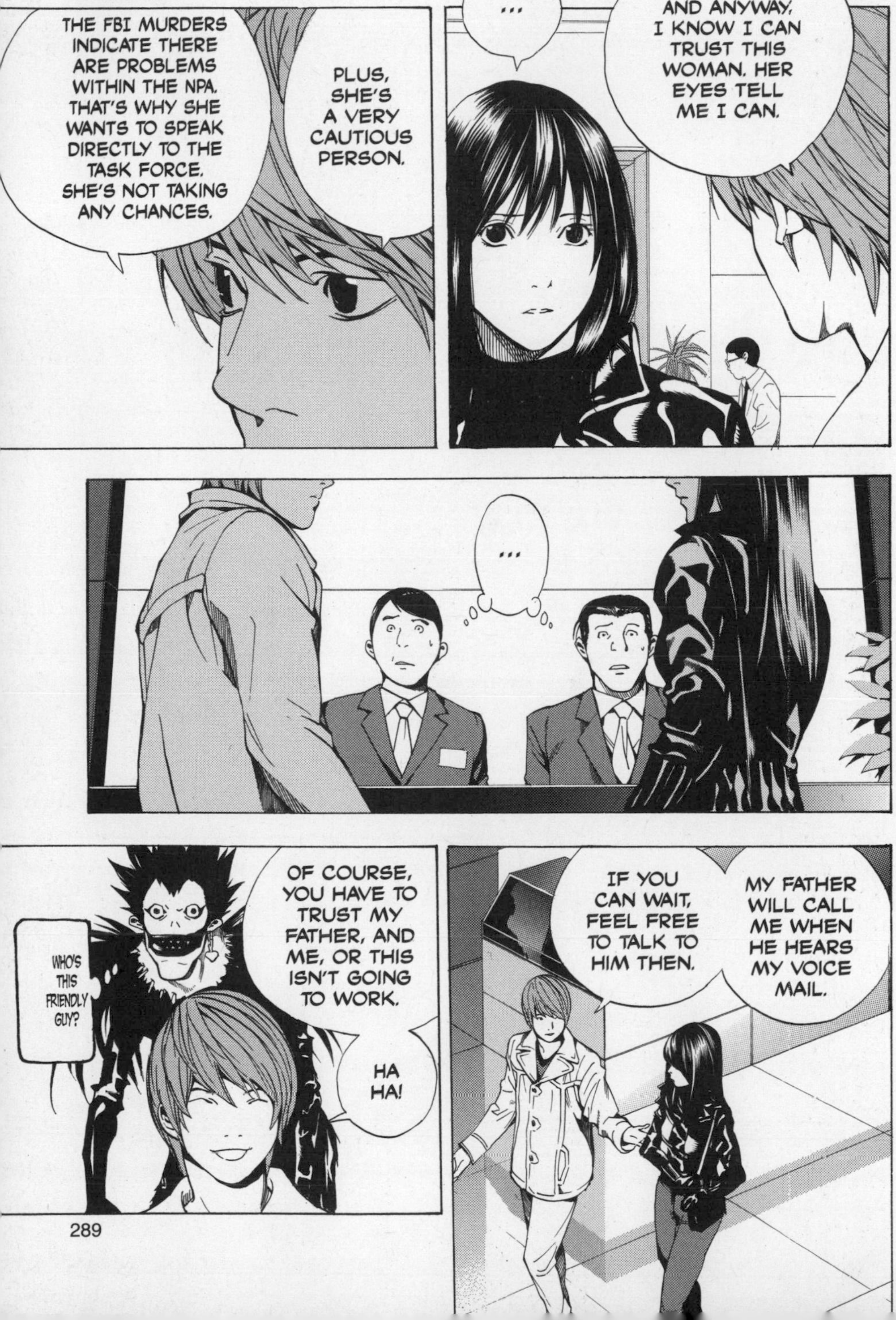
...
AND ANYWAY, I KNOW I CAN TRUST THIS WOMAN. HER EYES TELL ME I CAN.
THE FBI MURDERS INDICATE THERE ARE PROBLEMS WITHIN THE NPA. THAT'S WHY SHE WANTS TO SPEAK DIRECTLY TO THE TASK FORCE. SHE'S NOT TAKING ANY CHANCES.
PLUS, SHE'S A VERY CAUTIOUS PERSON.
...
MY FATHER WILL CALL ME WHEN HE HEARS MY VOICE MAIL.
IF YOU CAN WAIT, FEEL FREE TO TALK TO HIM THEN.
OF COURSE, YOU HAVE TO TRUST MY FATHER, AND ME, OR THIS ISN'T GOING TO WORK.
HA HA!
WHO'S THIS FRIENDLY GUY?

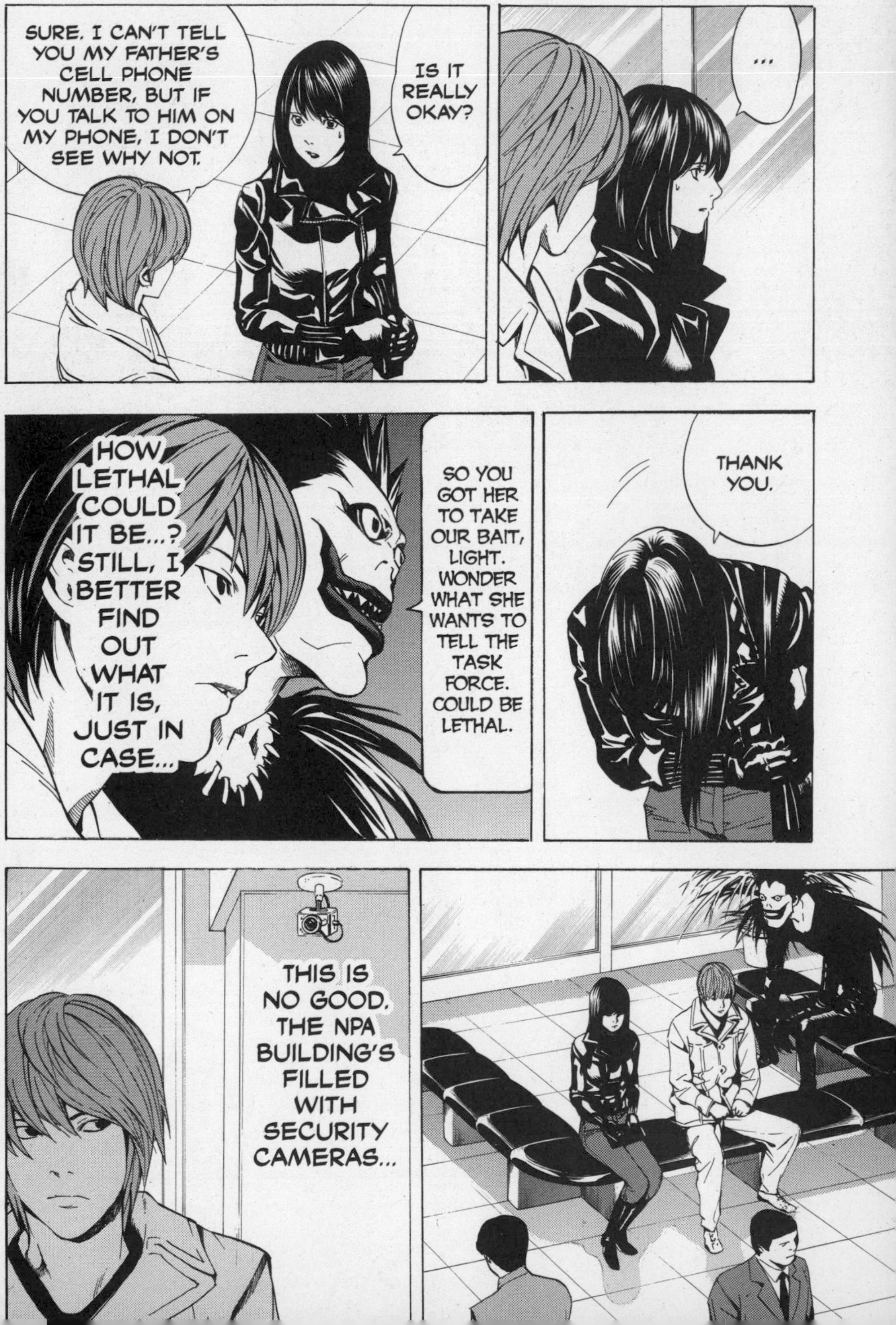
...
IS IT REALLY OKAY?
SURE. I CAN'T TELL YOU MY FATHER'S CELL PHONE NUMBER, BUT IF YOU TALK TO HIM ON MY PHONE, I DON'T SEE WHY NOT.
THANK YOU.
SO YOU GOT HER TO TAKE OUR BAIT, LIGHT. WONDER WHAT SHE WANTS TO TELL THE TASK FORCE. COULD BE LETHAL.
HOW LETHAL COULD IT BE...? STILL, I BETTER FIND OUT WHAT IT IS, JUST IN CASE...
THIS IS NO GOOD. THE NPA BUILDING'S FILLED WITH SECURITY CAMERAS...

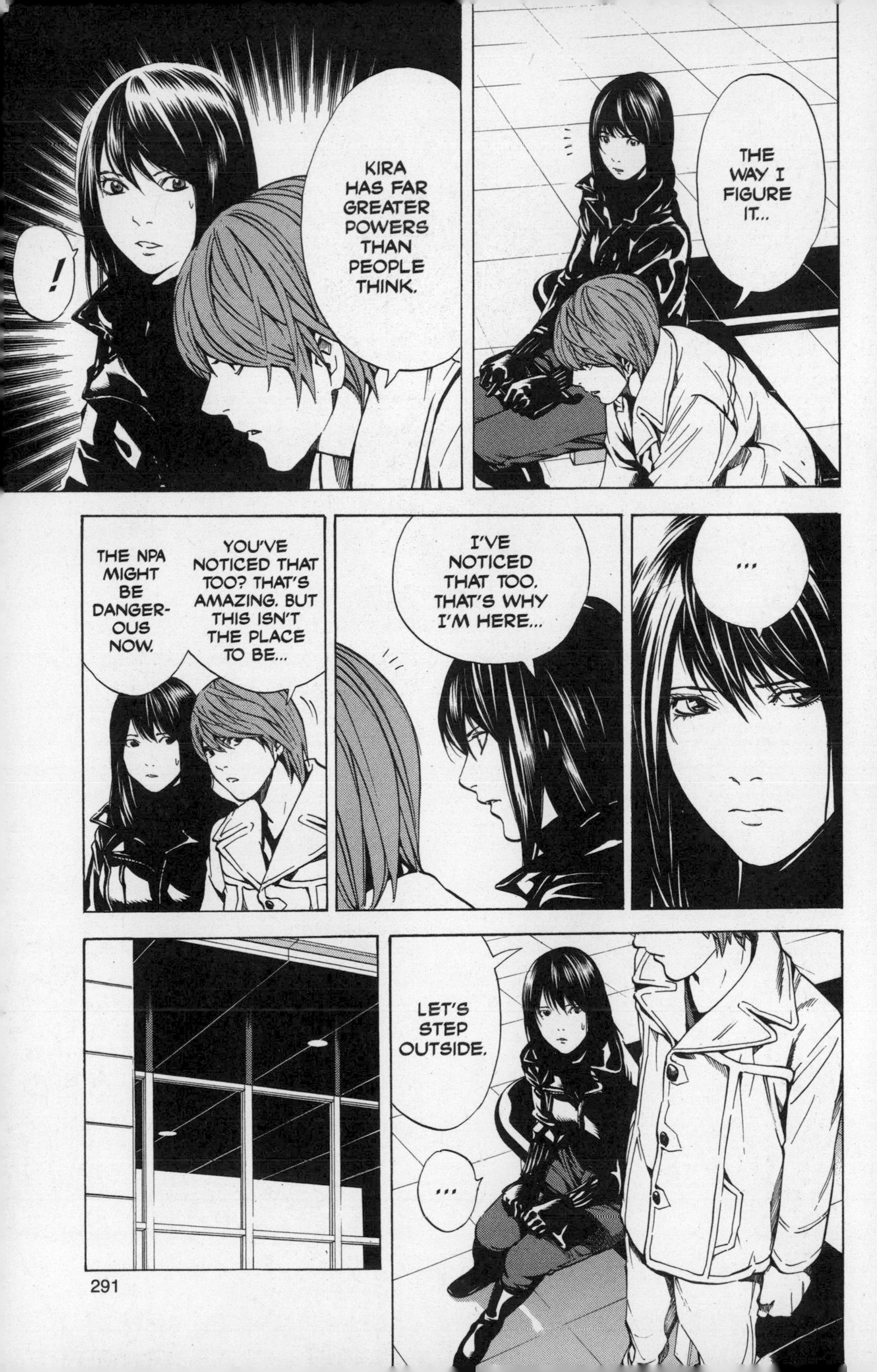
THE WAY I FIGURE IT...
KIRA HAS FAR GREATER POWERS THAN PEOPLE THINK.
!
...
I'VE NOTICED THAT TOO. THAT'S WHY I'M HERE...
YOU'VE NOTICED THAT TOO? THAT'S AMAZING. BUT THIS ISN'T THE PLACE TO BE...
THE NPA MIGHT BE DANGER-OUS NOW.
LET'S STEP OUTSIDE.
...

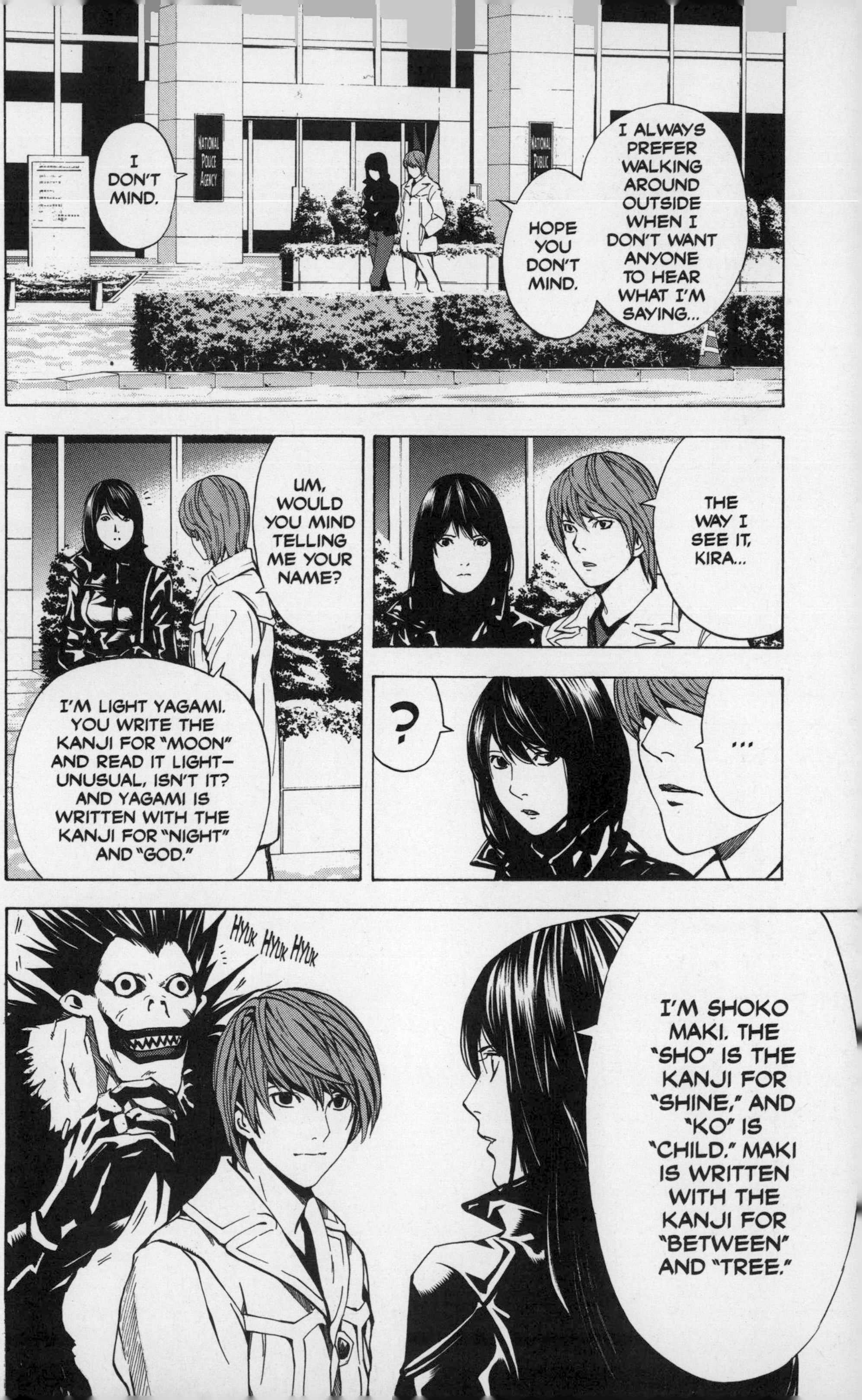
NATIONAL POLICE AGENCY
I ALWAYS PREFER WALKING AROUND OUTSIDE WHEN I DON'T WANT ANYONE TO HEAR WHAT I'M SAYING...
HOPE YOU DON'T MIND.
I DON'T MIND.
THE WAY I SEE IT, KIRA...
...
?
UM, WOULD YOU MIND TELLING ME YOUR NAME?
I'M LIGHT YAGAMI. YOU WRITE THE KANJI FOR "MOON" AND READ IT LIGHT—UNUSUAL, ISN'T IT? AND YAGAMI IS WRITTEN WITH THE KANJI FOR "NIGHT" AND "GOD."
I'M SHOKO MAKI. THE "SHO" IS THE KANJI FOR "SHINE," AND "KO" IS "CHILD." MAKI IS WRITTEN WITH THE KANJI FOR "BETWEEN" AND "TREE."
HYUK HYUK HYUK

READ THIS WAY

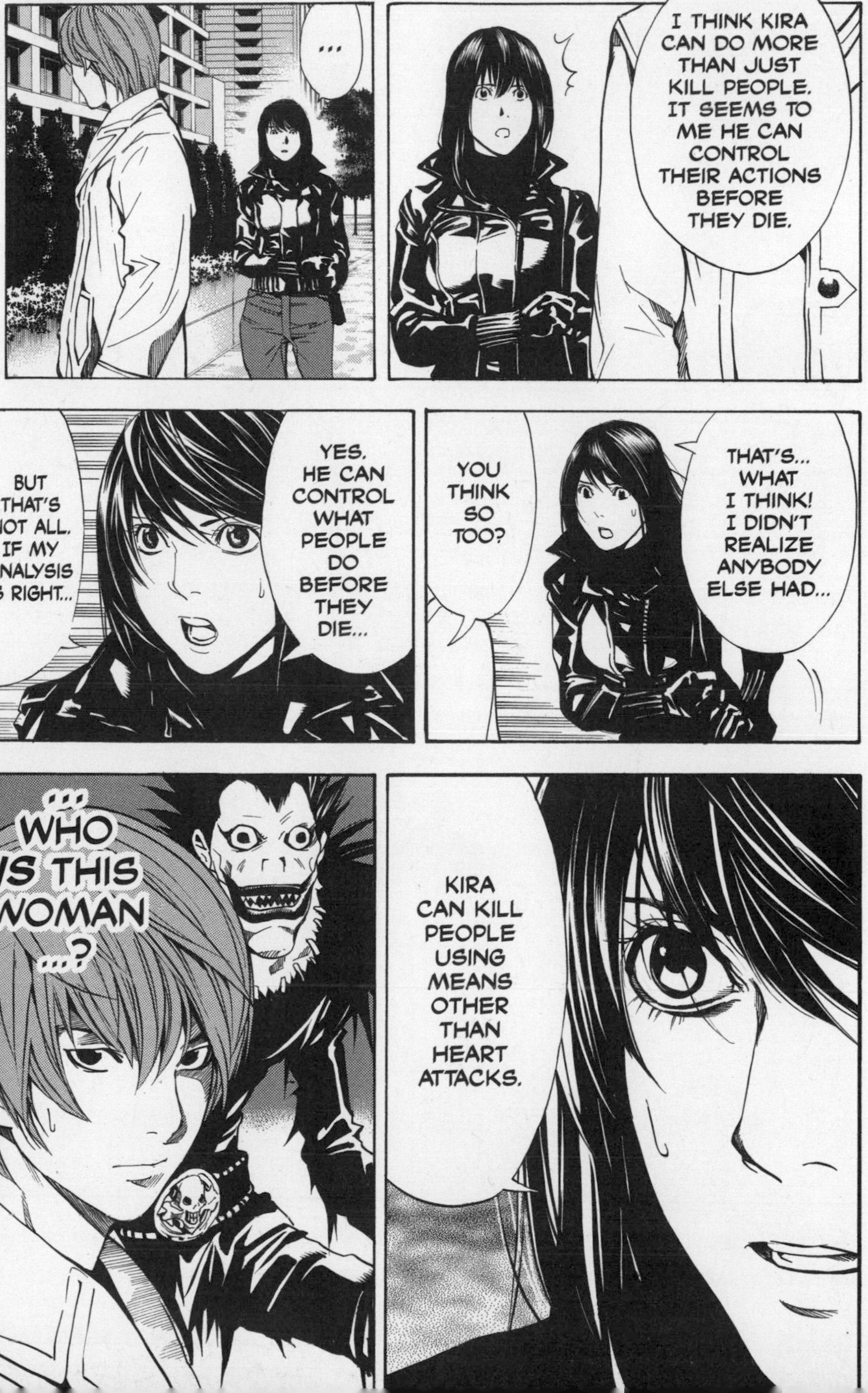
I THINK KIRA CAN DO MORE THAN JUST KILL PEOPLE. IT SEEMS TO ME HE CAN CONTROL THEIR ACTIONS BEFORE THEY DIE.
...
THAT'S... WHAT I THINK! I DIDN'T REALIZE ANYBODY ELSE HAD...
YOU THINK SO TOO?
YES. HE CAN CONTROL WHAT PEOPLE DO BEFORE THEY DIE...
BUT THAT'S NOT ALL. IF MY ANALYSIS IS RIGHT...
KIRA CAN KILL PEOPLE USING MEANS OTHER THAN HEART ATTACKS.
...WHO IS THIS WOMAN ...?

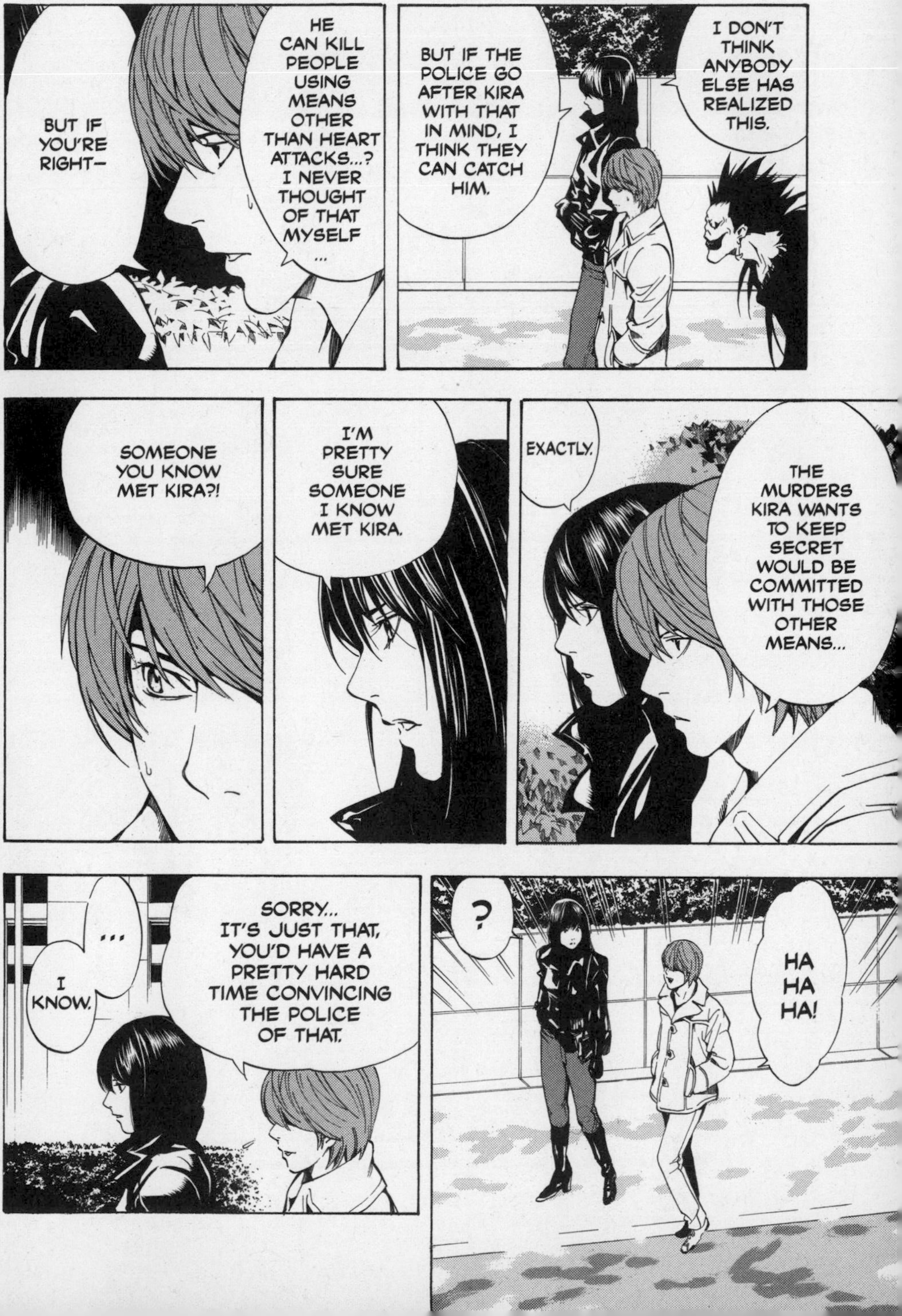
I DON'T THINK ANYBODY ELSE HAS REALIZED THIS.
BUT IF THE POLICE GO AFTER KIRA WITH THAT IN MIND, I THINK THEY CAN CATCH HIM.
HE CAN KILL PEOPLE USING MEANS OTHER THAN HEART ATTACKS...? I NEVER THOUGHT OF THAT MYSELF ...
BUT IF YOU'RE RIGHT—
THE MURDERS KIRA WANTS TO KEEP SECRET WOULD BE COMMITTED WITH THOSE OTHER MEANS...
EXACTLY.
I'M PRETTY SURE SOMEONE I KNOW MET KIRA.
SOMEONE YOU KNOW MET KIRA?!
HA HA HA!
?
SORRY... IT'S JUST THAT, YOU'D HAVE A PRETTY HARD TIME CONVINCING THE POLICE OF THAT.
...
I KNOW.

READ THIS WAY

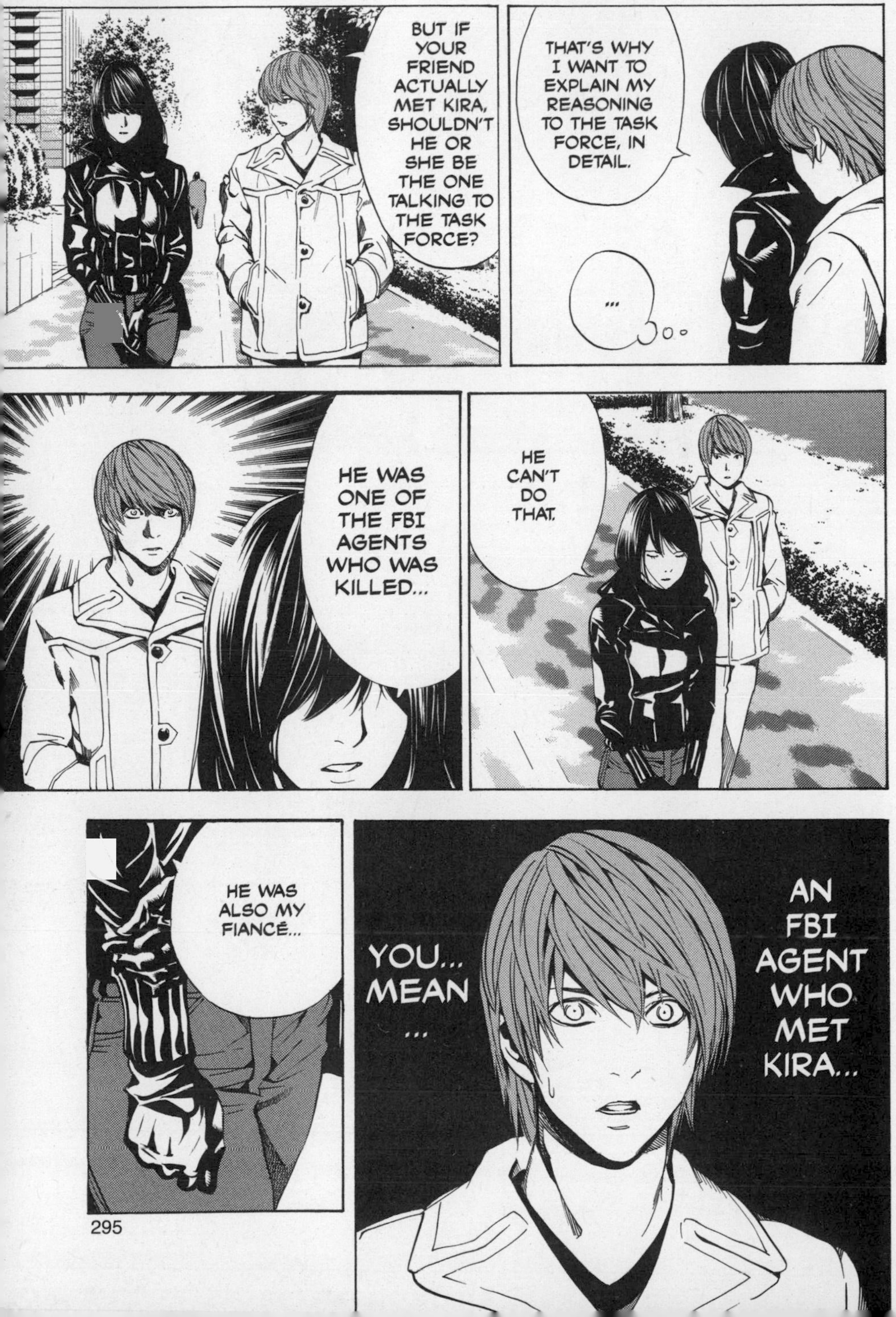
THAT'S WHY I WANT TO EXPLAIN MY REASONING TO THE TASK FORCE, IN DETAIL.
...
BUT IF YOUR FRIEND ACTUALLY MET KIRA, SHOULDN'T HE OR SHE BE THE ONE TALKING TO THE TASK FORCE?
HE CAN'T DO THAT.
HE WAS ONE OF THE FBI AGENTS WHO WAS KILLED...
AN FBI AGENT WHO MET KIRA...
YOU... MEAN ...
HE WAS ALSO MY FIANCÉ...

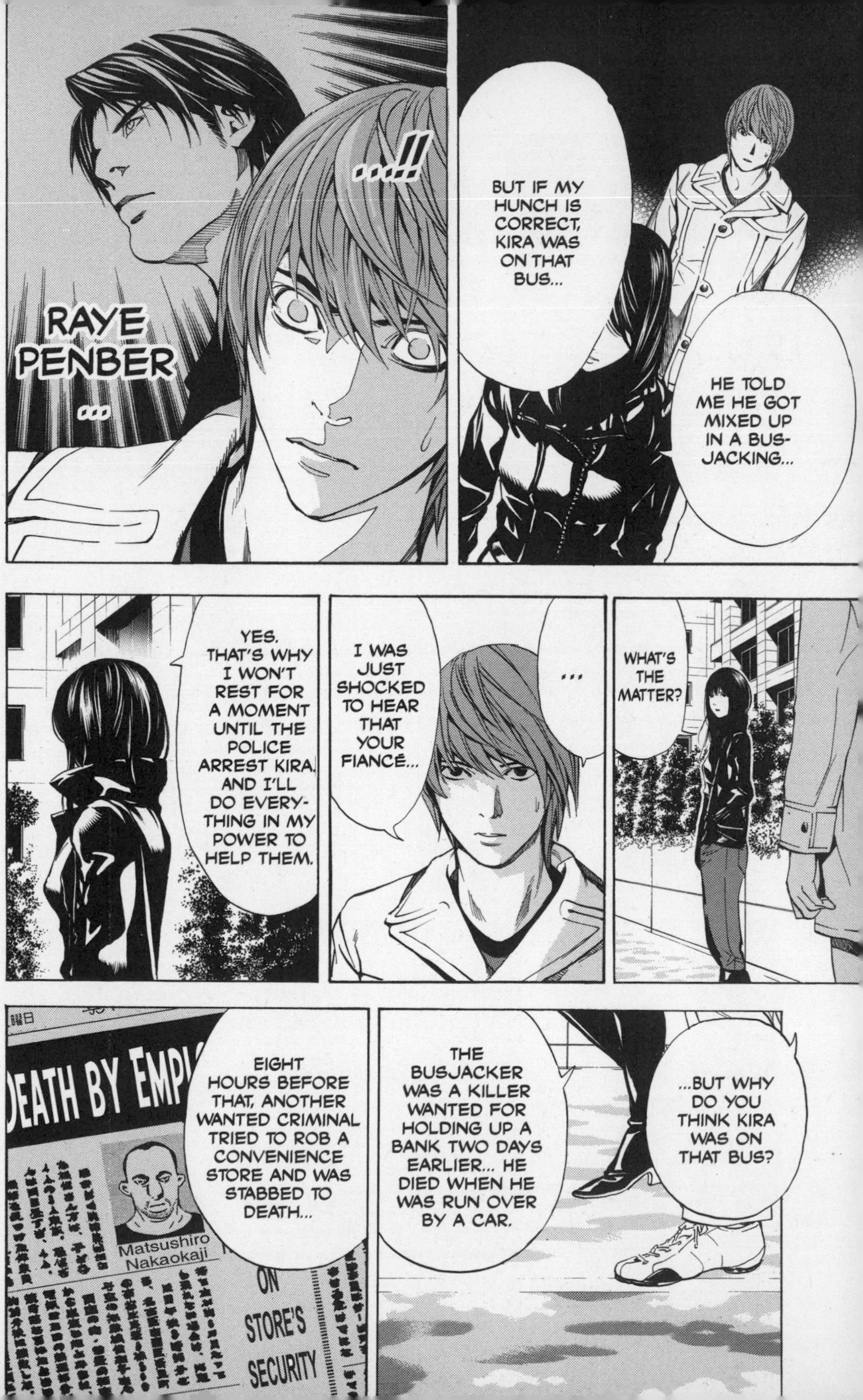
HE TOLD ME HE GOT MIXED UP IN A BUS-JACKING...
BUT IF MY HUNCH IS CORRECT, KIRA WAS ON THAT BUS...
...!!
RAYE PENBER ...
WHAT'S THE MATTER?
...
I WAS JUST SHOCKED TO HEAR THAT YOUR FIANCÉ...
YES. THAT'S WHY I WON'T REST FOR A MOMENT UNTIL THE POLICE ARREST KIRA. AND I'LL DO EVERY-THING IN MY POWER TO HELP THEM.
...BUT WHY DO YOU THINK KIRA WAS ON THAT BUS?
THE BUSJACKER WAS A KILLER WANTED FOR HOLDING UP A BANK TWO DAYS EARLIER... HE DIED WHEN HE WAS RUN OVER BY A CAR.
EIGHT HOURS BEFORE THAT, ANOTHER WANTED CRIMINAL TRIED TO ROB A CONVENIENCE STORE AND WAS STABBED TO DEATH...
DEATH BY EMPL
Matsushiro Nakaokaji
ON STORE'S SECURITY

READ THIS WAY

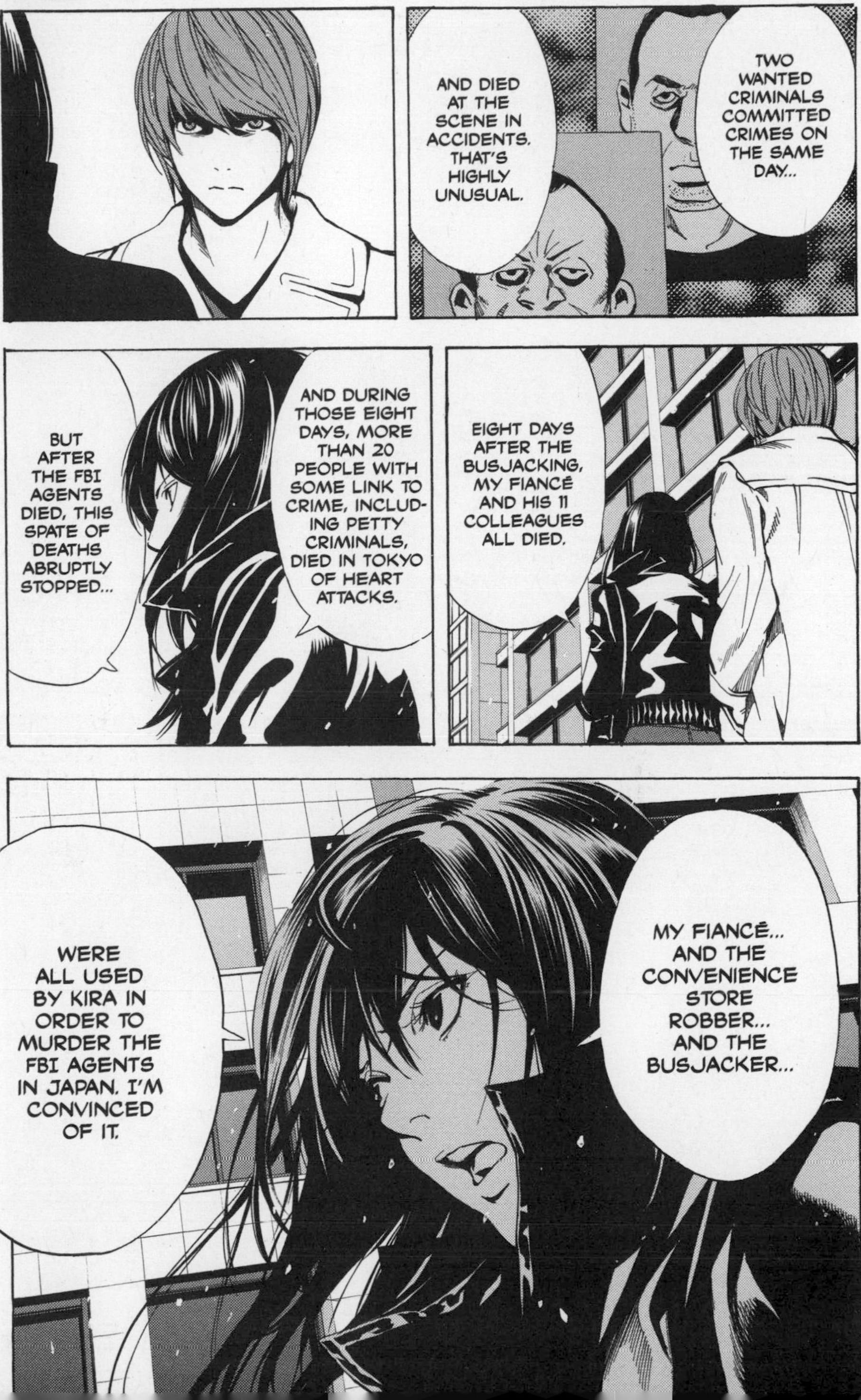
TWO WANTED CRIMINALS COMMITTED CRIMES ON THE SAME DAY...
AND DIED AT THE SCENE IN ACCIDENTS. THAT'S HIGHLY UNUSUAL.
EIGHT DAYS AFTER THE BUSJACKING, MY FIANCÉ AND HIS 11 COLLEAGUES ALL DIED.
AND DURING THOSE EIGHT DAYS, MORE THAN 20 PEOPLE WITH SOME LINK TO CRIME, INCLUDING PETTY CRIMINALS, DIED IN TOKYO OF HEART ATTACKS.
BUT AFTER THE FBI AGENTS DIED, THIS SPATE OF DEATHS ABRUPTLY STOPPED...
MY FIANCÉ... AND THE CONVENIENCE STORE ROBBER... AND THE BUSJACKER...
WERE ALL USED BY KIRA IN ORDER TO MURDER THE FBI AGENTS IN JAPAN. I'M CONVINCED OF IT.

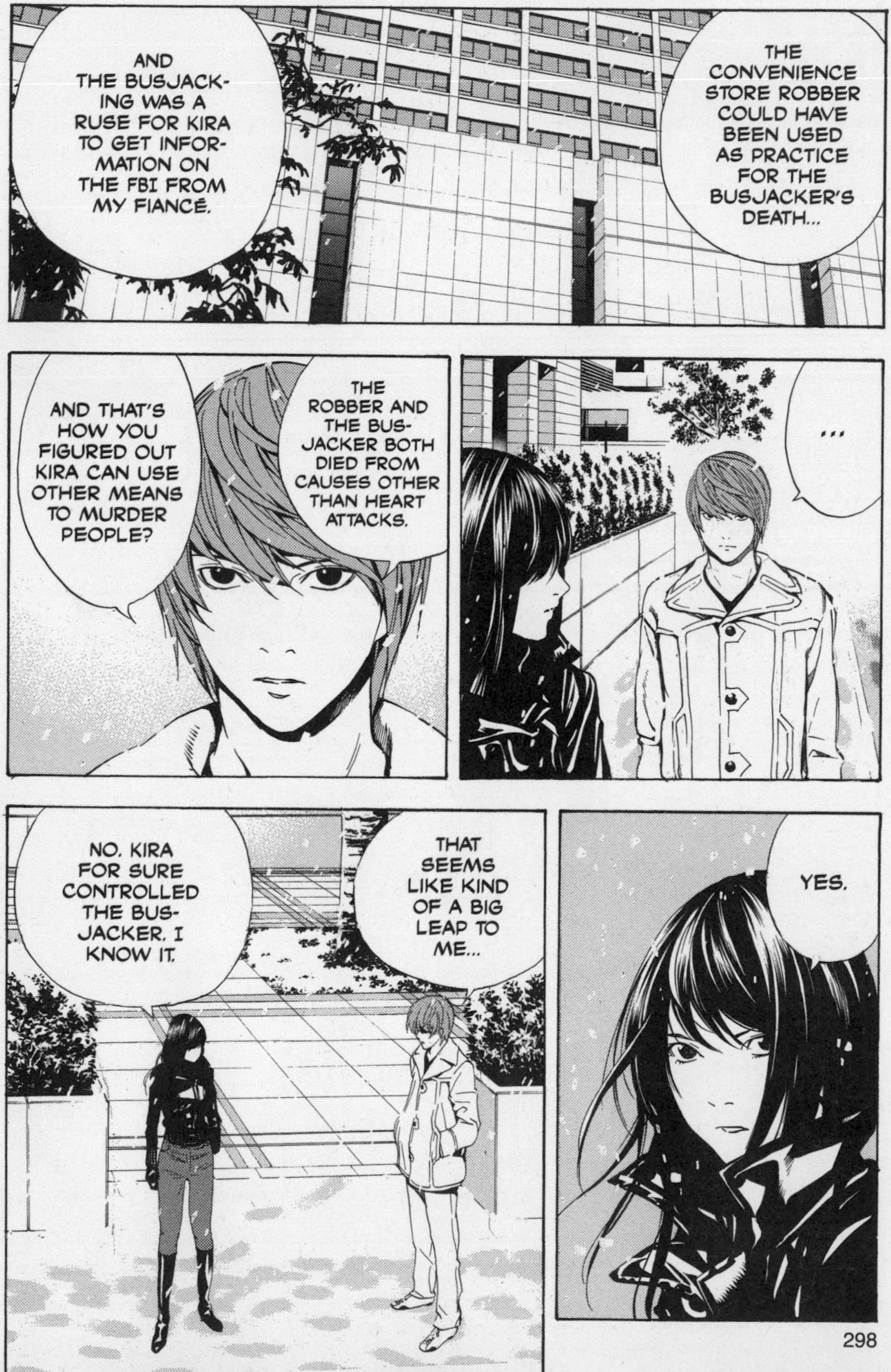
THE CONVENIENCE STORE ROBBER COULD HAVE BEEN USED AS PRACTICE FOR THE BUSJACKER'S DEATH...
AND THE BUSJACK-ING WAS A RUSE FOR KIRA TO GET INFOR-MATION ON THE FBI FROM MY FIANCÉ.
...
THE ROBBER AND THE BUS-JACKER BOTH DIED FROM CAUSES OTHER THAN HEART ATTACKS.
AND THAT'S HOW YOU FIGURED OUT KIRA CAN USE OTHER MEANS TO MURDER PEOPLE?
YES.
THAT SEEMS LIKE KIND OF A BIG LEAP TO ME...
NO, KIRA FOR SURE CONTROLLED THE BUS-JACKER. I KNOW IT.

READ THIS WAY

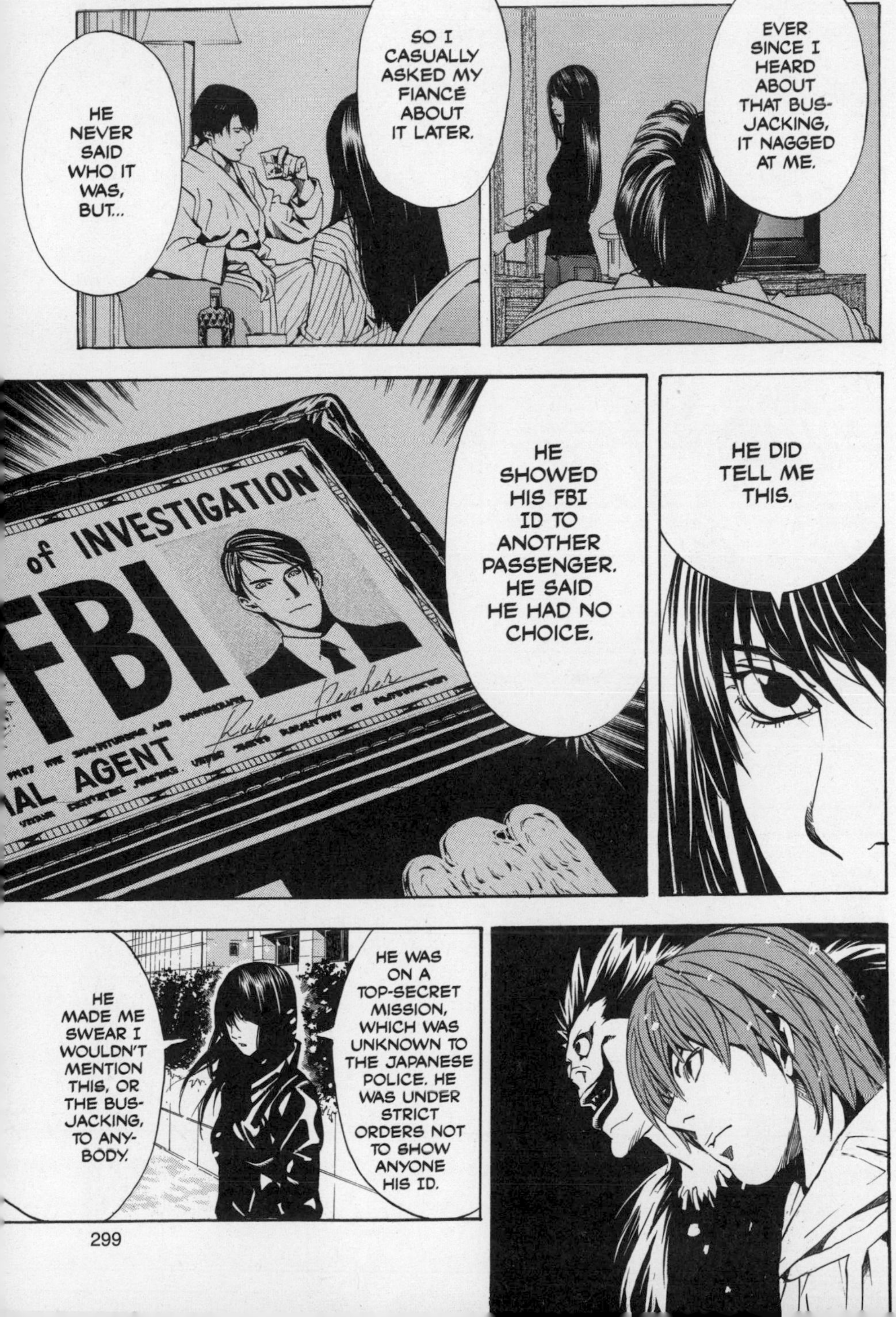

EVER SINCE I HEARD ABOUT THAT BUS-JACKING, IT NAGGED AT ME.
SO I CASUALLY ASKED MY FIANCÉ ABOUT IT LATER.
HE NEVER SAID WHO IT WAS, BUT...
HE DID TELL ME THIS.
HE SHOWED HIS FBI ID TO ANOTHER PASSENGER. HE SAID HE HAD NO CHOICE.
of INVESTIGATION
FBI
AGENT
HE WAS ON A TOP-SECRET MISSION, WHICH WAS UNKNOWN TO THE JAPANESE POLICE. HE WAS UNDER STRICT ORDERS NOT TO SHOW ANYONE HIS ID.
HE MADE ME SWEAR I WOULDN'T MENTION THIS, OR THE BUS-JACKING, TO ANYBODY.

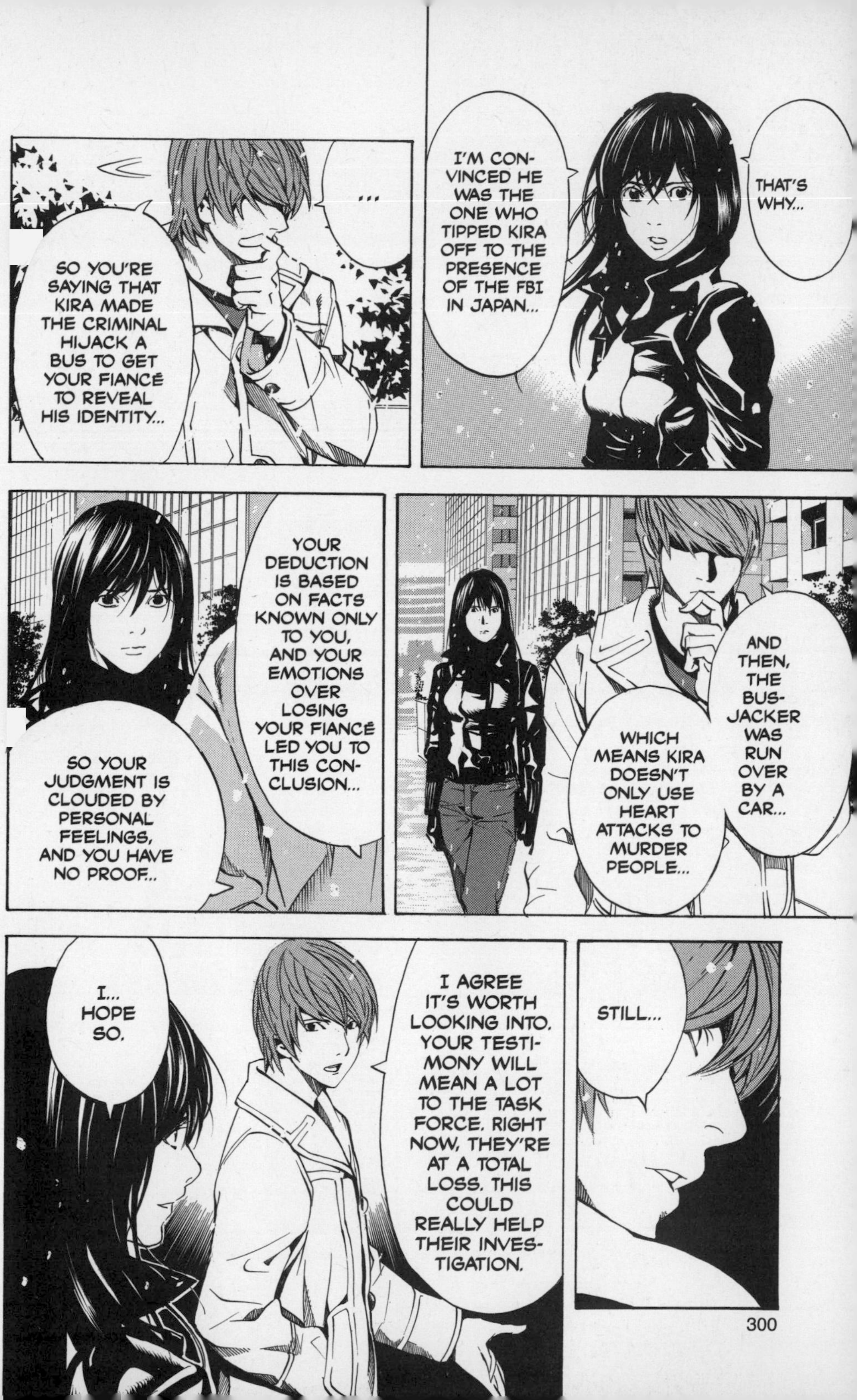
THAT'S WHY...
I'M CONVINCED HE WAS THE ONE WHO TIPPED KIRA OFF TO THE PRESENCE OF THE FBI IN JAPAN...
...
SO YOU'RE SAYING THAT KIRA MADE THE CRIMINAL HIJACK A BUS TO GET YOUR FIANCÉ TO REVEAL HIS IDENTITY...
AND THEN, THE BUS-JACKER WAS RUN OVER BY A CAR...
WHICH MEANS KIRA DOESN'T ONLY USE HEART ATTACKS TO MURDER PEOPLE...
YOUR DEDUCTION IS BASED ON FACTS KNOWN ONLY TO YOU, AND YOUR EMOTIONS OVER LOSING YOUR FIANCÉ LED YOU TO THIS CONCLUSION...
SO YOUR JUDGMENT IS CLOUDED BY PERSONAL FEELINGS, AND YOU HAVE NO PROOF...
STILL...
I AGREE IT'S WORTH LOOKING INTO. YOUR TESTIMONY WILL MEAN A LOT TO THE TASK FORCE. RIGHT NOW, THEY'RE AT A TOTAL LOSS. THIS COULD REALLY HELP THEIR INVESTIGATION.
I... HOPE SO.

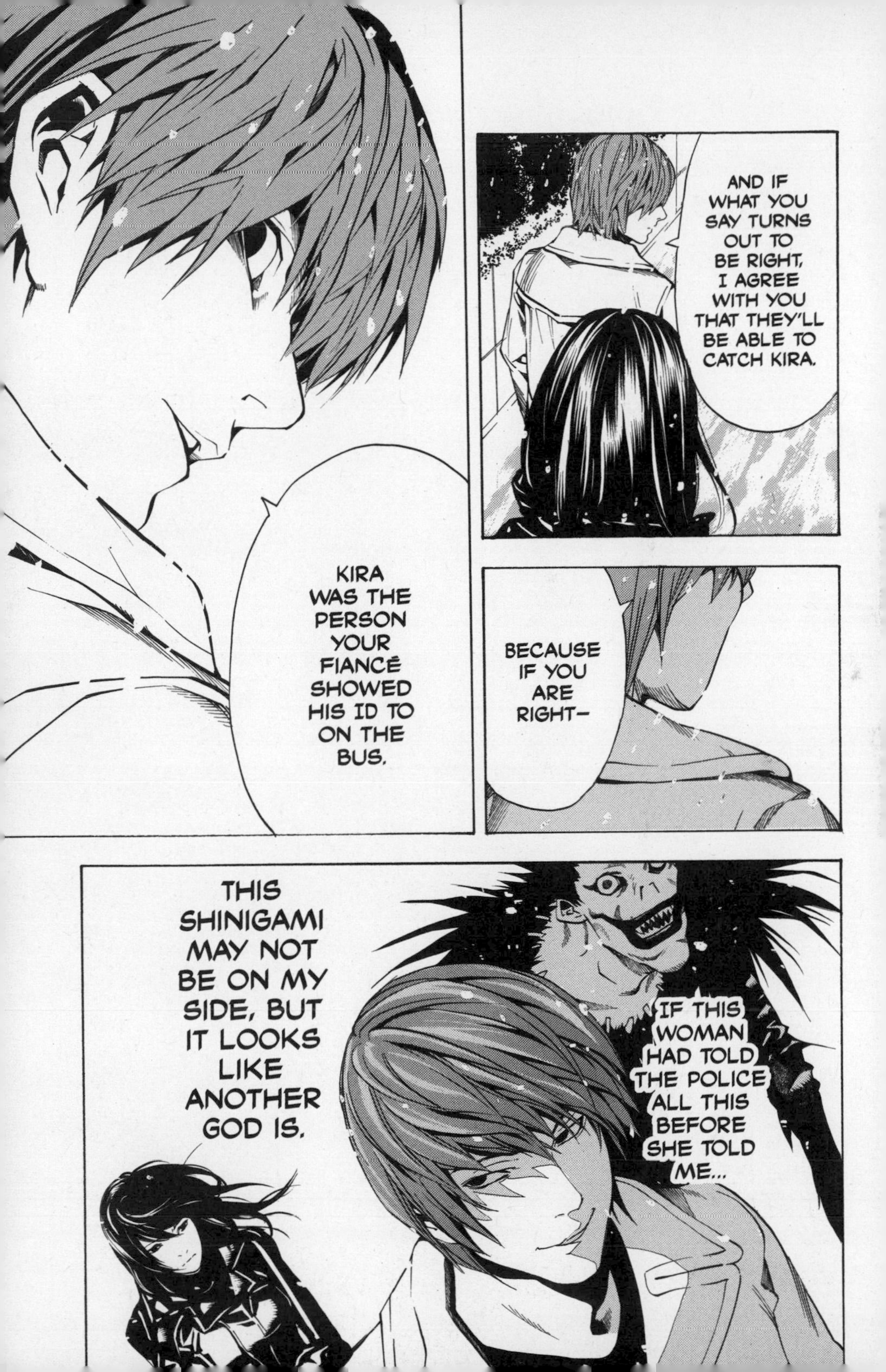
AND IF WHAT YOU SAY TURNS OUT TO BE RIGHT, I AGREE WITH YOU THAT THEY'LL BE ABLE TO CATCH KIRA.
BECAUSE IF YOU ARE RIGHT–
KIRA WAS THE PERSON YOUR FIANCÉ SHOWED HIS ID TO ON THE BUS.
IF THIS WOMAN HAD TOLD THE POLICE ALL THIS BEFORE SHE TOLD ME...
THIS SHINIGAMI MAY NOT BE ON MY SIDE, BUT IT LOOKS LIKE ANOTHER GOD IS.

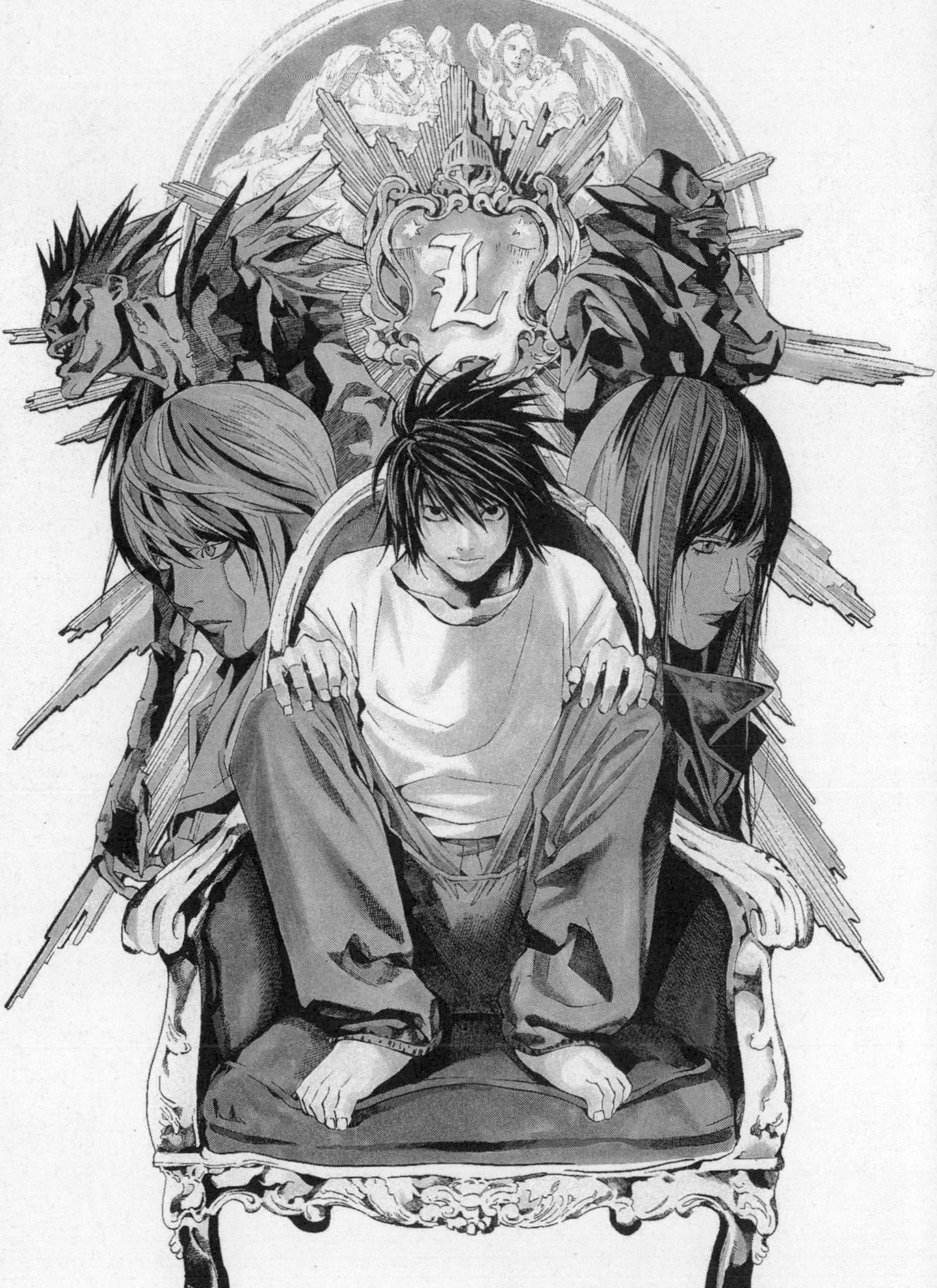

chapter 13 Countdown

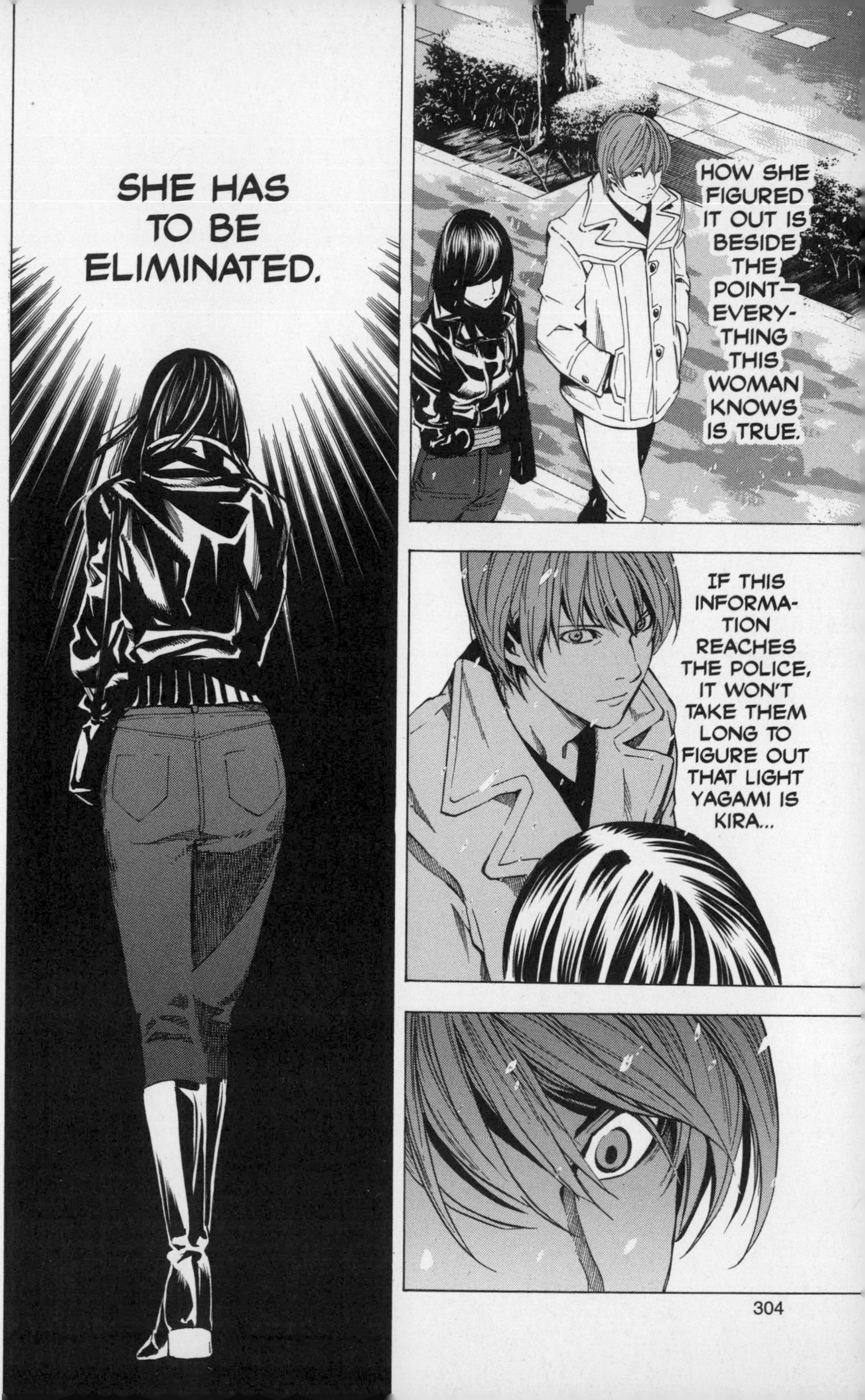
HOW SHE FIGURED IT OUT IS BESIDE THE POINT—EVERYTHING THIS WOMAN KNOWS IS TRUE.
IF THIS INFORMATION REACHES THE POLICE, IT WON'T TAKE THEM LONG TO FIGURE OUT THAT LIGHT YAGAMI IS KIRA...
SHE HAS TO BE ELIMINATED.

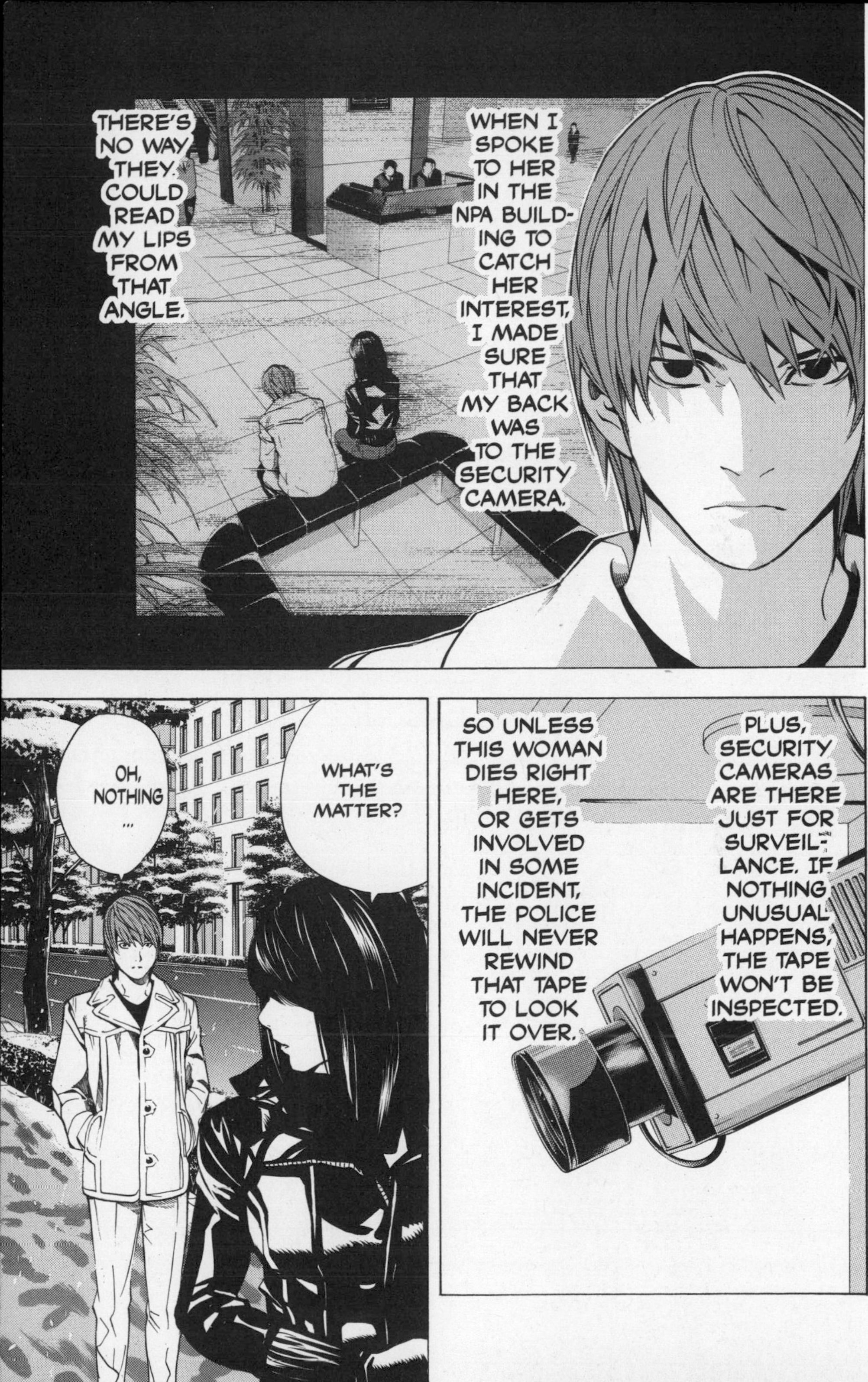
WHEN I SPOKE TO HER IN THE NPA BUILDING TO CATCH HER INTEREST, I MADE SURE THAT MY BACK WAS TO THE SECURITY CAMERA.
THERE'S NO WAY THEY COULD READ MY LIPS FROM THAT ANGLE.
PLUS, SECURITY CAMERAS ARE THERE JUST FOR SURVEILLANCE. IF NOTHING UNUSUAL HAPPENS, THE TAPE WON'T BE INSPECTED.
SO UNLESS THIS WOMAN DIES RIGHT HERE, OR GETS INVOLVED IN SOME INCIDENT, THE POLICE WILL NEVER REWIND THAT TAPE TO LOOK IT OVER.
WHAT'S THE MATTER?
OH, NOTHING ...

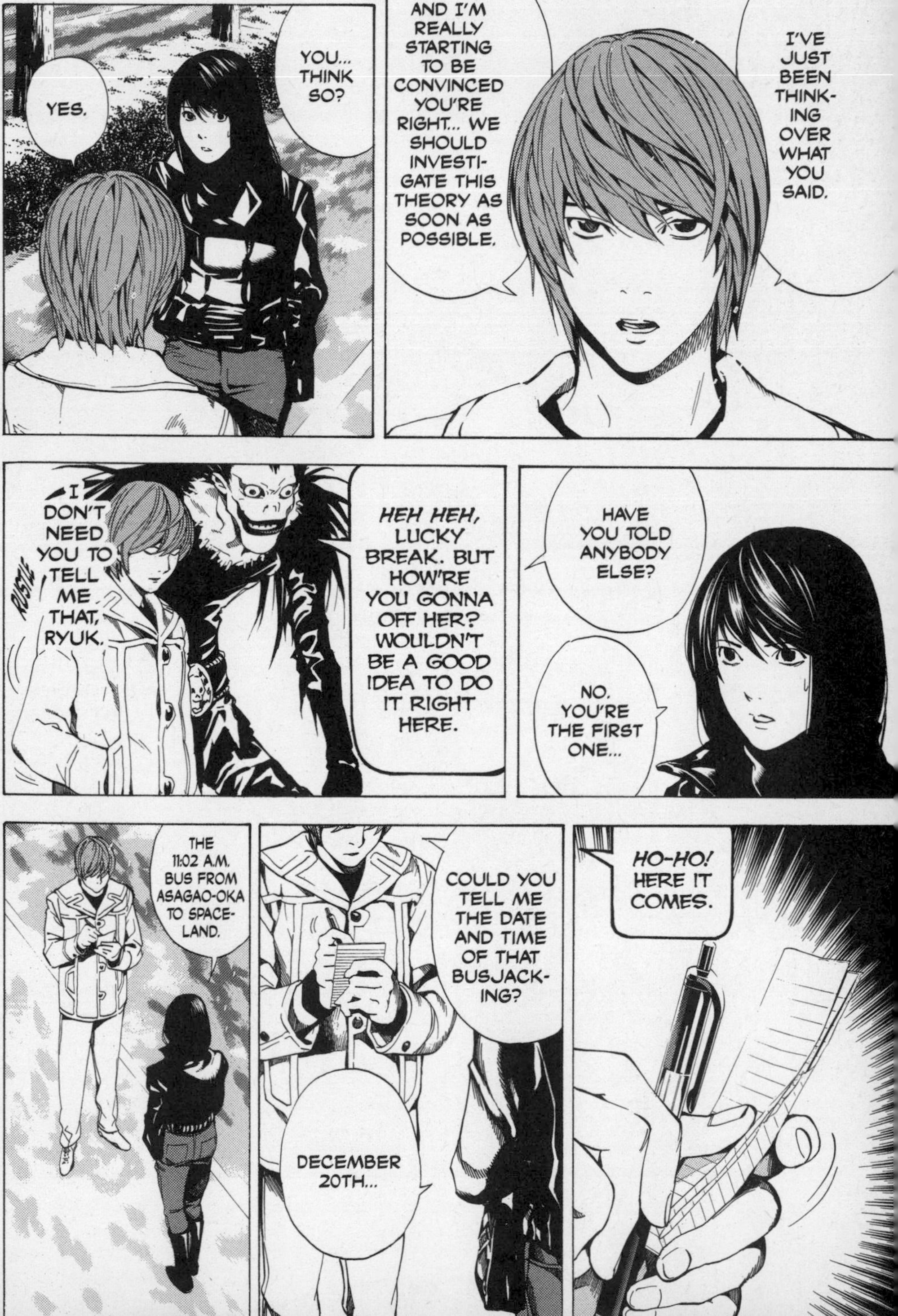
I'VE JUST BEEN THINKING OVER WHAT YOU SAID.
AND I'M REALLY STARTING TO BE CONVINCED YOU'RE RIGHT... WE SHOULD INVESTIGATE THIS THEORY AS SOON AS POSSIBLE.
YOU... THINK SO?
YES.
HAVE YOU TOLD ANYBODY ELSE?
NO. YOU'RE THE FIRST ONE...
*HEH HEH,* LUCKY BREAK. BUT HOW'RE YOU GONNA OFF HER? WOULDN'T BE A GOOD IDEA TO DO IT RIGHT HERE.
I DON'T NEED YOU TO TELL ME THAT, RYUK.
RUSTLE
*HO-HO!* HERE IT COMES.
COULD YOU TELL ME THE DATE AND TIME OF THAT BUSJACKING?
DECEMBER 20TH...
THE 11:02 A.M. BUS FROM ASAGAO-OKA TO SPACE-LAND.

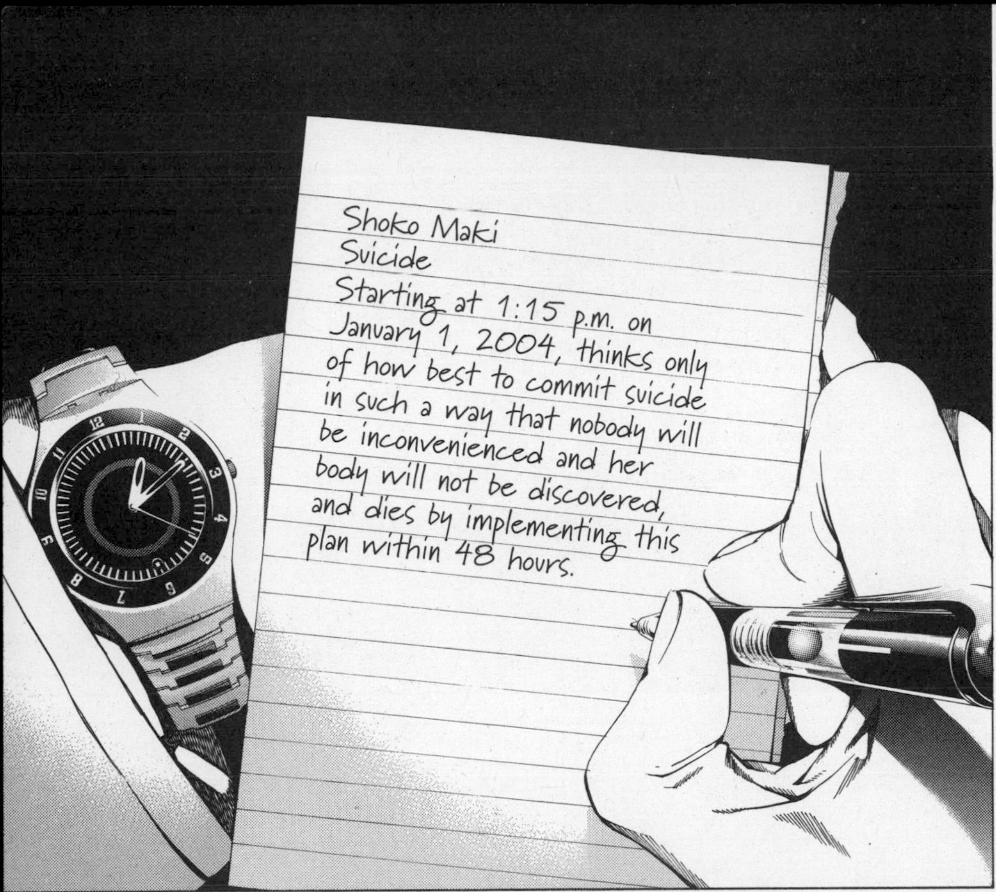
Shoko Maki
Suicide
Starting at 1:15 p.m. on January 1, 2004, thinks only of how best to commit suicide in such a way that nobody will be inconvenienced and her body will not be discovered, and dies by implementing this plan within 48 hours.

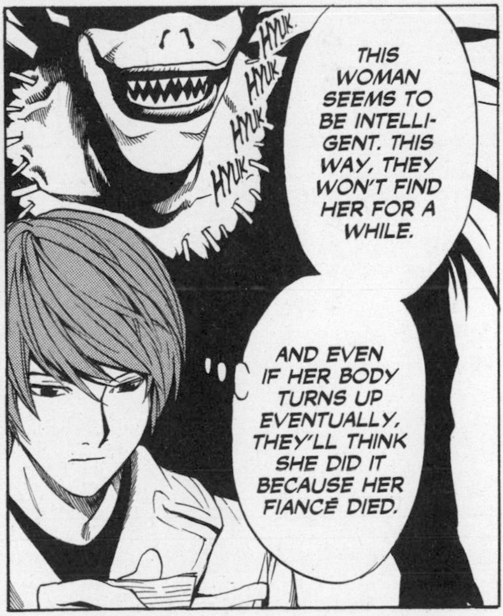
HYUK HYUK HYUK HYUK
THIS WOMAN SEEMS TO BE INTELLIGENT. THIS WAY, THEY WON'T FIND HER FOR A WHILE.
AND EVEN IF HER BODY TURNS UP EVENTUALLY, THEY'LL THINK SHE DID IT BECAUSE HER FIANCÉ DIED.

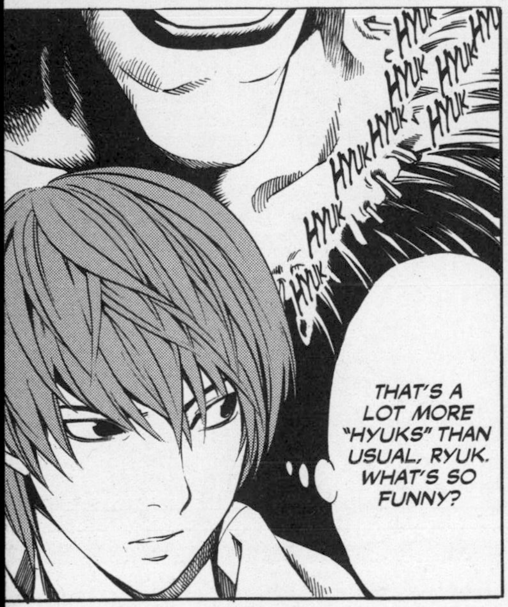
HYUK HYUK HYUK HYUK HYUK HYUK HYUK HYUK HYUK HYUK
THAT'S A LOT MORE "HYUKS" THAN USUAL, RYUK. WHAT'S SO FUNNY?

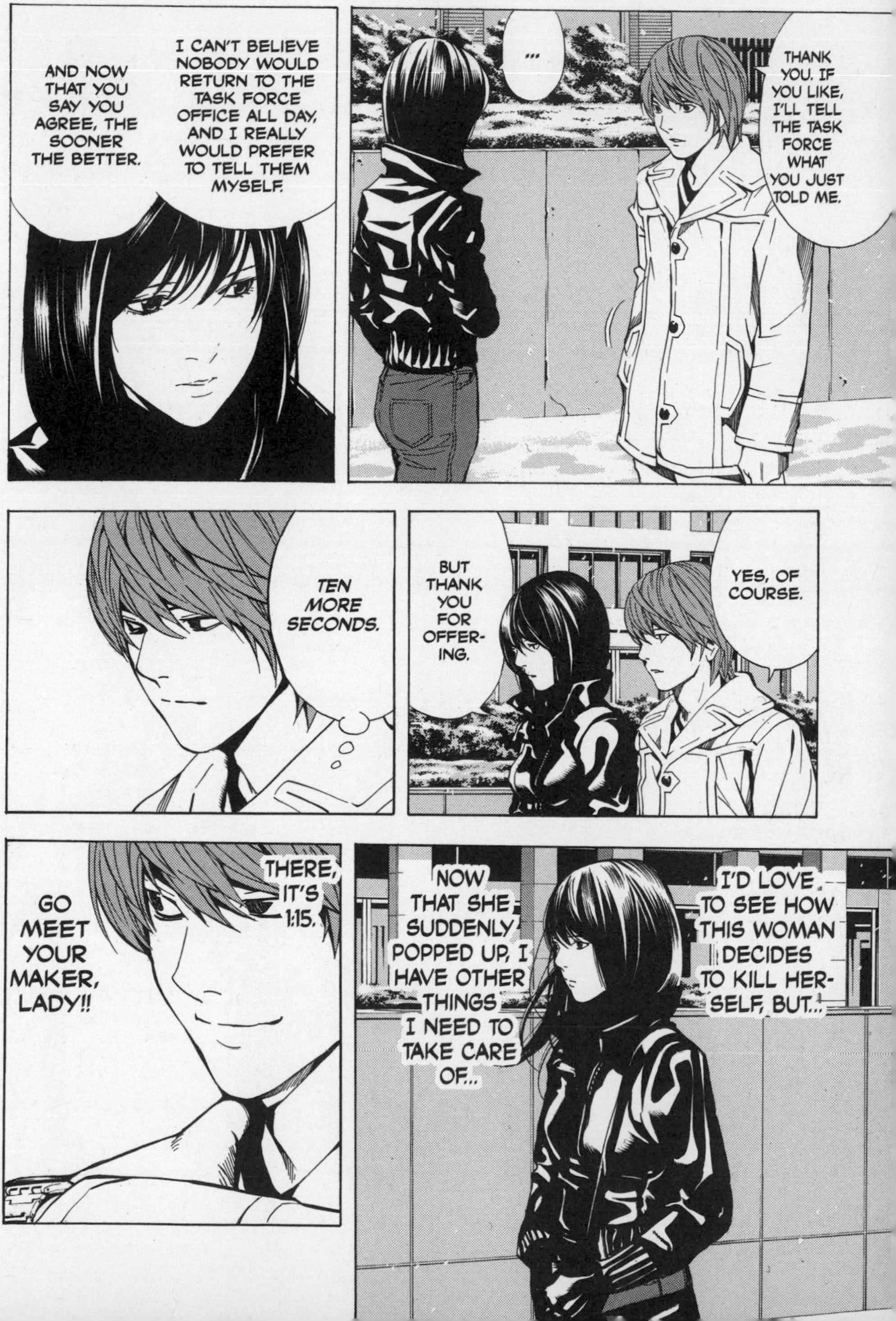
THANK YOU. IF YOU LIKE, I'LL TELL THE TASK FORCE WHAT YOU JUST TOLD ME.
...
I CAN'T BELIEVE NOBODY WOULD RETURN TO THE TASK FORCE OFFICE ALL DAY, AND I REALLY WOULD PREFER TO TELL THEM MYSELF.
AND NOW THAT YOU SAY YOU AGREE, THE SOONER THE BETTER.
YES, OF COURSE.
BUT THANK YOU FOR OFFER-ING.
*TEN MORE SECONDS.*
I'D LOVE TO SEE HOW THIS WOMAN DECIDES TO KILL HER-SELF, BUT...
NOW THAT SHE SUDDENLY POPPED UP, I HAVE OTHER THINGS I NEED TO TAKE CARE OF...
THERE, IT'S 1:15.
GO MEET YOUR MAKER, LADY!!

READ THIS WAY

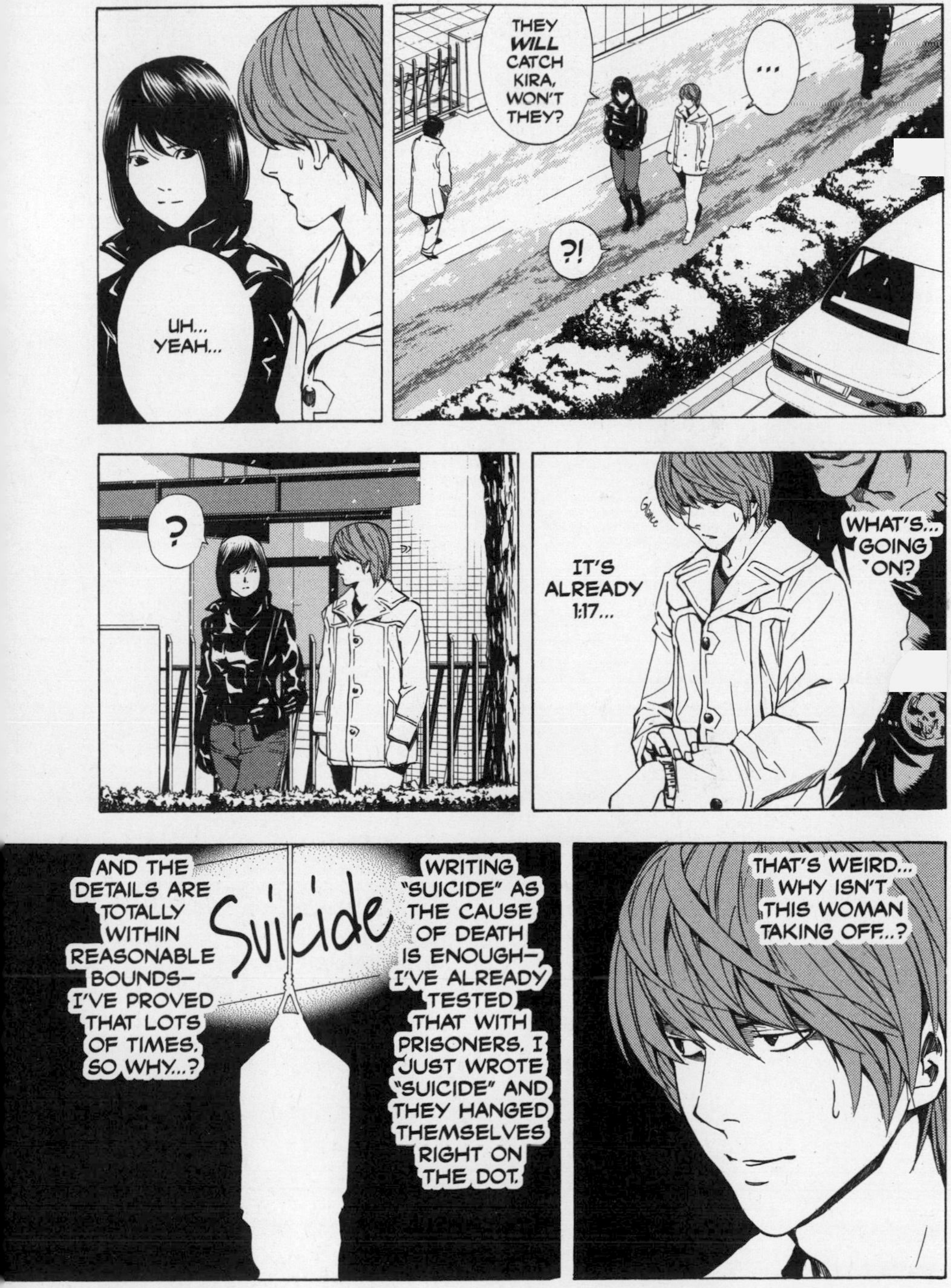

THEY *WILL* CATCH KIRA, WON'T THEY?
...
?!
UH... YEAH...
WHAT'S... GOING ON?
IT'S ALREADY 1:17...
Glance
?
THAT'S WEIRD... WHY ISN'T THIS WOMAN TAKING OFF...?
WRITING "SUICIDE" AS THE CAUSE OF DEATH IS ENOUGH— I'VE ALREADY TESTED THAT WITH PRISONERS. I JUST WROTE "SUICIDE" AND THEY HANGED THEMSELVES RIGHT ON THE DOT.
Suicide
AND THE DETAILS ARE TOTALLY WITHIN REASONABLE BOUNDS— I'VE PROVED THAT LOTS OF TIMES. SO WHY...?

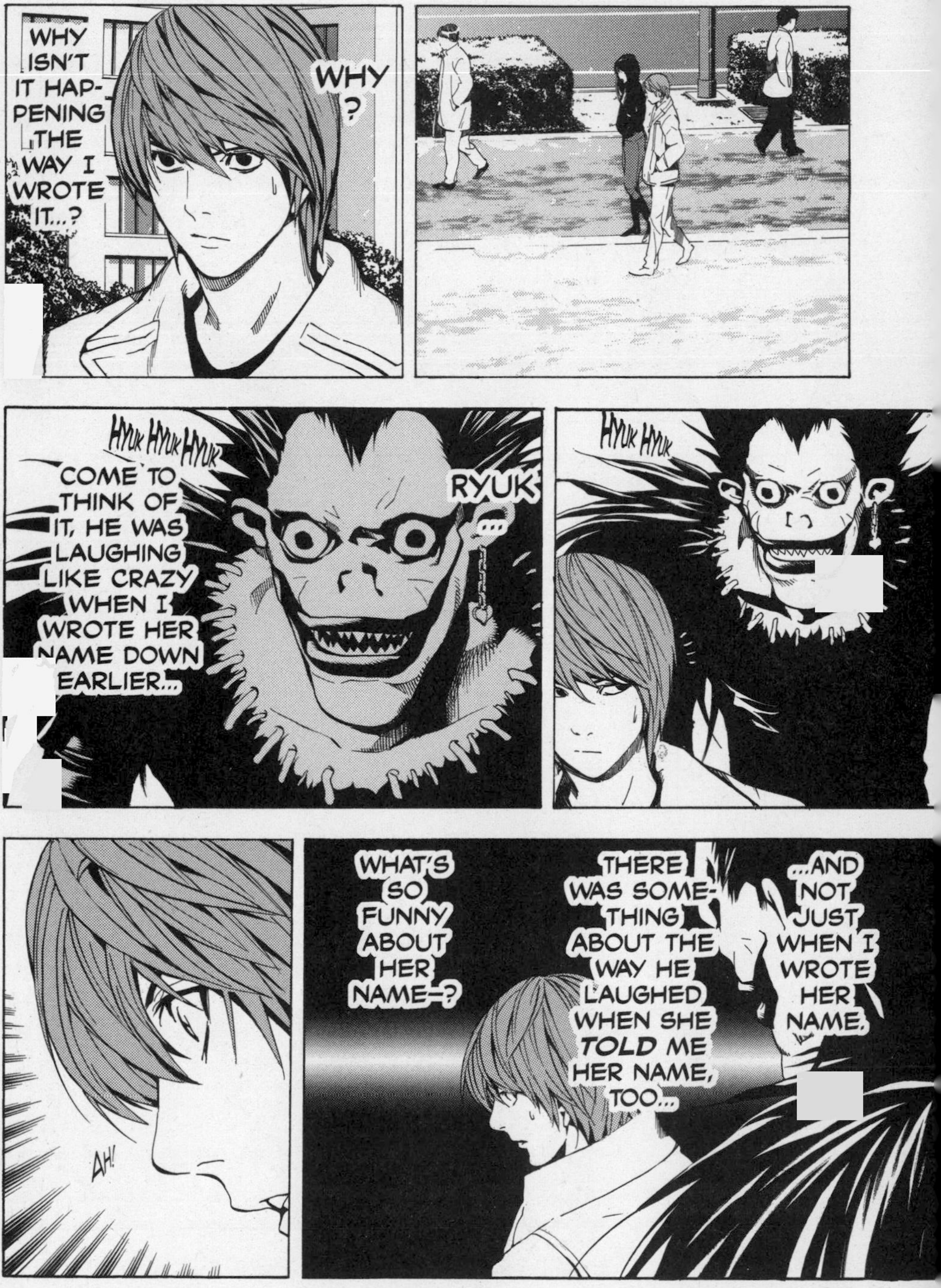
WHY ?
WHY ISN'T IT HAPPENING THE WAY I WROTE IT...?
HYUK HYUK
RYUK ...
HYUK HYUK HYUK
COME TO THINK OF IT, HE WAS LAUGHING LIKE CRAZY WHEN I WROTE HER NAME DOWN EARLIER...
...AND NOT JUST WHEN I WROTE HER NAME.
THERE WAS SOMETHING ABOUT THE WAY HE LAUGHED WHEN SHE *TOLD* ME HER NAME, TOO...
WHAT'S SO FUNNY ABOUT HER NAME—?
AH!

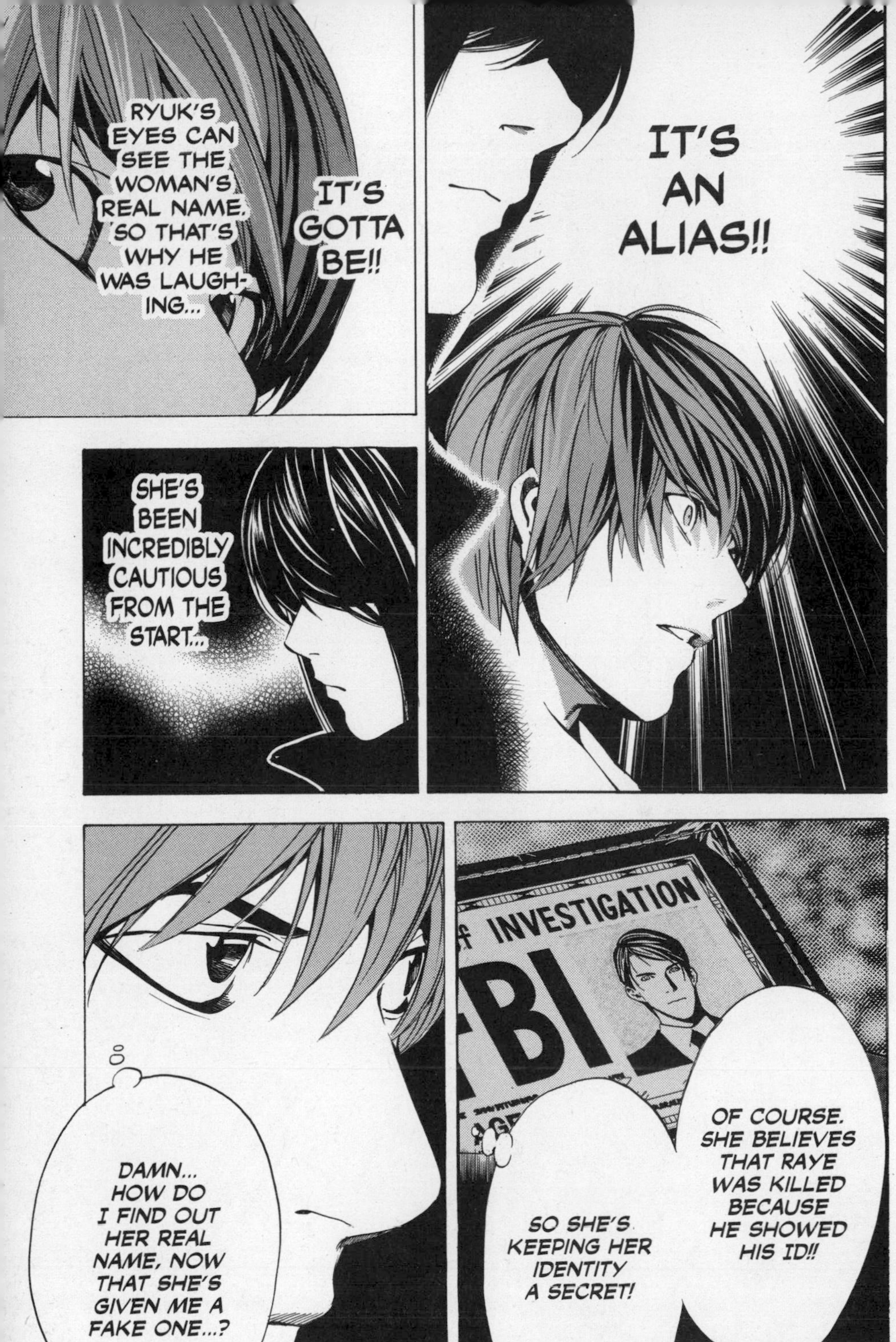
IT'S AN ALIAS!!
IT'S GOTTA BE!!
RYUK'S EYES CAN SEE THE WOMAN'S REAL NAME. SO THAT'S WHY HE WAS LAUGHING...
SHE'S BEEN INCREDIBLY CAUTIOUS FROM THE START...
INVESTIGATION
FBI
OF COURSE. SHE BELIEVES THAT RAYE WAS KILLED BECAUSE HE SHOWED HIS ID!!
SO SHE'S KEEPING HER IDENTITY A SECRET!
DAMN... HOW DO I FIND OUT HER REAL NAME, NOW THAT SHE'S GIVEN ME A FAKE ONE...?

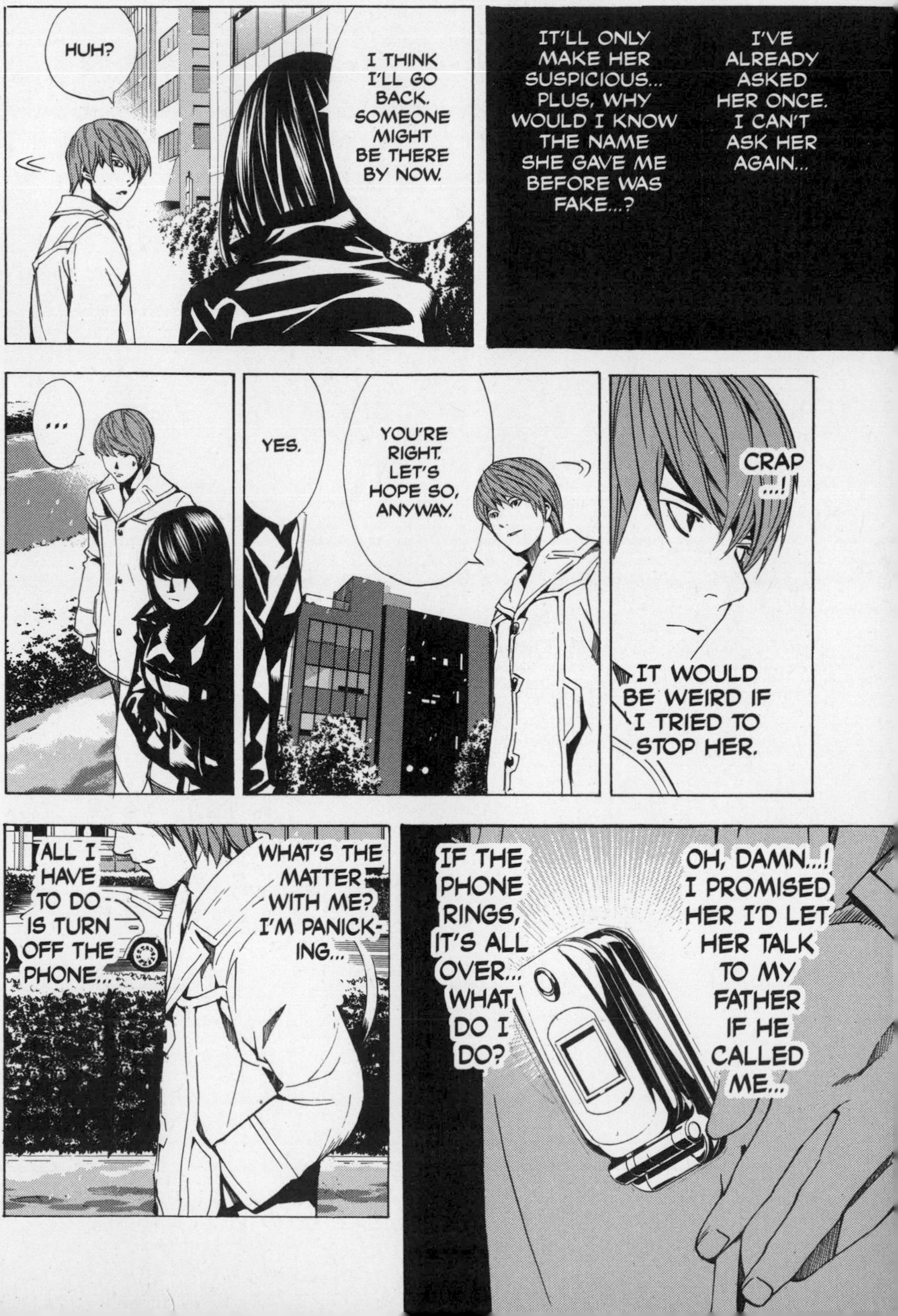
I'VE ALREADY ASKED HER ONCE. I CAN'T ASK HER AGAIN...
IT'LL ONLY MAKE HER SUSPICIOUS... PLUS, WHY WOULD I KNOW THE NAME SHE GAVE ME BEFORE WAS FAKE...?
I THINK I'LL GO BACK. SOMEONE MIGHT BE THERE BY NOW.
HUH?
CRAP ...!
IT WOULD BE WEIRD IF I TRIED TO STOP HER.
YOU'RE RIGHT. LET'S HOPE SO, ANYWAY.
YES.
...
OH, DAMN...! I PROMISED HER I'D LET HER TALK TO MY FATHER IF HE CALLED ME...
IF THE PHONE RINGS, IT'S ALL OVER... WHAT DO I DO?
WHAT'S THE MATTER WITH ME? I'M PANICK-ING...
ALL I HAVE TO DO IS TURN OFF THE PHONE...

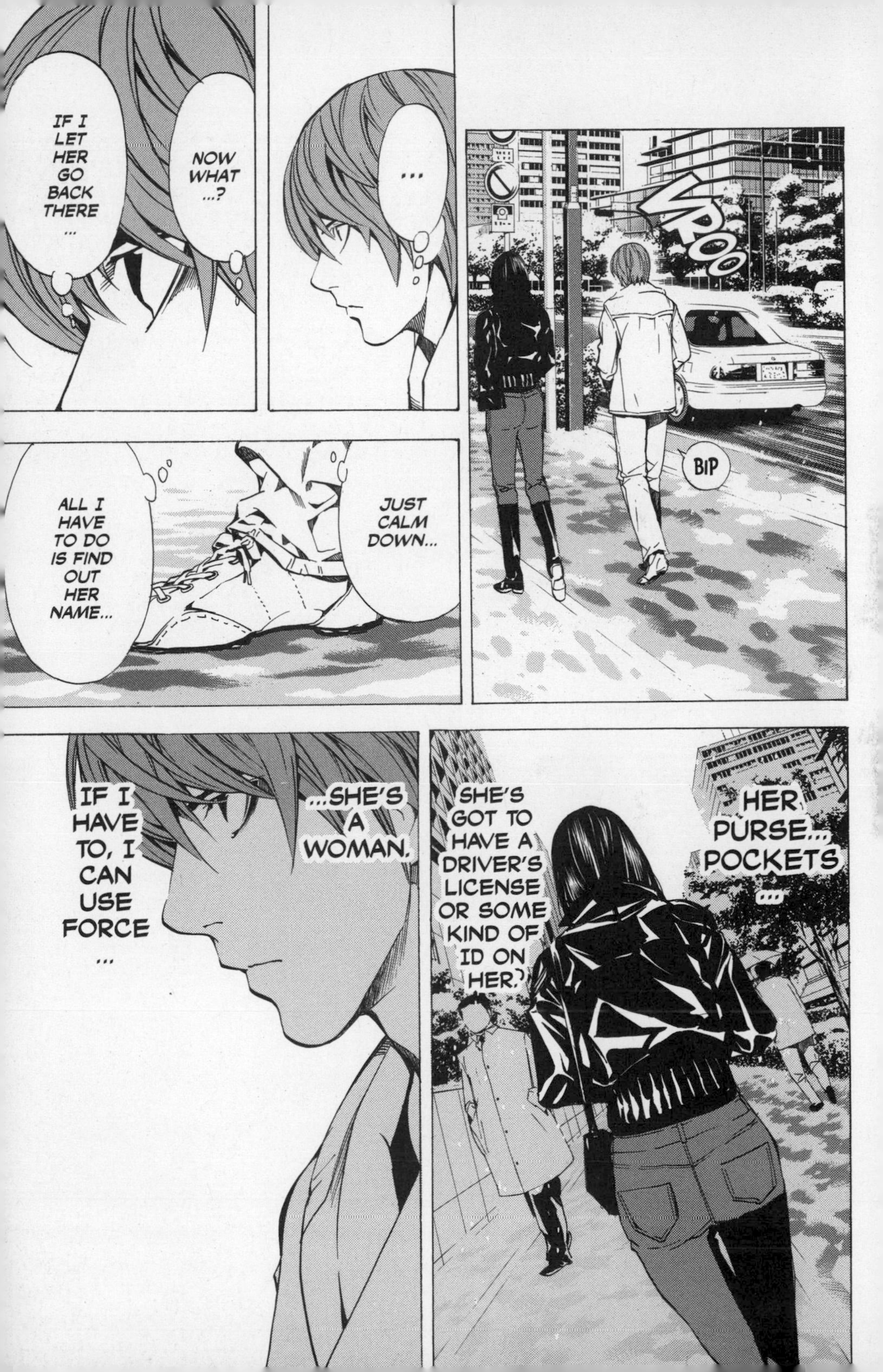
VROOO
BIP
...
NOW WHAT ...?
IF I LET HER GO BACK THERE ...
JUST CALM DOWN...
ALL I HAVE TO DO IS FIND OUT HER NAME...
HER PURSE... POCKETS ...
SHE'S GOT TO HAVE A DRIVER'S LICENSE OR SOME KIND OF ID ON HER.
...SHE'S A WOMAN.
IF I HAVE TO, I CAN USE FORCE ...

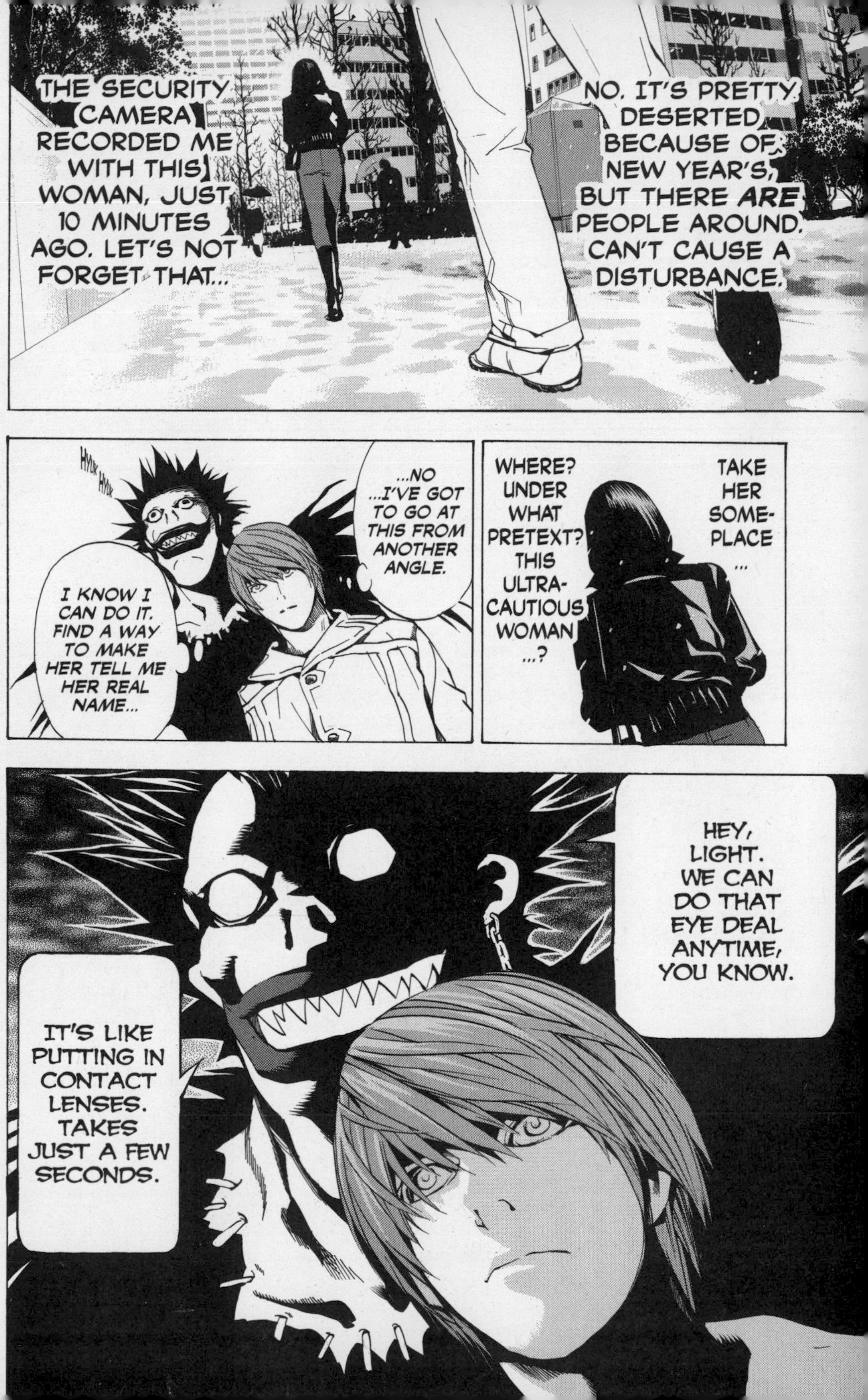
NO. IT'S PRETTY DESERTED BECAUSE OF NEW YEAR'S, BUT THERE *ARE* PEOPLE AROUND. CAN'T CAUSE A DISTURBANCE.
THE SECURITY CAMERA RECORDED ME WITH THIS WOMAN, JUST 10 MINUTES AGO. LET'S NOT FORGET THAT...
TAKE HER SOME-PLACE ...
WHERE? UNDER WHAT PRETEXT? THIS ULTRA-CAUTIOUS WOMAN ...?
...NO ...I'VE GOT TO GO AT THIS FROM ANOTHER ANGLE.
HYUK HYUK
I KNOW I CAN DO IT. FIND A WAY TO MAKE HER TELL ME HER REAL NAME...
HEY, LIGHT. WE CAN DO THAT EYE DEAL ANYTIME, YOU KNOW.
IT'S LIKE PUTTING IN CONTACT LENSES. TAKES JUST A FEW SECONDS.

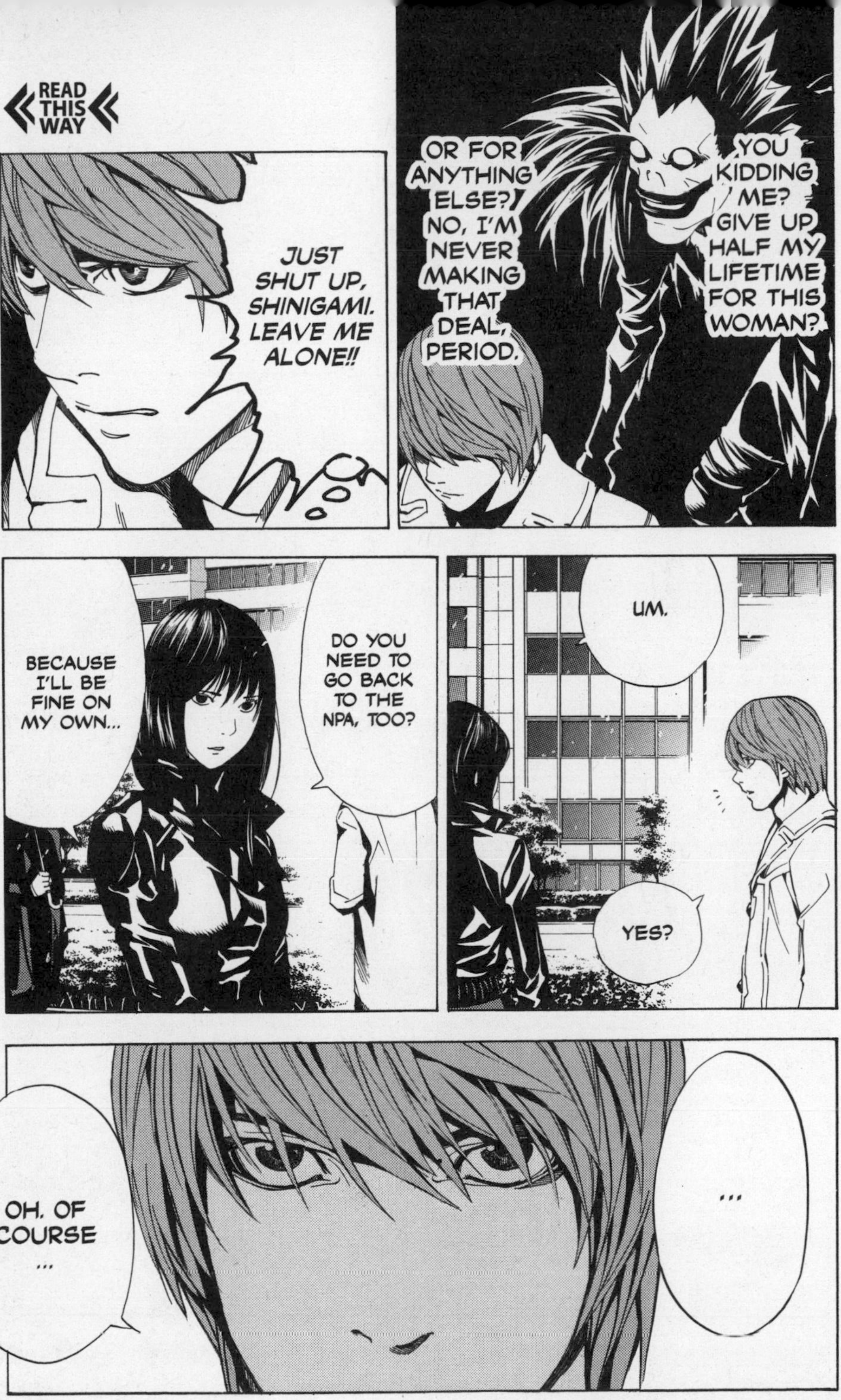

READ THIS WAY
YOU KIDDING ME? GIVE UP HALF MY LIFETIME FOR THIS WOMAN?
OR FOR ANYTHING ELSE? NO, I'M NEVER MAKING THAT DEAL, PERIOD.
JUST SHUT UP, SHINIGAMI. LEAVE ME ALONE!!
UM.
YES?
DO YOU NEED TO GO BACK TO THE NPA, TOO?
BECAUSE I'LL BE FINE ON MY OWN...
...
OH. OF COURSE ...

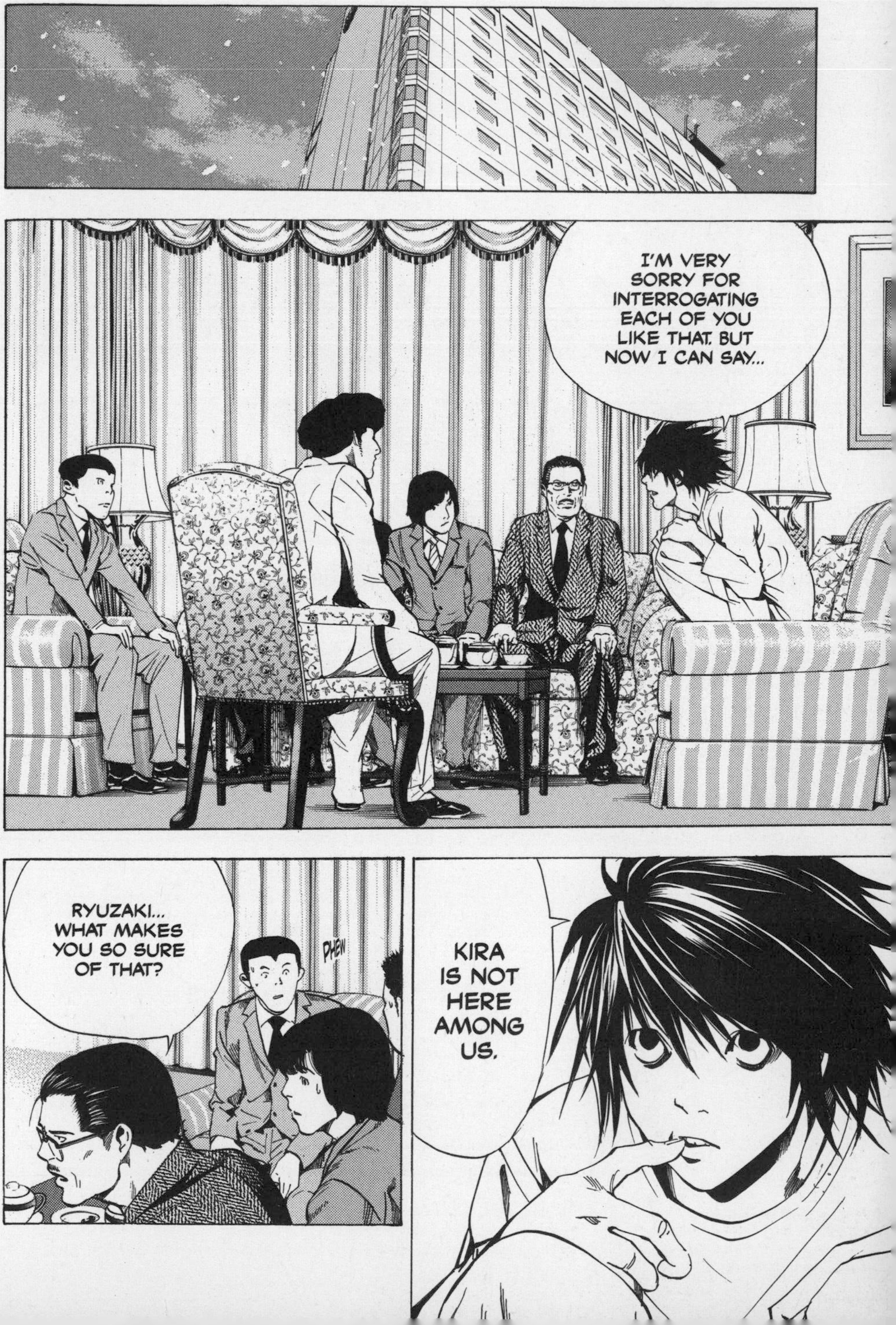
I'M VERY SORRY FOR INTERROGATING EACH OF YOU LIKE THAT. BUT NOW I CAN SAY...
KIRA IS NOT HERE AMONG US.
RYUZAKI... WHAT MAKES YOU SO SURE OF THAT?
PHEW

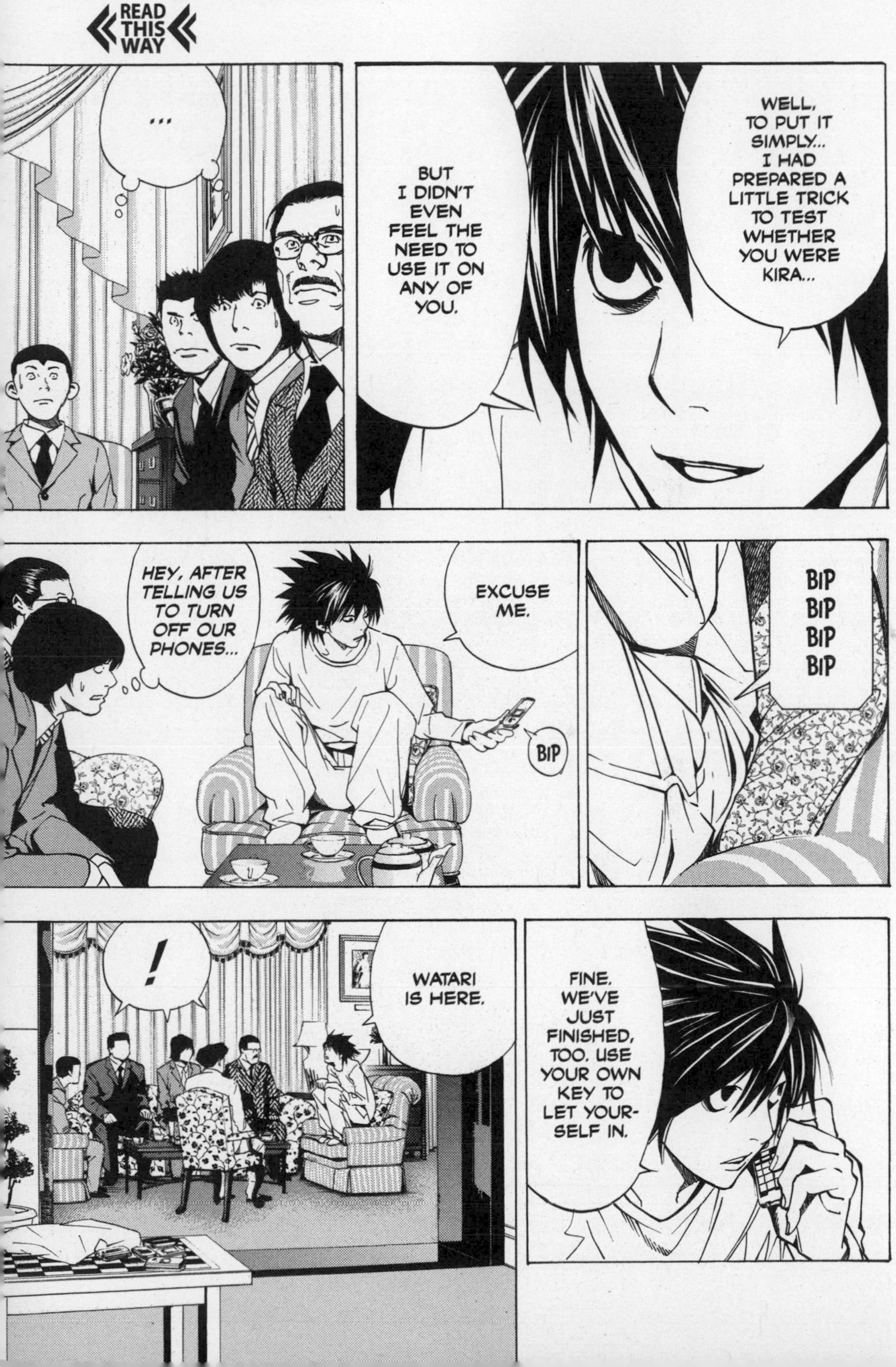
READ THIS WAY
WELL, TO PUT IT SIMPLY... I HAD PREPARED A LITTLE TRICK TO TEST WHETHER YOU WERE KIRA...
BUT I DIDN'T EVEN FEEL THE NEED TO USE IT ON ANY OF YOU.
...
BIP BIP BIP BIP
EXCUSE ME.
BIP
HEY, AFTER TELLING US TO TURN OFF OUR PHONES...
FINE. WE'VE JUST FINISHED, TOO. USE YOUR OWN KEY TO LET YOURSELF IN.
WATARI IS HERE.
!

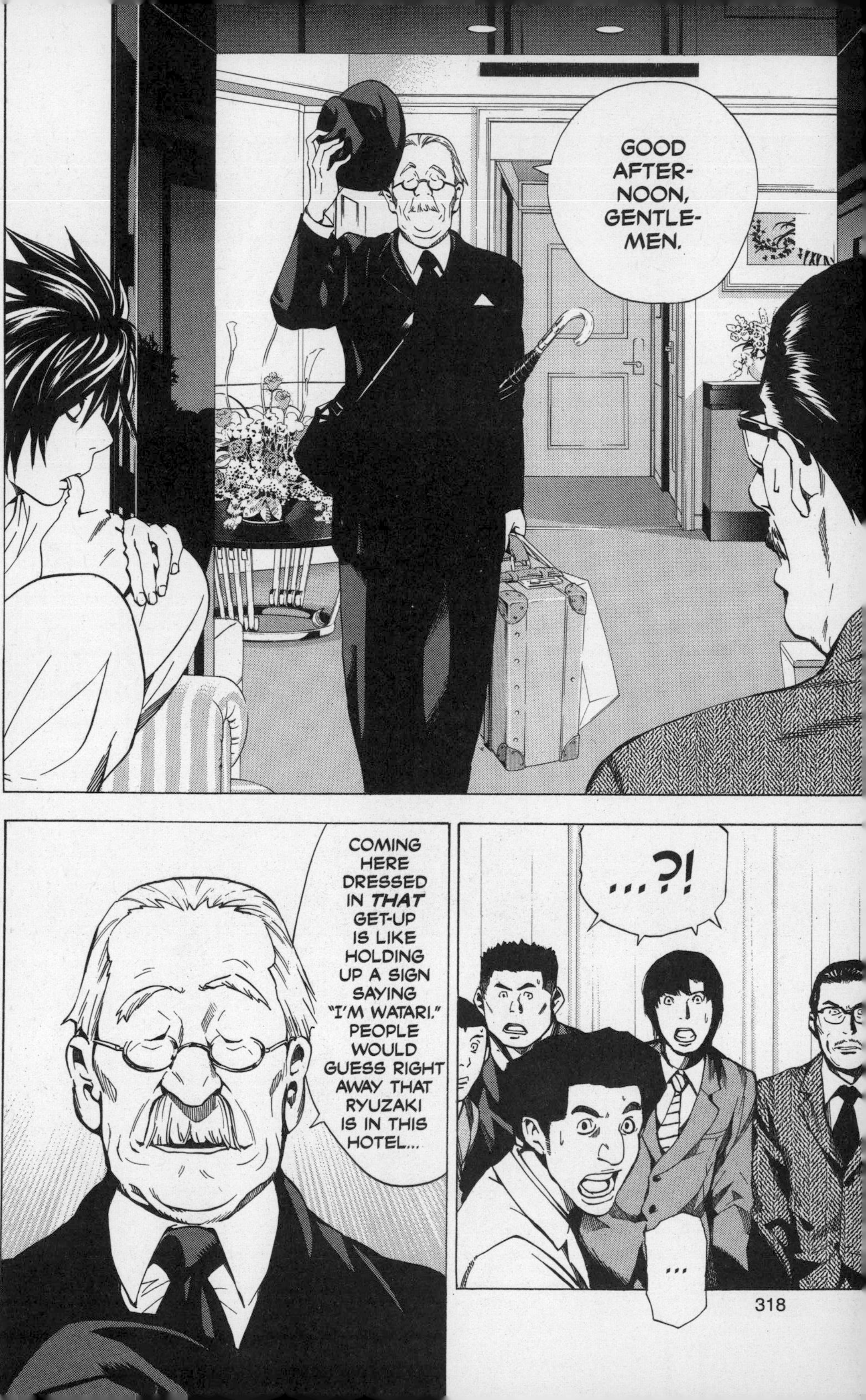
GOOD AFTER-NOON, GENTLE-MEN.
...?!
...
COMING HERE DRESSED IN *THAT* GET-UP IS LIKE HOLDING UP A SIGN SAYING "I'M WATARI." PEOPLE WOULD GUESS RIGHT AWAY THAT RYUZAKI IS IN THIS HOTEL...

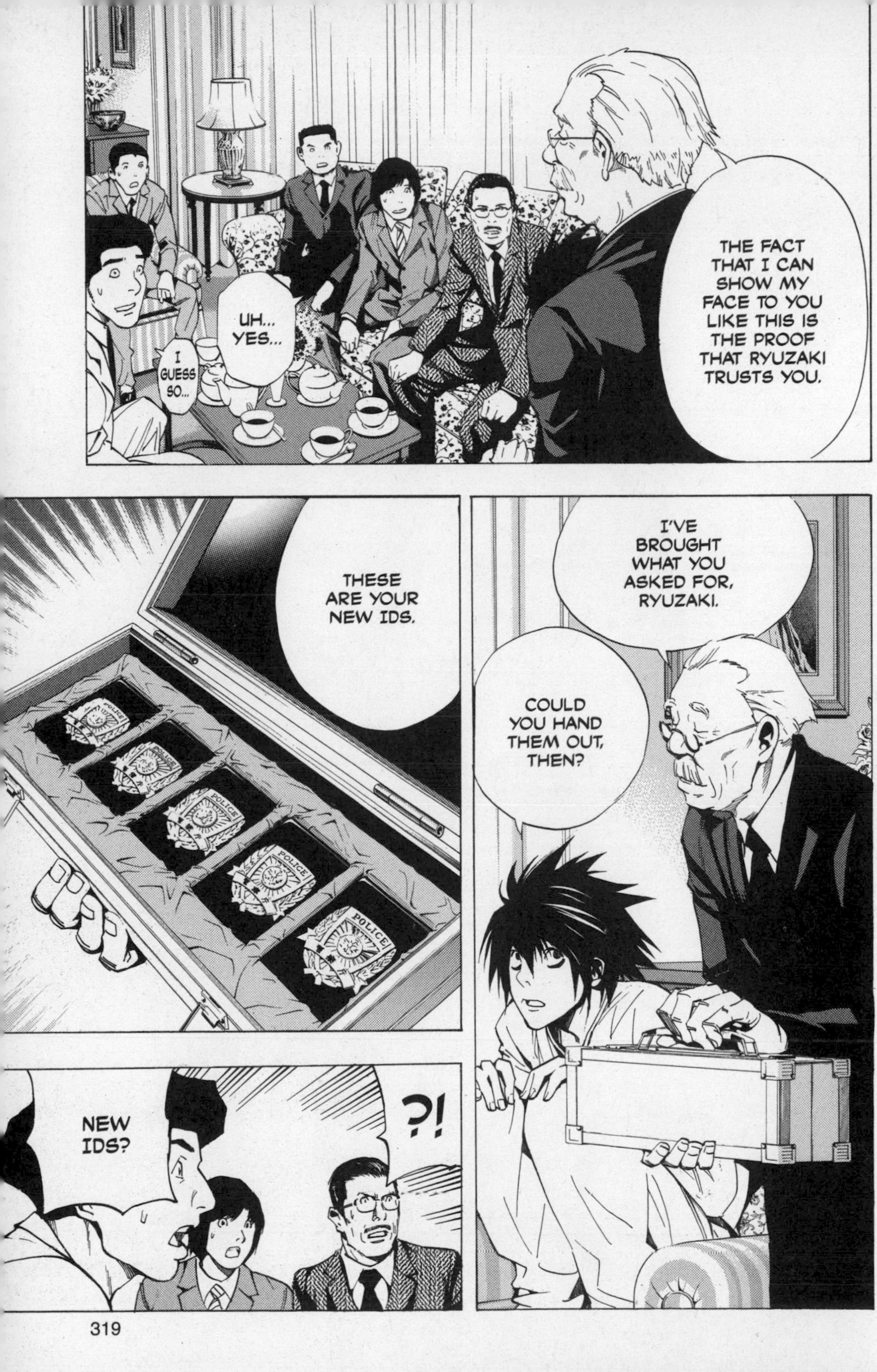
THE FACT THAT I CAN SHOW MY FACE TO YOU LIKE THIS IS THE PROOF THAT RYUZAKI TRUSTS YOU.
UH... YES...
I GUESS SO...
I'VE BROUGHT WHAT YOU ASKED FOR, RYUZAKI.
COULD YOU HAND THEM OUT, THEN?
THESE ARE YOUR NEW IDS.
?!
NEW IDS?

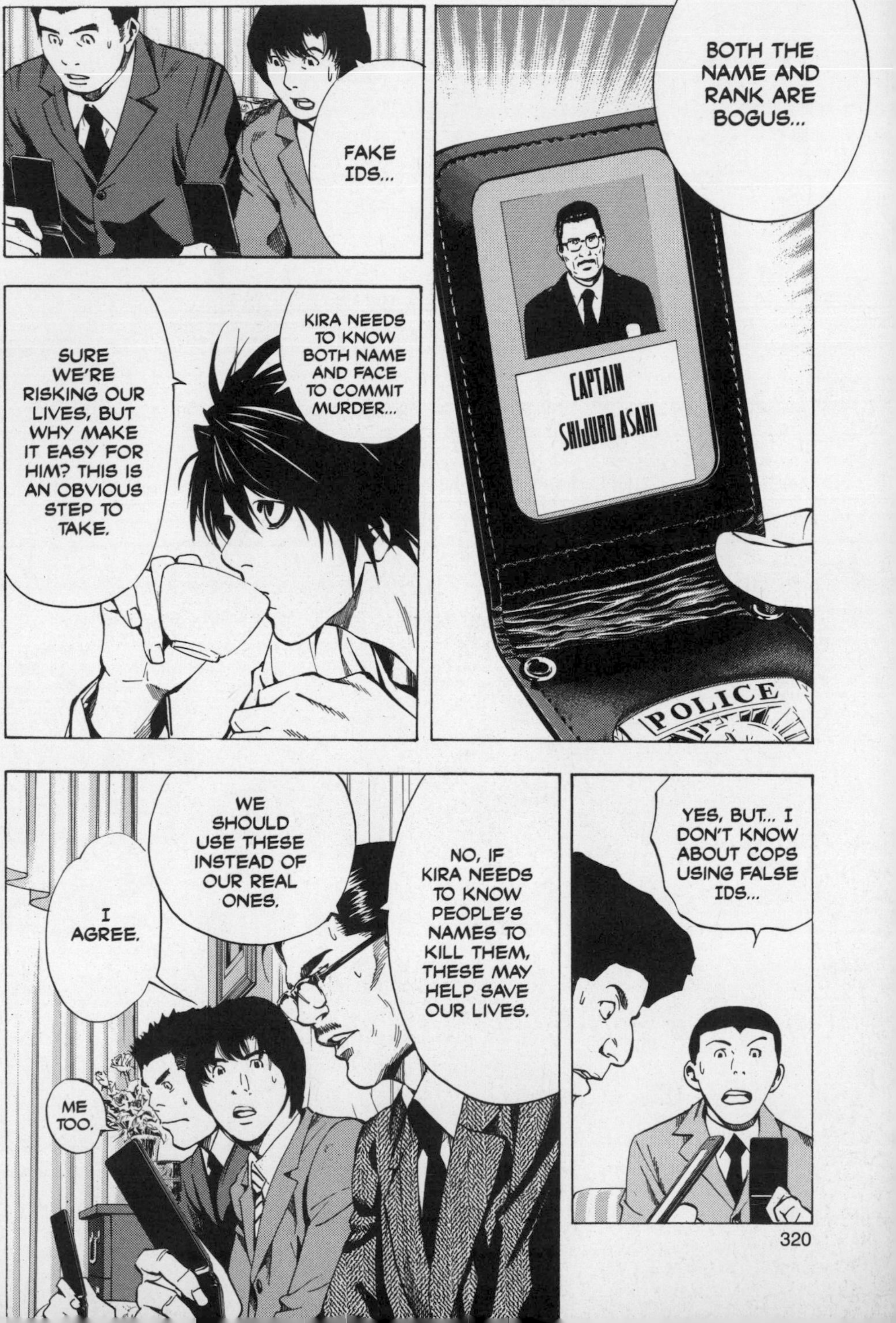
BOTH THE NAME AND RANK ARE BOGUS...
CAPTAIN
SHIJURO ASAHI
POLICE
FAKE IDS...
KIRA NEEDS TO KNOW BOTH NAME AND FACE TO COMMIT MURDER...
SURE WE'RE RISKING OUR LIVES, BUT WHY MAKE IT EASY FOR HIM? THIS IS AN OBVIOUS STEP TO TAKE.
YES, BUT... I DON'T KNOW ABOUT COPS USING FALSE IDS...
NO, IF KIRA NEEDS TO KNOW PEOPLE'S NAMES TO KILL THEM, THESE MAY HELP SAVE OUR LIVES.
WE SHOULD USE THESE INSTEAD OF OUR REAL ONES.
I AGREE.
ME TOO.

READ THIS WAY

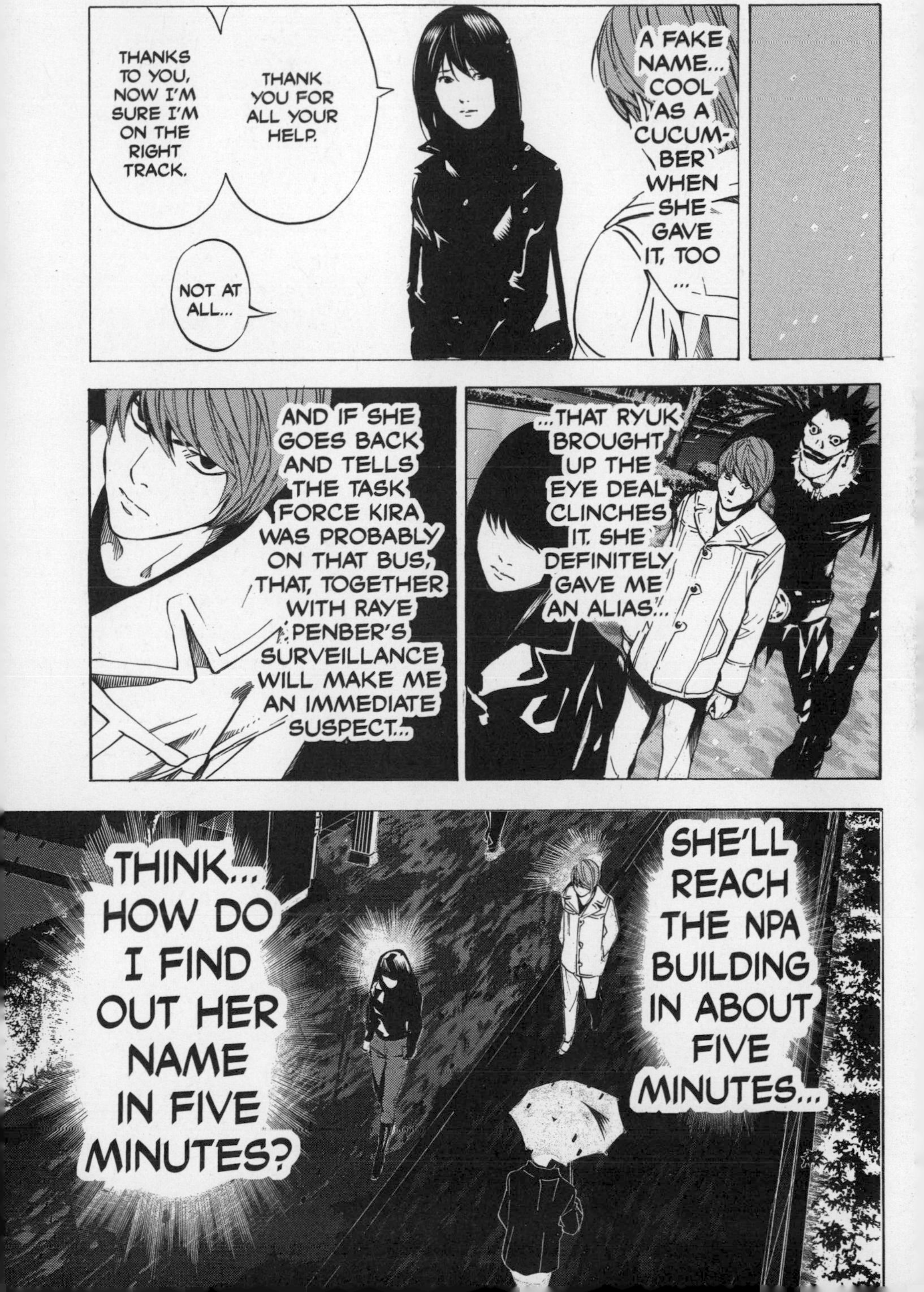
A FAKE NAME... COOL AS A CUCUMBER WHEN SHE GAVE IT, TOO...
THANK YOU FOR ALL YOUR HELP.
THANKS TO YOU, NOW I'M SURE I'M ON THE RIGHT TRACK.
NOT AT ALL...
...THAT RYUK BROUGHT UP THE EYE DEAL CLINCHES IT. SHE DEFINITELY GAVE ME AN ALIAS...
AND IF SHE GOES BACK AND TELLS THE TASK FORCE KIRA WAS PROBABLY ON THAT BUS, THAT, TOGETHER WITH RAYE PENBER'S SURVEILLANCE WILL MAKE ME AN IMMEDIATE SUSPECT...
SHE'LL REACH THE NPA BUILDING IN ABOUT FIVE MINUTES...
THINK... HOW DO I FIND OUT HER NAME IN FIVE MINUTES?

# DEATH NOTE
## How to use it
### IX

○ The DEATH NOTE will not affect those under 780 days old.

生後780日に満たない人間には、デスノートの効果は得られない。

○ The DEATH NOTE will be rendered useless if the victim's name is misspelled four times.

同一人物の顔を思い浮かべ、四度名前を書き間違えると、
その人間に対してデスノートは効かなくなる。

# chapter 14 Temptation

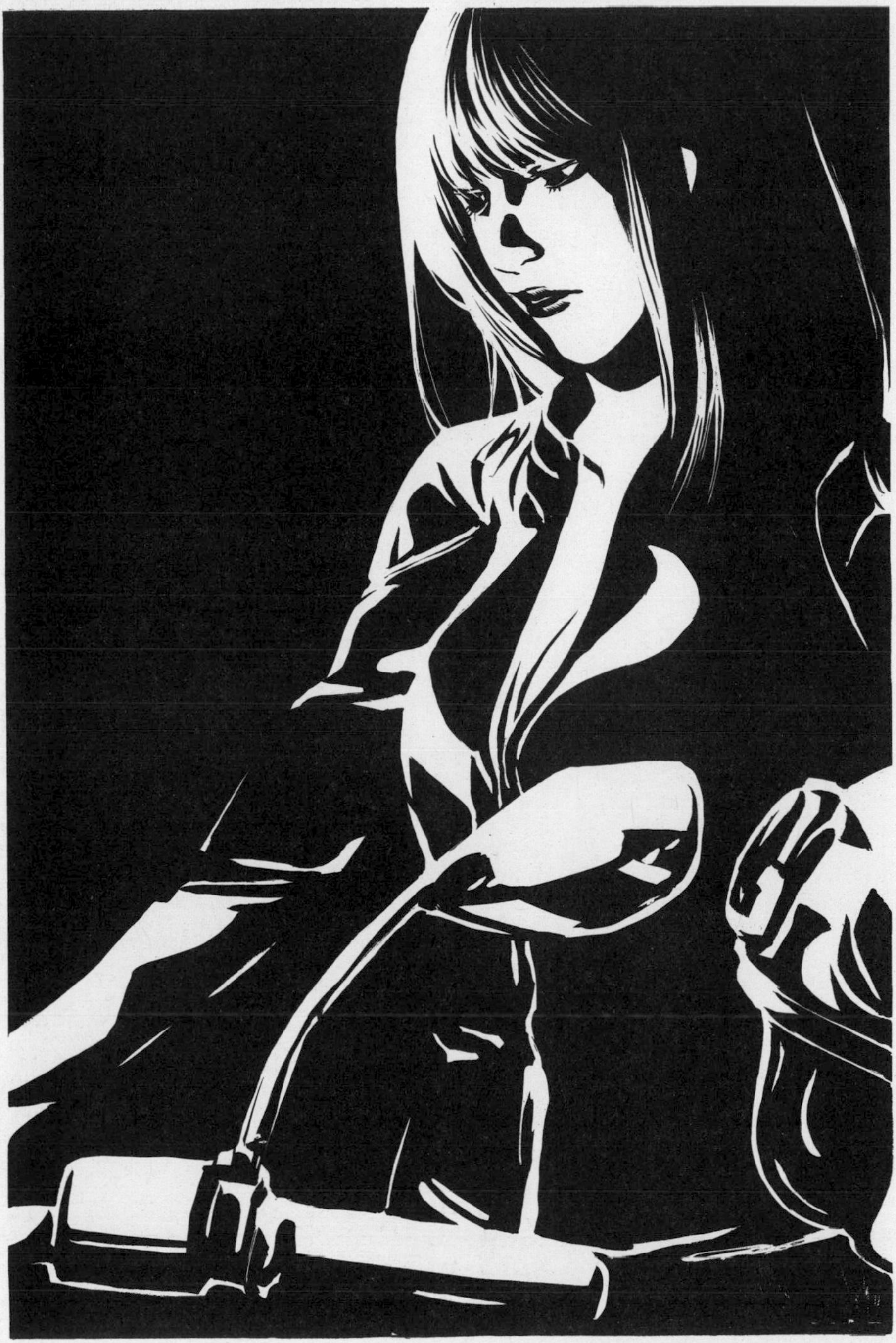

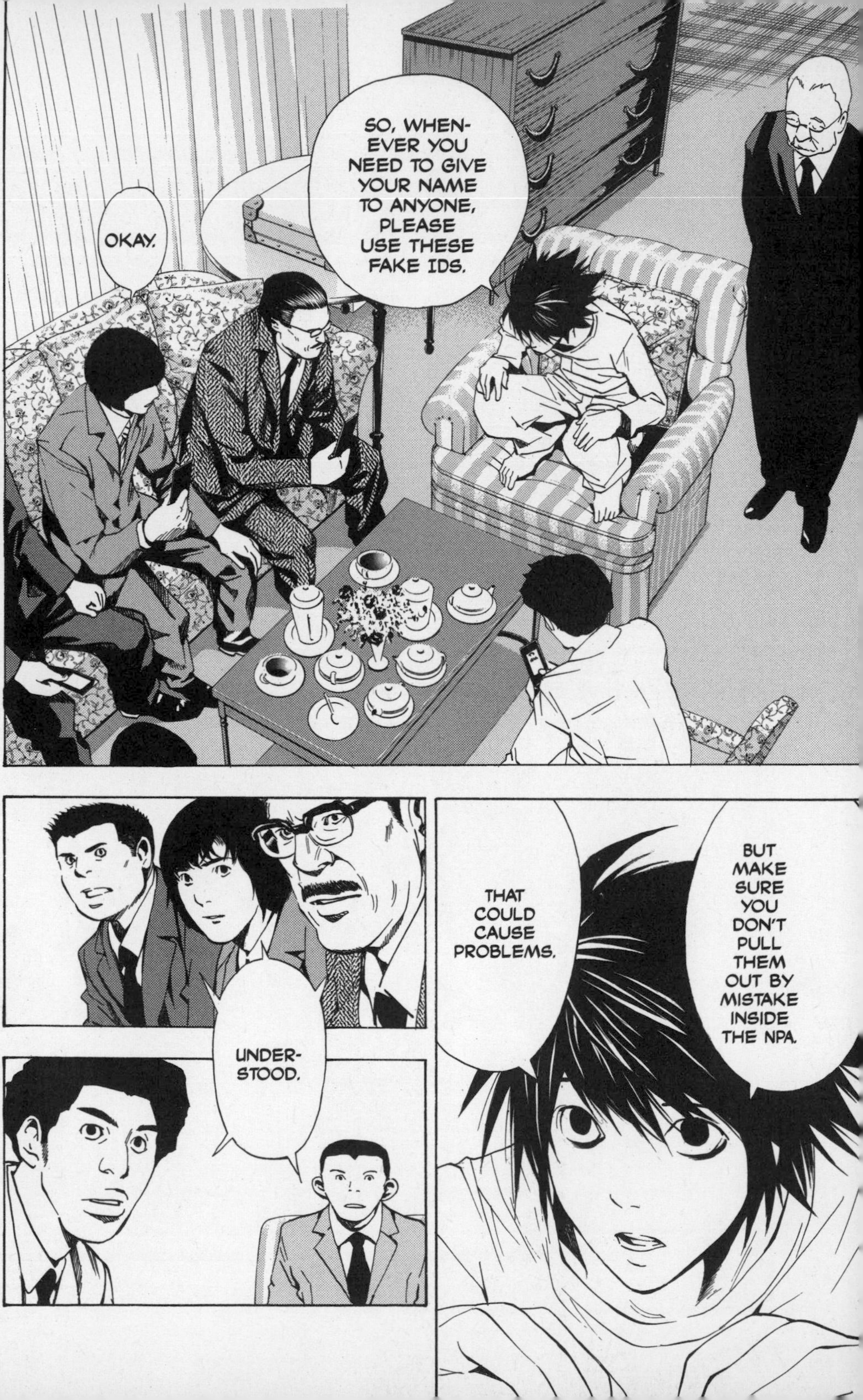
SO, WHEN-EVER YOU NEED TO GIVE YOUR NAME TO ANYONE, PLEASE USE THESE FAKE IDS.
OKAY.
BUT MAKE SURE YOU DON'T PULL THEM OUT BY MISTAKE INSIDE THE NPA.
THAT COULD CAUSE PROBLEMS.
UNDER-STOOD.

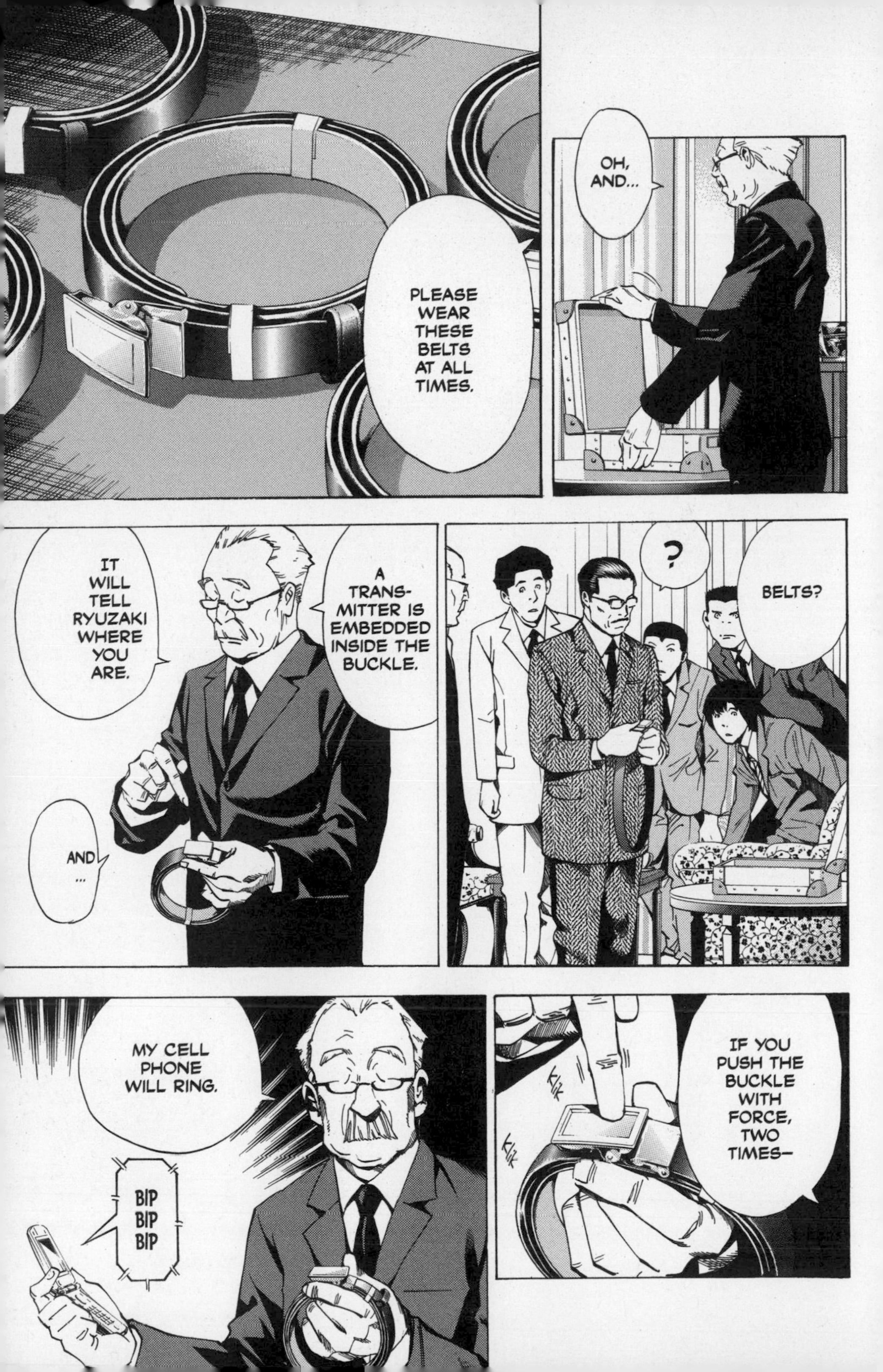
OH, AND...
PLEASE WEAR THESE BELTS AT ALL TIMES.
BELTS?
?
A TRANS-MITTER IS EMBEDDED INSIDE THE BUCKLE.
IT WILL TELL RYUZAKI WHERE YOU ARE.
AND...
IF YOU PUSH THE BUCKLE WITH FORCE, TWO TIMES—
KLIK
KLIK
MY CELL PHONE WILL RING.
BIP BIP BIP

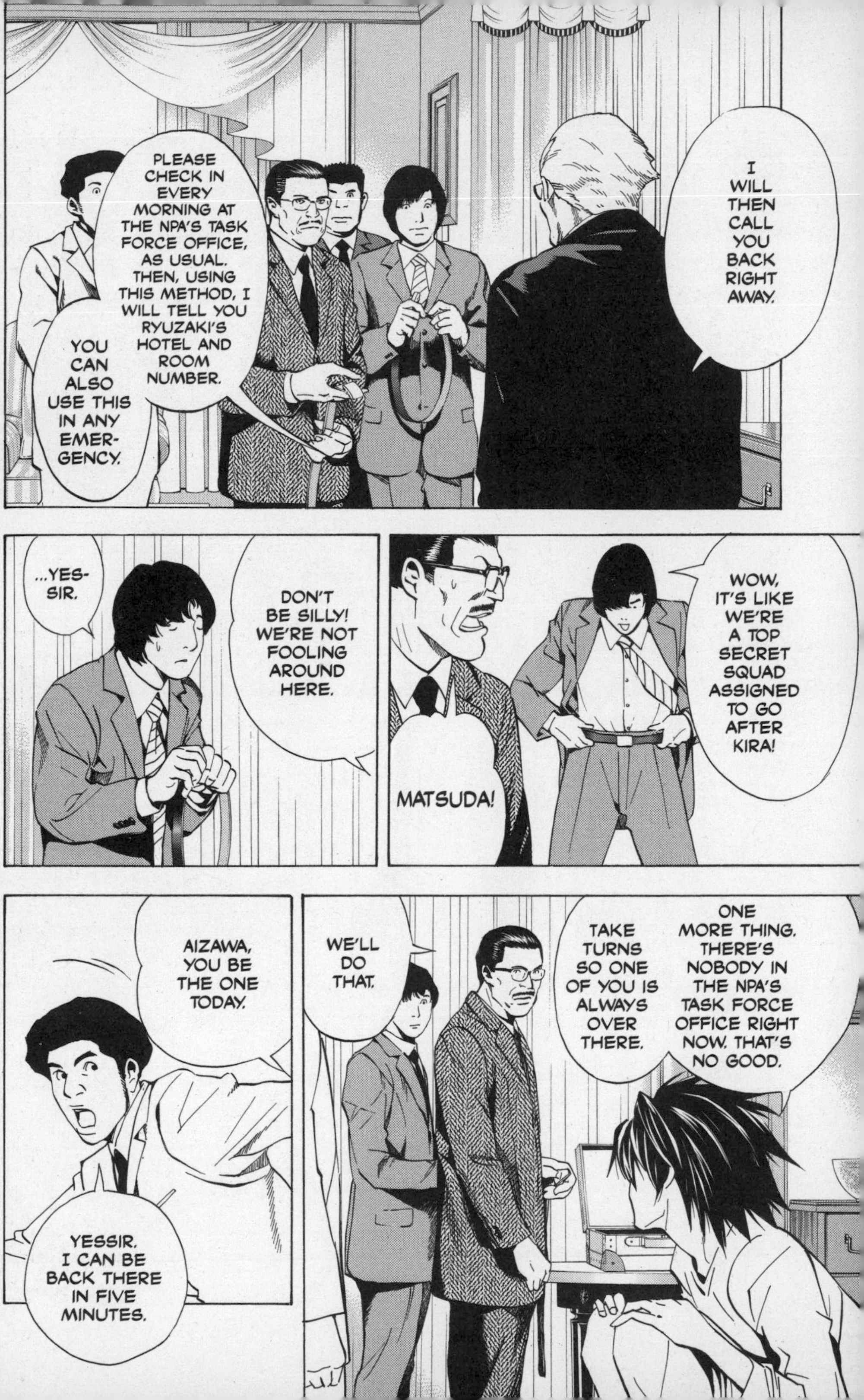
I WILL THEN CALL YOU BACK RIGHT AWAY.
PLEASE CHECK IN EVERY MORNING AT THE NPA'S TASK FORCE OFFICE, AS USUAL. THEN, USING THIS METHOD, I WILL TELL YOU RYUZAKI'S HOTEL AND ROOM NUMBER.
YOU CAN ALSO USE THIS IN ANY EMER-GENCY.
WOW, IT'S LIKE WE'RE A TOP SECRET SQUAD ASSIGNED TO GO AFTER KIRA!
MATSUDA!
DON'T BE SILLY! WE'RE NOT FOOLING AROUND HERE.
...YES-SIR.
ONE MORE THING. THERE'S NOBODY IN THE NPA'S TASK FORCE OFFICE RIGHT NOW. THAT'S NO GOOD.
TAKE TURNS SO ONE OF YOU IS ALWAYS OVER THERE.
WE'LL DO THAT.
AIZAWA, YOU BE THE ONE TODAY.
YESSIR. I CAN BE BACK THERE IN FIVE MINUTES.

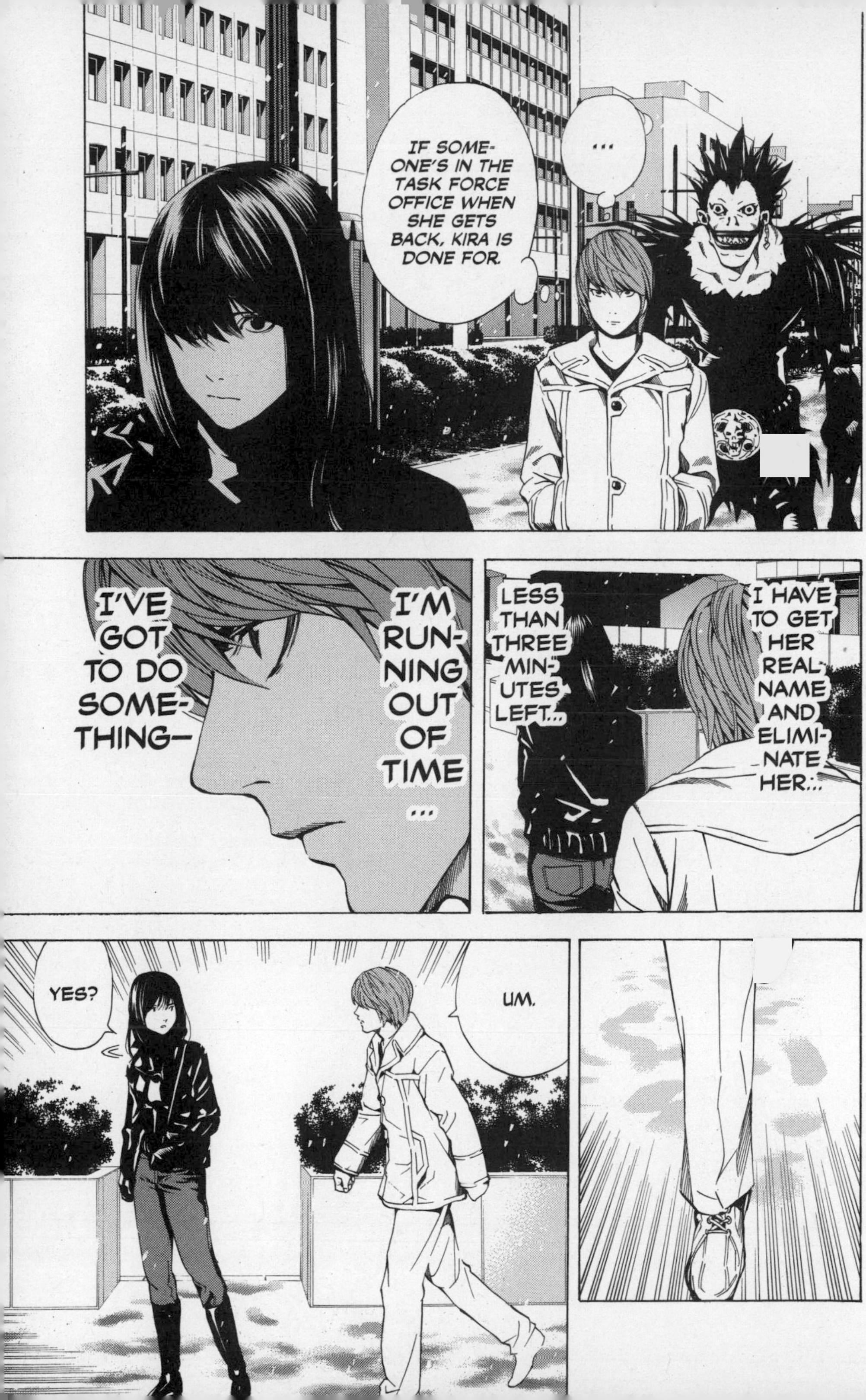
IF SOMEONE'S IN THE TASK FORCE OFFICE WHEN SHE GETS BACK, KIRA IS DONE FOR.
...
I HAVE TO GET HER REAL NAME AND ELIMINATE HER...
LESS THAN THREE MINUTES LEFT...
I'M RUNNING OUT OF TIME...
I'VE GOT TO DO SOMETHING—
UM.
YES?

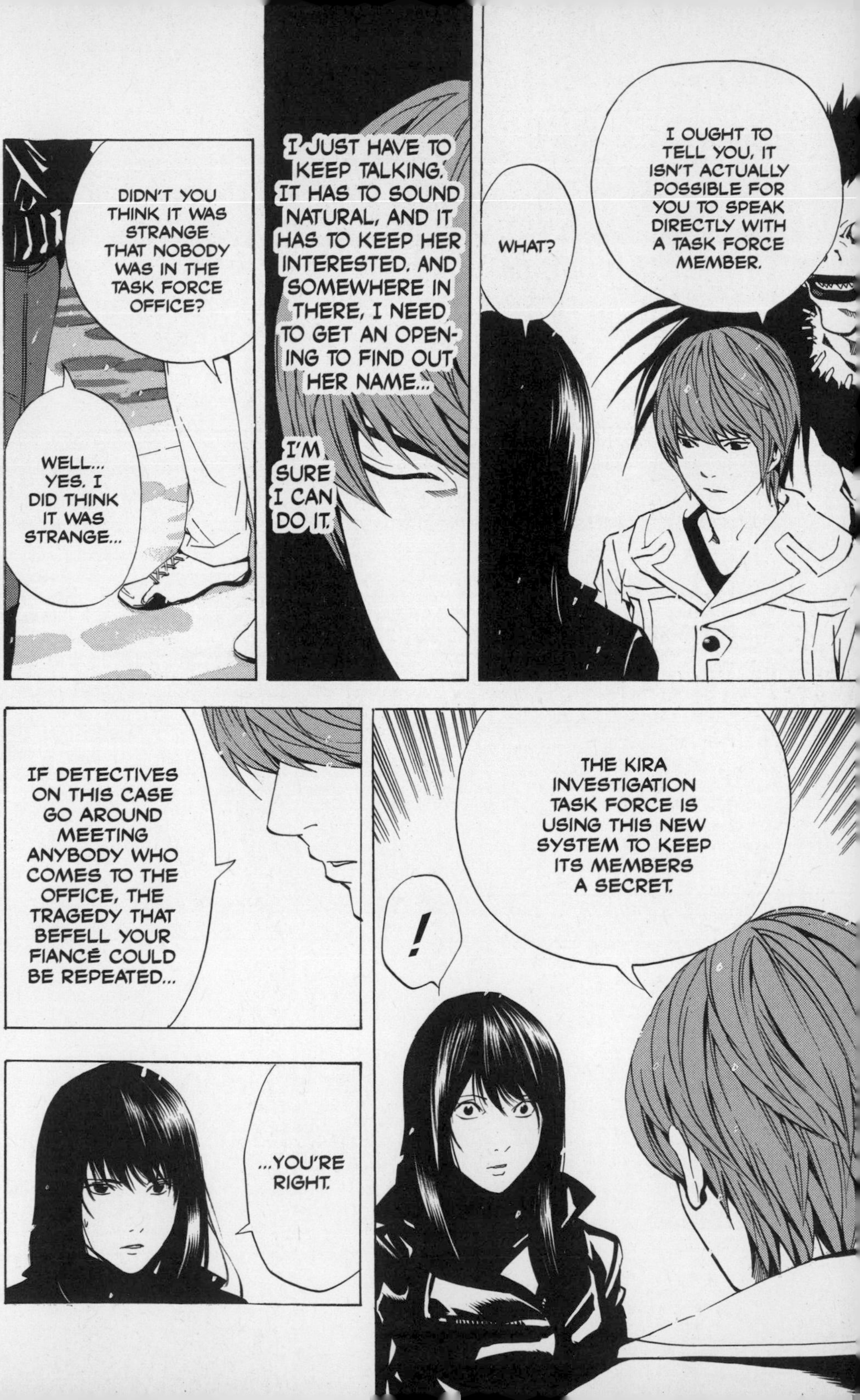
I OUGHT TO TELL YOU, IT ISN'T ACTUALLY POSSIBLE FOR YOU TO SPEAK DIRECTLY WITH A TASK FORCE MEMBER.
WHAT?
I JUST HAVE TO KEEP TALKING. IT HAS TO SOUND NATURAL, AND IT HAS TO KEEP HER INTERESTED. AND SOMEWHERE IN THERE, I NEED TO GET AN OPENING TO FIND OUT HER NAME...
I'M SURE I CAN DO IT.
DIDN'T YOU THINK IT WAS STRANGE THAT NOBODY WAS IN THE TASK FORCE OFFICE?
WELL... YES. I DID THINK IT WAS STRANGE...
THE KIRA INVESTIGATION TASK FORCE IS USING THIS NEW SYSTEM TO KEEP ITS MEMBERS A SECRET.
!
IF DETECTIVES ON THIS CASE GO AROUND MEETING ANYBODY WHO COMES TO THE OFFICE, THE TRAGEDY THAT BEFELL YOUR FIANCÉ COULD BE REPEATED...
...YOU'RE RIGHT.

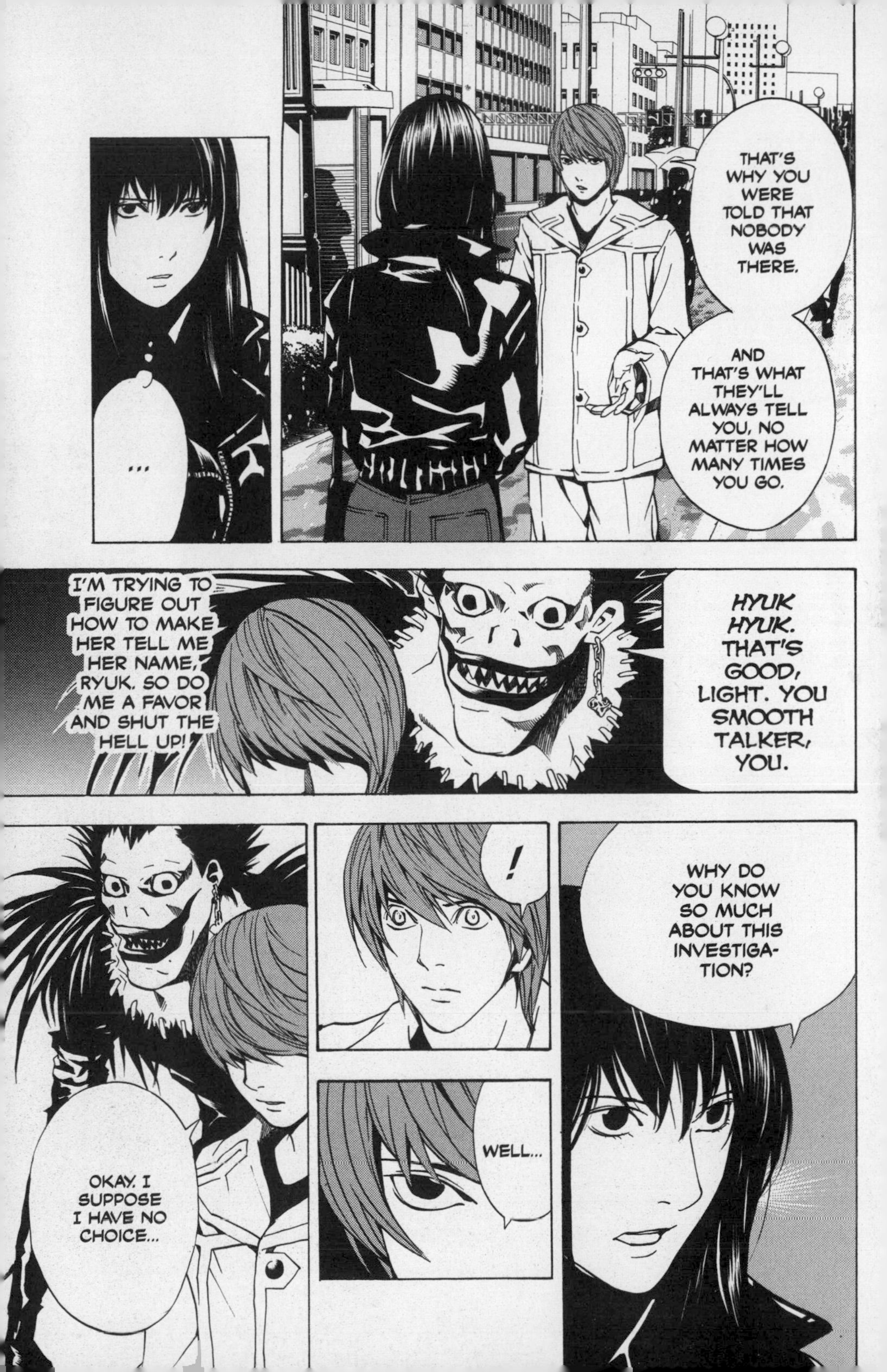
THAT'S WHY YOU WERE TOLD THAT NOBODY WAS THERE.
AND THAT'S WHAT THEY'LL ALWAYS TELL YOU, NO MATTER HOW MANY TIMES YOU GO.
...
*HYUK HYUK.* THAT'S GOOD, LIGHT. YOU SMOOTH TALKER, YOU.
I'M TRYING TO FIGURE OUT HOW TO MAKE HER TELL ME HER NAME, RYUK. SO DO ME A FAVOR AND SHUT THE HELL UP!
WHY DO YOU KNOW SO MUCH ABOUT THIS INVESTIGATION?
!
WELL...
OKAY. I SUPPOSE I HAVE NO CHOICE...

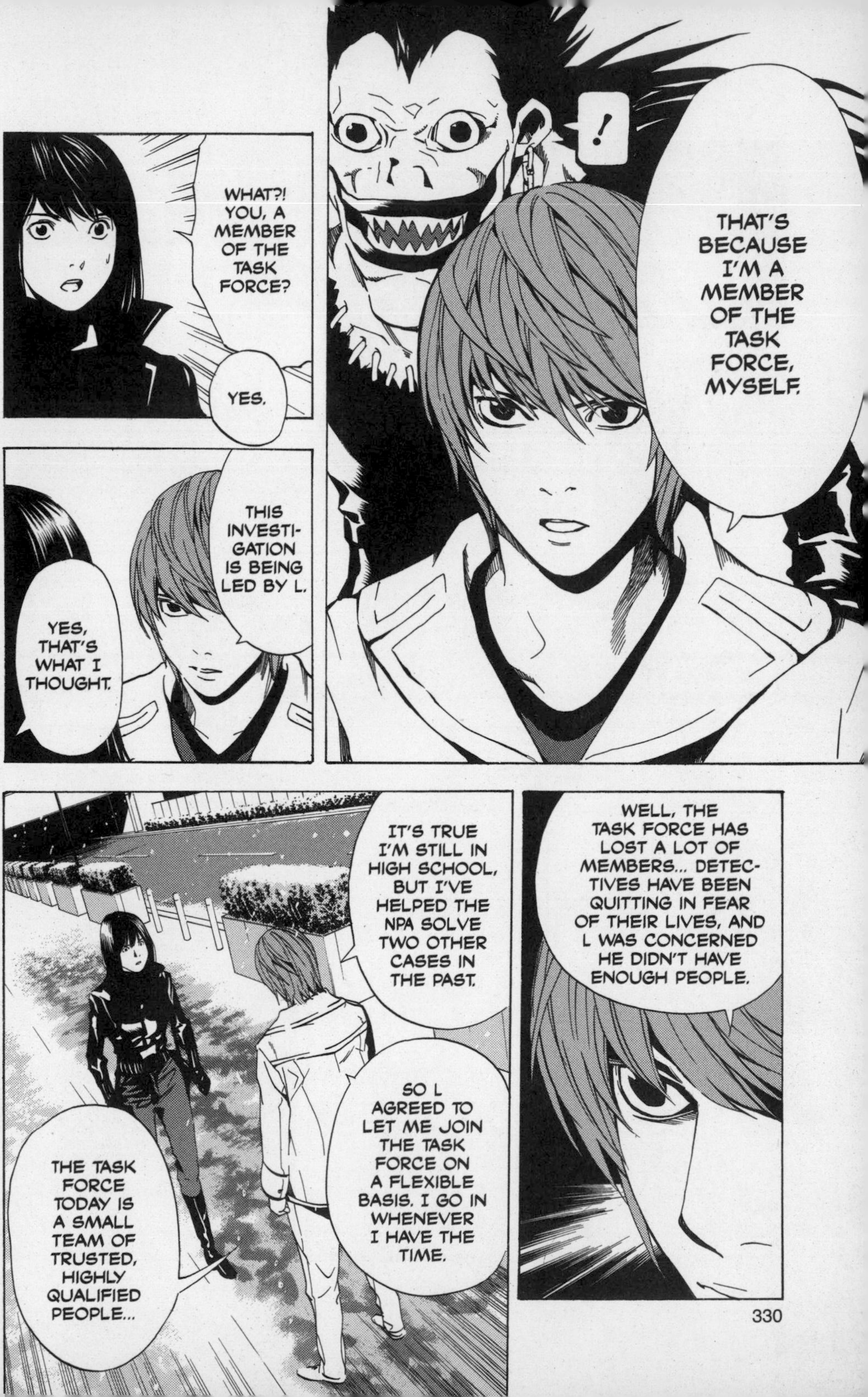
!
THAT'S BECAUSE I'M A MEMBER OF THE TASK FORCE, MYSELF.
WHAT?! YOU, A MEMBER OF THE TASK FORCE?
YES.
THIS INVESTIGATION IS BEING LED BY L.
YES, THAT'S WHAT I THOUGHT.
WELL, THE TASK FORCE HAS LOST A LOT OF MEMBERS... DETECTIVES HAVE BEEN QUITTING IN FEAR OF THEIR LIVES, AND L WAS CONCERNED HE DIDN'T HAVE ENOUGH PEOPLE.
IT'S TRUE I'M STILL IN HIGH SCHOOL, BUT I'VE HELPED THE NPA SOLVE TWO OTHER CASES IN THE PAST.
SO L AGREED TO LET ME JOIN THE TASK FORCE ON A FLEXIBLE BASIS. I GO IN WHENEVER I HAVE THE TIME.
THE TASK FORCE TODAY IS A SMALL TEAM OF TRUSTED, HIGHLY QUALIFIED PEOPLE...

READ THIS WAY

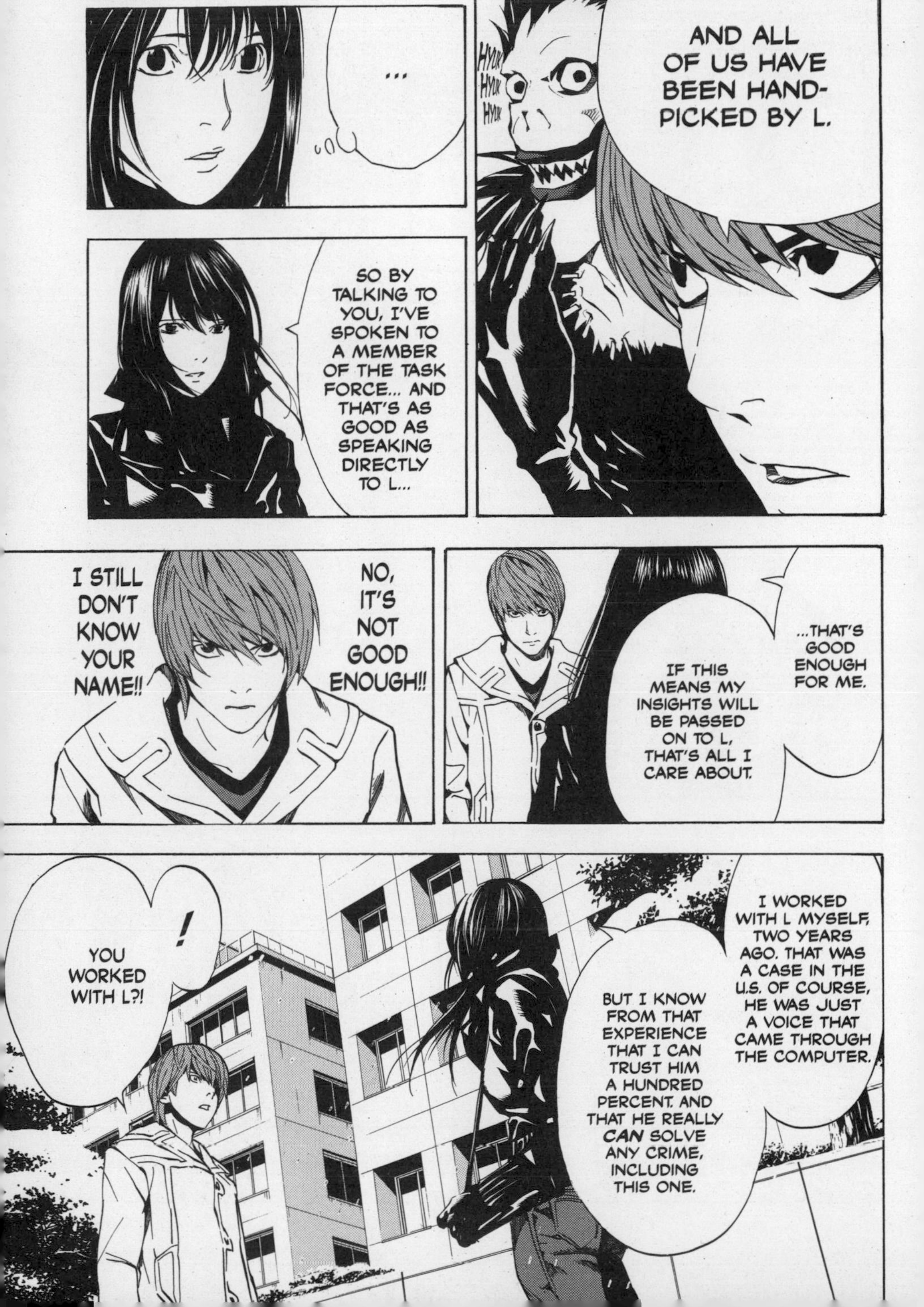

HYUK HYUK HYUK
AND ALL OF US HAVE BEEN HAND-PICKED BY L.
...
SO BY TALKING TO YOU, I'VE SPOKEN TO A MEMBER OF THE TASK FORCE... AND THAT'S AS GOOD AS SPEAKING DIRECTLY TO L...
...THAT'S GOOD ENOUGH FOR ME.
IF THIS MEANS MY INSIGHTS WILL BE PASSED ON TO L, THAT'S ALL I CARE ABOUT.
NO, IT'S NOT GOOD ENOUGH!!
I STILL DON'T KNOW YOUR NAME!!
I WORKED WITH L MYSELF, TWO YEARS AGO. THAT WAS A CASE IN THE U.S. OF COURSE, HE WAS JUST A VOICE THAT CAME THROUGH THE COMPUTER.
BUT I KNOW FROM THAT EXPERIENCE THAT I CAN TRUST HIM A HUNDRED PERCENT, AND THAT HE REALLY CAN SOLVE ANY CRIME, INCLUDING THIS ONE.
!
YOU WORKED WITH L?!

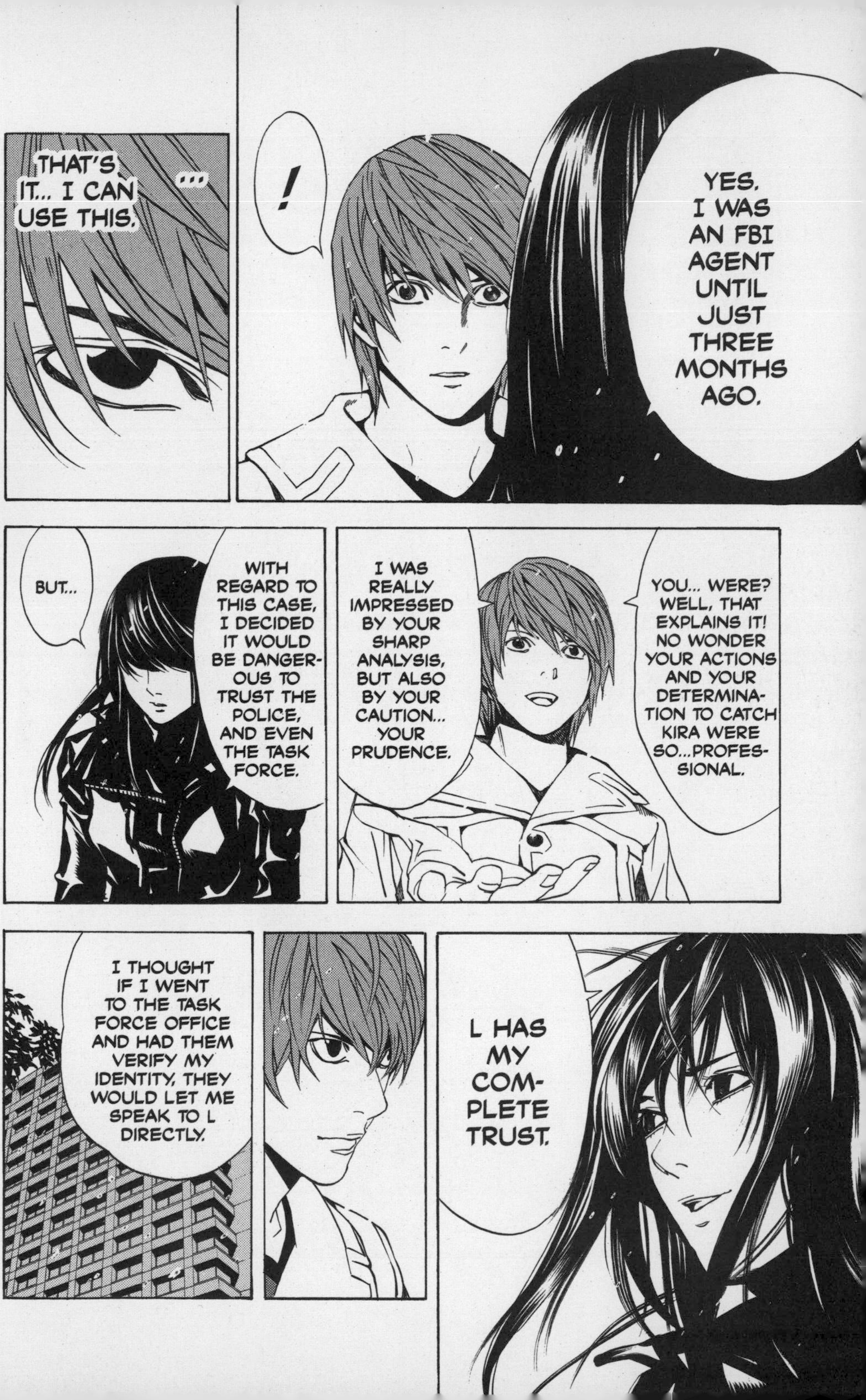
YES. I WAS AN FBI AGENT UNTIL JUST THREE MONTHS AGO.
!
...
THAT'S IT... I CAN USE THIS.
YOU... WERE? WELL, THAT EXPLAINS IT! NO WONDER YOUR ACTIONS AND YOUR DETERMINATION TO CATCH KIRA WERE SO...PROFESSIONAL.
I WAS REALLY IMPRESSED BY YOUR SHARP ANALYSIS, BUT ALSO BY YOUR CAUTION... YOUR PRUDENCE.
WITH REGARD TO THIS CASE, I DECIDED IT WOULD BE DANGEROUS TO TRUST THE POLICE, AND EVEN THE TASK FORCE.
BUT...
L HAS MY COMPLETE TRUST.
I THOUGHT IF I WENT TO THE TASK FORCE OFFICE AND HAD THEM VERIFY MY IDENTITY, THEY WOULD LET ME SPEAK TO L DIRECTLY.

READ THIS WAY

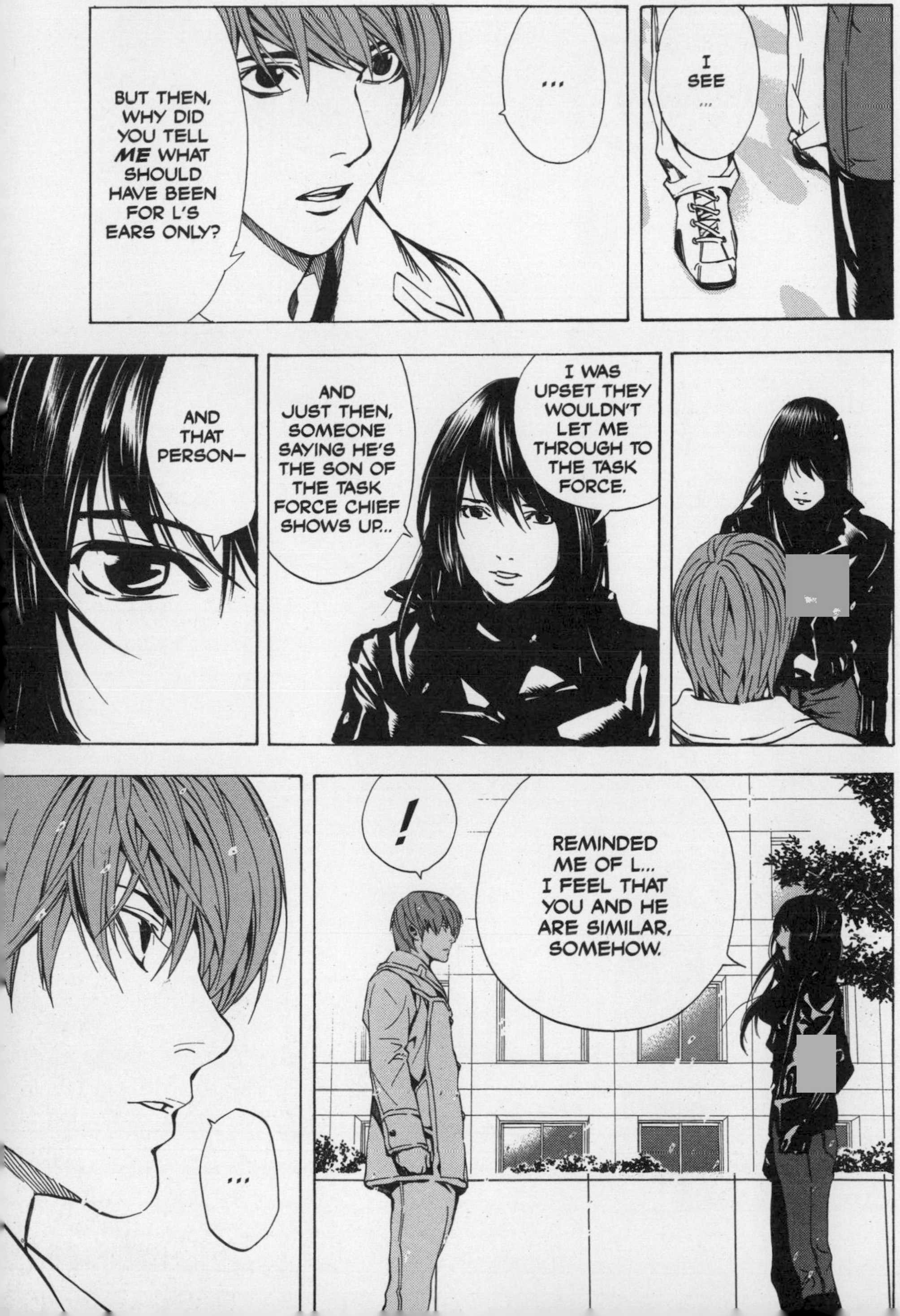
I SEE ...
...
BUT THEN, WHY DID YOU TELL *ME* WHAT SHOULD HAVE BEEN FOR L'S EARS ONLY?
I WAS UPSET THEY WOULDN'T LET ME THROUGH TO THE TASK FORCE.
AND JUST THEN, SOMEONE SAYING HE'S THE SON OF THE TASK FORCE CHIEF SHOWS UP...
AND THAT PERSON—
REMINDED ME OF L... I FEEL THAT YOU AND HE ARE SIMILAR, SOMEHOW.
!
...

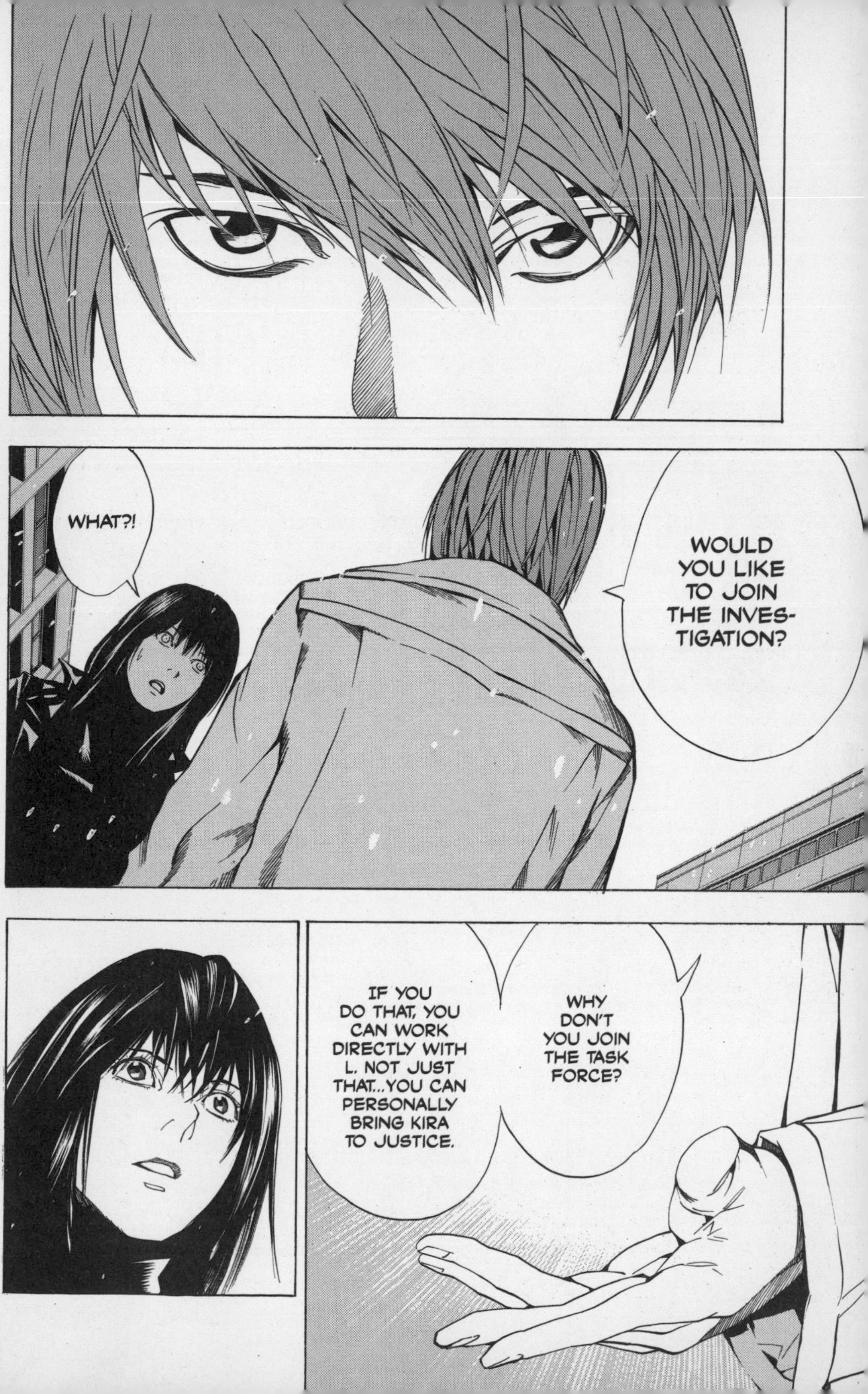
WOULD YOU LIKE TO JOIN THE INVES-TIGATION?
WHAT?!
WHY DON'T YOU JOIN THE TASK FORCE?
IF YOU DO THAT, YOU CAN WORK DIRECTLY WITH L. NOT JUST THAT...YOU CAN PERSONALLY BRING KIRA TO JUSTICE.

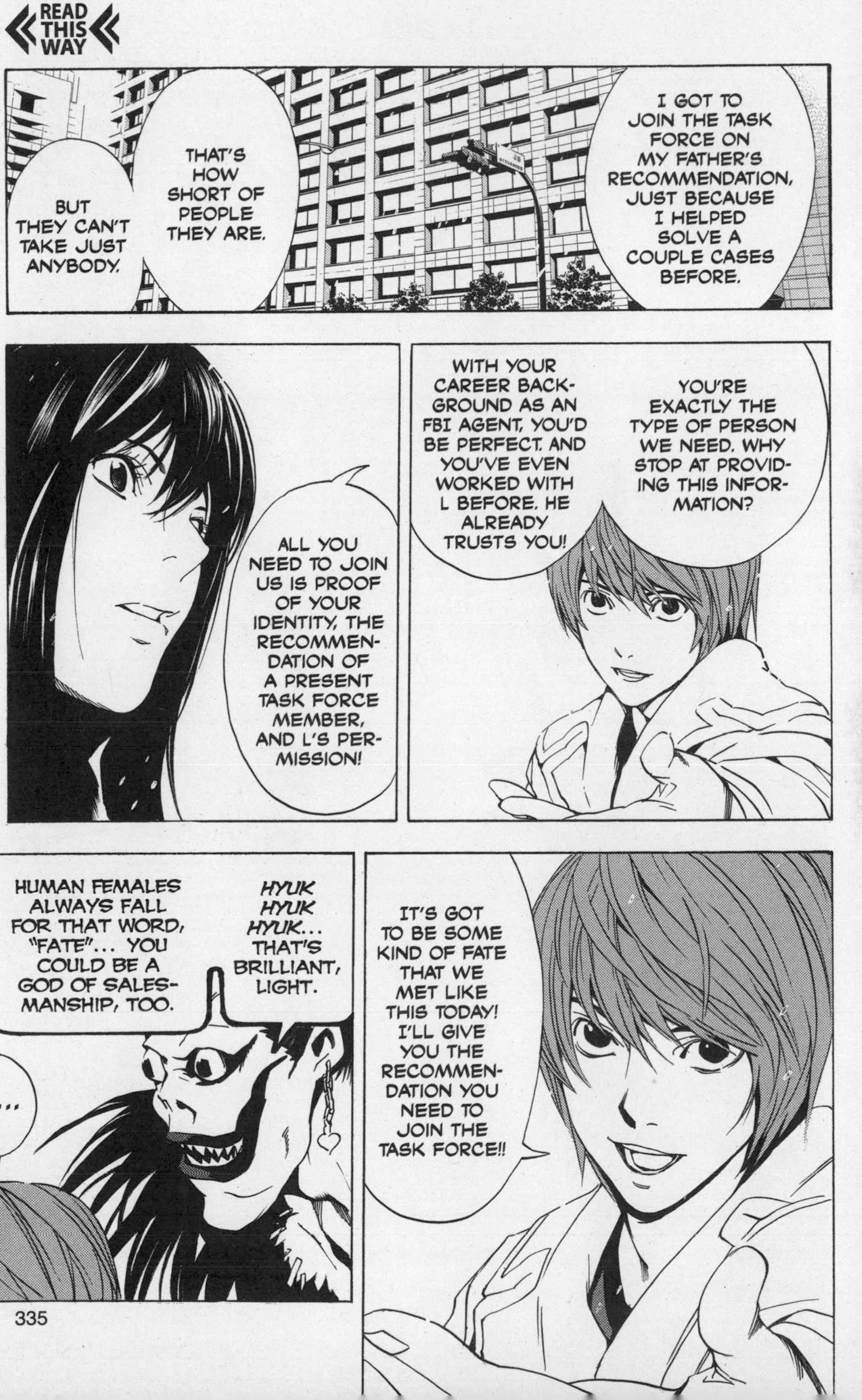
READ THIS WAY
I GOT TO JOIN THE TASK FORCE ON MY FATHER'S RECOMMENDATION, JUST BECAUSE I HELPED SOLVE A COUPLE CASES BEFORE.
THAT'S HOW SHORT OF PEOPLE THEY ARE.
BUT THEY CAN'T TAKE JUST ANYBODY.
YOU'RE EXACTLY THE TYPE OF PERSON WE NEED. WHY STOP AT PROVIDING THIS INFORMATION?
WITH YOUR CAREER BACKGROUND AS AN FBI AGENT, YOU'D BE PERFECT. AND YOU'VE EVEN WORKED WITH L BEFORE. HE ALREADY TRUSTS YOU!
ALL YOU NEED TO JOIN US IS PROOF OF YOUR IDENTITY, THE RECOMMENDATION OF A PRESENT TASK FORCE MEMBER, AND L'S PERMISSION!
IT'S GOT TO BE SOME KIND OF FATE THAT WE MET LIKE THIS TODAY! I'LL GIVE YOU THE RECOMMENDATION YOU NEED TO JOIN THE TASK FORCE!!
*HYUK HYUK HYUK*... THAT'S BRILLIANT, LIGHT.
HUMAN FEMALES ALWAYS FALL FOR THAT WORD, "FATE"... YOU COULD BE A GOD OF SALESMANSHIP, TOO.
...

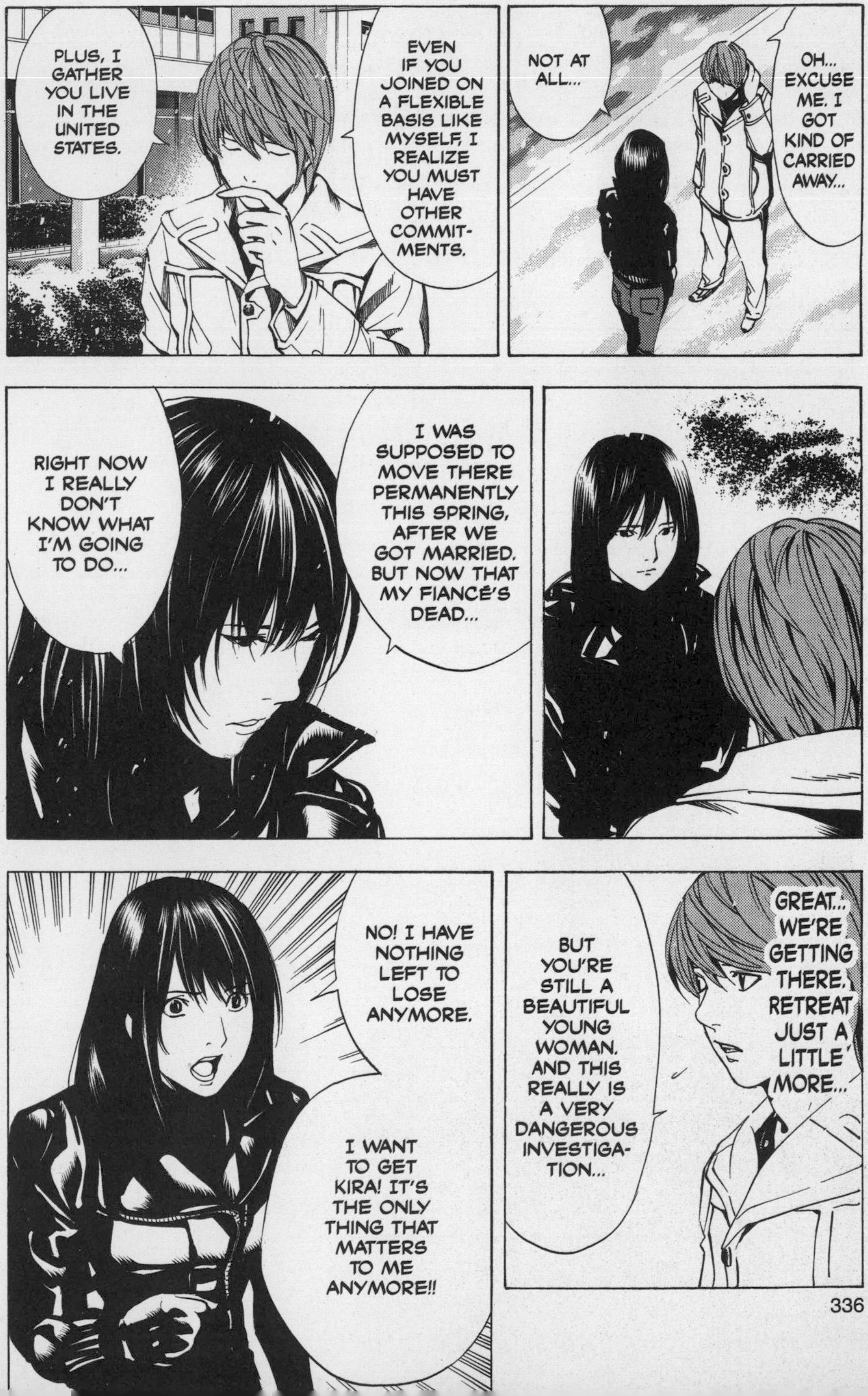
OH... EXCUSE ME. I GOT KIND OF CARRIED AWAY...
NOT AT ALL...
EVEN IF YOU JOINED ON A FLEXIBLE BASIS LIKE MYSELF, I REALIZE YOU MUST HAVE OTHER COMMIT-MENTS.
PLUS, I GATHER YOU LIVE IN THE UNITED STATES.
I WAS SUPPOSED TO MOVE THERE PERMANENTLY THIS SPRING, AFTER WE GOT MARRIED. BUT NOW THAT MY FIANCÉ'S DEAD...
RIGHT NOW I REALLY DON'T KNOW WHAT I'M GOING TO DO...
GREAT... WE'RE GETTING THERE. RETREAT JUST A LITTLE MORE...
BUT YOU'RE STILL A BEAUTIFUL YOUNG WOMAN. AND THIS REALLY IS A VERY DANGEROUS INVESTIGA-TION...
NO! I HAVE NOTHING LEFT TO LOSE ANYMORE.
I WANT TO GET KIRA! IT'S THE ONLY THING THAT MATTERS TO ME ANYMORE!!

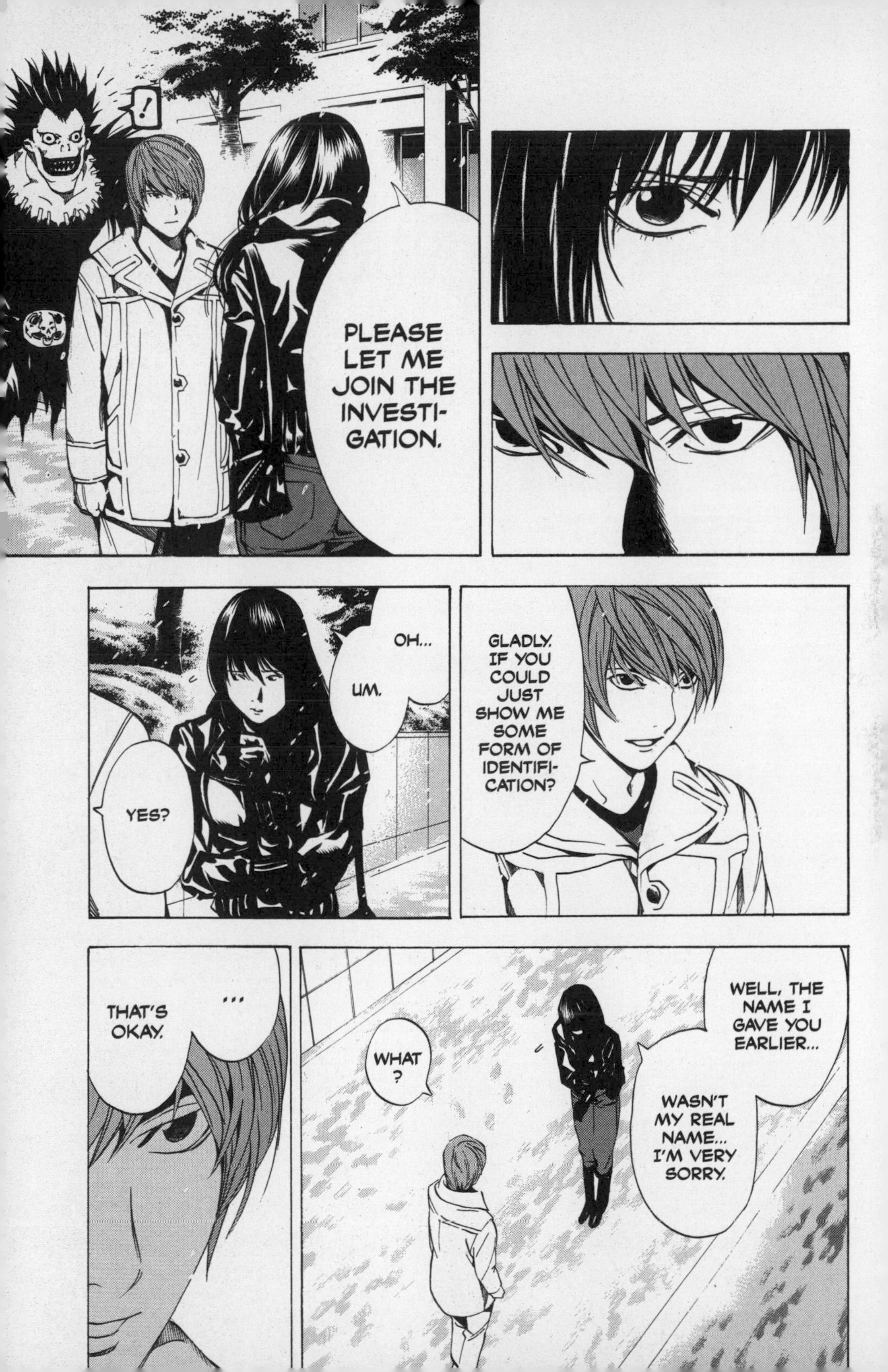
!
PLEASE LET ME JOIN THE INVESTI-GATION.
GLADLY. IF YOU COULD JUST SHOW ME SOME FORM OF IDENTIFI-CATION?
OH...
UM.
YES?
WELL, THE NAME I GAVE YOU EARLIER...
WASN'T MY REAL NAME... I'M VERY SORRY.
WHAT?
...
THAT'S OKAY.

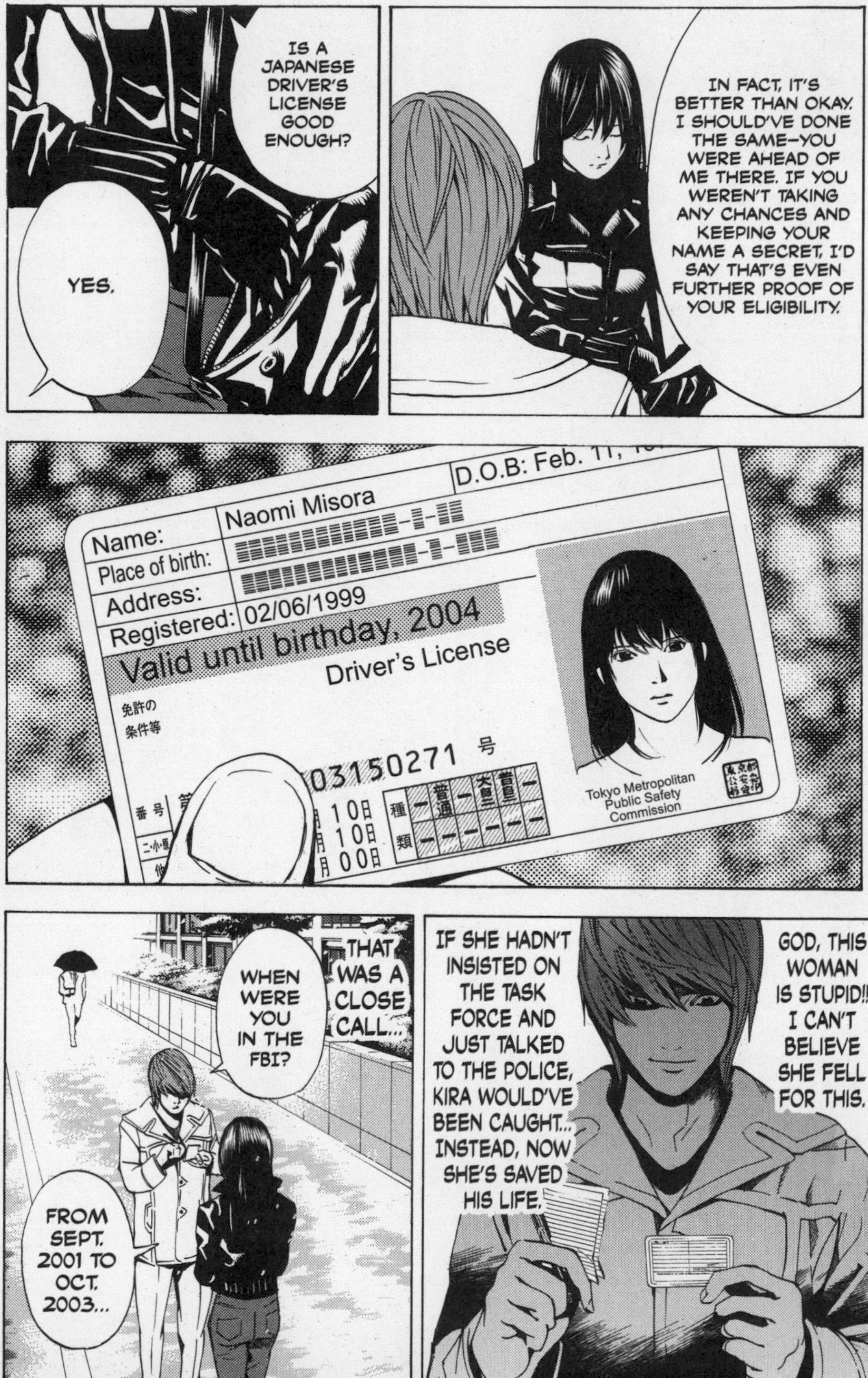
IN FACT, IT'S BETTER THAN OKAY. I SHOULD'VE DONE THE SAME—YOU WERE AHEAD OF ME THERE. IF YOU WEREN'T TAKING ANY CHANCES AND KEEPING YOUR NAME A SECRET, I'D SAY THAT'S EVEN FURTHER PROOF OF YOUR ELIGIBILITY.
IS A JAPANESE DRIVER'S LICENSE GOOD ENOUGH?
YES.
D.O.B: Feb. 11,
Name: Naomi Misora
Place of birth:
Address:
Registered: 02/06/1999
Valid until birthday, 2004
Driver's License
免許の
条件等
03150271 号
Tokyo Metropolitan Public Safety Commission
GOD, THIS WOMAN IS STUPID!! I CAN'T BELIEVE SHE FELL FOR THIS.
IF SHE HADN'T INSISTED ON THE TASK FORCE AND JUST TALKED TO THE POLICE, KIRA WOULD'VE BEEN CAUGHT... INSTEAD, NOW SHE'S SAVED HIS LIFE.
THAT WAS A CLOSE CALL...
WHEN WERE YOU IN THE FBI?
FROM SEPT. 2001 TO OCT. 2003...

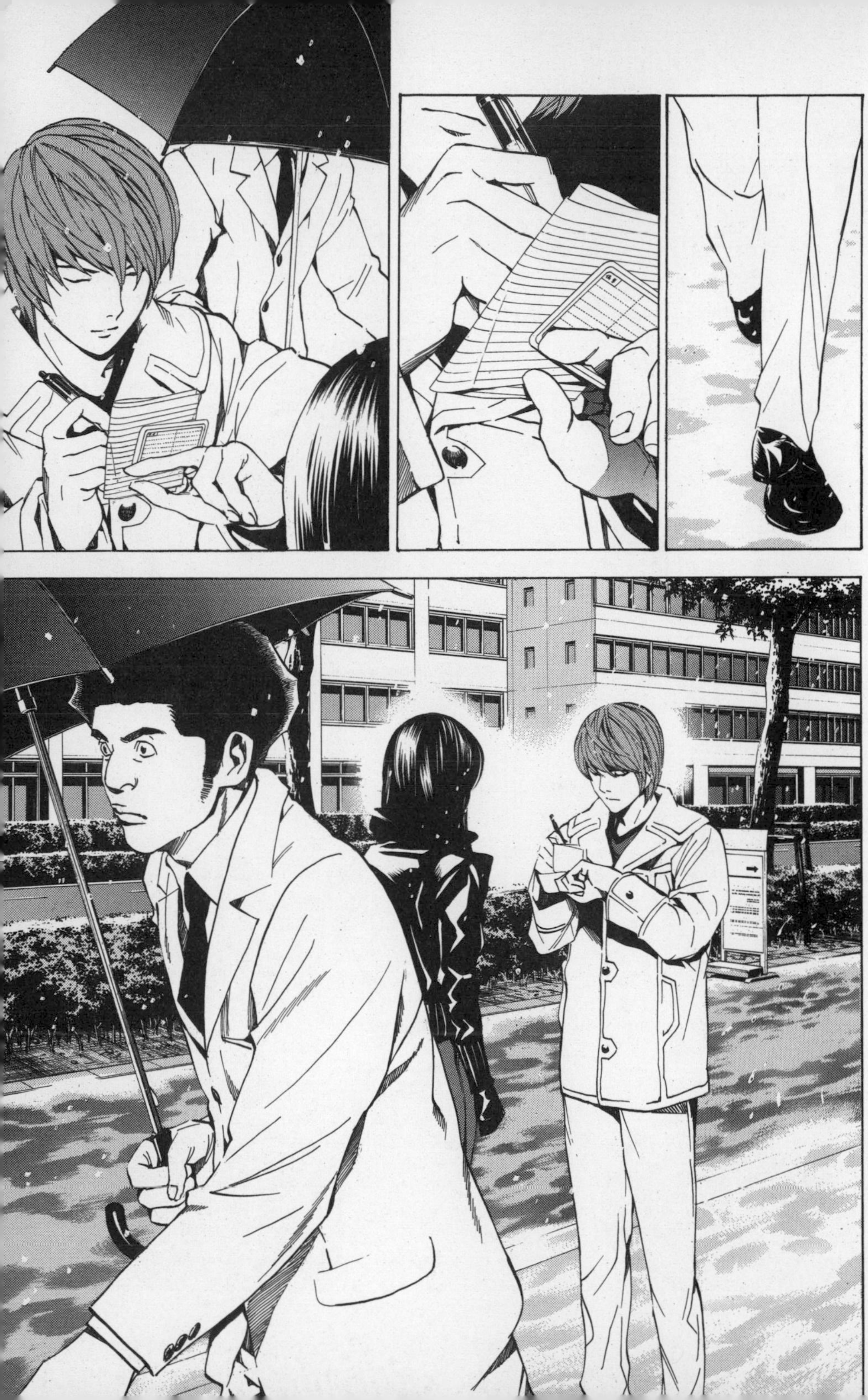

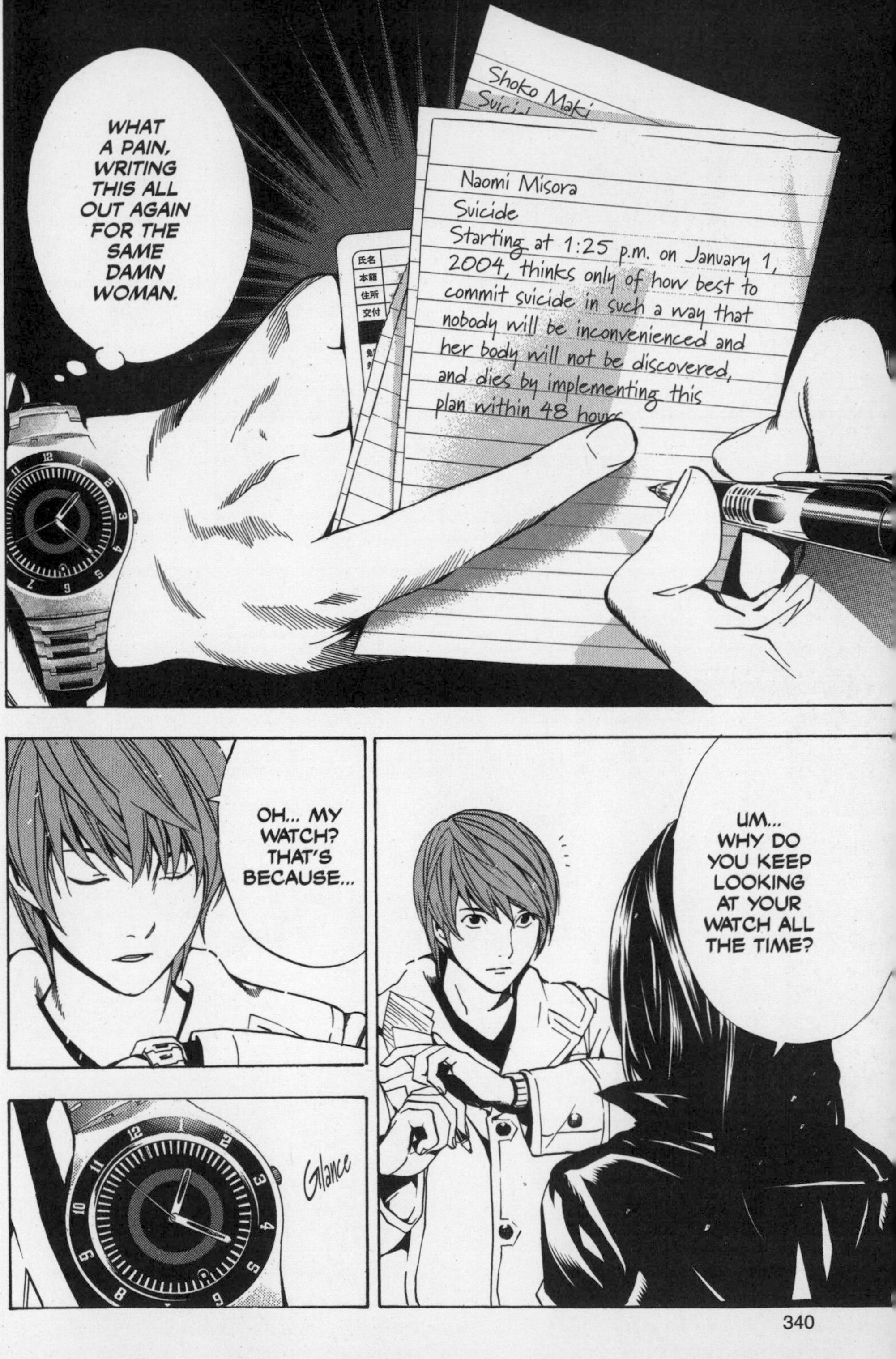
Shoko Maki
Naomi Misora
Suicide
Starting at 1:25 p.m. on January 1, 2004, thinks only of how best to commit suicide in such a way that nobody will be inconvenienced and her body will not be discovered, and dies by implementing this plan within 48 hour
氏名
本籍
住所
交付
WHAT A PAIN, WRITING THIS ALL OUT AGAIN FOR THE SAME DAMN WOMAN.
UM... WHY DO YOU KEEP LOOKING AT YOUR WATCH ALL THE TIME?
OH... MY WATCH? THAT'S BECAUSE...
Glance

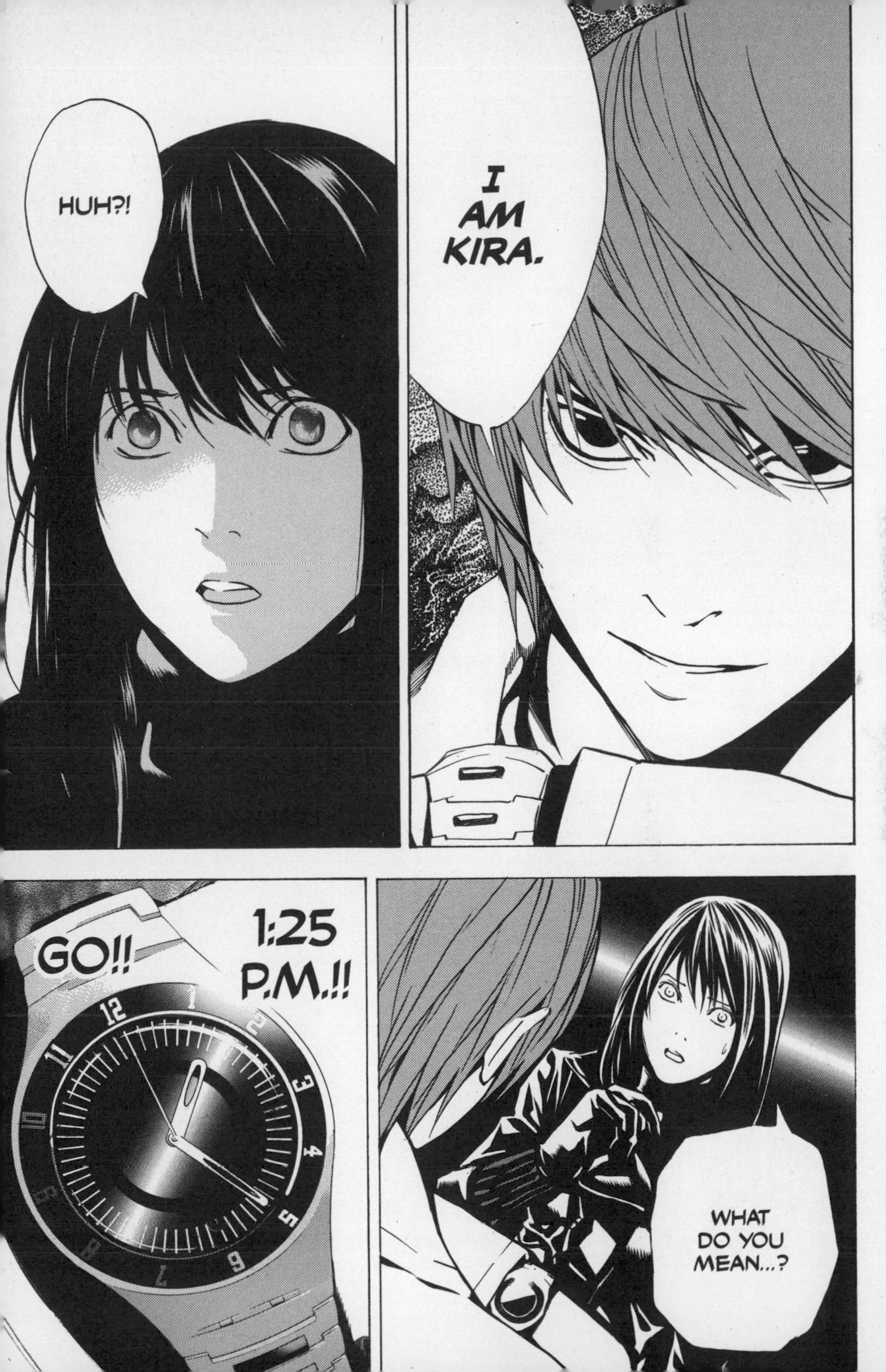
I AM KIRA.
HUH?!
WHAT DO YOU MEAN...?
1:25 P.M.!!
GO!!

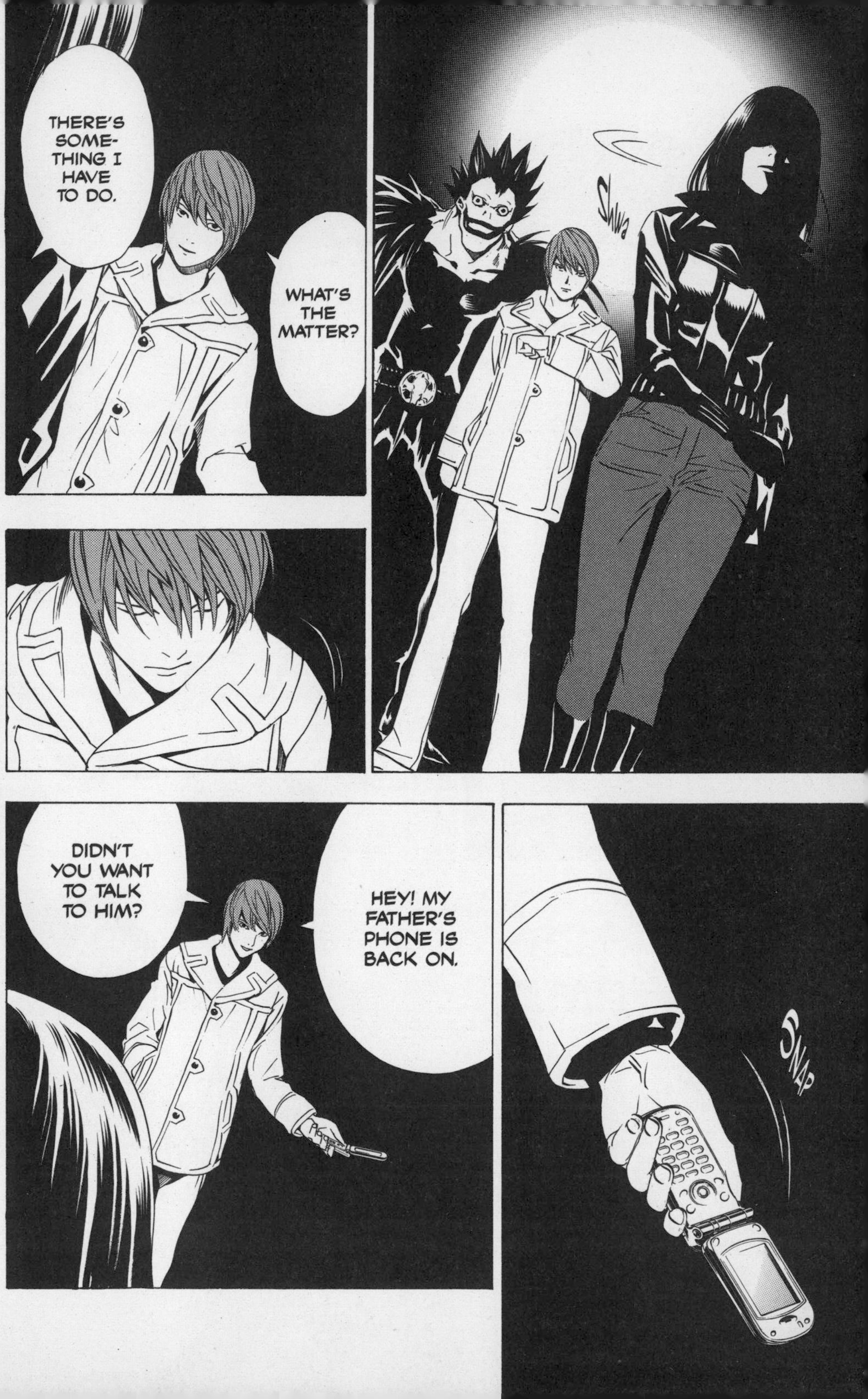
Shwa
WHAT'S THE MATTER?
THERE'S SOME-THING I HAVE TO DO.
SNAP
HEY! MY FATHER'S PHONE IS BACK ON.
DIDN'T YOU WANT TO TALK TO HIM?

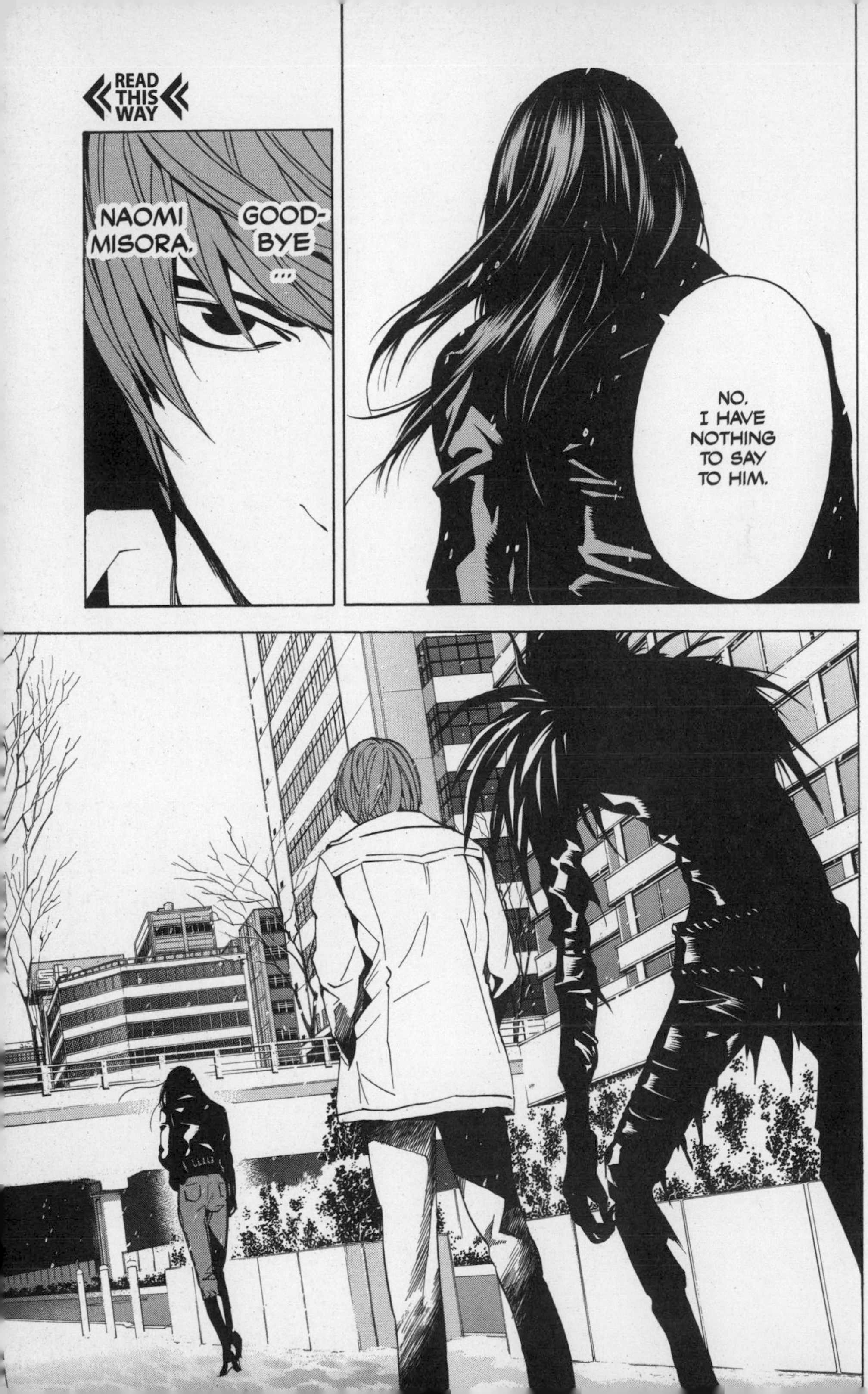
READ THIS WAY
NO. I HAVE NOTHING TO SAY TO HIM.
GOOD-BYE ...
NAOMI MISORA.

# DEATH NOTE
## How to use it
### X

○ "Suicide" is a valid cause of death.
Basically all humans are thought to possess
the possibility to commit suicide. It is,
therefore, not something "unbelievable to think
of".

死因に「自殺」は有効であり、ほぼ全ての人間に対し、自殺は可能性がある事
とされ、「考えもしない事」には入らない。

○ Whether the cause of the individual's death is
either a suicide or accident, If the death leads
to the death of more than the intended, the
person will simply die of a heart attack.
This is to ensure that other lives are not
influenced.

自殺でも事故死でも、名前を書かれた人間以外の死を
直接的に招く様な死に方をさせる事はできない。
他の人間の死を招く様であれば、
名前を書かれた者が第三者の死を招かない状況下で心臓麻痺となる。

# chapter 15 Phone Call

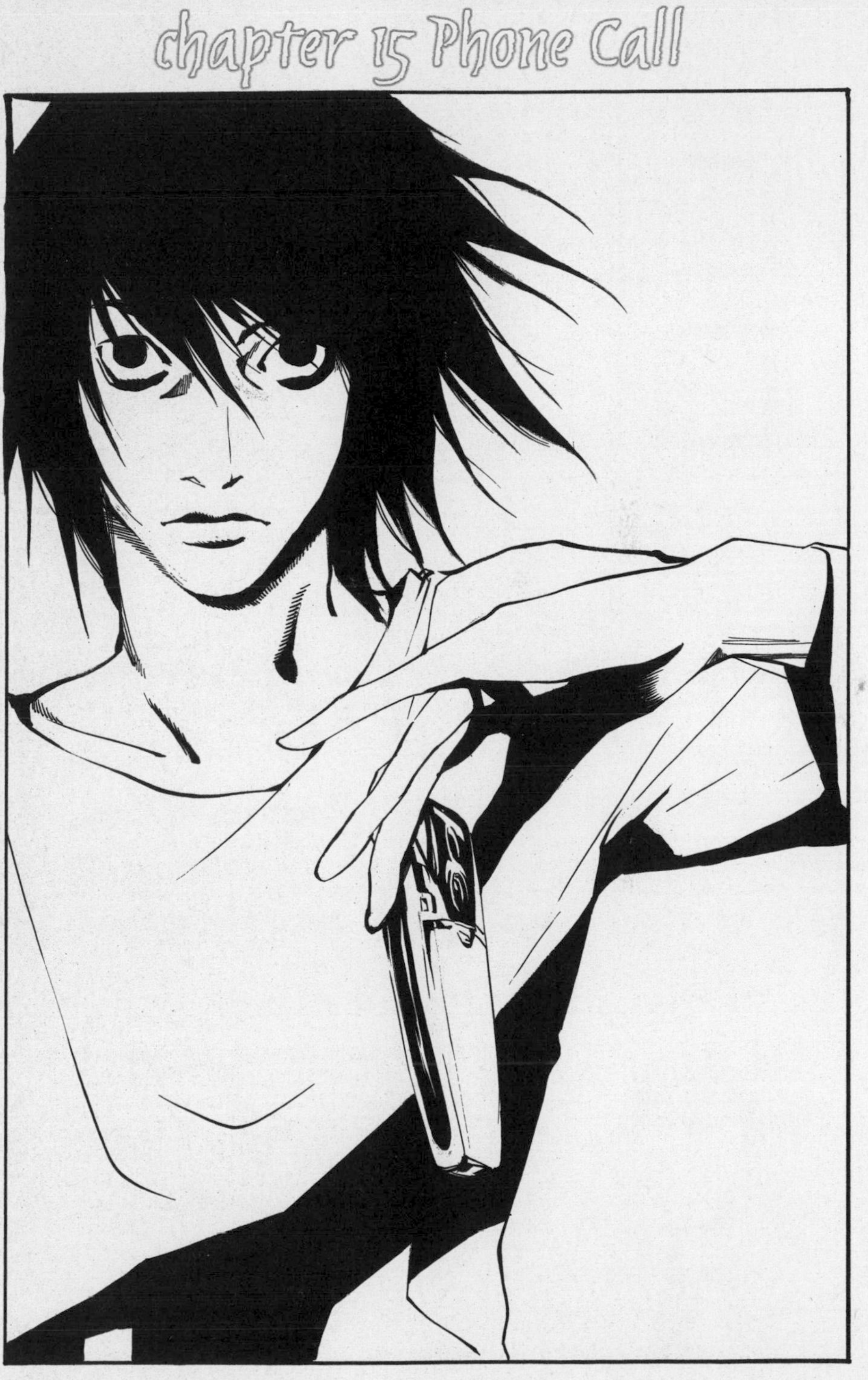

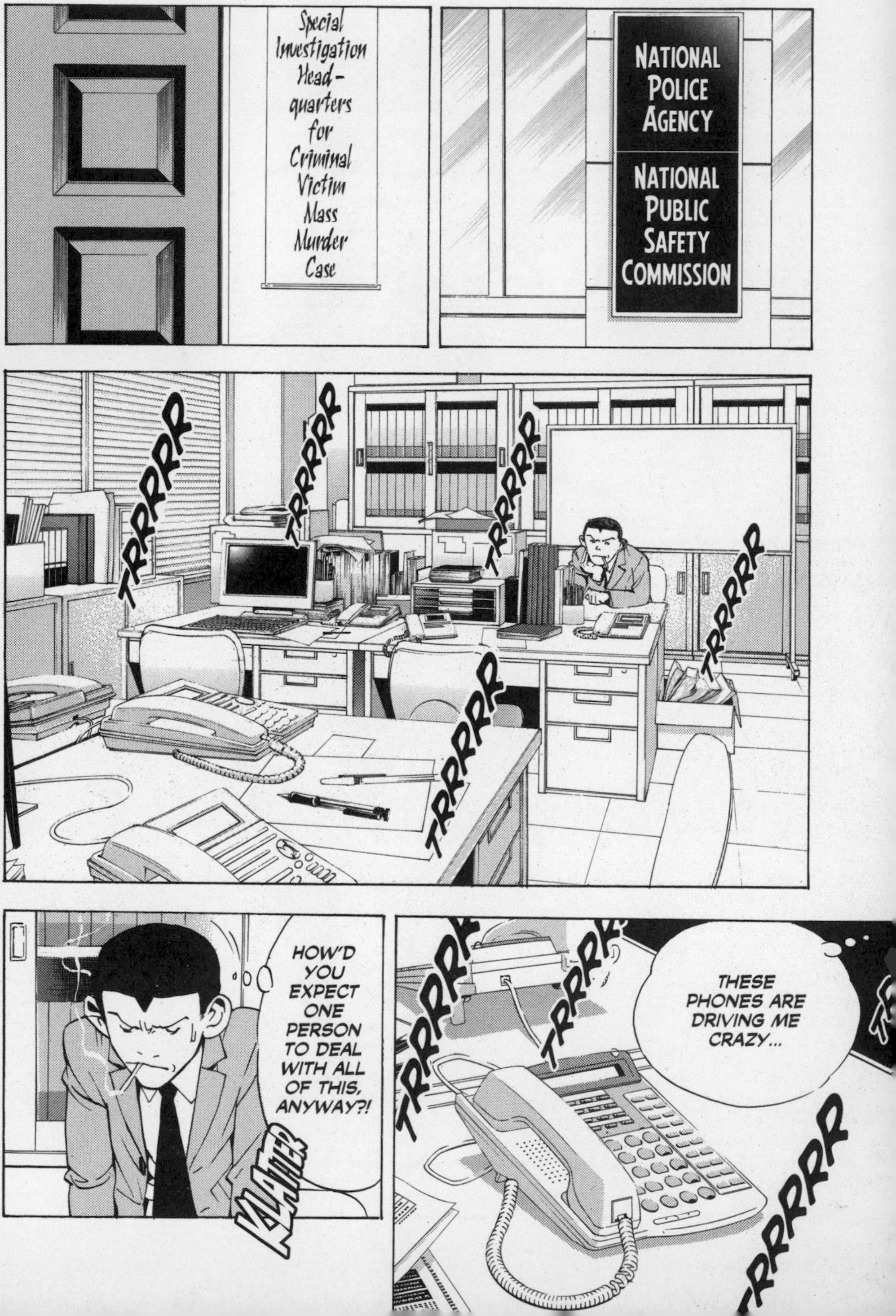
NATIONAL POLICE AGENCY
NATIONAL PUBLIC SAFETY COMMISSION
Special Investigation Head-quarters for Criminal Victim Mass Murder Case
TRRRR
TRRRRR
TRRRR
TRRRRR
TRRRRR
TRRRR
TRRRR
THESE PHONES ARE DRIVING ME CRAZY...
TRRRRR
HOW'D YOU EXPECT ONE PERSON TO DEAL WITH ALL OF THIS, ANYWAY?!
KLATTER

READ THIS WAY

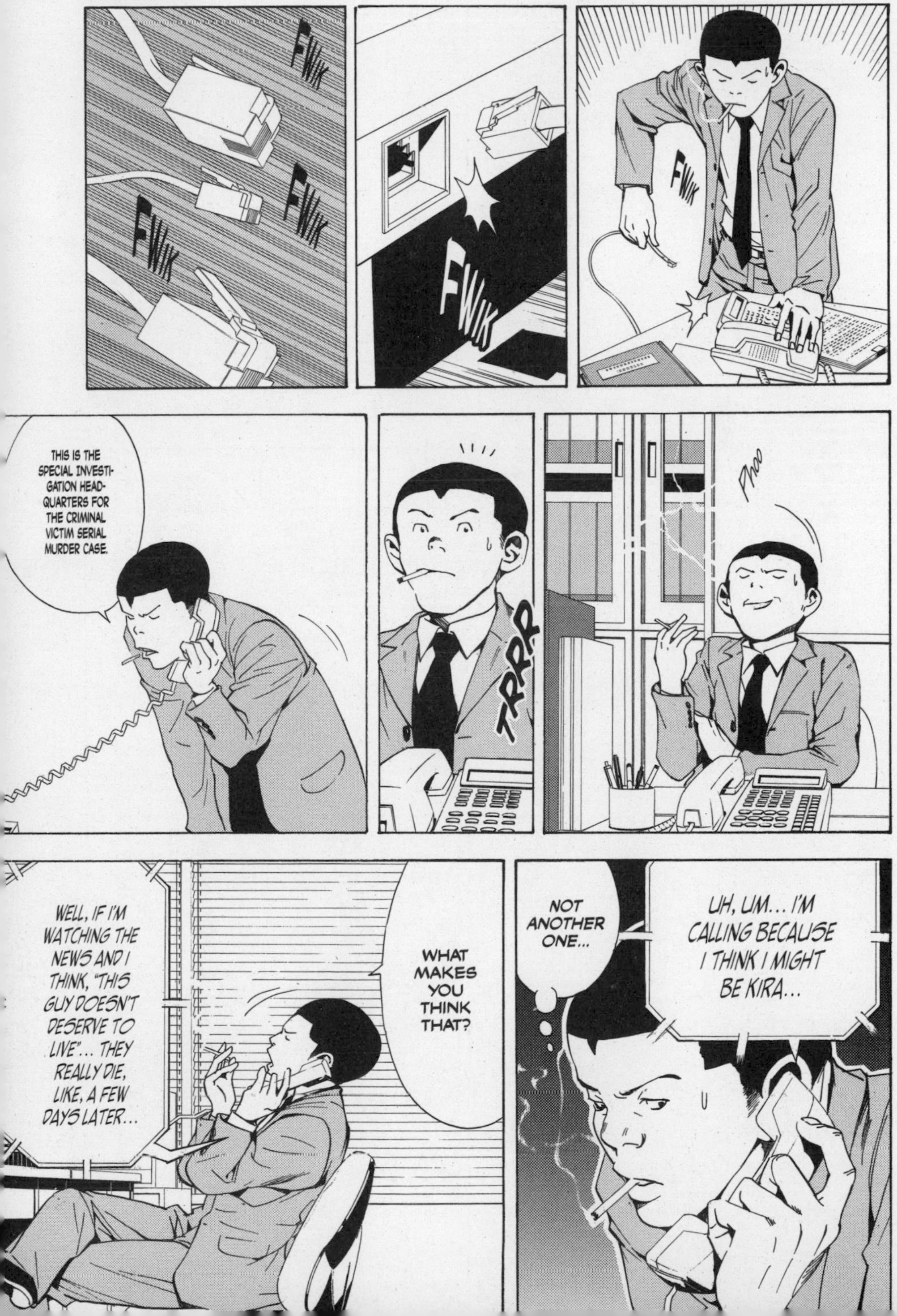
FWIK
FWIK
FWIK
FWIK
FWIK
Phoo
TRRR
THIS IS THE SPECIAL INVESTIGATION HEADQUARTERS FOR THE CRIMINAL VICTIM SERIAL MURDER CASE.
UH, UM... I'M CALLING BECAUSE I THINK I MIGHT BE KIRA...
NOT ANOTHER ONE...
WHAT MAKES YOU THINK THAT?
WELL, IF I'M WATCHING THE NEWS AND I THINK, "THIS GUY DOESN'T DESERVE TO LIVE"... THEY REALLY DIE, LIKE, A FEW DAYS LATER...

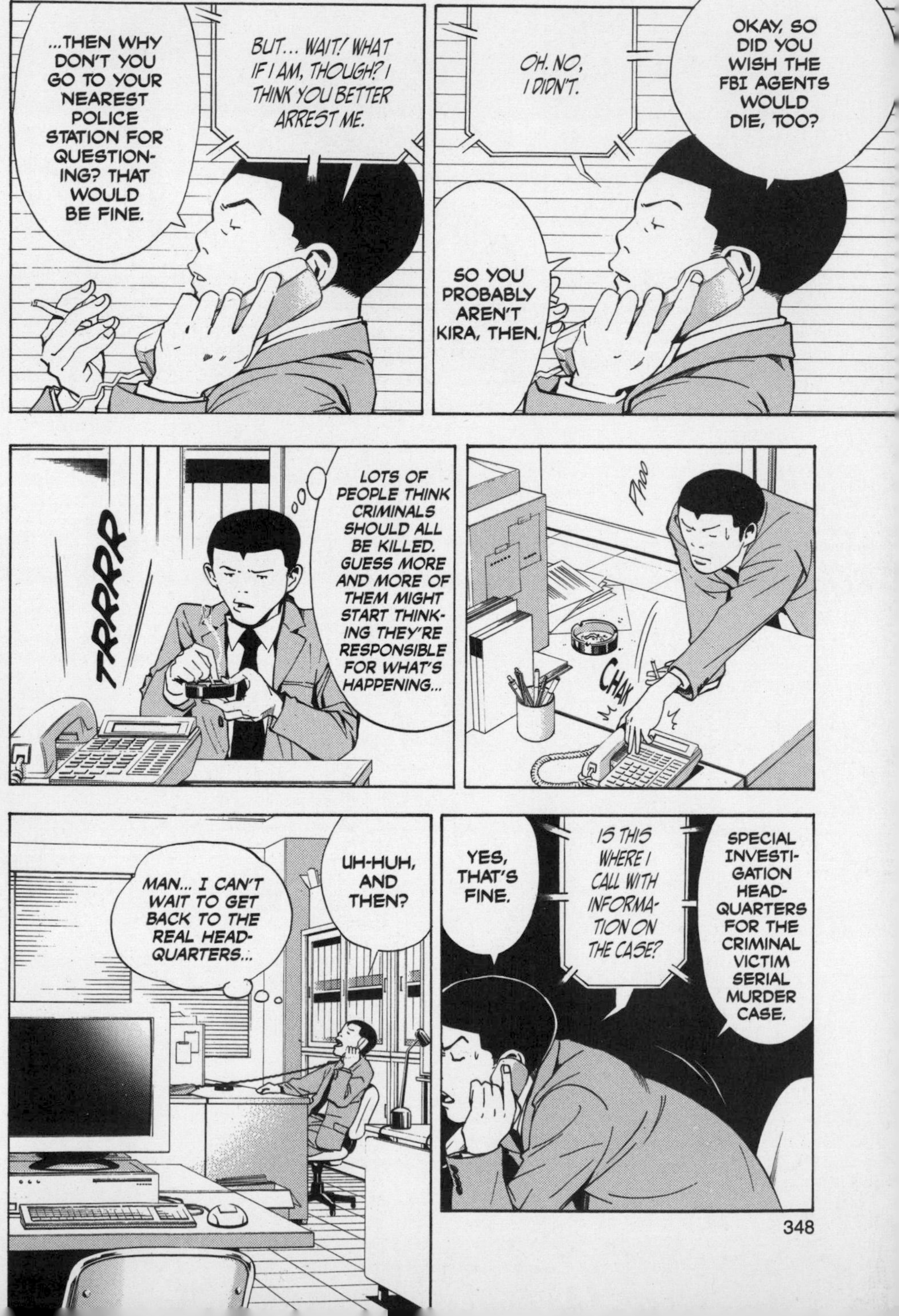
OKAY, SO DID YOU WISH THE FBI AGENTS WOULD DIE, TOO?
OH. NO, I DIDN'T.
SO YOU PROBABLY AREN'T KIRA, THEN.
BUT... WAIT! WHAT IF I AM, THOUGH? I THINK YOU BETTER ARREST ME.
...THEN WHY DON'T YOU GO TO YOUR NEAREST POLICE STATION FOR QUESTIONING? THAT WOULD BE FINE.
Phoo
CHAK
LOTS OF PEOPLE THINK CRIMINALS SHOULD ALL BE KILLED. GUESS MORE AND MORE OF THEM MIGHT START THINKING THEY'RE RESPONSIBLE FOR WHAT'S HAPPENING...
TRRRR
SPECIAL INVESTIGATION HEADQUARTERS FOR THE CRIMINAL VICTIM SERIAL MURDER CASE.
IS THIS WHERE I CALL WITH INFORMATION ON THE CASE?
YES, THAT'S FINE.
UH-HUH, AND THEN?
MAN... I CAN'T WAIT TO GET BACK TO THE REAL HEADQUARTERS...

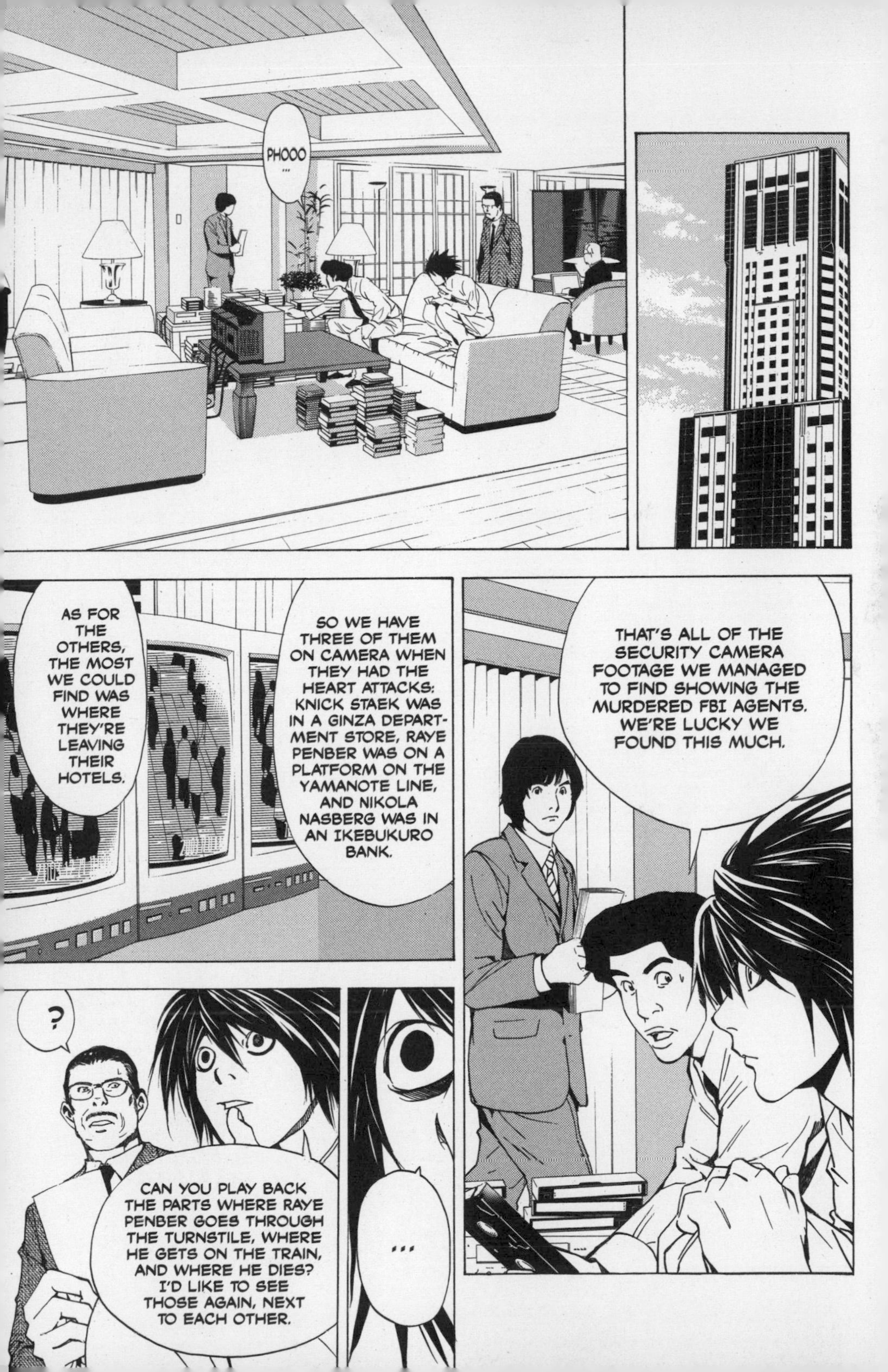
PHOOO ...
THAT'S ALL OF THE SECURITY CAMERA FOOTAGE WE MANAGED TO FIND SHOWING THE MURDERED FBI AGENTS. WE'RE LUCKY WE FOUND THIS MUCH.
SO WE HAVE THREE OF THEM ON CAMERA WHEN THEY HAD THE HEART ATTACKS: KNICK STAEK WAS IN A GINZA DEPARTMENT STORE, RAYE PENBER WAS ON A PLATFORM ON THE YAMANOTE LINE, AND NIKOLA NASBERG WAS IN AN IKEBUKURO BANK.
AS FOR THE OTHERS, THE MOST WE COULD FIND WAS WHERE THEY'RE LEAVING THEIR HOTELS.
...
?
CAN YOU PLAY BACK THE PARTS WHERE RAYE PENBER GOES THROUGH THE TURNSTILE, WHERE HE GETS ON THE TRAIN, AND WHERE HE DIES? I'D LIKE TO SEE THOSE AGAIN, NEXT TO EACH OTHER.

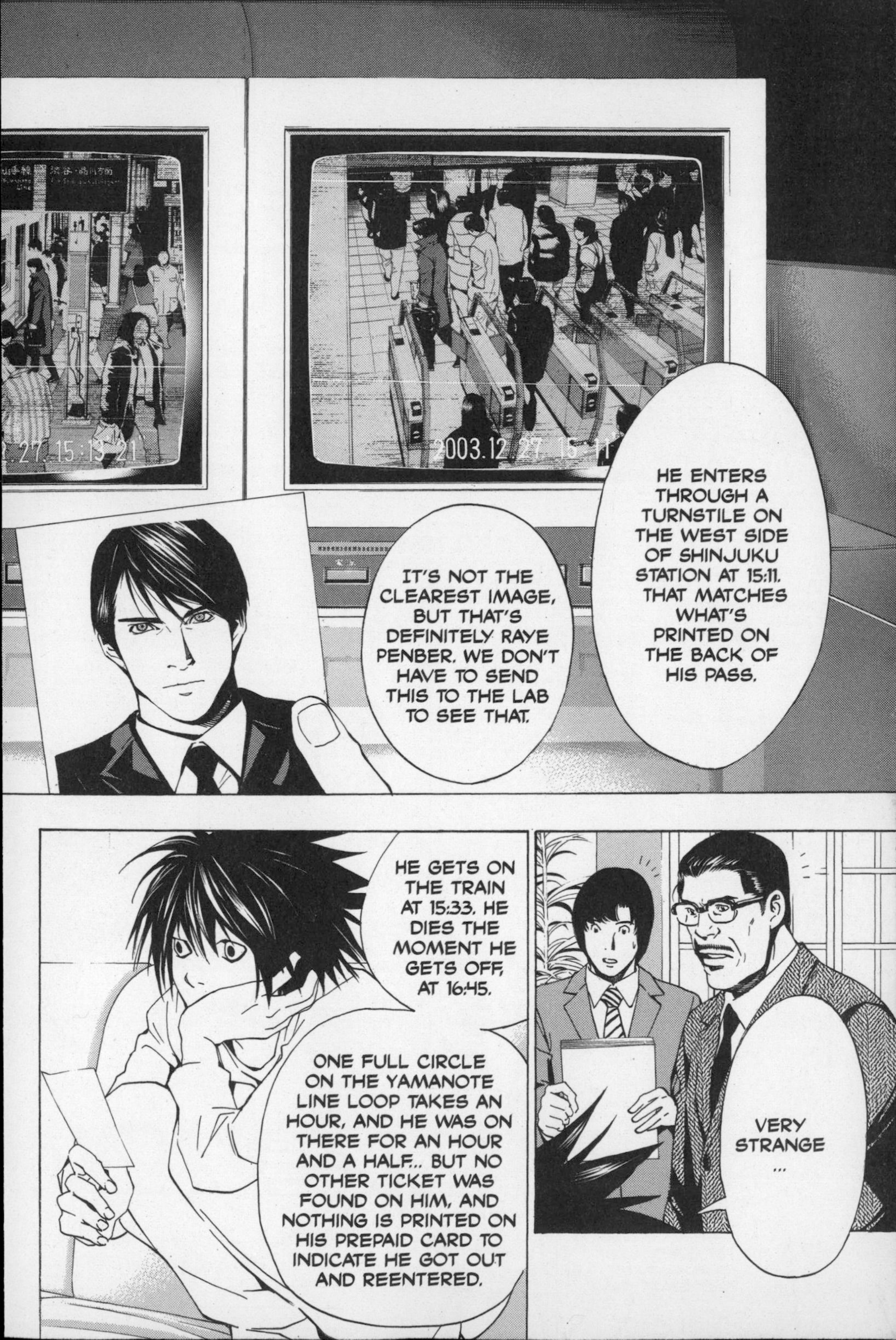
HE ENTERS THROUGH A TURNSTILE ON THE WEST SIDE OF SHINJUKU STATION AT 15:11. THAT MATCHES WHAT'S PRINTED ON THE BACK OF HIS PASS.
IT'S NOT THE CLEAREST IMAGE, BUT THAT'S DEFINITELY RAYE PENBER. WE DON'T HAVE TO SEND THIS TO THE LAB TO SEE THAT.
VERY STRANGE ...
HE GETS ON THE TRAIN AT 15:33. HE DIES THE MOMENT HE GETS OFF, AT 16:45.
ONE FULL CIRCLE ON THE YAMANOTE LINE LOOP TAKES AN HOUR, AND HE WAS ON THERE FOR AN HOUR AND A HALF... BUT NO OTHER TICKET WAS FOUND ON HIM, AND NOTHING IS PRINTED ON HIS PREPAID CARD TO INDICATE HE GOT OUT AND REENTERED.

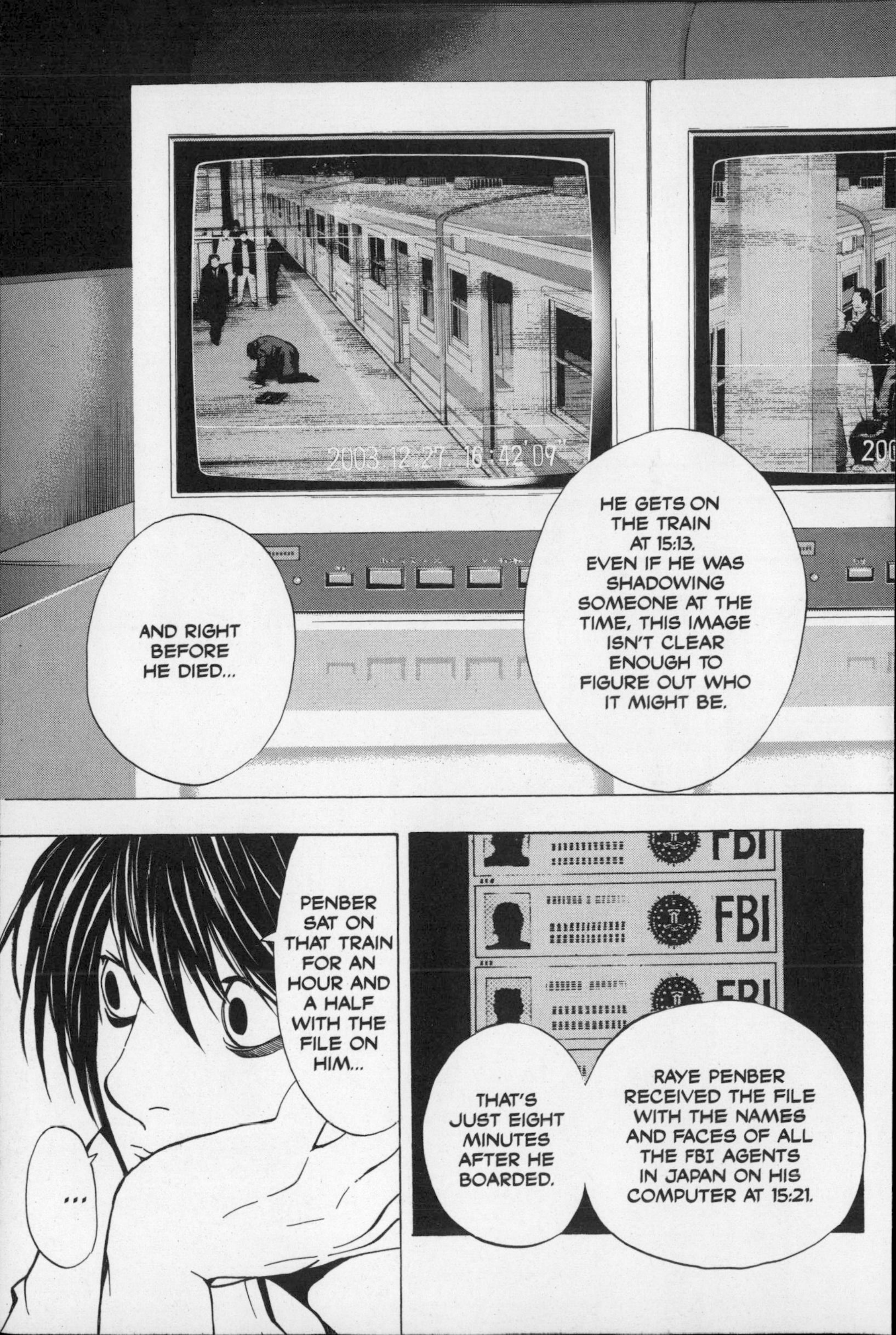
2003.12.27. 16:42'09''
HE GETS ON THE TRAIN AT 15:13. EVEN IF HE WAS SHADOWING SOMEONE AT THE TIME, THIS IMAGE ISN'T CLEAR ENOUGH TO FIGURE OUT WHO IT MIGHT BE.
AND RIGHT BEFORE HE DIED...
FBI
FBI
RAYE PENBER RECEIVED THE FILE WITH THE NAMES AND FACES OF ALL THE FBI AGENTS IN JAPAN ON HIS COMPUTER AT 15:21.
THAT'S JUST EIGHT MINUTES AFTER HE BOARDED.
PENBER SAT ON THAT TRAIN FOR AN HOUR AND A HALF WITH THE FILE ON HIM...
...

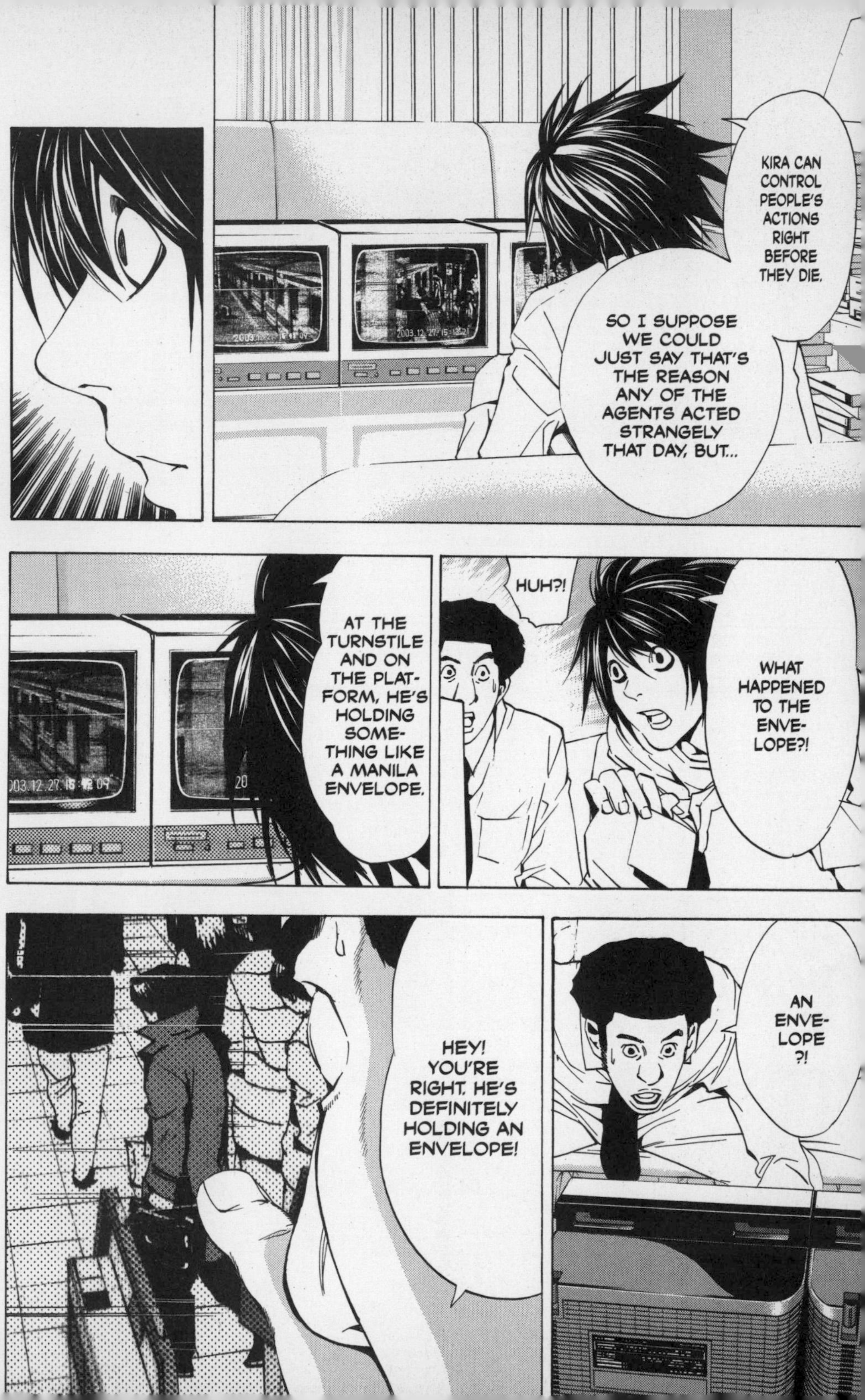
KIRA CAN CONTROL PEOPLE'S ACTIONS RIGHT BEFORE THEY DIE.
SO I SUPPOSE WE COULD JUST SAY THAT'S THE REASON ANY OF THE AGENTS ACTED STRANGELY THAT DAY, BUT...
WHAT HAPPENED TO THE ENVELOPE?!
HUH?!
AT THE TURNSTILE AND ON THE PLATFORM, HE'S HOLDING SOMETHING LIKE A MANILA ENVELOPE.
AN ENVELOPE ?!
HEY! YOU'RE RIGHT. HE'S DEFINITELY HOLDING AN ENVELOPE!

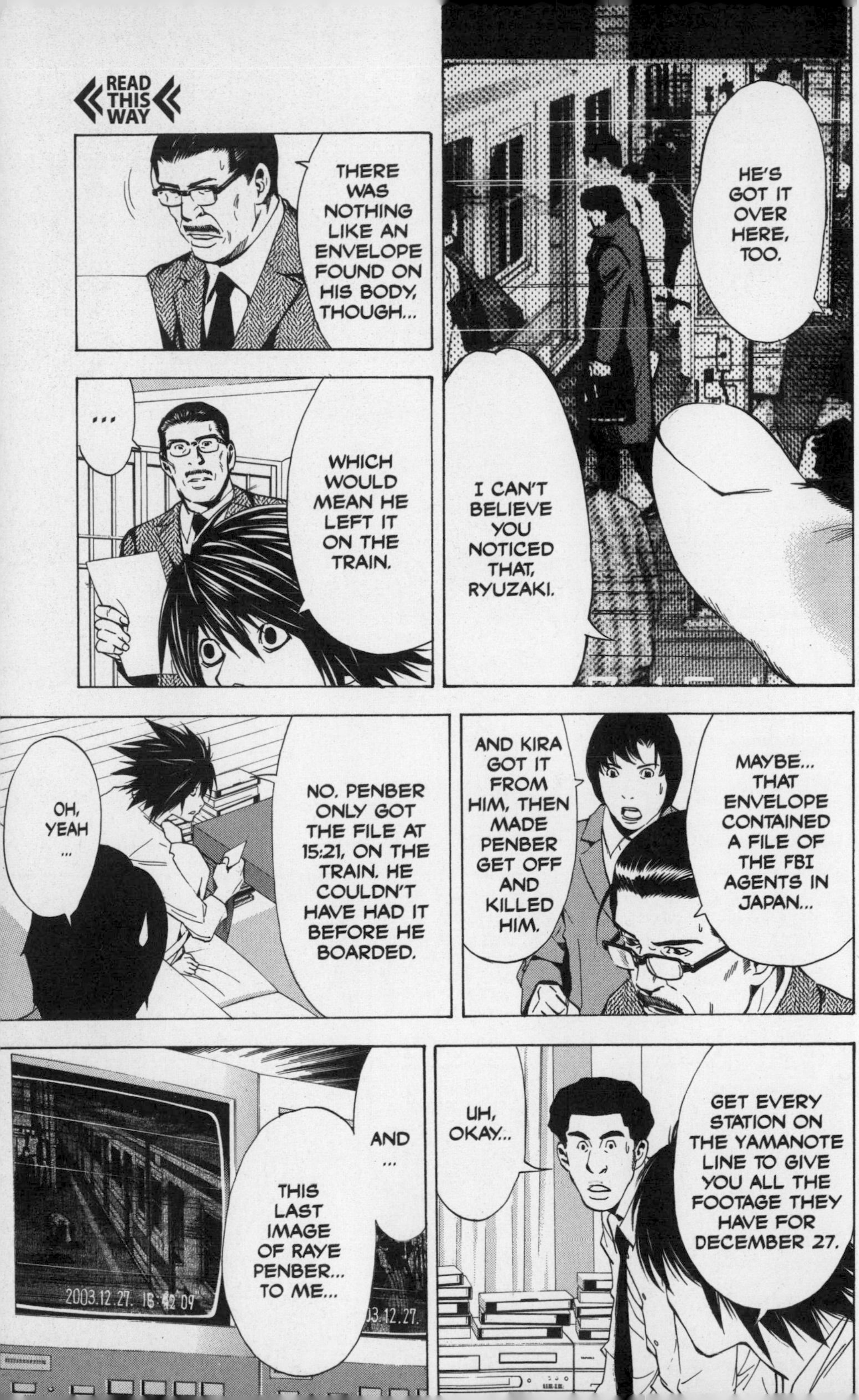
READ THIS WAY
HE'S GOT IT OVER HERE, TOO.
I CAN'T BELIEVE YOU NOTICED THAT, RYUZAKI.
THERE WAS NOTHING LIKE AN ENVELOPE FOUND ON HIS BODY, THOUGH...
WHICH WOULD MEAN HE LEFT IT ON THE TRAIN.
...
MAYBE... THAT ENVELOPE CONTAINED A FILE OF THE FBI AGENTS IN JAPAN...
AND KIRA GOT IT FROM HIM, THEN MADE PENBER GET OFF AND KILLED HIM.
NO. PENBER ONLY GOT THE FILE AT 15:21, ON THE TRAIN. HE COULDN'T HAVE HAD IT BEFORE HE BOARDED.
OH, YEAH ...
GET EVERY STATION ON THE YAMANOTE LINE TO GIVE YOU ALL THE FOOTAGE THEY HAVE FOR DECEMBER 27.
UH, OKAY...
AND ...
THIS LAST IMAGE OF RAYE PENBER... TO ME...
2003.12.27. 16:42 09
03.12.27.

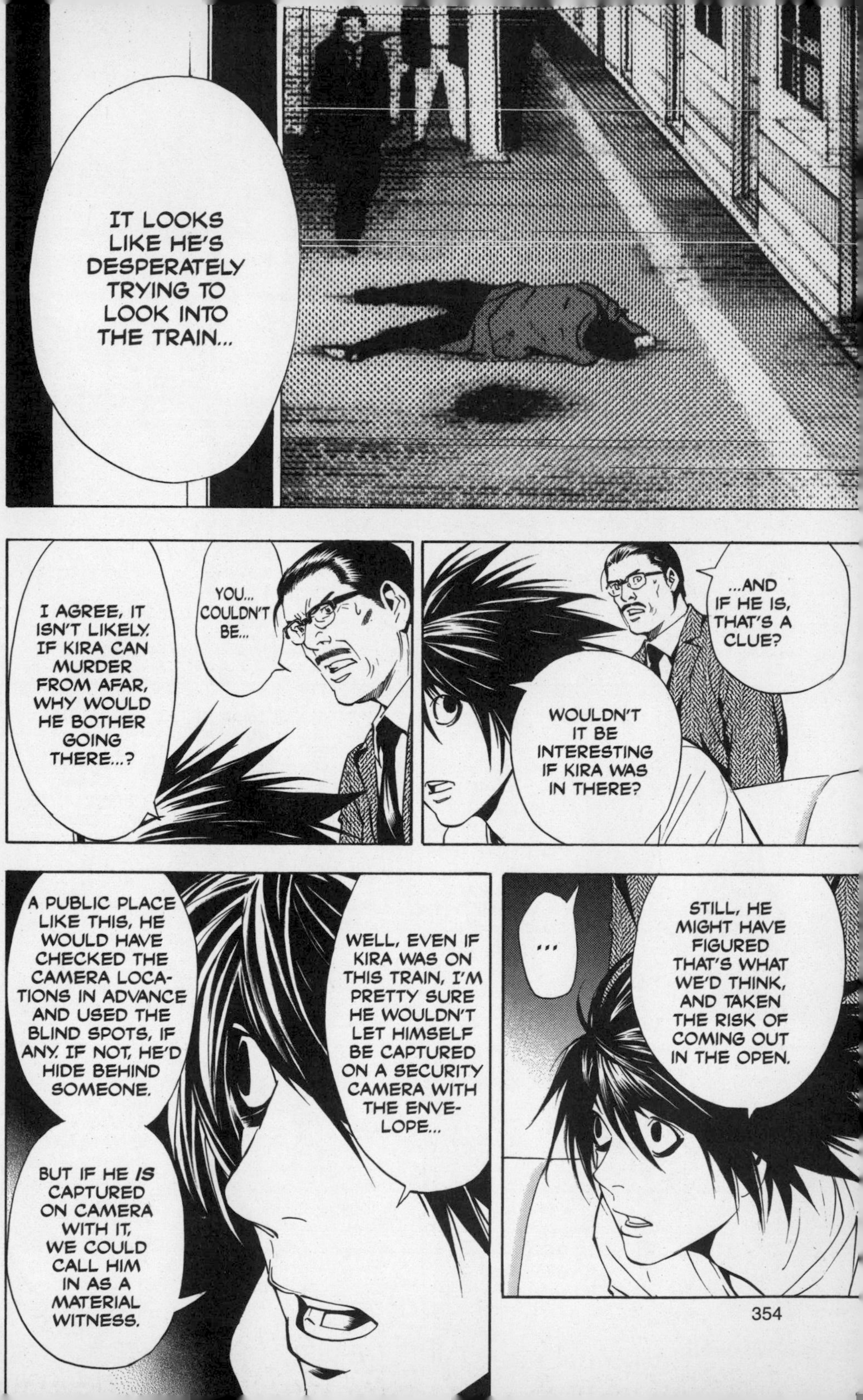
IT LOOKS LIKE HE'S DESPERATELY TRYING TO LOOK INTO THE TRAIN...
...AND IF HE IS, THAT'S A CLUE?
WOULDN'T IT BE INTERESTING IF KIRA WAS IN THERE?
YOU... COULDN'T BE...
I AGREE, IT ISN'T LIKELY. IF KIRA CAN MURDER FROM AFAR, WHY WOULD HE BOTHER GOING THERE...?
STILL, HE MIGHT HAVE FIGURED THAT'S WHAT WE'D THINK, AND TAKEN THE RISK OF COMING OUT IN THE OPEN.
...
WELL, EVEN IF KIRA WAS ON THIS TRAIN, I'M PRETTY SURE HE WOULDN'T LET HIMSELF BE CAPTURED ON A SECURITY CAMERA WITH THE ENVE-LOPE...
A PUBLIC PLACE LIKE THIS, HE WOULD HAVE CHECKED THE CAMERA LOCA-TIONS IN ADVANCE AND USED THE BLIND SPOTS, IF ANY. IF NOT, HE'D HIDE BEHIND SOMEONE.
BUT IF HE *IS* CAPTURED ON CAMERA WITH IT, WE COULD CALL HIM IN AS A MATERIAL WITNESS.

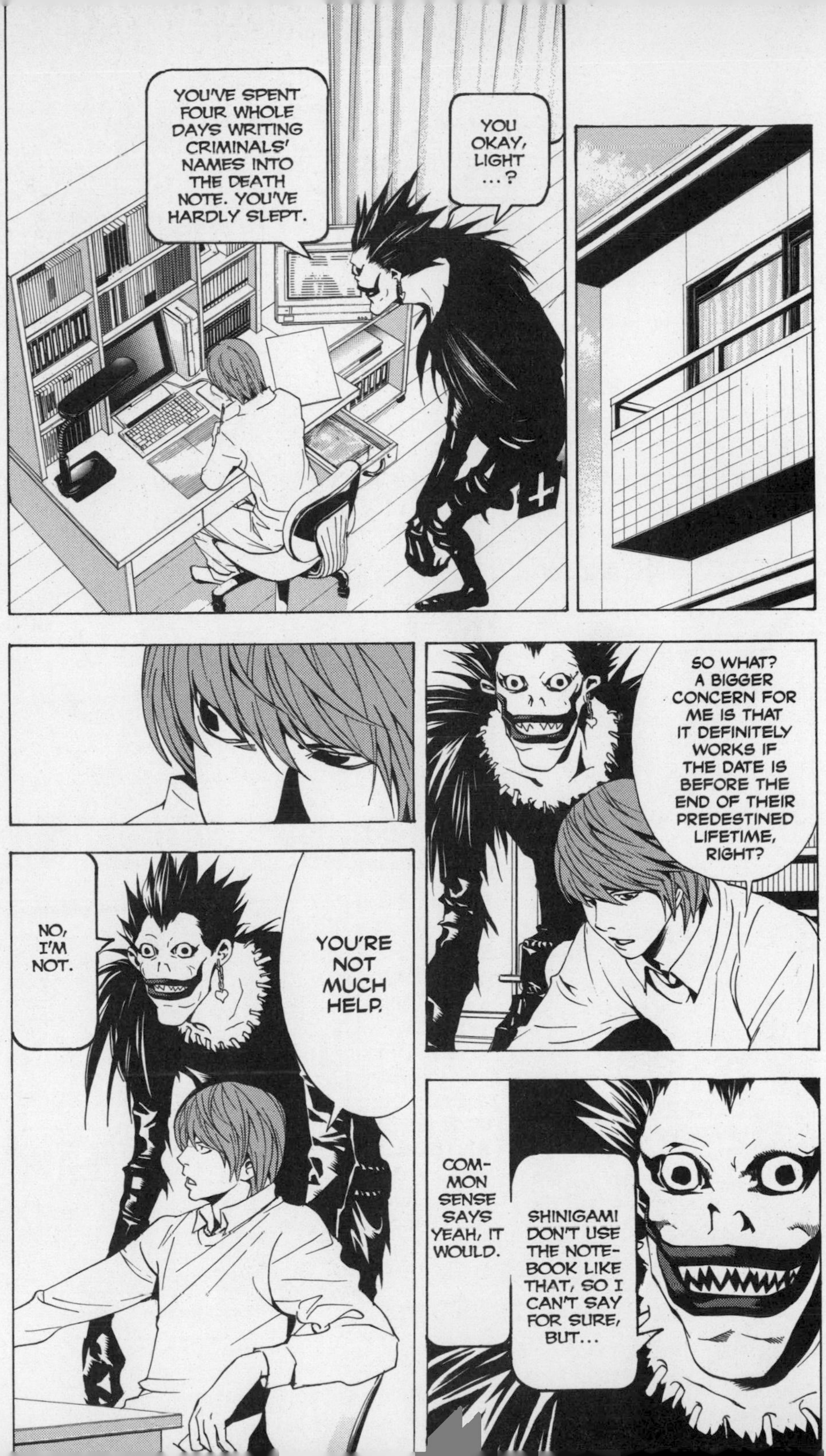
YOU OKAY, LIGHT ...?
YOU'VE SPENT FOUR WHOLE DAYS WRITING CRIMINALS' NAMES INTO THE DEATH NOTE. YOU'VE HARDLY SLEPT.
SO WHAT? A BIGGER CONCERN FOR ME IS THAT IT DEFINITELY WORKS IF THE DATE IS BEFORE THE END OF THEIR PREDESTINED LIFETIME, RIGHT?
SHINIGAMI DON'T USE THE NOTE-BOOK LIKE THAT, SO I CAN'T SAY FOR SURE, BUT...
COM-MON SENSE SAYS YEAH, IT WOULD.
YOU'RE NOT MUCH HELP.
NO, I'M NOT.

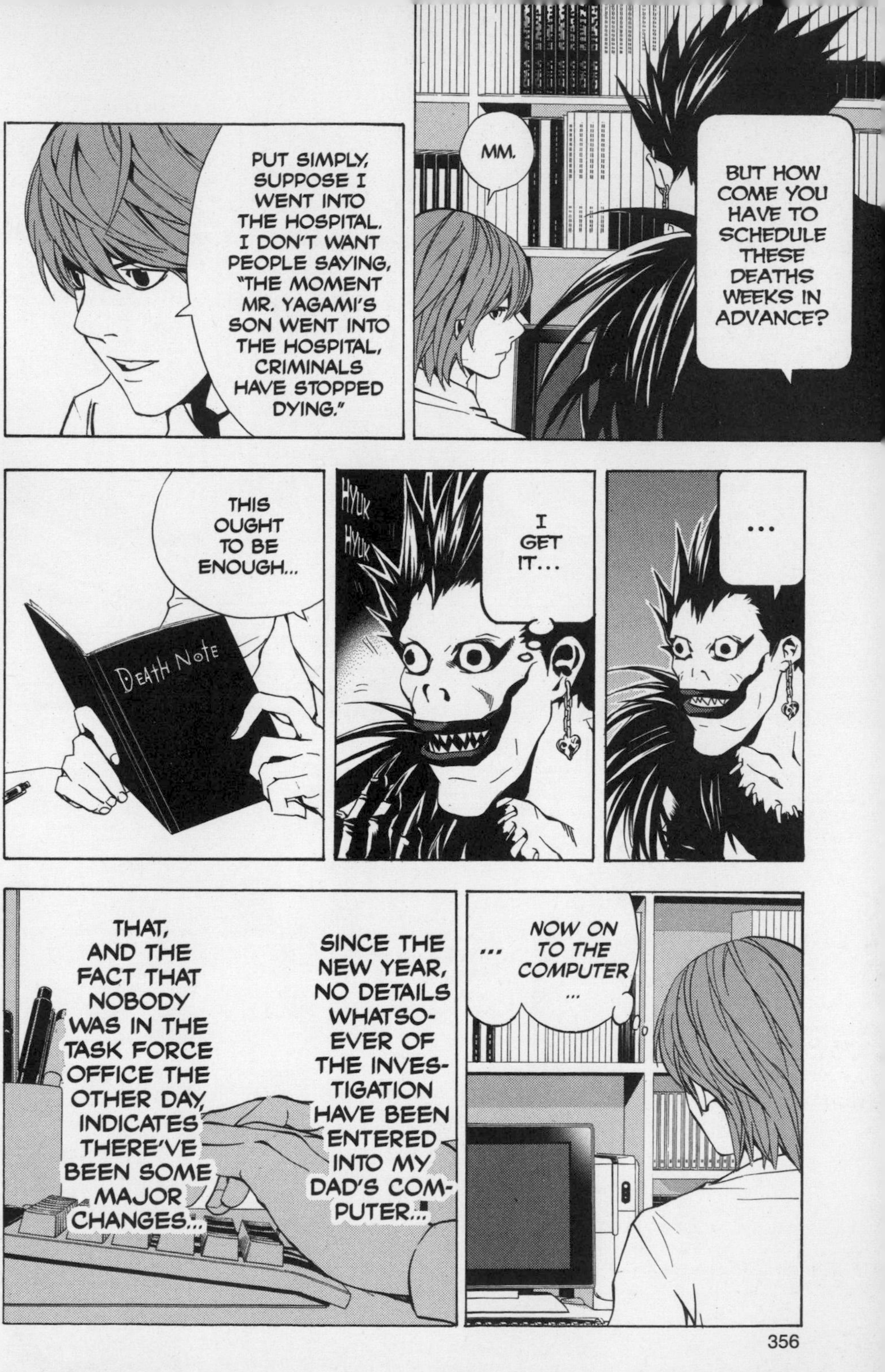
BUT HOW COME YOU HAVE TO SCHEDULE THESE DEATHS WEEKS IN ADVANCE?
MM.
PUT SIMPLY, SUPPOSE I WENT INTO THE HOSPITAL. I DON'T WANT PEOPLE SAYING, "THE MOMENT MR. YAGAMI'S SON WENT INTO THE HOSPITAL, CRIMINALS HAVE STOPPED DYING."
...
I GET IT...
HYUK HYUK
THIS OUGHT TO BE ENOUGH...
DEATH NOTE
...NOW ON TO THE COMPUTER...
SINCE THE NEW YEAR, NO DETAILS WHATSO-EVER OF THE INVES-TIGATION HAVE BEEN ENTERED INTO MY DAD'S COM-PUTER...
THAT, AND THE FACT THAT NOBODY WAS IN THE TASK FORCE OFFICE THE OTHER DAY, INDICATES THERE'VE BEEN SOME MAJOR CHANGES...

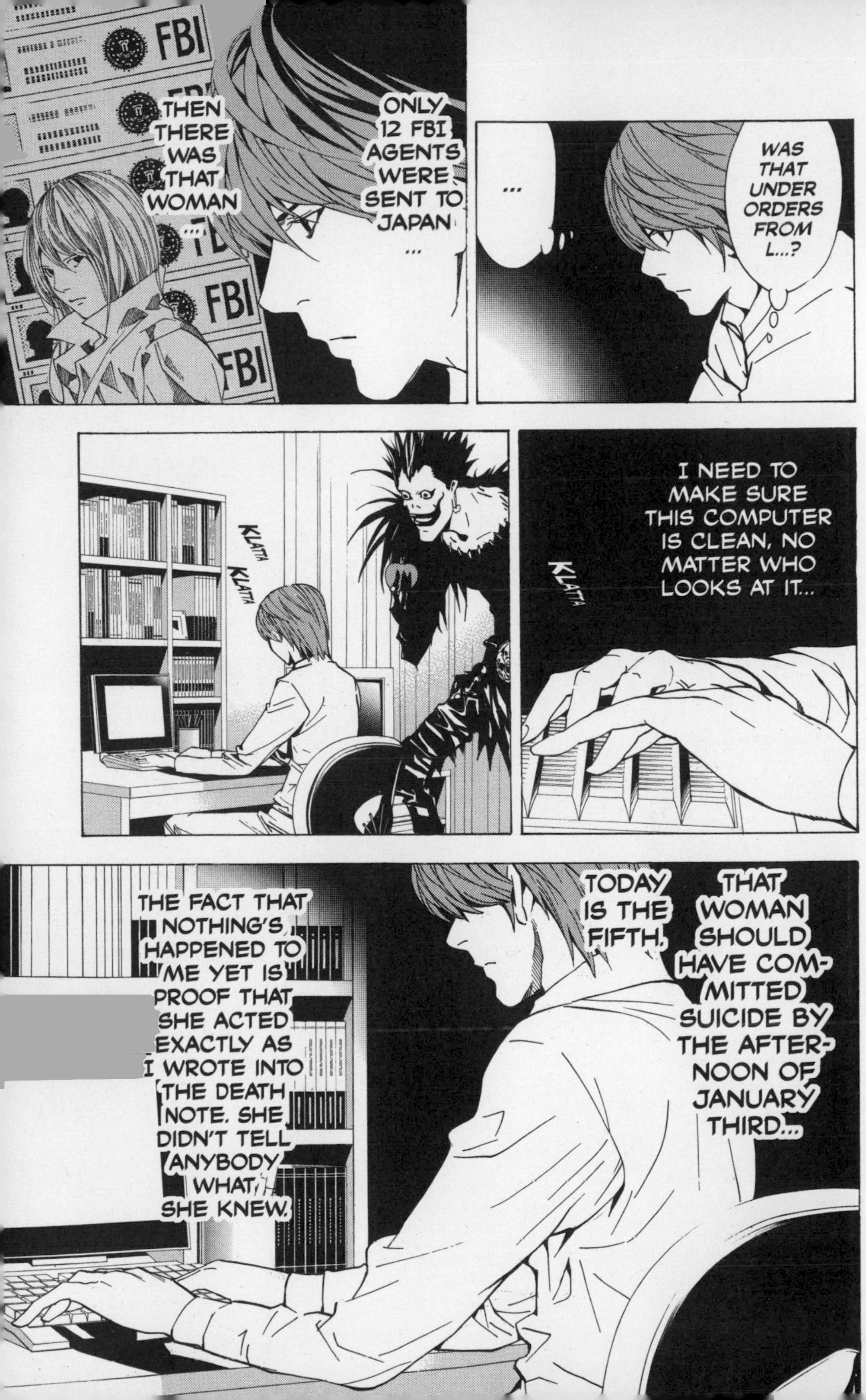
WAS THAT UNDER ORDERS FROM L...?
...
ONLY 12 FBI AGENTS WERE SENT TO JAPAN ...
THEN THERE WAS THAT WOMAN ...
FBI
I NEED TO MAKE SURE THIS COMPUTER IS CLEAN, NO MATTER WHO LOOKS AT IT...
KLATTA
KLATTA
KLATTA
THAT WOMAN SHOULD HAVE COM-MITTED SUICIDE BY THE AFTER-NOON OF JANUARY THIRD...
TODAY IS THE FIFTH.
THE FACT THAT NOTHING'S HAPPENED TO ME YET IS PROOF THAT SHE ACTED EXACTLY AS I WROTE INTO THE DEATH NOTE. SHE DIDN'T TELL ANYBODY WHAT SHE KNEW.

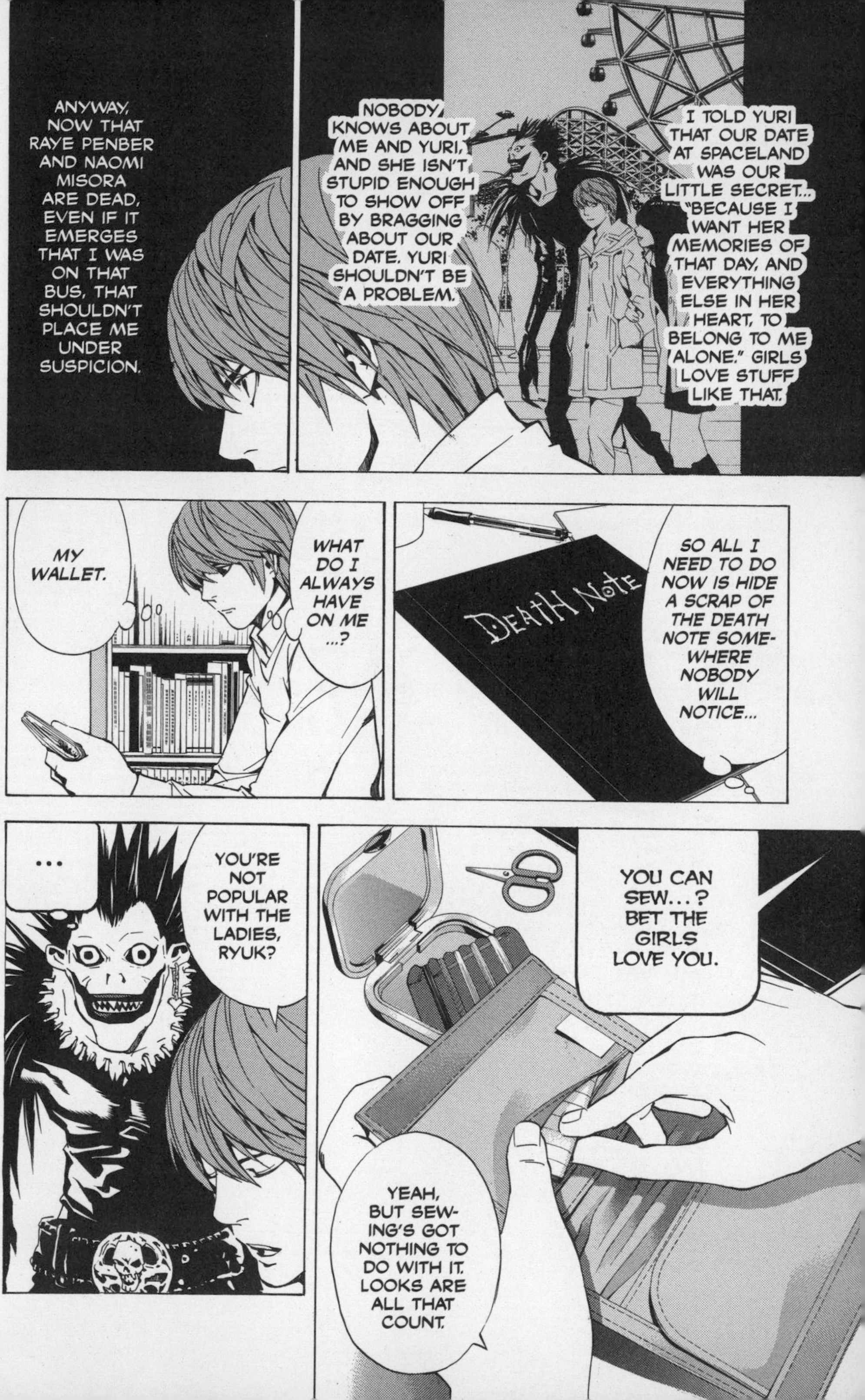
I TOLD YURI THAT OUR DATE AT SPACELAND WAS OUR LITTLE SECRET... "BECAUSE I WANT HER MEMORIES OF THAT DAY, AND EVERYTHING ELSE IN HER HEART, TO BELONG TO ME ALONE." GIRLS LOVE STUFF LIKE THAT.
NOBODY KNOWS ABOUT ME AND YURI, AND SHE ISN'T STUPID ENOUGH TO SHOW OFF BY BRAGGING ABOUT OUR DATE. YURI SHOULDN'T BE A PROBLEM.
ANYWAY, NOW THAT RAYE PENBER AND NAOMI MISORA ARE DEAD, EVEN IF IT EMERGES THAT I WAS ON THAT BUS, THAT SHOULDN'T PLACE ME UNDER SUSPICION.
SO ALL I NEED TO DO NOW IS HIDE A SCRAP OF THE DEATH NOTE SOME-WHERE NOBODY WILL NOTICE...
DEATH NOTE
WHAT DO I ALWAYS HAVE ON ME ...?
MY WALLET.
YOU CAN SEW...? BET THE GIRLS LOVE YOU.
YEAH, BUT SEW-ING'S GOT NOTHING TO DO WITH IT. LOOKS ARE ALL THAT COUNT.
YOU'RE NOT POPULAR WITH THE LADIES, RYUK?
...

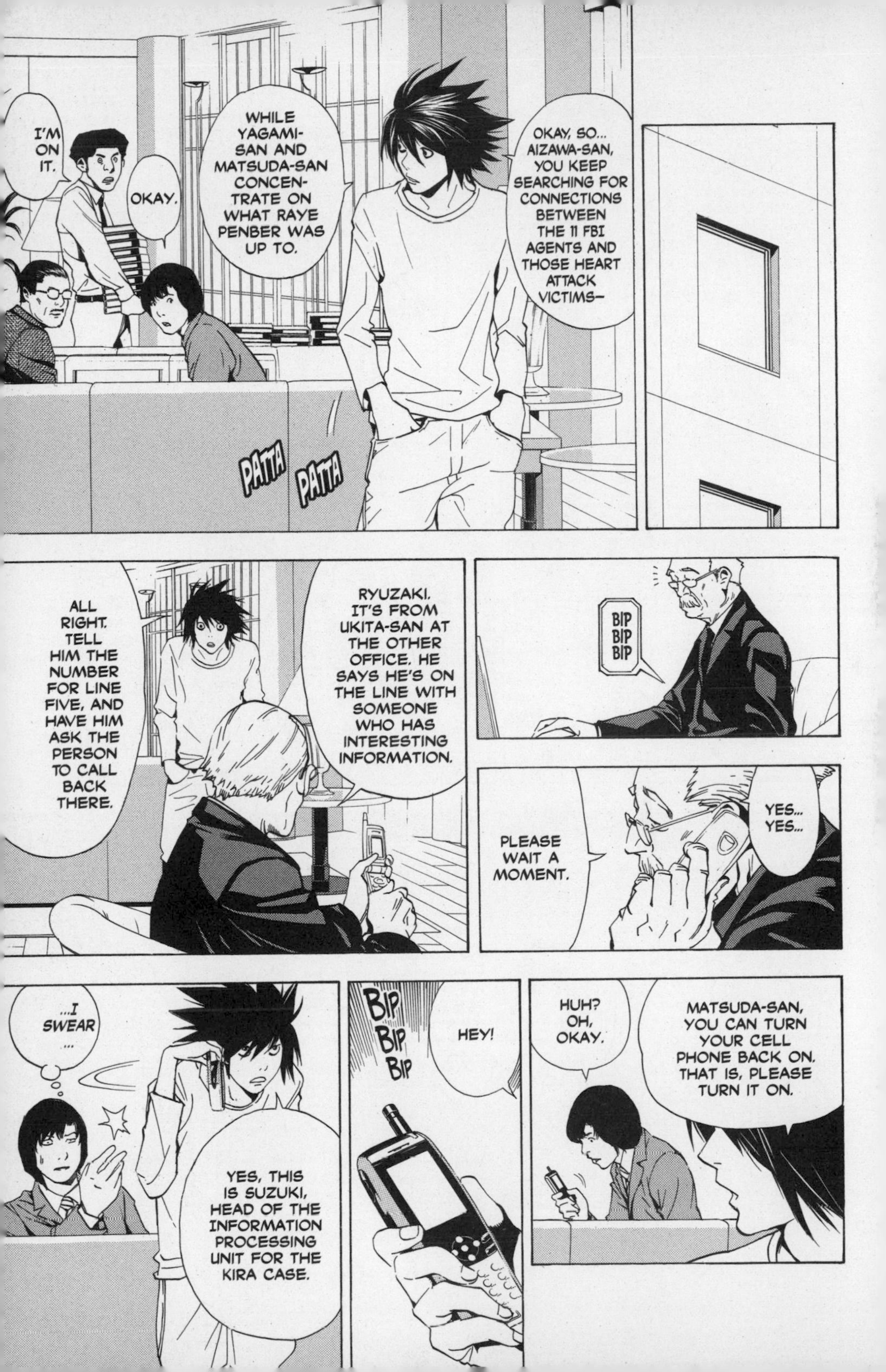
OKAY, SO... AIZAWA-SAN, YOU KEEP SEARCHING FOR CONNECTIONS BETWEEN THE 11 FBI AGENTS AND THOSE HEART ATTACK VICTIMS—
WHILE YAGAMI-SAN AND MATSUDA-SAN CONCENTRATE ON WHAT RAYE PENBER WAS UP TO.
OKAY.
I'M ON IT.
PATTA
PATTA
BIP BIP BIP
YES... YES...
PLEASE WAIT A MOMENT.
RYUZAKI. IT'S FROM UKITA-SAN AT THE OTHER OFFICE. HE SAYS HE'S ON THE LINE WITH SOMEONE WHO HAS INTERESTING INFORMATION.
ALL RIGHT. TELL HIM THE NUMBER FOR LINE FIVE, AND HAVE HIM ASK THE PERSON TO CALL BACK THERE.
MATSUDA-SAN, YOU CAN TURN YOUR CELL PHONE BACK ON. THAT IS, PLEASE TURN IT ON.
HUH? OH, OKAY.
HEY!
BIP BIP BIP
YES, THIS IS SUZUKI, HEAD OF THE INFORMATION PROCESSING UNIT FOR THE KIRA CASE.
...I SWEAR ...

THEY CAME TO JAPAN IN MID-DECEMBER AND WERE GOING TO COME VISIT US OVER THE NEW YEAR...

YES. OUR DAUGHTER, NAOMI MISORA, WAS ENGAGED TO BE MARRIED TO RAYE PENBER.

RAYE PENBER'S FIANCÉE?!

KLATTA KLATTA KLATTA

GLANCE

NAOMI MISORA? I'VE HEARD THAT NAME BEFORE.

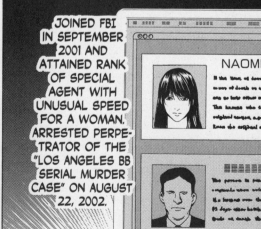

JOINED FBI IN SEPTEMBER 2001 AND ATTAINED RANK OF SPECIAL AGENT WITH UNUSUAL SPEED FOR A WOMAN. ARRESTED PERPETRATOR OF THE "LOS ANGELES BB SERIAL MURDER CASE" ON AUGUST 22, 2002.

NAOMI MISORA

KLIK

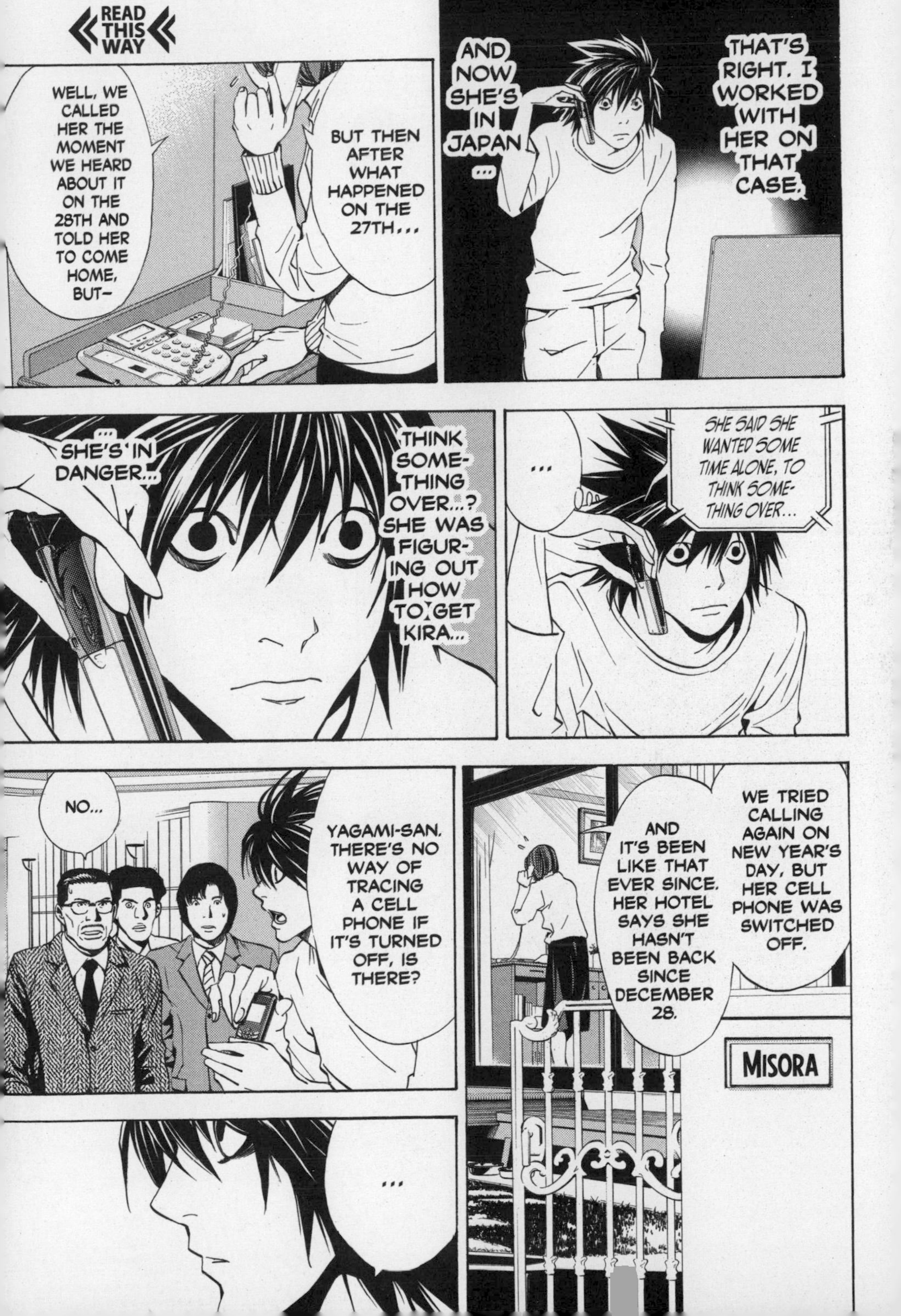
READ THIS WAY
THAT'S RIGHT. I WORKED WITH HER ON THAT CASE.
AND NOW SHE'S IN JAPAN...
BUT THEN AFTER WHAT HAPPENED ON THE 27TH...
WELL, WE CALLED HER THE MOMENT WE HEARD ABOUT IT ON THE 28TH AND TOLD HER TO COME HOME, BUT–
SHE SAID SHE WANTED SOME TIME ALONE, TO THINK SOME-THING OVER...
...
THINK SOME-THING OVER...? SHE WAS FIGUR-ING OUT HOW TO GET KIRA...
...SHE'S IN DANGER...
WE TRIED CALLING AGAIN ON NEW YEAR'S DAY, BUT HER CELL PHONE WAS SWITCHED OFF.
AND IT'S BEEN LIKE THAT EVER SINCE. HER HOTEL SAYS SHE HASN'T BEEN BACK SINCE DECEMBER 28.
MISORA
YAGAMI-SAN. THERE'S NO WAY OF TRACING A CELL PHONE IF IT'S TURNED OFF, IS THERE?
NO...
...

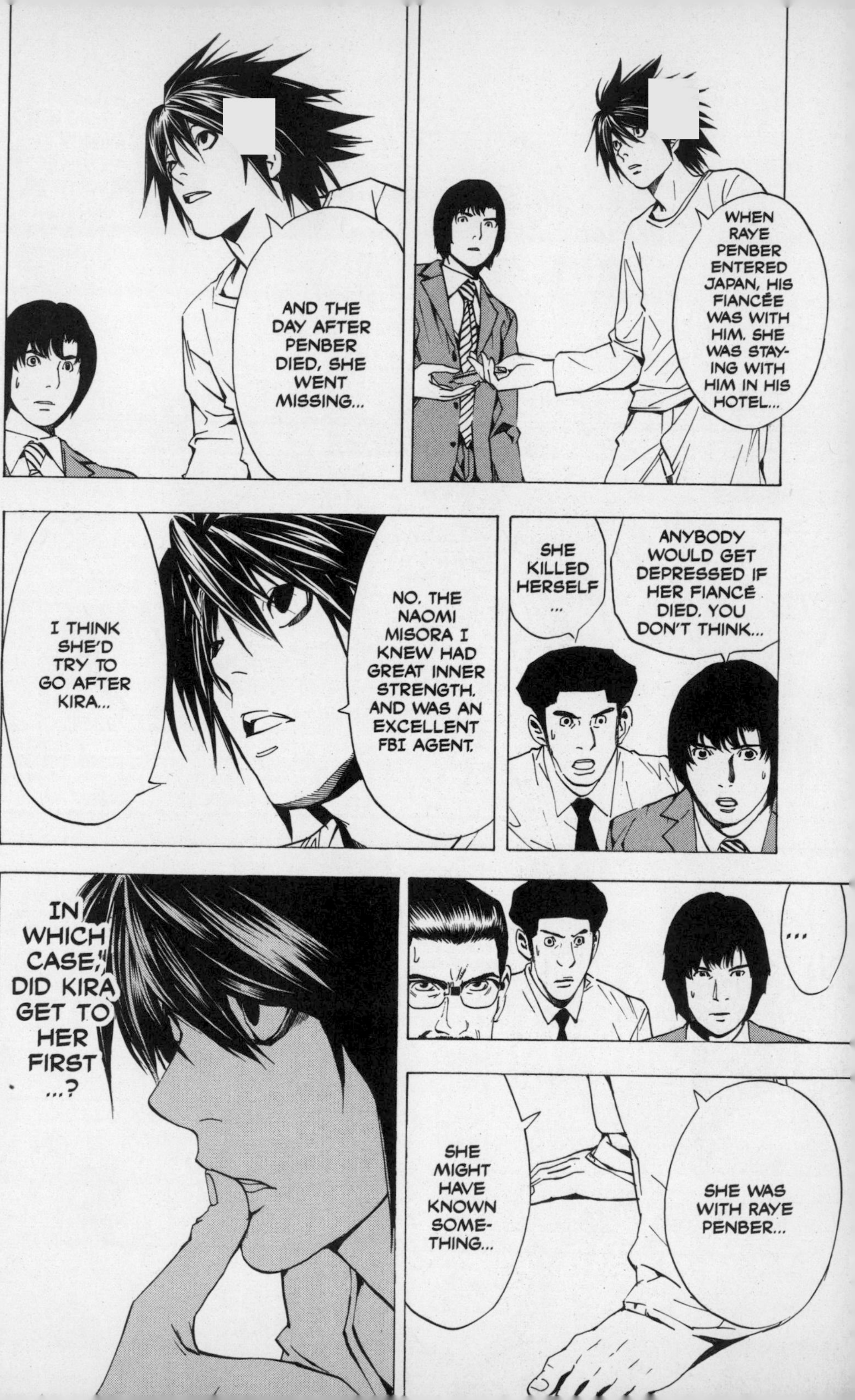
WHEN RAYE PENBER ENTERED JAPAN, HIS FIANCÉE WAS WITH HIM. SHE WAS STAYING WITH HIM IN HIS HOTEL...
AND THE DAY AFTER PENBER DIED, SHE WENT MISSING...
ANYBODY WOULD GET DEPRESSED IF HER FIANCÉ DIED. YOU DON'T THINK...
SHE KILLED HERSELF ...
NO. THE NAOMI MISORA I KNEW HAD GREAT INNER STRENGTH, AND WAS AN EXCELLENT FBI AGENT.
I THINK SHE'D TRY TO GO AFTER KIRA...
...
SHE WAS WITH RAYE PENBER...
SHE MIGHT HAVE KNOWN SOMETHING...
IN WHICH CASE, DID KIRA GET TO HER FIRST ...?

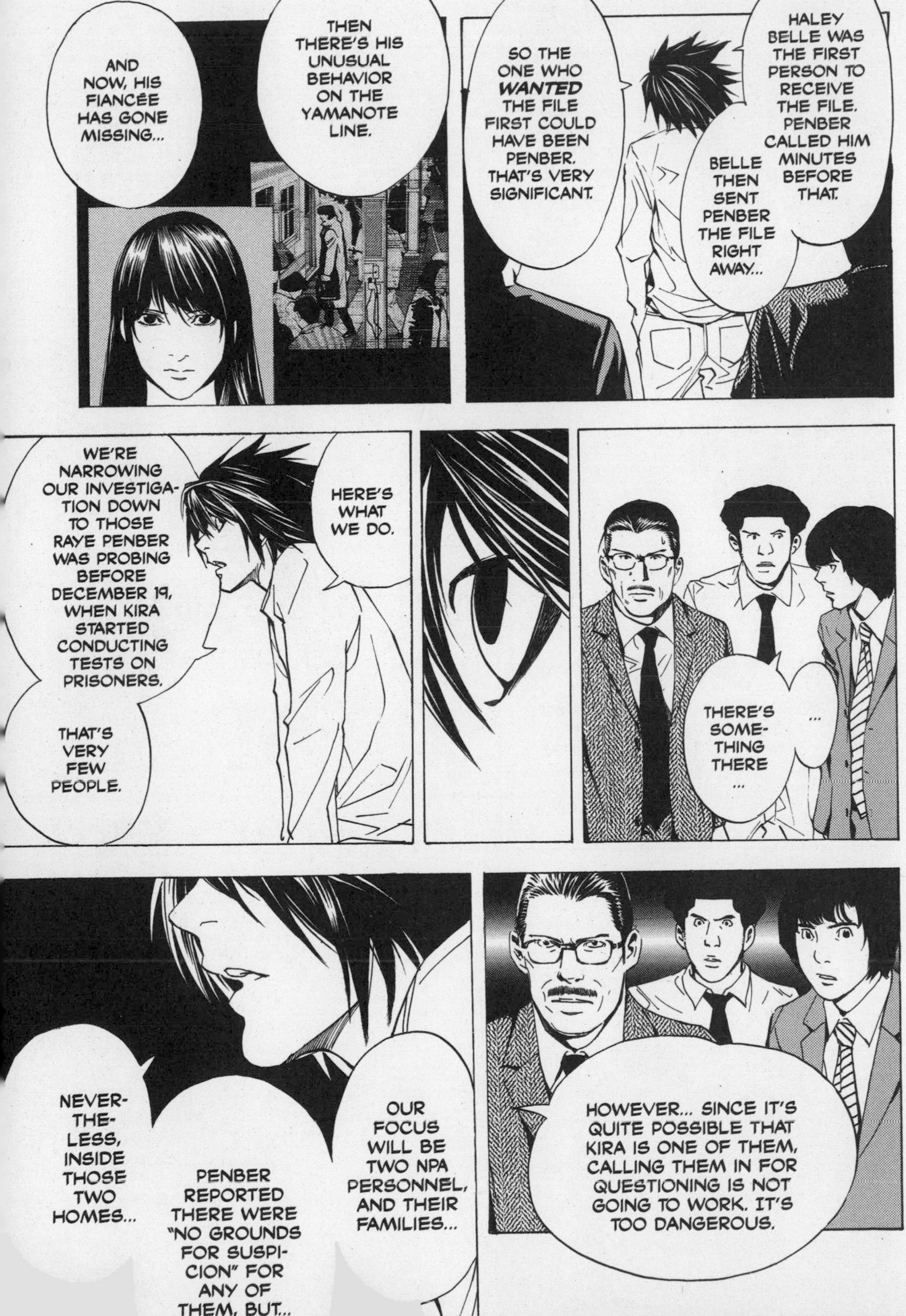
HALEY BELLE WAS THE FIRST PERSON TO RECEIVE THE FILE. PENBER CALLED HIM MINUTES BEFORE THAT.
BELLE THEN SENT PENBER THE FILE RIGHT AWAY...
SO THE ONE WHO ***WANTED*** THE FILE FIRST COULD HAVE BEEN PENBER. THAT'S VERY SIGNIFICANT.
THEN THERE'S HIS UNUSUAL BEHAVIOR ON THE YAMANOTE LINE.
AND NOW, HIS FIANCÉE HAS GONE MISSING...
...
THERE'S SOMETHING THERE...
HERE'S WHAT WE DO.
WE'RE NARROWING OUR INVESTIGATION DOWN TO THOSE RAYE PENBER WAS PROBING BEFORE DECEMBER 19, WHEN KIRA STARTED CONDUCTING TESTS ON PRISONERS.
THAT'S VERY FEW PEOPLE.
HOWEVER... SINCE IT'S QUITE POSSIBLE THAT KIRA IS ONE OF THEM, CALLING THEM IN FOR QUESTIONING IS NOT GOING TO WORK. IT'S TOO DANGEROUS.
OUR FOCUS WILL BE TWO NPA PERSONNEL, AND THEIR FAMILIES...
PENBER REPORTED THERE WERE "NO GROUNDS FOR SUSPICION" FOR ANY OF THEM, BUT...
NEVERTHELESS, INSIDE THOSE TWO HOMES...

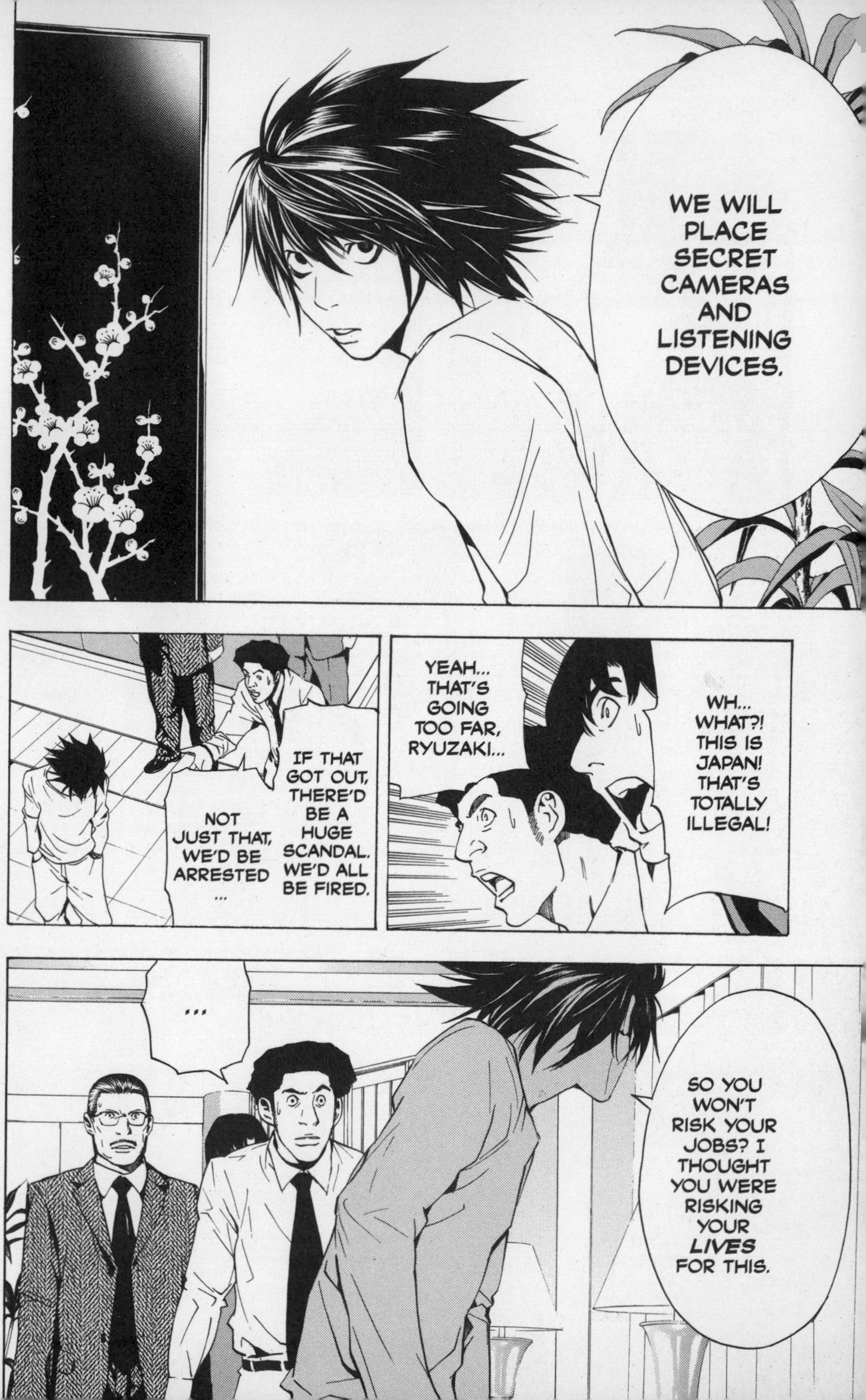
WE WILL PLACE SECRET CAMERAS AND LISTENING DEVICES.
WH... WHAT?! THIS IS JAPAN! THAT'S TOTALLY ILLEGAL!
YEAH... THAT'S GOING TOO FAR, RYUZAKI...
IF THAT GOT OUT, THERE'D BE A HUGE SCANDAL. WE'D ALL BE FIRED.
NOT JUST THAT, WE'D BE ARRESTED ...
SO YOU WON'T RISK YOUR JOBS? I THOUGHT YOU WERE RISKING YOUR *LIVES* FOR THIS.
...

READ THIS WAY

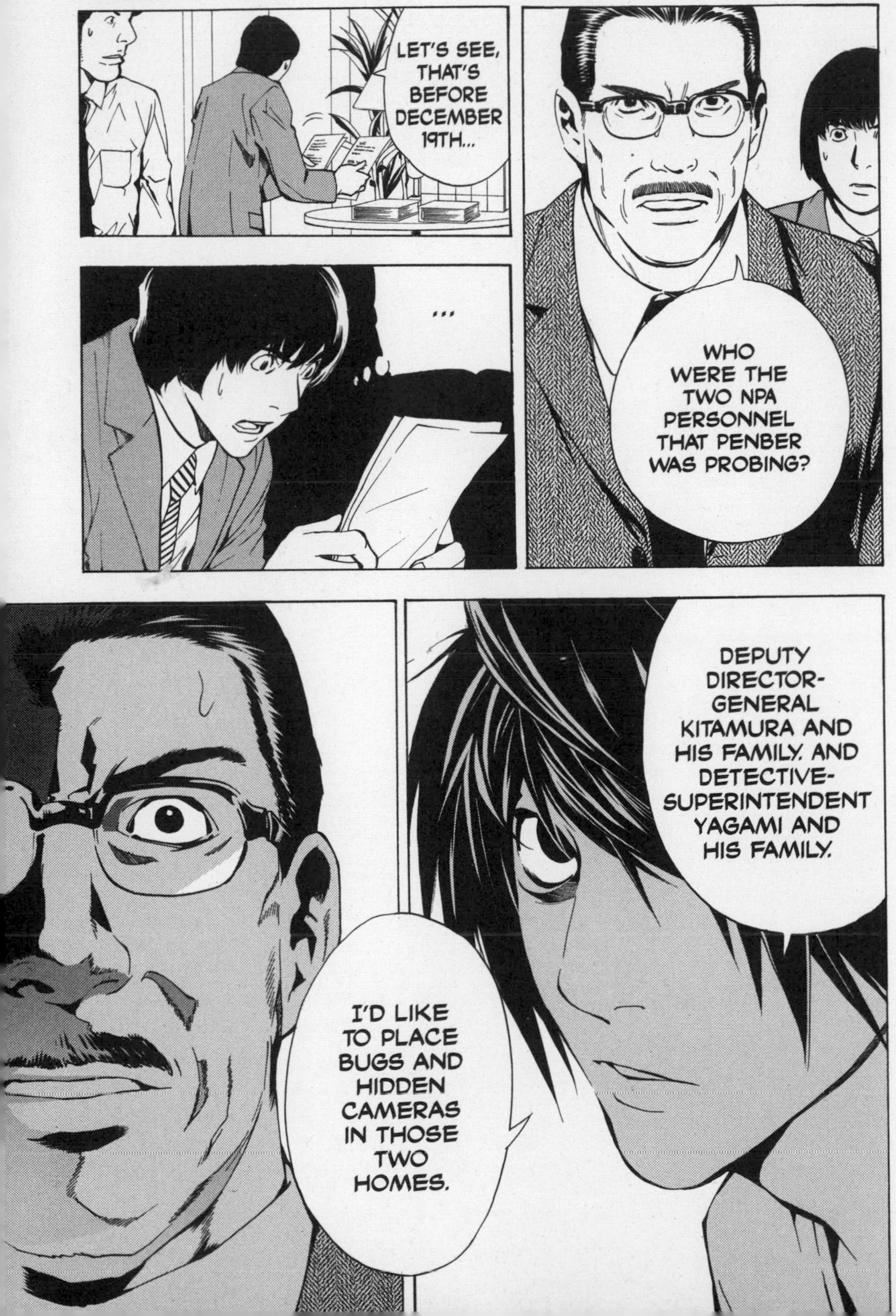
WHO WERE THE TWO NPA PERSONNEL THAT PENBER WAS PROBING?
LET'S SEE, THAT'S BEFORE DECEMBER 19TH...
...
DEPUTY DIRECTOR-GENERAL KITAMURA AND HIS FAMILY. AND DETECTIVE-SUPERINTENDENT YAGAMI AND HIS FAMILY.
I'D LIKE TO PLACE BUGS AND HIDDEN CAMERAS IN THOSE TWO HOMES.

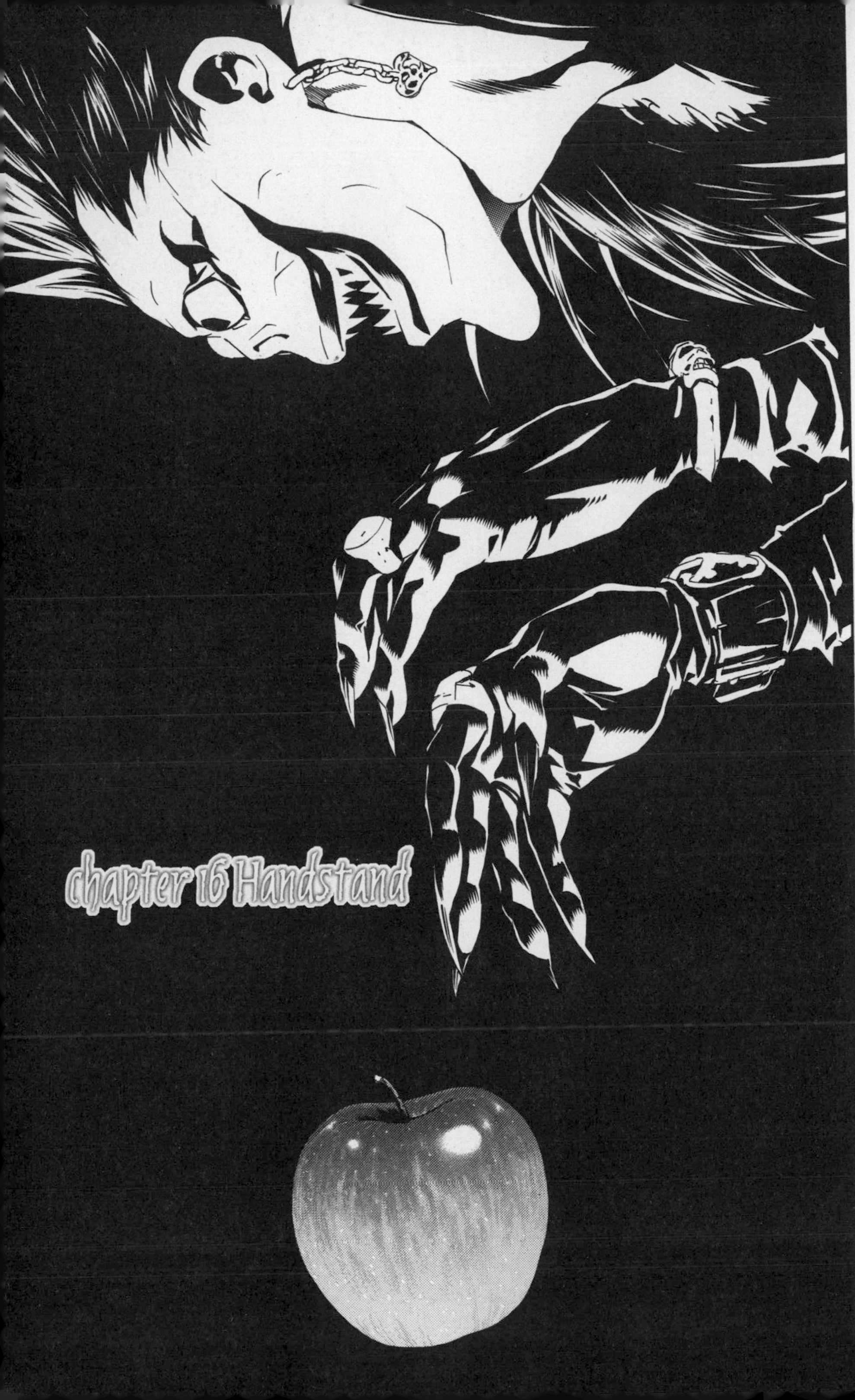
chapter 16 Handstand

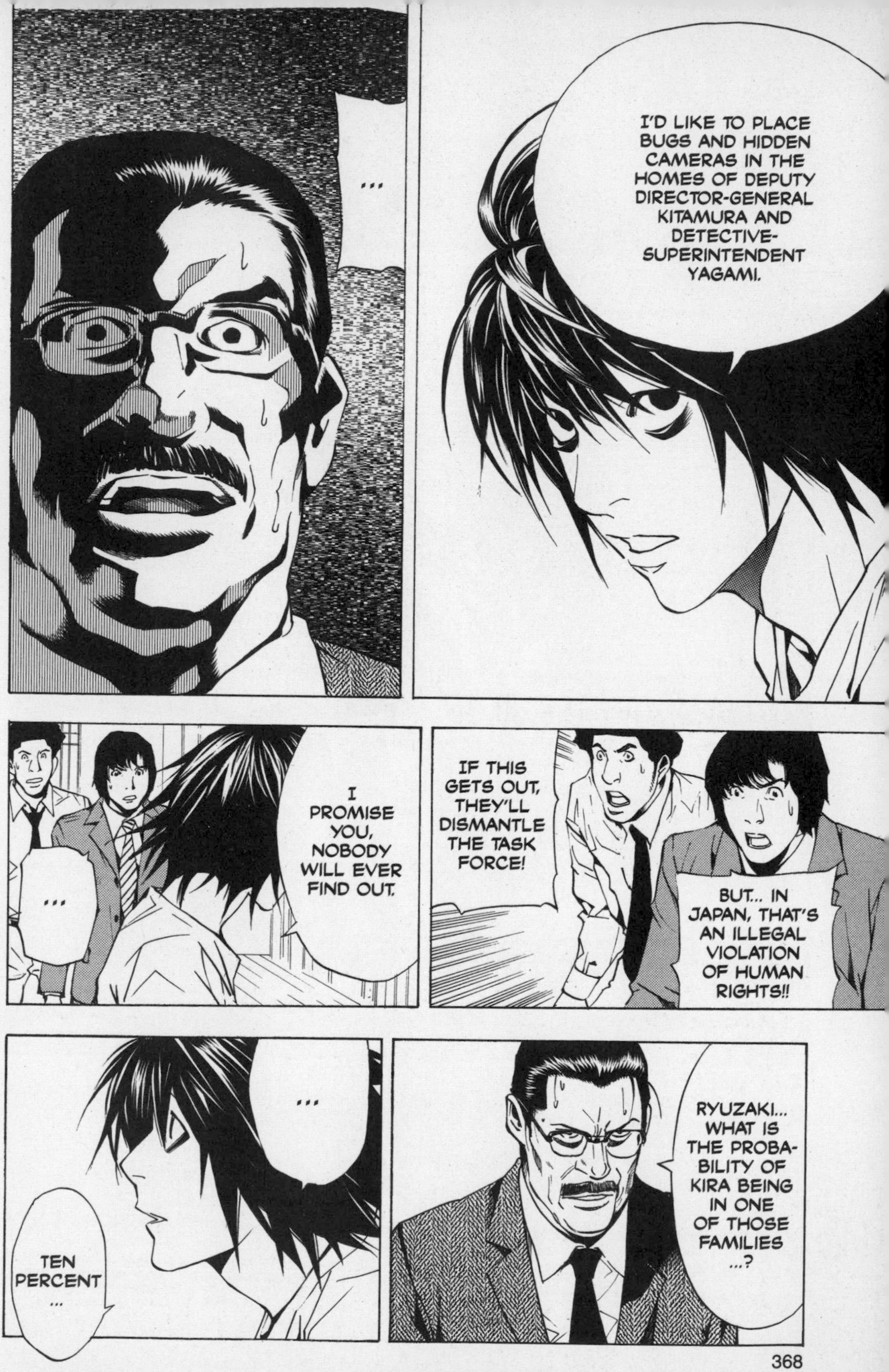
I'D LIKE TO PLACE BUGS AND HIDDEN CAMERAS IN THE HOMES OF DEPUTY DIRECTOR-GENERAL KITAMURA AND DETECTIVE-SUPERINTENDENT YAGAMI.
...
BUT... IN JAPAN, THAT'S AN ILLEGAL VIOLATION OF HUMAN RIGHTS!!
IF THIS GETS OUT, THEY'LL DISMANTLE THE TASK FORCE!
I PROMISE YOU, NOBODY WILL EVER FIND OUT.
...
RYUZAKI... WHAT IS THE PROBA-BILITY OF KIRA BEING IN ONE OF THOSE FAMILIES ...?
...
TEN PERCENT ...

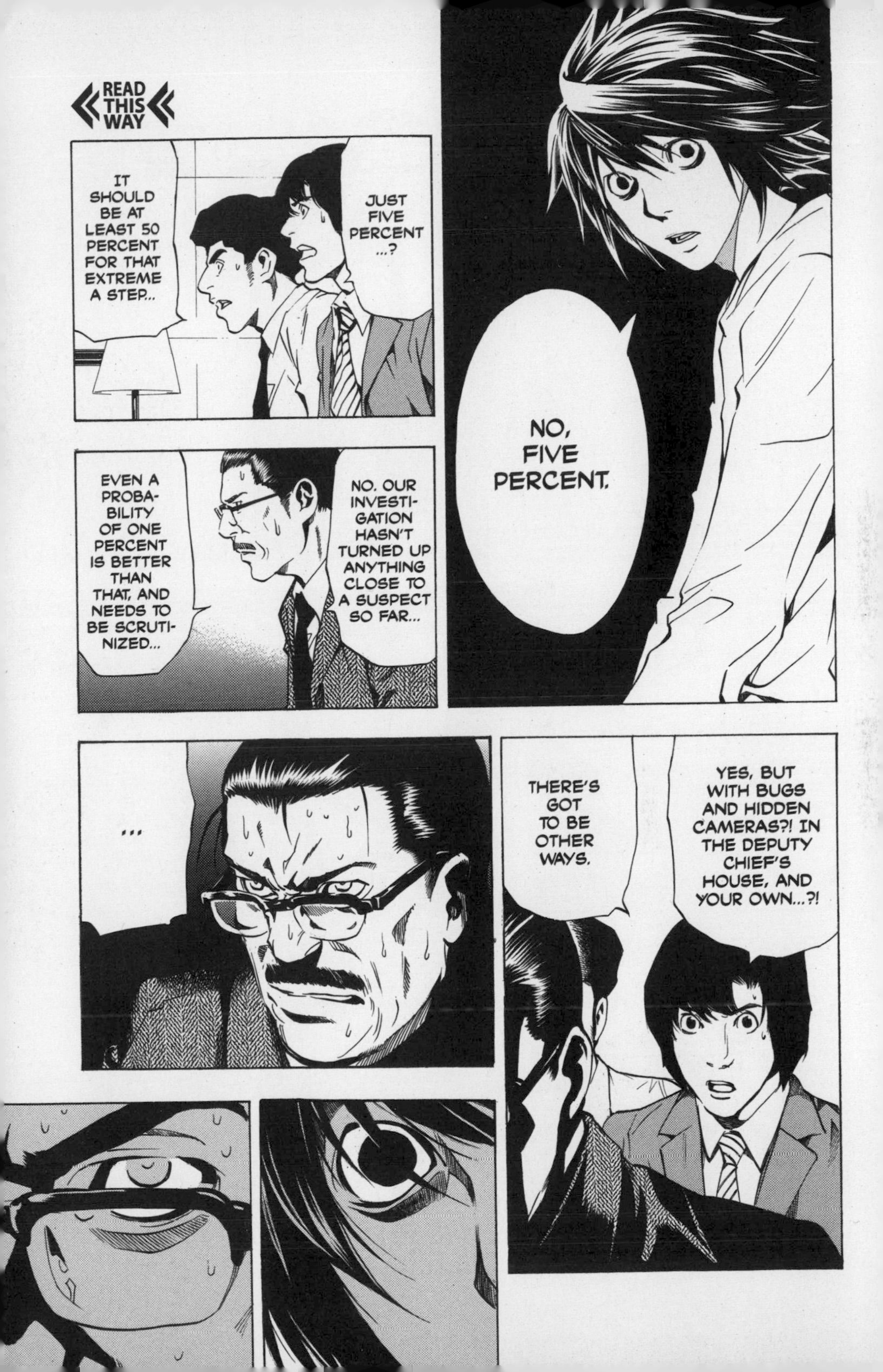
READ THIS WAY
NO, FIVE PERCENT.
JUST FIVE PERCENT ...?
IT SHOULD BE AT LEAST 50 PERCENT FOR THAT EXTREME A STEP...
NO. OUR INVESTIGATION HASN'T TURNED UP ANYTHING CLOSE TO A SUSPECT SO FAR...
EVEN A PROBABILITY OF ONE PERCENT IS BETTER THAN THAT, AND NEEDS TO BE SCRUTINIZED...
YES, BUT WITH BUGS AND HIDDEN CAMERAS?! IN THE DEPUTY CHIEF'S HOUSE, AND YOUR OWN...?!
THERE'S GOT TO BE OTHER WAYS.
...

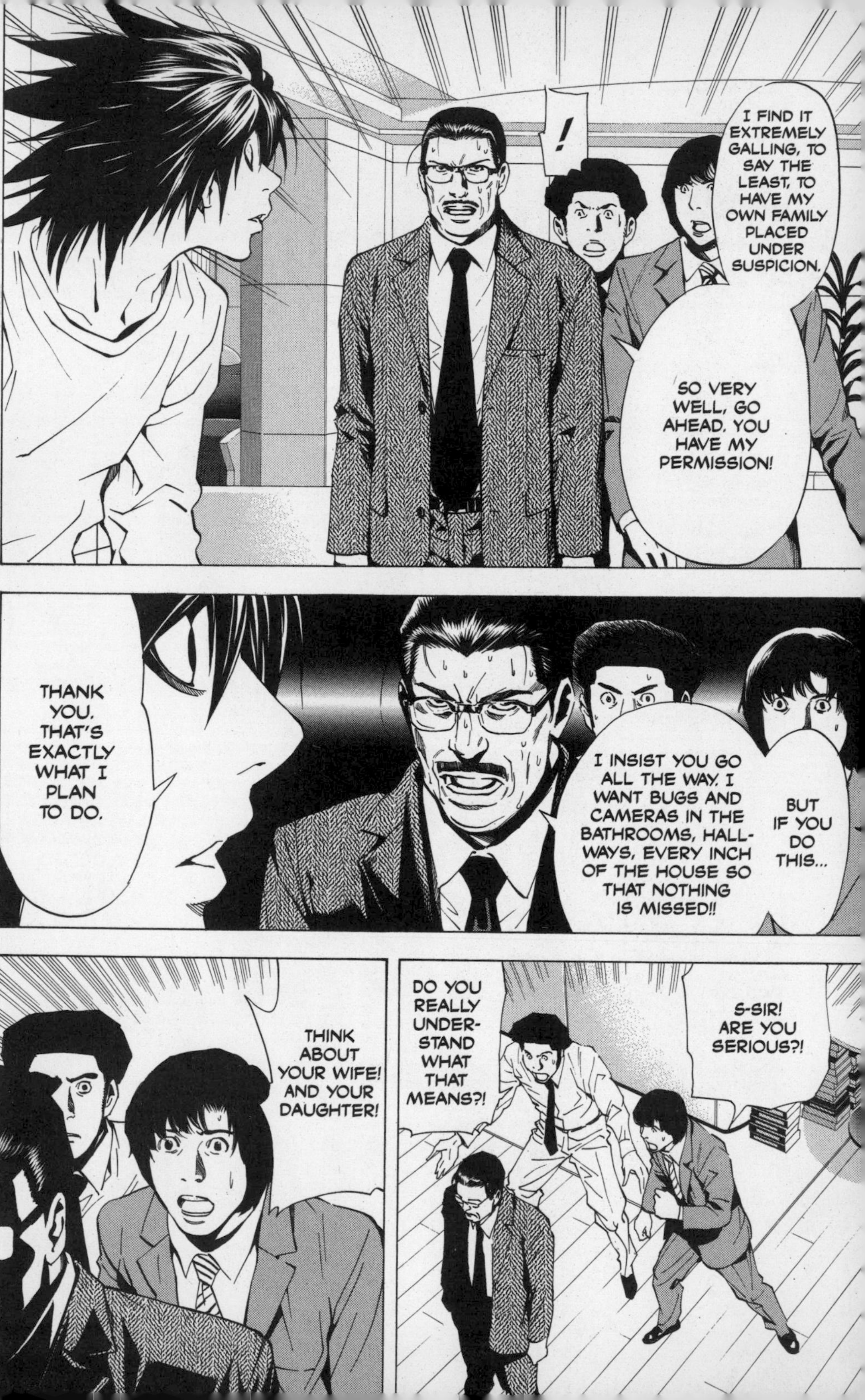
I FIND IT EXTREMELY GALLING, TO SAY THE LEAST, TO HAVE MY OWN FAMILY PLACED UNDER SUSPICION.
!
SO VERY WELL, GO AHEAD. YOU HAVE MY PERMISSION!
BUT IF YOU DO THIS...
I INSIST YOU GO ALL THE WAY. I WANT BUGS AND CAMERAS IN THE BATHROOMS, HALL-WAYS, EVERY INCH OF THE HOUSE SO THAT NOTHING IS MISSED!!
THANK YOU. THAT'S EXACTLY WHAT I PLAN TO DO.
S-SIR! ARE YOU SERIOUS?!
DO YOU REALLY UNDER-STAND WHAT THAT MEANS?!
THINK ABOUT YOUR WIFE! AND YOUR DAUGHTER!

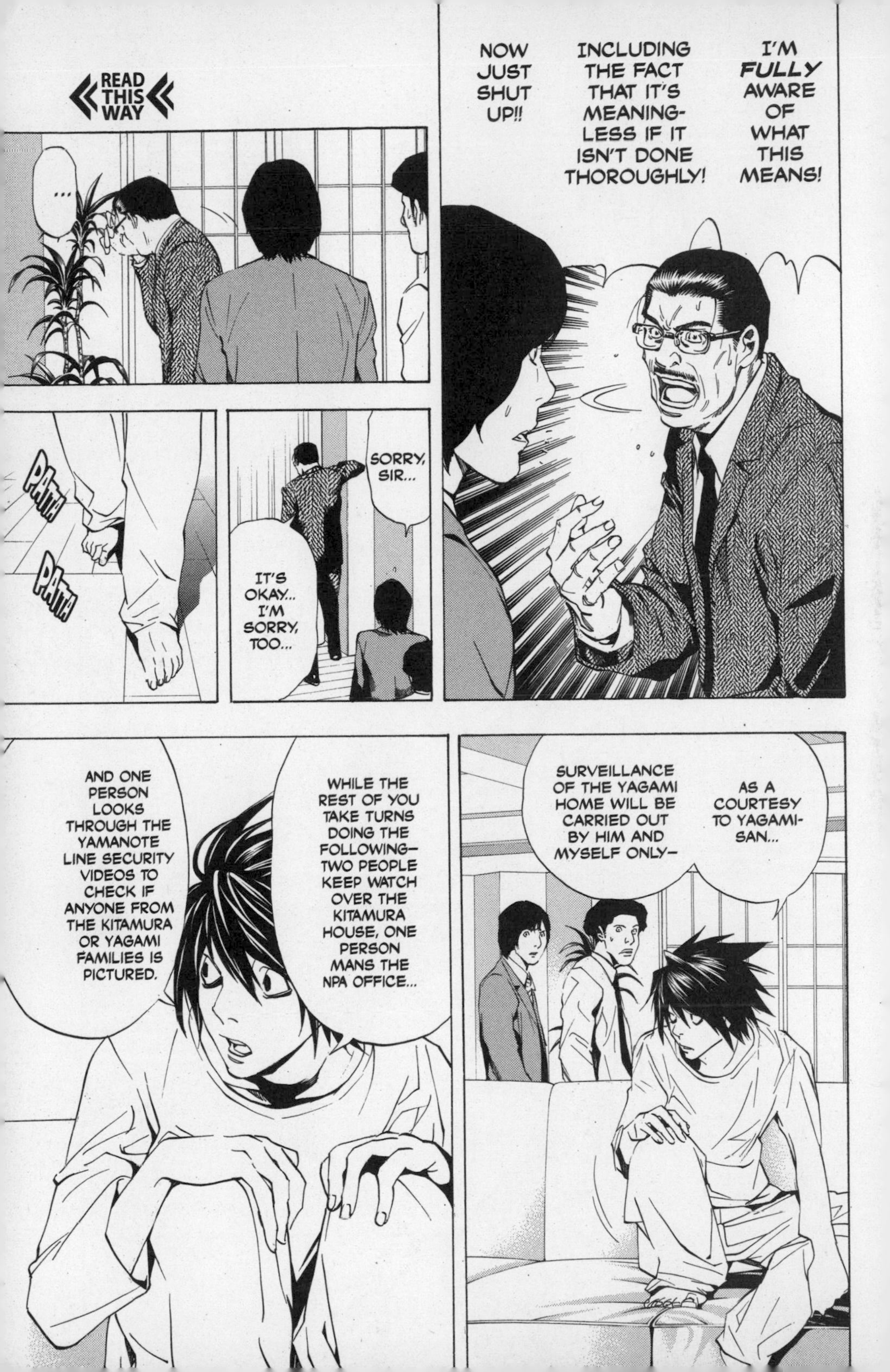
READ THIS WAY
I'M *FULLY* AWARE OF WHAT THIS MEANS!
INCLUDING THE FACT THAT IT'S MEANINGLESS IF IT ISN'T DONE THOROUGHLY!
NOW JUST SHUT UP!!
...
SORRY, SIR...
IT'S OKAY... I'M SORRY, TOO...
PATTA
PATTA
AS A COURTESY TO YAGAMI-SAN...
SURVEILLANCE OF THE YAGAMI HOME WILL BE CARRIED OUT BY HIM AND MYSELF ONLY—
WHILE THE REST OF YOU TAKE TURNS DOING THE FOLLOWING— TWO PEOPLE KEEP WATCH OVER THE KITAMURA HOUSE, ONE PERSON MANS THE NPA OFFICE...
AND ONE PERSON LOOKS THROUGH THE YAMANOTE LINE SECURITY VIDEOS TO CHECK IF ANYONE FROM THE KITAMURA OR YAGAMI FAMILIES IS PICTURED.

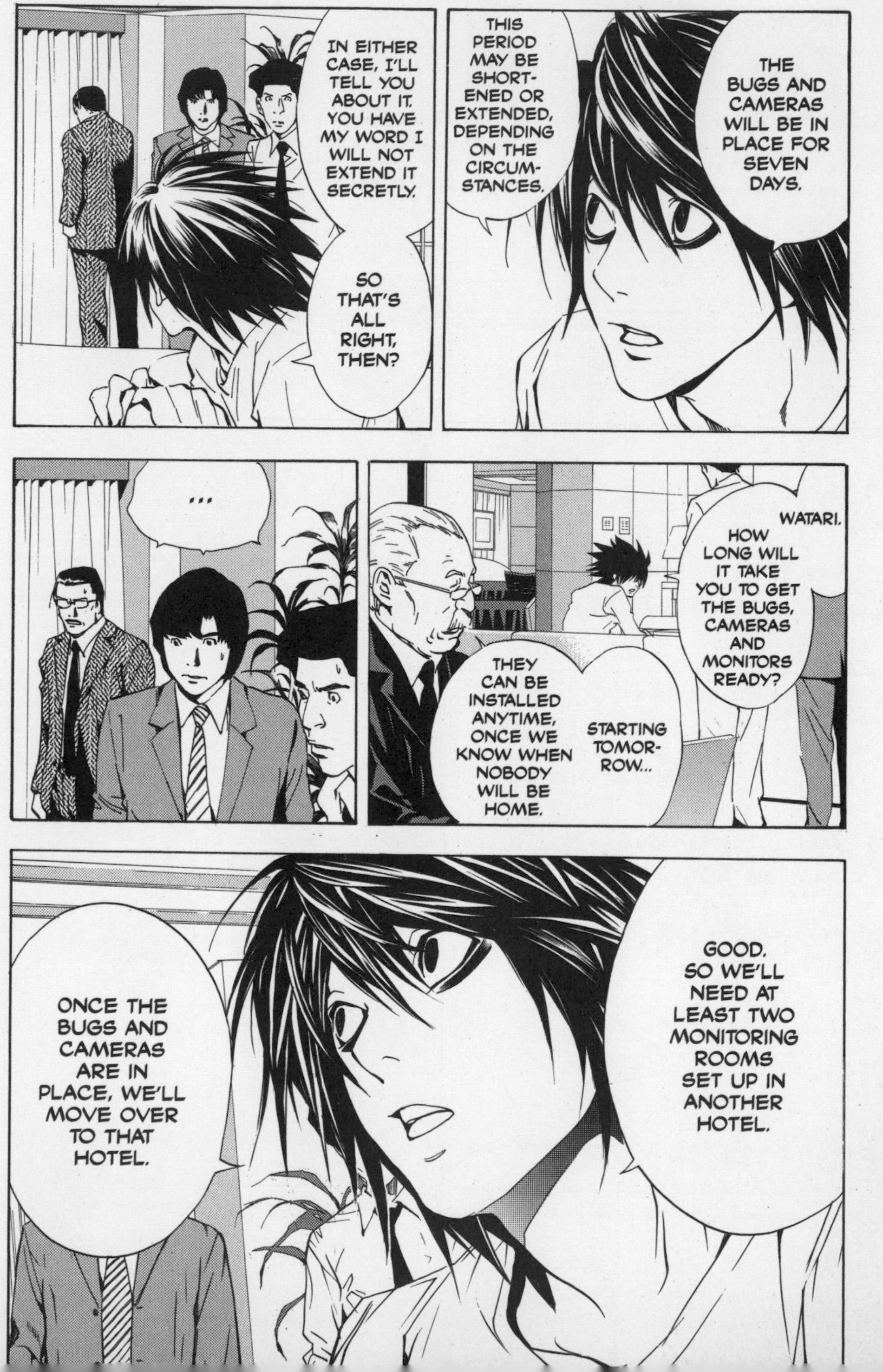
THE BUGS AND CAMERAS WILL BE IN PLACE FOR SEVEN DAYS.
THIS PERIOD MAY BE SHORTENED OR EXTENDED, DEPENDING ON THE CIRCUMSTANCES.
IN EITHER CASE, I'LL TELL YOU ABOUT IT. YOU HAVE MY WORD I WILL NOT EXTEND IT SECRETLY.
SO THAT'S ALL RIGHT, THEN?
WATARI.
HOW LONG WILL IT TAKE YOU TO GET THE BUGS, CAMERAS AND MONITORS READY?
STARTING TOMORROW...
THEY CAN BE INSTALLED ANYTIME, ONCE WE KNOW WHEN NOBODY WILL BE HOME.
...
GOOD. SO WE'LL NEED AT LEAST TWO MONITORING ROOMS SET UP IN ANOTHER HOTEL.
ONCE THE BUGS AND CAMERAS ARE IN PLACE, WE'LL MOVE OVER TO THAT HOTEL.

READ THIS WAY

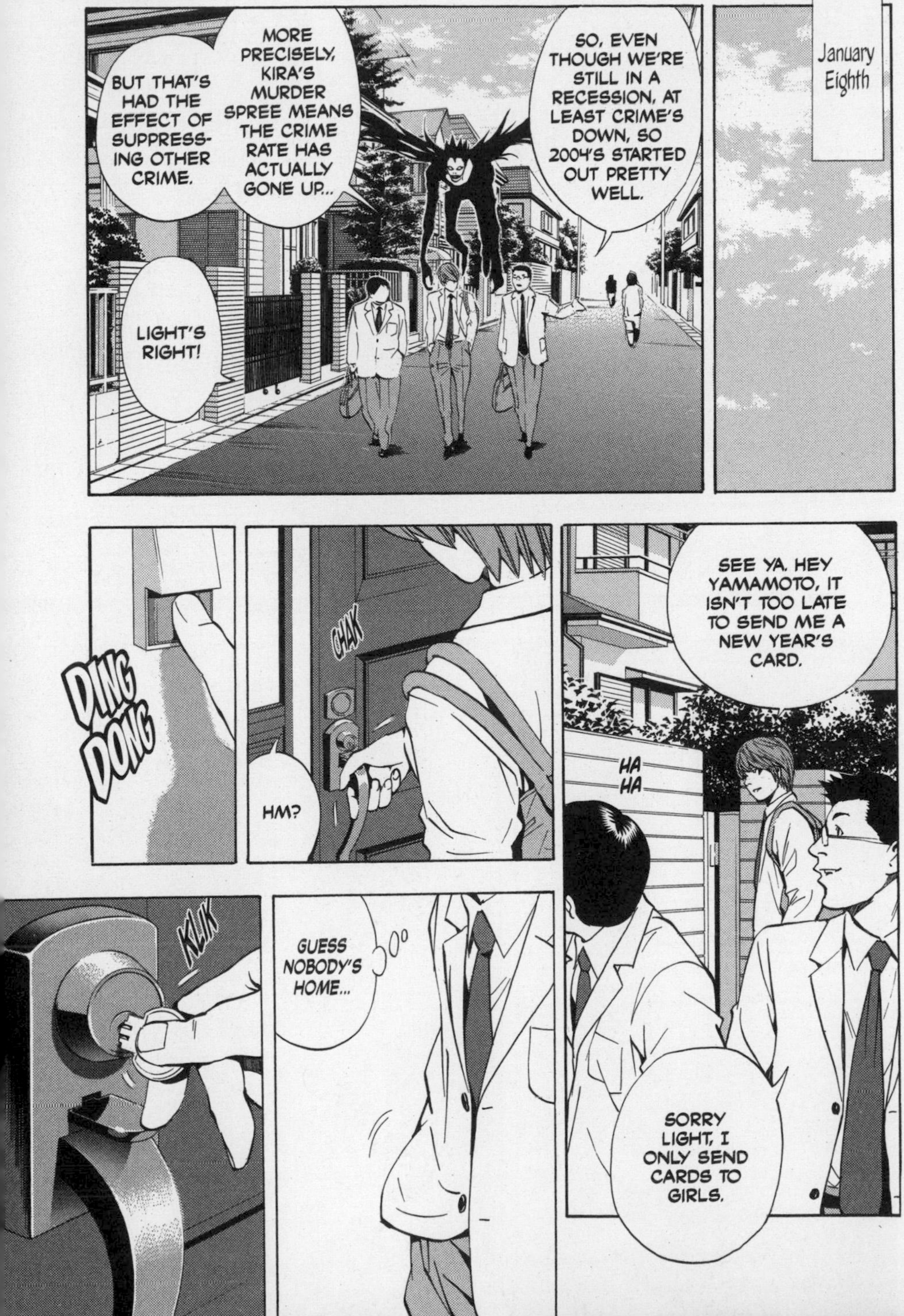

January Eighth
SO, EVEN THOUGH WE'RE STILL IN A RECESSION, AT LEAST CRIME'S DOWN, SO 2004'S STARTED OUT PRETTY WELL.
MORE PRECISELY, KIRA'S MURDER SPREE MEANS THE CRIME RATE HAS ACTUALLY GONE UP...
BUT THAT'S HAD THE EFFECT OF SUPPRESSING OTHER CRIME.
LIGHT'S RIGHT!
SEE YA. HEY YAMAMOTO, IT ISN'T TOO LATE TO SEND ME A NEW YEAR'S CARD.
HA HA
SORRY LIGHT, I ONLY SEND CARDS TO GIRLS.
CHAK
HM?
DING DONG
GUESS NOBODY'S HOME...
KLIK

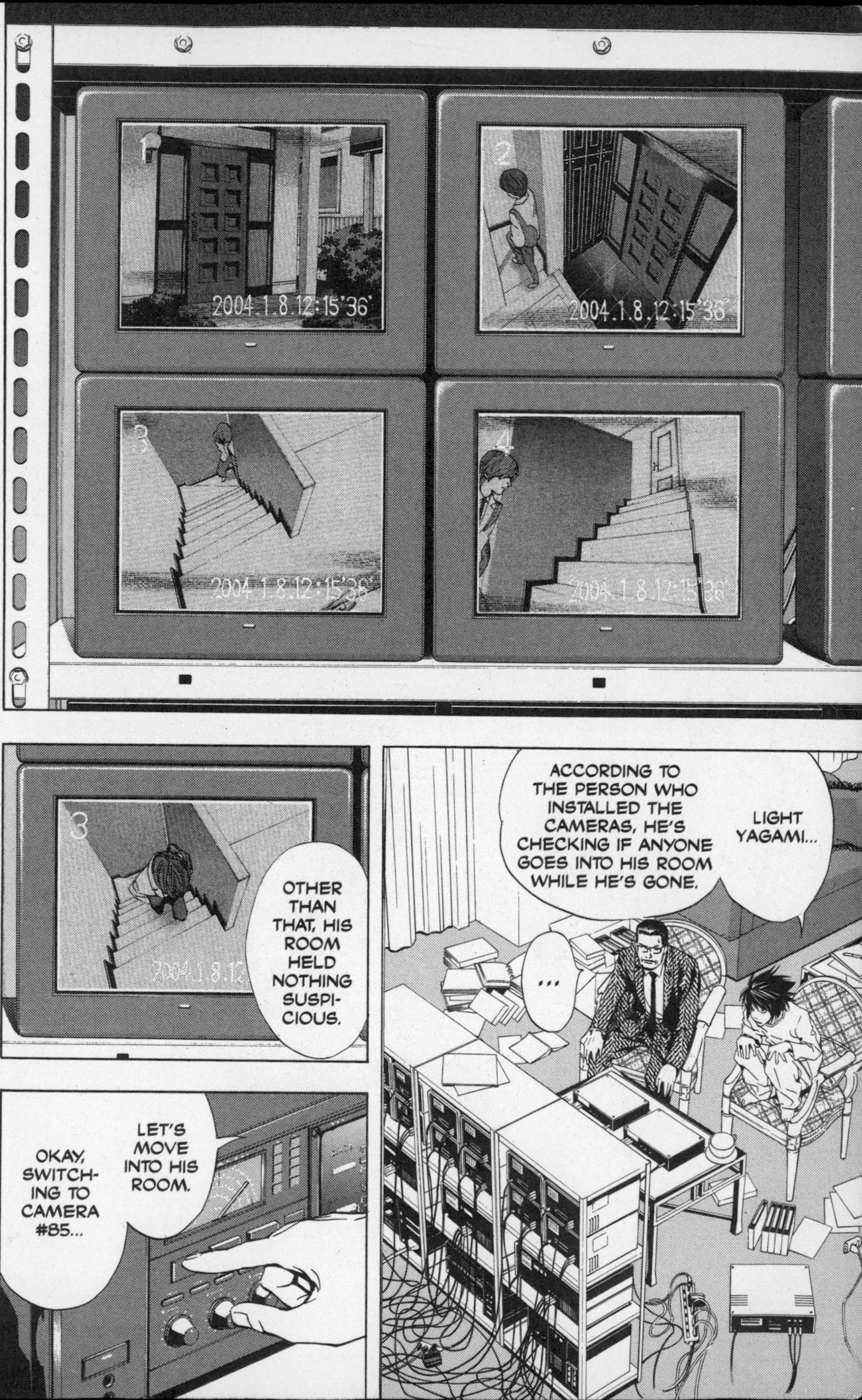
1
2004.1.8.12:15'36"
2
2004.1.8.12:15'36"
3
2004.1.8.12:15'36"
4
2004.1.8.12:15'36"
LIGHT YAGAMI...
ACCORDING TO THE PERSON WHO INSTALLED THE CAMERAS, HE'S CHECKING IF ANYONE GOES INTO HIS ROOM WHILE HE'S GONE.
...
3
OTHER THAN THAT, HIS ROOM HELD NOTHING SUSPICIOUS.
LET'S MOVE INTO HIS ROOM.
OKAY, SWITCHING TO CAMERA #85...

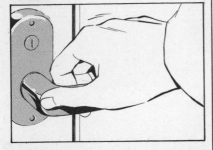

HEY LIGHT, SINCE NOBODY SEEMS TO BE HOME, HOW ABOUT WE PLAY A GAME OF MARIO GOLF?

BAM!

...

?

FLUTTER

KA-CHAK

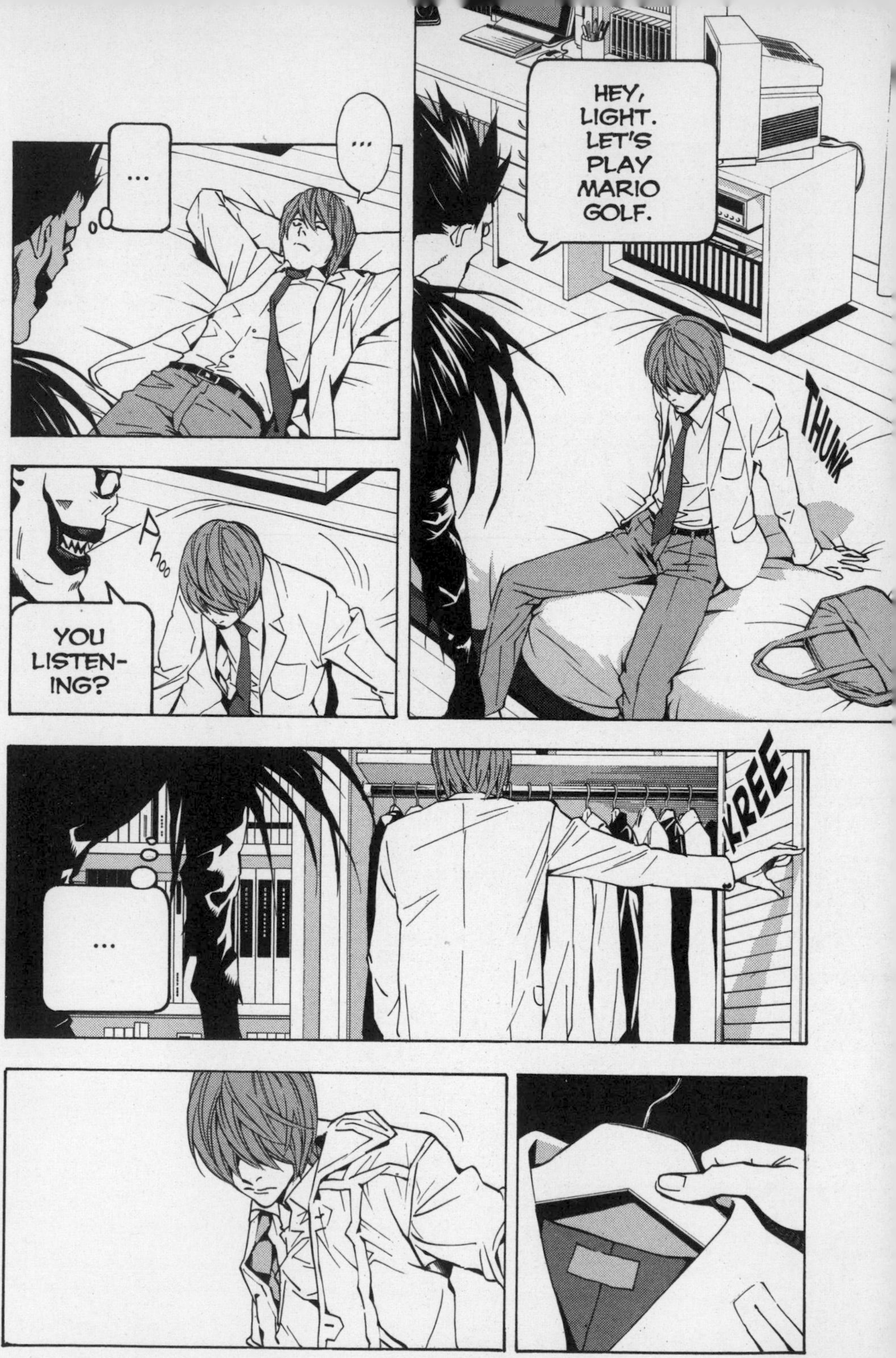
HEY, LIGHT. LET'S PLAY MARIO GOLF.
THUNK
...
...
Phoo
YOU LISTENING?
KREE
...

READ THIS WAY

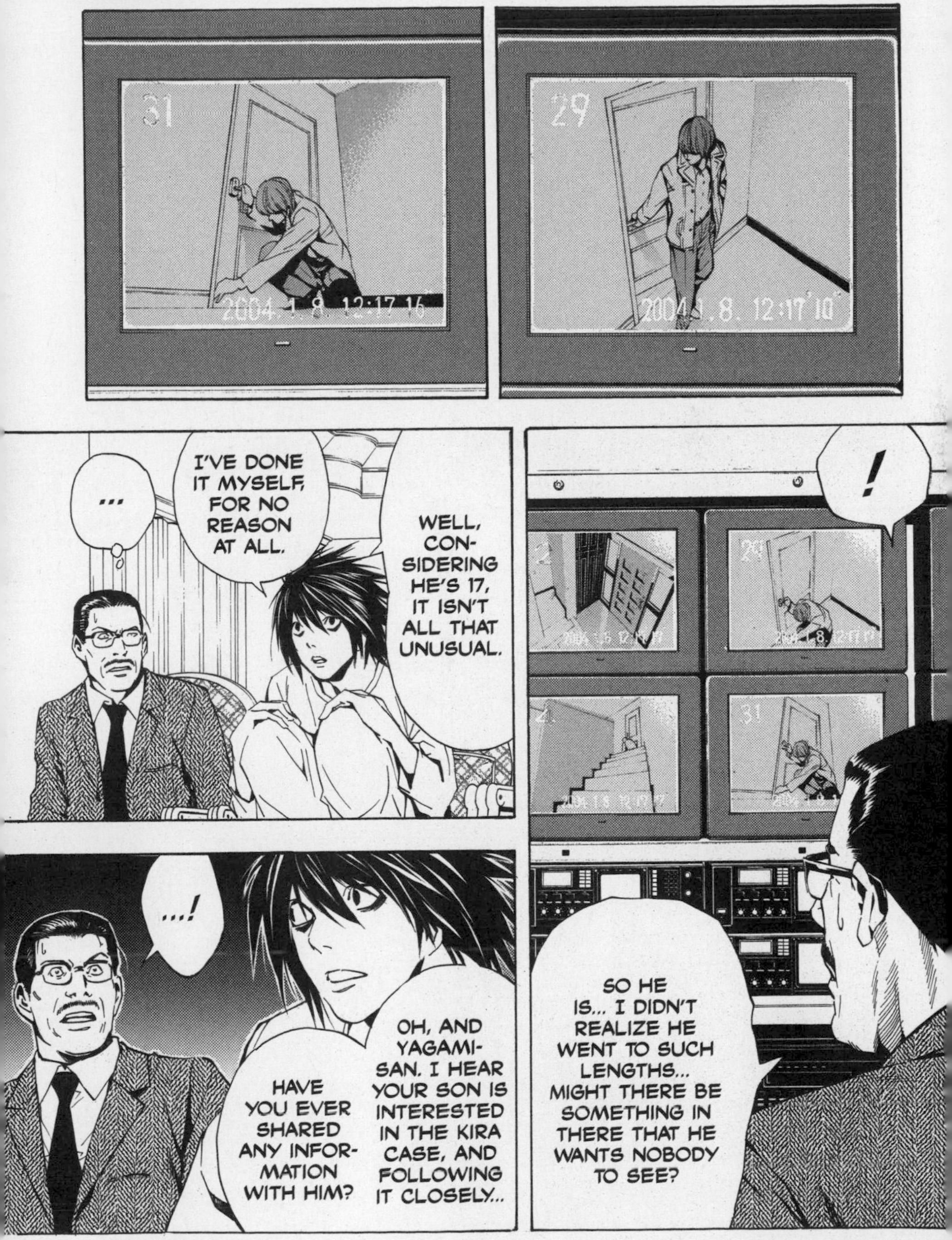
29
31
!
SO HE IS... I DIDN'T REALIZE HE WENT TO SUCH LENGTHS... MIGHT THERE BE SOMETHING IN THERE THAT HE WANTS NOBODY TO SEE?
WELL, CONSIDERING HE'S 17, IT ISN'T ALL THAT UNUSUAL.
I'VE DONE IT MYSELF, FOR NO REASON AT ALL.
...
OH, AND YAGAMI-SAN. I HEAR YOUR SON IS INTERESTED IN THE KIRA CASE, AND FOLLOWING IT CLOSELY...
HAVE YOU EVER SHARED ANY INFORMATION WITH HIM?
...!

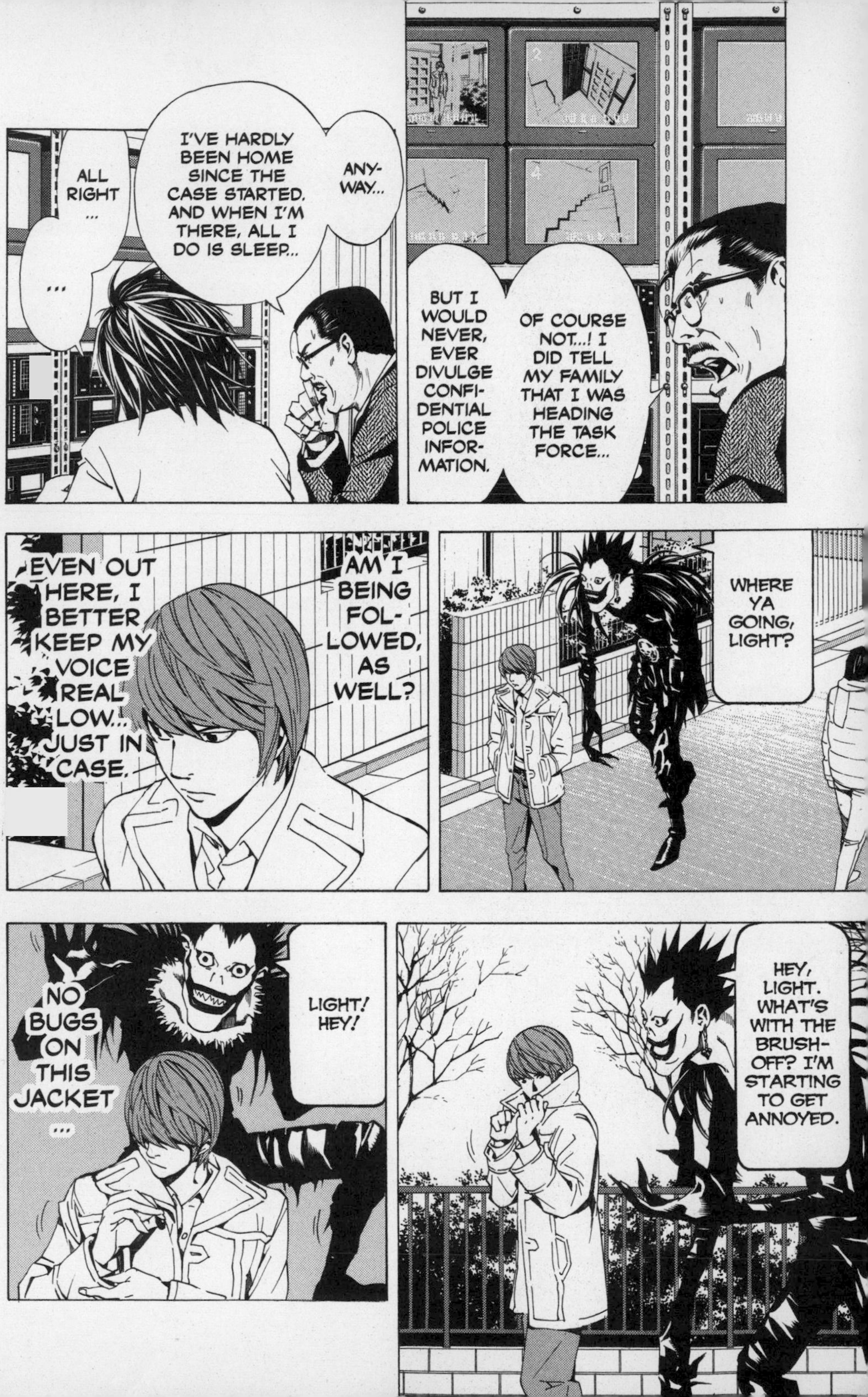
OF COURSE NOT...! I DID TELL MY FAMILY THAT I WAS HEADING THE TASK FORCE...
BUT I WOULD NEVER, EVER DIVULGE CONFIDENTIAL POLICE INFORMATION.
ANYWAY...
I'VE HARDLY BEEN HOME SINCE THE CASE STARTED. AND WHEN I'M THERE, ALL I DO IS SLEEP...
ALL RIGHT ...
...
WHERE YA GOING, LIGHT?
AM I BEING FOLLOWED, AS WELL?
EVEN OUT HERE, I BETTER KEEP MY VOICE REAL LOW... JUST IN CASE.
HEY, LIGHT. WHAT'S WITH THE BRUSH-OFF? I'M STARTING TO GET ANNOYED.
LIGHT! HEY!
NO BUGS ON THIS JACKET ...

READ THIS WAY

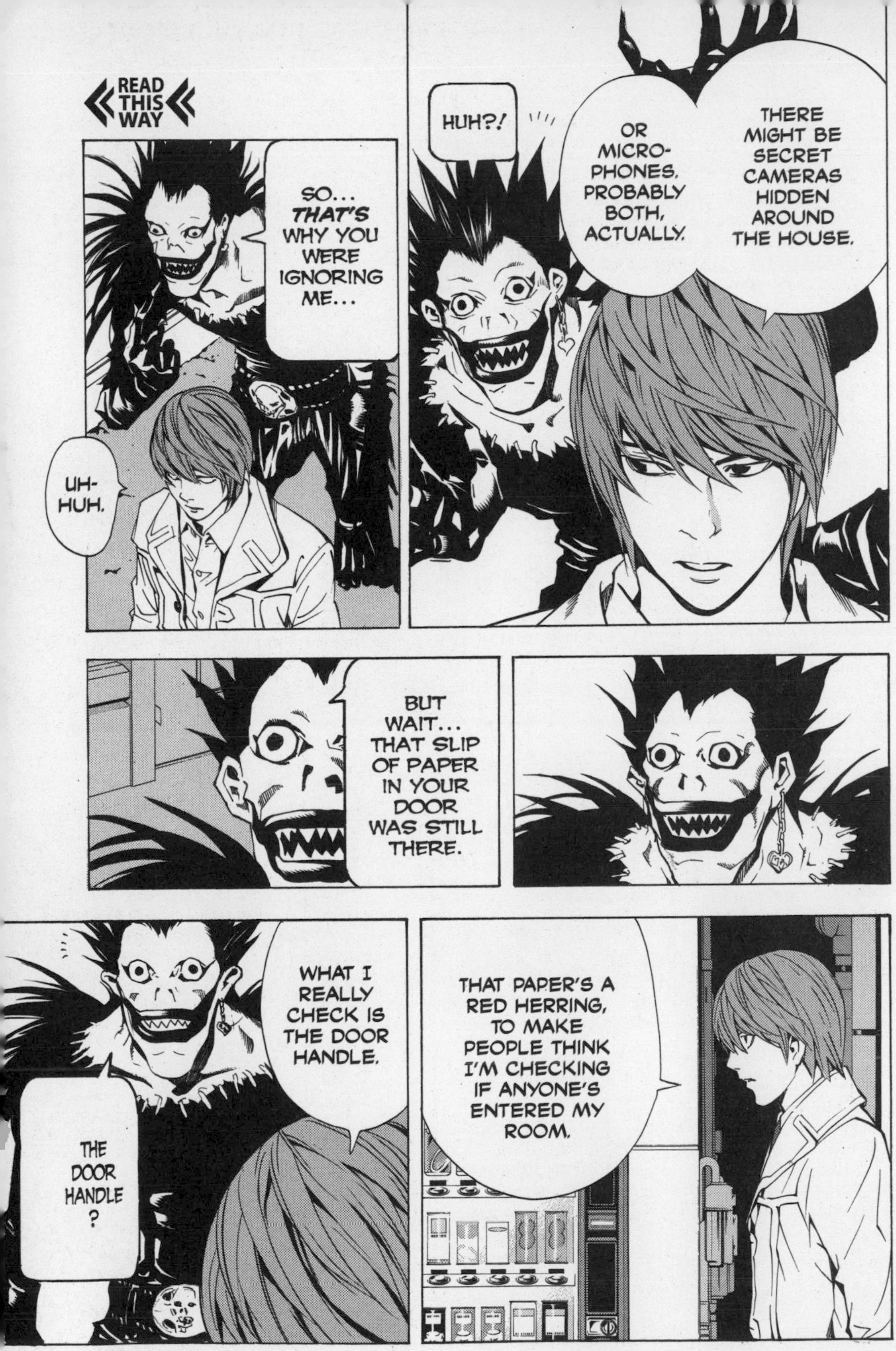
THERE MIGHT BE SECRET CAMERAS HIDDEN AROUND THE HOUSE.
OR MICROPHONES. PROBABLY BOTH, ACTUALLY.
HUH?!
SO... *THAT'S* WHY YOU WERE IGNORING ME...
UH-HUH.
BUT WAIT... THAT SLIP OF PAPER IN YOUR DOOR WAS STILL THERE.
THAT PAPER'S A RED HERRING, TO MAKE PEOPLE THINK I'M CHECKING IF ANYONE'S ENTERED MY ROOM.
WHAT I REALLY CHECK IS THE DOOR HANDLE.
THE DOOR HANDLE?

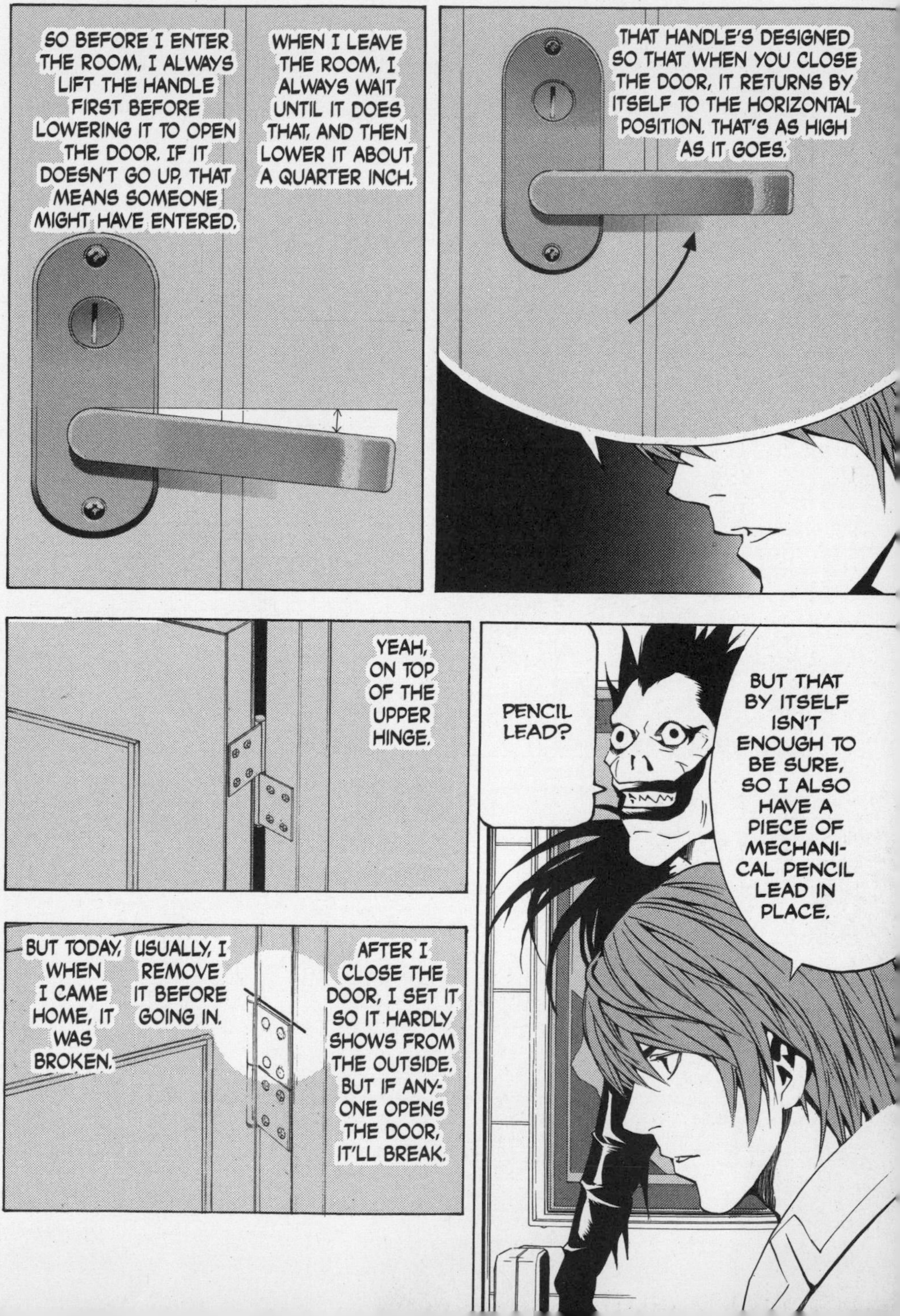
THAT HANDLE'S DESIGNED SO THAT WHEN YOU CLOSE THE DOOR, IT RETURNS BY ITSELF TO THE HORIZONTAL POSITION. THAT'S AS HIGH AS IT GOES.
WHEN I LEAVE THE ROOM, I ALWAYS WAIT UNTIL IT DOES THAT, AND THEN LOWER IT ABOUT A QUARTER INCH.
SO BEFORE I ENTER THE ROOM, I ALWAYS LIFT THE HANDLE FIRST BEFORE LOWERING IT TO OPEN THE DOOR. IF IT DOESN'T GO UP, THAT MEANS SOMEONE MIGHT HAVE ENTERED.
BUT THAT BY ITSELF ISN'T ENOUGH TO BE SURE, SO I ALSO HAVE A PIECE OF MECHANICAL PENCIL LEAD IN PLACE.
PENCIL LEAD?
YEAH, ON TOP OF THE UPPER HINGE.
AFTER I CLOSE THE DOOR, I SET IT SO IT HARDLY SHOWS FROM THE OUTSIDE. BUT IF ANYONE OPENS THE DOOR, IT'LL BREAK.
USUALLY, I REMOVE IT BEFORE GOING IN.
BUT TODAY, WHEN I CAME HOME, IT WAS BROKEN.

READ THIS WAY

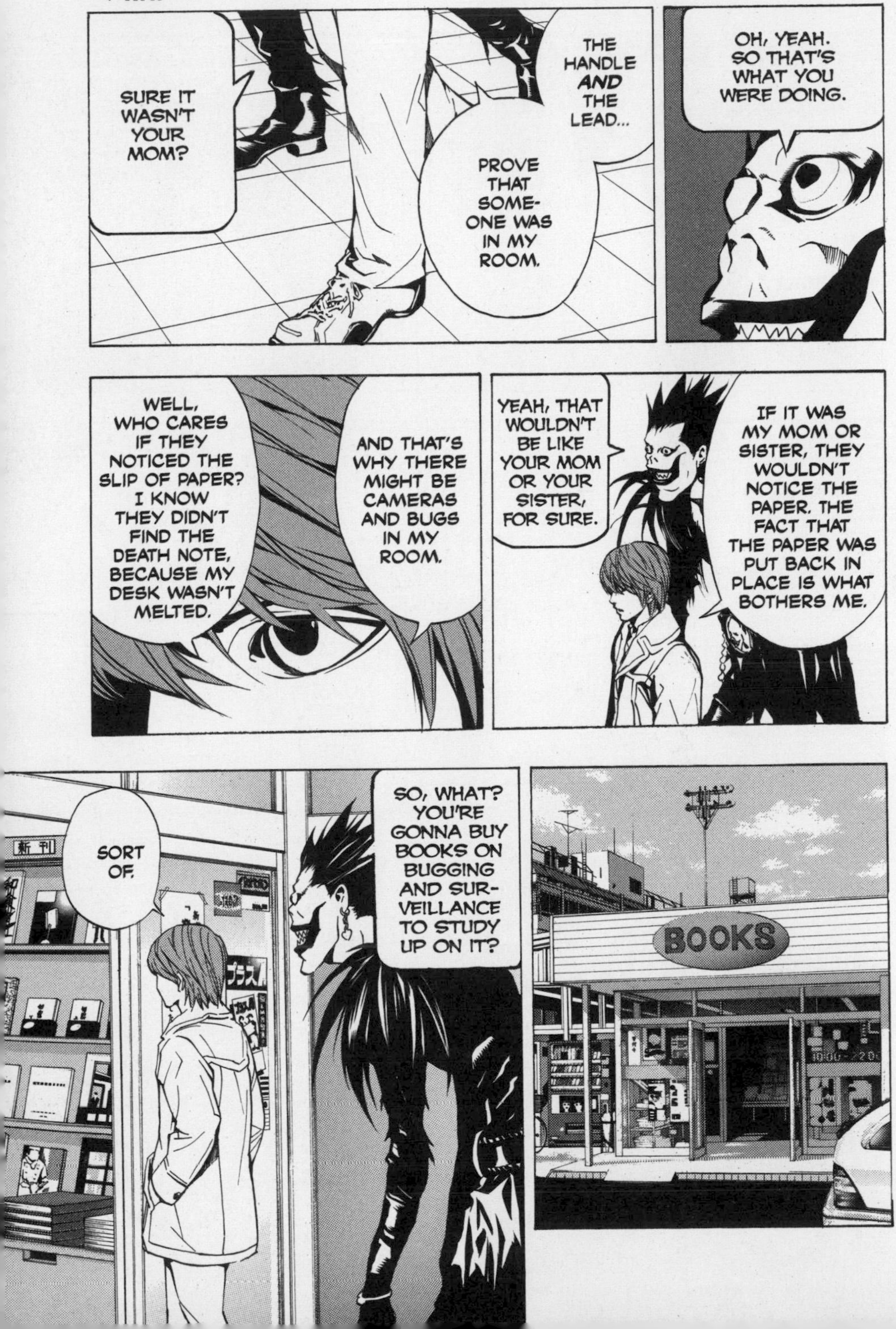
OH, YEAH. SO THAT'S WHAT YOU WERE DOING.
THE HANDLE AND THE LEAD...
PROVE THAT SOME-ONE WAS IN MY ROOM.
SURE IT WASN'T YOUR MOM?
IF IT WAS MY MOM OR SISTER, THEY WOULDN'T NOTICE THE PAPER. THE FACT THAT THE PAPER WAS PUT BACK IN PLACE IS WHAT BOTHERS ME.
YEAH, THAT WOULDN'T BE LIKE YOUR MOM OR YOUR SISTER, FOR SURE.
AND THAT'S WHY THERE MIGHT BE CAMERAS AND BUGS IN MY ROOM.
WELL, WHO CARES IF THEY NOTICED THE SLIP OF PAPER? I KNOW THEY DIDN'T FIND THE DEATH NOTE, BECAUSE MY DESK WASN'T MELTED.
BOOKS
SO, WHAT? YOU'RE GONNA BUY BOOKS ON BUGGING AND SUR-VEILLANCE TO STUDY UP ON IT?
SORT OF.

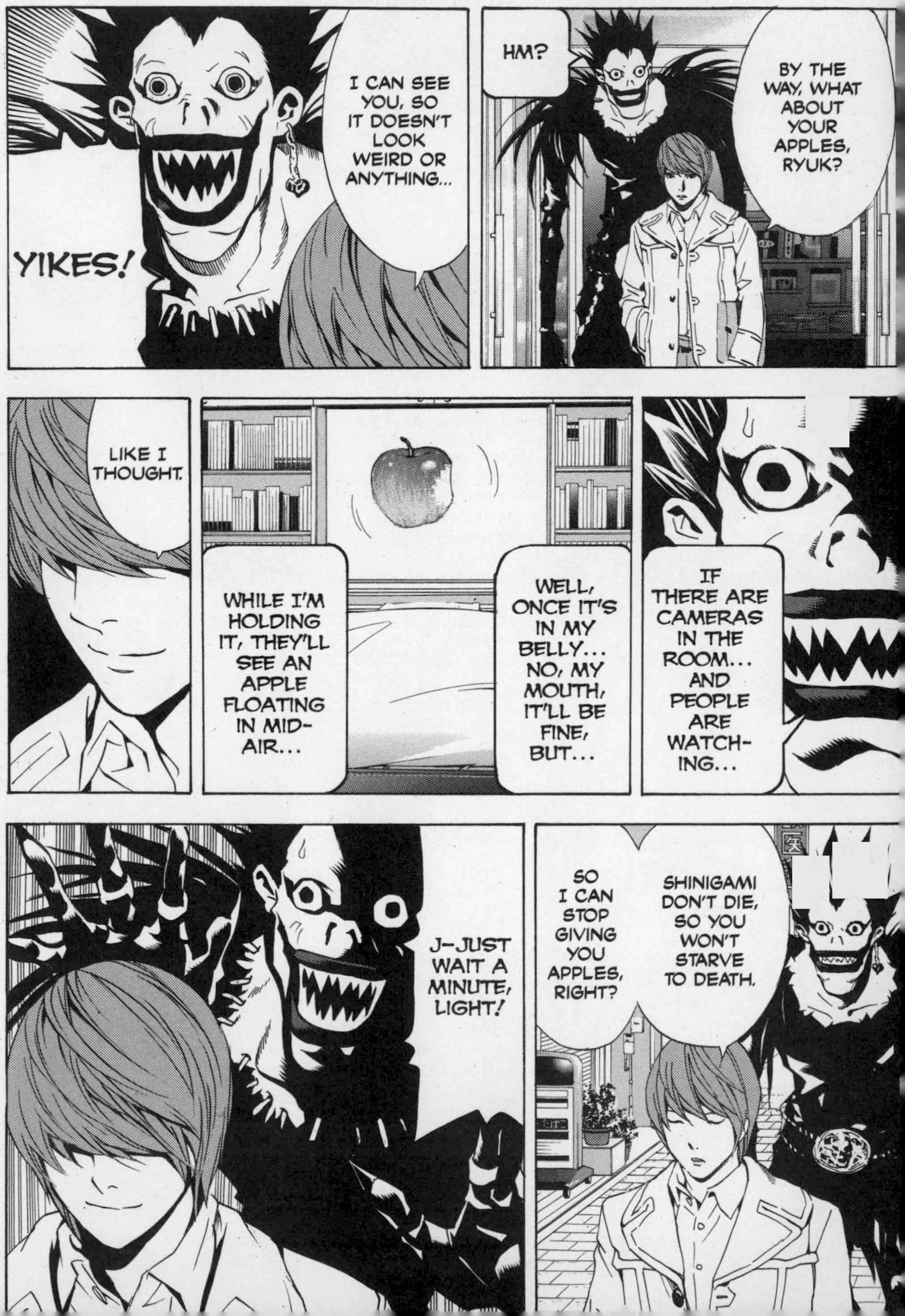
BY THE WAY, WHAT ABOUT YOUR APPLES, RYUK?
HM?
I CAN SEE YOU, SO IT DOESN'T LOOK WEIRD OR ANYTHING...
YIKES!
IF THERE ARE CAMERAS IN THE ROOM... AND PEOPLE ARE WATCHING...
WELL, ONCE IT'S IN MY BELLY... NO, MY MOUTH, IT'LL BE FINE, BUT...
WHILE I'M HOLDING IT, THEY'LL SEE AN APPLE FLOATING IN MID-AIR...
LIKE I THOUGHT.
SHINIGAMI DON'T DIE, SO YOU WON'T STARVE TO DEATH.
SO I CAN STOP GIVING YOU APPLES, RIGHT?
J-JUST WAIT A MINUTE, LIGHT!

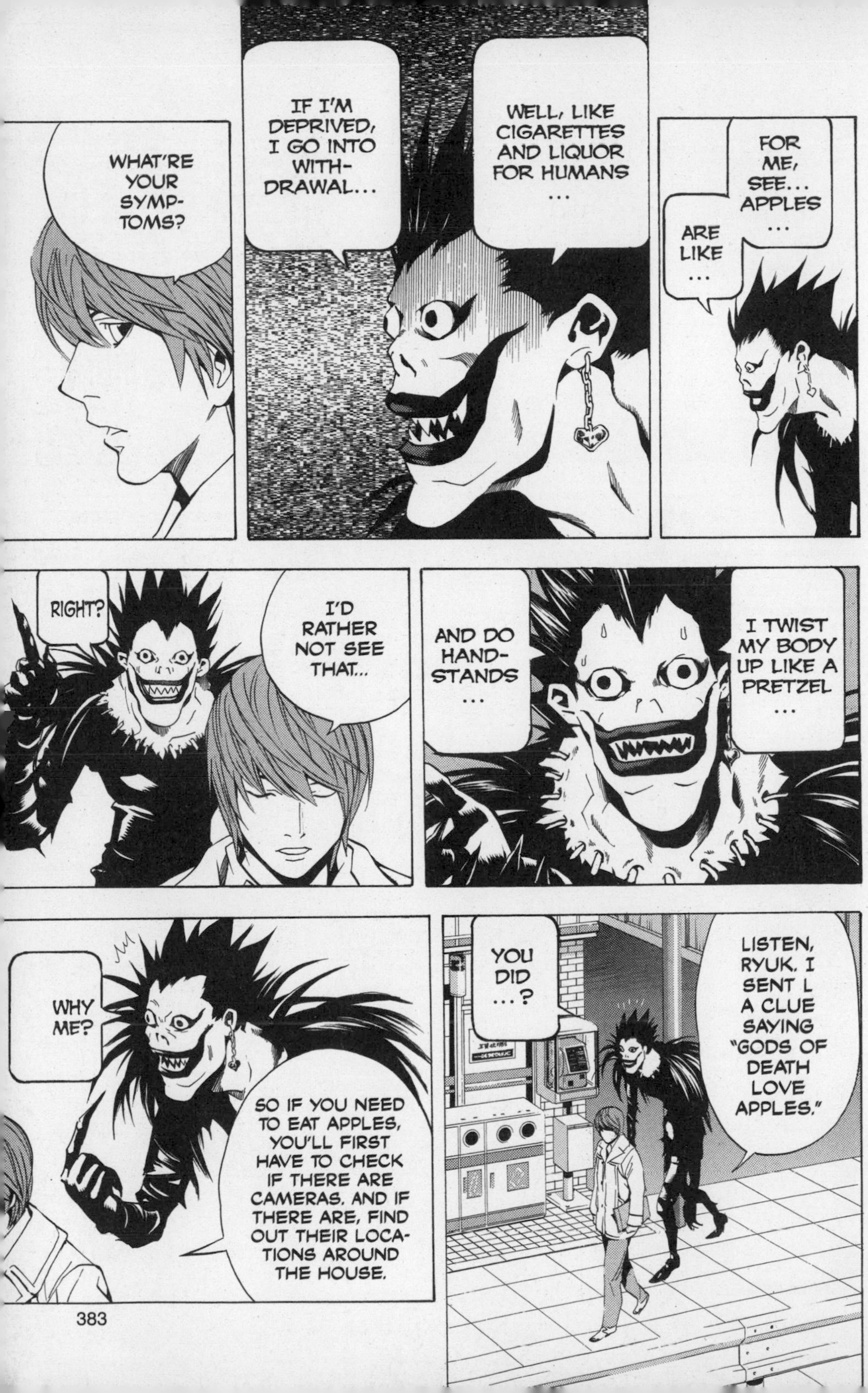
FOR ME, SEE... APPLES ...
ARE LIKE ...
WELL, LIKE CIGARETTES AND LIQUOR FOR HUMANS ...
IF I'M DEPRIVED, I GO INTO WITH-DRAWAL...
WHAT'RE YOUR SYMP-TOMS?
I TWIST MY BODY UP LIKE A PRETZEL ...
AND DO HAND-STANDS ...
I'D RATHER NOT SEE THAT...
RIGHT?
LISTEN, RYUK. I SENT L A CLUE SAYING "GODS OF DEATH LOVE APPLES."
YOU DID ...?
SO IF YOU NEED TO EAT APPLES, YOU'LL FIRST HAVE TO CHECK IF THERE ARE CAMERAS. AND IF THERE ARE, FIND OUT THEIR LOCA-TIONS AROUND THE HOUSE.
WHY ME?

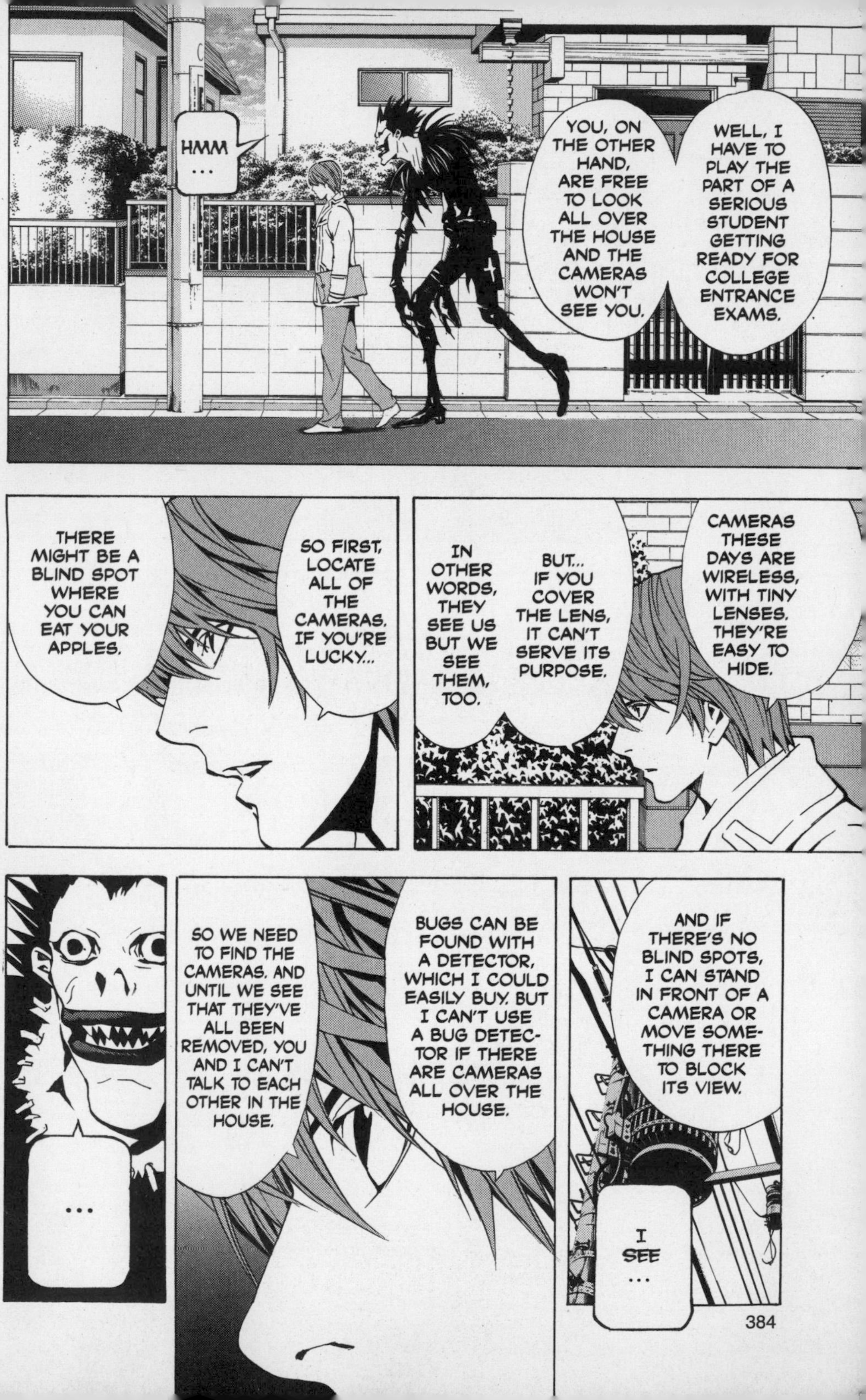
WELL, I HAVE TO PLAY THE PART OF A SERIOUS STUDENT GETTING READY FOR COLLEGE ENTRANCE EXAMS.
YOU, ON THE OTHER HAND, ARE FREE TO LOOK ALL OVER THE HOUSE AND THE CAMERAS WON'T SEE YOU.
HMM ...
CAMERAS THESE DAYS ARE WIRELESS, WITH TINY LENSES. THEY'RE EASY TO HIDE.
BUT... IF YOU COVER THE LENS, IT CAN'T SERVE ITS PURPOSE.
IN OTHER WORDS, THEY SEE US BUT WE SEE THEM, TOO.
SO FIRST, LOCATE ALL OF THE CAMERAS. IF YOU'RE LUCKY...
THERE MIGHT BE A BLIND SPOT WHERE YOU CAN EAT YOUR APPLES.
AND IF THERE'S NO BLIND SPOTS, I CAN STAND IN FRONT OF A CAMERA OR MOVE SOMETHING THERE TO BLOCK ITS VIEW.
I SEE ...
BUGS CAN BE FOUND WITH A DETECTOR, WHICH I COULD EASILY BUY. BUT I CAN'T USE A BUG DETECTOR IF THERE ARE CAMERAS ALL OVER THE HOUSE.
SO WE NEED TO FIND THE CAMERAS. AND UNTIL WE SEE THAT THEY'VE ALL BEEN REMOVED, YOU AND I CAN'T TALK TO EACH OTHER IN THE HOUSE.
...

READ THIS WAY

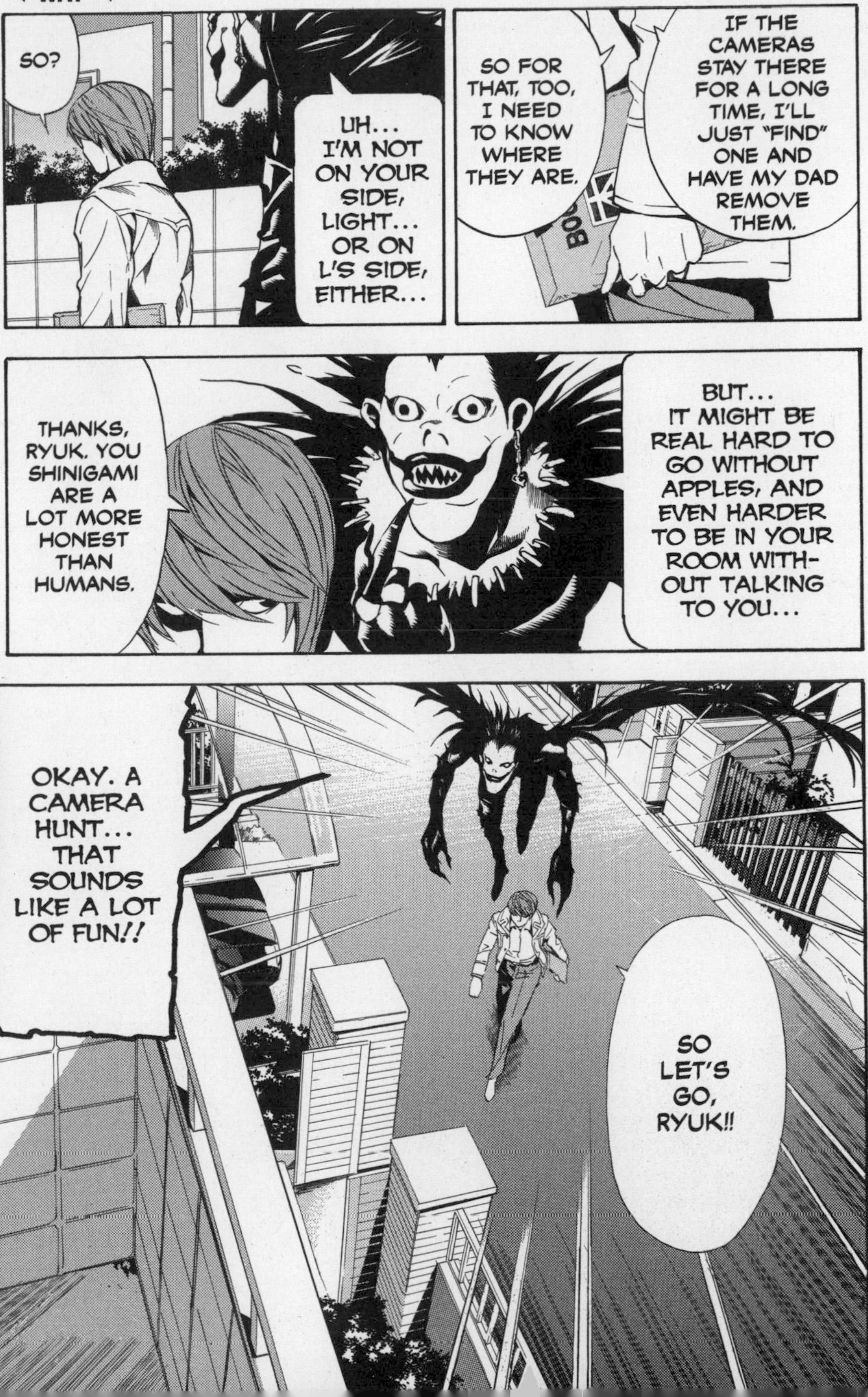
IF THE CAMERAS STAY THERE FOR A LONG TIME, I'LL JUST "FIND" ONE AND HAVE MY DAD REMOVE THEM.
SO FOR THAT, TOO, I NEED TO KNOW WHERE THEY ARE.
SO?
UH... I'M NOT ON YOUR SIDE, LIGHT... OR ON L'S SIDE, EITHER...
BUT... IT MIGHT BE REAL HARD TO GO WITHOUT APPLES, AND EVEN HARDER TO BE IN YOUR ROOM WITH-OUT TALKING TO YOU...
THANKS, RYUK. YOU SHINIGAMI ARE A LOT MORE HONEST THAN HUMANS.
SO LET'S GO, RYUK!!
OKAY. A CAMERA HUNT... THAT SOUNDS LIKE A LOT OF FUN!!

Is it okay to draw Shinigami?
Won't I be cursed for doing this?
I draw this manga with fear and trembling.

-Takeshi Obata

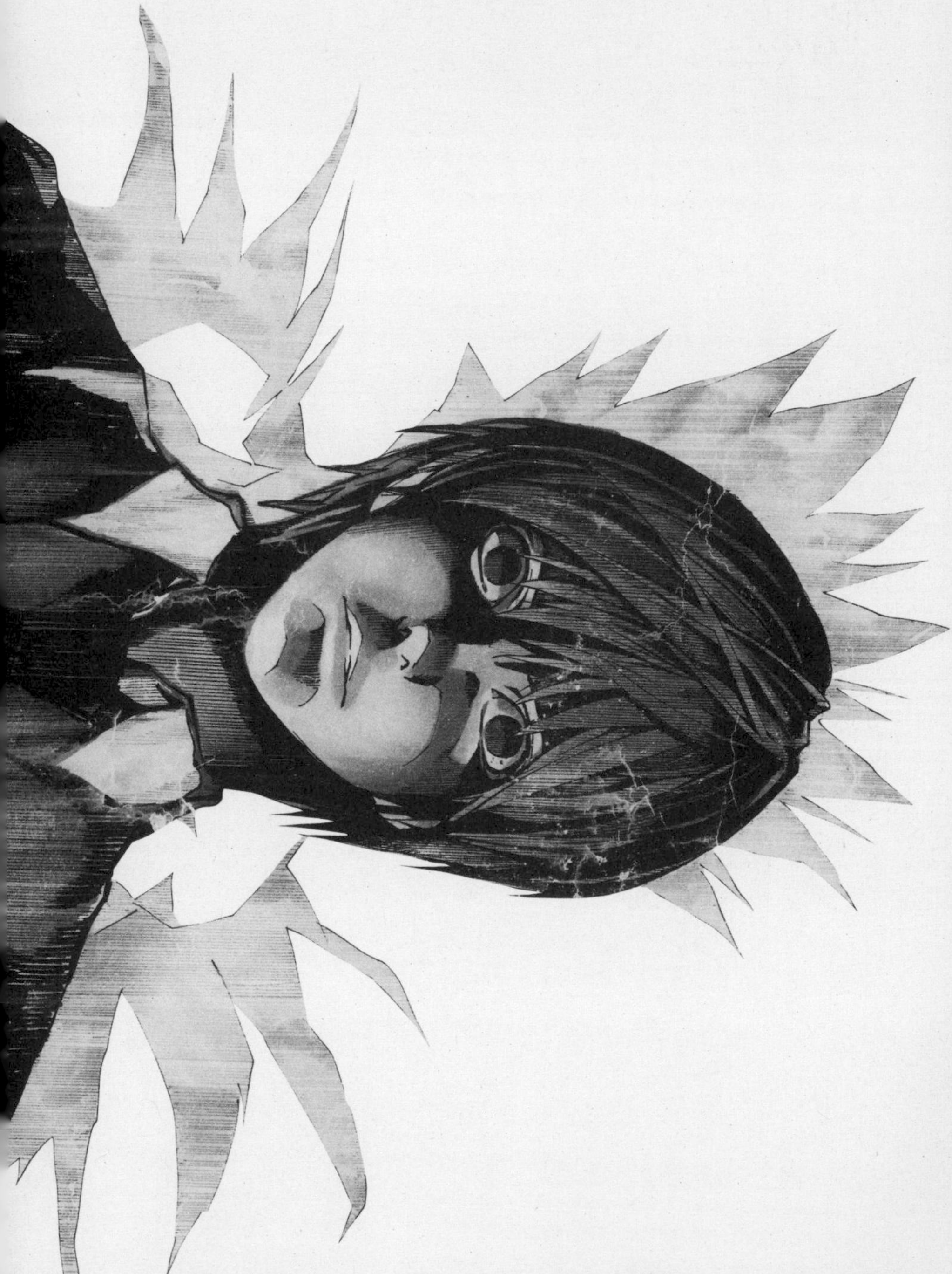

Story by Tsugumi Ohba  Art by Takeshi Obata

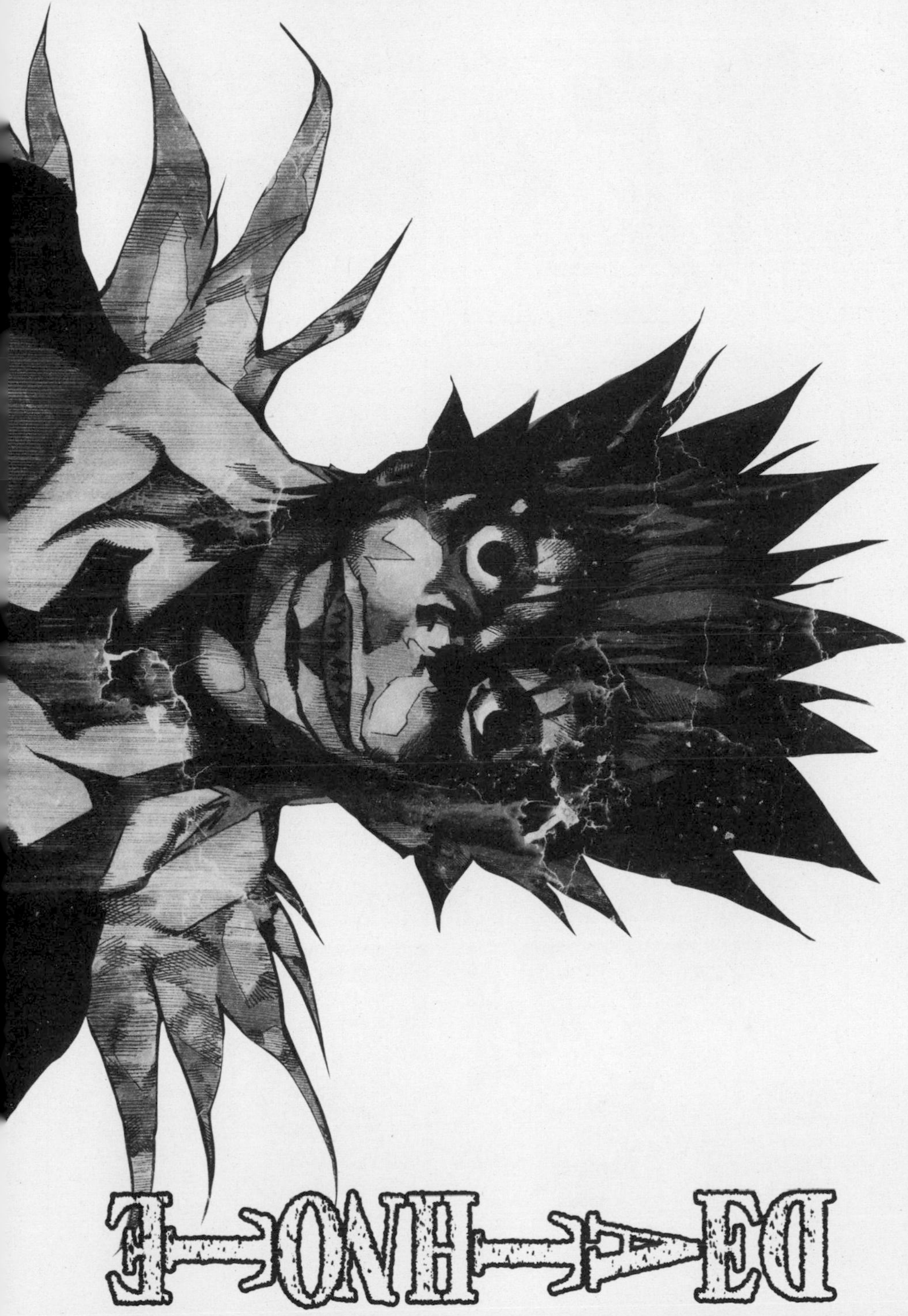

DEATH NOTE

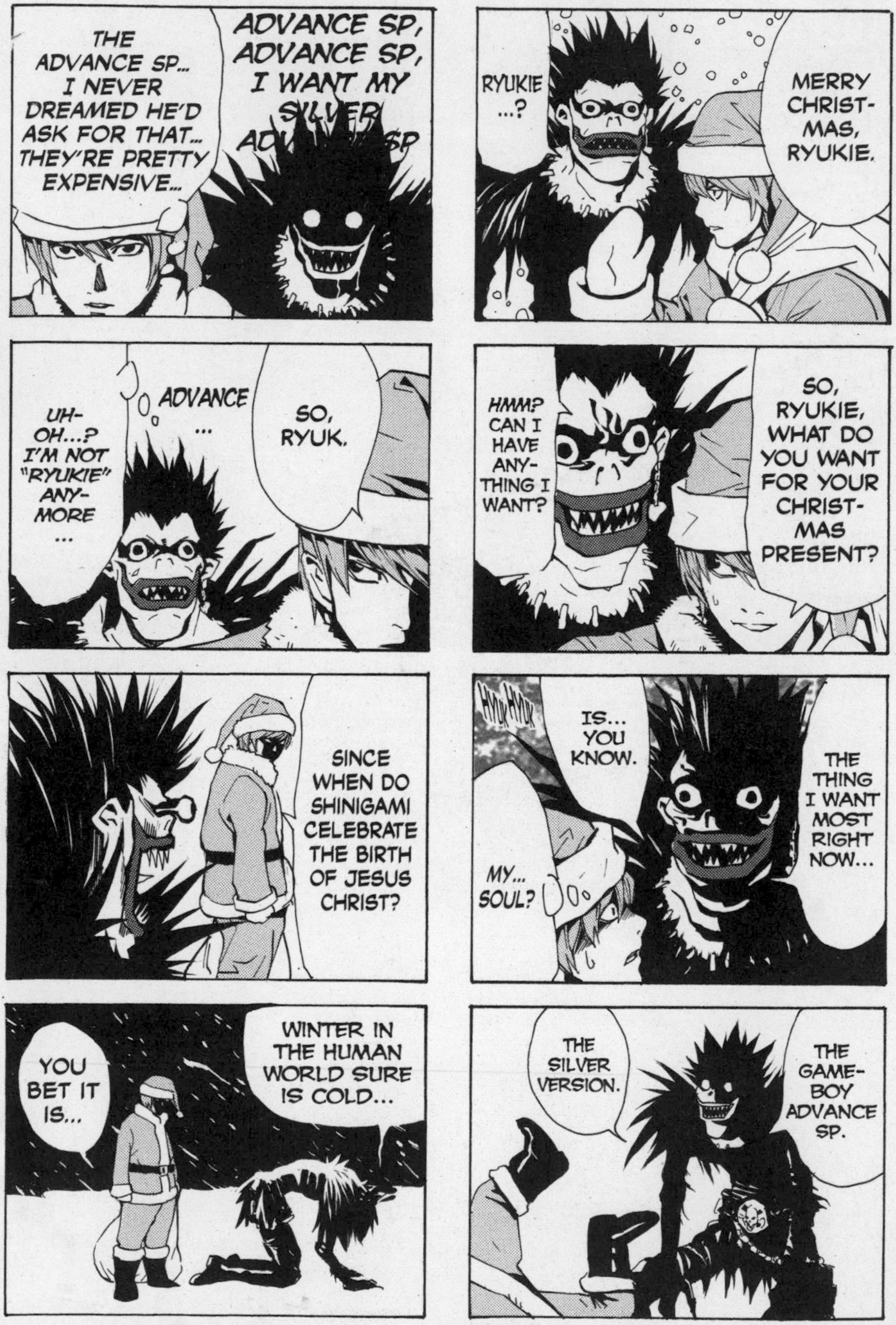
MERRY CHRIST-MAS, RYUKIE.
RYUKIE ...?
SO, RYUKIE, WHAT DO YOU WANT FOR YOUR CHRIST-MAS PRESENT?
HMM? CAN I HAVE ANY-THING I WANT?
THE THING I WANT MOST RIGHT NOW...
HYUK HYUK
IS... YOU KNOW.
MY... SOUL?
THE GAME-BOY ADVANCE SP.
THE SILVER VERSION.
SO, RYUK.
ADVANCE ...
UH-OH...? I'M NOT "RYUKIE" ANY-MORE ...
SINCE WHEN DO SHINIGAMI CELEBRATE THE BIRTH OF JESUS CHRIST?
WINTER IN THE HUMAN WORLD SURE IS COLD...
YOU BET IT IS...
ADVANCE SP, ADVANCE SP, I WANT MY SILVER
THE ADVANCE SP... I NEVER DREAMED HE'D ASK FOR THAT... THEY'RE PRETTY EXPENSIVE...

These four-panel cartoons originally appeared in "Weekly Shonen Jump" Vol. 4-5 (double issue), 2004.